ECE 2103

Literacy, Art and Music

Machado | Koster

CENGAGE
Learning·

Australia • Brazil • Japan • Korea • Mexico • Singapore • Spain • United Kingdom • United States

ECE 2103: Literacy, Art and Music

Early Childhood Experiences in Language Arts, 11th Edition
Machado

© 2016 Cengage Learning. All rights reserved.

Growing Artists, 6th Edition
Koster

© 2015 Cengage Learning. All rights reserved.

This book contains select works from existing Cengage Learning resources and was produced by Cengage Learning Custom Solutions for collegiate use. As such, those adopting and/or contributing to this work are responsible for editorial content accuracy, continuity and completeness.

Compilation © 2016 Cengage Learning

ISBN: 978-1-337-05418-8

Cengage Learning
20 Channel Center Street
Boston, MA 02210
USA

Cengage Learning is a leading provider of customized learning solutions with office locations around the globe, including Singapore, the United Kingdom, Australia, Mexico, Brazil, and Japan. Locate your local office at:
www.international.cengage.com/region.

Cengage Learning products are represented in Canada by Nelson Education, Ltd.

For your lifelong learning solutions, visit **www.cengage.com/custom.**

Visit our corporate website at **www.cengage.com.**

Brief Contents

1 Beginnings of Communication

Objectives

After reading this chapter, you should be able to:

1-1 Discuss the reciprocal behaviors of infants, parents, and caregivers.

1-2 Name four important influences that may affect an infant's language growth and development.

1-3 Compare two theories of human language emergence.

1-4 Name two areas of particular importance to infant care addressed in Developmentally Appropriate Practice (DAP) guidelines.

1-5 Discuss the behaviors and vocalizing efforts that infants use to communicate their needs and desires.

1-6 Describe what caregiver actions should take place when infants develop joint attentional focus.

1-7 Name and comment upon early reading and writing activities in late infancy.

1-8 Identify how infant centers monitor each infant's language and communicating behaviors.

naeyc NAEYC Program Standards

1A05 Teacher shares information with families about classroom expectations and routines.

1B01 Teaching staff foster children's emotional well-being by demonstrating respect for children and creating a positive emotional climate as reflected in behaviors, such as frequent social conversations, joint laughter, and affection.

1B11 Teaching staff engage infants in frequent face-to-face social interactions each day.

1B14 Teaching staff quickly respond to infants' cries or other signs of distress by providing physical comfort and needed care.

DAP Developmentally Appropriate Practice (DAP)

1A2 The infant's primary caregiver comes to know the child and family well, and so is able to respond to that child's individual temperament and needs and cues, and to develop a mutually satisfying pattern of communication.

1B1 Caregivers talk in a pleasant, calm voice, making frequent eye contact.

1C1 Caregivers often talk about what is going on with the infant.

1D2 Caregivers observe and listen and respond to sounds the infant makes.

1D3 Caregivers frequently talk to, sing to, and read to infants.

3B3 Appropriate games are played with interested infants.

COMMON Common Core State Standards for English Language Arts and Literacy

L.CCR 3 Apply knowledge to understand how language functions in different contexts.

A New Sign

Noah, 10 months, had a new sign for "cracker" that he had used a few times during the day at the infant center. He was very pleased when his "sign" resulted in someone bringing him a cracker. At pick-up time, one of the staff believed it important to talk to Noah's dad. Mr. Soares did not really understand what the teacher, Miss Washington, was talking about when she said "signing." Miss Washington gave Mr. Soares a quick explanation. He smiled proudly and then said, "That's great. I'll talk to his mom and let her know."

Questions to Ponder

1. Miss Washington had a new language-related topic for the next staff meeting. What would you suspect it was?

2. Did this episode tell you something about the language-developing quality of the infant center?

3. What do you know about male infants and their signing ability compared with that of female infants? Could you describe infant signing behavior?

   (If you are hesitating, this chapter provides answers.)

In this chapter the reader is acquainted with those elements in an infant's life that facilitate optimal growth in communication and language development. Socioemotional, physical, cognitive, and environmental factors that influence, promote, or deter growth are noted. Recommended interaction techniques and strategies are supported by research and reflect accepted appropriate practices and standards. As foundational aspects of infant communication are presented, *boxed* descriptions of the attuned and reciprocal behaviors caregivers make with infants are provided. Caregivers establish a relationship with each infant in their care, and the quality of that relationship serves to motivate each infant to engage in learning (McMullen & Dixon, 2006). Higher levels of warmth are connected to positive caregiver sensitivity. Gerber, Whitebook, & Weinstein (2007) note that the quality of caregiver practices has been linked to children's brain development and cognitive functioning.

For you to become the kind of educator children deserve, one who enhances language growth, you should begin by believing that most infants are able and natural communicators from birth onward unless some life circumstance has modified their natural potential. Infant care facilities with well-planned, positive, and growth-producing environments—that are staffed with skilled, knowledgeable, and well-trained adults who offer developmentally appropriate activities—provide a place where infants can and do thrive.

Each infant is a unique combination of inherited traits and environmental influences. Structural, hormonal, and chemical influences present before birth may have affected the growth and development of the fetus (Gould, 2002). Newborns seem to assimilate information immediately and are interested in their surroundings. Some suggest an infant possesses "the greatest mind" in existence and is the most powerful learning machine in the universe. During the third trimester of pregnancy, most mothers notice that their babies kick and move in response to music or loud noises. The sound of speech may draw a less spirited reaction, but there is little question that fetuses hear and react to a wide variety of sounds and seem to recognize the rhythm of their mother's voice.

Technology can now monitor the slightest physical changes in breathing, heartbeat, eye movement, and sucking rhythm and rates. Babies begin learning how to carry on conversations quickly and sucking patterns produce a **rhythm** that mimics that of give-and-take dialogues. Infants respond to very specific maternal signals, including tone of voice, facial changes, and head movements.

Greenspan (1999) suggests what may happen when interacting with a one- or two-month-old baby at a relaxed time after a nap or feeding:

> … when you hold him at arm's length and look directly into his eyes with a broad smile on your face, watch his lips part as if he's trying to imitate your smile. (p. 31)

Babies gesture and make sounds and seem to hold up their ends of conversations, but, at times, they appear to suppress output and channel their energy into seeing and hearing. Their eye contact with their caregivers, called **gaze coupling**, is believed to be one of their first steps in establishing communication. Infants can

---

rhythm — uniform or patterned recurrence of a beat, accent, or melody in speech.
gaze coupling — infant-mother extended eye contact.

shut off background noises and pay attention to slight changes in adult voice sounds.

An attuned adult responds with sensitivity and accuracy based on an understanding of an infant's (child's) cues.

an **ATTUNED** adult would:

- notice infant actions, including gestures, body positioning, noisemaking, eye gazing, and any shift from listening to watching.
- make face-to-face contact frequently.
- display admiration, affection, and pleasure and smile frequently.
- provide verbal and nonverbal communication.
- seek to maintain and prolong eye contact. ◂

McMillen (2013) posits babies are captivating, wondrous, and beguiling beings coming into the world fully equipped to enchant and draw us in. The qualities an infant inherits from parents and the events that occur in the child's life help shape the child's language development. Gender, temperament, and a timetable for the emergence of intellectual, emotional, and physical capabilities are all genetic givens. In the short four to five years after birth, the child's speech becomes purposeful and similar to adult speech. This growing language skill is a useful tool for satisfying needs and exchanging thoughts, hopes, and dreams with others. As ability grows, the child understands and uses more of the resources of oral and recorded human knowledge and is well on the way to becoming a literate being.

The natural capacity to categorize, to invent, and to remember information aids the child's language acquisition. Although unique among the species because of the ability to speak, human beings are not the only ones who can communicate. Birds and animals also imitate sounds and signals and are believed to communicate. For instance, chimpanzees exposed to experimental language techniques (American Sign Language, specially equipped machines, and plastic tokens) have surprised researchers with their language abilities. Some have learned to use symbols and follow linguistic rules with a sophistication that rivals that of some two-year-olds. Researchers continue to probe the limits of their capabilities. However, a basic difference between human beings and other species exists.

It is the development of the cerebral cortex that sets humans apart from less intelligent

▶❙❙ TeachSource Video 1-1

© 2016 Cengage Learning®

Observing and Monitoring Language Development in Infants: The Importance of Assessment

This video provides an example of a body motion play that is taking place with infants.

1. How long were the infants able to attend to the body play before they started turning away?
2. The babbling of a consonant was demonstrated by a child; do you know which consonant?
3. Did you notice infants imitating teacher actions?
4. Did teachers really understand why toddlers were distressed or did they have to guess?

animals. Our advanced mental capabilities, such as thought, memory, language, mathematics, and complex problem solving, are unique to human beings. Humans have the unique species-specific ability to test hypotheses about the structure of language. They can also develop rules for a particular language and remember and use them to generate appropriate language. Within a few days after birth, human babies recognize familiar faces, voices, and even smells and prefer them to unfamiliar ones.

Infant research has advanced by leaps and bounds to reveal amazing newborn abilities. Long before they can talk, for example, babies remember events and solve problems. They can recognize faces, see colors, hear voices, discriminate speech sounds, and distinguish basic tastes. When you combine the psychological and neurological evidence, it is hard not to conclude that babies are just plain smarter than adults. This is especially true when it comes to learning something new.

Begley (2009) urges teachers to be aware that a child's genes (inherited DNA) in themselves do not determine intelligence or any other complex human trait. An infant or child's appearance and temperament may elicit particular parent and teacher behaviors. These can include the adult's responsiveness and ability to pay attention to, interact with, speak with, and provide intellect-building interaction to the child. **naeyc**

Photo 1-1 "Wow, that is interesting!"

© 2015 Cengage Learning®

1-1 Infant Actions Prompt Caregiver Behaviors **naeyc**

The human face becomes the most significantly important communication factor for the infant, and the facial expressions, which are varied and complex, eventually will influence infant body reactions (interior and exterior). Caregivers strive to understand the infant's state of well-being by interpreting the infant's face and postures, as infants also search faces in the world around them.

Figure 1-1 identifies a number of signals infants use and their probable meanings. Response and intentional behavior become apparent as infants age and gain experience. Infants initially respond with various preprogrammed gestures, such as: smiling, intent and interested

Figure 1-1 Born communicators.

Infant Acts	Probable Meaning
turning head and opening mouth	feeling hungry
quivering lips	adjusting to stimuli
sucking on hand, fist, thumb	calming self, feeling overstimulated
averting eyes	tuning out for a while
turning away	needing to calm down
yawning	feeling tired/stressed
looking wide-eyed	feeling happy
cooing	feeling happy
appearing dull with unfocused eyes	feeling overloaded, needing rest
waving hands	feeling excited
moving tongue in and out	feeling upset/imitating

looking, crying, satisfied sucking, and snuggling. Soon these behaviors are followed by active demanding and attention-seeking patterns in which attempts to attract and solicit caregiver attention rapidly become unmistakable and intentional.

Researchers are studying the roles of facial expressions, gestures, and body movements in human social communication (Photo 1-1). Early expressions that look like smiling may occur minutes after birth and are apparent in the faces of sleeping babies, whose facial expressions seem to constantly change. When studying infant smiling during an infant's first week of life, observers note that infants smile during brief alertness periods, when drowsy, in active and quiet sleep, and randomly when nothing seems to provoke it. Many parents have noticed that smiling most often occurs in deep sleep.

Caregivers observe that infants search for the source of the human voice and face. An infant may become wide-eyed and crane his neck and lift his chin toward the source. His body tension increases as he becomes more focused and somewhat inactive. Most caregivers respond to these signals by picking up the infant and cuddling him. The National Association for the Education of Young Children in a 2013 publication, *Developmentally Appropriate Practice: Focus on Infants and Toddlers*, points out that it is a caregiver's responsibility to cultivate children's (infants' and toddlers') delight in exploring and understanding their world. They believe early childhood should be a time of laughter, love, play, and great fun.

- be aware of opportunities to soothe and touch and engage in some way with an infant.
- pick up and hold an infant gently while providing firm support.
- note an infant's well-being and comfort.
- attempt to interpret an infant's facial and body signals. <

1-1a Definitions

Language, as used in this text, refers to a system of intentional communication and self-expression through sounds, signs (gestures), or symbols that are understandable to others. Language also refers to a symbol-based, rule-governed, multidimensional system that is used to represent the world internally and to others through the process of communication (Pence, Justice, & Wiggins, 2008). The language-development process includes both sending and receiving information. Input (receiving) comes before output (sending); input is organized mentally by an individual long before there is decipherable output.

Communication is a broader term, defined as giving and receiving information, signals, or messages. A person can communicate with or receive communications from animals, infants, or foreign speakers in a variety of ways. Even a whistling teakettle sends a message that someone can understand. Infants appear to be "in tune," focused on the human voice, hours after birth.

Speech is much more complex than simple parroting or primitive social functioning. The power of language enables humans to dominate other life forms. The ability to use language secured our survival by giving us a vehicle to both understand and transmit language and to work cooperatively with others. Language facilitates peaceful solutions between people.

1-2 Influences on Development

A child's ability to communicate involves an integration of body parts and systems allowing hearing, understanding, organizing thoughts, learning, and using language. Most children accomplish the task quickly and easily, but many factors influence the learning of language.

Research suggests that babies instinctively turn their heads to face the source of sound and can remember sounds heard before birth. This has prompted mothers to talk to, sing to, and read classic literature and poetry to the unborn. Research has yet to document evidence of the benefits of these activities.

Of all sounds, nothing attracts and holds the attention of infants as well as the human voice—especially the higher-pitched female voice. "Motherese," a distinct caregiver speech, is discussed later in this chapter. Dietrich, Swingley, and Werker (2007) note:

> Infants begin to acquire their language by learning phonetic categories. At birth, infants seem to distinguish most of the phonetic contrasts used by the world's languages. However, over the first year, this "universal" capacity shifts to a language-specific pattern in which infants retain or improve categorization of native-language sounds but fail to discriminate many non-native sounds. (p. 16030)

Rhythmic sounds and continuous, steady tones soothe some infants. A number of commercial sound-making products that attempt to soothe can be attached to cribs or are imbedded in plush stuffed animals. Most emit a type of static or heartbeat sound or a combination of the two. Too much sound in the infant's environment, especially loud, excessive, or high-volume sounds, may have the opposite effect. Excessive household noise can come from televisions or other sources. Many have described sensory-overload situations when infants try to turn off sensory input by turning away and somehow blocking that which is at the moment overwhelming, whether the stimulus is mechanical or human. This blocking includes falling asleep.

Although hearing ability is not fully developed at birth, newborns can hear moderately loud sounds and can distinguish different pitches. Newborns' auditory systems are better developed than their sight systems, so the importance of language and voices to children's development is evident from the start (Galinsky, 2010). During the last weeks of pregnancy, a child's auditory system becomes ready to receive and remember sounds.

---

language — the systematic, conventional use of sounds, signs, or written symbols in a human society for communication and self-expression. It conveys meaning that is mutually understood.

communication — the giving (sending) and receiving of information, signals, or messages.

Photo 1-2 Sound-making toys attract attention.

Auditory acuity develops swiftly. Infants inhibit motor activity in response to strong auditory stimuli or when listening to the human voice, and attempt to turn toward it. Some researchers see this as an indication that infants are geared to orient their entire bodies toward any signal that arouses interest (Photo 1-2). Infants' body responses to human verbalizations are a rudimentary form of speech development (Figure 1-2).

Sensory-motor development, which involves the use of sense organs and the coordination of motor systems (body muscles and parts), is vital to language acquisition. Sense organs gather information through seeing, hearing, smelling, tasting, and touching. These sense-organ impressions of people, objects, and life encounters are sent to the brain, and each **perception** (impression received through the senses) is recorded and stored, serving as a base for future oral and written language.

Newborns and infants are no longer viewed as passive, unresponsive "mini-humans." Instead, infants are seen as dynamic individuals, preprogrammed to learn, with functioning sensory capacities, motor abilities, and a wondrous built-in curiosity. Families and caregivers can be described as guides who provide opportunity and act *with* newborns, rather than *on* them.

1-2a Beginning Socialization

A child's social and emotional environments play a leading role in both the quality and the quantity of beginning language. Many researchers

Figure 1-2 Auditory perception in infancy.

Age	Appropriate Hearing Behaviors
birth	awakens to loud sounds
	startles, cries, or reacts to noise
	makes sounds
	looks toward then looks away from environmental sounds
0–3 months	turns head to hear parent's or others' speech
	reacts to speech by smiling
	opens mouth as if to imitate adult's speech
	coos and goos
	seems to recognize a familiar voice
	calms down when adult's voice is soothing
	repeats own vocalizations
	seems to listen to and focus on familiar adults' voices
4–6 months	looks toward environmental noise (e.g., barking, vacuum, doorbell, radio, TV)
	attracted to noise-making toys
	babbles consonant-like sounds
	makes wants known with voice
	seems to understand "no"
	reacts to speaker's change of tone of voice
7–12 months	responds to own name
	may say one or more under-standable but not clearly articulated words
	babbles repeated syllables or consonant- and vowel-like sounds
	responds to simple requests
	enjoys playful word games like Peak-a-boo, Pat-a-cake, etc.
	imitates speech sounds frequently
	uses sound making to gain others' attention

auditory — relating to or experienced through hearing.

acuity — how well or clearly one uses the senses; the degree of perceptual sharpness.

sensory-motor development — the control and use of sense organs and the body's muscle structure.

perception — mental awareness of objects and other data gathered through the five senses.

describe communicative neonatal behaviors that evoke tender feelings in adults. Human children have the longest infancy among animals. Our social dependency is crucial to our individual survival and growth. Much learning occurs through contact and interaction with others in family and social settings. Basic attitudes toward life, self, and other people form early, as life's pleasures and pains are experienced. The young child depends on parents and other caregivers to provide what is needed for growth and **equilibrium** (a balance achieved when consistent care is given and needs are satisfied). This side of a child's development has been called the **affective sphere**, referring to the affectionate feelings—or lack of them—shaped through experience with others (Photo 1-3). Most experts believe that each time an infant takes in information through the

Photo 1-4 An infant who feels comfortable and whose needs are satisfied is alert to the world.

© 2015 Cengage Learning®

Photo 1-3 Care and attention in the early years influence language development.

© 2015 Cengage Learning®

senses, the experience is double-coded as both a physical/cognitive reaction and as an emotional reaction to those sensations.

Textbooks often speak indirectly about the infant's need to feel loved consistently, using words like *nurturance*, *closeness*, *caring*, and *commitment*. The primary goal of parents and caregivers should be handling the infant and satisfying the child's physical needs in a way that leads to mutual love and a bond of trust (Photo 1-4). This bond, often called **attachment**, is an event of utmost importance to the infant's progress. A developmental milestone is reached when a baby responds with an emotional reaction of his own by indicating obvious pleasure or joy in the company of a parent or caregiver (Figure 1-3). Attachment is formed through mutual gratification of needs

equilibrium — a balance attained with consistent care and satisfaction of needs that leads to a sense of security and lessens anxiety.

affective sphere — the affectionate feelings (or lack of them) shaped through experience with others.

attachment — a two-way process formed through mutual gratification of needs and reciprocal communication influenced by the infant's growing cognitive abilities. It is sometimes referred to as bonding or a "love affair" relationship.

Figure 1-3 Milestones in developing language behavior.

Infant's Age	Stages of Language Development
before birth	Listens to sounds. Reacts to loud sounds.
at birth	Birth cry is primal, yet individual—vowel-like. Cries to express desires (for food, attention, and so on) or displeasure (pain or discomfort). Makes eating, sucking, and small throaty sounds. Hiccups. Crying becomes more rhythmic and resonant during first days. Shows changes in posture—tense, active, or relaxed.
first days	Half cries become vigorous; whole cries begin to take on depth and range. Coughs and sneezes.
1 month	Three to four vowel sounds apparent. Seems to quiet movements and attend to mother's voice. Eating sounds mirror eagerness. Sighs and gasps. Smiles in sleep.
2–3 months	Coos and makes pleasurable noises (babbling) and blowing and smacking sounds. Most vowel sounds are present. Open vowel-like babbles may begin. Consonant sounds begin, usually the following—*b, d, g, h, l, m, n, p, t*. Markedly less crying. Smiles and squeals and may coo for half a minute. Peers into faces. Adults may recognize distinct variations in cries (i.e., cries that signal fear, tiredness, hunger, pain, and so on). Focuses on mother's face and turns head to her voice. May be frightened by loud or unfamiliar noise. May blow bubbles and move tongue in and out.
4–5 months	Sound play is frequent. Social smiling more pronounced. Can whine to signal boredom. May laugh. Reacts to tone of voice. Seems to listen and enjoy music. Likes adult vocal play and mimicking. Favorite people seem to induce verbalness. Babbles several sounds in one breath. Body gestures signal state of comfort or discomfort. Attracted to sounds. Approaching six months of age, may start to show understanding of words often used in household. Turns head and looks at speaking family members. Consonant sounds more pronounced and frequent.
6–8 months	Increased babbling and sound making; repeats syllables; imitates motions and gestures; uses nonverbal signals; vocalizes all vowel sounds; reduplication of utterances; more distinct intonation. Increases understanding of simple words. Enjoys making noise with toys and household objects. Repeats actions to hear sounds again. May blow toy horn. Delights in rhythmic vocal play interchange, especially those that combine touching and speaking. Twists and protrudes tongue, smacks, and watches mother's mouth and lips intently. May look at picture books for short period or watch children's television programs.
9–10 months	May make kiss sounds. Increasing understanding of words like *no-no*, *mommy*, *daddy*, *ball*, *hat*, and *shoe*. May play Pat-a-cake and wave bye-bye. May hand books to adults for sharing. Uses many body signals and gestures. May start jargonlike strings of sounds, grunts, gurgles, and whines. Listens intently to new sounds. Imitates.
11–14 months	Reacts to an increasing number of words. Speaks first word(s) (usually words with one syllable or repeated syllable). Points to named objects or looks toward named word. Makes sounds and noises with whatever is available. Imitates breathing noises, animal noises (like dog's bark or cat's meow), or environmental noises (like "boom" or train toot). Uses many body signals, especially "pick me up" with arms outstretched and reaching for another's hand, meaning "come with me." May understand as many as 40 to 50 words. At close to 15 months, one word has multiple meanings. Jargonlike strings of verbalness continue. The child's direction of looking gives clues to what the child understands, and the child may have a speaking vocabulary of 10 or more words. Uses first pretend play gestures such as combing hair with a spoon-shaped object, drinking from a pretend cup, pretending to eat an object, and pretending to talk with another on a toy telephone.

and reciprocal communication influenced by the infant's growing cognitive ability. The two-way nature of the attachment process is also referred to as bonding. The infant develops a beginning mental picture of the way people in his life interact with one another in systematic and loving relationships. Bardige (2009) describes early bonding in this way:

> Call it chemistry, natural attraction, or falling in love—babies lure adults from the start, and adults who tune in are easily lured. Bonding begins when parent and baby see each other for the first time—and it's a two-way street. With their large eyes and sweet expressions, babies are as cute as they are helpless. Adults naturally soften in their presence, and soon baby and parent are gazing into each other's eyes and forging a connection. (p. 20)

The special feelings an infant develops for a main caregiver later spread to include a group of beloved family members. If an attachment bond is evident and consistent care continues, the child thrives. Social interaction with an empathic and attuned caregiver plays the major role in the growth and regulation of the child's nervous system, and it helps the infant develop the strength needed to become socially competent (Gould, 2002).

Newborns seem to have an individual preferred level of arousal, a **moderation level**, neither too excited nor too bored. They seek change and stimulation and seem to search out newness. Each human may possess an optimal level of arousal—a state when learning is enhanced and pleasure peaks. Mothers and experienced caregivers try to keep infants at moderate levels of arousal, neither too high nor too low. One can perceive three states during an older infant's waking hours: (1) a state in which everything is all right and life is interesting; (2) a reactive state to something familiar or unfamiliar, when an observer can see an alert "what's that?" or "who's that?" response; and (3) a crying or agitated state. One can observe a switch from feeling safe or happy to feeling unsafe or unhappy in a matter of seconds (Photo 1-5). Loud noises can startle the infant and elicit distressed crying. Infants control input and turn away or turn off by moving their eyes and head or body and by becoming fussy or falling asleep.

Greenspan (1999) urges parents and caregivers of infants to improve their observational skills.

Photo 1-5 With tears still wet, this infant has moved on to observing another feature of his environment.

© 2015 Cengage Learning®

As you sharpen your observational skills and pay attention to the times when your baby seems to have more trouble becoming calm and sharing attention with you, you'll begin to assemble a truly revealing developmental profile of your child. You'll start recognizing whether an unpleasant smell, an unexpected hug or cuddle, or a piercing noise overwhelms your child. Don't forget, though, that even a crying, finicky baby is capable of a lot of looking and listening. You may receive some very expressive looks from your three-month-old when he's got a gas bubble in his stomach! If you rub his back while murmuring sympathetically, he may be encouraged to keep his looking and listening skills even when he's not feeling so good. He may be able to use your soothing sounds and touches to calm him. Practicing under slightly stressful conditions will make him into a stronger looker and listener later on. (p. 201)

an ATTUNED adult would:

- observe closely.
- assess infants' needs and work to satisfy them.
- notice reactions to room sounds—sound intensity or rhythm or other features.
- calm infants when necessary by trying a variety of strategies.
- use an attention-getting voice, voice variety, and/or high-pitched tones. ◂

---

moderation level — an individual preferred state of arousal between bored and excited when learning and pleasure peak.

1-2b Parent and Caregiver Attitudes and Expectations

As mentioned earlier, research indicates that parent and caregiver attitudes and expectations about infants' awareness and sensory abilities may be predictive of developmental growth.

> Certainly there are many possible explanations for developmental differences. But the fact remains: The earlier a mother thought her baby would be aware of the world, the more competent her baby grew to be. Why was this so? It is because the mothers treated the babies according to their expectations. In home visits, researchers observed that mothers who knew more about their infants' abilities were more emotionally and verbally responsive to their babies. They talked to them more. They provided them with more appropriate play materials and initiated more stimulating experiences. And they were more likely to allow their babies to actively explore the world around them. (Acredolo & Goodwyn, 2000, p. 102)

How we perceive children (infants) shapes how we treat them and therefore what experiences we give them (Begley, 2009). Eliot, a neuroscientist and author of *Pink Brain, Blue Brain* (2009), believes there is little solid evidence that sex differences exist in young children's brains. She maintains the sex differences in adult brains are the result of parent actions and expectancies and life experiences in infancy and childhood.

Eliot points out baby boys are often more irritable than girls, making parents less likely to interact with their thought-to-be nonsocial sons. She notes that, at four months, infant boys and girls differ in amount of eye contact, sociability, emotional expressivity, and verbal ability they exhibit. This, she feels, is not an innate trait but a self-fulfilling prophecy arising from an expectation that males are nonverbal and emotionally distant. Eliot entreats educators to not act in ways that make these perceived characteristics come true.

1-2c Growing Intellect

Other important factors related to the child's mental maturity or ability to think are ages, stages, and sequences of increased mental capacity that are closely related to language development. Language skill and intellect seem to be growing independently, at times, with one or the other developing at a faster rate. The relationship of intelligence and language has been a subject of debate for a long time. Most scholars, however, agree that these two areas are closely associated. Researchers suspect the mind's most important faculties are rooted in emotional experiences from very early in life.

The natural curiosity of humans requires discussion here. Curiosity can be defined as a compulsion (drive) to make sense of life's happenings. Over time, exploring, searching, groping, and probing by infants shift from random to controlled movements. At approximately eight months of age, infants begin to possess insatiable appetites for new things—touching, manipulating, and trying to become familiar with everything that attracts them. Increasing motor skill allows greater possibilities for exploration. Skilled caregivers of infants are kept busy trying to provide novelty, variety, and companionship while monitoring safety. The curiosity of infants seems to wane only when they are tired, hungry, or ill, but even then they are learning. Galinsky (2010) notes:

> Some people think babies aren't learning about talking until they start to babble or say actual words, but that couldn't be farther from the truth. (p. 112)

Cultural Ideas Concerning Infant Communication. Cultural and social forces affect language acquisition. They influence young lives through contact with group attitudes, values, and beliefs. Some cultures expect children to look downward when adults speak, showing respect by this action. Other cultures make extensive use of gestures and signaling. Still others seem to have limited vocabularies or believe that engaging in conversations with infants is inappropriate.

1-3 Theories of Language Emergence

Many scholars, philosophers, linguists, and researchers have tried to pinpoint exactly how language is learned. People in major fields of study—human development, linguistics, sociology, psychology, anthropology, speech-language pathology, and animal study (zoology)—have contributed to current theory. The following are major theoretical positions.

1-3a Behaviorist/Environmentalist (or Stimulus-Response) Theory

As parents and main caregivers reward, correct, ignore, or punish the young child's communication, they exert considerable influence over both the quantity and quality of language usage and the child's attitudes toward communicating. Under this theory, the reactions of the people in a child's environment have an important effect on a child's language development. In other words, positive, neutral, and negative reinforcement play a key role in children's emerging communicating behaviors.

The child's sounds and sound combinations are thought to be uttered partly as imitation and partly at random or on impulse, without pattern or meaning. The child's utterances may grow, seem to reach a standstill, or become stifled, depending on feedback from others (Photo 1-6). This theory is attributed to the work of B. F. Skinner, a pioneer researcher in the field of learning theory.

1-3b Maturational (Normative) Theory

This theory represents the position that children are primarily a product of genetic inheritance and that environmental influences are secondary. Children are seen as moving from one predictable stage to another, with "readiness" the precursor of actual learning. This position was

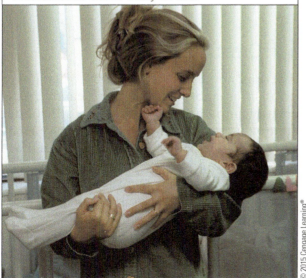

Photo 1-6 Enjoyable conversational interactions occur early in life.

© 2015 Cengage Learning®

widely accepted in the 1960s, when linguists studied children in less-than-desirable circumstances and discovered consistent patterns of language development. Using this theory as a basis for planning instruction for young children includes (1) identifying predictable stages of growth in language abilities and (2) offering appropriate readiness activities to aid children's graduation to the next higher level.

1-3c Predetermined/Innatist Theory

Under this theory, language acquisition is considered innate (a predetermined human capacity). Each new being is believed to possess a mental ability that enables that being to master any language to which he has been exposed from infancy. Chomsky (1968), a linguistic researcher, theorizes that each person has an individual language acquisition device (LAD). Chomsky also theorizes that this device (capacity) has several sets of language system rules (grammar) common to all known languages. As the child lives within a favorable family climate, his perceptions spark a natural and unconscious device, and the child learns the "mother tongue." Imitation and reinforcement are not ruled out as additional influences.

Chomsky notes that two- and three-year-olds can utter understandable, complicated sentences that they have never heard. More current theory also suggests that young children are equipped with an implicit set of internal rules that allows them to transform the sequences of sounds they hear into sequences of ideas—a remarkable thinking skill. Theorists who support this position note the infant's ability to babble sounds and noises used in languages the child has never heard.

1-3d Cognitive-Transactional and Interaction Theory

Under a fourth theory, language acquisition develops from basic social and emotional drives. Children are naturally active, curious, and adaptive and are shaped by transactions with the people in their environment. Language is learned as a means of relating to people. Others provide social and psychological supports that enable the child to be an effective communicator. L. S. Vygotsky's major work, *Thought and Language* (1986), suggests that children's meaningful social exchanges prepare them for uniting thought and speech into "verbal thought." This inner speech development, he theorizes, promotes oral communication and is the basis for written language. Drives stem from a need for love and care, and the need prompts language acquisition.

Children are described as reactors to the human social contact that is so crucial to their survival and well-being. They are natural explorers and investigators. The adult's role is to prepare, create, and provide environments and events. Children's views of the world consist of their mental impressions, which are built as new life events are fit into existing ones or as categories are created for new events. Language is an integral part of living; consequently, children seek to fit language into some pattern that allows understanding. With enough exposure and with functioning sensory receiving systems, children slowly crack the "code" and eventually become fluent speakers. There is a wide acceptance of this theory by early childhood professionals.

Vygotsky (1980) argues that language learning is, in part, biological, but that children need instruction in the zone between their independent language level and the level at which they can operate with adult guidance. The early childhood practitioner adopting Vygotsky's ideas would believe both the teacher's behaviors and the child's active physical manipulation of the environment influence and mediate what and how a young child learns or "constructs" mentally. In other words, without the teacher's social interaction, a child does not learn which characteristics are most important or what to notice and act upon. The teacher's role is to find out through thoughtful conversation, observation, and collaboration what concept a child holds during a jointly experienced happening and to aid the child to further mental construction(s). Consequently, under Vygotskian theory, teachers can affect young children's cognitive processes— the way they think and use language. Other individual and societal features that affect children's thinking are family, other children and people in their lives, and society at large, including language, numerical systems, and technology. Children learn or acquire a mental process by sharing or using it in circumstances with others, and then move forward in an independent manner.

1-3e Constructivist Theory

Proponents of constructivist theory propose that children acquire knowledge by constructing it mentally in interaction with the environment. Children are believed to construct theories (hypothesize) about what they experience and then put happenings into relationships. Later, with more life experiences, revisions occur and more adequate explanations are possible. Constructivists point to young children's speech errors in grammar. Internal rules have been constructed and used for a period of time, but with more exposure to adult speech, these rules change and speech becomes closer to adult forms. The rules young children used previously were their own construct and never modeled by adult speakers.

Planning for language development and early literacy using a constructivist perspective would entail offering wide and varied activities while emphasizing their interrelatedness. Teachers and parents are viewed as being involved jointly with children in literacy activities from birth onward. The overall objective of a constructivist's approach is to promote children's involvement with interesting ideas, problems, and questions. Teachers would also help children put their findings and discoveries into words, notice relationships, and contemplate similarities and differences. Children's hands-on activity is believed to be paired with mental action. A secure, unstressed environment encourages the development of children's ability to cooperate, respect one another, exercise curiosity, gain confidence in themselves, and figure things out on their own. They become autonomous learners.

1-3f Other Theories

There is no all-inclusive theory of language acquisition substantiated by research. Many relationships and mysteries are still under study. Current teaching practices involve many different styles and approaches to language arts activities. Some teachers may prefer using techniques in accord with one particular theory. One goal common among educators is to provide instruction that encourages social and emotional development while also offering activities and opportunities in a warm, language-rich, supportive classroom, center, or home.

Educators believe children should be included in talk and treated as competent language partners.

This text promotes many challenging activities that go beyond simple rote memorization or passive participation. It offers an enriched program of literary experience that encourages children to think and use their abilities to relate and share their thoughts. The text is based on the premise that children's innate curiosity, their desire to understand and give meaning to their world, and their predisposition equip them to learn language. Language growth occurs simultaneously in different-yet-connected language arts areas and all other curriculum offerings. Children continually form, modify, rearrange, and revise internal knowledge as experiences, activities, opportunities, and social interactions are encountered. Children's unconscious mental structuring of experience proceeds in growth spurts and seeming regressions, with development in one area influencing development in another.

1-4 Developmentally Appropriate Practice— Infant Care DAP

The National Association for the Education of Young Children's (NAEYC) 2013 Developmentally Appropriate Practice (DAP) guidelines for infants and toddlers are consistent with available research and have the acceptance and the consensus of most early childhood educators. The practice guidelines address the six areas of particular importance to young children's optimum development. These include: (1) relationships between caregivers and children, (2) environment, (3) exploration and play, (4) routines, (5) reciprocal relationships with families, and (6) policies. These guidelines have tried to capture the major aspects of practice that one might see in an excellent program rather than in a program that has not reached that level. Almost all recommended practice mentioned in the material affects young children's language development in some way. The author suggests teachers in training study the complete publication (NAEYC, 2013).

1-4a Research on Infants' Brain Growth naeyc

Researchers of **neurolinguistics** are making new discoveries about infants' and young children's brain growth and their early experience with their families and caregivers. Although awed by the brain's exceptional malleability, flexibility, and plasticity during early years and its ability to "explode" with new **synapses** (connections), scientists also warn of the effects of abuse or neglect on the child's future brain function. It is estimated that at birth, each neuron in the cerebral cortex has approximately 2,500 synapses, and the number of synapses reaches its peak at two to three years of age, when there are about 15,000 synapses per neuron.

A discipline called cognitive science unites psychology, philosophy, linguistics, computer science, and neuroscience. New technology gives researchers additional tools to study brain energy, volume, blood flow, oxygenation, and cross-sectional images. Neuroscientists have found that throughout the entire process of development, beginning even before birth, the brain is affected by environmental conditions, including the kind of nourishment, care, surroundings, and stimulation an individual receives. The brain is profoundly flexible, sensitive, and plastic and is deeply influenced by events in the outside world. The new developmental research suggests that humans' unique evolutionary trick, their central adaptation, their greatest weapon in the struggle for survival, is precisely their ability to learn while they are babies and to teach when grown-ups (Gopnik et al., 1999).

Early experience has gained additional importance and attention. New scientific research does not direct families to provide special "enriching" experiences to children over and above what they experience in everyday life. It does suggest, however, that a radically deprived environment could cause damage. Gould (2002) reports that various types of unpredictable, traumatic, chaotic, or neglectful environments can physically change the infant's brain by overactivating and/or stressing the brain's neural pathways. According to Gould, these changes may include a change in the child's muscle

---

neurolinguistics — a branch of linguistics that studies the structure and function of the brain in relation to language acquisition, learning, and use.

synapses — gap-like structures over which the axon of one neuron beams a signal to the dendrites of another, forming a connection in the human brain. They affect memory and learning.

tone, profound sleep difficulties, an increased startle response, and significant anxiety. Life experiences are now believed to control both how the infant's brain is "architecturally formed" and how intricate brain circuitry is wired. Infant sight and hearing acuity need to be assessed as early as possible given this new information. If a newborn's hearing disability is diagnosed and treated within six months, the child usually develops normal speech and language on schedule (Spivak, 2000). With new technology, hearing tests are far more accurate and can pinpoint the level of hearing loss in babies who are only a few hours old. (The American Academy of Pediatrics recommends that all infants be examined by six months of age and have regular checkups after age three.)

Infants are also far more sophisticated intellectually than we once believed. Babies, as young as four months old, have advanced powers of deduction and an ability to decipher intricate patterns. They have a strikingly nuanced visual palette, which enables them to notice small differences, especially in faces. This is an ability that adults or older children lose. Until a baby is three months old, he can recognize a scrambled photograph of his mother just as quickly as a photograph in which everything is in the right place.

Older debates about nature (genetic givens) versus nurture (care, experiential stimulations, parental teaching, and so on) are outdated (Figure 1-4). Nature and nurture are inseparably intertwined. Genetics lays out our neurological blueprints, but parents and life experiences wire infants' brain (Raftery, 2009).

Many scientists believe that in the first few years of childhood there are a number of critical or sensitive periods, or "windows," when the brain demands certain types of input. If a child's brain is not stimulated during a specific window of time, consequences occur. For example, researchers posit vision will not be normal if by approximately six months, an infant is not seeing things in the world around him. In neurobiological literature, these special periods are described as "critical periods" or "plastic periods," and they are believed to be one of nature's provisions for humankind to be able to use environmental exposure to change the anatomy of the brain and make it more efficient. A span of time from about nine months of age to roughly five years of age is believed to be a period when a natural human opportunity to acquire new skills and use higher cognition exists. This includes learning a second language. This silent and invisible infant language ability is used when a mother or family is bilingual and converses consistently in both languages around the infant. As the child ages he or she may become a functioning bilingual. Increasingly research is showing that the brains of people who know two or more languages are different from monolinguals. Bilinguals can be better at reasoning, multitasking, and grasping and reconciling conflicting ideas (Kluger, 2013). Kluger believes bilinguals are not smarter, they just have more flexible and resourceful brains.

Explosive language growth takes place during the early years and is scattered throughout the brain, but as early as toddlerhood, a pruning

Figure 1-4 Rethinking the brain.

Old Thinking . . .	New Thinking . . .
How a brain develops depends on the genes you are born with.	How a brain develops hinges on a complex interplay between the genes you are born with and the experiences you have.
The experiences you have before age three have a limited architecture impact on later development.	Early experiences have a decisive impact on the architecture of the brain and on the nature and extent of adult capacities.
A secure relationship with a primary caregiver creates a directly favorable context for early development and learning.	Early interactions do not just create a context; they affect the way the brain is "wired."
Brain development is linear: the brain's capacity to learn and change grows steadily as an infant progresses toward adulthood.	Brain development is nonlinear: there are prime times for acquiring different kinds of knowledge and skills.
A toddler's brain is much less active than the brain of a college student.	By the time children reach age three, their brains are twice as active as those of adults. Activity levels drop during adolescence.

Brain Connection

Brain Researchers' Recommendations

- Providing excellent child care for working parents.
- Talking to babies frequently.
- Cuddling babies and using hands-on parenting.
- Using **parentese**, the high-pitched, vowel-rich, sing-song speech. The way we typically talk to infants—speaking more slowly, enunciating words, pausing between sounds, and varying the pitch of our voice—makes learning language much easier (Galinsky 2010).
- Giving babies freedom to explore within safe limits.

- Providing safe objects to explore and manipulate.
- Giving babies regular eye examinations and interesting visual opportunities.
- Providing loving, stress-reduced care for the child's emotional development.
- Believing an infant's brain is actively seeking meaning in speech sounds and is trying to understand the actions, intentions, and behaviors of others.

or scaling back action happens, making the brain more cognitively and categorically efficient. This is a "use it or lose it" phenomena and is important to bilingual parents who speak a language other than English. They should be continuing to use their native language around their children if they wish them to become true bilinguals. Many educators support programs for early second language learning. Second language learning creates new neural networks that increase the brain's capacity for all sorts of future learning, not just language learning.

Gopnik (2013) notes the newest research suggests infants and toddlers are designed to be especially open to experience and are not encumbered by the executive function of older children's and adults' brains. This makes very young children vividly conscious of every common sight that habit has made invisible to adults. Babies and toddlers are enchanted with the world around them, including things the adult doesn't find the least bit fascinating, like a water bottle, or a butterfly, or the sound of a small horn. Educators and families agree that infant care should be provided by knowledgeable adults who realize that early experiences and opportunities may have long-term developmental consequences (Photo 1-7). Caregivers should also provide rich, language-filled experiences and opportunities and recognize delayed development. Experts describe possible infant learning difficulties related to brain function:

- 0–3 months: Infant does not turn head toward a speaker or try to make vocal sounds.
- 4–6 months: Infant does not respond to *no* or note changes in other's tone of voice. Does

not search for sources of sounds or babble and make consonant-like sounds.

- 7–12 months: Infant does not react to his name; imitate speech sounds, or use actions or sounds to gain attention.

Photo 1-7 Knowledgeable teachers respond with attention and warmth.

© 2015 Cengage Learning®

---

parentese — a high-pitched, rhythmic, singsong, crooning style of speech. It is also known as motherese or baby talk.

Greenspan's (1999) observations suggest that certain kinds of emotional nurturing propel infants and young children to intellectual and emotional health and that affective experience helps them master a variety of cognitive tasks. He states:

> As a baby's experience grows, sensory impressions become increasingly tied to feelings. It is the **dual coding** of experience that is the key to understanding how emotions organize intellectual capacities and indeed create the sense of self. (p. 78)

Coles (2004), a reviewer of brain research, also points out that growing evidence suggests that thinking is an inseparable interaction of both **cognition** and emotion (feelings, desires, enthusiasms, antipathies, etc.). Interactive emotional exchanges with caregivers and their reciprocal quality are increasingly viewed as being critical to human infants' growth and development, including language development. Early childhood caregivers realize:

> . . . the adult a baby will someday become is the end result of the thousands of times a parent or caregiver comforted her when she cried, helped her to play well with others in the sandbox and sang just one more lullaby before she finally closed her eyes for the night. Each of these seemingly simple acts gently shapes a child's growing sense of self. (Kantrowitz, 2000, p. 6)

The importance of environmental feedback is considerable. Feedback by caregivers includes giving words of approval and providing caregiver attention, and it promotes the emotional satisfaction an infant feels when he is successful in doing something he set out to do.

Some developers of infant materials, equipment, books, and services suggest they can speed brain development. Families may feel they need to find ways to accelerate early childhood experiences and believe that it is up to them to find products and services. Most educators believe this is unnecessary and suggest spending time with infants and providing natural parenting, such as playing, engaging in reciprocal talk, and simply putting plastic mixing bowls on the floor. Honig (2007) concurs and points out that when an infant shakes a bell or pulls a toy on a string to make it move, he is delightedly learning he can get a specific effect. She notes scientists use these same strategies in their laboratories every day.

1-5 Communicative Abilities in Infancy

COMMON CORE

Newborns quickly make their needs known. They cry and their parents or caregivers respond. Adults feed, hold, and keep infants warm and dry. The sounds of footsteps or voices or a caring touch often stops infants' crying. Babies learn to anticipate. The sense perceptions they receive begin to be connected to stored impressions of the past.

Infants are very powerful in shaping relationships with significant caregivers. They are a wonderful combination of development, potential development, and cognitive flexibility. An infant can perceive from caregivers' behavior a willingness to learn from the infant and respond to his patterns of behavior and rhythms of hunger. This is accomplished by a caregiver's close observation of the infant's vocal and body clues, which indicate the child's state of being. At some point, the caregiver notices that a pattern of mutual gazing is established. Then a type of proto-conversation begins with caregiver vocalizations followed by infant response and noisemaking. Two important developmental tasks that confront infants are: learning to regulate and calm themselves, and learning to interact and "play" with caregivers. The first may be difficult for some infants, but the second seems to come naturally.

The infant is a noisemaker from birth. The child's repertoire includes sucking noises, lip smacking, sneezes, coughs, hiccups, and, of course, different types of cries. As an infant grows, he makes vocal noises, such as **cooing** after feeding. During feeding, slurping and guzzling sounds indicate eagerness and pleasure. Cooing seems to be related to a child's comfort and satisfaction. Cooing consists of relaxed, low-pitched vowel sounds that are made in an open-mouthed way; for example, *e* (as in see), *e* (get), *a* (at), *ah*, and *o, oo, ooo*. The infant appears to be in control of this sound making. Discomfort, by comparison, produces consonant sounds, made in a tense manner with the lips partly closed and

---

dual coding — the belief that infants' experiences and emotions influence cognition.

cognition — the process that creates mental images, concepts, and operations.

cooing — an early stage during the prelinguistic period in which vowel sounds are repeated, particularly the *u-u-u* sound.

the tongue and the ridge of the upper or lower jaw constricting airflow.

Families who attend to infant crying promptly and who believe that crying stems from legitimate needs rather than attempts to control, tend to produce contented, trusting infants. Advice for families of colicky babies consists of holding and carrying the infant more frequently in an effort to soothe. Infants differ in numerous ways from the moment of birth. In speaking to parents about the unique differences in infants, Greenspan (1999) notes the following:

> For most babies, swaddling (gently but firmly bundling the baby's arms and legs in a receiving blanket wrapped around their bodies) is soothing. Other babies enjoy a body massage in which their limbs are gently flexed and extended.
>
> Up until recently, scientists assumed that all human beings experienced sensations in similar ways. We now know that individuals perceive the same stimulus very differently. Your feathery touch could feel tickly and irritating on your newborn's skin, while another baby might take delight in the same caress. (p. 91)

The individual pace of development varies. Whether an infant reaches developmental milestones on the early or late side of normal seems to bear little relation to either cognitive skills or future proficiency (Raymond, 2000). However, in most cases, milestones in language development are reached at about the same age and in a recognizable sequence (Figure 1-5 and Photo 1-8).

Babies learn quickly that communicating is worthwhile because it results in action on the part of another. Greenspan (1999) warns that unless a child masters the level we call two-way intentional communication, normally achieved by an eight-month-old infant, the child's language, cognitive, and social patterns ultimately develop in an idiosyncratic, piecemeal, disorganized manner. There is a high degree of relationship between a caregiver's responsiveness and a child's language competence. By 9 to 18 months of age, the more responsive mothers promoted greater language facility and growth.

Infants quickly recognize subtle differences in sounds. This helps infants to calm down and pay attention—in other words, to listen. Infants move their arms and legs in synchrony to the rhythms of human speech. Random noises, tapping sounds, and disconnected vowel sounds do not produce this behavior.

Figure 1-5 Examples of the typical order of emergence of types of nonword vocalizations in the first year.

Age	Nonword Vocalizations
newborn	cries
1–3 months	makes cooing sounds in response to speech (oo, goo) laughs cries in different ways when hungry, angry, or hurt makes more speechlike sounds in response to speech
4–6 months	plays with some sounds, usually single syllables (e.g., ba, ga)
6–8 months	babbles with duplicated sounds (e.g., bababa) attempts to imitate some sounds
8–12 months	babbles with consonant or vowel changes (e.g., badaga, babu) babbles with sentencelike intonation (expressive jargon/conversational babble) produces protowords

Photo 1-8 Infants often babble to toys: especially ones that make noise.

There is a difference between people in an infant's life. Some talk and touch. Others show delight. Some pause after speaking and seem to wait for a response. The child either "locks on" to the conversationalist, focusing totally, or breaks eye contact and looks away. It is almost as though the infant controls what he wants to receive. Of course, hunger, tiredness, and other factors also influence this behavior and may stop the child's interest in being social.

The special people in the infant's life adopt observable behaviors when "speaking" to him or her, just as the infant seems to react in special ways to their attention. Talking to babies differs from other adult speech in that the lyric or musical quality of speech seems more important than words. Infants listening to these long, drawn-out vowels experience an increase in heart rate. At the same time, it speeds up the brain's ability to recognize connections between words and objects. Educators believe "baby-talk" speech modifications can vary among cultures. The attention-holding ability of this type of adult speech may help the infant become aware of the linguistic function of vocalizations (Sachs, 1997). Mothers sometimes raise voice pitch to a falsetto, shorten sentences, simplify syntax and vocabulary, use nonsense sounds, use a slower tempo, and use longer pauses than in adult conversations. They maintain prolonged eye contact during playful interchanges. Most infants are attracted to high-pitched voices, but a few infants seem to overreact and prefer lower speech sounds. Infants can pick up higher-pitched sounds better than lower-frequency ones, which may be why they are entranced by the high-pitched coos and singsong nature of parent talk. Parents' voices when talking to their infants can be described as playful, animated, warm, and perhaps giddy. Falk (2004) proposes that parent talk forms a scaffold for infants' language acquisition, and caregivers often use vocal means to placate and reassure. They attempt to control their infant's state of well-being. Falk notes that vowels are lingered over, phrases are repeated, and questions carry exaggerated inflections.

A mutual readiness to respond to each other appears built-in to warm relationships. The infant learns that eye contact can hold and maintain attention and that looking away usually terminates both verbal and nonverbal episodes. They learn a great deal about language before they ever say a word. Most of what they learn at a very early age involves the sound system of language.

1-5a Crying

Crying is one of the infant's primary methods of communication. Cries can be weak or hearty, and they provide clues to the infant's general health. Crying may be the only way an infant can affect his situation of need or discomfort. Infants begin early in life to control the emotional content of their cries. Many parents believe they can recognize different types of crying, such as sleepy, frightened, hungry, and so on, especially if infant body actions are observed concurrently. Researchers have discovered that parents do indeed accurately infer the intensity of an infant's emotional state from the sound of the cry itself, even if the baby is not visually observed. Even adults inexperienced with infants seem to possess this ability.

Child development specialists advise adult alertness and responsiveness to minimize crying. Crying will take place in the best of circumstances, and research has indicated that there are some positive aspects of crying, including stress reduction, elimination of toxin in tears, and reestablishment of physical and emotional balance. However, although crying may have its benefits, it is not recommended that infants be left to cry, but rather that adults continue to attempt to soothe and satisfy infants' needs. Narvaez (2012) believes the "cry it out" strategy adopted by some parents and sometimes endorsed by infant pediatricians can have negative effects on a child's moral and cognitive development. She suggests the practice can threaten the child's sense of safety and security. Stepping in to comfort a crying infant every two or so minutes allows a child a period to calm down. This has been called the "every few minutes approach." It may result in reducing stress that allows sleep—a preferred alternative to crying it out. Most caregivers check for conditions that might cause discomfort or distress periodically as a preventative measure.

A baby's crying may cause strong feelings in some adults, including anger, frustration, irritation, guilt, and rejection. Successful attempts at soothing the infant and stopping the crying give the infant and the caregiver satisfaction, feelings of competence, and a possible sense of pleasure.

Photo 1-9 A child may fall asleep while being soothed.

© 2015 Cengage Learning®

When out-of-sorts infants cease crying, alertness, attentiveness, and visual scanning usually happen and/or the infants fall asleep (Photo 1-9). Infant-caregiver interaction has been described as a rhythmic drama, a reciprocal dance, and a family melody. All of these touch on the beauty and coordination of sound-filled moments between the adult and child.

Emotions are expressed frequently in crying as the infant nears his first birthday. Fear, frustration, uneasiness with novelty or newness, separation from loved ones, and other strong emotions can provoke crying through childhood and beyond. Infant care providers in group programs engage in frank staff discussions concerning infant crying. Normal and natural staff feelings concerning crying need to be openly discussed so that strategies can be devised in the best interests of both the infants and the staff members. Many techniques exist to minimize crying and also to monitor the crying

levels of individual infants so that health or developmental problems can be spotted quickly.

1-5b Smiling and Laughing

True smiling can occur before six months of age and is usually associated with a caretaker's facial, auditory, or motor stimuli. Laughter may occur as early as four months of age and is believed to be a good predictor of cognitive growth. Some developmental experts suggest that the earlier the baby laughs, the higher the baby's developmental level is. In the second half of the first year, infants smile at more complex social and visual items. Laughter at this age may be full of squeals, howls, hoots, giggles, and grins. Incongruity may be noticed by the infant, and laughter follows. If an infant laughs when he sees the family dog in the driver's seat with its paws on the wheel, the child may be showing recognition of incongruity—the child has learned something about car drivers.

Responsive caregivers promote infant smiling. Ainsworth and Bell (1972) concluded that **responsive mothers**, those who are alert in caring for the infants' needs, had babies who cried less frequently and had a wider range of different modes of communication (Photo 1-10). These responsive mothers created a balance between showing attention and affording the infant autonomy (offering a choice of action within safe bounds) when the infant became mobile. They also provided body contact and involved themselves playfully at times.

Photo 1-10 A quick adult response to crying is appropriate and recommended.

© 2015 Cengage Learning®

responsive mothers — mothers who are alert and timely in responding to and giving attention to infants' needs and communications.

an **ATTUNED** adult:

- notices infant reactions to auditory stimuli.
- is aware of infant preferences.
- notices if an infant has an attachment to a caregiver and/or expresses pleasure in another's company.
- seeks to help the infant maintain a state of balance and a comfort level.
- is attentive and consistent in recognizing and satisfying a child's needs.
- has sufficient energy and seeks to engage frequently with an infant.
- monitors an infant's health and safety and observes closely.
- provides a variety of experience and sensory materials for exploration.
- uses words to accompany child and adult actions.
- records milestones in development and uses them to guide caregiver interactions.
- is playful, gives attention, and provides feedback to an infant's efforts. <

1-5c Infant Imitation and Babbling

Acredolo and Goodwyn (2000) suggest that infants as young as one or two days old may imitate parent head movements and facial behaviors; they explain:

> This inborn push to mimic others gets babies into a problem-solving mode from the very beginning. And as we mentioned earlier, babies thrive on problem solving. The payoff is such a pleasant one—Dad sticks around to interact some more, and baby is amused. Imitation is such an important developmental component that Mother Nature has not left it up to chance. She has made sure that each of us begins life's journey with a necessary tool in hand. (p. 185)

Early random sound making is often called **babbling**. Infants the world over babble sounds they have not heard and that they will not use in their native language. This has been taken to mean that each infant has the potential to master any world language. Close inspection shows repetitive sounds and "practice sessions" present. Babbling starts at about the fourth to sixth month and continues in some children through the toddler period. However, a peak in babbling is usually reached between 9 and 12 months. Periods before the first words are spoken are marked by a type of babbling that repeats syllables, as in *dadadada*. This is called **echolalia**. Infants seem to echo themselves and others. Babbling behavior overlaps the stages of making one and two or more words, and may end for some children at about 18 months of age.

Infants who are deaf also babble. In play sessions, they will babble for longer periods without hearing either adult sound or their own sounds, as long as they can see the adult responding. However, these children stop babbling at an earlier age than do hearing children. It is not clearly understood why babbling occurs, either in hearing or hearing-impaired children, but it is thought that babbling gives the child the opportunity to use and control the mouth, throat, and lung muscles. Researchers trying to explain babbling suggest that infants are not just exercising or playing with their vocal apparatus. Instead, they may be trying out and attempting to control their lips, tongues, mouths, and jaws to produce certain sounds. A child's babbling amuses and motivates the child, acting as a stimulus that adds variety to the child's existence. Meltzoff et al. (2009) suggest the language background of the home is continually being collected, digested, sorted, and analyzed by the infant's computer-like brain. Consequently, it is forming patterns of sounds that may be practiced or reproduced during later babbling periods.

In time, the child increasingly articulates clear, distinct vowel-like, consonant-like, and syllabic sounds. *Ba* and *da* are acquired early because they are easy to produce, whereas *el* and *ar* are acquired late because they require a sophisticated ability to articulate sounds. Although babbling includes a wide range of sounds, as children grow older, they narrow the range and begin to focus on the familiar language of the family. Other sounds are gradually discarded.

Physical contact continues to be important. Touching, holding, rocking, and engaging in other types of physical contact bring a sense of security and a chance to respond through sound making. The cooing and babbling sounds infants make may also draw caregivers into "conversations." Babies learn to wait for the adult's response after they have vocalized, and both infants and adults are constantly influencing

---

babbling — an early language stage in sound production in which an infant engages in vocal play with vowel and consonant sounds, including some sounds not found in his or her language environment.

echolalia — a characteristic of the babbling period. The child repeats (echoes) the same sounds over and over.

Photo 1-11 Infants' vocal and playful interactions with caregivers are the precursors of conversation.

one another in establishing conversation-like vocal interactions (Photo 1-11).

Bardige (2008) points out babies need to hear everyday language during their babbling period. She suggests adults talk about what the baby and they themselves are doing and continue to make language part of their daily care as they bathe, change, feed, play, and soothe the infant.

The active receiving of perceptions is encouraged by warm, loving parents who share a close relationship. Secure children respond more readily to the world around them. Children who lack social and physical contact or those who live in insecure home environments fall behind in both the number and range of sounds made; differences start showing at about six months of age. Sound imitation eventually becomes syllable imitation, and short words are spoken near the end of the child's first year.

1-5d Stages of Vocalization

There is a definite progression of infant production and vocalization ability that early educators focusing on their development notice. Progress may include a blending of steps as infants move forward. The reflective vocalizations of infants during their first few months include sound making such as fussing, crying, burping, miscellaneous sounds, and a few vowel like sounds that meld into a stage of sound production that indicates a mellowing during comfort and feeding satisfaction situations. This can include cooing,

giggles, and laughs. In the next few months a wider repertoire of vocalization emerges. It is full of voice changes indicating a playful nature exists. Loud and soft sounds happen during the day along with squeals of delight and what seems to be vowel – making episodes. This is typical in the months before and infants' first half year of age.

The appearance of babbling takes hold next. This period produces an increase in the variety of sound making and includes sequences of both consonant and vowel blended episodes. Parents and educators may believe they recognize a few almost words in infants sound making. Deaf infants can appear to be limited in their babbling efforts while infants with normal hearing ability may be reinforced by the vocal enjoyment they share with others and increase babbling. Real words, though few at first, begin to appear.

1-5e A Shared Developmental Milestone

Almost immediately after birth, infants display a critical cognitive skill. It is their ability to focus their attention on the features of their environment, especially to voices and sounds. By the last half of the first year, children begin to take part in a new type of interaction with their caretakers. They share attention given to objects with another person by following that individual's gaze or pointing, responding to the individual's emotional reaction to an event, and imitating that person's object-directed actions (Nelson & Shaw, 2002). This gives adults who notice this behavior a chance to pair words with objects, actions, events, and people. First words or sounds are usually simple associates of objects or situations. The infant simply voices a shared reference. Nelson and Shaw note that the leap from shared reference associations to meaningful language requires the child to integrate skills with communicative patterns and conceptual knowledge. The child is then standing on a first communicative step.

1-5f Infant Signing (Signaling) and Beginning Understanding

At a few months of age some infants realize that some of their simple actions cause caregivers to focus their attention on them. Waving arms, kicking legs, and banging objects may promote adult reactions, such as speaking to them. During the latter part of the first year, alert caregivers notice hand and body positions that suggest the child is attempting to communicate. Researchers suggest that parents pair words with easy-to-do gestures. At the age of one year, children cannot gain enough mastery over their tongues to form many words. Gesturing with their fingers and hands is simpler. For example, infants as young as seven months may bang on a window to get a family cat's attention or reach out, motion, or crawl toward something or someone they want. The use of signs continues until the child's ability to talk takes off. Some educators believe **signing** may spark other critical thinking skills and lead to better intelligence quotient (IQ) scores when testing begins. This has led to overeager commercial advertisers making unproven assertions and claims concerning signings' present and future educational advantages. Most educators believe that promoting the practice isn't harmful, in fact it seems to give infants confidence and satisfaction. They recognize that many parents are enthusiastic proponents. Only further research can substantiate signing benefits.

Toward the end of the child's first year, pointing becomes goal oriented—the infant will point to a desired object. As time progresses, more and more infant body signaling takes place. Signals are used over and over, and a type of sign language communication emerges. It can be a "signal and sound system" understood by caregivers. When caregivers respond appropriately, the infant easily progresses to word use and verbal aptitude. Signing by infants and young toddlers is believed to stimulate brain development, particularly brain areas involved in language, memory, and concept development.

Some studies of communication gestures note that infants with more advanced gestures have larger vocabularies and that girls seem slightly more advanced in gesturing than do boys. (This paragraph offered an answer to one of the questions in this chapter's beginning vignette. The next paragraph answers another.)

Well-meaning parents or caregivers may choose not to respond to infant gestures and signals, thinking this will accelerate or force the use of words. The opposite is thought to be true. Alert parents who try to read and receive signals give their infant the message that communication leads to fulfillment of wishes. Successful signaling becomes a form of language—a precursor of verbal signals (words). Some experts believe baby signers by age two are better at both expressing themselves and understanding others' speech and, on average, have slightly larger vocabularies than their peers who do not sign. Sitting down at the child's level at times when the infant is crawling from one piece of furniture to another may facilitate the adult's ability to pick up on signaling. Watching the infant's eyes and the direction the infant's head turns gives clues. Infants about eight months old seem fascinated with the adult's sound-making ability. They often turn to look at the adult's lips or want to touch the adult's mouth.

Early childhood educators employed by infant-toddler centers need to know their center's position regarding expected educator behaviors. Most centers expect educators to actively pair words with adult or child signs, encourage child use of signs, and learn and respond to each child's individual sign language.

Most babies get some idea of the meaning of a few words at about six to nine months. At about 10 months of age, some infants start to respond to spoken word clues. Somewhere between eight and 13 months, the child's communication, whether vocal or a type of gesture, becomes intentional. The child makes a connection between his behavior and the parent's or early childhood educator's response (Photo 1-12). Children seem to recognize a prime caregiver's change of voice tone and also that some of their caregiver's nonverbal behaviors may communicate a message. Infants are becoming aware of adult actions that may affect them. A game such as Pat-a-cake may start the baby clapping, and "bye-bye" or Peek-a-boo brings about other imitations of earlier play activities with the parents. The child's language is called passive at this stage, for he primarily receives (or is receptive). Speaking attempts will soon become active (or expressive). Vocabulary provides a small portal through which adults can gauge a little

---

signing — a body positioning, sound, action, gesture, or combination of these undertaken by an infant in an effort to communicate a need, desire, or message.

Photo 1-12 This infant has learned to respond to the adult's pointing gestures.

of what the child knows. There is a point at which children expand nonverbal signals to true language.

Older infants still communicate with their caregivers through many nonverbal actions; one common way is by holding up their arms, which most often means, "I want to be picked up." Other actions include facial expression, voice tone, voice volume, posture, and gestures such as "locking in" by pointing fingers and toes at attention-getting people and events.

Although infants at this stage can respond to words and changes in caregivers' facial expressions, voice tone, and voice volume, actions and gestures also carry feelings and messages important to infants' well-being. Understanding the tone of caregivers' speech comes before understanding the words used.

Gopnik et al. (1999) describe what happens when infants are about one year old.

> One-year-old babies know that they will see something by looking where other people point; they know what they should do to something by watching what other people do; they know how they should feel about something by seeing how other people feel. (p. 243)

Research suggests infants at 20 months have what Galinsky (2010) calls *language sense*. This means they can detect statistical patterns in which speech sounds go together in their native language (or languages) to determine the beginnings and endings of words (p. 2). She also suggests new research theorizes another infant sense, *people sense*, exists in infancy as infants focus on people's intentions rather than seeing what people do as random movements.

1-5g First Words

Before an understandable, close approximation of a word is uttered, the child's physical organs need to function in a delicate unison and the child must reach a certain level of mental maturity. Close to 12 months of age, the speech centers of the brain have developed the capacity to enable the infant to produce his first word—a great accomplishment and milestone. The child's respiratory system supplies the necessary energy. As the breath is exhaled, sounds and speech are formed with the upward movement of air. The larynx's vibrating folds produce voice (called **phonation**). The larynx, mouth, and nose influence the child's voice quality (termed **resonation**). A last modification of the breath stream is **articulation**—a final formation done through molding, shaping, stopping, and releasing voiced and other-than-voiced sounds that reflect language heard in the child's environment.

Repetition of syllables such as *ma, da,* and *ba* in a child's babbling occurs toward the end of the first year. If *mama* or *dada* or a close copy is said, parents and caregivers show attention and joy. Language, especially in the area of speech development, is a two-way process; reaction is an important feedback to action.

The term *protoword* is often used for the invented words a child may use during the transition from prespeech to speech. During this transition, a child has acquired the difficult concept that sounds have meaning and is unclear only about the fact that one is supposed to find out what words exist instead of making them up.

Generally, first words are nouns or proper names of foods, animals, or toys; vocabulary may also include *gone, there, uh-oh, more,* and *dat* ("what's that?"). Greetings, farewells, or other social phrases, such as *peek-a-boo,* are also among the first recognizable words.

Monolingual (one-language) children utter their first words at approximately 11 months of age; the range is from about 9 months to about 16 months. At about a year and a half, the child learns approximately one new word every three days. Most experts believe that talking alone shows no link to mental development at age two, but a child's comprehension of words is paramount. Experts conclude that there is little scientific evidence to suggest that late talkers will become less fluent than early talkers. Some children acquire large numbers of object names in their first 50 to 100 words. The first spoken words usually contain *p, b, t, d, m,* and *n* (front of the mouth consonants), which require the least use of the tongue and air control. They are shortened versions, such as *da* for "daddy," *beh* for "bed," and *up* for "cup." When two-syllable words are attempted, they are often strung together using the same syllable sound, as in *dada* or *beebee.* If the second syllable is voiced,

the child's reproduction of the sound may come out as *dodee* for "doggy" or *papee* for "potty."

At this stage, words tend to be segments of wider happenings in the child's life. A child's word *ba* may represent a favorite, often-used toy (such as a ball). As the child grows in experience, any round object seen in the grocery store, for instance, will also be recognized and called *ba.* This phenomenon has been termed *over-extension.* The child has embraced "everything round," which is a much broader meaning for ball than the adult definition of the word.

Following is a list of words frequently understood between 8 and 12 months of age: *mommy, daddy, bye-bye, baby, shoe, ball, cookie, juice, bottle, no-no,* and the child's own name and names of family members.

A child finds that words can open many doors. They help the child get things and cause caregivers to act in many ways. Vocabulary quickly grows from the names of objects to words that refer to actions. This slowly decreases the child's dependence on context (a specific location and situation) for communication and gradually increases the child's reliance on words—the tools of abstract thought. Children learn very quickly that words not only name things and elicit action on another's part but also convey comments and express individual attitudes and feelings.

an **ATTUNED** adult:

- nurtures infant curiosity.
- uses words and gestures in communication.
- builds a sign language relationship with infants.
- tries to judge the intensity of infants' emotions.
- offers a choice of child actions and explorations within safe limits.
- responds to and promotes reciprocal communication.
- pairs words with actions and objects.
- observes the direction of infants' gazes for clues to infants' moment to moment interests.
- continues to be at eye level when possible.
- expects and recognizes invented words.
- encourages first word use by repeating word back to child and connecting the child's word to objects or actions as appropriate.
- guesses frequently about a child's meaning in communication.
- works toward a child's success at using words to fulfill his desires, needs, and interests. <

---

phonation — exhaled air passes the larynx's vibrating folds and produces "voice."

resonation — amplification of laryngeal sounds using cavities of the mouth, nose, sinuses, and pharynx.

articulation — the adjustments and movements of the muscles of the mouth and jaw involved in producing clear oral communication.

Figure 1-6 Approximate frequency of child utterances from 6 to 12 months.

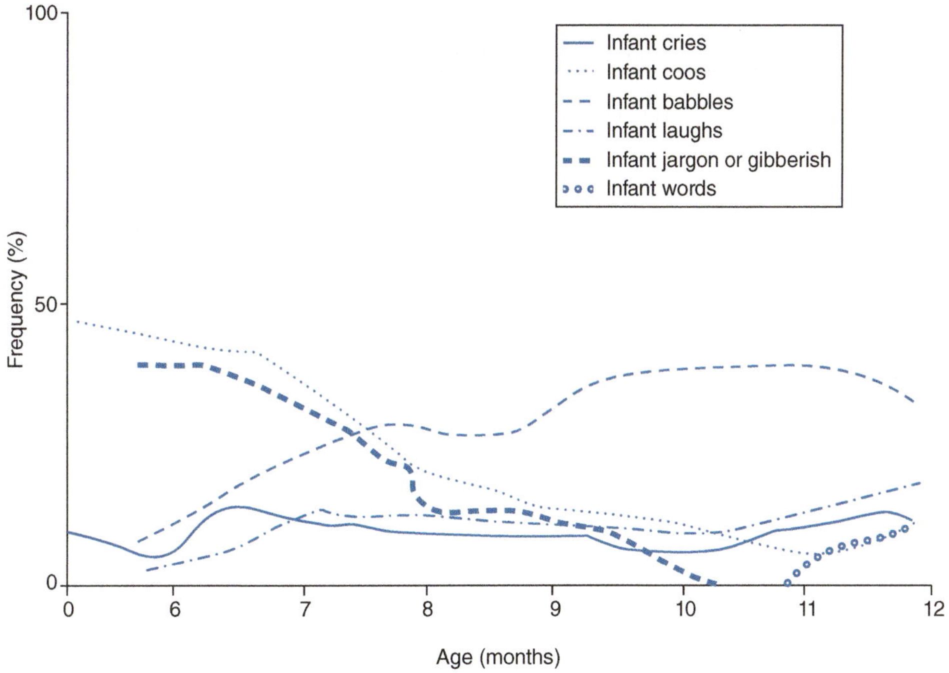

Toddlerhood begins, and the child eagerly names things and seeks names for others. The child's single words accompanied by gestures, motions, and intonations are called **holophrases**. They usually represent a whole idea or sentence.

While the child is learning to walk, speech may briefly take a backseat to developing motor skill. At this time, the child may listen more intently to what others are saying. The slow-paced learning of new words (Figure 1-6) is followed by a period of rapid growth. The child pauses briefly, listening, digesting, and gathering forces to embark on the great adventure of becoming a fluent speaker.

1-6 Implications for Infant Center Staff Members

The importance of understanding the responsive, reciprocal nature of optimal care-giving in group infant centers cannot be overestimated. The soothing, calming, swaddling, rocking, sympathizing, and responding behaviors of infant care specialists help infants maintain a sense of security and a relaxed state, calmness, and equilibrium.

The emotional well-being of infants has been given increased attention as research on infant development uncovers its importance. Physician Chet Johnson (2005) points out:

The research shows how powerful emotional well-being is to a child's future health. A baby who fails to meet certain key "emotional milestones" may have trouble learning to speak, read, and later, do well in school. By reading emotional responses, doctors have begun to discover ways to tell if a baby as young as three months is showing early signs of possible psychological disorders, including depression, anxiety, learning disabilities and perhaps autism. Instead of just asking if they're crawling or sitting we're asking more questions about how they share their world with their caregivers. (p. 35)

See Figure 1-7 for infants' emotional milestones.

At about four months, babies begin to gaze in the direction in which caregivers are looking. Caregivers are able to follow the line of vision of babies as well. Well-trained caregivers will naturally comment and offer language labels and a running commentary. This process is known as *joint attentional focus*. When adults know that the infant does not yet understand language,

---

holophrases — the expression of a whole idea in a single word. They are often found in the speech of children at about 12 to 18 months of age.

Figure 1-7 Emotional milestones and social skill characteristics.

Age	Emotional/Social Characteristics
Birth to around 3–4 months	At birth, the infant is able to feel fear and contentment and is self-absorbed. During first three to four months, infant becomes aware of the environment around him and is attentive and interested; seems able to calm self at times; develops deliberate responses; focuses on the faces of people and smiles at them; eyes may widen in anticipation; may react to strong scents or odors; has a developing sense of security; holding and touching may reduce stress, and rhythmic motion may soothe; may enjoy swaddling; pays attention and reacts to sounds (some infants are oversensitive to some types of sounds). Reacts to visual cues, especially from care provider's face.
Around 5–6 or more months	Displays emotions such as surprise, joy, and frustration. Falls in love with care provider; beams with delight at times; able to see the pattern formed by features on care provider's face; smiles in recognition; may display sorrow and annoyance; builds a stronger relationship with primary care provider; begins to realize he can make things happen; is comforted by physical closeness; develops feelings of being loved, valued, and esteemed by others; easy to tell when infant is happy; sense of self is a reflection of care provider's emotional interactions with infant; may experience jealousy.
Around 10 or more months	Initiates two-way communication; notices where care provider looks and often follows by also looking; tries to catch care provider's eye and gives physical cues to others to obtain a desired action, such as being held; may use signs and signals to make things happen; may respond to rhythm with rhythmic movements; expects his action will prompt a reaction; may mimic gestures; may express fear, anger, anticipation, caution, and surprise with strangers; responds to name, words, and sounds, and attempts to imitate them; Is curious and perhaps assertive and negative at times; May experience a sense of loss at something removed; May show fear if care provider looks angry, frowns, or stares (not recommended). Seeks pleasure and enjoys stimulating self (for example, touching toes and participating in adult-infant games that involve moving or touching body parts, such as "This Little Piggy." Note: This is not intended to be a complete inventory of emotional milestones; research in identifying infant emotional development and capacity is still in its infancy. Notice social skill and emotional response is intertwined and dependent on environmental and human experience.

most adults behave as if the child's response is a turn in the conversation. Adult caregivers need to read both nonverbal and vocalized cues and react appropriately (Photo 1-13). They need to be attentive and loving. Learning to read each other's signals is basic to the quality of the relationship. Liberal amounts of touching, holding, smiling, and looking promote language and the child's overall sense that the world around him is both safe and fascinating. Recognizing the child's individuality, reading nonverbal behaviors, and reacting with purposeful actions are all expected of professional infant specialists, as is noticing activity level, mood, distress threshold, rhythms of the body, intensity, sense of adventure, distractibility, adaptability, and attention span.

There are many skills that well-trained caregivers possess, beginning with holding the infant firmly yet gently and making soft, gentle sounds while moving smoothly and holding the infant close. Gillespie and Hunter (2011) suggest caregivers' laughter helps children form connections and signal a safe and loving environment. Leong and Bodrova (2012) note that as infant educators interact and react to infant's growing communication ability, emotional bonds form. Educators, consequently, prepare infants to learn from them. Adults in early childhood centers become play partners and perhaps become an infant's first play mentor other than their family members. Other caregiver skills are identified in the following list.

Photo 1-13 It is easy to tell these infants are focused and eager activity participants.

© 2016 Cengage Learning®

an **ATTUNED** adult:

- talks in a pleasant, soothing voice; uses simple language; and makes frequent eye contact.
- emphasizes and expects two-way "conversation"; hesitates; and pauses for an infant response.
- makes a game out of the infant's smiles, sounds, and movements when the infant is responsive.
- speaks clearly.
- explains what is happening and what will happen next.
- is consistently attentive.
- does not interrupt the infant's vocal play, jargon, or self-communication.
- engages in word play, rhyme, chants, and fun-to-say short expressions.
- is an animated speaker and a responsive companion.
- may, with an older infant, attempt to offer simple finger plays.
- plans real and concrete participatory activities with textures, sights, and sounds.
- encourages sound making and provides noisemaking and musical toys.
- labels objects, happenings, actions, and emotions.
- uses highly intonated speech that may be high pitched at times with very young infants.
- speaks distinctly with clear enunciation to help children identify phonemes.
- emphasizes, at times, one word in a sentence.
- uses repetition but avoids overdoing it.
- gives feedback by responding with both words and actions.
- creates and pursues game-like strategies and techniques.
- serves as a co-explorer. <

Being playful and initiating singing conversations with infants can be enjoyable and may lay the foundation for later musical activities. Both recorded and live musical sounds are part of an auditory-rich environment for infants. For identified early childhood goals and additional caregiver activities, see Figure 1-8.

Williams (2008) urges caregivers to explore the world outside the classroom or home with older infants and toddlers. Children are born with a desire to understand the environment around them, and they possess incessant curiosity that compels them to explore it (Medina, 2008). Their discoveries can bring joy. Like an addictive drug, Medina believes, exploration creates the need for even more discovery. Think about watching or feeling raindrops, experiencing mud, touching a caterpillar, smelling flowers, or hearing birds. The reality and beauty of natural landscapes surrounds us, and there are multiple ways to experience it safely.

Remember that infants are alike yet uniquely different. Some sensitive infants may appear overwhelmed and require little stimuli to maintain equilibrium. Others will thrive in an environment that provides a multitude of people, sights, sounds, and new activities. Each infant provides a challenge one must "puzzle out" to decide best courses of action—what works, what does not work, and what is best. Bardige (2009) suggests adult-infant connection may not always go smoothly.

> Some babies are fussy and hard to soothe, some are so sensitive that they have to be approached carefully and given lots of support before they can engage, and some are challenged in one modality (e.g., hearing or sight) but hyperacute in another. Some babies are flexible by nature, but others are fearful or feisty. Babies also differ in their natural activity levels and in their rates of development. Some babies give clear signals when they need food or play or comfort or rest; others are much harder to read. (p. 23)

Figure 1-8 Adult goals and activities for language development during infancy.

Age	Adult Goals	Adult Activity
birth to 2 months	1. to create a trusting, intimate relationship 2. to take pleasure in the reciprocal infant-adult interactions 3. to help infant calm and regulate himself 4. to verbally communicate and promote a two-way pattern of responses 5. to maintain eye contact and spend time face to face 6. to seek to create an appropriate environmental moderation level	1. anticipate and satisfy infant needs 2. show interest and provide positive reactions and joy in the infant's presence and communicative attempts 3. provide sights, sounds, touches, and playful companionship 4. talk, croon, whisper, sing, and mimic infant gesture 5. repeat infant sounds 6. provide a comfortable environment that satisfies the child's needs
2–6 months	1. to keep alert to infant attempts to communicate distress or needs 2. to strengthen growing bond of enjoyment in adult-infant "together time" and explorations 3. to recognize child individuality, moods, likes and dislikes, uniqueness 4. to encourage "you talk" and "I talk" behaviors 5. to see infant gestures as possibly purposeful 6. to hold child's eye contact when speaking and gain child's attention with animated speech 7. to use clear and simple speech	1. provide adult-infant play time and joint new experiences 2. provide infant exploring of sights, sounds, music, and play materials and indoor and outdoor environments 3. offer "talking" opportunities with others 4. name child's actions, toys, happenings while changing, bathing, and feeding 5. play baby games such as Pat-a-cake 6. use talk and touch as a reward for the child's communication attempts 7. repeat child sounds and gestures
6–12 months	1. to pursue infant interests, tailoring your talk to child focus 2. to promote the idea that language is used for naming and describing 3. to play with rhythm and rhyme in adult-infant communications 4. to speak clearly, emphasizing new words when appropriate 5. to show delight in child's verbal and physical accomplishments 6. to pair your words with actions, happenings, and objects 7. to recognize and respond appropriately to child signaling and words 8. to make sure sound level and noise is appropriate 9. to listen for intent, not perfection 10. to provide safe environment conducive to child exploring and action	1. expand the child's world with neighborhood trips, people, playthings, and experiences 2. name and describe happenings, emotions, actions, and environments as things take place 3. introduce and read board books to the child, letting child explore them himself 4. sing songs, perform finger plays, play word games with visual and touching actions 5. listen and pause for infant response 6. name body parts, colors, and objects 7. tell simple stories 8. delight in the world and its joyful pursuits with the child

Because infants' first sensory experiences are part of emotional relationships with caregivers, caregivers' efforts to provide developmental care go hand in hand with providing positive emotional support in daily reciprocal exchanges between the child and adult. The terms *child-centered* and *child-focused* need to be coupled with reactive, observant, playful, and nurturing adult behaviors. This type of infant care is nearly impossible when adult-infant ratios are inadequate.

Generally, the types of adults who promote language are those who are alert to the child's achievements, notice them, and enjoy interacting, as well as adults who can offer novelty, assistance, and enthusiasm in addition to focusing on the child's interests. Mangione (2010) believes the emotional security infants derive from positive caring relationships with primary and secondary care providers, provides infants with a buffer for the negative stresses he might encounter in daily experiences.

1-6a Baby Games and Explorations

Almost daily, infants seem to increase the ways they can explore and enjoy verbal-physical games. Birchmayer, Kennedy, and Stonehouse (2008) urge caregivers to explore creative ways to communicate with infants to sustain their interest.

> For very young children, spoken language can be extended through face and body games and rhymes. Though infants still will not understand many or even most words used, they will nevertheless enjoy the sound, rhythm, and tone of the language and other creative elements of the experience. (p. 31)

Most adults know that holding an infant and singing or dancing with him are good ways to comfort the fussy child or to foster interest in place of boredom. Since some infants are newly experiencing game play at a center, watching for stress signs and tenseness is important. Some infants adapt readily and enjoy immediately. Others are more cautious and need a slow introduction to any bouncing or other baby movements. Infants may also register boredom or tiredness when the game is no longer fun signaling they will need a new activity or rest.

Infant educators create their own games and activities that are enjoyable to both infants and caregivers. They become aware of their infants' focus and reactions. Games that deal with child anticipation often elicit smiles or giggles. Playing classics such as Peek-a-boo or Johnny Jump Up or hiding an object under a cloth has delighted generations of children. More newly devised activities include tying a soft tinkling bell to the wrist or leg of an infant or connecting a soft ribbon from an infant's ankle to an overhead mobile (under adult supervision).

Experts recommend that, from a baby's earliest days, caregivers begin with simple imitation games during face-to-face interaction, making sure to pause long enough for the infant to take in the information and mount a response. The best distance for these games is 8 to 12 inches away from the child's face. Imitation of the baby's movement or vocal efforts is also suggested, as is rewarding the baby's effort with attention or smiles.

The following classic language and body action play has brought delight to generations of infants. The most enjoyed play activities include tickling, bouncing, and lifting with accompanying words and rhymes.

This Little Piggy

(Each line is recited while holding a toe, moving toward the pinkie.)

This little pig went to market. This little pig stayed home. This little pig had roast beef. This little pig had none. This little piggy cried, "Wee, wee, wee, wee!" all the way home.

(First published in 1728.)

Pat-a-Cake

(Recited while helping the child with hand clapping.)

Pat-a-cake, pat-a-cake, baker's man.

Bake me a cake as fast as you can.

Pat it and prick it and mark it with a "B."

And put it in the oven for baby and me.

So Big

Say, "Look at you—so big!" Slowly raise both of the infant's arms up, extending them over the child's head while saying, "[child's name] is so-o-oh big" and then slowly bring the arms down.

Repeat.

Say the child's name slowly as you raise the infant close to your face at eye level. Then say, "So-o-oh big." Then gently say, "Wow, wow, wow—what a baby. A so-o-oh big baby!" with a big smile.

1-6b Musical Play

Music, singing, and musical expression appear to be a central part of the crucial interaction that occurs between caregivers and infants as infants develop over the first year of life. Two types of musical or singing interaction take place: (1) a soothing go-to-sleep lullaby-style interaction and (2) a playful, upbeat adult behavior that might be described as rhythmic and joyful. The first style is seen as caregivers attempt to regulate or promote a particular infant state (such as relaxation, contentment, or sleep), and the second style, the communication of emotional information (such as mutual enjoyment and love of music).

Experts believe babies as young as three months can distinguish between certain melodies. Musical infant babbling has been described as tonal and rhythmic babble. Tonal babble is babbling in a single pitch, the babble sounding like a monotone singer. In rhythmic babble the child's body or voice displays a rhythmic beat or quality. Geist, Giest, and Kuznik (2013) believe research implies that even the youngest children have the potential to inherently respond to music and also mathematical constructs. Music contains beats, rhythm, tempo, and steady beats, which often make up a rhythmic pattern that infants and toddlers pay attention to. Often caregiver's rock infants to soothe them using an accompanying music or song. This can involve simple to complex musical patterns. These patterning experiences support later literacy learning, it is believed.

Nursery, cultural, and folk tunes can be introduced in intimate and pleasant settings. Simple, safe musical instruments are enjoyed, and moving to music is natural to young children. Wolf (2000) suggests that educators start with songs they love, ones sung to them as children. Others suggest using children's music recorded by well-known performers. Some educators recommend Bach preludes and Vivaldi's *Springtime* Symphony along with other classical pieces. Yet others recommend popular children's bouncy selections. Two benefits of musical activities for some older preschoolers and primary children are believed to be enhanced abstract reasoning and **spatial-temporal reasoning**.

Scientists are finding that the human brain may be "prewired" for music. They suspect that some forms of intelligence are heightened by music. Although controversial at present, some researchers believe learning musical skills in childhood can help children do better at mathematics.

Schmid (2010) confirms the beliefs of many educators.

> Words and music are such natural partners that it seems obvious they go together. Now science is confirming that those abilities are linked in the brain, a finding that might even lead to better stroke treatment. (p. A6)

Only more studies with more children will prove whether music produces specific or lasting benefits in cognition.

See Additional Resources at the end of this chapter for favorite musical and movement activities and song books.

1-7 Early Reading and Writing Practices

Common Core State Standards in the English Language Arts and Literacy in History/Social Studies, Science, and Technical Subjects (2010) are affecting language and literacy instruction at all educational levels and may modify or change how caregivers interact with children in Pre-K programs, as well as the curriculum to be planned for them. Although the standards are designed for grade levels K–12, they are sure to prompt Pre-K programs to examine how they align to preschool practices. The standards have been adopted by most states and the recommended instructional goals are being exercised in almost all curriculum areas, including the English language arts.

Giving young children the idea that they are capable communicators starts with alert infant caregivers who provide attention to and are aware of the infant's nonverbal communicative actions. What is at first an infant caregiver's guesswork concerning an infant's state of being, be that

---

spatial-temporal reasoning — the mental arrangement of ideas and/or images in a graphic pattern indicating their relationships over time.

hunger, tiredness, or distress or well-being, leads to the adult's ability to spot infants' communicating behaviors and act effectively and in a reciprocal manner. The infant soon begins to understand that he can influence how others (mother and teachers) interact with him. He becomes even more successful at communicating his wants or needs.

Educators' and early childhood caregivers' goals include more than teaching language and literacy. They aim to create a child's learning habit and disposition that develops from the joy and excitement of learning. This is encouraged by the exploring, engaging, and discovering that happens in activities and experiences during his early years. Hopefully, a love of learning will be retained in future schooling. Many early childhood centers are developing new ways to equip children to be successful when they enter common core kindergarten classrooms.

1-7a Reading to Infants

Some parents read books aloud during a mother's later stages of pregnancy, believing the practice will produce some positive results. Some infants remember and give greater attention to stories read to them before their birth. Conclusive research evidence has yet to verify this. Zambo and Hansen (2007) suggest that from birth to three months, read-alouds are purely an emotional connection between the infant and caregiver.

> Being held, feeling good, and having a familiar, comforting voice are more important than the kind of book or the content of the story. Lullabies, singsong stories, and other repetitive, rhythmic experiences bring joy and comfort to infants and establish a special time together for child and caregiver. (p. 34)

Between 6 and 12 months, some infants will sit and look at a picture book with an adult. It is the sound of the reader's voice that gets the young child's attention, even before the child's focus shifts to the pictures. The warmth and security of being held and the reader's voice make for a very pleasurable combination.

The child may want to grab pages and test the book in his mouth or try to turn pages. His head may swivel to look at the adult's mouth. If the child has brought a book to the adult, he will usually want to sit on the adult's lap as both go through the book. Children get ever more adept at turning pages as their first birthday nears (Photo 1-14). Familiar objects in colorful illustrations set on white or plain backgrounds and large faces seem to be particularly fascinating. Infants seem to respond well to and enjoy the rhyme they hear.

Photo 1-14 Ryan is trying to turn a page.

Adult-reading to infants younger than 12 months of age is increasingly recommended, for researchers believe the infant is learning about the sound patterns in words and how words are formed. Book-reading techniques include reading something the adult enjoys with average volume and expression, using gesturing or pointing when called for, promoting child imitation, letting the child turn sturdy pages, and making animal or sound noises. A good rule of thumb is to stop before the child's interest wanes. Adults may find that many infants enjoy repeated reading of the same book. Some parents are very adept at sharing picture books. These parents find **cues** in book features, such as familiar objects, events depicted, sounds, colors, and so on, that give the infant pleasure, as may be evidenced by the adult saying, "It's a dog like our Bowser!" Skilled early childhood educators realize it is the colorful illustrations that attract, so they name and point to features and when possible relate words to like objects found in the classroom. They also attempt to make illustrations relevant to the child's past experience.

Colorful books with sturdy or plastic-coated pages or cardboard books are plentiful. Books of cotton fabric and ones with flaps to lift and peek under, soft furry patches to feel, rough sandpaper to touch, and holes to look through or stick a finger through are books that include enjoyable sensory exploration. Homemade collections of family photographs have delighted many young children. Faces and common household objects in illustrations catch infants' attention. Picture books with simple, large illustrations or photos that are set against a contrasting background and books that are constructed to stand on their own when opened are also popular.

There are a number of literary classics (although not all experts agree to the same titles) that most children in our culture experience. Many of these involve rhyme and rhythm. They have, over time, become polished gems passed onto succeeding generations.

1-7b Recordings

Growing numbers of CDs, tapes, tablet activities, and videos are being produced for infants. Infants watch, listen, and sometimes move their bodies rhythmically. Research has yet to confirm the educational or language-developing benefits claimed by manufacturers of audios or visuals. In *The Journal of Pediatrics*, Interlandi (2007) reports on a new study that included a group of 1,000 families and reviewed the use of infant DVDs; this report suggests that babies who watch recordings fared worst with DVDs than with several other types of programming in terms of educational or language-developing benefits.

> Exposure to educational shows, like "Sesame Street," and noneducational ones, like "SpongeBob SquarePants," had no net effect on language, researchers said—but for every hour that infants 8 to 16 months spent watching the baby DVDs, they understood six to eight fewer words, out of a set of 90, than infants who didn't watch. (p. 14)

1-7c Early Experiences with Writing Tools

As early as 10 to 12 months, infants will watch intently as someone makes marks on a surface or paper. They will reach and attempt to do the marking themselves. Large chalk, thick crayons, or large crayon "chunks" are recommended for exploring, but caregivers are reminded to supervise closely because of infants' tendency to put small objects in their mouths. Large-sized paper (for example, torn flat grocery brown bags) taped at the edges to surfaces and chalkboards work well. The child may not realize the writing tool is making marks but may imitate and gleefully move the whole arm. Many believe it is simply not worth the effort to supervise very young children during this activity and save this activity until the children are older.

1-8 Monitoring Infant Development

Stark, Chazen-Cohen, and Jerald (2002) point out that normal paths of development within various domains serve as reference points to assess infant competence. Infant assessments undertaken by educators try to identify strengths and developmental areas where the infant and/or family may need supportive assistance to

---

cues — prompts or hints that aid recognition, such as a parent pointing to and/or saying "teddy bear" when sharing a picture book illustration. This is done because the infant is familiar with his own teddy bear.

promote optimal infant growth. Maternal health histories sometimes provide clues, as do home visits and daily or periodic educator-family interactions. An examination of whether the school's schedules, activities, staff, and curriculum need to change or adapt takes place frequently so that each child's individual needs have every chance of being met.

Infants should be observed daily with an eye toward assessing developmental milestones and mental and physical health, and educators must be knowledgeable of ages and stages. In a busy center, making dated notes for individual files is suggested as new, questionable, or important behaviors are observed. A notepad in a handy pocket is recommended. Frequent staff meetings should discuss individual infant language behaviors and development. This is followed by planning sessions that create individual learning plans and family consultation when necessary.

Eiserman and associates (2007) note that hearing loss may be an "invisible" condition. Dramatic improvements in hearing screening technology and growth in the number of hospitals that do at-birth screenings have occurred in the past 10 years.

1-8a Implications for Families

Family attitudes about their infant's communicating abilities may influence the infant's progress, in part by affecting how the family responds to the infant. These attitudes are the early roots of the critical partnership between adult and child and the child's sense of feeling lovable and powerful. Consequently, they influence the child's self-assessment.

Special infant projects to promote later school success have provided information in this area. Positive home factors mentioned include the following:

- a lot of attention by socially responsive caregivers
- little or no disruption of bonding attachment between the infant and his primary caregiver during the first year
- availability of space and objects to explore
- good nutrition
- active and interactive exchanges and play time
- parent knowledge of developmental milestones and the child's emerging skills

- parent confidence in infant handling
- maintenance of the child's physical robustness
- positive attention and touching in play exchange

Parent (or family) stress and less-than-desirable quality in child-parent interactions seem to hinder children's language development. Because most families face stress, a family's reaction to stress, rather than stress itself, is the determining factor. In today's busy families, time spent interacting and talking to infants and young children needs to remain a family priority.

Good advice for families includes not worrying about teaching as much as creating a rich and emotionally supportive home atmosphere. A rich atmosphere is one that offers opportunity and companionship rather than expensive toys and surroundings. Current research indicates that families who spontaneously speak about what the child is interested in and who zoom in and out of the child's play as they go about their daily work are responsive and effective families. Also, families should know early and late "talkers" usually show little difference in speaking ability by age three. The variation between children with respect to the onset and accomplishment of most human characteristics covers a wide range when considering what is normal and expected.

Munir and Rose (2008) describe healthy social behavior in infancy, as well as infants who display possible early autistic behaviors.

> Healthy infants as young as six or eight months do communicate and respond nonverbally to social cues. Most look up or turn at the sound of their name. By 12 months, they typically babble and point at objects. By 16 months, they say single words; by 24 months, two-word phrases. In contrast, children with autism seldom make meaningful eye contact or respond to familiar voices. They may never speak. Their play is often repetitive and characterized by limited imagination. Others may simply flap their hands in excitement or disappointment.
>
> On their own, none of these signs means a child has autism or another development disorder. Nevertheless, if a child has any of these signs, he or she merits evaluation. (p. 64)

Regardless of the setting, the experts agree the primary need of infants and toddlers is emotional connection (Lloyd-Jones, 2002). Human relationships are the key, and emotional development is critical for growth. Children of the poor, who are considered to be at-risk, may escape at-risk status if they share the following commonalities. They live in large, extended families that provide supportive language stimulation and encouragement, and they have no other social or biological risks present. Their families manage to safeguard their infants' and older children's health. Intervention and social service programs may also be accessible. It is the isolated poor families with multiple risk factors, including abusive home environments, whose children are the most negatively affected.

Summary

1-1 Discuss the reciprocal behaviors of infants, parents, and caregivers.

Caregivers and other adults observe and interpret an infant's state of well-being, try to understand both general and specific behaviors. They identify child signals and clues and are responsive and alert companions who interact, communicate, and provide consistent care. Caregivers attempt to provide language and intellect-building comments during daily routines and play periods.

Infants search adult faces for facial expression and gain information through their sense organs. Basic attitudes form through contact and interactions. With consistent, affectionate care that satisfies infant needs, attachment bonds form. This is a two-way process. The quality and quantity of caregiver attention becomes an important factor in infant communication and language growth.

1-2 Name four important influences that may affect an infant's language growth and development.

Important influences in infant language growth and development include the care and attention infants' experience, the integration of their bodies' growth systems, the growing cognitive ability and intellectual understandings they possess, their sensory organ development, their emerging ability to recognize language-specific patterns in the speech they hear around them, and also whether they make early attempts to categorize speech sounds. The social and emotional environment can influence the achievement of equilibrium and attachment in infants. Adult attitudes and expectations may affect infant language growth along with other cultural and social factors.

1-3 Compare two theories of human language emergence.

In comparing two theories of human language growth mentioned in the text one would have to display a knowledge of the identifying characteristics of two of the following theoretical positions: Behaviorist/Environmentalist theory, Maturational (Normative) theory, Predetermined/Innatist theory, Cognitive – Transactional (Interaction) theory, or Constructivist theory.

1-4 Name two of the areas of particular importance to infant care addressed in Developmentally Appropriate Practice (DAP) guidelines.

The six areas of particular importance addressed in developmentally appropriate practice are: (1) relationships between caregivers and children, (2) the environment, (3) exploration and play, (4) routines, (5) reciprocal relationships with families, and (6) policies.

1-5 Discuss the behaviors and vocalizing efforts that infants use to communicate their needs and desires.

Infant behaviors and vocalizing efforts start with crying, body movements, and body positions. They develop mutual gazing behavior and early proto-conversations with caregivers begin. Infants respond with noisemaking and eye contact. Infant noises include sucking, sneezing, coughing, and feeding noises. Later these early noises are accompanied with cooing and vowel-like sounds or discomfort noises and sounds. Infants usually display a pleasure in engagement with others and an eagerness to communicate. Infants find their actions and vocalizations can result in caregiver attention and sometimes action.

1-6 Describe what caregiver actions should take place when infants develop joint attentional focus.

When infants gain the ability to focus jointly with caregivers, their caregivers are responsive and seek reciprocal interactions. Caregivers seek to offer optimal opportunities for speech and language development. This includes teacher pointing, pairing and connecting words with objects or events, and perhaps imitating an infant's object-directed actions. Emotional reactions to an event are shared and noted by teachers. Shared reference associations lead to eventual meaningful language usage. First words or sounds are usually simple associates of objects or situations.

1-7 Name and comment upon early reading and writing activities in late infancy.

Early reading activities in late infancy include teacher activities, such as reading books, offering lullabies, songs, storytelling experiences, and other language developing experiences. The text suggested that reading material and activities should contain repetitive, musical, and rhythmic features to attract older infants. Reading books aloud is also designed to promote child enjoyment and social–emotional togetherness. When possible book features were to be related to children's life experiences and naming illustrative features and pointing to objects together was suggested. Early writing activities mentioned in the text included safe writing tools and sturdy taped-down paper for a child to scribble upon.

1-8 Identify how infant centers monitor each infant's language and communicating behaviors.

Infant centers monitor each child's progress in a number of ways, including: conducting assessments, creating health histories, and continually observing if each infant's developmental needs have been met. Developmental milestones are recorded and individual growth files are developed. The center's program and schedules are adjusted and reviewed during planning sessions to assure quality care is offered each infant. Continual communication with parents and families is undertaken and the school encourages positive home language growth—producing features, activities, and experiences.

Additional Resources

Readings

Anderson, N. A. (2007). *What Should I Read Aloud? A Guide to 200 Best-Selling Picture Books*. Newark, DE: International Reading Association.

Bjorklund, D. F. (2011). *Children's Thinking: Cognitive Development and Individual Difference*. Belmont, CA: Cengage Learning.

Karp, H. (2002). *The Happiest Baby on the Block*. New York: Bantam Dell.

Murray, C. G. (2007). *Simple Signing with Young Children: A Guide for Infant, Toddler, and Preschool Teachers*. Beltsville, MD: Gryphon House.

Infant Books

Aston, D. H. (2006). *Mamma Outside, Mama Inside*. New York: Henry Holt.

Bauer, M. D. (2003). *Toes, Ear, and Nose*. New York: Little Simon.

Boyton, S. (2004). *Moo Baa, La La La!* New York: Simon & Schuster.

Hindley, J. (2006). *Baby Talk: A Book of First Words and Phrases*. New York: Candlewick Press.

Intrater, R. G. (2002). *Hugs and Kisses*. New York: Scholastic.

Saltzberg, B. (2004). *Noisy Kisses*. San Diego: Red Wagon.

Infant Play Games

Silberg, J. (2012). 125 *Brain Games for Babies*. Beltsville, MD: Gryphon House

Infant Music, Movement Activities, and Song Books

Beaton, C. (2008). *Playtime Rhymes for Little People*. Cambridge, MA: Barefoot Books (CD and book).

Charmer, K., Murphy, M., & Clark, C. (2006). *The Encyclopedia of Infant and Toddler Activities*. Beltsville MD: Gryphon House.

Long, S. (2002). *Hush Little Baby*. San Francisco: Chronicle Books.

Helpful Websites

Better Brains for Babies

http://www.fcs.uga.edu

Current research in infant brain development.

National Parent Information Network

http://npin.org

Contains readings and parenting resources.

Sensory Awareness Foundation

http://www.sensoryawareness.org

Lists available infant experiences.

The Program for Infant/Toddler Care

http://www.pitc.org

Responsive care guides.

2 The Tasks of the Toddler

Objectives

After reading this chapter, you should be able to:

2-1 Name four conventions of the English language that toddlers are learning about speaking.

2-2 Describe how toddlers move from using first words to using sentences.

2-3 Identify three common characteristics of toddler language.

2-4 State two criteria for selecting books and describe four recommended techniques when reading books to toddlers.

2-5 Identify three suggestions for toddler teachers and parents concerning toddler opportunities to explore and experience their environment.

 NAEYC Program Standards

1C02 Support children's development of friendship; provide opportunities for children to play and learn from each other.

1B13 Adjust interactions to toddlers' various states and levels of arousal.

1B15 Talk frequently with children and listen to children with attention and respect.

1B15 Use strategies to communicate effectively and build relationships with every child.

2E02 Toddlers have varied opportunities to experience books, songs, rhymes, and routine games.

Developmentally Appropriate Practice (DAP)

1A2 Know the child and family well and respond to child's individual temperament, needs, and cues and develop a mutually satisfying pattern of communication with child and family.

1B1 Caregivers use pleasant, calm voices as well as simple language and nonverbal cues.

1B3 Caregivers frequently read to toddlers and sing, do finger plays, and act out simple stories and folktales with children participating actively.

1B6 To satisfy toddlers' native natural curiosity caregivers give simple, brief, accurate responses.

1C1 Adults initiate conversations with a toddler giving ample time to respond. They attentively listen and respond verbally.

Common Core State Standards for English Language Arts and Literacy

L.CCR 4 Determine or clarify the meaning of unknown and multiple meaning words and phrases.

The Toddler Teacher

Kelsa (26 months) and her grandfather entered the classroom. He drew me aside after his granddaughter had run off to the housekeeping area. With a smile he shared what Kelsa had done and said to him. "We were watching TV, and I commented on something," he said. "She got up and stood right in front of me. Next, she cupped my cheeks with her hands and said, 'Look at me when you say words.'" He laughed. I explained, "Sometimes with toddlers we can understand their words only if they speak right into our face."

Questions to Ponder

1. Is this a teacher strategy that helps toddlers?
2. Was the teacher's explanation to Kelsa's grandfather sufficient, or would a longer explanation have been better?
3. Is Kelsa's language acquisition advanced or about average for her age?

Photo 2-1 Exploring a small slide is a toddler adventure.

© 2015 Cengage Learning®

If you were amazed at the infant's and the one-year-old's ability, wait until you meet the toddler! Toddlerhood marks the beginning of a critical language-growth period. Never again will words enter the vocabulary at the same rate; abilities emerge in giant spurts almost daily. When children stop and focus on things, from specks on the floor to something very large, concentration is total—every sense organ seems to probe for data.

Toddlerhood begins with the onset of toddling (walking), a little before or after the child's first birthday. The toddler is perched at the gateway of a great adventure, eager to proceed, investigating as she goes, and attempting to communicate what she discovers and experiences (Photo 2-1). "The bags are packed" with what has been learned in infancy. The child will both monologue and dialogue as she ages, always knowing much more than can be verbally expressed. During toddlerhood she uses words whose meanings have been rooted in social acts and may have significance.

Toddlers are action-oriented. They simultaneously act on and perceive the environment around them. Toddlers' thoughts become a sensorimotor activity. As they age higher-level thinking happens, and toddlers begin to think first and then act.

By the age of two, toddlers' brains are as active as those of adults. The metabolic rate keeps rising, and by the age of three, toddlers' brains are two and a half times more active than the brains of adults—and they stay that way throughout the first decade of life (Shore, 1997). One can compare the working rate of a toddler's mind to an adult's mind as that of supercomputer to an abacus.

An important milestone during the toddler period occurs when the toddler uses symbolic (speech) communication rather than communicating primarily through body actions and gestures. This is made possible by the child's growing mental capability and the richness of the child's affective and life experiences.

Many experts believe that a warm, close relationship with a caregiver promotes the child's communication ability and provides satisfaction in itself. Experts agree that the primary need of toddlers (and infants) is emotional connection.

From a few spoken words, the toddler will move to purposeful speech that gains what is desired, controls others, allows personal comments, and accompanies play. It becomes evident that the toddler recognizes the give and take of true conversation. She also realizes the difference between being the speaker and being the one who listens and reacts—the one who persuades or is persuaded, the one who questions or is questioned. Toddlers become aware that everything has a name and that playfully trying out new sounds is an enjoyable pursuit. The child's meanings for the few words she uses at the start of the toddler period may or may not be the same as common usage. As children age, they will continually and gradually modify their private meanings of the words in their speaking vocabulary to conform to public meanings.

Cambourne (1988) describes the enormous complexity of learning to talk:

> When one has learned to control the oral version of one's language, one has learned literally countless thousands of conventions. Each language spoken on the Earth today (some three or four thousand) comprises a unique, arbitrary set of signs, and rules for combining those signs to create meaning. These conventions have no inherent "rightness" or "logic" to them, just as driving on the right or left side of the road has no intrinsic rightness or logic to it. Yet each language is an amazingly complex, cultural artifact, comprising incredibly complex sets of sounds, words, and rules for combining them, with equally numerous and complex systems for using them for different social, personal, and cognitive purposes. (p. 252)*

Even though toddlers have an innate predisposition for learning to communicate, they face four major tasks in learning the rule systems of language: (1) understanding phonology (the sound system of a language); (2) learning syntax (a system of rules governing word order and combinations that give sense to short utterances and sentences, often referred to as *grammar*); (3) learning semantics (word meanings); and (4) learning pragmatics (varying speech patterns depending on social circumstances and the context of situations). The understanding of these rule systems takes place concurrently—one area complementing and promoting the other. Rule systems form without direct instruction as toddlers grope to understand the speech of others, to express themselves, and to influence others both verbally and nonverbally. We can think of the toddler as one who tests many hypotheses—the kind of thinker who over time can unconsciously discover and formulate the rules of language.

Language emergence is but one of the toddler's achievements. Intellectually, toddlers' process, test, and remember language input. They develop their own rules, which change as they recognize what are and are not permissible structures in their native language. Other important developmental achievements intersect during late toddlerhood as children increasingly shift to symbolic thinking and language use. Gains in social, emotional, and physical development are apparent, as are issues of power and autonomy.

2-1 Learning the English Language naeyc DAP COMMON CORE

Toddlers learn the **phonology** of their native language—its phonetic units and its particular and sometimes peculiar sounds. This is no easy job! An enormous growth in phonology learning occurs between birth and age five. The young language learner must sort sounds into identifiable groups and categories while she is possibly experiencing the speech of a variety of people in various settings. Because spoken language is characterized by a continuous flow of word sounds, this makes the task even more difficult.

After the child learns sounds, she learns sound combinations. It is prudent to point out here that not every sound in one language exists in another. Consequently, English language learners may be unfamiliar with new sounds in English.

A **phoneme** is the smallest unit of sound that distinguishes one utterance from another—implying a difference in meaning. Standard American English has approximately 39 phonemes; of these 15 are vowels and 24 are consonants. Not all experts agree on these numbers. Language from a phonetic perspective might be conceived as a continuous sequence of sounds produced when air is pushed through the throat and mouth, and then received and recognized by sensitive ear structures.

Languages are divided into vowels and consonants. When pronouncing vowels, the breath stream flows freely from the vocal cords; when pronouncing consonants, the breath stream is blocked and molded in the mouth and throat

---

* From Brian Cambourne, *The Whole Story*. Copyright ©1988.

phonology — the sound system of a language and how it is represented with an alphabetic code.

phoneme — the smallest unit of speech that distinguishes one utterance from another.

Figure 2-1 Average age of consonant sound production.

Learned by	
Age 1 to 3 =	h, m, n, p, w.
Age 2 to 4 =	b, d, g, k.
Age 2-1/2 to 4 =	f, y.
Age 2 to 6 =	t, ng.
Age 3 to 6 =	r, l.
Age 3 to 8 =	s, z.
Age 3-1/2 to 7 =	ch, sh.
Age 4 to 7 =	j.
Age 4 to 8 =	v.
Age 4-1/2 to 7 =	th (unvoiced)
Age 5 to 8 =	th (voiced)
Age 6 to 8 =	zh.

area by soft tissue, muscle tissue, and bone, with the tongue and jaw often working together. The child focuses on those sounds heard most often. The toddler's speech is full of repetitions and rhythmic speech play. Toddler babbling of this type continues and remains pleasurable during early toddlerhood. Sounds that are combinations of vowels and consonants increase. Vowel production is reasonably accurate by age three. Low, unrounded vowels (that is, *i, o, u*) are favored during infancy. Consonant sounds that are difficult to form will continue to be spoken without being close approximations of adult sounds until the child reaches five or six years of age or is even slightly older (Figure 2-1). Early childhood teachers realize that, in many instances, they will have to listen closely and watch for nonverbal clues to understand child speech.

It is a difficult task for the child to make recognizable sounds with mouth, throat, and breath control working in unison. Perfecting the motor control of speech-producing muscles is a sophisticated skill that comes ahead of many other physical skills. It requires precise and swift movements of the tongue and lips. This is all but fully developed when most other mechanical skills are far below levels of their future accomplishment.

Much of early speech has been described as unintelligible or gibberish. The toddler seems to realize that conversations come in long strings of sound. Rising to the occasion, the child imitates the rhythm of the sound but utters only a few understandable words.

Toddlers hear a word as an adult hears it. Sometimes, they know the proper pronunciation but are unable to reproduce it. The child may say "pway" for *play*. If the parent says "pway," the child objects, showing confusion and perhaps frustration. Toddler talk represents the child's best imitation, given present ability. Parents and teachers are urged to look at toddlers' speech mistakes as evidence that children are learning in an intelligent way.

Adult-to-child talk can be defined as "child-directed speech," that is, a set of speech modifications commonly found in the language adults use to address young children. Most speech researchers divide adult-child language into five main categories: pedagogy, control, affection, social exchange, and information. The pedagogy mode is characterized by slow adult speech that is over enunciated or overemphasizes one or two words. This type of adult speech is "tailor-made" for one- or two-year-olds trying to segment the speech stream into comprehensible units. Many adults tend to label happenings and objects with easy-to-learn, catchy variations, such as *choo-choo*, *bow-wow*, and so forth. Additional parental language techniques include the following:

1. Labeling themselves as "Mommy" or "Daddy," instead of "I" or "me" in speech.

2. Limiting topics in sentences.

3. Using short and simple sentences.

4. Using repetition.

5. Expanding or recasting children's one-word or unfinished utterances. If the toddler says "kitty," the parent offers "Kitty's name is Fluff."

6. Using a wide range of voice frequencies to gain the child's attention and initiate a communication exchange.

7. Carrying both sides of an adult-child conversation. The adult asks questions, and then answers them too. This technique is most often used with infants but is also common during the toddler period. The adult is modeling a social exchange.

8. Echoing a child's invented word. Many toddlers adopt a special word for a certain object (Photo 2-2). The whole family may use the child's word in conversational exchanges also.

Photo 2-2 The teacher's comments concentrate on the hat when the hat is the object of children's attention.

▶❚❚ **TeachSource** Video 2-1

Observing and Monitoring Language Development in Toddlers: The Importance of Assessment

This displays a toddler classroom in action and teacher behaviors to increase child language.

1. Would you describe most of the teachers in this video as being at eye level when they're talking with children?

2. Were the demonstrations teachers were providing toddlers along with words effective?

3. Did you notice teachers tending to talk about the children's agendas and follow their interests?

4. Would you say that toddlers were understandable in their speech some of the time or most of the time?

When adults feel infants and toddlers are able communicators, it is reflected in their actions and speech. This can, and usually does, increase children's communicative abilities and opportunities. Early childhood educators believe caregivers should treat toddlers as communicating children, and avoid childlike or cutesy expressions. They offer simple forms of speech and easy-to-pronounce words whenever possible, especially when they introduce new words.

Views on adult use of baby talk after the infancy period stress the idea that the practice may limit more mature word forms and emphasize dependency. On the other hand, adults may offer simplified, easily pronounced forms, such as *bow-wow* for a barking poodle. They later quickly switch to harder-to-pronounce forms when the child seems ready. In the beginning, though, most adults automatically modify their speech when speaking with toddlers by using short sentences and stressing key words.

Children progress with language at their individual rates and with varying degrees of clarity. Some children speak relatively clearly from their first tries. Other children, who are also progressing normally, take a longer time before their speech is easily understood. All basic sounds (50, including diphthongs) are perfected by most children by age seven or eight.

2-1a Morphology

A **morpheme** is the smallest unit of language standing by itself with recognized meaning. It can be a word or part of a word. Many prefixes (*un-*, *ill-*) and suffixes (*-s*, *-ness*, *-ed*, *-ing*) are morphemes with their own distinct meanings. The study of morphemes is called **morphology**. There are wide individual differences in the rates toddlers' utter morphemes. It is unfortunate if early childhood teachers or families attempt to compare the emerging speech of toddlers or equate greater speech usage with higher ability, thus giving the quiet toddler(s) perhaps less of their time. Between the ages of two and four years, children gradually include a variety of different morphemes in their

---

morpheme — the smallest unit in a language that by itself has a recognizable meaning.

morphology — the study of the units of meaning in a language.

spontaneous utterances. There seems to be a common sequence in their appearance.

2-1b Syntax

Languages have word orders and rules, and young children speak in word order and follow the rules of their native tongue. Children typically acquire the rules of grammar in their native language, with little difficulty, from normal communicative interactions with adults.

The rules for ordering words in sentences do not operate on specific words, but on classes of words such as nouns, verbs, and adjectives, and a relatively small number of syntactical rules can account for the production of a very large number of sentences. In some languages, the subject of a sentence follows the verb; in other languages, it precedes the verb.

Modifiers (descriptive words) in some languages have gender (male and female forms), but in others they do not. Plurals and possessive forms are unique to each language. Young speakers will make mistakes, but adults marvel at the grammar the child does use correctly, having learned the rules without direct instruction. One can compare children's mastery of **phonetics** to their mastery of **syntax**. The child's mastery of phonology is gradual, but the child's use of correct syntax is almost completely mastered from early beginning attempts.

By age two, and sometimes as early as 18 months, children begin to string together two or more holophrases and have thereby arrived at the telegraphic stage. All telegraphic speech consists of acceptable grammatical sequences that are the precursors of the sentence.

From all the perceptions she has received and the words spoken to and about her, the child has noted regularities and has unconsciously formed rules, which are continually revised. Chukovsky (1963) describes this task:

> It is frightening to think what an enormous number of grammatical forms are poured over the poor head of the young child. And he, as if it were nothing at all, adjusts to all the chaos, constantly sorting out in rubrics the disorderly elements of words he hears, without noticing as he does this, his gigantic effort. If an adult had to master so many grammatical rules within so short a time, his head would surely burst. (p. 31)

Grammar involves the way sounds are organized to communicate meaning. With grammatical knowledge, the young child can produce and understand a wide range of new, novel, grammatically correct, and meaningful sentences. As the child learns to talk during preschool years, she may construct many ungrammatical sentences and use words in unusual ways. The errors of the two-year-old disappear as the child gains more control over language, but new kinds of errors appear in three-year-olds, who are trying new forms of expression. An understanding of the general rules of grammar develops before an understanding of the exceptions to the rules. Correct grammar forms may change to incorrect forms as the child learns new rules. *First past tenses of the irregular verbs may have been correct. Then when a child starts using and adding -ed endings for regular verb past tenses, her "came" may become "camed," or her "broke" to "broked it," or her "went" to "wented." The child has replaced the correct irregular past tense form with an incorrect **over-generalization**. The child may not return to correct forms until she ages and hears more English spoken around her. Even though the correct forms may have been practiced for several months, they are driven out of the child's speech by* **overregularization**.

In later years, during elementary school, the child will formally learn the grammar rules of the English language. What the child has accomplished before that time, however, is monumental. The amount of speech that already conforms to the particular syntactical and grammatical rules of language is amazing. The child has done this through careful listening and by mentally reorganizing the common elements in language that have been perceived. The toddler's growing use of

---

modifiers — words that give a special characteristic to a noun (e.g., a large ball).

phonetics — pertaining to representing the sounds of speech with a set of distinct symbols, each denoting a single sound.

syntax — the arrangement of words as elements in a sentence to show their relationship.

grammar — the rules of a specific language that include both written and spoken utterances and describe how that specific language works and the forms of speech that conform to the rules that well-schooled speakers and writers observe in any given language.

over-generalization — the act of presuming something to be true of all members of a particular class of words.

overregularization — the tendency on the part of children to make the language regular, such as using past tenses like -ed on verb endings.

Photo 2-3 Mara's teacher knows the child frequently does not maintain eye contact when speaking.

© 2016 Cengage Learning®

intonation and **inflections** (changes in loudness of voice) adds clarity, as do nonverbal gestures. The child is often insistent that adults listen.

The toddler's system of nonverbal signals, body postures, and motions that were used in late infancy continues and expands, becoming part of the toddler's communication style (Photo 2-3). Many signals translated by mothers or care providers to strangers leave strangers bewildered as to how the mother or another adult could possibly know what the child wants. It may seem impossible based on what the stranger observed and heard.

English sentences follow a subject-verb-object sequence. The three fundamental properties of sentences are verb-object, subject-predicate, and modification, and almost all human languages have rules for these basic sentential structures. Learning grammar rules helps the toddler express ideas, and her understanding of syntax

helps the child to be understood. Our knowledge of the rules of combination determines how we construct and understand an infinite number of sentences from a finite vocabulary. Syntax gives language its power.

A person who listens closely to the older toddler will sometimes hear the child self-correct speech errors. Toddlers talk to themselves and to their toys often. It seems to aid the storage of words and memory. The toddler understands adult sentences because the child has internalized a set of finite rules or combinations of words.

2-1c Semantics

Semantics is the study of meanings and acquisition of vocabulary. It probes how the sounds of language are related to the real world and life experiences. The toddler absorbs meanings from both verbal and nonverbal communication sent and received. The nonverbal refers to expressive associations of words, such as rhythm, stress, pitch, gesture, body position, facial change, and so on. Adults perform important functions in the child's labeling and concept formation by giving words meaning in conversations.

The toddler who comes from a home that places little emphasis on expressing ideas in language may be exposed to a relatively restricted range of words for expressing conceptual distinctions. Every early childhood center should offer opportunities for children to learn a rich and varied vocabulary to refer to various experiences and to express ideas (Photo 2-4).

Photo 2-4 Toddlers begin to engage in social interactions with others.

© 2016 Cengage Learning®

---

inflections — the grammatical "markers," such as plurals. Also, a change in pitch or loudness of the voice.

semantics — the study of meanings associated with words and the acquisition of vocabulary.

In toddler classrooms, teachers have many opportunities to name objects and happenings as the day unfolds. Using teacher gesturing along with words (or pointing to illustrations and photographs in simple picture books or classroom signs) helps the toddler form a connection between what is seen and heard. Repeating words with voice stress can be done in a natural way while monitoring whether the child is still interested.

Word meanings are best learned in active, hands-on experiences rather than "repeat-after-me" situations. Meanings of words are acquired through their connotations, not their denotations, that is, in situations that consist of feelings and verbal and nonverbal messages with physical involvement. The word *cold* for instance, means little until physically experienced. Toddlers assume that labels (words) refer to wholes instead of parts (the creature, not the tail) and to classes instead of items (all horses, not one horse) (Cowley, 2000).

When an older infant is first learning to talk, the same sound often serves for several words; for instance, *bah* can mean "bottle," "book," "bath," and "bye." And sometimes infants use one sound to name an object and also to express a more complicated thought; for example, a child may point to a ball and name it, but later may say the same word and mean, "I want to play with the ball. Roll it to me."

The child's **concept** building is an outgrowth and result of a natural human tendency to try to make sense of the surroundings. Attending to and pondering about the relationships, similarities, and differences in events and happenings, and mentally storing, remembering, and retrieving those ideas and impressions are important aspects of concept development. With young children's innate curiosity, drive, and desire to explore and experience, concepts are continually being formed, reformed, and modified.

Examples of toddler behavior demonstrate that conceptual conclusions happen daily in group and home care settings. When a child blows a whistle-shaped toy, licks and bites a plastic fruit, tightly clings to an adult when a dog barks, or says "hot" when pointing to a water faucet, one can see past experiences are basic to the child's concept development.

To understand how concept development is individual and based on life experiences, ask yourself what makes a cup a cup. How many distinguishing features can you list? Ask another adult to do the same. You will both probably list some of the following characteristics:

- has a handle
- holds liquids and substances
- is often round on top, tapering to a smaller round base or can be cylindrical
- is used as a standard measurement in cooking (8 ounces)
- is made from clay, plastic, glass, metal, or other solid substances
- can be used to drink liquids

Adults speaking about cups understand one another because they usually recognize the same distinguishing characteristic(s). If asked to get the cup on the shelf, they won't get a glass. A toddler using the word cup often means his personal drinking cup.

A toddler may overuse concepts in new situations. Perhaps a bandage on the tip of a brother's finger will be called a thimble. For a short time, all men are daddies, a cow may be called a big dog, and all people in white are feared. As mental maturity and life experiences increase, concepts change; small details and exceptions are noticed. Toddlers may use a word to refer to a smaller category than would adults. An example of this phenomenon is the toddler's use of the word *dog* only in reference to the child's pet rather than all dogs encountered.

Concepts, often paired mentally with words, aid categorizing. Concept words may have full, partial, or little depth of meaning. The toddler's level of thought is reflected in speech. When counting to three, the toddler may or may not know what "three" represents. Words are **symbols**. Young children acquire word meaning and also begin to understand the symbolic nature of words. The meaning of a word is known and learned from other speakers of a common language. A word is a sign that signifies a referent. Infants' first words are almost always nouns that are common, familiar objects or people. In an English-speaking family a one year old infant who becomes familiar with hearing the word "doggie" being used when

---

concept — a commonly recognized element (or elements) that identifies groups or classes; usually has a given name.

symbols — things that stand for or suggest (such as pictures, models, word symbols, and so forth).

referring to the hairy, little critter who barks, will use the word doggie when she speaks about it or calls it. The dog is the referent. If the same dog is given away to a Spanish speaking family and lives around that family's infant and becomes a familiar object, it is still a referent, but the word the child uses will be that family's word for the dog. This arbitrary relationship between the referent and the sign for the word is symbolic. A few words in English are not arbitrary but have a sound associated with its referent such as hiss, tinkle, and woof.

A toddler's firsthand sensory experiences are very important. Stored mental perceptions are attached to words. Words are only as rich as the experiences and depth of understanding behind them. The activities and experiences found in subsequent chapters will help the early childhood teacher enrich the child's concepts by providing deeper meanings in a wide range of language arts. Every activity for young children—a total school program—gives them a language arts background full of opportunities to explore by handling, tasting, using their bodies, smelling, and touching, as well as by seeing and listening.

2-1d Common Core State Standards and Children's Vocabulary

A rich and varied vocabulary will be necessary if kindergartners are to function successfully and reach the expectations of the *Common Core State Standards for English language arts & literacy in history/social studies, science, and technical subjects-K-12*, (National Governors Association Center for Best Practices and Council of Chief State School Officers, 2010). It has been adopted in most state school systems. Without words learned in the toddler-preschool period, the ideas found in kindergarten books and early readers may escape children's comprehension. Children will also need an abundant repertoire of content words gained through an early childhood curriculum that not only built language, literacy skills, and background knowledge, but also promoted a specific and detailed vocabulary in other core domains.

In picture book readings, toddler teachers emphasize and explain, as simply as possible, new words and how they relate to toddlers' past experiences. Educators will also need to clarify and review words enough times for children

to become familiar with them and understand their meanings. Word learning will not be left to chance, but rather will be teacher promoted.

2-1e Pragmatics

The subtleties of our language are multifaceted. **Pragmatics** is the study of how language is used effectively in a social context, or the practical aspect of oral communication. It is the study of who can say what, in what way, where and when, by what means, and to whom (Figure 2-2). Language is a tool in questioning, ordering, soothing, ridiculing, and engaging in other social actions. One can request quiet in the form of a question such as, "Can't anyone get a peaceful moment around here?" or talk longingly about the candy in a store for the purpose of obtaining it without making a direct request, as in, "Oh, they have my favorite kind of chocolate bar!"

The language that young children use to express desires, wishes, concerns, and interests becomes a reflection of their social selves. When a toddler communicates effectively, the toddler receives feedback from others. Many times, a sense of well-being elicited by positive events helps the child shape a feeling of competency and self-esteem. Not yet socially subtle in speech, the toddler has not learned the pragmatically useful or appropriate behaviors of older children. Toddlers seem to have just one goal: to get messages across by gaining adult attention regardless of

Figure 2-2 Pragmatic skills.

Pragmatic Skills

1. taking turns in a conversation with another
2. knowing you are supposed to answer when a question is asked
3. noticing nonverbal body cues, signals, gestures, and signs and then responding
4. introducing a topic in a conversation for the listener to understand
5. having the ability to stay on the subject of a conversation
6. maintaining the right amount of eye contact; not staring or turning away too frequently
7. using different communicative styles that suit different communicative partners
8. learning that in certain situations talking is inappropriate

pragmatics — the study of how language is used effectively in a social context; varying speech patterns depending on social circumstances and the context of situations.

who is present and in what situation. The world, from the toddler's perspective, revolves around the toddler and her need to communicate.

2-2 Attachment and Development of Language Skills

Attachment problems can slow communicative development. Observers describe infants and toddlers in less-than-adequate care situations as fearful, apathetic, disorganized, and distraught. If responsive social interaction and adult feedback exchanges are minimal, limited, frightening, or confusing, the infant or toddler may display a marked lack of interest in holding or obtaining adult attention. During toddlerhood these children can fall behind in speech development. Lally (1997) describes the importance of toddler social interaction:

> Infants and toddlers develop their sense of who they are from the adults who care for them. They learn from their caregivers what to fear, what behaviors are appropriate, and how their communications are received and acted upon. They learn how successful they are at getting their needs met by others, what emotions and intensity levels of emotions to safely display, and how interesting others find them. (p. 288)

Toddlers are sometimes shy with newcomers, so caregivers cast their eyes to the side rather than searching a toddler's face at first meeting. They bend or squat to toddler eye level. When more comfortable conversing takes place, teachers comment on toddler movements while watching for child wariness and/or acceptance. They react and respond to all of toddlers' verbal overtures including babble, gestures, miscellaneous sound making, hand or body signs, or words. Teachers are enthusiastic and joyful companions celebrating toddler accomplishments with attentive and appreciative feedback. They explain what is happening between themselves and the toddler and also what is occurring in the environment around them. naeyc DAP

2-2a First Words

Any time between 10 and about 22 months is considered within the normal range for first words. A vocabulary growth spurt happens around 18 to 22 months (Strickland & Schickedanz, 2004).

Photo 2-5 Gestures often indicate a child's desire or need.

© 2015 Cengage Learning®

First words and content words carry a lot of meaning. They usually consist of names of important people or objects the toddler encounters daily and include functional words such as *up*, *out*, *night-night*, and *bye-bye* used in social contexts (Photo 2-5). Easy-to-pronounce words are more likely to be included in toddlers' early expressive vocabularies.

Single words can frequently go further than naming by representing a meaningful idea (a holophrase). The task of the adult includes both being responsive and guessing the child's complete thought. This may sound simple, but many times it is difficult and frustrating. Many factors influence the degree of adult responsiveness and talkativeness, particularly in child center settings—room arrangements, adult-child ratios, level of staff training, and other emotional and environmental factors. The greatest inhibitor of adults' speaking and responding to children seems to be adults' talking to one another instead of the children. Professionals save chatting for breaks and after school meetings. The nature of the work in a group care program can easily be described as emotion packed and demanding, in addition to rewarding and challenging. On the surface, the general public may not see or understand skilled verbal interactions taking place between toddlers and caregivers. What seems to be random, natural playfulness and verbal responsiveness can be really very skilled and professionally intentional behavior. The same, of course, is true regarding family behavior.

Adults sometimes question the practice of responding to toddlers' grunts and "uhs"; instead they respond only to toddlers' spoken words. Many toddlers seem to understand everything said to them and around them but get by and satisfy most of their needs with sounds and gestures. The points for adults to consider are that the child is performing and learning a difficult task and that speech will soon follow. The message that responsive adults relay to children when rewarding their early attempts with attention is that children can be successful communicators and that further attempts at speech will get results.

2-2b From Egocentric Speech to Inner Speech

During the toddler period, observers notice that words or short phrases spoken by adults are remembered and spoken out loud. The toddler's "hot," "no," "kitty," or similar words accompany the child's actions or a simple viewing of objects at hand. Vygotsky (1986) has called this "egocentric" speech, which is ultimately and usefully tied to the toddler's thinking.

As the child matures, this type of speech slowly becomes **inner speech**; part of the child's thinking process. Egocentric speech is regulatory, that is, useful in helping the child regulate (manage) her own behavior. As adults, we see examples of this regulatory function when we talk ourselves through particular perplexing situations. For example, "First the key goes in the lock, then turn the handle, and the bar moves to the left."

2-2c Symbolic Gesturing

It is old-fashioned to believe that real communication does not exist before a child's first words. Researchers have helped us understand that gestures and signs (signals) occur in tandem with early vocalizing. Young toddlers can possess a rich repertoire of signals, and female infants tend to rely on or produce them with slightly greater frequency than male infants. Signs have been defined as nonverbal gestures symbolically representing objects, events, desires, and conditions that are used by toddlers to communicate with those around them. They literally can double a young toddler's vocabulary.

Toddlers' interest in learning hand signals (signing) varies greatly. Conducting an infant-toddler program in which signing is a regular part of the curriculum has become popular. Some toddlers may use 20 or more signs for various objects, feelings, and needs; other toddlers mixed only a few gestures with their beginning words. Both would be displaying normal development.

The use of words and symbols to influence other people in predictable ways requires the child to represent mentally the relationship between the symbol (word or gesture), the *meaning* for which it stands, and the intended effect on the other person. A symbol—a word, a picture, a dance—exists because of human intention to infuse some tangible form—a sound, a mark, a movement—with meaning and thereby to comment on or take action in the social world.

Various researchers have studied a child whose parents felt that their child was capable of learning nonverbal as well as verbal labels. The parents informally concocted hand or body signs on the spot for new events without any reference to a formal sign language system. Figure 2-3, from a study by Acredolo and Goodwyn (1985), describes the signs and gives the age the signs appeared in the child's communicative behaviors and the age the child said the word represented by the sign. The list of signs includes the signs the child learned with and without direct parent teaching.

Gestures are integral companions of toddler verbalizations. Adults may have modeled the gestures in their adult-child interactions. A family's signals are "read" by toddlers, and a hand held palm up is usually read as "give it to me." Toddlers show their understanding by behaviors. Toddlers can and do invent new gestures; consequently, signing is not simple, imitative behavior. Pointing is probably the most commonly used gesture of toddlers. Eventually, words are preferred and gesturing remains as an accompaniment of speech. We have all slipped back into a gesturing mode as we search for words in conversation, and hand gestures are used automatically to convey the word(s) that we cannot quite express.

Early childhood educators employed by infant-toddler centers need to know their centers' position regarding expected language-developing behaviors. Most centers expect educators to pair words with adult hand signs, to encourage toddler use of signs, and to learn and respond

---

inner speech — mentioned in Vygotsky's theory as private speech that becomes internalized and is useful in organizing ideas.

Figure 2-3 Symbolic signs, in order of acquisition, produced by case study subject.

Signs	Description	Age of Sign Acquisition (Months)	Age of Word Acquisition (Months)
flower	sniff, sniff	12.5	20.0
big	arms raised	13.0	17.25
elephant	finger to nose, lifted	13.5	19.75
anteater	tongue in and out	14.0	24.0
bunny	torso up and down	14.0	19.75
Cookie Monster	palm to mouth plus smack	14.0	20.75
monkey	hands in armpits, up-down	14.25	19.75
skunk	wrinkled nose plus sniff	14.5	24.00
fish	blow through mouth	14.5	20.0
slide	hand waved downward	14.5	17.5
swing	torso back and forth	14.5	18.25
ball	both hands waved	14.5	15.75
alligator	palms together, open-shut	14.75	24.0
bee	finger plus thumb waved	14.75	20.00
butterfly	hands crossed, fingers waved	14.75	24.0
I dunno	shrugs shoulders, hands up	15.0	17.25
hot	waves hand at midline	15.0	19.0
hippo	head back, mouth wide	15.0	24.0
spider	index fingers rubbed	15.0	20.0
bird	arms out, hands flapping	15.0	18.5
turtle	hand around wrist, fist in-out	15.0	20.0
fire	waving of hand	15.0	23.0
night-night	head down on shoulder	15.0	20.0
X-mas tree	fists open-closed	16.0	26.0
mistletoe	kisses	16.0	27.0
scissors	two fingers open-closed	16.0	20.0
berry	"raspberry" motion	16.5	20.0
kiss	kiss (at a distance)	16.5	21.0
caterpillar	index finger wiggled	17.5	23.0

to each child's individual sign language. To do this, teachers must be alert to children's cues, in particular noticing what in the environment attracts them so that words can be supplied and the children's intentions can be "read." Teachers' behaviors should reflect their awareness, intentional efforts, and attention to toddlers' efforts to communicate. Their continual goal is to establish a warm, emotionally fulfilling connection to each child in their care.

Toddlers are very interested in exploring. Teachers should hang back when toddlers interact with other toddlers and try not to interrupt play. Becoming social with peers is given priority and promoted. Teachers of toddlers do a lot of word modeling. They attempt to be both calm and fun companions. Most will tell you that after a full day with toddlers they look forward to conversing with adults.

2-2d First Sentences

The shift from one word to a two-word (or more) stage at approximately 18 months is a milestone. At that time, the toddler has a speaking vocabulary of about 50–75 words; by 36 months, upward of 1,000 words. It is crucial in talking about vocabulary to acknowledge that children not only acquire new words as they get older but also expand their understanding of old words.

If one looks closely at two-word utterances, two classes of words become apparent. The smallest group of words is made up of what are called "pivot words." Examples of toddlers' two-word sentences, with pivot words underlined, are shown in Figure 2-3. Pivot words are used more often than other words, and seem to enter the vocabulary more slowly, perhaps because they are stable and fixed in meaning. In analyzing two-word toddler comments, one finds they are both subject-predicate and topic-comment in nature. Frequently stressed syllables in words and word endings are what toddlers' first master, filling in other syllables later. At times, toddlers use -*um* or -*ah* as placeholders for syllables and words. They replace these with correct syllables and words as they age.

Understanding of grammar rules at this two-word stage is displayed even though many words are missing. Toddlers frequently use a simple form and, almost in the same breath, clarify by expansion (by adding another word). The invention of words by toddlers is common. One 18-month-old had her own private word for "sleep," consistently calling it "ooma." Families trying to understand their toddlers get good at filling in the blanks. They then can confirm the child's statement and can add meaning at a time when the child's interest is focused.

2-2e Toddler – Adult Conversations

Toddlers control attending or turning away when interacting with others, as do infants. At about one year, they understand many words and begin to display turn-taking in conversation, with "you talk, I answer" behaviors. **Joint attention** starts around nine- to 10-months of age. At this time infants develop intentional communication and willingly share emotions, intentions, and interest in the outside world. To do this, the child has to be sure that both she (the speaker) and her intended receiver is focused on the same thing. She does this by capturing another's attention, establishing the topic of conversation, and maintaining attention on the topic by looking back and forth. Her communication usually consists of one or more of the following: looking, pointing, gesturing, showing, giving, making sounds, and changing her facial expression.

Toddlers learn that speech deserves attention and that speech is great for getting adults to notice them. They seem to revel in the joint-endeavor aspect of conversations. Toddlers are skillful communicators. They converse and correct adult interpretations, gaining pleasure and satisfaction from language exchanges. The following incident shows more than toddler persistence:

> A first-time visitor to the home of a 20-month-old toddler is approached by the toddler. The visitor eventually rises out of his chair, accompanies the toddler to the kitchen, gets a glass of water, and hands it to the child. The toddler takes a tiny drink, and returns, satisfied, to the living room. Parents were not involved. Thirst, itself, was unimportant. The pleasure gained by the child seemed to motivate her actions.

For the child to accomplish her ends, the following actions occurred. The visitor:

1. focuses attention on child.
2. realizes a "talking" situation is occurring.
3. listens and maintains a receiver attitude.
4. corrects his own behavior, guesses at the child's meaning, and tries new actions.
5. realizes the conversation is over.

While the toddler:

1. stands in front of visitor; searches face to catch eye; makes loud vocalization, dropping volume when eye contact is made; observes visitor behavior.
2. repeats first sound (parents understand, visitor does not) and observes visitor reaction.
3. grabs visitor's hand, vocalizes loudly, and looks in visitor's eyes.
4. tugs at hand, uses insistent voice tone, and gestures toward the kitchen.
5. pulls visitor to sink and uses new word (visitor does not understand); corrects through gestures when visitor reaches for the cookie jar.
6. corrects visitor's guess (milk), gestures toward water, and holds out hand.
7. drinks a small sip and hands back the glass, smiles, and walks away.

joint attention — child's awareness that he or she must gain and hold another's focus during communicational exchanges to get his or her message understood.

Photo 2-6 Children seek out people willing to show interest in what they are doing.

This type of behavior has been called *instrumental expression* because vocalization and nonverbal behaviors were used to obtain a certain goal. The toddler seeks people willing to listen and learns from each encounter (Photo 2-6). Toddlers' subject matter in conversations is commonly concerned with recent memorable happenings in toddler's lives. Adults modify and adapt their speech based on the abilities they observe in the child. This is done intuitively by use of shorter and less complex comments, and it changes when adults notice increased capacity.

Many experienced caregivers describe a time when some toddlers in their care remain very close. During this time, the toddler's behavior is characterized by clinging to a primary caregiver, watching adult lips intently, showing decreased interest in toys or playing independently, frequently bringing objects to the caregiver, and attempting to say words. The duration and appearance of these behaviors is unique to each toddler, and some do not display them at all. Families can worry about spoiling the toddler, if these behaviors persist, and educators urge families to satisfy children's needs for increased attention and language input. Usually the child will emerge with a longer attention span and branch out to explore a wider world.

2-3 Characteristics of Toddler Language

The speech of young children speaking in two-word, or longer, sentences is termed **telegraphic** and **prosodic**. It is telegraphic because many words are omitted because of the child's limited ability to express and remember large segments of information; the most important parts of the sentence are usually present. Prosodic refers to the child's use of voice modulation and word stress with a particular word or words to give special emphasis and meaning. Telegraphic speech can be defined as utterances that are devoid of function words and resemble messages sent by telegraph, for instance, "Jimmy truck" could represent "That truck belongs to Jimmy" or "Give me my truck." Meanings often depend on context and intonation of the utterance. For additional toddler language characteristics that may appear before the child's third birthday, see Figure 2-4.

No discussion of older toddlers' language would be complete without mentioning the use of "no." There seems to be an exasperating time when children say "no" to everything—seemingly testing whether there is a choice. Young children first use "no" to indicate nonexistence. Later it is used to indicate rejection and denial. Even when the child can speak in sentences longer than three words, the "no" often remains the first in a sequence of words. A typical example is "No want go bed." Soon, children insert negatives properly between the subject and the verb into longer utterances, as sentence length increases. Of all speech characteristics adults remember, toddlers' use of negatives and their avid energetic demands to be "listened to" stick in the memories of their caregivers.

2-3a Aids to Toddler Speech Development

The swift rate of new words entering toddlers' vocabularies indicates that educators caring for them should begin to become increasingly specific with descriptive terms in their speech. If a truck is blue, a comment like "The blue truck rolled in the mud" is appropriate. If an object is

---

telegraphic speech — a characteristic of young children's sentences in which everything but the crucial word or words are omitted, as if for a telegram.

prosodic speech — the child's use of voice modulation and word stress to give special emphasis and meaning.

Figure 2-4 Toddler language characteristics.

Toddler Language Characteristics

- Uses two- to five-word sentences.
  "Baby down."
  "Baby boom boom."
  "No like."
  "No like kitty."
  "Me dink all gone."
  "See me dink all gone."
- Uses verbs.
  "Dolly cry."
  "Me going."
  "Wanna cookie."
- Uses prepositions.
  "In car."
  "Up me go."
- Adds plurals.
  "Birdies sing."
  "Gotta big doggies."
  "Bears in dat."
- Uses pronouns.
  "Me big boy."
  "He bad."
- Uses articles.
  "The ball gone."
  "Gimme a candy."
- Uses conjunctions.
  "Me and gamma."
- Uses negatives.
  "Don't wanna."
  "He no go."
- Runs words together.
  "Allgone," "gotta," "gimme," "lookee."
- Asks questions.
  "Wa dat?"
  "Why she sleep?"
- Does not use letter sounds or mispronounces spoken words.
  "Iceam," "choo" (for shoe), "member" (for remember), "canny" (for candy).
- Sings songs.
- Tells simple stories.
- Repeats words and phrases.
- Enjoys word and movement activities.

on the bottom shelf, in the top drawer, or under the table, those words can be stressed. A color, number, or special quality, like fast or slow, big or little, or many other adjectives and adverbs, can be inserted in simple comments. Playing detective to understand toddlers will always be part of adults' conversational style. Teachers may request that toddlers look directly at them when they communicate so that teachers can better hear each word and determine intent.

Many experts offer adults advice for providing an optimal toddler environment for language stimulation. The following are some specific tips.

- Expose the child to language with speech neither too simple nor too complex, but just slightly above the child's current level (Photo 2 - 7).
- Stay in tune with the child's actual abilities.
- Omit unreasonable speech demands, yet encourage attempts.
- Remember that positive reinforcement is a more effective tool than negative feedback.
- Accept the child's own formulation of a language concept.
- Provide a correct model.
- Make a point of being responsive.
- Follow the child's interest by naming and simple discussion.

Photo 2-7 "I see you found a green block!"

Photo 2-8 Shea croons and repeats "up, down, up, down," as he turns the doll upside down and then turns it to an upright position again.

Other suggested pointers follow.

- Explain what you are doing as you work.
- Describe what is happening.
- Display excitement for the child's accomplishments (Photo 2-8).
- Talk about what the child is doing, wanting, or needing.
- Pause and listen with ears and eyes after you have spoken.
- Encourage toddler imitation of gestures and sounds.
- Imitate the child's sounds playfully at times.

Language and self-help skills blossom when two-year-olds have opportunities to participate in "real" activities, such as cutting bananas (using a plastic knife), emptying baskets, sponging off the table, and helping sweep the floor.

The following selected passages of recommended adult behaviors are included in developmental appropriate practices identified by the National Association for the Education of Young Children (NAEYC) in *Developmentally Appropriate Practice: Focus on Infants and Toddlers* (Copple, Bredekamp, & Charner, 2013). A few others were listed on this chapter's first page. **DAP**

- Caregivers spend most of the day in one-to-one, face-to-face conversations with toddlers. The tone of the interactions is warm and caring: caregivers use pleasant calm voices as well as simple language and nonverbal cues. [*p. 67*]
- Caregivers learn each toddler's cues and respond consistently in ways that are caring and specific to each child, which lets the child explore, knowing he can trust the adults to be there for help or comfort as needed. [*p.67*]
- Caregivers frequently read to toddlers—to one child individually or to groups of two or three—always in close physical contact. Caregivers sing with toddlers, do finger plays, and act out simple stories or folktales, with children participating actively. [*p.68*]
- Caregivers create an emotionally and physically inclusive classroom. They give every toddler warm, responsive care. They make sure that spatial organization, materials, and activities are planned such that all children can participate actively (e.g., a child with a physical disability eats at the table with other children). [*p.68*]
- To satisfy toddlers' natural curiosity, caregivers give simple, brief, accurate responses when children stare at or ask questions about a person with a disability or other differences. [*p.68*]

- Caregivers respect toddlers interest in objects—to carry objects around with them, collect objects, move them from one place to another, and to roam around or sit and parallel play with toys and other objects. [p.69]

- An adult initiating a conversation with the toddler gives the child ample time to respond. Caregivers also listen attentively for children's verbal initiations and respond to these. [p.70]

- Caregivers label or name objects, describe events, and reflect feelings ("Youre angry that Yvette that took the block.") to help children learn new words. Caregivers simplify their language for toddlers who are just beginning to talk. Then as children acquire their own words, caregivers expand on the toddler's language (Child: "Mark sock." Adult: "Oh, that's Mark's missing sock, and you found it"). [p.70]

- Caregivers ask the family what sounds, words, and nonverbal cues their toddler uses to better understand what the child means when she uses beginning speech or a home language that is not understood by the caregivers. [p.70]

- Caregivers learn what each child's cries mean (e.g., fear, frustration, sleepiness, pain) and when to wait (e.g., to see if the child solves his own problem) or take action. They respond promptly to toddler's cries or other signs of distress.[p.70] (NAEYC, 2013)

The above passages are from a larger body of material and selected because of their relationship to toddler's language and literacy growth. Teachers aware of developmentally appropriate practice put it in action during the course of a toddler's day as they interact and participate in a wide range of both planned and unplanned teacher activities. Toddler teacher actions that commonly take place in centers can include:

- setting out two or three familiar objects and asking the child to get one.

- calling attention to interesting things you see, hear, smell, taste, or feel.

- showing and labeling your facial features and the child's in a mirror.

- labeling and pointing to objects around a room.

- verbally labeling items of clothing as the child is dressing and undressing.

- labeling the people in the toddler's world.

Frequent teacher-child exchanges using language and movement play are recommended by many experts. One classic play activity follows.

Take Your Little Hands

Take your little hands and go clap, clap, clap.

Take your little hands and go clap, clap, clap.

Take your little hands and go clap, clap, clap.

Clap, clap, and clap your hands.

Take your little foot and go tap, tap, tap.

Take your little foot and go tap, tap, tap.

Take your little foot and go tap, tap, tap.

Tap, tap, and tap your foot.

Take your little eyes and go blink, blink, blink.

Take your little eyes and go blink, blink, blink.

Take your little eyes and go blink, blink, blink.

Blink, blink, and blink your eyes.

Take your little mouth and go buzz, buzz, buzz.

Take your little mouth and go buzz, buzz, buzz.

Take your little mouth and go buzz, buzz, buzz.

Buzz like a bumblebee.

Take your little hand and wave bye, bye, bye.

Take your little hand and wave bye, bye, bye.

Take your little hand and wave bye, bye, bye.

Wave your hand bye-bye.

2-3b Language with Music

Toddlers are music lovers. If a bouncy melody catches their ear, they move. They obtain plenty of joy in swaying, clapping, or singing along. Young children can anticipate a pattern when a song is familiar. They usually first recognize its rhythm or beat and then its words. Often children watch others first before joining in. With teacher encouragement and enough repetitions they learn the song and actions completely and may improvise and make additions.

Many can sing short, repeated phrases in songs, and some toddlers will create their own repetitive melodies (Photo 2-9). Adult correction is not necessary or appropriate. Playful singing and chanting by adults is a recommended language-development technique.

Photo 2-9 Making music is a popular preschool activity.

© 2015 Cengage Learning®

Educators can encourage young children's creativity with music. If teachers always focus on everyone singing the same words and/or doing the same actions, they may not be using music to promote creative expression. Fortunately, with the uninhibited and exuberant toddler this is not a problem; teachers are going to see some fantastic "moves" and hear some unique lyrics and takeoffs on songs and dances. The author remembers the time a two-year-old composed his own song: "Zipper your do da."

The social component in musical games is also a language facilitator. Joining the fun with others gradually attracts even the youngest children (Photo 2-10). A toddler can be introduced to the joy of moving to a new song with others; mutual musical listening and participation in music experiences at small group times add new avenues for language growth.

One technique educators frequently engage in with music is to verbally describe how a particular child is moving to music. ("Johnny is lifting his knee high up to his tummy.") This encourages children's movement to music and should be used when appropriate. The adult can extend two index fingers for the shy or wobbly child to grip, thereby creating a dance partnership. This allows the child to release

at any time. Gently swaying or guiding movements to the music may increase the child's enjoyment.

The following criteria for selecting sing-along songs, recorded music, and songbook selections are recommended. Choose a short selection for toddlers, repetitive phrases, reasonable, range (C to G or A), and simple rhythms. Try to find pieces that represent the ethnic and cultural diversity of attending children and include folk music.

2-3c Symbolic Play

What often looks like random play during the toddler period is actually experimentation that may produce new understandings. Children's cause and effect knowledge can be enhanced by manipulating features of the environment. For toddlers this might be pots and pans, toys, art materials, large rocks, or about anything they have gained access to. Objects can be sorted, lined up, and classified in some manner during play and particular attributes of playthings may be noticed. An alert teacher can casually or purposefully supply fitting words, labels for objects, or simple action words describing child action as they enjoy toddler's company.

Photo 2-10 The right book can hold a toddler's attention.

At approximately 12 to 15 months, toddlers will begin to engage in symbolic (pretend) play. This important developmental leap allows the child to escape the immediate and firsthand happenings in her life and use symbols to represent past experiences and imagine future possibilities. Medina (2008) explains:

> Symbolic reasoning is a uniquely human talent. It may have arisen from our need to understand another's intentions and motivations, allowing us to coordinate within a group. (p. 47)

The acts of toddler pretend play observed by adults are widely diverse and depend in part on the child's life experiences. Greenspan (1999) describes a parent observing a young toddler's symbolic play:

> . . . he tenderly puts his teddy bear to be inside an empty shoe box, and the parent recognizes the child is starting to grasp that one thing can stand for, or symbolize, another. Because he can picture what a bed looks and feels like in his mind, he is able to pretend that a hollow, rectangular box is

really a symbol for a bed. When the parent comments that his teddy bear "is sleeping in his bed," he will eventually comprehend that the word "sleeping" stands for the bear's activity in the bed. As soon as he can articulate the sounds, the toddler will himself use the word symbol "sleeping" to describe an elaborate pattern of behaviors that he has observed. (p. 200)

One can always find toddlers who will talk into toy phones, spank dolls, grab the wheel of toy vehicles, and accompany motor movements with sounds, speech, and *vrooms*. Some reenact less common past experiences that are puzzling to their teachers. Gowen (1995) suggests the teacher techniques listed in Figure 2-5.

2-3d Making Friends

Toddlers seem to have a strong need for both individual identity and autonomy and social connectedness. At times they display the ability to help others and are sympathetic or empathetic. They may venture out toward peers and retreat back to the security, closeness, physical comfort of caring adults. They are constantly learning from their first contacts and relationships with "other small people" and new adults.

Wittmer (2008) believes that teachers cannot underestimate the importance of their relationships with toddlers. Social competence and emotional control development predict school readiness. Caring adults can be instrumental in helping toddlers figure out, experiment with, and understand new ways to interact and communicate with peers and also in learning the rules of physical contact and socialization.

Each toddler entering group care differs not only in personality, capability, culture, and gender but also in past human relationships, memories, and their expectations of others. Past experience may or may not include attachment to significant adults or positive social interactions with other like-age children. Some toddlers may avoid peers, or express hostility and aggression, or ignore them. Toddler communication skills also vary. Vocal ability can range from utter silence to being a chatterbox.

Often, toddler play is side-by-side play. A toddler may watch what a neighboring peer is doing and may sometimes imitate the peer's actions. However, two toddlers playing cooperatively in an organized, shared-goal play situation is infrequent. Toddlers are usually in-their-own-

Figure 2-5 Teacher's response to toddlers' symbolic play.

1. <u>Mirror the child's sounds, words or actions.</u>
   (Child is rocking a doll while humming.)
   Teacher picks up a doll, rocks it, while saying
   "Go to sleep, baby."
   (Child is putting blocks together.)
   Teacher sits with child and puts one block on top
   of another and says "Blocks."

2. <u>Describe the child's actions.</u>
   (Child is climbing stairs.)
   Teacher says "One foot on the step, two feet
   on the step."
   (Child feeds doll with toy bottle.)
   Teacher says "You are giving your baby a drink of
   milk. Um, um, that tastes good."
   "Your ball is bouncing up, and down, up and
   down. Down it goes; up it goes. You picked up
   the ball, Will."

3. <u>Suggest a child action.</u>
   (Child has rolled a toy car across the rug.)
   Teacher says "Let's push our cars under the table
   and park them," as she grabs another toy car
   pushes it and parks it.
   (Child has picked up small floor pillows and is
   carrying them.)
   Teacher says "I'll get the wagon so you can put
   the pillows inside."

4. <u>Request or suggest an action or vocalization.</u>
   (Child is putting a plastic bowl on his head.)
   "Robin (child's name) has a new hat." teacher says.
   Then sitting next to him and picking up another
   bowl, she says,
   "Teacher needs a new hat too. Put it on my head,
   please."

5. <u>Make a positive statement.</u>
   (Child pats doll's back putting it upon her shoulder.)
   Teacher says "Your dolly feels better now. What a
   good mommy you are."
   (Child puts pretend play iron over the play ironing
   board.)
   "You are ironing your family's clothes so they look
   neat and pretty.
   (Child tries to feed teacher a plastic apple.)
   Teacher says "That apple tastes good. I was
   hungry. Thank you very much."

6. <u>Model an action or word(s) for the child to copy.</u>
   With stuffed dog and baby blanket, teacher says,
   "My dog is cold today. I'm going to wrap him up
   so he can take a nap."
   While on the play yard a loud airplane has attracted
   children's attention overhead.
   "I'm an airplane flying to grandma's house."
   Teacher pretends to fly.

world-of-discovery people, but they do at times pick up play ideas from one another. Social graces may be absent, yet some beginning empathy for others may be apparent when one toddler communicates by patting or hugging a crying peer or handing over a toy. Poole (1999) describes the difficulties toddlers face in building peer friendships:

> It's hard work for toddlers to learn how to play with one another. At first, some may examine their playmates as if they were inanimate objects, such as a doll or a ball, pinching and poking without understanding that their actions can hurt. Toddlers also don't always have control over their strong emotions.

> It takes time to learn not to hug too hard or to say "Hello" rather than swipe at a friend's face. Even when toddlers begin to sense that such behavior is frowned upon, they may continue testing the limits. (p. 37)

Wittmer (2008) reminds teachers that it takes time for toddlers to become interested in peers, feel comfortable playing with them, and develop their growing ability to be a caring friend.

> Children's sense of *self* and other, which they bring to their interactions with peers, begins to develop in their first relationships with significant adults. A self that is full of confidence, capable of being intimate with others, and convinced that others are likely to be enjoyable and responsive (or not) emerges from these first relationships. Infants and toddlers develop their beginning sense of other as kind, trustworthy, helpful, and fun in the embrace and enfolding (figuratively and literally) of the mother, father, and other special adults. (p. 10)

By 15 to 18 months of age, many toddlers participate in joint physical activities and may more fully enjoy others' company. By age two, they often pair off with a peer and have favorite companions. Young toddlers' emotions may erupt when sharing classroom playthings, causing friendships to change quickly. It is then, at age two, that words can help children attract companions and repel others. Two-year-olds mimic increasingly and use words a friend uses.

Early childhood teachers are better able to identify accelerated, normal (average), and delayed speakers at about 18 months of age. What causes diversity is too complex to mention here, but some factors can be inferred, and others have been previously mentioned. Families' and caregivers' responses to children's nonverbal and verbal attempts to communicate toward the end of the first year and into the second year can be a determining factor.

Birckmayer, Kennedy, and Stonehouse (2010) urge caregivers to observe and discover each child's particular way of communicating, which may be crying, smiling, making noises, hand and body actions, or other behaviors that the child employs to convey thoughts and feelings. Then responsive caregiver feedback should occur so the toddler learns making sounds and/or other overtures prompts the receiver (adult) to make sounds and/or actions back.

Language growth differences, in particular their vocabulary growth, can relate to a child's temperament. Temperament can affect interactions with peers and adults. A number of temperament traits become somewhat stable during toddlerhood and catch the teacher's eye. A child's activity level might range between highly active to relaxed. A child's typical behavior can appear cautious or withdrawn when faced with new activities or people. Teacher may notice moodiness, even temper, or a positive or negative attitude developing toward certain classroom activities. Persistence and sticking to a new task varies in children. When faced with a problem or hurdle some children may give up quickly while others do not. Individuality can enhance toddlers' learning opportunities or block them. They may also cause caregivers to limit or modify their own verbal interaction. A teacher's attitude or expectations can change. Well-trained early educators when recognizing child temperaments that are in some way affecting language growth and development act after gathering more information to confirm their observations. They try to discover if the behavior is new, only happens under certain circumstances, or is typical and somewhat stable behavior. In other words, they assess the situation and act accordingly using strategies and techniques that might facilitate the child's language growth in a positive way. Actions might include attempting to increase a child's social integration, social competence, play skills, or his group inclusion. Children's general well-being is observed and monitored by all staff involved. Children are not labeled, but studied. Teachers analyze their own attitudes and child expectations always aware of how their verbal comments, teaching behaviors, and program planning might produce the best educational results for each child.

2-4 Introducing Toddlers to Books and Other Activities

Toddlers show an interest in simple, colorful books and pictures and enjoy adult closeness and attention. Pointing and naming can become an enjoyable game. Sturdy pages that are easily turned help the toddler. A scrapbook of favorite objects mounted on cardboard individualizes the experience. Clear contact paper and lamination will add life and protection.

Board books (usually stiff, coated, heavy cardboard) for toddlers allow exploratory play and may offer colorful, close-up photographs or illustrations of familiar, everyday objects. These books promote the child's naming of pictures and active participation at book-reading times.

Toddler books are plentiful, and school collections include both fiction and nonfiction. Experts and librarians recommend volumes that are colorful, simple, inviting, realistic, and contain opportunities that encourage child involvement. With durable, glossy, wipe-clean page coating and smaller-than-average picture-book size, board books allow small and sometimes sticky hands to explore without tearing sturdy covers or pages. Oversized and big books with giant illustrations can also be enjoyable.

Because a toddler may move on quickly to investigating other aspects of the environment, adults offering initial experiences with books need to remember that when interest has waned, it is time to respect the search for other adventures (Photo 2-11).

Other hints concerning the introduction of books, from Kupetz and Green (1997), are as follows:

- Do not expect to quiet a rambunctious toddler with a book.
- Pick a time when the child seems alert, curious, and interested.
- Establish a special reading time (although books can be read anytime).

Photo 2-11 Toddlers often name what they see in book illustrations.

Photo 2-12 Certain toys promote early scribbling behavior.

- Use your voice as a tool to create interest.

- Be responsive.

- React positively to all of the child's attempts in naming objects, turning pages, or attempting any form of verbalization (Photo 2-12).

Toddlers with past experiences with picture books may have certain expectations for adult-child book sharing. They may want to cuddle with a blanket, sit in adult laps, turn pages for themselves, point to and question book features, name objects, watch the adult's mouth during reading, and so on. Exhibiting flexibility and following the child's lead reinforces the child's social enjoyment of the book.

Educators should be cautioned about the practice of requiring a group of toddlers to sit and listen to a story together. The key words are group and require. Toddler group times are of short duration and planned for active child participation. As toddlers age, they maintain focus for longer periods. Educators of toddlers might try sharing a picture book with a few children. When they do so, they endeavor to keep the experience warm, comfortable, and intimate.

Jalongo (2004) suggests the following when reading to a small group:

- Choose developmentally appropriate titles with simple text, larger size, familiar objects, and with available child "join in" opportunities.

- Adjust your expectations of toddler behavior. Coach patiently and offer needed support as they settle down.

- Use a routine signal to begin story time and be aware the shared reading time (or looking time) may be some children's initial experience. Slow down and urge assisting adults to offer the comfort of a lap.

- Pace reading to maintain child focus.

- Alternate active movement and quiet times during group time by using singing, finger play, or physical movement, which is suggested by oral or textual material (p. 122).

What can toddlers begin to understand during the reading of picture books? Besides knowing that photographs and illustrations are between the covers of books, the toddler gathers ideas about book pleasure. As the child touches pictured objects, the child may grasp the idea that the objects depicted are representations of familiar objects. The toddler can notice that books are not handled as toys. According to Cohen (2013), research suggests reading aloud to toddlers may dramatically increase their receptive and expressive language abilities. These are pre-reading skills necessary for success when reading instruction begins.

Very young children's reading-like behaviors may surprise their teachers especially when they observe the independent activity of toddlers with their favorite books. Almost as soon as the older toddler becomes familiarized with particular books through repetitive readings, he begins to play with them in reading-like ways. Attracted by the familiar object with which she has such positive associations, the toddler picks up the book, opens it, and begins attempting to retrieve some of the language and its intonations. Almost unintelligible at first, this reading-like play rapidly becomes picture-stimulated, page-matched, and story-related.

Near two years of age, the toddler probably still names what is pictured but may understand stories. The toddler may grasp the idea that book characters and events are make-believe. If a particular book is reread to a child, the child can know that the particular stories in books do not change, and what is to be read is predictable. Sometimes the toddler finds that she can participate in the telling by singing, repeating character lines, and making physical motions to represent actions; for example, "knocking on the door" and saying "moo."

2-4a Selecting Toddler Books

Books for toddlers should be:

- repetitive and predictable.
- rhythmical.
- illustrated with simple, familiar, easy-to-identify colorful objects, animals, toys, and so on.
- fiction or nonfiction.
- filled with feel, touch, and smell opportunities.
- sturdy, with easy-to-turn pages.
- set with few words on each page.
- relatively short, with simple, concise story lines about common, everyday life and environmental experiences.
- full of common, everyday activities toddlers can imitate such as waving goodbye, tooth brushing, face washing, using a spoon, wiping face with napkin, door knocking, stair climbing, or movement activities such as kissing, blowing, clapping, bouncing, stepping, jumping, stretching, and so on.
- simple and illustrate elementary concepts such as black and white, big and little, on and off, up and down, over and under, large and small, inside and outside, and so on.
- formatted with illustrations matched to the text on each page.

Bardige (2009) suggests selecting toddler books that include big, noisy things, such as garbage trucks, airplanes, farm and zoo animals, or small intriguing things such as birds, bugs, butterflies, baby animals, and balls. This type of book often offers specific content vocabulary.

Additional desirable features of toddler-appropriate books often include simple, uncomplicated storylines; colorful, well-spaced illustrations or photographs; opportunities for the toddler to point and name familiar objects; sensory features; predictive books (ones allowing the child to guess or predict successfully); and strong, short rhymes or repetitive rhythms. "Touch and feel" books are particularly enjoyed, as are sturdy, heavy board pages. Novelty books that make noise, pop-up books, and books with easy-to-use moving parts capture a toddler's attention. Now is the time to also share the strong rhyming rhythms of Mother Goose and introduce two classics: *Mary Had a Little Lamb* and *Pop Goes the Weasel*.

Adults sing with toddlers, do finger plays, act out simple stories like *The Three Bears* with older toddlers participating actively, or tell stories using a flannel board or magnetic board, and allow children to manipulate and place figures on the boards. This is an age when book-handling skills begin. This includes how to hold a book, where to look for illustrations, and how to open it. These skills can be modeled and discussed while adults point, ask questions, gesture, stress words, follow child interest or note lack of it, and enthusiastically enjoy the shared book experience.

2-4b Electronic Books

Books with electronic features provide another way to engage toddlers with stories and print. Each book differs, but many have colorful illustrations that move, flash, "talk," or make musical sounds and noises. Pressing an area, button, icon, or symbol activates prerecorded features. But the research of Zimmerman and Christakis (2007) alerts early childhood educators to possible ill effects of early media exposure, particularly children's media viewing before the age of three. Their study conclusions note that viewing of either violent or nonviolent entertainment television before age three was significantly associated with subsequent attention problems in school five years later. The viewing of any content type at ages four to five was not associated with attentional problems. Another research study by the same researchers (Christakis and Zimmerman, 2007) examined violent television viewing during preschool years and its associated increased risk of children's antisocial behavior during school-age years. Other researchers (Dworak et al., 2007) have concluded that a link exists between television and computer game exposure and children's sleep patterns, diminished verbal cognitive performance, and their learning and memory abilities. Dworak and associates' research was conducted with a small group of school-age children. More extensive research is needed to probe preschoolers' entertainment viewing and their educational game playing.

Most educators and parents agree that electronic books, games, and television programs do attract toddlers, but that interest usually wanes quickly unless the media is shared with a responsive adult. Educators understand how easily clever television commercials and television programs sometimes capture and engage toddlers. They advise families to limit or omit toddler viewing time. Toddlers may respond to catchy tunes, animation, and flashing colorful images with physical movement such as singing, dancing, and clapping. It looks like toddlers are learning, but the television program can't interact, build on a child's response, or expand interest with language-developing feedback. Overexposure to the medium actually crowds out and subtracts from time spent in more positive human contact and/or conversation in which language is really learned. Chapter 16 includes a discussion on a joint position statement developed by the National Association for the Education of Young Children and the Fred Rogers Center for Early Learning and Children's Media (2012). This publication offers current and well-respected recommendations for early childhood educators.

2-4c Scribbling

In most home environments, toddlers see others writing and want to try it themselves. Large, chunky crayons and nontoxic markers are easily manipulated by toddlers at about 18 months of age. They usually grasp them in their fist and use a scrubbing motion. They have some difficulty placing marks where they might wish, so it is best to use very large sheets of sturdy paper taped to a tabletop. Brown bags cut flat or untreated shelf paper work well. The act of scribbling can serve several useful purposes, including enhancing small muscle coordination, exercising cognitive abilities, promoting social interaction, and allowing emotional release. It can also be seen as a precursor to an interest in symbols and print. An important point in development is reached when the child moves from linear scribbles to enclosed shapes and at a later age begins realistic, representational drawing. Some Asian families may place a high emphasis on drawing activities for young children, and their children's work at school often reflects more comfort and experience with art materials and writing tools.

During toddlerhood, some children gain general knowledge of books and awareness of print. This is viewed as a natural process, which takes place in a literate home or early learning environment. Immersing toddlers in language activities facilitates their literacy development. It is possible to establish a positive early bonding between children and book-sharing times—a first step toward literacy. Some toddlers, who show no interest in books will, when exposed to books at a later time, find them as interesting as other children. Parents need to understand that a literary interest can be piqued throughout early childhood. The fact that a toddler may not be particularly enamored with books or book-sharing times at a particular stage is not a matter of concern. It may simply be a matter of the child's natural, individual activity level and her ability to sit and stay focused in an environment that holds an abundance of features to explore.

2-4d Musical Activities

Musical play with toddlers can help promote literacy skills. Activities can include:

- focused listening experiences.
- play that focuses on or highlights discrimination of loud and soft and fast and slow, rhythms, repeated patterns, tones, words, and so on.
- the use of repetitive beats, catchy melodies or words, clapping, tapping, rocking, galloping, marching, motions, and body actions.

- coordination of movement and music in some way.
- creative and imaginative opportunities.
- experiences with a variety of simple, safe musical instruments.
- the singing of age-appropriate songs.

Music activities often can be used to create an affectionate adult-child bond. Singhal (1999) describes toddlers participating in adult and child music activities:

> Toddlers are beings in motion, and music is the perfect vehicle for directing and freeing their movements. They feel and internalize the steady beat of adult motions. Contrary to popular belief, toddlers can also be excellent listeners. They are fascinated by sound, whether it's a bee buzzing or a clarinet melody. The different shapes, feel, and sounds of simple rhythm instruments also mesmerize toddlers. Being able to make a steady sound on his own on an instrument such as the drum is very empowering to a young child who wants to "do it myself!"
>
> Even though at this age children may not be willing to echo back chanted tonal and rhythm patterns, it is still important that they hear them. The patterns are being "recorded" in their minds for future reference.
>
> Singing, listening, and music-making are a completely natural and enjoyable part of a young child's being. (p. 22)

2-4e Toys

Certain types of toys have a strong connection to toddlers' emerging language development (Photo 2-12). Musical toys, dolls, and stuffed animals that make noises or talk, and alphabet toys, including magnetic alphabet letters, can be described as language-promoting toys. Noise-making toys or recordings, both audio and visual, capture the toddler's attention. Manipulative toys for toddlers are becoming increasingly available.

2-5 Freedom to Explore

Greenspan (1999) emphasizes how toddler problem solving develops and describes its relationship to "freedom to explore" (within supervised limits).

An ability to solve problems rests on the even more basic skill of seeing and deciphering patterns. It is the ability to understand patterns that lets a toddler know if she takes two steps here and two steps there that she'll be able to reach her favorite toy. She becomes a successful navigator not only because her muscles are coordinated, but also because her growing brain now enables her to understand patterns. Toddlers learn to recognize how one room leads to another, and where you are in relation to them. They can meaningfully explore the world long before they are able to express their wishes and thoughts in words.

2-5a The Comical Toddler— Exploring Humor

Adults may not realize that children begin honing their own comedic skills at impressively early ages. They point out that a child's reaction to physical stimuli, seen in activities such as tickling and bouncing, take a new form sometime after the first birthday by becoming visual or oral rather than tactile. Toddler silliness or "joking" behavior can be seen as rudimentary attempts at humor and can be appreciated as child-initiated attempts to get others' reactions to the ridiculous and unexpected. They may playfully mimic adult words or actions, wear a pot for a hat, make a funny face, or wholeheartedly enjoy participating in an "All Fall Down" activity.

2-5b Advice to Toddler Teachers

Bardige (2009) concludes that the quality of care, especially language-developing care, for toddler-to-three-year-olds in the United States needs improvement.

> At the critical age for language learning, public investments in children's education are lower than they will be at any time during childhood. Caregivers and teachers on the frontlines, who are doing their best to provide safe, loving, growth-promoting care, are not doing enough talking. (p. 219)

She concludes that with appropriate supports, caregivers and teachers will be able to maintain language-rich environments and provide care attuned to the needs of the individual child and the group as a whole. Under these conditions children will thrive, but more financial program support is necessary.

Brain Growth Approach

Teaching involves the active engagement of the child's mind using purposeful teaching strategies based on principles derived from research and neuroscience. Teachers and caregivers are encouraged to consider the nature of the brain to make better decisions concerning instructional methods useful in reaching more learners.

Teachers using a brain growth approach realize the brain is a mass of highly connected areas with one brain area affecting others. The brain is also a whole entity that is highly adaptable and designed to respond to environmental input.

Early childhood educators have made special efforts to plan and equip classrooms that provide language and literacy opportunities that are both functional and responsive to the developmental needs of children's bodies and minds. Carefully designed classrooms help teachers to fulfill job duties while promoting children's full potential.

Young children's brains are busy routing and filtering environmental input gained through their sensory organs. Input is sent to specific brain areas for processing. If the information gathered is deemed by the brain to be of sufficient importance, it is organized and indexed and stored. There is no single brain pathway, but rather different shared and unique pathways for different types of learning, such as emotional, social, spatial, vocabulary, and other brain areas. This statement should remind the reader of the work of Howard Gardner (1993), a well-known theorist and psychologist, whose work focused on multiple intelligences.

> No discussion of brain activity can exclude the fact that there are different types of brain cells. A brain neuron is a basic structural and processing unit of the nervous system. It continuously fires, integrates, and generates information across gaps called *synapses* linking one cell to another and acts as a conduit for information. As a rule, the more connections one's cells make, the better (Jensen, 2008, p. 13). A two-year-old has twice the number of neurons as an adult.

Toddlers may seem cute and naïve when they refer to all males as daddy or when they attempt to bite a toy that resembles a banana. Their behavior illustrates toddler global (macro) thinking prior to their further experience when they notice details and exceptions that refine their understandings. The brain can be thought of as acting like a muscle. The more activity that takes place, the larger and more complex it can become. What a child experiences intellectually and physically changes what his/her brain looks like. The brain can wire and rewire depending on environment, life choices available, and also the individual choices that are made, such as choosing to learn to play a musical instrument or learning how to move the body to play a physical sport (Medina, 2008, p. 58).

2-5c Consulting with Families

Verbally responsive and playful people, and a "toddler-proof" home equipped with objects and toys the toddler can investigate, will help facilitate a toddler's emerging language skills. An adult sitting on the floor or on a low chair near a toddler at play can promote toddler communication and also help the adult see things from the child's vantage point.

Objects and toys need not be expensive and can be designed and created at home. Social contact outside the home is important also. Toddlers enjoy branching out from the home on excursions into nature and community with caring adults. Local libraries may offer toddler story hours, and play groups are increasingly popular and sponsored by a wide number of community groups. Exposing the toddler to supervised toddler play groups gives the child "peer teachers" and promotes social skills. Typically, toddlers play side-by-side rather than cooperatively, but beginning attempts at sharing and short give-and-take interactions take place.

Some toddlers may frequently ask for the names of things and can be insistent and impatient about demands. Words will be learned during real events with concrete (real) objects. Children continue to generate language when their early efforts are accepted and reinforced. Situations that involve positive emotions and those that involve multiple sensory experiences also evoke child language production.

Regularly involving toddlers in educative conversations with educational toys and simple books prompts language growth. Patience and interest—rather than heavy-handed attempts to teach—are best. Getting the most from everyday experiences is a real art that requires an instructive yet relaxed attitude and the ability to talk about what has captured the child's attention. A skilled adult who is with a toddler who is focused on the wrapping paper rather than the birthday present will add comments about the wrapping paper. Or at the zoo, in front of the bear's cage, if the child is staring at a nearby puddle, the adult will discuss the puddle. Providing words and ideas along the child's line of inquiry, and having fun while doing so, becomes second nature after a few attempts.

Skilled adults tend to modify their speech according to the child's ability. They speak clearly, slowly enunciate and slightly exaggerate intonation, and pause between utterances. They may end their sentences with the "focused-on" new word and emphasize it in pitch and stress. They also add to sentence length and complexity, providing that which is just a little beyond the child's level. Parent talk that sensitively and effectively suggests and instructs primes the child's language growth. If the home language is not English, supporting children's development of that language by using it extensively around the home is a wise course of action for it serves as a foundation for the later learning of a second language (in this case, English). This is aided by a strong school-home partnership and the families' active role in their child's education (Figure 2-6).

Parents may need to become aware of the consequences that can result from home or center environments where toddlers experience chaos,

Figure 2-6 Checklist for working with non-English speaking families.

Do	Don't
Make sure parents know it is acceptable to stay with their toddlers for an adjustment period before leaving the toddler on his/her first day or week.	constantly push English word learning by turning most of your teaching interactions or handling of a toddler into an English lesson.
Encourage parents to tour the early childhood center and stay a few hours before enrollment. This allows the child and parent to feel more comfortable.	neglect the importance of promoting the family's use of home language and their feeling of pride in their culture.
Secure a volunteer or a staff member who speaks the toddler's home language. Hearing the home language bolsters the toddler's sense of security.	forget to invite parents to share cultural songs, poetry, and stories at school or record them for school use.
Create a welcoming display or bulletin board outside the classroom, which uses print and photos of non-English-speaking communities, neighborhoods and neighborhood activities. Print captions in multiple languages.	
Find family members or seek volunteers who can develop a key word vocabulary list in the home language of all attending children with words such as "mama," "hello," "help," "bathroom," "drink," "no more," "bottle," "water," "yes," "no," etc. for teacher use.	
Learn to be an expert at reading children's gestures, cues, body positions, state of well-being, or distress, etc.	
Stress key English words calmly and simply and use gestures often to accompany words or phrases. Simple teacher gestures if repeated this way become a visual clue to what is happening next.	
Repeat a nonverbal gesture in the child's home language, for example, pretend to drink while saying water. The toddler will eventually connect the word water with your pretend gesture.	
Invite parents to volunteer and use their native language at school. They become great teachers for teachers trying to learn a child's language.	

unpredictability, violence, and frightening experience as a daily reality. Honig (1999) describes these toddlers as quick to be startled, aroused, angry, defiant, fearful, or withdrawn. She describes the chemical activity in their brains as abnormal. Building intimate, warm, trusting relationships is the best way to teach a child's brain that it need not send the body messages to release high levels of stress hormones. Experts recommend that nurturing providers offer each child interpretable, orderly, soothing, and loving experiences daily to support optimal brain development.

Summary

2-1 Name four conventions of the English language that toddlers learn about speaking.

Toddlers are sorting the sounds they hear in spoken words around them. They attempt group and categorize spoken sounds and develop beginning understandings of, the phonology of their native language. An understanding of the rules of grammar is also happening with exposure to oral speech experiences and listening to others while observing their actions. Grammar rules form and reform as the child gets closer to reproducing mature speech patterns. Toddlers are learning about word order in sentences (syntax). Toddlers also learn the meanings of some words and nonverbal communications. Morphemes enter toddler speech. They are learning to notice regularities and the meanings of words and gestures (semantics). They gain new vocabulary. Pragmatics, the study of how language is used effectively in social contexts, begins to be understood by toddlers. This promotes the toddler's ability to express his needs, wants, ideas, and concerns successfully.

2-2 Describe how toddlers move from using first words to using sentences.

Toddler's first words relate to significant and important people, and objects in their daily lives. Parents and caregivers conversations with toddlers together with firsthand exploration using their sense organs provides depth and meaning to toddlers' new words. Toddlers are active in conversations, speaking and listening, sometimes correcting themselves when trying to get their message across to whomever will listen. Sentences are barely recognizable at first but gain more and more clarity as children age.

Functional action words used in social exchanges appear. Toddlers talk to themselves and their toys in one-word and then two-word (or more) sentences. Easy to pronounce words are added and gestures accompany words adding clarity. One word in a two word sentence is often a pivot word. Toddler sentences become condensed containing only important words or parts of words because of their limited vocabulary and ability to express them (telegraphic and prosodic speech). Understanding the child's meaning often depends on context and the child's voice intonation. Longer sentences appear when children add more verbs, and prepositions, pronouns, articles, and conjunctions.

2-3 Identify three common characteristics of toddler language.

- Toddlers use telegraphic and prosodic speech at times and sentences may be devoid of function words.
- Two to five word sentences are typical.
- Verbs, prepositions, plurals, pronouns, articles, and conjunctions begin to appear in speech.
- Negatives are used.
- Words are often run together and mispronounced alphabet letter sounds are commonplace.
- Gestures accompany many words.
- Toddlers initiate conversations with others and use verbalization to gain adult attention.
- Egocentric speech is frequent and commonplace.
- Toddlers understand much more than they can express.

2-4 State two criteria for selecting books and describe four recommended techniques for reading books to toddlers.

Simple and colorful illustrations or photographs of familiar, everyday objects and situations are appropriate in toddler books. Durable coatings on board books extend use and paperweight facilitates the toddler's handling and page turning. Both fiction and nonfiction books are to be considered. Books containing sensory items to explore were recommended and also books with content that allowed toddlers to interact in some way. Recommended toddler teacher presentation techniques include:

- Select a reading time when a child is curious.
- Don't attempt to use books as a focusing mechanism or a calming down tool during high activity periods.
- Use teacher enthusiasm to entice child interest.
- React by providing recognition for children's positive behaviors such as page turning, naming, or pointing.
- Expect occasional or frequent loss of toddler focus during reading times, for interest may wane quickly and switch to something else.
- Set a special reading time and location for book readings.

2-5 Identify three suggestions for toddler teachers and parents concerning toddlers' opportunities to explore and experience their environment.

- Toddler problem solving is encouraged when toddlers are able to explore and experience their environment with adult supervision.
- Toddlers' growing brains allow them to observe and understand patterns and relationships before they are able to express or describe them.
- Social interactions, playfulness, experiencing instances of cause-and-effect, and investigating objects and people expand children's mental capabilities and verbal skills.
- A language-rich environment with interesting objects coupled with verbally responsive adults promotes speech growth and development.
- Skilled adults modify their comments to a toddler's ability and they speak clearly. An adult may focus upon and emphasize new words that are important aspects of any situation at hand that is interesting to the child.
- Toddlers are able to thrive in and out of the classroom, in nature, and in the community when adults arrange supervised excursions and play groups.

Additional Resources

Readings

Barbro, J. (2013). *Foundations of Responsive Caregiving: Infants, Toddlers, and Twos*. St. Paul, MD: Redleaf Press.

Falasco, D. (2010). *Teaching Twos and Threes: A Comprehensive Curriculum*. St. Paul, MN: Redleaf Press.

Pan, B. A., Rowe, M. L., Singer, J., & Snow, C. E. (2005). Maternal correlates of toddler vocabulary production in low income families. *Child Development*. 76 (4), 765–782.

Toddler Books

Cowley, J. (1999) *Mrs. Wishy-Washy*. East Rutherford, NJ: Philomel Books. (Board book.)

Davenport, Z. (1995). *Toys*. New York: Ticknor & Fields. (Common toys and objects.)

Elya, S. M. (2006). *BeebeGoes Shopping*. New York: Harcourt.

Fleming, D. (2006). *The Cow Who Clucked*. New York: Henry Holt. (Sounds and silliness that delight.)

Kindersley, D. (2003). *Are Lemons Blue?* New York: Author. (Playful.)

Low, W. (2009). *Machines Go to Work*. New York; Henry Holt.

Manushkin, F. (2009). *The Tushy Book*. New York: Macmillan.

Oxenbury, H. (1988). *Tickle, Tickle*. New York: Macmillan.

Priddy, R. (2002). *My Big Animal Book*. New York: St. Martin's Press.

Wattenberg, J. (2007). *Mrs. Mustard's Baby Faces*. San Francisco: Chronicle Books.

Whitford, R. (2005). *Little Yoga: A Toddler's First Book of Yoga*. New York: Holt, Henry Books for Young Readers. (Expect to try yoga positions with toddlers.)

Helpful Website

National Parent Information Network

http://npin.org

Provides related websites for parents and teachers.

3

Preschool Years

Objectives

After reading this chapter, you should be able to:

3-1 Identify three characteristics of younger preschoolers' speech and communication.

3-2 Describe three pieces of recommended advice to a family concerned about a preschooler's speaking abilities.

3-3 Describe conversational skills necessary for an older preschooler to maintain a true conversation.

3-4 Discuss older preschoolers' manipulation and playful use of words.

3-5 List reasons for planning sensory, motor skill activities; cognitive, building activities; or social, emotional growth activities, to promote language development.

naeyc NAEYC Program Standards

C03 Teaching staff support children as they practice skills and build friendships.

1F01 Teaching staff actively teach children social, communication, and emotional regulation skills.

1F02 Teaching staff help children use language to communicate needs.

2A10 The curriculum guides teachers to incorporate content, concepts, and activities that foster language and literacy.

DAP Developmentally Appropriate Practice (DAP)

1A2 Teachers help children learn how to establish positive, constructive relationships with others.

2B3 Teachers help children acquire new skills and understandings using a range of strategies.

2B6 Teachers frequently engage children in planning or reflecting on their experiences, discussing past experiences, and working to represent them.

2B7 Teachers promote children collaborating to work through ideas and solutions.

2D2 Teachers use verbal encouragement and acknowledge effort with specific comments.

3G2 Teachers make sure that children have plenty of opportunities to use large muscles.

3G4 Teachers provide for fine motor skill development.

COMMON CORE Common Core State Standards for English Language Arts and Literacy

L.CCR 5 Demonstrate understanding of figurative language, word relationships, and nuances in meaning.

SL.CCR 4 Present information, findings, and supporting evidence such that listeners can follow the line of reasoning and the organization, development, and style that are appropriate to task, purpose, and audience.

R.CCR 7 Integrate and evaluate content presented in diverse media and format, including visually and quantitatively, as well as in words.

On And On And On . . .

Wilford is four and eager to speak in groups. He rambles, goes on and on, and both bores and loses his audience. Renee, his teacher, waits, patiently listening, but occasionally interrupts him to say, "Thank you, Wilford, for sharing with us." Sometimes this stops him, but often it does not.

Questions to Ponder

1. Is this "stream of consciousness" talking typical of four-year-olds? Is this a behavior found in some adults?

2. What teacher strategies might help Renee?

3. Describe three program activities that might help Wilford.

The preschool child's speech reflects sensory, physical, and social experiences, as well as thinking ability. Teachers accept temporary limitations, knowing that almost all children will reach adult language levels. During the preschool years, children move rapidly through successive phases of language learning. By the time youngsters reach their fifth year, the most challenging hurdles of language learning have been overcome.

An understanding of typical preschool speech characteristics can help the teacher interact skillfully and provide appropriate learning opportunities and activities, as does classroom experience and child study. This chapter pinpoints language use during preschool years. Although speech abilities are emphasized, growth and change in other areas, as they relate to speech, are also covered. In addition to school, the child's home environment and playing with other children are major factors influencing language development. Finding friends in his age group is an important benefit of attending an early childhood center. In a place where there are fascinating things to explore and talk about, language abilities blossom (Photo 3-1).

It is almost impossible to find a child who has all of the speech characteristics of a given age group, but most children possess some age-typical characteristics. There is a wide range within normal age-level behavior, and each child's individuality is an important consideration. For simplicity's sake, the preschool period is divided into two age groups: young, or early,

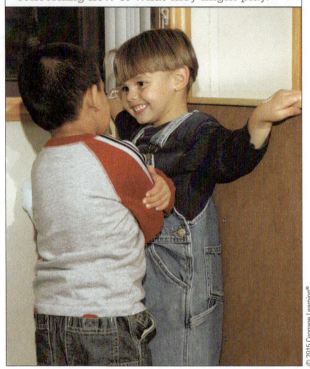

Photo 3-1 Children often share their ideas concerning how or what they might play.

© 2015 Cengage Learning®

preschoolers (two- and three-year-olds) and older preschoolers (four- and five-year-olds).

3-1 Young Preschoolers

Preschoolers communicate needs, desires, and feelings through speech and action. Close observation of a child's nonverbal communication can help uncover true meanings. Raising an arm, fiercely clutching playthings, or lying spread-eagle over as many blocks as possible may express more than the child is able to put into words. Stroking a friend's arm, handing a toy to another child who has not asked for it but looks at it longingly, and following the teacher around the room are behaviors that carry other meanings. One can expect continued fast growth and changing language abilities, and children's understanding of adult statements is surprising. They may acquire six to 10 new words a day. Figure 3-1 displays children's stunning vocabulary growth from ages one to seven.

Figure 3-1 Vocabulary growth.

Vocabulary Growth

10–14 months	first word	First words are usually nouns instead of verbs.
12–18 months	two words a week; close to 50 by 18 months	Child looks at something (or someone), points, and then says one or two words. Mispronunciations are common.
18–24 months	200 words	Some toddlers constantly ask "What dat?" or just "Dat?" They want objects named.
2–3 years	500 words	Questions, questions, questions! Mispronunciations still happen, and consonants may be substituted for one another in some words.
3–4 years	800 words	Preschoolers start to use contractions ("won't," "can't") as well as prepositions ("in," "on") and time expressions ("morning," "afternoon"). They may also make up words.
4–5 years	1,500 or more words	Children speak with greater clarity, can construct five- and six-word sentences, and make up stories.
5–7 years	11,000 words	Children retell and discuss stories. They have many words at hand and will know more than 50,000 as adults.

Squeals, grunts, and screams are often part of play. Imitating animals, sirens, and environmental noise is common. The child points and pulls to help others understand meanings. Younger preschoolers tend to act as though others can read their thoughts because, in the past, adults anticipated what was needed. A few children may have what seems to be a limited vocabulary at school until they feel at home there.

A difference between the child's **receptive** (or **comprehension**) **vocabulary** and his **expressive** (or **productive**) **vocabulary** is apparent, with the productive vocabulary lagging behind the receptive vocabulary. The receptive vocabulary requires that the child hears a word and anticipates or reacts appropriately; the production of a word means the child speaks the word at an appropriate time and place.

Children begin to acquire the more complex forms of grammar during this time period, including past tenses, embedded clauses, and passive constructions. Creative mistakes happen, such as "he breakeded my bike," which indicates that the child is noticing consistent patterns and applying them to the language system as he understands it.

The words used most often are nouns and short possessives: *my, mine, Rick's*. Speech focuses on present events, things are observed in newscaster style, and "no" is used liberally.

As preschoolers progress in the ability to hold brief conversations, they must keep conversational topics in mind and connect their thoughts with those of others. This is difficult for two-year-olds, and true conversational exchange with playmates is brief, if it exists at all. Although their speech is filled with pauses and repetitions in which they attempt to correct themselves, early preschoolers are adept at conversational turn taking. Talking over the speech of another speaker at this age occurs only about five percent of the time.

Speech may be loud and high-pitched when the child is excited, or it may be barely audible and muffed when the child is embarrassed, sad, or shy. Speech of two- and three-year-olds tends to be uneven in rhythm, with comments issued in spurts rather than in an even flow like the speech of older children (Photo 3-2). There seems to be an important step forward in the complexity of content in children's speech at age two. They may begin making comments about cause and effect and sometimes use conjunctions, such as *'cause, 'ah*, and *'um*, between statements. Young preschoolers' talk is self-focused and mostly concerned with their intentions and feelings. Why they wanted or did not want to do certain things, or what they wanted other people to do. Statements such as "I'm painting" or "I'm not climbing!" are commonplace.

receptive (comprehension) vocabulary — the comprehension vocabulary used by a person in listening (and silent reading).
expressive (productive) vocabulary — the vocabulary a person uses in speaking and writing.

Much of the time very young preschoolers' play focuses on recreating the work of the home and family—cooking, eating, sleeping, washing, ironing, infant care, and imitations of family events and pets (Photo 3-3). Play of slightly older preschoolers is more interactive. The child continues self-play and also explores other children, adults, environments, and actions. Eventually, most preschoolers understand that it is usually worth their while to share toys and take turns because when other playmates are around it is more fun. Two-year-olds may believe, as one preschooler remarked to his teacher, that "share means you give it away." When children begin exploring these other play options, "what's happening" in play becomes a speech subject, along with brief verbal reactions to what others are saying and doing.

Photo 3-2 Speech can be limited when children are very interested.

A desire to organize and make sense of their experiences is often apparent in young preschoolers. Colors, counting, and new categories of thought emerge in their speech. There is a tendency for them to live out the action words they speak or hear in the speech of others. An adult who says "We won't run" may motivate a child to run; in contrast, an adult who says "Walk" might be more successful in having the child walk. This is why experienced teachers tell children what they want children to do rather than what they do not want them to do.

3-1a The Subdued Two-Year-Old

In any given group of young children, a few may appear subdued and quiet, having a tendency toward what many might call shyness. These children may possess a natural inclination that tends to inhibit spontaneous speech. Strong emotions can cause muscle tension, including tension in the larynx. Some adults asked to speak in front of a group experience this phenomenon. It can also affect speech volume. Most preschool teachers

Photo 3-3 Teachers encourage the verbalizations of preschoolers.

have worked with children whose speech was difficult to hear. Often, these children seem restrained when faced with unfamiliar situations. As older preschoolers, they may become more outgoing and talkative or may continue to be less talkative and somewhat subdued when compared with their more boisterous counterparts. Teachers respect these children's natural inclinations and tendencies, but try to build the children's trust and their play opportunities with others.

3-1b Verb Forms

In English, most verbs (regular forms) use *-ed* to indicate past tense. Unfortunately, many frequently used verbs have irregular past-tense forms, such as *came, fell, hit, saw, took,* and *gave.* Because the child begins using often-heard words, early speech contains correct verb forms. With additional exposure to language, children realize that past events are described with *-ed* verb endings. At that point, children tack the *-ed* on regular verbs as well as on irregular verbs, creating words such as *broked, dranked,* and other charming past-tense forms. This beautiful logic often brings inner smiles to the adult listeners. Verbs ending with *-ing* are used more than before. Even auxiliary verbs are scattered through speech—"Me have," "Daddy did it." Words such as *wanna, gonna,* and *hafta* seem to be learned as one word, and stick in children's vocabulary, to be used over and over.

A term for children's speech behavior that indicates they have formed a new internal rule about language and are using it is **regularization**. As children filter what they hear, creating their own rule systems, they begin to apply the new rules. An expected sequence in forming rules for past-tense verb usage follows.

- Uses irregular tense endings correctly (e.g., *ran, came, drank*).
- Forms an internal rule when discovering that *-ed* expresses past events (e.g., *danced, called, played*).
- Over-regularizes; for example, adds *-ed* to all regular and irregular verbs that were formerly spoken correctly (e.g., *camed, dided, wented, goed*).
- Learns that both regular and irregular verbs express past tense, and uses both.

In using plural noun forms, the following sequence is common.

- Remembers and uses singular forms of nouns correctly (e.g., *ball, dog, mouse, bird*).
- Uses irregular noun plurals correctly (e.g., *men, feet, mice*).

- Forms an internal rule that plurals have "s" or "z" ending sounds.
- Applies rule to all nouns (e.g., *balls, mens, dogs, feets, birds, mices, or ballsez, dogsez, feetsez*).
- Achieves flexible internal rules for plurals, memorizes irregular plural forms, and uses plurals correctly.

3-1c Key-Word Sentences and Questioning

The two-year-old omits many words in sentences, as does the toddler. The remaining words are shortened versions of adult sentences in which only the essentials are present. These words are key words and convey the essence of the message. Teachers attempt to relate questionable child utterances to concurrent child activity to grasp a child's meaning. Sentences at this stage are about four words long. Some pronouns and adjectives, such as *pretty* or *big*, are used. Very few, if any, prepositions (*by, on, with*) or articles (*a, an, the*) are spoken. Some words are run together and are spoken as single units, such as "whadat?" or "eatem," as are the verb forms mentioned earlier. The order of words (syntax) may seem jumbled at times, as in "outside going ball," but basic grammar rules are observed in most cases.

Pronouns are often used incorrectly and are confused, as in "Me finish milk," and "him Mark's." Concepts of male and female, living things, and objects may be only partly understood, as shown in the example of the three-year-old who says of a special toy she cannot find, "Maybe it is hiding!" This probably indicates she hasn't yet learned that hiding can be done only by an animate object.

Questions (where, what, why, who) begin to appear in the speech of the young preschooler. During the toddler period, rising voice inflection and simple declarative utterances such as "Dolly drink?" are typical. At this stage, questions focus on location, objects, and people. Occasionally, their questions display a special interest in causation (why), process (how), and time (when). This reflects more mature thinking that probes purposes and intentions in others. Encouraging children's questions is an important job skill and allows early childhood teachers to at times to answer 'I don't know." A teacher might say, "That's

---

regularization — a child's speech behavior that indicates the formation and internalization of a language rule (regularity).

Figure 3-2 Question development.

Age	
age 2	raises voice pitch at sentence ending: "Me go?" "All gone?" uses short "what" and "where" questions: "Whas dat?" "Where kitty?"
age 3	asks yes-no questions begins to use "why" questions begins to use auxiliary verbs in questions: "Can I have gum?" "Will you get it?" begins to use "how" questions: "How you do that?"
age 4	adds tag endings: "Those are mine, okay?" "You like it, huh?" "That's good, isn't it?" inverts auxiliary verbs in questions: "Why are you sad?" "Why aren't we staying with gramma?" begins to use complex and two-part questions and statements: "I will tell him how to do it if you like." "What can I do when he won't come?" "I don't know what to do." "Why does it fall down when the door slams?"

a good question," or if speaking with a younger preschooler, they can follow the child's question with an open ended question of their own such as "what happened?" This can lead to seeking the answer together. Teachers often call attention and point to features purposefully letting children in on their thoughts and observations. Sometimes this practice prompts children's questions. Nurturing children's questions can increase their sense of wonder and curiosity leading to further vocabulary development and support for a further search for answers or solutions. Figure 3-2 shows one child's question development. Questions are frequent, and the child sometimes asks for an object's function or the causes of certain events. It is as if the child sees that things exist for a purpose that in some way relates to him. The answers adults provide stimulate the child's desire to know more. Questions about words and word meanings appear, such as "Why is his name Ang?" Vocabularies of the young preschooler range from 250 to more than 1,000 words (Figure 3-3). An average of 50 new words enters the child's vocabulary each month.

Figure 3-3 Growth of vocabulary.

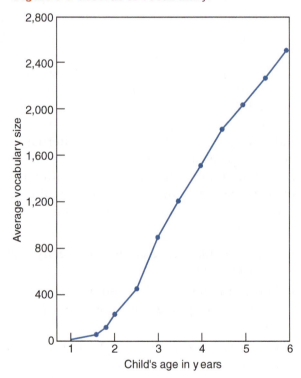

3-1d Categories in Children's Thinking

Children organize a tremendous amount of sensory data and information gained though life experiences by forming mental categories. Studies point out that young children can be quite sophisticated in how they group objects and think about their groupings. Young preschoolers' categories differ from those of older children. The young preschooler tends to focus on superficial properties such as the "look" of something and where it is found. A younger child may focus on the teacher's fuzzy sweater by wanting to touch and rub it and saying "soft." An older preschooler may talk about its number of buttons, or patterns, or its similarity to his own sweater or other sweaters he has seen. Preschoolers often put items together in terms of their visual similarities rather than grouping items according to more fundamental likenesses.

Figure 3-4 Common overextensions used in a child's first three years.

First Word	Word Was Used to Identify an Object, Person or Event	Later Word Was Applied to
dada	daddy	store clerk, doctor, mailman, football player, teenager.
moo	moon	cookie, melon, letter O, clock, pizza pan, button.
ah	soft	fuzzy sweater, dog's fur, flower petal, plush doll.
em	worm	pasta, caterpillar, licorice ropes, string, rice.
wh	sound of train	vacuum cleaner, mixer, wind, fast vehicles. motor noise.
ba	ball	oranges, meatballs, yarn, coconut, overhead light, lollypop, bubbles.

Younger preschoolers commonly call all four-footed furry animals "dog," and all large animals "horse." This reflects **overextension**, in which the child has overextended and made a logical conclusion because these animals have many of the same features, can be about the same size, and therefore fit the existing word. This phenomenon is seen in the examples given in Figure 3-4.

Concept development, defined in Chapter 2 as the recognition of one or more distinguishing features or characteristics, proceeds by leaps and bounds during preschool years and is essential to meaningful communication. The details, exceptions, and discrepancies are often discussed in four-year-olds' conversations. The younger preschooler can be described as a "looker and doer" who engages in limited discussion of the features of situations. The excitement of exploration and discovery, particularly of something new and novel, is readily apparent in preschool classrooms. Children typically crowd around to see, touch, experience, and make comments about objects and events. Teachers notice the all-consuming focusing and the long periods of watching or touching, usually followed by verbalizing and questioning an event or experience.

As they age, young children can find that learning not only brings them pleasure, but also perhaps mastery and satisfaction. Medina (2008) suggests this breeds the confidence it takes to take intellectual risks. A young preschooler who learns to button his sweater, tie his shoe, ride a bike, or count to five, usually wants to share his accomplishment with anyone who will listen and will repeat the physical actions over and over just to prove he can do them.

3-1e Running Commentaries and Repetition

As children play, their actions are sometimes accompanied by a running self-commentary or "stream of consciousness" talking concerning what they are doing or what is happening (Figure 3-5). It can be described as a kind of verbal thought process, like mentally talking to oneself such as "Now, where did I put that key?" It seems to increase in complex play situations as the child problem solves and talks it through.

Researchers suggest multiple reasons for preschoolers' private speech. These include the following: (1) talking to themselves is a way of giving themselves directions for their intended actions, (2) they need a sensorimotor activity as a reinforcer or "crutch" because their cognitive schemes are not yet well developed, and (3) it is more efficient for them to talk their ideas through in words rather than silently.

Self-talk may help children sequence actions, control their own behavior, use more flexible modes of thinking, and manipulate the goals they are trying to achieve in their play. Talking to self and talking to another can occur alternately. Toys, animals, and treasured items still receive a few words. Statements directed to others do not usually need answers. Private speech rarely considers another's point of view. A conversation between young preschoolers may sound like two children

---

overextension — in the early acquisition of words and their meanings, the application of a word to include other objects that share common features, such as "water" being used to describe any liquid.

Figure 3-5 Conversation during play activity.

Situation: Four- and five-year-old girls playing with water

	Commentary	Characteristic
Debbie:	"Two of those make one of these." (playing with measuring cups)	Talking to self.
Debbie:	"Two cups or three cups . . . whoops it went over."	Talks about what happened.
Tifine:	"Stop it or else I'll beat you up." (said to Debbie)	Does not respond to another's speech.
Debbie:	"This is heavy." (holding the 2-cup measuring container full of water)	Describes perception.
Christine:	"Is it hot?" (Christine just dropped in)	
Debbie:	"Feel it and see."	Hears another; answers appropriately.
	"It's not hot." (feeling the water)	Child talking to self.
Debbie:	"I'm finished now. Oh this is awfully heavy—I'm going to pour it into the bottle."	Talking about what she perceives and what she is doing.

talking together about different subjects. Neither child is really listening or reacting to what the other says. When a very young preschooler does wish to talk directly to another child, it is sometimes done through an adult. A child may say, "I want truck," to an adult, even if the child playing with the truck is standing close by.

Other researchers who have examined self-talk suggest a number of possible developmental benefits. These include:

- practicing newly recognized language forms (Photo 3-4).

- obtaining pleasure through play with word sounds.
- exploring vocal capacities.
- reliving particular significant events.
- creating dialogue in which the child voices all participants' parts, perhaps helping the child later fit into social settings.
- experimenting with fantasy, thereby accommodating the creative urge.
- attending objectively to language.
- facilitating motor behavior in a task or project.

Photo 3-4 Trying to put the peg into the hole, Valerie utters, "Goes in."

Whatever its benefits, self-talk is natural, common behavior. By the age of five, the child's self-talk is observed infrequently. As children approach the age of three, both dialogue and monologue are apparent. Observers of play conversations find it difficult to determine just how much of each is present.

Teachers who conduct group times with younger preschoolers are familiar with children who ramble on and on; the teachers deal with this behavior by using a variety of techniques. Teachers try to encourage "my turn, your turn" behaviors. Kitchen timers, a ping-pong paddle held by one speaker and then passed to another, or a turned-on flashlight used to signal a child that his speaking turn is over are strategies teachers have devised. Teachers also try to draw focus back to the subject at hand by saying, "Amy, yes, dogs do use their tongues when they drink. It is Jeremy's turn to tell us about his dog now."

Repetition in speech is common. Sometimes it happens randomly at play, and at other times it is done with a special purpose. A young child may repeat almost everything said to him. Most young preschoolers repeat words or parts of sentences regularly. Children's growing language skills allow them to create repetitions that rhyme, as in "oogie, woogie, poogie bear," which greatly please them. They quickly imitate words that they like; sometimes, excitement is the cause. Rhyming words or rhyming syllables may promote enjoyable mimicking and younger preschoolers are particularly fascinated and attracted to words that rhyme. Repetition of rhyming words seems to help children remember things such as "Get up at eight and you won't be late." Free associations (voiced juggling of sounds and words) occur at play and at rest and may sound like babbling. Many times, it seems as though, having learned a word, the child must savor it or practice it, over and over (Photo 3-5).

3-1f Lack of Clarity

About one in every four words uttered by the young preschooler is not readily understandable. This lack of clarity is partially caused by an inability to control the mouth, tongue, and breathing and an inability to hear subtle differences and distinctions in speech. Typically, articulation of all English speech sounds, especially some **consonant** blends, is not accomplished until age seven or eight. Young preschoolers are only 40 to 80 percent correct in their articulation of words. This lack of intelligibility can be partly attributed to the complexity of the task of mastering the sounds. Although children may be right on target in development, their speech may still be difficult to understand.

Photo 3-5 Elsa Beth calls this "bussing" her teeth.

© 2015 Cengage Learning®

The young preschooler may have difficulty with the rate of speech, phrasing, inflection, intensity, syntax, and voice stress. Faulty articulation and defective sound making can also contribute to the problem. The child who attempts to form the longest utterances is the one who is hardest to understand. The child who omits sounds is less clear than the one who distorts them. As a rule, expect omissions, substitutions, and distortions in the speech of two- and three-year olds, for they will be plentiful.

By three years of age, children's pronunciation patterns are not yet fully like those of adults, but the basic features of the adult phonological system are present. Most children can produce all of the **vowel** sounds and nearly all of the consonant sounds in at least a few words, but their productions are not 100 percent accurate.

Young children typically omit sounds at the ends of words, saying, for example, *ba* for "ball." Middle consonants in longer words are also passed over lightly—*ikeem* for "ice cream" or *telfone* for "telephone." Even beginning sounds may be omitted, as in *ellow* for "yellow."

Substitutions of letter sounds are also common, for example, *aminal* and *pasghetti*. Until the new sound is mastered, one consonant may even

---

consonant — (1) a speech sound made by partial or complete closure of the vocal tract, which obstructs air flow; (2) an alphabet letter used in representing any of these sounds.

vowel — (1) a voiced speech sound made without stoppage or friction of air flow as it passes through the vocal tract; (2) an alphabet letter used in representing any of these sounds.

▶❚❚ TeachSource Video 3-1

Preschool: Communication Development through Language and Literacy Activities

The video focuses on preschoolers' dramatic play and role playing as well as songs, stories, and prewriting opportunities that are language and literacy-building.

1. What dramatic play scenarios might be commonly initiated by a full classroom of preschoolers living in a rural farm community? And how might their teachers plan to accommodate it? How about a classroom full of inner-city urban preschoolers?

2. In what way might early childhood educators connect alphabet letter recognition or print awareness opportunities with preschoolers' dramatic play?

© 2016 Cengage Learning®

take the place of another; *wabbit*, *wun*, and *wain* are common examples. Children who cannot yet produce all of the speech sounds accurately can generally hear the differences such as the difference between *w* and *r*, or *t* and *th*, when they are pronounced by others.

Short play sequences that involve acting or imitating the behavior of family begin at home and school. Speech usually accompanies the reenactments. Although young children at this age play side-by-side, most of this dramatic play starts as solitary activity. Common play themes include talking on the phone, caring for a baby, or cooking. Dolls, toys, and dress-up clothes are usually part of the action and may serve to initiate this type of play. Observers of two- and three-year-olds in classrooms find it hard to determine whether children are engaged in joint planning

of play or are simply playing in the same area with the same kinds of playthings. Preschools purposely purchase multiple dolls so that many children can feed and rock "their babies" when they see others doing it.

3-2 Advice for Families and Early Childhood Educators DAP

Families sometimes fret about a child who stops, stammers, or stutters when speaking. Calling attention to this speech and making demands on the child cause tension, making the situation worse. All children hesitate, repeat, stop, and start in speaking—it is typical behavior. Searching for the right word takes time, and thoughts may come faster than words. Adults need to relax and wait. Speech is a complex process of sending and receiving. Maintaining patience and optimism and assuming a casual "I'm listening" stance is the best course of action for the adult. Many schools routinely send home informational material to alert families to age-level speech characteristics and the need to check child's hearing frequently due to colds and upper respiratory infections.

Teachers frequently encounter child statements that are seemingly illogical and they suspect, if they acknowledge them, that the child will soon provide more information. Child logic is there, but teachers know that they are not privy to inner thought processes or children's past experiences. With more information, what at first appeared illogical turns out to have beautiful logic.

Frequently, a listening teacher will feel on the edge of understanding what a child is trying to say. This happens with both younger and older preschoolers struggling at times to put into words what they are thinking (Photo 3-6). Acceptance and interest are appropriate.

Attentive interaction with positive feedback is recommended for adults who live or work with two- and three-year-olds. Reacting to the intent of the child's message is more helpful than concentrating on correctness. In other words, focus on what is said rather than the way it is said. A lot of guessing is still necessary to determine what the child is trying to say. The adult's model of speech will override temporary errors as the child hears more and more of it.

Photo 3-6 "Me eatem!"

By simply naming objects, adults can encourage children to notice how different items are similar and can help children gain new information about the world. Helping children see the details and relationships in what they encounter is useful if done in a matter of fact rather than a pressured way or an "I'm trying to teach you something" manner. Connecting past events to present events may aid their understanding.

3-2a Books for Younger Preschoolers

Many picture books are available for younger preschoolers. Experts suggest books for this age group that have:

- themes, objects, animals, or people that are familiar and within their range of life experience.
- clarity of content and story line.
- clear, simple illustrations or photographs with backgrounds that do not distract from the intended focus.
- themes concerning everyday tasks and basic human needs.

Most two- and three-year-olds enjoy actively participating in story reading, but they can be very good listeners as well. Participation can include pointing, making noise, repeating dialogue, or performing imitative body actions. Books that are repetitive and predictable offer the enjoyment of anticipating what will come next. For children who are used to being read to at bedtime,

the calming effect of listening to the human voice becomes very apparent during story reading when heads nod or children act sleepy. Chapter 8 covers the topic of introducing preschool children to literature.

3-3 Older Preschoolers

As younger preschoolers get older, adults can expect the following:

- longer sentences with more words per sentence
- more specificity
- more "ing" endings on verbs
- increased correctness in the forms of the verb "to be"
- use of more auxiliary verbs
- more facility with passive-voice verbs, including "did" and "been"
- changes in negative sentences, from "No want" to "I don't want"
- changes in question forms, from "Car go?" to "Where did the car go?"
- changes in mental categories
- additional clarifications in articulation of speech sounds

By the time they are between four and five years of age, most preschoolers' speech is similar to adult use; their sentences are longer, with almost all words present rather than only key words (Photo 3-7).

Preschoolers' play is active and vocal, and they copy each other's words and manner of speaking. A word such as "monster," or more colorful words, may swiftly become of interest and spread rapidly from child to child. Remember the joy that both younger and older children exhibited with the phrases: "zip-a-dee-doo-dah," "bibbidi-bobbidi-boo," "scoobidoobi-do," "blast off," "fuzzy-wuzzy," and "ooey-gooey"? Every generation of preschoolers seems to have their own favorite sayings, and new ones are constantly appearing.

The older preschooler's social speech and conversations are heard and interpreted to a greater degree by others of the child's age. The child learns and practices the complexities of social conversation, including (1) gaining another's attention by making eye contact, touching, or using words or catch-phrases like "Know what?"; (2) pausing and listening; (3) correcting himself; (4) maintaining attention and word flow by not pausing, so as not to let another speaker jump in; (5) taking turns in conversing by developing patience and trying to listen while still holding in mind what he wants to say. Being more social

now, four- and five-year-olds' self-talk has almost completely disappeared. He now plans, monitors ideas, and evaluates silently, but he has yet to stop talking about his accomplishments and discoveries and still displays a "look at me" need.

3-3a Friendships and Group Play

The young preschooler may develop a new friend or find another he prefers to play near or with. At ages two and three, friendships are usually temporary, changing from day to day. Friendships of older preschoolers are more stable and lasting. By ages four and five, there seems to be a desire to remain compatible and work out differences, therefore creatively maintaining a type of play acceptable to both. Negotiation, clarification, and open-mindedness flourish during play. A friend's needs and requests are handled with sensitivity, and flexibility characterizes conversations. Needless to say, spats, "blowups," and the crushed feelings accompanying rejection sometimes occur. Verbal interaction between children adds a tremendous amount of verbal input and also promotes output.

Joint planning of play activities and active make-believe and role-playing take on new depth in older preschoolers. Most four- and five-year-olds' main concern seems to be interacting with age-mates. Twosomes and groups of play companions are typical in older preschoolers' classrooms and play yards (Photo 3-8). As speech blossoms, friendships blossom and disintegrate (Photo 3-9). Speech is used to discourage and disallow entrance to play groups when running from newcomers is impossible. Speech is found to be effective in hurting feelings, as in statements such as "I don't like you" or "No girls." Children find that verbal inventiveness may help them join play or initiate play.

In group play, pretending is paramount. Make-believe play appears to be at its zenith. Many children grow in the ability to (1) verbally suggest

Photo 3-7 Rene is explaining why she selected a certain puzzle piece.

© 2015 Cengage Learning®

Photo 3-8 Twosomes may become stable or disintegrate.

new directions and avenues of fantasy, (2) engage in verbal negotiation, (3) compromise, (4) argue, and (5) become a group's leader by using the right words. Popular children seem to be those who use speech creatively and become enjoyable companions to others. Violent statements such as "I'm going to shoot you" or "cut you up" are sometimes heard, and these tend to reflect television viewing or media drama. The reality-fantasy dividing line may become temporarily blurred in some play situations, causing some children considerable anxiety.

Older preschoolers talk "in character" as they elaborate their dramatic play. If a scenario calls for a mother talking to a baby or teenagers talking, preschoolers routinely adopt appropriate speech. Imitations of pop singers or cartoon characters are common. Role-taking is an important skill in mature communication, indicating that

Photo 3-9 Group play encourages social development and social connectiveness.

social and dramatic play and improvisation are effective means of facilitating growth in communicative competence.

Four-year-olds seem to boast, brag, and make lots of noise. However, apparently boastful statements such as "Look what I did" may just be the child's attempt to show that he is capable and to share his accomplishments. Although preschoolers enjoy being with their peers, they quickly and easily engage in quarreling and name-calling. Sometimes, they do battle verbally. Typically, three- to five-year-olds disagree over possession of objects or territory, and verbal reasons or verbal evidence may help them win arguments. Many conflicts are resolved and lead to continued play. Speech helps children settle their affairs with and without adult help.

As a child develops an enhanced sense of humor, giggling becomes part of the noise of play. Silliness often reigns. One preschool boy thought it hilarious to go up to a teacher named Alice and say, "What's your name, Alice?" and then run off laughing—quite mature humor for a four-year-old! Preschoolers may distort and repeat what a caregiver says, making changes in sounds and gleefully chanting the distorted mes-

sage. Teachers who want to cultivate children's ability to understand and appreciate humor try to plan activities and present materials that challenge children's ability to interpret humor. Getting a joke often depends on understanding a play on words or ideas. Slapstick humor is still the most popular form with older preschoolers.

Argument, persuasion, and statements aimed at controlling others are frequently heard during play. Older preschool children are able to state reasons (Photo 3-10), request information, give explanations, utter justifications for their behavior, and verbally defend themselves. At times, establishing authority in disagreements seems paramount to compromising.

3-3b Exploring the Conventions of Conversation

Children learn language by reinventing it for themselves, not by direct instruction. They crack the code through exposure and opportunities to converse. They actively, although unconsciously, ingest and discover the rules of the system. Their speech errors often alert adults to the inner rules of language being formed.

Conversations have unwritten rules and expectations, the "you-talk-I-talk" sequence being the most apparent. Some preschoolers (three- and four-year-olds) may delight in violating or "playing" with the conventions of conversation. Sometimes preschoolers deliberately mislead (usually to tease playfully) or use "taboo" bathroom talk, nonsense talk, or unexpected tone when they are capable of verbally responding at a more mature level. Most teachers sense the child may be asserting independence by rejecting conversational convention. One teacher termed this "going into the verbal crazies"—to reject what another child or adult is saying, therefore attempting to change or control the situation. By violating conversational convention, children may clarify how conversational interaction should take place.

3-3c Relational Words

More and more relational words appear as the child begins to compare, contrast, and revise stored concepts with new happenings. The following teacher-recorded anecdote during a story-telling activity shows how the child attempts to relate previously learned ethics to a new situation.

Photo 3-10 Look at what I caught!

© 2015 Cengage Learning®

During storytelling Michael repeated with increasing vigor, "He not berry nice!" at the parts of the story when the wolf says, "I'm going to blow your house down." Michael seemed to be checking with me the correctness of his thinking based on his internalized rules of proper moral conduct. (Machado, 2011, p. 16)

Perhaps because adults stress bad and good or because a young child's inner sense of what is and what is not proper is developing, teachers notice that preschoolers often describe feelings and people within narrow limits. One is pretty or ugly, mean or nice. Shades of meaning or extenuating circumstances seem yet to be understood. Preschoolers are focused on the here and now. Their senses actively probe by touching, smelling, observing, and listening to sounds. Around age four, conceptual dimensions begin to be understood, and they question the function and use of items, make comparisons, and discover relationships. They are beginning to categorize their environment differently:

> Although the words "big" and "little" are commonly used by preschoolers, they are overused. Many other comparison words give children trouble, and one hears "biggerer," "big-big-big," and "bestus one" to describe size. Time words elicit smiles from adults as children wrestle with present, past, and future, as in "zillion days" or "tomorrower." Number words are difficult for some children to handle, and expressions such as "whole bunches" and "eleventeen" are sometimes heard.

Although four-year-olds are able speakers, many of the "plays on words," double meanings, and connotative language subtleties that are important in adult speech are beyond children's understanding. Their creative uses of words at times seem metaphoric and poetic and are valiant attempts to put thoughts into words. Half-heard words and partially or fully learned words are blended together and are, at times, wonderfully descriptive. The author still laughs about the four-year-old who called her "Mrs. Eye Shadow."

3-3d Creative, Impact Words and Vocal Manipulation

There is tremendous variety in the ways children can modify their voices, and they may speak in a different pitch or rhythm when speaking to different people. They can whine, whisper, change volume, and distort timing and pronunciation. Some children discover that by increasing volume or changing tone they can affect others' behavior. They find that speech can show anger or sarcasm and can be used aggressively to hurt others.

Preschoolers may mimic the speech of "bad guy" media characters. Acts of aggression, clothed in the imitated speech and actions of a movie, television, or video character, can become part of this type of play. Purposeful echoing or baby talk can irritate or tease. Excessive talking is sometimes used to get one's way, and "talking back" may occur. Some children find that silence can get as much attention from adults as loud speech. Tattling on another may simply be a way of checking for correctness, or it can be purposeful.

Through trial and error and feedback, the child finds that words can hurt, gain friends or favor, or satisfy a wide range of needs. Because preschoolers are emotion-packed human beings, their statements range from expressions of "you're my buddy" to "you're my enemy" within a matter of minutes. What may appear to be violent statements may be just role-playing or make-believe competition. To some adults, preschooler speech may appear loud and wild. Their speech seems overly nasal and full of moisture that sprays outward. A young child may have frequent nasal colds and congestion during this period. Preschoolers tend to stand close to others and their volume increases when they feel strongly about their subjects.

Impact Words. Not all speech used by older preschoolers is appreciated by adults. Name-calling and offensive words and phrases may be used by active preschoolers to gain attention and reaction from both adults and children. Children discover that some phrases, sentences, and words cause unusual behavior in others. They actively explore these and usually learn which of these are inappropriate and when they can be used. Children recognize that most of this type of talk has "impact value." If certain talk makes people laugh or gives the children some kind of positive reward, it is used over and over.

Bathroom words seem to be explored and used as put-downs and attention getters. As every parent and teacher knows, young children experiment with language related to the body, and particularly to the private parts, going to the bathroom, and sexuality. In fact, children's use of sexual words can make it seem as if they know more than they do. Giggles and uproarious laughter can ensue when these words are used, adding to the child's enjoyment, and new teachers may not know how to handle these situations. The school's policy regarding this matter can be a subject for staff discussion. Generally, newly spoken bathroom talk should be ignored unless it is hurtful, or the child should be told that the place to use the word is in the bathroom. This often remedies the behavior because the child's enjoyment of it is spoiled without an audience. Alternatively, it might suffice to firmly say, "That's a word that hurts. His name is Michael," or in a calm but firm voice, "That kind of talk is unacceptable." Preschoolers love using forbidden words, especially when they play together. What parents and teachers can control is what is said in their presence.

Sound Words. In our culture, children are particularly fond of repeating conventionalized sounds reputedly made by animals ("arf-arf," "meow," "baa") as well as action sounds for toy vehicles ("putt-putt," "beep," "varoom"). When a child is playing the baby in home reenactment dramatic play, "wa-wa" will be heard frequently. Rough-and-tumble outside play may be accompanied by cartoon-strip sounds like "pow," "bam," and "zap." In addition, a good number of four-year-olds can distinguish rhyming words, and they enjoy creating them.

Created Words. Created words such as "turner-overer" for pancake turner, "mudpudders" for rain boots, or "dirt digger" for spade are wonderfully descriptive and crop up occasionally in child speech, perhaps as a means of filling in gaps in their vocabularies. Many cite young children's fascination with the functions of objects in their environment as the reason such words are created. Children enjoy nonsense words, and may revel in their newly gained abilities to use them.

Displaying Creativity. Being creative is not a problem for most preschoolers. Most display their growing ingenuity and imaginative thought and see relationships outside of conventional categories as they manipulate, discover, and investigate their environment and the new experiences their teachers plan and introduce. Many school activities are carefully rigged for children's manipulation and first-hand exploration. In classrooms where children have learned their ideas are welcomed and listened to, discussion can lead to clarification and further dialogue. In an activity planned to

help children cross a street safely, a teacher will no doubt get many practical and illogical suggestions including asking an adult for help, looking and listening carefully, and perhaps creative solutions such as riding an elephant borrowed from the zoo.

3-4   Word Meanings

During later preschool years children often become focused on what words mean and they begin to think and wonder about words. They begin to understand that words are arbitrary symbols with no intrinsic connection to their meaning but rather are representatives of meaning. The young child who says, "Templeton has a big name; my name is small," is displaying a recognition of word length or number of syllables.

3-4a   Reality, Nonsense, and Speech Myths

Some preschool children can enjoy the absurd, nonsensical, and ridiculous in their experiences and find humor in the unexpected. Others, at a different stage in their cognitive development with another orientation, insist on knowing the right way—the real, the accepted, the "whys and wherefores"—and will see no humor in what confuses them or contradicts the "usual order of things." A number of preschoolers view life and surroundings seriously, literally. Others can "play" in speech with the opposite of what they know to be true. We know this is true in some adults also. Some simply do not seem to enjoy what most of us may find humorous.

There is considerable "language play" in nursery rhymes, fairy tales, and classic stories and children discover wonderful, fun ways to repeat things that story characters say. They may gleefully stomp up a hallways saying, "Fee, fi, fo, fum, here I come!" They may build bridges with blocks and make play figures "trip, trap, trip, trap" across them. Teachers are careful not to suppress a child's delight in absurdity by insisting on exact or literal renditions of things. Teachers encourage nonsense play by appreciating a child's inventions or nonsensical propositions. They may model some silliness or nonsense themselves. For example, the teacher might invert words in a sentence well known to the children to evoke child laughter by saying, "And the dogs go meow and cats say bowwow." And then the teacher would hope the children would either correct her or join in the game, producing their own inversions.

A large and mature vocabulary at this age may lead teachers to think a child has superior intelligence. Making conclusions about children based on language ability at this age has inherent pitfalls considering the many factors that could produce limited or advanced vocabulary, particularly when one considers cultural differences, bilingualism, and the child's access to "language-rich environments." At later ages language usage does seem to be related to school success.

3-4b Common Speech Patterns of Older Preschoolers

Four-year-olds often rhyme words in their play and speech, as previously mentioned. Older preschoolers engage in less frequent self-chatter. They continue to make errors in grammar and in the use of the past tense of verbs ("He didn't caught me"), adjectives ("It's biggerer than yours") (Figure 3-6), time words ("The next tomorrow"), and negatives ("I didn't did it"). But preschoolers' skills increase, and their use of forms of the irregular verb "to be" improves such as "I am so," or "Mine are hot, and yours are cold." Sentence structure comes closer to adult usage, including use of relative clauses and complex and compound sentence forms. Articulation of letter sounds is still developing; about 75 percent of English letter sounds are made correctly. Omissions of letter sounds ('merca for "America") and substitutions (udder for "other") are still present.

Older preschoolers may have a vocabulary larger than 1,500 words. They are learning new words and new concepts while they also enrich and solidify their knowledge of known words by establishing multiple links among words and concepts. Four-year-olds' attention and memory improve as they gain a greater understanding of concepts, strategies, and relationships that are associated with their first-hand manipulation and real experiences (Thomlinson & Hyson, 2009).

Many older preschoolers are very concerned about the correct names of things and detect errors in the speech of others. Being an active explorer, his questions can indicate his interest in natural phenomena such as "Why is the moon in the sky?" The four-year-old becomes a problem solver and tends to explain things through visually noted attributes; for example, "A cow is called that 'cause of its horns."

Additional speech and language characteristics include:

- Preschoolers may not be able to talk about their solutions to problems. Although they can respond to and solve questions posed verbally, they may not be able to explain their thinking.

- Four-year-old children enjoy books, stories, and more of their time is spent on them leading to a greater interest in words.

- A best friend's speech or his nonverbal gesturing might be copied for a period of time.

- Older preschooler's basic mental categories become elaborated as experience and details and specifics are noticed and understood. The basic category animals eventually includes a subcategory, cats, and then may include a smaller category such as Persian or Siamese.

A wide range of individual speech behavior is both normal and possible. Some younger preschoolers may have the speech characteristics of older preschoolers, whereas some older preschoolers have the characteristics of younger preschoolers or kindergarteners. Each child is unique in his progress and rate of acquiring language skills.

3-4c Standards & Early Childhood Special Needs

As early as 15 months, environmental factors, including the socioeconomic group in which the child resides, may have depressed the child's vocabulary development. By age three, there may be a significant and noticeable gap in the number of words in a child's vocabulary. This may only widen before the child enters kindergarten. Since preschool years are the years of the highest vocabulary growth, it is a crucial time to intervene and use instructional vocabulary building strategies and other planning to increase both quantity and quality of children's receptive and expressive vocabulary. *The Common Core State Standards in English Language Arts and Literacy in History/Social Studies, Science, and Technical Subjects* (2010) (CCSS), only identifies what language arts' outcomes kindergartners should attain, but does not do so for the preschool years. If one was to decide what experiences and

Figure 3-6 Developmental language-related milestones at ages two through five.

Child's Age

2–2½ years	joins words in sentences of two or more words knows name has vocabulary of more than three words understands long spoken sentences and simple commands begins using plurals and past tense changes pitch and/or loudness for specific meaning begins using forms of verb "to be" uses a few prepositions uses "I," "me," and "you"	uses about 25 phonemes articulates about 10 to 12 vowel types and about 12 to 15 consonants points to and names objects in pictures names five to eight body parts enjoys rhythm in words, nursery rhymes, finger plays, and simple stories understands and responds to almost all of adult speech generalizes by calling round objects ball, and so on
2½–3 years	begins to use negatives, imperatives, and commands shows variety in question types adds as many as two to three words to vocabulary daily names items in signs and books uses three- or four-word sentences enjoys fun with words	follows simple directions points to body parts when asked names many common objects uses an increasing number of nouns, verbs, and pronouns draws lines and circular forms in artwork knows words or lines from books, songs, and stories
3–4 years	asks why, what, where, how, and when questions loves word play makes closed figures in art begins using auxiliary verbs tells sex and age utters compound sentences with connecting "and . . . er . . . but," and so on engages in imaginary play with dialogue and monologue says full name follows two- and three-part requests relates ideas and experiences uses adverbs, adjectives, and prepositions answers who, what, and where questions names some colors and is interested in counting	looks at books while alone and enjoys reading times talks about relationships memorizes a short song, poem, finger play, or story repeats three digits and two to three nonsense syllables if asked uses adjectives and pronouns correctly can copy a recognizable circle or square well if shown a model can imitate a clapping rhythm starts to talk about the function of objects can find an object in group that is different can find missing parts of wholes can classify using clear, simple distinctions knows names of common shapes
4–5 years	has vocabulary of more than 1,500 words uses sentences of five to six (or more) words may use impact, shock, and forbidden words may use words of violence argues, convinces, and questions correctness shares books with friends acts out story themes or recreates life happenings in play has favorite books likes to dictate words notices signs and print in environment uses etiquette words, such as "please," "thank you," and so on enjoys different writing tools knows many nursery rhymes and stories	may add alphabet letters to artwork creates and tells long stories can verbally express the highlights of the day knows many colors can repeat a sentence with six or more words may pretend to read books or may actually read others' name tags holds writing tools in position that allows fine control traces objects with precision classifies according to function asks what words mean is familiar with many literary classics for children knows address and phone number can retell main facts or happenings in stories uses adultlike speech

Metalinguistic Awareness and Brain Growth

Metalinguistic awareness is a child's knowledge of the nature of language as an object. Children begin to notice words as objects and later become able to manipulate them to learn to read and write and to accomplish a host of other ends, such as using metaphors, creating puns, and using irony. Pan and Gleason (1997) observe:

> Before children can engage in flexible uses of words, they must have an implicit understanding that words are separate from their referents. Young children often consider the name of an object another of its intrinsic attributes. They believe, for instance, that if you called a horse a cow, it might begin to moo. Later children learn that words

themselves are not inherent attributes of objects, which allows them to move beyond literal word use and adopt a metaphoric stance. (p. 327)

A critical restructuring of the brain begins at about age four, when a surge in learning is happening. The brain is beginning to eliminate weak connections but is still eagerly seeking information from the senses. Early childhood educators and many researchers are urging that a national emphasis and priority be given to early childhood education, especially in the key areas of language learning, mathematics, music education, and problem-solving skill development.

---

activities should be offered to children identified as needing special instruction to equip them to enter a CCSS kindergarten, the author's recommendations are found in the Appendix.

3-5 Additional Growth Systems Affect Language Development

All body systems need a minimum level of movement (exercise) to keep the body in good working order and to stimulate brain growth. Food, living conditions, and emotional security can also affect a child's acquisition of language. A preschool center intent on developing language skills focuses on satisfying both physical and emotional needs, while offering intellectual opportunity and challenge.

3-5a Physical Growth

Early childhood teachers are aware of fundamental physical changes that take place in young children. Physical development can affect children's perceptions of themselves, as well as the way they are treated by others. A slightly taller, physically active, strong, and well-coordinated child who can ride a two-wheel bike and dropkick a football may be admired by peers. These two skills are not

often witnessed during preschool years, but occasionally a child accomplishes these physical skills. A wide range of physical abilities in individual children exists within any preschool group.

Preschoolers grow at a rate of two to three inches in height and add three to four pounds in weight a year. At about 18 to 24 months, the child's thumb is used in opposition to just one finger. The ability to use some tools and drawing markers with a degree of skill emerges. The nutritional quality of the child's diet exerts an influence on both body and neural development. Illness during an accelerated growth period may produce conditions affecting language development if it damages necessary body systems. Hearing loss and vision difficulties can also impair the child's ability to receive communications and learn a native language.

3-5b Planned Physical Activities

Planned physical movement opportunities and activities prepare children for academic learning. Movement stimulates learning physiologically, and helps young children experience concepts so they can process them cognitively. Teachers often offer children opportunities to solve movement problems by urging them to invent their own solutions and activities. Abstract concepts like over and under are made concrete if the teacher asks children to physically

---

metalinguistic awareness — a conscious awareness on the part of a language user of language as an object in itself.

Physical Movement and Cognition

Brain-based learning advocate, Eric Jensen (2008), emphasizes the benefits and needs of physical movement for children. He believes exercise triggers the release of a brain-derived factor that enhances cognition by boosting the ability of neurons to communicate with one another. Jensen urges early childhood educators to:

- facilitate hand movements each day with clapping games, dancing, puzzles, and manipulative objects.

- engage learners in cooperative activities and group work.
- offer novel activities in a variety of learning locations, and plan child activities and choices connected to the learning that require moving the body in some way. (p. 39).

---

experience them. Teachers can urge children to talk aloud about a motor task at hand while they are performing it. According to a study by Winsler, Manfra, and Diaz (2007), both kindergarteners and preschoolers respond to a teacher's speech instructions and "performance on motor sequencing and counting tasks improved when children are able to speak out loud" (p. 28).

3-5c Perception and Perceptual Skills

Seeing and trying to touch or act upon the environment are the work of infancy. This early physical stage precedes and develops into the child's **mental image** of his world, and this makes later verbal labeling and speech possible. As the child matures, perceptual acuity increases; finer detail is seen. Most children achieve 20/20 vision (adult optimum) at age 14. From ages two to five, vision is in the 20/45 to 20/30 range. It is estimated that 20 to 25% of preschoolers have some eye problem that, if uncorrected, could delay learning or cause vision loss. Experts advise watching for an eye that slightly turns in or out, squinting, eye closing, or head turning when the child is focusing, avoidance of coloring activities or books, and clumsiness or frustration during play. Vision tests should be performed by professionals.

Young children are noted for their desire to get their hands on what they see that interests them. If a new child with a particularly noticeable hair style joins a group, hands and fingers are sure to try to explore its texture. If a teacher wears bright or shiny jewelry, some children will want to touch it. Perceptions are gathered with all sense organs. Experts believe the main purpose

of receiving, organizing, and interpreting what one encounters perceptually is to achieve constancy—a stable, constant world. Development involves changes or shifts in the way a person organizes experience and copes with the world, generally moving from simpler to more complex, from single to multiple and integrated ways of responding.

Young children, as they age, get better at focusing on one aspect of a complex situation. They become selective in focusing their attention, and they ignore the irrelevant and distracting. Individual differences exist in the way children explore their environment and react to it.

Visual Literacy. The process of visual perception involves several basic parts, including the sensing of information along dual pathways in the brain. An understanding of this process is essential to realizing the power of visual images to move us emotionally and behaviorally and to influence our conscious thought. Visual literacy is a basic human capacity that aids learning and problem solving and is useful across many educational disciplines. It involves young children's understanding and use of symbolic representation. It refers to a group of vision competencies. The development of these competencies is fundamental to normal human learning. When developed, they enable a visually literate person to discriminate and interpret the visible actions, objects, and symbols that the person encounters in the environment.

Literacy in the 21st century is primarily visual—pictures, graphics, images of every kind—and students must learn to process both words and pictures and shift back and forth between

---

mental image — a "perceptual representation" or mental picture of a perceptual experience, remembered or imagined.

them. Teachers can help children become more knowledgeable and more skilled in their use of verbal communications, and can also help them gain skill in using and understanding visual images. Children will need to know how to make meaning, not just from text, but also from vast amounts of information conveyed through images.

Perceptual-Motor Skills. Perceptual-motor, or sensory-motor, intelligence has been defined as an action-oriented knowledge, not to be confused with the intelligence that invokes thinking and logic. Intelligence grows during preschool years and beyond when children think about and know without acting out in a physical way. During preschool years, the development of motor skills is as important as the development of language skills. Just as there is gradually increasing control over language, movement, and body control in the preschool years, there is also a similar continuing increase in the ability to scan new material, organize one's perception of it, remember it, and perhaps refer to it by some label or assign meaning in some other way. The close ties between motor activities and thought processes indicate that the child needs motor activity involving the five sense organs, as well as large muscle use. Figure 3-7 describes perception activities that promote perception skills.

Figure 3-7 Perceptual activities.

Experiences Dealing with	Possible Materials and Equipment
Visual Discrimination	
long, longer, longest	felt or paper strips; sticks; ribbons
small, smaller, smallest	nested boxes; blocks; buttons; measuring cups
big, little	blocks; jars; buttons; balloons; toys
tall, short	felt figures; stuffed toys
wide, narrow	pieces of cloth and paper; scraps of wood; boxes
high, low	jump rope; small ball; see-saw made from small board with tiny block in middle
above, below	felt pieces to place above and below a box with colored stones
Auditory Discrimination	
quiet, noisy	two boxes: one containing something that rattles (such as stones or beads) and one containing cloth or paper
bell sounds	bells of varying shapes and sizes for a variety of tones
falling sounds	feather; leaf; stone; block of wood; cotton
shaking sounds	maracas; baby rattle; pebbles inside coffee can
musical sounds	variety of rhythm instruments
Tactile Discrimination	
textures	sandpaper; tissue; stone; waxed paper; tree bark; velvet; wool; fur; cotton
outline of shapes	thin wooden circle, square, triangle, rectangle; letters cut from sandpaper
recognition of objects	four different-shaped objects, each tied in end of sock—children guess what each is by feeling it (change objects often)
hard, soft	handkerchief; rock; cotton batting; nail; sponge
Taste Discrimination	
identifying food: sweet, salty, sour	small jars: filled with salt, sugar, unsweetened lemonade
trying new foods	variety of vegetables children may not know; samples of fruit juices; honey, molasses, maple syrup
Smell Discrimination	
identifying object by smell	cake of soap; vial of perfume; pine sprig; onion; vials of kitchen spices; orange
Kinesthetic Discrimination	
lifting, racing downhill, swinging, throwing, running, jumping, climbing, bending, stretching, twisting, turning, spinning, balancing	yard and motor play materials

3-5d Motor Skill Development and Activities

Motor skills develop in an orderly, predictable head to toe fashion. Neck, head, and upper body muscles are controlled first (large muscles before small muscles), and center-of-body muscles are coordinated before extremities (fingers and toes). Handedness (left or right) is usually stable by age five or six. Child limitations can occur if motor and sensory motor experience is limited. A child who has had limited experience may not be prepared for the finer adjustments that are required in the motor skills of eye movement and hand-eye coordination in the early grades of school. Many educators who study the Montessori approach (1967) to early childhood education are influenced by her ideas. Montessori believed an obvious advantage was to be obtained by enlarging children's perception skills. She suggested that intellect is built by experience, firsthand contact, and other exploration of the environment.

Preschools are full of appealing equipment (Photo 3-11), and programs offer planned approaches to the development of sensory motor skills. They are seen as integral parts of the curricula. There seems to be no clearly accepted or definite separate place within the preschool curriculum for sensory skill development. Yet almost all centers include them in their instructional goals and identify a series of sequential activities and label them perceptual or sensory motor activities. Every activity in which the child moves can be classified as an activity that develops perceptual-motor skill. Commonly, music activities and physical games are so classified, for they often deal with physical coordination and endurance.

Early childhood programs often plan for perceptual-motor activities within their language arts curriculum. What remains important is that this type of emphasis is part of every center's program. The following list of objectives (goals) is designed to promote and refine perceptual-motor skills. It is drawn from a number of schools' and centers' goal statements.

- awareness of self in space
- awareness of self in relation to objects
- flexibility
- body coordination
- posture and balance
- awareness of spatial relationships
- rhythmic body movements
- ability to identify objects and surfaces with the eyes closed
- awareness of temperatures by touch
- ability to trace form outlines with fingers
- ability to discriminate color, shapes, similar features, different features, sizes, textures, and sounds

Photo 3-11 Bicycles are a popular outside play equipment choice.

© 2016 Cengage Learning®

- ability to match a wide variety of patterns and symbols
- ability to identify parts of figures or objects when a small part of a whole is presented
- eye-hand coordination
- familiarity with the following terms: same, different, long, longer, longest, small, smaller, smallest, big, little, tall, short, wide, narrow, high, low, above, below, on, in, hard, soft, sweet, salty, sour
- ability to identify food by tasting
- ability to identify smells of various items
- ability to identify common sounds

3-5e Cognitive Development

There are opposing views concerning the link between language and thought. One view holds that language is the foundation of thought and vital to a person's awareness of the world. Another view suggests that language is dependent on thinking; as intelligence grows, language grows, reflecting thoughts. Most educators agree that language and thought are closely associated. Educators also tend to agree that preschool children are much more capable of learning than previously believed. Therefore, educators attempt to provide a variety of experiences and opportunities for children's self-discovery, and they encourage thoughtful classroom discussions and teacher-child interactions.

Experience changes the brain, but then those very changes alter the way new experience affects the brain. Children who have lived in unfortunate circumstances and have been passive viewers of life rather than active listeners, explorers, and conversationalists, may lack both auditory analysis skill and logical and sequential reasoning skills. The idea that the reciprocal emotionally charged interactions between young children and caregivers influence their cognitive development is not new, but increasingly it is given close attention by anyone working with the young.

Problem-solving ability has been associated with the preschool literacy experiences that come before conventional reading and writing. Once children become higher-level symbolic thinkers, they are able to piece together the mental processes used in everyday problem solving with the symbols needed for reading and writing. As mentioned previously, intellect is rooted in each particular child's stored perceptual and sensory-motor experiences. Each child interprets happenings and attempts to connect each to what she already knows. If it fits, the child understands and it all falls together. Children classify what they encounter, including events, people, and objects before they have words for them. Each mental grouping is distinguished by a set of distinct features, and objects yet to be classified are examined for the presence of these features. Later, a word or language symbol can be attached to a class or category, which makes it possible for the child to communicate about what the class or category means to the child or how the child feels about it. Preschool teachers observe differences between the feelings and meanings expressed by each child. For example, the way that a child reacts when meeting a new large animal may demonstrate what she knows and feels about large animals. One child's reaction might be entirely different from another's.

Putting events and experiences into classes and categories is innate—a natural mental process. The motivation to engage actively with the environment—to make contact, to have an impact, and to make sense of experience—is built into human beings. The mind yearns for order and knowledge is built within from what is experienced. Children construct theories or hypotheses about objects and phenomena by putting things into relationships. A child's knowledge is constantly changing, for children are curious and are constantly searching for a variety of experience, and to fight boredom. A new or novel idea or event may greatly affect a child by adding to or changing all a child knows and feels on a particular subject.

As a child's language ability develops, mental classes, categories, and concepts are represented symbolically by words. Words become an efficient shortcut that eliminates the need to act out by gesturing or signaling to make something known to another. Thoughts can be analyzed and evaluated internally as the child grows older. If a common language system exists between the child and others, it can be used to reveal the child's unique self.

Piaget's (1952) terms **assimilation** and **accommodation** describe what happens when children experience something new. Each individual

---

assimilation — the process that allows new experiences to merge with previously stored mental structures.

accommodation — the process by which new experiences or events change existing ideas or thought patterns.

unconsciously structures (internally builds and organizes) what is perceived. If a new experience or event is perceived, it is assimilated into what already mentally existed. If it changes or modifies those existing structures, the new is accommodated. In other words, children attend to features that make sense to them, and learning involves adding to what is already known or modifying what is known. The brain structures of some children may be developing more slowly than those of others, which might affect their ability to learn and cause teachers to compare them unfairly with children of the same age who have developed more quickly. Figure 3-8 lists children's emerging intellectual skills.

What a teacher may at first consider an error in thinking, may, upon deeper analysis, be seen as quite mature and understandable and not just random guesses. When a child says a camel is a horse with a hump, the child should be given credit for seeing the similarity, rather than being merely corrected. "It has four legs like a horse, but this animal has a hump on its back and it is called a camel" a teacher can say.

3-5f The Teacher's Role

The teacher's role in intellect building not only includes the teacher's provision of materials and equipment that promote exploring and experiencing, but also involves teacher interactions.

Figure 3-8 The child's emerging intellectual skills.

1. seeking information (focusing)
2. seeking word labels (concept building)
3. naming, classifying, categorizing, and grouping experiences mentally—objects, ideas, etc. (general to specific; revising concepts)
4. responding and remembering (memorizing and recalling)
5. comparing and contrasting information (abstracting)
6. making inferences and predicting in general ways (predicting)
7. generalizing (inductive thinking)
8. applying known information to new situations (transferring)
9. making hypotheses (educated guesses) and predicting in specific ways (deductive thinking)

A "zone of proximal development" is what Vygotsky (1980) calls the area between what a child can solve alone when faced with the problem or experience, and what a child can possibly solve or come to know with the help of a teacher or another. When adults name and explain happenings and talk about relationships, this is seen as a stimulant to both language and mental growth. It is also important that adults know when not to interrupt children's thoughts when they are deeply engaged, but rather show interest and wait for the child to put happenings into words. Dialogue makes much more sense when children seek adult help or when teachers are companions in activities. Teachers can talk about both meaning and feelings. Each intellect-building encounter and interaction starts with supportive acceptance and caring. Teachers promote further discovery, and they listen and observe closely. Listening may expose aspects of the child's thinking, logic, concepts, and feelings. Children can ask many questions on any given day. Teachers may sometimes answer a question with a question and often provide answers the child cannot discover herself. Skillful questioning and sensitive responses preserve children's feelings about expressing worthwhile ideas and make a child more willing to speak, share, and ask again. Teachers can also support children as they converse by encouraging them to step outside their own perceptions to become aware of larger, more generalized patterns in the things they observe. The process of questioning, predicting, and testing possibilities can be learned firsthand as children solve their own problems. Early childhood educators facilitate children's ability to come to their own conclusions and relate those conclusions to observable evidence when possible. A teacher may also ask children to compare their ideas with one another in group conversations (Photo 3-12).

Children may gain **metalinguistic skills** during their preschool years. They are then able to think about language as a separate entity, and some children make comparisons between spoken and written words or analyze words into individual parts. Some may also judge what correct word usage is and what it is not, or playfully manipulate words.

---

metalinguistic skills — the ability to think about language as a separate entity.

Photo 3-12 A teacher attempts to extend children's discussion of a discovered bug in the sandbox.

3-5g Social and Emotional Growth and Connectedness

Interaction with other people is always a major factor in a child's language learning. Children who have positive feelings about themselves—feelings of self value and security—tend to speak frequently. New contacts with adults or children outside of the home can run smoothly. Gallagher and Mayer (2008) suggest the school day should begin with feelings of warmth and comfort as children transition from family. This is a time when responsive teachers make an effort to recognize each child's individual presence by welcoming and greeting them.

How to be in a relationship may be the most important skills children learn (Gallagher and Mayer, 2008). Research suggests children able to form high-quality and secure relationships display better language usage, Problem-solving ability, **social connectedness**, and they acquire harmonious play skills. Young children watch and learn from their teachers and others. The tone set in a caring and supportive school environment can lead to feelings of acceptance. Each child should feel he or she is a valued member of a group of others. Social connectedness has been

defined as a characteristic of people with stable and secure lives, supportive families and friends, and close ties to community. They are accepted as a worthy individual part of a group. They are the children who seem to be able to weather life's stresses and possess a sense of individual identity.

During preschool years, children form ideas of self-identity. It becomes difficult for children to believe in themselves, or their language abilities, if self-esteem is constantly undermined. A teacher's behavior and response when communicating with children can promote a variety of social skills (Figure 3-9). Social development must not be ignored when planning and conducting language activities or in trying to manage groups. Structure and rules are necessary for group living. An individual child's status in the eyes of the group can be enhanced through the sharing and appreciation of the child's ideas and accomplishments and by providing frequent opportunities for the child to lead or help lead the group in activities, at times. This is almost always a confidence- and status-building experience.

Through activities, preschoolers begin to learn labels for feelings, such as happy, sad, jealous, fearful, and so on, and many begin to think of others' feelings. The conscience is forming, and interest

social connectedness — a term associated with the following human characteristics: is stable and secure, develops close relationships with others, has supportive family and friends, and is deemed a worthy individual by others. Often seen by others as able to transcend stress and possess an individual identity.

Figure 3-9 Teacher behaviors that are helpful to the child's social growth.

In communication, the teacher:
- cares and is ready to give of self.
- listens, intent on understanding.
- adds simple words when the child cannot.
- does not correct speech when this might break down willingness to speak further.
- is available for help in clarifying ideas or suggesting new play and exploring possibilities.
- senses child interests and guides to new real experiences.
- is available when problems and conflicts happen.
- enjoys time spent in child activities.
- establishes friendships with each child.
- talks positively about each child's individual uniqueness.
- is an enthusiastic and expressive communicator.
- offers friendly support while redirecting undesirable social behavior or stating rules.
- notices and respects each child's work.

Photo 3-13 Being left out feels like the end of the world.

© 2015 Cengage Learning®

in right and wrong is being expressed. Teachers who speak of their own feelings as adults set an example and provide a classroom climate in which children's feelings are accepted and understood.

Most children explore social actions and reactions. They want to have friends (Photo 3-13). In play, they learn to make plans, negotiate, and communicate. Strong emotions accompany much of children's behavior; their total being speaks. When a child feels left out, life becomes an overwhelming tragedy; on the other hand, a party invitation may be a time to jump for joy. It is through symbolic and pretend play that young children are most likely to develop both socially and intellectually, so many play opportunities and room areas are set up for it. Planned play periods are a daily event. Play activities can also help children develop a sense of self.

The following is a list of social ability goals that serve as a strong foundation for future schooling. These are promoted throughout a school's day. Children should be able to

- get and hold the attention of adults in a variety of socially acceptable ways.

- express affection or mild annoyance to adults and peers when appropriate.
- use adults as resources after determining that a task is too difficult to handle alone.
- show pride in achievement.
- both lead and follow children of the same age.
- compete with age mates.

Teachers strive to supply a center atmosphere in which a sense of trust and security thrives. Children need to learn to trust people in their world, or else they reject all that these people want to teach them. They need to have faith in those who respect them and accept their feelings, and also learn to trust themselves. Whether young children see themselves as valued identities depends on their interactions with others.

Summary

3-1 Identify three characteristics of younger preschoolers' speech and communication.

Younger preschoolers' speech is often unclear, but close teacher observation may uncover meaning. Frequent gestures and body motions accompany words. Young children understand teacher's speech with apparent ease and they daily acquire new vocabulary. Vocal noises often accompany their play and they may limit speech output when adjusting to new situations. Younger preschoolers possess receptive and expressive vocabulary and are acquiring more complex forms of English grammar. They are noticing consistent speech patterns and applying them to their developing language system. Their most frequently spoken words are nouns. And "no" is liberally used. They engage in short conversations and their speech can be uneven with pauses and repetitions. At times, they correct their own speech. Excitement elevates their speech volume and pitch, but some may be shy, using a barely audible voice. Cause-and-effect statements are appearing. Self-talk is commonplace and often reflects what they are physically performing. Their short sentences may include only key words. Questions are frequently asked, and their new words may be practiced and repeated over and over.

3-2 Describe three pieces of recommended advice to a family concerned about their preschooler's speaking abilities.

1. Calling a child's attention to his speech or making demands causes child tension, making the situation worse rather than better. Families were advised to wait and relax. A child often needs time to speak the words he wishes to.

2. Speaking is a complex process, so families were advised to remain patient and optimistic while assuming an "I'm here to listen" stance.

3. Children's illogical comments in conversations are frequently cleared up when the child adds more information. Families were advised to gain more information by asking questions. Advice implied this is an age level characteristic.

4. Families were advised to be accepting and interested as a child struggles to express himself.

5. Families were advised to react to the intent of the child's messages, rather than his word usage.

6. Families were advised to help children see the details and relationships.

3-3 Describe conversational skills necessary for an older preschooler to maintain a true conversation.

In a functional conversation, a child needs skill in gaining the attention of the listener, turn taking, pausing to listen to the speaker, which encourages the conversational partner to talk, correcting himself if necessary, maintaining word flow and not pausing long enough for the other to jump in, and holding in mind what he wants to say or answer as he continues listening.

3-4 Discuss older preschoolers manipulation and playful use of words.

Some preschoolers may enjoy absurd, nonsensical, and ridiculous word use. They may repeat catchy phrases or words that are funny to them. They may use silly or nonsense words in their play or invert words in sentences or state the opposite of what they know to be true. Words in nursery rhymes may delight them because they are fun to say. These children see humor in using words unconventionally.

3-5 List reasons for planning sensory, motor skill activities; cognitive, building activities; or social, emotional growth activities to promote language development.

1. Motor activity involves the five sense organs. Educators believe a strong connection exists between the development of mental and physical skill development. The sharpening of perceptual-motor skill offers a solid foundation for intellectual growth. A preschool child with limited perceptual-motor skill may not be as successful in the small motor skills necessary for the eye movement and hand-eye coordination called for in kindergarten.

2. Language growth is viewed by many educators as being dependent on or related to a child's thinking. As language grows, intelligence grows. Offering children problem solving associated with literacy experiences, aids learning to read and write. Preschoolers classify life experiences and add words to them. This can take place in an early childhood center through teacher interaction and planned activities. Teachers supply activity materials and verbal comments during activities to promote child exploration and discovery. Discussing classroom happenings and relationships that exist in any given situation stimulates both language and mental growth.

3. Teachers start the day by welcoming and greeting individual children and they try to create a classroom of comfort and warmth for the child. They realize that young children are forming a self-image partially based on how they are treated in the classroom. Planned activities have built in social rules for group living. Teachers offer activities that provide labels for feelings and model feelings of their own. They promote each child's status in the group and give attention to children's ideas and accomplishments. Teachers are aware of each child's social connectedness and promote it whenever possible. Play activities are offered, particularly pretend play experiences, and room area furnishings are set up to encourage child participation.

Additional Resources

Readings

Christ, T., & Wang, X.C. (2012). Supporting preschoolers' vocabulary learning: Using a decision making model to select appropriate words and methods. *Young Children, 67*(2): 74–80.

Sharapan, H. (2013). From STEM to STEAM: How early childhood educators can apply Fred Rogers' approach. In C. Copple, S. Bredekamp, D. Loralek, & K. Charner (Eds.). *Developmentally Appropriate Practice: Focus on Preschoolers*. (pp.158–163). Washington, DC: National Association for the Education of Young Children.

Siegler, R. S., & Alibali, M.W. (2005). *Children's Thinking*. Upper Saddle River, NJ: Prentice Hall.

Helpful Websites

National Child Care Information Center

http://nccic.org

Staff will research your questions and connect you with information on young children's language and literacy.

National Network for Child Care

http://www.nncc.org

Ages and stages of three-and four-year-olds is provided. Select Articles & Resources and then select Child Development.

International Visual Literacy Association

http://www.ivla.org

Contains articles and information on research and conferences.

National Child Care Information Center

http://www.nccic.org

Lists ages and stages of growth.

4 Understanding Differences

Objectives

After reading this chapter, you should be able to:

4-1 Describe a safe and sensitive classroom environment for children with language or cultural differences.

4-2 Discuss the similarities and differences between Standard English and American dialects.

4-3 Identify common strategies second-language learners use to learn Standard English on their own.

4-4 Discuss program planning for second-language learners.

4-5 Name two common school program types for second language learners.

4-6 Identify young children's common speech problems.

4-7 Name at least four characteristics of language-advanced preschoolers.

naeyc NAEYC Program Standards

2A02 The curriculum allows for adaptations and modifications to ensure access for all children.

2D03 Children have varied opportunities to develop competence in verbal and nonverbal communications by responding to questions, communicating needs, thoughts, and experiences, and describing things and events.

2D04 Children have varied opportunities to develop vocabulary through conversations, experiences, field trips, and books.

2A04 The curriculum can be implemented in a manner that reflects responsiveness to family home values, beliefs, experiences, and language.

2D02 Children are provided opportunities to experience oral and written communications in a language their family uses or understands.

DAP Developmentally Appropriate Practice (DAP)

3H5 Teachers support dual language learners and their home language as well as promoting their English.

3H4 Teachers attend to the particular needs of dual language learners and children behind in vocabulary and other aspects of language learning.

3H7 Teachers help children use communication and language as tools for thinking and learning.

A Problem Solved

It was the first song at circle time.

> Good morning, I like the shoes you've got on. / In fact, I like 'em so much, I'm gonna put 'em in a song. / In a song, in a song, / I'm gonna put you and your shoes in a song.

A boy asked if we could put hair in. "Good morning, I like the hair you've got on. . . ." The boy stopped singing. We finished the verse. The boy leaned toward me and said quietly, "But what about Mr. Baker?" "Who's Mr. Baker?" I asked. The boy lifted one hand from his lap and pointed to his left. I saw Mr. Baker, one of the father volunteers who came to tell stories. He was totally bald and trying not to laugh. None of the children found it funny. To leave Mr. Baker out was not funny. A girl whispered loudly to the boy, "Say skin." He leaned toward me and said, "Sing skin this time." The cloud left the boy's face. . . . and Mr. Baker gave him a thumbs-up, as if to celebrate another problem solved (Hunter, 2003).

Questions to Ponder

1. What is this reading an example of? What do you like about this song activity?

2. Could this vignette's song be used in a planned unit of study on diversity? If so, explain how?

The United States is a multicultural society. It is a vast array of people of different backgrounds and ethnicities. Members of families may be married, remarried, single, gay, straight, birth parents, adoptive parents, and/or unrelated individuals.

Children's families also differ substantially in size, resources, values, goals, languages spoken, educational attainment, child-raising practices, past experiences along with immigration status, countries of origin, and length of time in the United States. Families have broken almost all traditional rules for what makes a family, but continue to affirm the most basic definition of family: a bond reinforced by love and caring.

Experienced teachers throughout the United States report that the children they teach are more diverse in their backgrounds, experiences, and abilities than were those they taught in the past. Projections suggest that by the year 2025, more than half of the children enrolled in America's schools will be members of "minority" groups, not of European-American origin. Diversity is the new norm and immigrant families are widely dispersed. Garcia and Jensen (2009) note two to three million children, ages birth to eight in the United States are learning English as a second language. Many reside in families with culturally different backgrounds. Early childhood programs and elementary grade levels are enrolling more Spanish-speaking and non-English speaking children in parts of the country with little or no history of ethnic or racial diversity. This trend is stronger at early childhood levels where Hispanic preschoolers under age five account for over 20 percent of the preschool population (Collins & Ribeiro, 2004).

Some young children enter school with addictions, diseases, and disorders, such as fetal alcohol syndrome, and without having had sufficient sleep, food, or supervision at home. Teachers have found themselves virtually unprepared to deal with the vastly different linguistic and life experiences and abilities of language-diverse children (Photo 4-1).

Early childhood educators recognize that DAP extra efforts made early in some young children's lives can prevent problems with learning to read. Children who are poor and nonnative speakers are considered much more likely to fail to learn to read adequately. As with other educators, you will be searching for ways to meet young children's varied educational needs. Since play opens children to expression, it will be an integral part of any early childhood program.

Barrett (2003) reviewed research concerning preschool enrollment and later reading achievement. His findings led him to believe that:

- Preschool programs can have an important short-term impact on general cognitive development and academic abilities including reading achievement.

- Effects appear to be larger for intensive, high-quality educational programs targeting children in poverty.

- School success (primarily grade repetition and special education placement) is dependent on verbal

Photo 4-1 Ethnic and cultural diversity is commonplace in America's classrooms.

© 2015 Cengage Learning®

abilities; in particular, reading plays an important role in accessing new knowledge from textbook readings and other schoolwork. (p. 57)

Barrett concluded that preschool education in a variety of forms improves general cognitive abilities during early childhood and produces long-term increases in reading achievement.

4-1 Child-Focused and Child-Sensitive Approaches

Au (2006) describes what is important to consider when a classroom includes children of diverse backgrounds. Establishing positive relationships with children is key:

> It may be helpful for the teacher to have an understanding of the students' cultural backgrounds and the values they bring to school. Once positive relationships and open communication have been established, students will accept the teacher as a role model and as a model of literate behavior. (p. 197)

Program planners are experimenting and refining instructional models. These new approaches are described as child-focused and child-sensitive approaches (Figure 4-1). A child focused-approach is based upon the individual child observations and inferences the teacher makes concerning a child's learning style, needs, classroom interactions, and the attitudes a child possesses that tend to promote learning and school success. Child-sensitive approaches are similar but primarily involve a teacher's knowledge of what is respectful and appropriate in light of a child's cultural and experiential background.

Figure 4-1 Wall chart.

Kids Are Different

Kids are different

They don't even look the same

Some kids speak different languages

They all have a different name

Kids are different

But if you look *INSIDE* you'll see

The one with brown hair, black hair, red hair or blond hair,

Is just like you and me.

Author Unknown

A safe classroom environment using these approaches is one that respects differences and uniqueness and energizes young children's ability to communicate desires, fears, and understandings.

In 1996 the NAEYC recognized and recommended the following child-sensitive suggestions that have continued to gain increased importance:

> For the optimal development and learning of all children, educators must accept the legitimacy of children's home language, respect (hold in high regard) and value (esteem, appreciate) the home culture, and promote and encourage the active involvement and support of all families, including extended and nontraditional family units. (p. 42)

Teachers realize that children whose language skills or patterns are different are just as intelligent and capable as those who speak Standard English. An early childhood educator's goal is (1) to help all young children and (2) to help in such a way that it will not actually make matters worse. The teacher's sensitivity to and knowledge of a particular cultural group and its different language patterns can aid a particular child's growth. Preserving the child's feelings of adequacy and acceptance is the teacher's prime goal; moving the child toward the eventual learning of standard forms is a secondary goal.

Early childhood educators strive, through professional associations, individual efforts, and attention to standards, to increase program quality. In doing so, each center needs to examine its program to ensure language learning is not seen as occurring only at language time but from the moment teachers greet each child at the beginning of the day. Every child-adult interaction holds potential for child language learning. The key question is whether each child is receiving optimum opportunity during group care to listen and speak with a savvy adult skilled in natural conversation that reinforces, expands, and extends.

Language acquisition is more than learning to speak; it is a process through which a child becomes a competent member of a community by acquiring both the linguistics and sociocultural knowledge needed to learn how to use language in that particular community. It is particularly important that every individual have equal access to educational and economic opportunity, especially those from groups who have consistently been found on the bottom of the educational, social, and economic heap: African-Americans, Latinos, and Native American people.

4-2 Standard English

Standard English is the language of elementary schools and textbooks. It is the language of the majority of people in the United States. Increasingly, preschool programs enroll children whose speech reflects different past experiences and a cultural (or subcultural) outlook. When attending a preschool or center, these children become aware of the group's values, attitudes, food preferences, clothing styles, and so on, and gain acceptance as group members by practicing and copying the enrolled group's way of speaking. Some theorize that group membership influences children's manner of thinking about life's experiences. Standard English usage is advantageous and a unifying force that brings together cultures within cultures, thereby minimizing class differences.

Dialect, as used here, refers to language patterns that differ from Standard English. Dialects exist in all languages and fall into two categories: (1) regional and geographical and (2) social and ethnic. Dialect is a regional or social variety of language distinguished by pronunciation, grammar, or vocabulary, especially a variety of speech differing from the standard literary language or speech pattern of the culture in which it exists. Diverse dialects in the United States include African-American English, Puerto Rican English, Appalachian English, and varieties of Native American English, Vietnamese English, and others. Dialects are just as highly structured, logical, expressive, and complex as Standard English.

Boser (2006) notes that experts have been predicting the imminent demise of American dialects for decades because of increased mass media exposure, but the opposite seems true. Boser notes his conclusion is drawn from the work of expert linguists who are compiling a multi-volume

---

Standard English — substantially uniform formal and informal speech and writing of educated people that is widely recognized as acceptable wherever English is spoken and understood.

dialect — a variety of spoken language unique to a geographical area or social group. Variations in dialect may include phonological or sound variations, syntactical variations, and lexical or vocabulary variations.

reference North American English called the *Dictionary of Regional English*. This reference, which plots all major speech patterns in the continental United States and Canada, shows that regional dialects have become more pronounced. Boser points out that although mountains of data have been collected on *how* dialects are changing, understanding of *why* they change remains elusive.

African-American preschoolers who speak **Black English** (African-American English) use advanced and complex syntax, such as linking two clauses, as do their Standard English-speaking peers. Black English is a systematic, rule-governed dialect that can express all levels of thought. African-American English, Black English, and the term **Ebonics** refer to a grammatically consistent speech whose key features include not conjugating the verb "to be" and the dropping of some final consonants from words (Figure 4-2). In the past, many debated whether African-American English is a distinct language or a dialect; the controversy still exists today. Elevating African-American English to the status

Figure 4-2 Some features of African-American vernacular English.

1. extreme reduction of final consonants ("so" for "sold," "fo" for "four," "fin" for "find," "ba" for "bad")
2. phonological contrasts absent, such as -th versus -f at word endings ("baf" for "bath," "wif" for "with")
3. "l" or "r" deleted in words ("pants" for "parents," "doe" for "door," "he'p" for "help")
4. verb "be" used to indicate extended or continuous time ("I be walkin")
5. deletion of some "to be" verb forms ("He sick" or "She talk funny")
6. deletion of s or z sounds when using third person singular verbs ("He work all the time" or "She say don't go")
7. elimination of s in possessives ("Mama car got crashed")
8. use of two-word subjects ("Ben he be gone")
9. use of "it" in place of "there" ("It ain't none pieces left" for "There are no pieces left")

of a language has evoked emotional reaction nationwide from both African-Americans and others. Early childhood professionals have mixed opinions.

Many educators believe that the professional teacher's primary task is to preserve children's belief that they are already capable speakers and that teachers also should provide the opportunity for children to hear abundant Standard English speech models in classrooms. Linguists and educators do agree on the desperate need to teach some African-American children Standard English, but there is little agreement on how best to do so. Although it has long been suggested that the dialectic features of African-American vernacular English and its phonology create additional challenges for learning to read English, limited efforts to test this hypothesis have been undertaken. It should also be made clear that many African-American children speak Standard English, not African-American English.

Relatively minor variations in vocabulary, pronunciation, and grammatical forms are apparent in most dialects. Speakers of a particular dialect form a speech community that reflects the members' lifestyles or professional, national, family, or ethnic backgrounds. Certain common features mark the speech of the members, and no two members of a particular community ever speak exactly alike because each person's speech is unique. Unfortunately, to some, the term dialect can connote less-than-correct speech. Speech accents differ in a number of ways and are fully formed systems. Children from other than mainstream groups enter school with a set of linguistic and cultural resources that in some respects differ from, and even conflict with, rather than resemble, those of the school culture.

Individuals react to dialects with admiration, acceptance, ambivalence, neutral feelings, or rejection based on value judgments. Many Americans have just a superficial acquaintance with stereotypes of American Southern or New York varieties of English. People make assumptions about an individual's ethnicity, socioeconomic status, and competence based on the way he or she speaks, and unfortunately discrimination is not uncommon.

Black English — a language usually spoken in some economically depressed African-American homes. A dialect of non-Standard English having its own rules and patterns, it is also called African-American English.

Ebonics — a nonstandard form of English, a dialect often called Black English that is characterized by not conjugating the verb "to be" and by dropping some final consonants from words.

Just as a child who meets another child from a different part of the country with a different **accent** might say, "You sound funny!" Others may think of dialectic speech as crude or reflecting a lack of education. Early childhood teachers are trained to remain nonjudgmental and accepting. Dialect-speaking teachers, aides, and volunteers (working with children and families of the same dialect) may offer children a special degree of familiarity and understanding (Photo 4-2). A Standard English-speaking teacher may sound less familiar, but affords the child a model for growth in speaking the dominant language of our society, which is important to his life opportunities.

Although a dialect (or accent) may be an advantage in one's community, it may be a disadvantage outside of that community. When someone begins to learn English, others may feel betrayed because they feel the individual has denied his or her identity and joined forces with those who are rejecting group values.

4-2a The Teacher's Role: Working with Dialect-Speaking Families

Many early childhood centers employ DAP staff members who have dialects that the children can easily understand so that children feel at home. Teachers who speak the children's dialect may be eagerly sought and in short supply. Additional insight into the child's culture and the particular meanings of their words is often an advantage for teachers who have the same dialect as the children. They may be able to react to and expand upon ideas better than a Standard English-speaking teacher.

It is important for teachers to know whether the children are speaking a dialect and to understand dialectic differences. The four most common dialectic differences between Standard English and some common dialects occur in verb forms. These differences occur in the following areas:

- Subject-verb agreement
- Use of the verb "to be"
- Use of present tense for past tense
- Use of "got" for "have"

In some areas where a language other than English is spoken, part of the rules of the second language may blend and combine to form a type of English different from the standard. Two examples of this are (1) English spoken by some Native American children and (2) English spoken in communities close to the Mexican-American border.

Photo 4-2 An assistant teacher who speaks the same dialect can often form a special relationship with a child.

© 2015 Cengage Learning®

accent — prominence or emphasis given to a word or syllable through one or more of the following factors: loudness, change of pitch, and longer duration (Harris & Hodges, 1995).

There are differing opinions about the teaching of preferred Standard English in early childhood centers. In most centers, however, preserving the child's native dialect, while moving slowly toward Standard English usage, is considered more desirable than providing immediate, purposeful instruction in standard forms. Joint family and center discussions can help clarify program goals.

Understanding dialectic differences is important to the teacher's understanding of each child. To give young children the best model possible, the early childhood teacher should speak Standard English. The federal government mandates that all children attending American public schools learn English, and instruction in English always begins at some point during the elementary school years.

Many successful teachers have speech accents and also possess other characteristics, abilities, and useful techniques that aid young children's development of language and literacy. It matters very little to children whether the teacher speaks a bit differently from the way they speak. The teacher's attitude, warmth, and acceptance of the dialect and the children themselves are very important considerations (Photo 4-3).

Teachers are in a unique position to build bridges rather than walls between cultures. Teachers' essential task is to create new and shared meanings with the children—new contexts that give meaning to the knowledge and skills being taught. The challenge is to find personally interesting and culturally relevant ways of creating new contexts for children, contexts in which school skills are meaningful and

Photo 4-3 A teacher builds a warm relationship with each child.

© 2016 Cengage Learning®

rewarding. Competence is not tied to a particular language, dialect, or culture. Professional educators realize that language instruction or any other part of the planned curriculum should not reject or be designed to be a replacement of children's language or culture, but rather be viewed as language expansion and enrichment.

Early childhood teachers may receive little instruction (teacher training) in the types of language behaviors to expect from diverse speakers; training in how to affect growth in language competencies also may be lacking. Teachers themselves will need to do their own classroom observation and research to identify cultural variations and differences that affect attending children's speech growth and development. Young preschoolers have learned the social speech expectations of their homes and possibly their communities. They know when to speak and when to be silent. At school they infer what is appropriate based on what they hear and observe there. When children begin to use a second language or second dialect, they tend to use words in syntactic constructions found in their native speech or dialect. Because many cultures, including Asian and some Native American communities, expect children to learn from listening, young children from these cultures may be relatively silent compared with children encouraged to be verbal from birth. Hawaiian children observed by researchers often did not like to be singled out for individual attention and tended to give minimal answers when questioned. In some cultures, children may be encouraged to use "yes" and interrupt adult speech to signify that they are in tune with the speaker.

Some facial expressions or gestures acceptable in one culture may be highly insulting in another. Even the acceptable distance between speakers of different languages varies. Teachers may interpret various child language (or lack of it) as disrespectful without considering cultural diversity. Misunderstandings between children, humorous as they may be to teachers, require sensitive handling.

A child may be a very good speaker of his particular dialect or language, or he may be just a beginner. Staff members working with the young child respect the child's natural speech and do not try to stop the child from using it. The goal is to promote the child's use of natural speech in his native dialect. Standard English can be taught by having many good speaking models available at the center for the child to hear. Interested adults, play activities, other children, and a rich language arts program can provide a setting where children listen and talk freely. Teachers refrain from correcting children's oral language errors and look for meaning and intention. They stress cooperation, collaboration, and frequent conversation.

The teacher should know what parts of the center's program are designed to increase the child's use of words. Teachers can show a genuine interest in words in their daily conversations with the children. Teachers can also use the correct forms of Standard English in a casual way, using natural conversation. Correcting the children in an obvious way could embarrass them and stop openness and enthusiasm.

Delpit (1995) points out that constant teacher correction and a focus on correctness impedes the child's "unconscious acquisition" of a language by raising the child's anxiety level and forcing him to cognitively monitor his every word. She provides an example of one four-year-old's resistance to being taught to answer the teacher's morning greeting with a specific "I'm fine, thank you" response. Delpit's example (1995) follows.

Teacher: Good morning, Tony. How are you?

Tony: I be's fine.

Teacher: Tony, I said, How are you?

Tony: (with raised voice) I be's fine.

Teacher: No Tony, I said, How are you?

Tony: (angrily) I done told you I be's fine. I ain't telling you no more. (p. 94)

Careful listening, skillful response, and appropriate questions during conversations help the child learn to put thoughts into words. The child thinks in terms of his own dialect or language first and, in time, expresses words in Standard English. Delpit (1995) recommends that teachers provide students with exposure to an alternative form and allow children the opportunity to practice that form in contexts that are not threatening, have real purpose, and are intrinsically enjoyable.

Preschool teachers must face the idea that children's language and appearance may unconsciously affect their attitudes about those children and, consequently, teacher behaviors. A new or unsure teacher may tend to seek out and communicate with children whose speech and appearance is most similar to her or his own. Extra effort may be necessary to watch this tendency and converse and instruct all attending children. Staff-parent meetings and additional planning are musts to meet the needs of children with diverse language patterns. Pronunciation guides helping teachers say children's names correctly are gathered from families at admitting interviews. This is just a small first step.

Sensitive, seasoned teachers will not put some children on the spot with direct questions or requests at group times. They may include additional storytelling or demonstration activities with young children whose native cultures use this type of approach. "Rappin" and words-to-music approaches may appear to a greater extent in some child programs. Drama may be a way to increase language use in other classrooms. To be sure, with the great diversity in today's early childhood classrooms, teachers will be struggling to reach and extend each child's language competence. This is not an easy task. Teachers who work with other than mainstream children learn that their own views of the world, or ways of using language in that world, are not necessarily shared by others.

Accepted instructional strategies used when working with dialect speaking children and families include:

1. Treating individual dialects with immediate acceptance and avoiding any pressure to hurry children toward Standard English usage. Over time, as exposure increases and children explore and gain experience, their speech will change.

2. Recognizing that trial and error are a part of the learning process. Children should be able to practice language skills on their own and have teachers who both listen and converse.

3. Realizing new language skills are added to existing linguistic skills while young children retain their native dialect and culture.

4. Providing a stimulating language environment full of the functional uses of language and meaningful social interactions. Grammar will improve over time.

5. Using teacher observations to guide the children or adults learning a language other than their native language, their speech is planning of program activities,

a teacher should guard against:

- correcting children in a way that makes them doubt their own abilities.
- giving children the idea that they are not trying hard enough to correct or improve their speech.
- discouraging children's speaking.
- allowing teasing about individual speech differences.
- interrupting children who are trying to express an idea.
- hurrying a child who is speaking.
- putting children on stage in an anxiety-producing way.

4-3 Second-Language Learners

Non-English-speaking children, like nonstandard dialect speakers, tend to come from lower socioeconomic backgrounds and attend schools with disproportionately high numbers of children in poverty; however, many will not fit this description. A large group of professional, foreign-born technology workers' families reside in some urban areas. In the world today, in many countries it is "natural" to grow up speaking more than one language. More than 70 percent of the world's population does so.

Second-language learners are children who speak their native language in social and cultural contexts out of school and have developed the necessary communicative competence. Second-language learners are also referred to as **bilingual** learners, English as a second-language students, students with limited English proficiency, language-minority learners, English-language learners, dual language learners, cultural learners, and linguistically diverse students.

Second-language learners are being introduced, in substantive ways, to another language. In this discussion, it is English. Cummins (2011) suggests it usually takes about two years for students to become reasonably fluent in conversational English. When second-language learners their speech is characterized by high-frequency vocabulary words and common grammatical constructions. A child is usually described as "balanced bilingual" when she possesses age-appropriate competence in both languages.

How many years will it take a child to gain second-language proficiency? The answer depends on whether oral or academic proficiency is being assessed. Hakuta, Goto Butler, and Witt (2000) calculate two to three years for oral proficiency, and four to seven years for academic English proficiency with school-age children. Most seasoned early childhood teachers will estimate fewer years for preschoolers who seem to learn English at an amazing rate.

There are two main categories of second-language learners who speak no or very little English. The first category consists of those children who come to this country at a very young age or are born here to immigrants who have lived in areas of the world where language as well as the culture, systems of government, and social structures are quite unlike those of the United States. The second group of learners is native born, such as Native Americans or Alaskan native born children, but speak a different language and are members of a different culture than the mainstream American culture.

4-3a Bilingual learners

A bilingual child can be described as a child younger than three who learns two (sometimes more) languages at the same time, or a child who learns a second language after age three. Sequential acquisition describes what occurs when a child starts to learn a second language after the first language is only partially established—such as when a young child enrolls in a school where his native language is not spoken.

Many researchers believe that some individuals may have a natural aptitude for learning language (Photo 4-4). Research emphasizes that the experience of becoming bilingual *itself* may make learning an additional new language easier (Marian, 2009). A bilingual advantage is also likely to be generalized beyond word learning to other kinds of language learning and an ability to better maintain verbal information.

---

bilingual — refers to an individual with a language background other than English who has developed proficiency in the primary language and a degree of proficiency in English.

Photo 4-4 Arianne speaks Spanish, German, and English.

It is not unusual to find enrolled preschool children who are learning English and also possess different degrees of proficiency in two or more other languages (Photo 4-4). Bilingual children initially might have smaller vocabularies when each language is considered separately. But when one considers that the memory capacity of young children is limited and this restricts their rate of vocabulary acquisition, it is understandable. Bilingual children have two sets of vocabularies to learn. At any particular point during development, one would expect them to know fewer vocabulary items in each language but approximately the same number when both languages are considered.

Many experts suggest that if more than one language is spoken in the home and both languages are spoken well, the infant should be exposed to both from the beginning. However, if, as is so often the case, the first language is spoken exclusively in the home, research indicates the child should be encouraged to develop expertise in a wide range of language functions in the first language with the expectation that these will easily transfer to the second language (English). Learning his native language allows the child's phonemic sensitivity to develop, which may allow him to gain an alphabetic insight that is needed for learning to read with ease.

4-3b Assessing Second-Language Learners

The most immediate question the teacher of a bilingual child must face is deciding how well the child is progressing in all of the languages the child is learning. A full language assessment with respect to the child's first language and with respect to the child's knowledge of English will probably show that the child's difficulties are limited to the acquisition of English. The testing of young children in multicultural and economically diverse classrooms is a **DAP** growing practice.

Teachers attempt to continually gauge if children are learning new vocabulary and gaining concept knowledge. Gaining a clear picture of each child's progress is, at times, difficult. Neuman and Wright (2013) note that second-language learners are likely to go through a silent period that indicates a lack of comfort in trying out new words.

Simple game-like testing after planned activities can reveal a lack of vocabulary learning or concept knowledge, which may indicate the need for more repetition of new vocabulary and content. One teacher's assessment game consisted of giving children a small flag on a stick to wave when they heard their teacher make a mistake. It was an assessment game that the children enjoyed. Objects and photos were among teacher's props for this game. "This is a turkey because it has colorful feathers," the teacher said. The teacher was showing a photo of a parrot. "You're waving flags, why?" the teacher asked. Another example is when the teacher said, "I'm holding a small shovel. You are waving because you don't think I can't dig a hole with this. How can I use it?" (The teacher was holding a small rake.) "Wave your flag if this is called a rake as Brooke has just told us." Both examples are a fast visual check to assess what wasn't retained and who didn't profit from instruction. The examples given suited children with English language ability. The game-like assessment might also be used for the names of common classroom or environment words or objects that second-language learners are learning.

Tests of language always reflect aspects of culture, so it is impossible to construct a single test that is absolutely culturally sensitive and incorporates aspects of all cultures to which children belong. The phrase "culturally sensitive" refers to whether a test is responsive to social and cultural differences among test takers. Any intelligence test with many questions about farm animals would be considered insensitive if one was trying to test the knowledge of inner city preschoolers.

When working with English language learners it is important that the learner receives input that is not only comprehensible, but that is just slightly beyond his or her current level of competence. Knowing common strategies that young children use to learn English as a second language helps teachers. Children may:

- assume that what people are saying is directly related to the ongoing situation.
- learn a few stock expressions or formulaic speech and start to talk.
- search for patterns that recur in the language.
- make the most of the language they already have.
- spend their major effort on getting across meaning and save refinement for later.

Recommended strategies that teachers of language learners use follow. Teachers:

- should build on what the child already knows.
- should not rush instruction, but rather should go slow enough to aid understanding.
- should use scaffolding and combine new words with some kind of gesture or action.
- design room area hideaways that provide child comfort and safety.
- plan frequent activities with no or minimal expectations of a child having to speak.
- encourage English-speaking children by suggesting ways to communicate with second-language peers.
- expand and extend children's limited word use.
- talk about present and at hand classroom happenings.
- restate their comments in more simplified terms at times and offer consistent routines.
- ensure children's inclusion by inviting a child by name to small-group activities.

Most educators realize it will take time for most second-language learners to become competent users of English and children will also need to develop a knowledge and mastery of formal schooling practices. Educators believe all children can attain high levels of achievement if provided with a rich, challenging curriculum and appropriate forms of assistance.

An effective early childhood curriculum for second-language should provide for frequent and diverse opportunities for speaking and listening that offer **scaffolding** to help guide the child through the learning process. The curriculum also should encourage children to take risks when speaking, construct meaning, and reinterpret knowledge within comfortable social contexts. Pairing students as language partners and coworkers in projects is being given increased classroom emphasis.

The dilemma that second-language learners may face in early school experiences is likened to a situation in which you can't win. To learn the new language, one needs to be socially accepted by those speaking the language; however, to be socially accepted, one has to be able to speak the new language. Young children often hurdle this bind by using various strategies, including gestures to invite others to play and accept their company. Crying, whimpering, pointing, miming, and making other nonverbal requests may also be tried. Children collect information by watching, listening, and speculating. They may talk to themselves and experiment with sounds or rehearse what they have heard. Telegraphic and formulaic language develops and they may say "Hey!" or "Lookit" over and over to gain attention.

Preschool dual language learners (DLLs) may exhibit temporary disruptive, challenging or inappropriate coping behaviors in classrooms. These behaviors may occur as a reaction to the difficulty or stress of learning languages both at home and school. Educators routinely examine all children's behaviors and possible causes that might be responsible for new or persistent behavior that can interfere with learning. They use informal and varied professional assessments and conduct family consultations to develop instructional planning strategies and individual plans that may affect a change of unwanted behaviors.

Monolingual and bilingual speakers make inferences about social and linguistic appropriateness based on continued interaction in diverse

---

scaffolding — a teaching technique helpful in promoting languages, understanding, and child solutions. It includes teacher-responsive conversation, open-ended questioning, and facilitation of children's initiatives. Also defined as instruction in which a teacher builds upon what the child already knows to help the child accomplish a task and/or suggests breaking a task down into simpler components to promote accomplishment.

According to Schwartz (2011), regular high-level use of more than one language may actually improve early childhood brain development He notes:

> According to several different studies, command of two or more languages bolsters the ability to focus in the face of distraction, decide between competing alternatives,

and disregard irrelevant information. These essential skills are grouped together, known in brain terms as executive function. The research suggests they develop ahead of time in bilingual children, and are already evident in kids as young as 3 or 4." (p. 26)

social situations. Learning a second language includes a number of difficult tasks. The child must:

- produce sounds that may not be used in the native language.
- understand that native speech sounds or words may have different meanings in the new (second) language.
- learn and select appropriate responses.
- sort and revise word orders.
- learn different cultural values and attitudes.
- control the flow of air while breathing.

Experts have identified four stages in learning English: (1) home language use, (2) an observational and listening period, (3) telegraphic and formulaic speech, and (4) fluid language use. Many factors may have an impact on how quickly young children acquire a second language: motivation, exposure, age, personality, aptitude, consistency, attitude, learning style, opportunity and support, and the individual characteristics of the home and family environment. Snow (2011) states research is clear. Children who are dual-language learners show the best gains in English when their teacher uses their home language in conjunction with English. An important technique—admitting and recognizing that a child is a classroom resource when it comes to explaining other ways of naming and describing objects or other ways of satisfying human needs—should be utilized by educators. Printed word cards in both languages can be added to the classroom to reinforce this idea.

Bilingual youngsters have not encountered a lifelong setback, but instead, they may be more imaginative, better with abstract notions, and more flexible in their thinking than monolingual children. They also have been described as more creative and better at solving complex problems. Compared with monolingual children, bilingual children may develop more awareness concerning the nature of language and how it works. Horz (2012) suggests that being bilingual enhances cognitive development. He posits bilinguals are better able to pay attention, identify spoken syllables, and display an enhanced working memory.

Some English-only parents, particularly more affluent ones, seek tutors or early childhood programs that offer their monolingual children the opportunity to become second-language learners. Nationally many legislators believe bilingual programs should be available for all children, but this is yet to become a national priority.

Youngquist and Martinez-Griego (2009) conclude that when a *strong foundation* is developed in a child's native language, he will learn to read, write, and speak in English faster than a child without one. These authors emphasize the importance of involving families and community to support the school's efforts. This *has* become a national priority recognized by professional associations, such as NAEYC and the International Reading Association (IRA). It is also considered a priority in Head Start programs and the No Child Left Behind legislation, and it is mentioned in most state standards that promote quality.

Pandey (2012) suggests functional bilingualism strengthens children's interpersonal and academic skills, and their understanding of people and customs (p. 96). In Pandey's 2010 publication, *The Child Language Teacher*, she states that familiarity with more than one language enhances children's academic and problem-solving skills and helps them maintain healthy, confidence-boosting ties with at least two communities. On the other hand, some educators worry that a young child's bilingualism may cause family distress. Educators have raised concerns about placing young English-language learners in English-only preschools and believe that this may result in the children losing the ability to communicate effectively in their native language. This, they feel, may adversely affect family relationships and the young child's conceptual development.

4-4 Program Planning for Second-Language Learners

Educators urge program planners who provide second-language learning opportunities to realize that the child's exposure, comfort level, motivation, familiarity, and practice in real communicative contexts are all important considerations. Curriculum developers in early childhood programs that enroll other-than-English-speaking children will have to decide their position on the best way to instruct. A debate rages. One end of the debate espouses native language use, native cultural instruction, and academic learning in the child's native language before instruction in English begins. At the other end, advocates would present English on the child's first day of schooling, with minimal use of the child's native language. Those on this side of the argument believe that the earlier English is introduced and confronted, the greater the child's linguistic advantage. Others disagree, saying no research evidence supports the idea that there is a neural window on second-language learning, and deferring instruction for a year or two is not a disadvantage. Policy recommendations put forth by the National Institute for Early Education Research in 2006 say that support for English language learners should be provided in both the home language and English, where feasible.

Educators note the different points of view concerning English language learners, but may choose to create their own programs by using innovative curricula and other instructional techniques because no comprehensive studies clearly chart the right path for educators to take when teaching preschool ELLs (English language learners) (Freedson-Gonzales, 2008). Each teacher and each educational leader must decide what will work for the children they have enrolled in the context of the curriculum they use and the standards that guide them (Nemeth,

2009). Nemeth and Endosi (2013) note some programs schedule home language times and English-only times each school day. This might mean English-only during play times and home language during meals and snack times. They recommend teachers use props, a tone of voice, body language, pictures, and visuals to clarify new word meanings.

Above all, most educators agree that other-than-English-speaking children need to be perceived as intellectually able, and their teachers should hold high achievement and academic expectations for them as they do for all enrolled children. Teachers are aware that planning well for each child means gathering and knowing as much as one can about the child's culture, home environment, family, and community.

Au (2006) recommends that in any curriculum approach, educators need to realize that one factor that handicaps the academic advancement of English language learners is some teachers' tendency to be overly concerned about the surface features of language, such as correct pronunciation of English, rather than the content of the ideas students are trying to communicate. She also points out that if students believe that what they have to say is important, they will have the confidence to learn the language needed to express those ideas. Most programs approach the differences existing between home and school cultures by promoting children's biculturalism. This allows children to have successful experiences both in their families, where one set of values and behaviors prevails, and in school, where another set of values and behaviors may be expected. In a culturally sensitive approach, early childhood professionals would use modeling with culturally diverse children and slowly introduce and increase the practice of teaching via direct inquiry, particularly using verbal questions while they continue to use modeling. This practice would help increase children's verbal skills and their ability to follow directions.

Planned activities that relate to the experiences of children's everyday lives are also important. For example, cooperative learning activities that involve a small group of young children working together helps develop social skills and positive group relations. Jones and Shue (2013) describe how one preschool teacher's approach to instruction evolved from her desire to implement a classroom project approach. The project was to be interesting enough to engage all children attending. Noticing that native English-speaking children spoke and played with only others like themselves and Spanish-speaking children did the same, the teacher believed a project approach could integrate her group: particularly the hands-on activities planned when the class endeavored to create a classroom pizza parlor. Both groups had home and community pizza experiences in common. The pizza project she planned became an effective method of introducing a curricular topic where joint problem-solving and teamwork occurred. This was done by both child consulting and planning meetings and resulting exploration of hands-on activities that promoted cooperation, language use, and vocabulary. Concept development opportunities occurred frequently.

Early childhood educators working with enrolled English language learners have studied the *Common Core State Standards for English Language Arts* (2010), which is used in all but a few states. They realize kindergarten outcomes will be a huge challenge for English language learners. Educators, therefore, are re-examining how best to increase children's attainment of these ambitious expectations with appropriate preschool-level instruction. Kindergarten curriculum outcomes aim to ensure children can demonstrate a beginning level of Standard English grammar and its conventions when speaking or writing at the end of the school year.

4-4a Classroom Activities

The importance of opportunities for English language learners to engage in pretend play early in their preschool attendance period is emphasized by Roskos and Christie (2007) and Cheatham and Ro (2010). Teacher support can promote and extend children's play periods. When reading and writing play materials are suggested and supplied by a teacher during child-selected (or teacher suggested) play scenarios, child play has a chance for added literacy depth. Many read-alouds lead naturally to possible pretend play and reenacting of the story. Role-playing, whether based on book characters or child-chosen scenario characters, provides an additional benefit resulting in higher measures of child creativity and enhanced ability to analyze situations from different perspectives (Bronson & Merryman, 2010).

Photo 4-5 The introduction of English picture books benefit second-language learners.

© 2015 Cengage Learning®

The value of exposing second-language learning children to quality books cannot be overlooked (Photo 4-5). Story times and one to-one, adult-child book readings can supply vocabulary and meaning in a way that conversational models alone cannot accomplish. Songs and music can also present language-learning opportunities. Print use in the center environment is another vehicle to promote literacy development. Above all, opportunities for abundant play and interaction with English-speaking children are critical. The most successful methods for teaching a second language include the same techniques mentioned in the monolingual child's learning of his first language—warm, responsive, articulate adults involved with children's everyday, firsthand exploration of the environment.

Additional suggested teacher strategies and techniques follow.

- Provide a safe, accepting classroom environment.
- Respond to meaning, rather than speech technicalities or specifics.
- Promote sharing and risk taking.
- Make classroom activities inviting, interesting, meaningful, and successful.

- Emphasize and repeat key words in sentences.
- Point at objects or touch them while naming them, when possible.
- Learn how to correctly pronounce the child's name.
- Include the child in small groups where there are other child models to follow.
- Help the child realize he is unique and special, exactly "as is."
- Learn a few useful words in the child's language (for example, *bathroom, eat, stop, listen*).
- Gesture and use objects and pictures that give children additional clues, such as a picture-based daily schedule.
- Provide activity choices in which the child does not have to interface with others—so-called safe havens.
- During activity times, provide enough staff so that teachers can work closely with children and materials.
- Use a running commentary technique in interactions. "Serena is painting with red paint." "I'm pinning a name tag on your sweater."
- Choose predictable books to share.
- Work with a small group at story-reading times.
- Use repeated presentations of the same songs at group times.
- Link up English-speaking "partners" in noncompetitive games.
- Take the time to look children in the eye, showing you value your interaction (Nemeth, 2009).
- Check classroom noise levels to assure English-language learners will have no difficulty distinguishing English speech sounds.

When teachers work with second-language learners, they make adjustments similar to those families make when talking to their very young children; these include organizing talk around visual references (real objects, actions, happenings, people, and so on), using simple syntax, producing many repetitions and paraphrases, speaking slowly and clearly, checking often for comprehension, and expanding and extending topics introduced by the child. The teacher can develop a list of survival words in both English and the native language of attending children such as eat, help, bathroom, play, rest, and so on for her own and the children's use. Figure 4-3 is a list of some

survival words in Spanish. Professional education associations recommend that teachers faced with many different languages in their classrooms consider grouping together, at specific times during the day, children that speak the same or similar languages so that children can construct knowledge with others who speak their home language.

Playmates of second-language learners can be encouraged not only to be aware and accepting of other children but to approach and invite them to play. Through discussion, example, and modeling, children can learn to use gestures, to use simple sentences, to speak slowly, and to repeat themselves or use different words when they think their "friends" do not quite understand. Teachers stress that these new classmates may need help. One classroom regularly scheduled a short picture book reading time when family members shared a book in a language other than English. Children could choose whether to attend. The book would then

Figure 4-3 Survival words and phrases in English and Spanish.

English Word or Phrase	Spanish Word or Phrase
Hello	Hola
Teacher	la maestra
Bathroom	el bano
Eat	comer
Play	jugar
Drink	beber
Wash	lavar
Please sit down	Sientese, por favor
Welcome to school	Bienvenidos a la escuela
Take a rest	Tome un descanso
Do you need help?	Necesita ayuda?
My name is	Mi nombre es…
Join us, please	Por favor unase a nosotros.
We are friends	Somos amigos
Does that hurt?	Te duele?
Pleased to meet you	Mucho gusto!
Let's go outside	Salamos fuera
Are you cold?	Esta frio?
Time to clean up	Momento de la limpieza
Time to pick up	Hora de recogida
Thank you	Igracias
Your mom will be here soon.	Tu mama volvera pronto

be repeated in English by their regular teacher, and a discussion period examined how children both attempted to understand and felt during the first reading.

Second-language learners can be ignored and left out of peer play. Even when trying to communicate nonverbally, they can be treated as "babies" or as invisible. They may be cast as the infant in dramatic play situations or be the object of a mothering child's attention—perhaps unwanted attention. Other children may speak to them in high-pitched voices and in shortened and linguistically reduced forms as they have observed adults sometimes do with very young children who are learning to speak. Teachers should monitor these peer behaviors and discourage them if necessary.

4-4b Reaching Families

Home-school instructional support programs have provided books, electronic media, "borrowed" materials and equipment, and "take home" suggestions for homes with limited access to English-language models and storybooks. Encouraging families to continue to maintain their first language and their home language literacy activities, and perhaps increase everyday conversations, is a common practice. Schools usually ask families questions about what types of language exposure a child has had since birth and what types of literacy experiences have been associated with them. Designing room features and planning curriculum activities that welcome a family's participation in classroom activities are both important considerations.

Early childhood educators who speak more than one language and are culturally knowledgeable are an invaluable resource in the early childhood setting. Many experts and researchers advocate recruiting teacher assistants and classroom volunteers who speak children's native tongue. A classroom interpreter may frequently be necessary and considered an invaluable staff member in many programs.

Teachers can expect a Spanish-speaking child to have a problem producing consonant sounds that do not exist in his native language, such as *d, j, r, v, sh, th*, and *s*; beginning-of-word blends, such as *st, sp*, and *sm*; and word endings of *r* blends, such as *-rd, -rt*, and *-rs*. A few other word sounds also will be difficult.

Second-language learners may reach a stage when they seem to repeat words, focus intently, and rehearse words. This happens not for the purpose of communication, but rather so the child can practice through repetition, which is reminiscent of younger preschoolers' private speech or self-talk during play situations. These rehearsing behaviors are usually done at a low volume. The first unintelligible utterances that second-language learners issue may be sound experimentation.

4-4c Providing Targeted Support

English language learners are just as unique as native speakers, and they often profit from the targeted supportive assistance teachers offer. Motivation to learn a new language when separate from family overwhelms some children, and they may have a problem initiating play with others. The social actions and reactions of teachers and other children can help or impact their desire to learn the classroom's language. Teachers should design activities, environments, and classroom situations that attempt to increase children's motivation in a number of ways. Capturing a child's curiosity, enhancing children's feelings of acceptance and safety, or developing trust helps. Most teachers get clever when offering targeted teaching strategies to influence a child's adjustment and ability to choose to participate and engage. Teaching a child a few common English vocabulary words and gestures can be a first positive step in the child's ability to communicate his needs and desires. Beginning vocabulary words are usually labels for objects and people or short social phrases such as "Hi," "Play," and "Please." The child's receptive vocabulary grows at a faster pace as she understands additional words to name things in both languages. Noticing Alfaro's minimal understanding of English words, his teacher planned targeted support activities and one-on-one instruction.

Teachers can plan more effectively if they have background information concerning the second-language learners. Getting the answers to the following questions would help. Answers and information is gained through observation at school and by interviewing parents and families during intake interviews or at a later time:

- Is there any special speech (either native or English) that the child uses during the school day? If so, when, where, and with whom?

- Does the child participate in nonverbal play with peers?
- Does the child seek out native-speaking peers or native-speaking adults in the classroom that the child feels comfortable with?
- Do parents describe the child as talkative at home? Or verbally limited or having a recognized problem speaking with neighborhood children?
- Is the child being ignored, teased, or laughed at during school?
- When does the child appear happy at home and at school?
- Are there times of day when the child speaks more often or that are particularly difficult for the child at school?
- Does the child use any headsets for listening activities at school?
- Are there people who use his home language at school?
- Will the child join in during a song in his home language at school or home?
- If given a sign or signal to use to gain help, will the child use it at school?
- Has using a school buddy system had any success?
- When was the child's last eye and ear physical exam?

- At school, how many English directions does the child follow? When?
- What classroom areas or materials interest him the most?
- Does he use nonverbal communication at home or school? Is it successful?

4-5 Promoting Cultural Awareness

Teachers interested in studying the cultures of enrolled children can start by identifying components of culture. These components include family structure; definitions of stages, periods, or transitions during a person's life; roles of adults and children; their corresponding behavior in terms of power and politeness; discipline; time and space; religion; food; health and hygiene; history; traditions; holidays; and celebrations (Photo 4-6).

In some cultures it is believed that children are not appropriate conversational partners for adults. Children may not be encouraged to initiate conversations about themselves or their interests, and adult talk may not be child-centered. Children may have learned that it is impolite to look directly at adults when talking. Some children grow up learning that cooperation is more highly valued than competition; others do not.

Photo 4-6 Children's food preferences are often discussed with parents.

© 2016 Cengage Learning®

▶❚❚ TeachSource Video 4-1

Multicultural Lessons: Embracing Similarities and Differences

Shelley Outwater, a literacy coach, discusses her philosophy for helping her students become aware of cultural similarities and differences in her classroom.

1. Discuss how multicultural learning and language learning can go hand-in-hand in a classroom such as Shelly's classroom or in a preschool classroom.

2. In the video's read-aloud segment, what teacher techniques and strategies are used in the adult-child conversation to increase child understanding and comprehension?

Cultures are complex and changing, so understanding cultural similarities and differences can be a life's study in itself. **Culture** is defined here as all the activities and achievements of a society that individuals within that society pass from one generation to the next.

Ethnic origin is often a basic ingredient in subcultural groupings. **Subculture** is defined as other than a dominant culture. Class structure also exists in societies consisting of upper, middle, and lower income groups. Often, patterns of child-rearing vary between cultures and classes.

Practitioners may have to field questions from children about another child's speech. Answering in an open, honest fashion with accurate information gives the adult an opportunity to affirm diversity and perhaps correct a child's biased ideas. Negative stereotypes can be diminished or

dismissed. Before answering, it is a good idea to clarify what the child is really asking. Examples of teacher statements follow:

"Yes, Paloma speaks some words you don't understand. Her family comes from Guatemala and they speak the Spanish language. Paloma is learning lots of new words at school in the language of her new country—English."

"Quan doesn't talk to you because he doesn't know our words yet. He speaks a different language at his house. He is listening, and one day he will speak. While he is listening and learning words to speak, he wants to play. Show him with your hands and words what you want him to do. He will understand."

Teachers working with culturally diverse children need to watch and listen closely. Children's behavior and movements will give clues to their well-being and feelings of safety in the group. Teachers may need to ease into situations in which unpleasant remarks or actions are directed at a newly enrolled child who speaks a different language and express sadness, such as: "Ricardo has heard some unkind and unfriendly words from you boys in the loft. He is new at school and doesn't know what our school is like. I'm going to try and help Ricardo enjoy his first day in our room."

An adult's inability to modify their speech to a child's level, neutral or negative environments, family arrangements that require children to be alone for long periods, frequent situations in which children are expected to be quiet or cannot gain adult attention, and a lack of books or early reading experiences are all factors that can affect speech growth. Families are the primary language teachers during the early years, and language competence grows out of familiar situations, such as seeking help or establishing joint attention—situations that provide frameworks in which children learn to make their intentions plain and to interpret the intentions of others.

4-5a Planning Cultural Awareness Language Activities

In planning language activities of all types, every effort must be made to make children aware of cross-cultural similarities while exploring

---

culture — all the activities and achievements of a society that individuals within that society pass from one generation to the next.

subculture — an ethnic, regional, economic, or social group exhibiting characteristic patterns of behavior sufficient to distinguish it from others within an embracing culture or society.

differences. Language arts programming should draw on the linguistic, cultural, and personal experiences of language-diverse children. When planning instructional activities, it is important to provide opportunities that are familiar to children from their family and community life. Parents and extended family members can be invited to share family stories and artifacts relating to theme units, learning centers, or other program components.

Young children can be exposed to the idea that people eat, sleep, wear clothing, celebrate, dance, sing, live in groups, and speak to one another in common languages, and that they do these things in ways that may be either the same as or different from the ways their families do these things. Planned activities can make comparisons, treating diversity with the dignity it deserves. Skin color, hairstyles, food preferences, clothing, and music are starting points for study. Modeling friendship and cooperation between cultures and planning activities showing dissimilar individuals and groups living in harmony is a good idea. Stories exist in all languages and in most dialects. Some centers ask children and parents to contribute family photos to use to construct a classroom "My Family" book. Each child is asked to dictate a caption for each family photo. The book is permanently placed in the class library collection. When a new child enrolls, new family photos are added. (Identifying quality multicultural and multiethnic picture books is discussed in Chapter 8.) Room displays, bulletin boards, and learning centers should also reflect the cultural diversity of attending children.

It is important to plan language arts programs that incorporate different cultural styles of dramatic play, storytelling, and chanting. Librarians can help teachers discover picture books and other materials written in dialects or two-language translations.

4-5b Families as Partners

A strong connection between home and school should exist with families playing a role in program planning and as assistants or teachers in classrooms. When family literacy rates are depressed, teachers have to proceed carefully with suggestions concerning reading to children. Wordless books and parent's oral stories are alternatives. Reading books aloud at home in a bilingual child's primary language is also recommended. (Family literacy programs are discussed in Chapter 18.)

Volk and Long (2005) have the following suggestions, which can help educators honor children's home and school literacy resources.

- Guard against a **deficit perspective** that distorts the educator's vision when working with marginalized families.
- Gain the perspective that homes, families, cultures, and communities possess "funds of knowledge," that is literacies and individuals with valuable skills.
- Understand that children become literate in many ways.
- Recognize that most families value education and believe it is important.
- Recognize that families may use different yet various and effective methods to support literacy.
- Believe that children participate in many literacy interactions at home (Figure 4-4).
- Realize that children may be surrounded by abundant human and literary resources including networks of support and people of varying ages and abilities.
- Recognize that peers help each other and may clarify the teacher's statements.

4-5c Program Types

Controversy exists concerning which type of program is best suited to the child learning English as a second language. There are various program types, such as

- Bilingual programs: Two languages are used for instruction.
- Transitional bilingual programs: Children's first language is used as a medium of instruction until they become fluent enough to receive all of their instruction in English.
- Newcomer programs: Recent immigrant children are provided a special academic environment for a limited period. They provide a welcoming classroom environment and use instructional strategies to orient children to American life and culture. Bilingual staffs are secured when possible.
- Developmental bilingual programs: Equal status is given to English and another language,

---

deficit perspective — an attitude or belief that attributes children's school failures to children themselves, or to their family or culture.

Figure 4-4 How families can increase child literacy with home activities.

Dear Families,

Many parents ask how they can help develop their child's literacy skills at home.

A families' daily activities can be literacy-building and might include:

- Reading letters from their country of origin together.
- Consulting on children's homework.
- Jointly reviewing school assignments.
- Reading all school-home written communication with children.
- Reading and discussing all kinds of books such as phone book, dictionaries, encyclopedias, address books, recipe books, and reference books in their home language or English.
- Practicing new school skills or family skills that require reading such as instruction manuals, bills, announcements, advertisements, junk mail, milk and cereal cartons, and so on.
- Reading age-level appropriate books to their child in English or home language and discussing narrative, or naming actions or objects in illustrations.
- Discussing electronic or digital media they experience it together. Selecting educational content when possible.
- Playing games with and without electronic media especially games with cards, numbers, alphabet letters and rules.
- Participating in writing, singing, listening, viewing activities connected to their home or the American culture.
- Reading or listening to material concerned with the family's religious orientation and experience.
- Providing writing and art materials in a home area that is comfortable and supplied with a variety of paper, notebooks, coloring books, etc. and different kinds of writing tools—pens, markers, crayons, etc.
- Talking about print in the neighborhood such as street signs, house numbers, window ads, posted ads and announcements, menus, and so on.
- Enacting books, plays, events, or common and important family occasions with role playing.

Sincerely,
Your child's teacher

Digital Download

promoting full proficiency in two languages. Mixing and translating language is avoided but acceptable at social times.

- Two-way immersion programs: This type of program provides integrated language and academic instruction for native English speakers and native speakers of another language. This enables English speakers to develop second-language proficiency. Both groups' families must have an interest in bilingualism.
- Tutor-assisted programs: A special tutor (or teacher) works with a child for a portion of the school day.
- Full-immersions: A full-immersion program offers an age-appropriate curriculum in a language foreign to the child. August and Shanahan (2006) point out full immersion in English that gives no attention to children's native language has not been shown to offer any advantage for later academic schooling.

Frequently mentioned features of successful English-language learner programs include:

- ongoing and guided parental involvement.
- professional development for early childhood educators.
- the promotion of growth and proficiency in both first and secondary languages.
- the use of assessment that is linked to instructional objectives to inform instructional planning and delivery.
- developmentally appropriate and culturally sensitive curriculum.
- high standards for language acquisition and academic achievement.
- strong staff joint planning and leadership.
- sheltered instruction, an approach that integrates language and content instruction.
- academic instruction in English.
- the adoption of strategies to make content (in activities) meaningful and comprehensive.

In addition, visuals and images (pictorial representations) used while the teacher is interacting improves student listening comprehension and may reduce recall errors.

4-6 Assessment and Types of Special Needs DAP

Assessment is usually undertaken when teachers suspect that a child has difficulty communicating and could profit from specialized instruction. The goal is to identify whether a child's language is more or less advanced than that of other children his age (delayed language) or is deficient when compared with performance on social and/ or intellectual tasks (language deficit) or whether the child fits other categories. Screening tests should be conducted by trained professionals.

The California State Department of Education (2009) suggests teachers should team up with professionals knowledgeable about second-language acquisition to sort out which child behaviors are caused by second-language learning and other causes. Behaviors that can be misinterpreted include the following:

- speaks infrequently
- speaks excessively (either in home language or in English)
- refuses to answer questions
- confuses similar sounding words
- is unable to tell or recall stories
- has poor general recall
- uses poor pronunciation
- uses poor syntax and grammar
- does not volunteer information (p. 64)

4-6a Types of Special Needs and Language Development

Special language-development preschool centers with expert personnel are available in most communities for children with easily identifiable communication deficiencies, such as hearing loss, visual impairment, and obvious speech impairments. Other children in need of special help may not be identified at the preschool level and may function within the wide range of children considered to be average or typical for preschool ages. In language arts, learning disability is a term that refers to a group of disorders manifested by significant difficulties in the acquisition and use of listening, speaking, reading, or writing. Most programs are reticent to label children as having language learning problems because of their lack of expertise to screen and evaluate children in a truly professional manner. Referral to speech-language pathologists or local or college clinics is suggested to families when a question exists concerning a particular child's progress. Early childhood teachers are not speech or language pathologists and therefore should not be expected to diagnose language problems or prescribe therapy. Communication disorders are usually divided into two main categories—**hearing disabilities** and speech and language disabilities.

Speech and language disabilities can affect the way people speak and understand; these range from simple sound substitutions to not being able to use speech and language effectively. Many children in the United States have experienced some kind of expressive speech problem, delay, or disability; the most common problems involving articulation, language, voice, and fluency disorders, or a combination of these. Most articulation problems not caused by physical, sensory, or neurological damage respond to treatment. Nonorganic causes of problems include:

- lack of stimulation.
- lack of need to talk.
- poor speech models.
- lack of or low reinforcement.
- insecurity, anxiety, crisis.
- shyness or lack of social confidence

4-6b Language Delay

Language delay may be connected to syntax, semantics, morphology, pragmatics, vocabulary, and remembering and discussing happenings in the right order. Language delay is characterized by a marked slowness in the development of the vocabulary and grammar necessary for expressing and understanding thoughts and ideas. It may involve both comprehension and the child's expressive language output and quality. It is wise for families to consult a speech-language pathologist if the delay is more than six months, so language therapy begins if recommended.

---

hearing disabilities — characterized by an inability to hear sounds clearly. This may range from hearing speech sounds faintly or in a distorted way, to profound deafness.

speech and language disabilities — communication disorders that affect the way people talk and understand; range from simple sound substitutions to not being able to use speech and language at all.

A complete study of a child includes first looking for physical causes, particularly hearing loss, and then examining other structural (voice-producing) conditions. Neurological limitations come under scrutiny, as do emotional development factors. Home environments and family communication styles are also examined.

A language-delayed child may have a small vocabulary and may use short and simple sentences with many grammatical errors. He may have difficulty maintaining a conversation and may often talk about the immediate present rather than future happenings. He can have difficulty understanding others and in making himself understood. Besides linguistic problems, a language-delayed child may have problems classifying objects and recognizing similarities and differences. He also may ignore opportunities to play with others.

Additional behaviors a teacher might notice in a language-delayed child include:

- less variety in sentence structure
- simple two- and three-word sentences
- less frequent speech
- frequent occurrence of playing alone
- less adept participation in joint planning with classmates

Early childhood educators concerned about the speech and socialization of "late talkers" should discuss their suspicions with their teaching team and supervisors. Teachers might readily agree with the following sample description of a language-delayed child: "Speaks markedly less well than other children of the same age and seems to have normal ability in intellectual, motor, sensory, and emotional control areas, but may be rejected by peers."

The quantity of parent talk with their young children can differ greatly between two families—a child from one family could hear 700 utterances each day while a child from another family hears 11,000 utterances. Children in the first category can seem to possess lower-level language skills not caused by any innate problem, but rather by an environmental situation.

Teachers working with language-delayed children use the following interactive techniques:

- gaining attention with tempting, interest-catching activities
- being at eye level, face-to-face, if possible
- establishing eye contact
- displaying enthusiasm and playfulness
- establishing a play activity involving "my turn, your turn" interaction
- verbalizing single words, short phrases, or short sentences, depending on the child's verbal level
- pausing, waiting, and looking expectantly, encouraging the child's turn to talk
- repeating teacher statements and pausing expectantly
- copying the child's actions or verbalizations
- following the child's focus of interest with joint teacher interest
- probing the child's interest with logical questions
- maintaining close, accepting physical contact and a warm interactive manner

A few children may make a conscious decision not to try to learn Standard English or a new language when they are confronted with a language other than their native language or dialect. A number of reasons for their choice are possible. If others enrolled or teachers speak their native language, they may believe it is not necessary or simply not worth the effort. Families may not give a high priority to learning the new language, or children's enrollment may consist of only a few mornings a week. A child's decision can be temporary or long-term.

Cloistered Children. Some teachers and educators describe children with inadequate language due to lack of human interactive environments. To be "cloistered" connotes isolation, separation, limited experience, meager human contact, a narrow view of the world, small or sparsely furnished living quarters, and perhaps a time-consuming devotion to spiritual contemplation and prayer. In the cloistered child, spiritual contemplation and prayer is replaced with the passive pursuit of hours and hours of never discussed screen watching. The cloistered child often displays language delay and may also display one or many of the following characteristics:

- limited attention span.
- inability to express ideas.
- limited language and vocabulary.
- inability to draw on past knowledge.

- inability to listen.
- impulsiveness (says first thing that pops into mind).
- lack of perseverance ("It's work. It's too hard.").
- blunted interest and curiosity.
- disorganization.
- impatience, inability to wait.
- poor conversation skills.

To develop what is seen as "missing language and missing experience," experts recommend a curriculum that includes lots of talk, active involvement, time and play with others, and exposure to literature. Some educators recommend opportunities to play with peers and plan actions, which facilitate the child's seeing himself in control, along with the promotion of child resourcefulness in seeking help from others.

Overstressed Children. There are many different reasons why some children have stressful living situations. When young children's stress is connected to new adults, new situations, groups of peers, books and book-reading times, or conversations with an adult, teachers will notice child anxiety, aversion behavior, and reluctance in speaking out in groups. O'Leary, Newton, Lundz, Hall, O'Connell, Raby, and Czarnecka (2002) describe degrees of stress and possible causative factors teachers should avoid.

> Mild stress enhances conscious learning, but too much stress, especially for too long a time, prevents it. Stress speaks primarily to the emotional learning system, and there it works primarily in a negative way.
>
> Extreme stress, caused by too much different information, unrelated information, or information too rapidly introduced or presented within too short a space of time, adds to a negative emotional reaction and clicks in a fear response. This memory is engraved below the level of awareness and becomes conscious as an attitude toward or feeling about the situation or topic. (p. 46)

Fortunately, when no pressure and stress exist and a safe school environment is experienced, many children who display an initial aversion to certain school activities, including language arts activities, venture forth slowly and their attitudes change. Most early childhood teachers have been acquainted with children who avoid book-sharing times, yet listen from another area in the classroom. After a period, they move closer, and eventually they join the read-aloud group.

4-6c Expressive and Receptive Language Difficulties

Educators begin suspecting problems in language development when they observe attending children in a variety of classroom situations, including group times, play times, adult-child exchanges, and social interactions. In lower elementary school grades, including kindergarten, the following characteristics are cause for concern:

1. limited use of language.
2. trouble starting and/or responding to conversation.
3. heavy reliance on gesture or nonverbal communication.
4. limited or nonspecific vocabulary.
5. inappropriate grammar.
6. difficulty in sequencing rhymes or stories.

Teachers handling preschoolers may think many of these characteristics are typical of younger preschoolers and that they will be corrected as the child approaches kindergarten age. Their program planning and teacher-child interactions aim to erase difficulties, and they would be concerned if growth in a preschooler's language ability and skill was not observable and apparent over time.

4-6d Articulation

Articulation disorders involve difficulties with the way sounds are formed and strung together, usually characterized by substituting one sound for another, omitting a sound, or distorting a sound. If consonant sounds are misarticulated, they may occur in the initial (beginning), medial (middle), or ending positions in words. It is prudent to point out again that normally developing children do not master the articulation of all consonants until age seven or eight.

Most young children (three- to five-years-old) hesitate, repeat, and re-form words as they speak. Imperfections occur for several reasons:

(1) a child does not pay attention as closely as an adult, especially to certain high-frequency consonant sounds; (2) the child may not be able to distinguish some sounds; or (3) a child's coordination and control of his articulation mechanisms may not be perfected. For example, the child may be able to hear the difference between *Sue* and *shoe* but cannot pronounce them differently. About 60 percent of all children with diagnosed articulation problems are boys.

Articulation characteristics of young children include the following.

- Substitution: One sound is substituted for another, as in "wabbit" for "rabbit" or "thun" for "sun."

- Omission: The speaker leaves out a sound that should be articulated. He says "at" for "hat," "ca" for "cat," "icky" for "sticky," "probly" for "probably." The left out sound may be at the beginning, middle, or end of a word.

- Distortion: A sound is said inaccurately, but is similar to the intended sound.

- Addition: The speaker adds a sound, as in "li-it-tle" for "little" and "muv-va-ver" for "mother."

- Transposition: The position of sounds in words is switched, as in "hangerber" for "hamburger" and "aminal" for "animal."

- Lisp: The *s, z, sh, th, ch,* and *j* sounds are distorted. There are two to 10 types of lisps noted by speech experts.

Articulation problems may stem from a physical condition, such as a cleft palate or hearing loss, or they can be related to problems in the mouth, such as a dental abnormality. Many times, articulation problems occurring without any obvious physical disability may involve the faulty learning of speech sounds. Some children will require special help and directed training to eliminate all articulation errors; others seem to mature and correct articulation problems by themselves.

Teacher behavior that helps a child with articulation problems includes not interrupting or constantly correcting the child and making sure that others do not tease or belittle. Modeling misarticulated words correctly is a good course of action. Simply continue your conversation and insert the correctly articulated word in your answering comment.

4-6e Voice Quality and Fluency Disorders

Teachers sometimes notice differences in children's voice quality, which involves pitch, loudness, resonance, and general quality (breathiness, hoarseness, and so on). The intelligibility of a child's speech is determined by how many of the child's words are understandable. One can expect 80 percent of the child's speech to be understandable at age three.

Stuttering and cluttering are categorized as fluency disorders. Stuttering involves the rhythm of speech and is a complicated, many-faceted problem. Stuttering speech is characterized by abnormal stoppages with no sound, repetitions, or prolonged sounds and syllables. There may also be unusual facial and body movements associated with efforts to speak. This problem involves four times as many males as females and can usually be treated. All young children repeat words and phrases, and this tends to increase with anxiety or stress. It is simply typical for the age and is not true stuttering. A teacher should wait patiently for the child to finish expressing himself and should resist the temptation to say "slow down." An adult talking at a slow, relaxed rate and pausing between sentences can give a child time to reflect and respond with more fluency. Keeping eye contact and not rushing, interrupting, or finishing words is also recommended. Classmates should be prohibited from teasing a peer who stutters.

Trautman (2003) identifies the following causes of stuttering:

- *Genetics*: approximately 59 percent of all people who stutter have family members who stutter.

- *child development*: children with speech, language, cognitive, or development delays are more likely to stutter.

- *neurophysiology*: research has shown that some people who stutter process speech and language in different areas of the brain than people who do not stutter.

- *family dynamics*: fast-paced lifestyles and high expectations can contribute to stuttering.

Trautman notes that most stuttering starts between the ages of two and four, and about 20 percent of children in that age group are affected. Many others in this age group go through a temporary lack of fluency and outgrow it. She points out that if stuttering lasts longer than three months and begins after age three, the child will likely need therapy to correct it. Most children make a full recovery. The disorder continues in a few, affecting about one percent of the adult population. Studies suggest that genetics plays a role in about half of stuttering cases (Rubin, 2010). A speech-language pathologist is the appropriate person to evaluate and plan improvement activities. The National Stuttering Association provides support, education, advocacy, and current research information.

Cluttering involves the rate of speaking, and it includes errors in articulation, stress, and pausing. Speech seems too fast with syllables and words running together. Listener reaction and good speech modeling are critical aspects of behavior for teachers when a child lacks fluency. Adults who work with a young child refrain from criticizing, correcting, acting negatively, or calling a speech problem to the child's attention. They create a warm adult-child relationship if possible, and try to eliminate any factors or conditions that increase problems in fluency. They work to protect the child's expectation of normal fluency and build the child's self-confidence as a speaker.

Approximately 25 percent of all children go through a stage of development during which they seem to stutter or clutter when excited or are searching for a word to express their thoughts. This may be temporary lack of fluency associated with learning to speak. Only a minority persists in early childhood stuttering, whereas in the majority of cases, stuttering is temporary and an often short-lived disorder that disappears without formal intervention, apparently on its own.

4-6f Selective (Elective) Mutism

Occasionally, early childhood teachers encounter silent children. Silence may be temporary or lasting, in which case it will be a matter for teacher concern. Children with **selective (elective) mutism** are described simply as children who can speak but do not. They display functional speech in selected settings (usually at home) and/or

choose to speak only with certain individuals (often siblings or same-language speakers). Researchers believe selective mutism, if it happens, commonly occurs between ages three and five years. Because child abuse may promote delayed language development or psychological disorders that interfere with communication, such as selective mutism, teachers need to be concerned. School referral to speech professionals leads to assessment and individual treatment programs. School administrators prefer that families make appointments and usually provide families with a description of local resources.

Teachers can help professionals by providing observational data to describe the child's behavior and responses in classroom settings. Many factors can contribute to a particular child's silence or reduced speech. Consequently, teachers are cautioned to avoid a mutism diagnosis. A child's teasing or any other action that causes the embarrassment of a child with a language or speech difference should be handled swiftly and firmly by preschool staff members. **DAP**

4-6g Other Conditions

Frequent crying. Occasionally, frustrated children will cry or scream to communicate a need. Crying associated with adjustment to a new situation is handled by providing supportive attention and care. Continual crying and screaming to obtain an object or privilege, on the other hand, calls for the following kinds of teacher statements:

"I don't understand what you want when you scream. Use words so I will know what you want."

"Sara does not know what you want when you cry, Ethan. Saying 'Please get off the puzzle piece' with your words tells her."

These statements let the child know what is expected and help him see that words solve problems.

Avid talkers and shouters. Occasionally, children may discover that talking incessantly can get them what they want. In order to quiet children, others sometimes give in. This is somewhat

---

cluttering — rapid, incomplete speech that is often jerky, slurred, spoken in bursts, and difficult to understand; nervous speech.

selective (elective) mutism — a behavior that describes child silence or lack of speech in select surroundings and/or with certain individuals.

different from the common give and take in children's daily conversations or children's growing ability to argue and state their cases.

Language for these children becomes a social weapon instead of a social tool. A child may find that loudness in speech can intimidate others and will out-shout the opposition. If a child behaves this way, it is prudent to have the child's hearing checked. Teachers often change this type of behavior through discussions of "inside" (the classroom) voices and "outside" voices (which may be used on the playground), and also by mentioning how difficult it is to hear a "too loud" voice.

Questioners.
At times, children ask many questions, one right after another. This may be a good device to hold or gain adults' attention: "Why isn't it time for lunch?" or "What makes birds sing?" or "Do worms sleep?" The questions may seem endless to adults. Most of the questions are prompted by the child's natural curiosity or an attempt to gain attention. Educators' help children find out as much as possible and strive to fulfill the needs of the individual child. Along the way, there will be many questions that may be difficult or even impossible to answer.

Learning Disabilities.
Children with learning disabilities may exhibit the following in their language use and behavior. They may:

- start talking later than other children
- have pronunciation problems
- display slow vocabulary growth; be unable to find the right word
- have trouble learning numbers, the alphabet, the days of the week
- display difficulty rhyming words
- seem extremely restless and easily distracted
- have trouble with peers
- exhibit poor ability to follow directions or routines
- avoid puzzles, drawing, and cutting activities

Experts point out that the sooner a problem can be identified and treated, the better the outcome is likely to be. Most programs handling children with learning difficulties strive to pinpoint causative factors, and to assess children's present level of functioning. Then programs and/or professional consultants develop individual learning plans (IEPs).

Hearing Problems and Hearing Disabilities.
A screening of young children's auditory acuity may uncover hearing loss. Rones (2004) estimates that two to three infants of every 1,000 are born with significant and/or permanent hearing loss and about 70 percent get their ears checked before leaving the hospital. The seriousness of hearing loss is related both to the degree of loss and the range of sound frequencies that are most affected. Because young children develop ear infections frequently, schools alert families when a child's listening behavior seems newly impaired.

Hearing disabilities are characterized by an inability to hear sounds clearly. Disabilities range from the ability to hear faint sounds to profound deafness. Approximately one out of every 300 children is born with permanent loss (Eiserman, Shisler, Foust, Buhrmann, & White, 2007). Appropriate intervention before the age of six months can significantly improve language and cognitive development in some milder cases of loss. The American Speech-Language-Hearing Association is a recommended teacher and family resource.

Otitis media is a medical term that refers to any inflammation of the middle ear. There are two types of otitis media: (1) a fluid-filled middle ear without infection and (2) an infected middle ear. Researchers believe that otitis media may affect babbling and interfere with an infant's ability to hold on to a string of utterances in working memory long enough to draw meaning. Many preschoolers have ear infections during preschool years, and many children have clear fluid in the middle ear that goes undetected. Even though the hearing loss caused by otitis media may be small and temporary, it may have a serious effect on speech and language learning for a preschool child. The common cold outranks child ear infection, and a teacher can expect one child in three to be affected on any given day during some seasons of the year.

---

otitis media — inflammation and/or infection of the middle ear.

If undetected hearing distortion or loss lasts for a long period, the child can fall behind. Children who have a history of middle ear disease are often enrolled in speech and language treatment programs. General inattentiveness, wanting to get close to hear, trouble with directions, irritability, or pulling and rubbing of the ear can be signs a teacher should heed. Other signs to look for include:

- difficulty hearing word endings such as -*ed*, -*ing*, and -*s*.
- problems interpreting intonation patterns, inflections, and stress.
- distractibility.
- inattentiveness.
- asking adults to repeat.
- confusion with adult commands.
- difficulty repeating verbally presented material.
- inappropriate responses to questions.
- watching for cues from other children.
- complaints about ears.
- persistent breathing through the mouth.
- slowness in locating the source of sounds.
- softer or "fuzzier" speech than others.
- aggressiveness.
- loss of temper.*

Preschool staff members who notice children who confuse words with similar sounds may be the first to suspect **auditory processing** difficulties or mild to moderate hearing loss.

Mild hearing impairment may masquerade as:

- stubbornness.
- lack of interest.
- a learning disability.

With intermittent **deafness**, children may have difficulty comprehending oral language. Severe impairment impedes language development and is easier to detect than the far more subtle signs of mild loss. Most infected ears cause considerable pain, and parents are alerted to the need for medical help. However, if the ear is not infected or if the infection does not cause pain, the problem is harder to recognize.

4-6h Suggestions and Strategies for Working with Children with Disabilities and Special Needs

The following suggestions and strategies are useful with typically developing children, but also help children with disabilities and special needs. They apply to educators, administrators, and families.

- Investigate whether a child is receiving supportive services at school and/or at an out-of-school location.
- Investigate equipment and media used or developed for specific problems or needs.
- Create and provide visual aids that depict or clarify instructional intent, such as posters and signs with pictures, drawings, or photographs.
- Use gestures that clarify words.
- Place children next to others who can provide help.
- Use cues such as a flashing light or music to gain attention, if necessary.

The Individuals with Disabilities Education Act, through federal and state mandates, ensures that children who have educationally significant hearing loss and certain other disabilities receive free, appropriate, public education. Programs develop a team approach that includes families or others familiar with the child's personality and interests, and professionals who are knowledgeable. This group creates individualized learning plans. Classroom environments are designed to promote learning and child comfort (Katz & Schery, 2006).

If a child's speech or language lags behind expected development for the child's age, school staff members should observe and listen to the child closely to collect additional data. When speech is unusually difficult to understand—rhythmically conspicuous, full of sound distortion, or consistently difficult to hear—this may indicate a serious problem. Professional help is available to preschool programs and families through a number of resources. Most cities have speech and hearing centers and public and

---

auditory processing — the full range of mental activity involved in reacting to auditory stimuli, especially speech sounds, and in considering their meanings in relation to past experience and to their future use.

deafness — hearing is so impaired that the individual is unable to process auditory linguistic information, with or without amplification.

private practitioners specializing in speech-language pathology and audiology. Other resources include:

- city and county health departments.
- universities and medical schools.
- state departments of education offices.
- the American Speech-Language-Hearing Association, as mentioned previously.

Experts give the families of hearing-impaired children the following advice:

- Help the child "tune in" to language.
- Talk.
- Provide stimulation.
- Read picture books.
- Enroll the child in an infant-stimulation program during infancy.
- Schedule frequent doctor examinations.
- Join parent organizations with a hearing-impairment focus.
- See the child simply as a child, rather than "a hearing-impaired child."

4-7 Advanced Language Achievement

Each child is unique. A few children speak clearly and use long and complex sentences at two, three, or four years of age. They express ideas originally and excitedly, enjoying individual and group discussions. Some may read simple primers (or other books) along with classroom word labels. Activities that are commonly used with kindergarten or first-grade children may interest them. Although educational experts' suspect eight to 15 percent of young children might be identified as displaying significantly advanced abilities, it is estimated that only two to three percent are recognized by teachers in the early grade of schooling (McGee & Hughes, 2011). These advanced abilities may or may not be connected to language giftedness.

Singson and Mann (1999), researchers exploring possible factors associated with precocious reading ability, found that phonological awareness and parent's emphasis on letter sounds were significant predictors of early childhood ability. A few early readers may be sight readers with an exceptional memory for words. Educators aware of current research believe young children's knowledge of both alphabet letter names and sounds will aid their reading instruction.

Just as there is no stereotypical average child, language-talented children are also unique individuals. Inferring that these language-precocious children are also intellectually gifted is not at issue here. Young children with advanced language development may:

- attend to tasks in a persistent manner for long periods.
- focus deeply or submerge themselves in what they are doing.
- speak maturely and use a larger-than-usual vocabulary.
- show a searching, exploring curiosity.
- ask questions that go beyond immediate happenings.
- demonstrate an avid interest in words, alphabet letters, numbers, or writing tools.
- remember small details of past experiences and compare them with present happenings.
- read books (or words) by memorizing pictures or words.
- prefer solitary activities at times.
- offer ideas often and easily.
- rapidly acquire English skills, if bilingual, when exposed to a language-rich environment.
- tell elaborate stories.
- show a mature or unusual sense of humor for age.
- possess an exceptional memory.
- exhibit high concentration.
- show attention to detail.
- exhibit a wide range of interests.
- demonstrate a sense of social responsibility.
- show a rich imagination.
- possess a sense of wonder.
- enjoy composing poems or stories.
- use richly descriptive expressions in talking
- be highly attentive listeners who remember exceptionally well.
- read print in the classroom environment.
- write recognizable words or combinations of words.

- have sophisticated computer skills.
- express feelings and emotions, as in storytelling, movement, and visual arts.
- use rich imagery in informal language.
- exhibit originality of ideas and persistence in problem solving.
- exhibit a high degree of imagination.

According to Spencer and Stamm (2008), characteristics of possible giftedness in children under age three include:

- meeting verbal milestones early (speaking full sentences by 18 months, for instance).
- a long attention span (30 minutes is long for toddlers).
- being able to do complicated mental tasks early (like putting together puzzles with many pieces).
- creativity in thinking and problem solving.
- an early, avid interest in books.
- responsiveness to music.
- an interest in sorting, organizing, and seeing patterns.
- asking lots of questions.
- memory for detail and how to get to many locations.
- creative play (both in art and imaginative play, including having imaginary friends).
- a preference for older children.
- a marked interest in people.
- a less-than-typical need for adult help and guidance in activities.

Preschoolers may recognize letters early and show an early focus on printed matter. They may be interested in foreign languages and also exhibit correct pronunciation and sentence structure in their native language. Young children may show an advanced vocabulary and may begin reading before they start preschool.

Unfortunately, young children who may be quiet, noncompetitive, and nonassertive; who are slow to openly express feelings; who rarely make direct eye contact, ask questions, or challenge something they know is incorrect; and who are acting appropriately according to their home culture may not be identified as gifted or talented. Native American and Alaskan native children may be more likely to fall into this category.

Most experts recommend planning activities within the regular curriculum that promote advanced children's creative thinking. Suggestions include providing the following opportunities:

- Fluency. Promoting many different responses, for example, "What are all the ways you can think of to . . ."
- Flexibility. Having the facility to change a mind-set or see things in a different light, for example, "If you were a squirrel how would you feel . . ."
- Originality. For example, "Make something that no one else will think of."
- Elaboration. Embellishing of an idea or adding detail, for example, presenting a doodle or squiggle and asking, "What could it be?"

Some educators believe that teachers can help ward off problems for advanced students by grouping language-advanced children with others of high ability or shared interests. Other educators feel doing so robs peers of the sparkle and insight some peers possess. Arranging situations in which the child's gifts or talents are seen as a group asset is another tactic, as is promoting individual special assignments and varied projects.

If teachers believe, as does Gardner (1993, 2000), in the theory of multiple intelligences (one of which is linguistic intelligence) and in the occurrence of "crystallizing experiences," those teachers will notice the young children who take particular interest in and react overtly to some attractive quality or feature of a language arts activity. These children will tend to immerse themselves and focus deeply. This may be the child who loves to act in dramatic play, collects words, is fascinated with books or alphabet letters, creates daily rhymes, or displays similar behaviors. The child may persist and spend both time and effort on his chosen pursuit and displays a definite intellectual gift.

4-1 Describe a safe and sensitive classroom environment for children with language or cultural differences.

The classroom will:

- have program goals that reflect the needs and interests of diverse children.
- use Standard English in instructional and planned activities.
- design activities that respect language and cultural differences.
- preserve children's feelings of adequacy and acceptance and value children's home culture.

4-2 Discuss the similarities and differences between Standard English and American dialects.

- Standard English is the language of America's elementary schools and its textbooks. It is the majority language in the United States. Dialects refer to the language patterns used in regional or geographical locations or those having social and ethnic variety. Dialects are distinguished by pronunciation, grammar, vocabulary, and especially a variety of speech differing from the standard literary language or speech patterns of the American culture. Widely recognized dialects are a Southern accent, the speech of some speakers in New England, and some African-American English speakers (Black English).

4-3 Identify common strategies second-language learners use to learn Standard English on their own.

- Commonly second language learners believe what is being said around them refers to the ongoing present classroom situation they find themselves in. They learn to use gestures and use a few familiar conversational phrases or words in their interactions. They begin to recognize language patterns that recur in daily speech and try to communicate their intended meanings

with their limited English vocabulary using a major effort to do so. They use gestures frequently.

4-4 Discuss program planning second-language learners.

- Second-language instruction may differ from school to school depending upon the belief of the teaching staff, the administration, and the school sponsors.

4-5 Name two common school program types for second-language learners.

- Bilingual programs, transitional programs, newcomer programs, developmental bilingual programs, two-way immersion programs, tutor-assisted programs, and full immersion programs are common program types used for child instruction in Standard English.

4-6 Identify young children's common speech problems.

- Common childhood speech problems include poor pronunciation, limited vocabulary or speech output, poor syntax or grammar, poor hearing, unintelligible speech, language delay, poor articulation, and stuttering.

4-7 Name four characteristics of language advanced preschoolers.

- Advanced language achievement may be present when a child displays long and complex sentences, mature idea expression, reading ability, persistent attention to tasks, deep focus, and may know all letter names and sounds. Other characteristics include being highly creative with words, having an extensive vocabulary, having an excellent memory for words, displaying a vivid imagination, preferring older mature children as playmates, demonstrating an interest in words and numbers, and during testing exceeds age level norms.

Additional Resources

Readings

Alanis, I. (2011). Learning from each other: Bilingual pairs in dual language classrooms. *Dimensions of Early Childhood. 39*(1), 21–28.

Gadrikowski, A. (2013, May). Differentiation strategies for exceptionally bright children. *Young Children, 68*(2), 8–14.

Helm, J. H. & Katz, L. G. (2011). *Young Investigators: The Project Approach in the Early Years.* New York: Teachers College Press, & Washington, DC: National Association for the Education of Young Children.

Helpful Websites

American Educational Research Association (AERA)

http://www.aera.net

Information on the academic achievement of second-language learners (search Publications).

The Association for the Gifted (TAG)

http://www.cectag.org

Assists parents and professionals with advanced children.

*From Center for Research on Education, Diversity, & Excellence. (2001). Some program alternatives for English language learning. Practitioner's Brief #3.

6 ⟩ Promoting Language and Literacy

Objectives

After reading this chapter, you should be able to:

6-1 List three roles of a teacher in early childhood language instruction.

6-2 Discuss ways teachers model positive language behaviors.

6-3 State three reasons why teachers should use specific and detailed speech.

6-4 Describe how and why a teacher uses extension techniques to build child language.

6-5 Discuss two ways a teacher acts as a balancer.

naeyc NAEYC Program Standards

3G04 Teachers support and challenge children's learning during interactions or activities that are teacher initiated and child initiated.

3G07 Teachers use their knowledge of content to pose problems and ask questions that stimulate children's thinking.

3G07 Teachers help children express their ideas and build on the meaning of their experiences.

DAP Developmentally Appropriate Practice (DAP)

3A8 Teachers draw on their knowledge of the content, awareness of what is likely to interest children of that age, and understanding of the cultural and social contexts of children's lives.

3A9 Teachers plan curriculum that is responsive and respectful to the specific context of children's experiences.

3A11 Teachers connect curriculum topics with children's interests and with what children already know and can do.

COMMON CORE Common Core State Standards for English Language Arts and Literacy

SL.CCR 3 Evaluate a speaker's point of view, reasoning, and use of evidence in rhetoric.

Children's Literacy Portfolios

Miss Powell, a kindergarten teacher, planned a home visit to each entering child in her fall kindergarten class. At one home, a mother proudly shared the child's preschool literacy portfolio. Miss Powell was able to sit with both her soon-to-be student and the child's mother as they both commented on items in the binder. She found the child was reading a few words and had a huge interest in cats. Although she knew her district would test each child after school started, she was delighted with this home visit.

Questions to Ponder

1. How can Miss Powell put to good use the information she now has about this child?
2. Would you suggest that a child literacy portfolio be part of this child's kindergarten experience also?

A good description of a skilled early childhood educator is a "responsive opportunist" who is enthusiastic, who enjoys discovery, and who is able to establish and maintain a warm, supportive environment. An educator is also one who tries to build language, literacy, brain power, and emotional connection (Bardige, 2009). When a reciprocal relationship between a child and teacher is based on equality, respect, trust, and authentic dialogue (real communication), child language learning is promoted. Speech is at the foundation of a child's learning life. Teachers need to create a classroom atmosphere where children can expect success, see the teacher as a significant person, are allowed choice, and are able to make mistakes. Ideally, children should join in planned activities eagerly. These activities should end before the child's capacity to focus is exhausted. The child should be able to expect the teacher to listen and respond to the child's communication in a way that respects the child's sense of the importance of the communication.

In whatever preschool activities and learning experiences a child encounters, the following is taking place.

> There are events happening in the individual "cognitive apparatus" (child's mind) of the learner as he or she struggles to understand and remember the subject that is being learned; but it is also the case that much, if not most, effective learning occurs in social settings, as learners communicate or engage in collaborative activity with other individuals. Furthermore, when a person learns, or develops, or changes cognitively, these individual and social domains are intimately interrelated (Phillips & Soltis, 2009, p. 66).

Early childhood language arts foundational skills educators should keep in mind during daily activities and adult-child interactions include the child's growing

- phonological awareness.
- phonemic awareness and word recognition ability.
- comprehension of the world around him.
- ability to collaborate with others.
- conversational success.
- question-asking ability.
- expression of thoughts and ideas.
- Standard English usage.
- vocabulary.
- engagement success.

Studies examining the quality of language environments in American preschools found that many preschools serving poor children scored in the inadequate range. High-quality group book experiences, cognitively challenging conversation, and teacher use of a wide vocabulary were associated with quality environments and young children's subsequent language and literacy development. It is impossible to overemphasize the importance of adult-child *interaction*. In schools and centers of questionable quality, some children may rarely interact with a preschool teacher and may receive little or no individualized attention. They may be unable to make a socially satisfying and trusting emotional connection to the teacher or peers. These schools fail the children who most need a quality literacy environment to prepare them for later schooling. Teacher behaviors conducive to the development of positive teacher-child relationships identified in research include providing responsive individualized attention, being consistent and firm, supporting children's positive behaviors, and incorporating elements of children's culture and language in planned activities (Gillanders, 2007).

6-1 Teaching Strategies and Behaviors

Three specific teaching functions that encourage the development of language arts and literacy are discussed in this chapter.

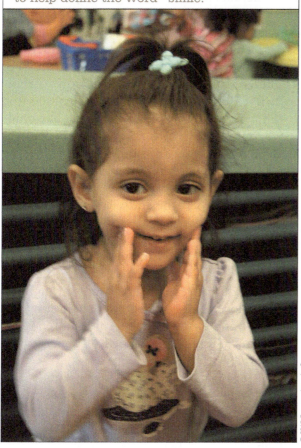

Photo 6-1 Lucia is showing her teacher that she can make a big smile by pulling her cheeks up as her teacher has done herself to help define the word "smile."

© 2015 Cengage Learning®

1. The teacher serves as a *model* of everyday language use. What is communicated and how it is communicated are important.

2. The teacher is a *provider* of experiences. Many of these events are planned; others happen in the normal course of activities.

3. The teacher is *one who facilitates (interacts)*. She creates sharing experiences and builds a trusting connection with the children while encouraging conversation (Photo 6-1).

These three functions should be balanced, relative to each child's developmental level and individual needs. The teaching role requires constant decision making: knowing when to supply or withhold information to help self-discovery and when to talk or listen (Figure 6-1). Basically, sensitivity can make the teacher the child's best ally in the growth of language skills. The importance of teachers' attitudes toward children's talk and teachers' recognition of children's thinking is critical. Researchers studying teacher-child interactions have found that teachers with more education are more responsive and sensitive. Teachers interested in maximizing each child's language development and potential will

- try to increase each child's language usage so language serves needs, desires, and well-being.

Figure 6-1 Range of teaching styles.

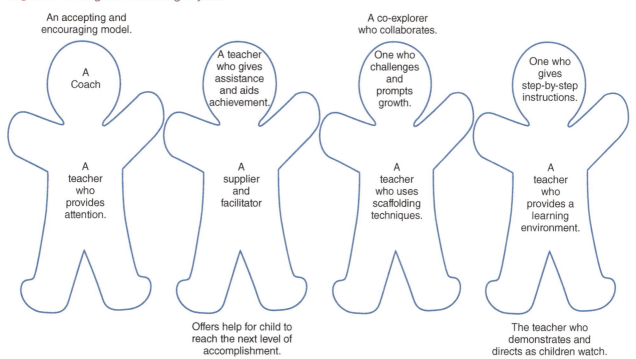

An accepting and encouraging model.

A Coach

A teacher who gives assistance and aids achievement.

A co-explorer who collaborates.

One who challenges and prompts growth.

One who gives step-by-step instructions.

A teacher who provides attention.

A supplier and facilitator

A teacher who uses scaffolding techniques.

A teacher who provides a learning environment.

Offers help for child to reach the next level of accomplishment.

The teacher who demonstrates and directs as children watch.

- encourage children's exploration and experimentation with language.
- promote children's use of language for a variety of different purposes.
- encourage child conversations and word usage with others.
- encourage the child's ability to share personal experiences and stories.
- strive to supply words and their definitions when necessary to promote a child's vocabulary growth.
- encourage curiosity, imagination, and the child's questioning ability, speaking ability, and the ability to relate what he has discovered by putting it into his own words.
- thoughtfully use sentences of increasing length and complexity offering a little above what each child might accomplish on his own.

Newer, stricter licensing regulations and standards regarding the training of early childhood educators in most states aim to improve the quality of teacher-child interactions. Zaslow and Martinez-Beck (2006) studied five teacher training models designed to build literacy expertise and enhance a teacher's ability to support children's early childhood literacy development. Their findings suggest as new teachers gain classroom experience and management skills they move around their classrooms and engage children in productive conversations that link teacher interactions to curriculum planning and classroom organization. Preschool teachers in the study seemed to want to learn more about focused and didactic learning approaches and how to use strategies that foster literacy using accepted standards as guides. Teacher reflection was promoted when teachers recorded and analyzed their conversations with children.

6-1a The Observer Teacher

Observing all elements of a program, as well as children's behavior and progress, involves watching, listening, and recording. This can be the most difficult part of teaching because of time constraints and supervisory requirements. In-depth observation is best accomplished when a teacher is relieved of other responsibilities and can focus without distractions. Many teachers who do not have duty-free observation time must observe while on duty. Observation often unearths questions regarding children's difficulties, talents, and a wide range of special needs that can then be incorporated into plans and daily exchanges.

Learners are most likely to remember and understand what they are learning if they are challenged to make the connection to their own lives (Burman, 2009). Your role as the teacher is to provide experiences that challenge young learners' thinking so new connections can be made. In the best situations, the teacher has background knowledge about each child's unique prior experience and knowledge so instruction can be individualized. Knowing children's interests, present behaviors, and emerging skills helps the teacher perform the three aforementioned functions, based on group and individual needs. Teachers must be part detective and part researcher, sifting through the clues children leave, collecting data, testing hypotheses, and examining the way children really are to make a credible record of their growth and development.

Listening intimately is highly advisable. Providing an environment that is conducive to growth depends partially on being on a child's or group's wavelength. Conversations are more valuable when teachers try to converse and question based on the child's line of thought. Activities provided should increase children's ability to think and rethink and therefore make sense from what they encounter.

Unplanned teacher talk can be just as important as talk during teacher-guided activities. If a child brings you a leaf found in the play yard, that's the time for both of you to discuss its characteristics, where or how he found it, or some other features of the leaf. The listening and observing behavior of teachers increases the quality and pertinence of teachers' communicative interactions.

6-2 The Teacher as a Model

Teachers model not only speech, but also attitudes and behaviors in listening, writing, and reading. Children watch and listen to adults' use of grammar, intonation, and sentence patterns and imitate and use adults as examples. Consider the different

Figure 6-2 Adult verbal styles.

Example A

Child: "It's chickun soup."
Teacher: "That's right."

Example B

Child: "It's chickun soup."
Teacher: "Yes. I see chicken pieces and something else."
Child: "It's noodles."
Teacher: "Yes, those are long, skinny noodles. It's different from yesterday's red tomato soup."
Child: "Tastes good. It's 'ellow."
Teacher: "Yellow like the daffodils in the vase." (Pointing.)

Example C

Child: "Baby cry."
Adult: "Yes, the baby is crying."

Example D

Child: "Baby cry."
Adult: "You hear the baby crying?"
Child: "Uh-huh."
Adult: "Maybe she's hungry and wants some milk."
Child: "Wants bottle."
Adult: "Let's see. I'll put the bottle in her mouth."
Child: "Her hungry."
Adult: "Yes, she's sucking. The milk is going into her mouth. Look, it's almost gone."

and similar ways teachers verbally interact with young children by examining Figure 6-2. Can you see how examples B and D offer the child more language growth?

An early and classic study by Bernstein, who studied British families in 1962, concluded that a recognizable style of verbal interaction based on social class exists. Children living in poverty, depressed economic circumstances, or in homes with significantly less enriching, educative, communicative encounters may have families that use a type of speech providing limited speech specificity and short conversational interchanges. These families' speech characteristics may be

- specific to a current physical context.
- limited.
- stereotyped.
- condensed.
- inexact.
- nonspecific.
- short in sentence length.
- vague and indefinite.

Middle-class families, on the other hand, more typically use speech that elaborates and is more differentiated, more precise, not specific to a particular situation or context, and affords opportunities for more complex thought.

Speakers' styles of communication can be powerful factors in the young child's development of cognitive structures and modes of communication, and they can result in educational advantages or disadvantages in school settings in which a different type of speech predominates. The major assumption behind this view is that middle-class ways of talking with children support literacy. Children profit when the adults in their lives engage in conversational exchanges that offer opportunities to draw conclusions, infer cause-and-effect relationships, plan together, evaluate consequences, evaluate happenings, and at times label things, provide information, and promote children's close observation. These are strategies you will want to use.

It is suggested that early childhood teachers who aim to be good speaking models focus on studying their ability to use **explanatory talk** in child-teacher verbal exchanges. Explanatory talk consists of conversations concerning some connection between objects, events, concepts, and/or conclusions that one speaker is pointing out to another (Photo 6-2). Teachers typically explain their intent and actions to children and provide explanations in response to child comments and questions. This is a preferred behavior in early childhood teachers' verbal interactive exchanges. Some examples follow.

- "The blocks go on the shelf. We will know where to find the blocks when we want to use them again, and no one will trip on them."
- "The window was open, and the wind blew into our classroom. It knocked over the small cups where our seeds were planted."
- "I'm putting my snack dish in the tub on the table when I'm finished. Mrs. Gregorio will come and get the tub after snack time."

explanatory talk — a type of conversation characterized by a speaker's attempt to create connections between objects, events, concepts, or conclusions to promote understanding in the listener.

Photo 6-2 This teacher is using explanatory talk to make connections as the children listen.

© 2016 Cengage Learning®

Photo 6-3 The teacher comments on skills she observes once work has been successfully completed.

© 2016 Cengage Learning®

This explanatory style sometimes carries over into teachers' personal lives. Teachers report family members often say to them, "Yes, I know why you're doing that!"

Adults should use clear, descriptive speech at a speed and pitch easily understood. Articulation should be as precise as possible. However, keep in mind that a good model involves more than merely speaking clearly, slowly, and appropriately. A good model uses a variety of facial expressions and other forms of nonverbal communication; associates talking with understanding and affection; provides happy, pleasant experiences associated with talking; and takes advantage of various timely situations. **DAP**

Teachers also need to be sure that reward in the form of attention is present in their teaching behavior as they deal with young children's attitudes, skills, and behaviors in language arts activities (Photo 6-3). Developmentally appropriate practice lists teacher acknowledgment among their excellent teaching strategies (Copple, Bredekamp, Koralek, Charner, 2013b). Most of us remember a teacher who did so by using positive comments, or a smile, or a thumbs up from across the classroom. Doing so perfectly suits the needs of preschoolers who want badly to share their discoveries and accomplishments and frequently utter "look at me" statements.

Educators should use language patterns with which they feel comfortable and natural and should analyze their speech, working toward providing the best English model possible. Familiar language patterns reflect each teacher's personality and ethnic culture. Knowing what kind of model one presents is important, because

knowing that there is room for improvement can help a teacher become more professional.

Modeling the correct word or sentence is done by simply supplying it in a relaxed, natural way rather than in a corrective tone. The teacher's example is a strong influence; when a teacher adds courtesy words ("please" and "thank you," for instance), these words appear in children's speech. Finishing an incomplete word by adding an ending or beginning may be appropriate with very young speakers. (The child may say "na na"; the teacher would provide "banana.") Completing a phrase or offering complete sentences in Standard English suits older speakers. Although adult modeling has its limits in facilitating spontaneous language, it is an essential first step in learning language.

After hearing corrections modeled, the child will probably not shift to correct grammar or usage immediately. It may take many repetitions by teachers and adults over time. What is important is the teacher's acceptance and recognition of the child's idea within the verbalization and the addition of pertinent comments along the same line.

To build children's vocabulary knowledge, the classroom needs to introduce and expose children to new words, and to provide these words in the context of situations. Definitions are offered using terms that are understandable and relate when possible to children's past experience. Opportunities will arise because of children's innate curiosity and interest in the world around them. As children mature, they develop independent strategies to figure out a word's meaning. Dictionary use is introduced and educators provide assistance and are interested word collectors themselves. Being "word conscious" happens when children's interest is piqued and they seek new word meanings (Christ & Wang, 2010). Christ and Wang point out knowing a word's meaning includes knowing what the word refers to and gaining the ability to use the word in accurate examples.

When adults focus on the way something was said (grammar) rather than the meaning, they miss opportunities to increase awareness and extend child interest. Overt correction often ends teacher-child conversation. Affirmation is appropriate; the teacher should emphasize the child's intended message.

Adults can sometimes develop the habit of talking and listening to themselves rather than to the children; it is hypnotic and can be a deterrent to really hearing the child. If one's mind wanders or if one listens only for the purpose of refuting, agreeing, or jumping to value judgments, it interferes with receiving communication from others. Teachers need not be afraid of silences and pauses before answering. The following listening suggestions are recommended:

- Work as hard to listen as you do to talk.
- Try to hear the message behind the words.
- Consciously practice good listening.

One teaching technique that promotes language skill is simple modeling of grammar or filling in missing words and completing simple sentences. This is called **expansion**. It almost becomes second nature and automatic after a short period of intentional practice. When using an expansion, the adult responds to the child by expanding the syntactic composition of the child's utterance. For example, the child's "It is cold" might be followed by "The window pane felt cold when you pressed your nose against it." The teacher's expansion is contingent and responsive, focusing on what the child was experiencing. Although using the strategy of expansion is a widely accepted and practiced teacher behavior, Crawford (2005) notes there is little research evidence that it has any positive effect. Evidence showing a negative effect is also yet to be found. Even without research validating the technique, many educators believe that the practice is still valuable, and when additional research takes place it will confirm their actions. While using

expansion, the teacher can also promote wider depth of meaning or spark interest by contributing or suggesting an idea for further exploration. Additional conversation usually occurs.

The teacher is a model for listening and speaking. Children will copy words, expressions, pronunciations, and gestures, too. A quiet teacher may have a quiet classroom; an enthusiastic, talkative teacher (who also listens) may have a classroom where children talk, listen, and share experiences. The way children feel about themselves is reflected in their behavior. When teachers listen closely, children come to feel that what they say is worthwhile.

Modeling good printing is also important. Children seem to absorb everything in their environment, so it is necessary to provide correctly formed alphabet letters and numerals on children's work, charts, bulletin boards, and any displayed classroom print. This is discussed at length in Chapter 14. Teachers' use and care of books are modeled, as are their attitudes toward story and nonfiction book experiences. Through their observations of teachers' actions, children begin to develop ideas about how books should be handled and stored. One teacher who wanted to model storytelling of personal stories divided a large paper into eight sections; in each section she drew a picture of different stages in her life. She showed this to her class and asked them to pick a picture, which she then related in storytelling. Teachers also model poetry reading and its use, dramatization, puppet play, and many other language arts activities.

What we are communicates far more eloquently than anything we say or do. This is an old saying that was not written expressly for teachers of young children; nonetheless it is a good addition to this discussion. A teacher models attitudes and ways of approaching a problem. If teacher says "Let's take a closer look at this problem," she is modeling an attitude that is catching. According to Au (2006), teachers must demonstrate the kind of literacy they want students to show. They must see themselves as readers and writers and convince students of the value of reading and writing. In doing so, they help young children gain an appreciation for literacy in their own lives. With picture books, some of the ways this is accomplished is

---

expansion — a teaching technique that includes the adult's (teacher's) modeling of words or grammar, filling in missing words in children's utterances, or suggesting ideas for child exploration.

by selecting and sharing books with an obvious enjoyment factor, by building on children's interests, and by discussing enjoyed book sections as these relate to individual children. An educator on any teaching day can model his or her thinking by talking aloud to promote children's thinking along the same lines. This is often done when sharing a book, but there are many additional opportunities.

- "Today we have three boys sitting together in our circle whose names start with the letter 'J' . . . Jacob, Joseph and Joshua."
- "You made a new color when your yellow paint touched the blue paint."
- "I hear the same sound at the end of Emma, Olivia, and Isabella's names—Emma, Olivia, Isabella. And in Isabella's name I hear the sound two times."
- "If I pour too much juice into this cup, it will spill. I don't want to do that so I'll stop a little way below the top."

6-3 The Teacher as Provider

As providers, preschool teachers strive to provide experiences that promote literacy. Fortunately, the number of interesting language arts activities one can offer children is almost limitless. Teachers rely on both their own creativity and the many resources available to plan experiences based on identified goals and what they observe and feel is necessary for child growth and needs. Early childhood resource books, other teachers, teacher magazines, workshops, the Internet, and conferences all contribute ideas.

Many beginning teachers gather activity ideas and store them in a personal resource file, so they can keep track of all of the activity ideas they come across. An activity file can include new or tried-and-true activity ideas. Developing a usable file starts with identifying initial categories (file headings) and then adding more headings as the file grows. Whatever the file size, teachers find that files are very worthwhile when it comes to daily, weekly, and monthly planning. Often, files are helpful when ideas on a certain subject or theme are needed or when a child exhibits a special interest. A file collection is not used as the basis for activity planning, but rather as a collection of good ideas or ideas one might like to try that might suit the particular needs of a group of children. Many activity ideas are presented in following chapters. Your creativity can produce many others.

As a provider of materials, a teacher must realize that every classroom object can become a useful program tool to stimulate language. From the clock on the wall to the doorknob, every safe item can be discussed, compared, and explored in some way (Photo 6-4). Because most school budgets are limited, early childhood teachers

Photo 6-4 Madison has an interest in insects so her teacher supplies both opportunity and equipment.

© 2015 Cengage Learning®

find ways to use available equipment and materials to their fullest.

Most teachers are pleasantly surprised to see how avidly their classes respond to their personal interests. When the teacher shares enthusiasm for out-of-school interests, hobbies, projects, trips, and individual talents, she can help introduce children to important knowledge. Almost anything appropriate can be presented at the child's level. Whether the teacher is an opera buff, scuba diver, gourmet cook, stamp collector, or violin player, the activity should be shared in any safe form that communicates special interest and love of the activity, and the specific vocabulary and materials relating to the activity should be presented. Enthusiasm is the key to inspired teaching.

6-3a Providing for Abundant Play

Abundant opportunities for play are important to the child's language acquisition. Play is usually divided into four types: motor play, pretend play, construction play, and games. All involve varying kinds of language usage and can overlap and combine with children's constantly changing play scenarios. Child's play is more complex than it is commonly believed. It provides a rich variety of experiences: communication with other children, verbal rituals, topic development and maintenance, turn taking, intimate speech in friendships, follower-leader conversations, and many other kinds of language exchanges. Except when the children's safety is in question, children's natural ability to pretend should be encouraged, and the flow of this kind of play, if safe, should proceed without the teacher's interference. Children will want to talk to teachers about their play, and the teacher's proper involvement is to show interest and be playful themselves at times.

According to Burman (2009), intellectual conflict, when something conflicts with a learner's existing schema and shakes up thinking, is a necessary requirement for learning. Teachers see preschool peers in frequent serious discussions. When this happens, children may shift their understanding because a playmate has offered an alternate perspective or a different idea. In the playhouse area this might be as simple as a child saying "Daddies don't cook!" and a peer replying "My dad cooks pancakes." They may even check the validity of their new understanding by running it by teacher for confirmation and/or further discussion.

If a child has chosen to engage a teacher in conversation instead of play or during play, the teacher should be both a willing listener and a competent, skillful conversationalist. As young children talk about their experiences, the talking itself aids their organization of thoughts. At times, younger children monologue in our presence. They are not really asking for our reaction, but rather, they are listening to themselves think while they also enjoy our physical closeness.

Young children explore constantly. They want to do what they see others doing. Play opportunities usually involve manipulating something. When deeply involved in play, children may seem to be momentarily awestruck in their search for meanings, but soon they will approach others with questions or comments.

They gain skills in approaching other children and asking if they can play or just nonverbally joining a play group in progress. They begin to understand what attracts others to them, how to imitate another child's actions or words, how to express affection or hostility, how to assume a leadership role, how to negotiate, and how to follow or refuse playmates' requests. These and other play skills help them stay engaged in a play group for a longer period of time. Preschoolers at play may even argue over correct language use. Some observers believe that the majority of language teaching that takes place in the four-year-olds' classroom is child-to-child teaching.

A resourceful teacher will strive to provide a variety of play by regarding all of a center's area (and furnishings) as a possible place (or object) for safe and appropriate play. Creative use can be made of each foot of floor space. Children need large blocks of uninterrupted time to construct knowledge and actively explore their problem-solving options in an environment thoughtfully and carefully prepared by the teacher.

6-3b Outside Play and Literacy

Interacting to promote literacy during outdoor play challenges educators, but it is possible to offer some materials and activities that include a literacy feature. Probably the most common way is to try to read books on a blanket, in the shade, in the playhouse, or under a tree. Sidewalk chalk activities and games can be fun and might include printing names to jump on or over, or printing simple directions that read "Stamp your feet" or "Follow this line." Snapping instant photos and writing captions with the photographed child is a favorite activity. Occasionally labeling bikes A, B, C, etc. with hang-on cards might improve letter recognition, but caution is needed here. Overzealous teachers whose aim is to "teach on all occasions" should skip this discussion because children need lots of undirected time and freedom to pursue their own agendas, particularly when out of doors and using their own creative play ideas.

Trawick-Smith (2012) notes a preschool curriculum that encourages children's pretend play through adult introduction and child-child play interactions promotes higher scores on language and literacy measures. Teacher can support this type of play by providing ideas, suggestions, physical props and materials, and, at times, companionship. Teacher actions and behaviors can supplement child play scenarios rather than directing or dominating them. Not inhibiting the free flow of children's play choices, with the exception of safety concerns, is important. Not all young children are able to play independently; and regardless of the cause of this behavior, teachers should realize adult help and involvement can model how to pretend and make believe. This helps make the same behavior appear in the child (p. 264).

6-3c Providing Accurate and Specific Speech in All Content Areas

Although this text concentrates on teacher-child interactions in the subject field of language arts, other content areas, such as mathematics (numbers), social studies, health and safety, art, music, movement, and so on, will be subjects of teacher-child conversations and discussions. The same teacher techniques that are useful in building children's language competence and vocabulary in language arts are equally useful for other content areas. Every subject area has its own vocabulary and common terms that can overlap other fields of study. For example, teacher comments will include number words whether children are focused on the number of muffins on a tray or on whether there are enough scissors to go around.

There are more than two schools of thought concerning an educator's role in offering vocabulary to preschoolers. It is possible for an educator to use both of the strategies mentioned next.

The first emphasizes a teacher's use of rich, specific, and sometimes unusual words in daily instruction and conversation that are a little above children's common daily usage. Children adopt and savor them and incorporate them into their working vocabulary. If the teacher has an extensive knowledge of flowers, their names, care, and other information, she could add considerable vocabulary in a natural way without overdoing it. The second strategy involves consciously using or planning to use vocabulary root words or key words found in read-aloud books and themes. Root words are words or parts of words that children will encounter in early readers when their reading instruction begins. These are words identified as being words that are frequently used in beginning reading primers. Several high frequency word lists have been published over time, such as those developed by Dolch (1948) or Biemiller and Slonim (2001). Kindergarten teachers can also be good resources for beginning word lists. See Figure 6-3 for additional tips for increasing vocabulary.

Teacher comments should be as accurate and specific as possible in light of what the teacher believes the children might already know or have experienced. Purposeful teacher conversation adds a little more information than the children already know, and reinforces and adds depth to words already in the children's vocabulary. When working with numerals or other subjects, the teacher should use terminology that is appropriate to the subject area but at a level the children will understand. For example, the teacher might say "Let's count the muffins" or "The tool in your hand is a wire whip" or "The metal cylinder attached to the wall is a fire extinguisher. Fire extinguishers have something inside that can be sprayed out to put out fires." In movement or music activities, many descriptive terms can be added to teacher directions and conversations, such as hop, jump, stretch, soft, loud, high, and low. These are easily understood while the child is in the process of experiencing them. The quality of the words children hear is crucial for their later school and language performance (Kalmar, 2008). Children build meaning as adults and teachers make comments, provide information, comfort them, guide them, praise and encourage their efforts, and display excitement and enthusiasm for the world around them. Sometimes, teachers are reluctant to use big, new words such as the word *hibernate* (Neuman & Roskos, 2007). Neuman and Roskos

Figure 6-3 Teaching tips for vocabulary instruction.

Instruction Method	Teaching Tip
Provide purposeful exposure to new words	**Teach thematically to provide multiple exposures to words throughout the day, through read-alouds, conversations, centers, and projects.** • Select books for read-alouds in which illustrations and text provide clues to word meanings. • Use an interactive read-aloud style and engage children in cognitively challenging discussions about books. • Create media centers where children view DVDs, explore electronic books, and listen to interactive read-alouds on DVD that use new vocabulary.
Intentionally teach word meanings	**Use a variety of direct teaching strategies.** • Ask eliciting and noneliciting questions during readalouds to prompt children to think about new words and their meanings. • Provide an embedded definition when exposing children to a new word whose meaning is important for them to understand. • Use extended instruction to help children gain a nuanced understanding of a word's meaning.
Teach word-learning strategies	**Teach word-learning strategies while reading aloud.** • Use the three steps for strategy instruction: model, guide, and practice. • Select books in which both text and illustrations give clues to a word's meaning.
Offer opportunities to use newly learned words	**Provide a variety of opportunities for children to use newly learned vocabulary.** • Use concept-mapping activities to organize pictures and props related to a classroom theme or project. • Have children retell, buddy read, or act out texts that have been read in the classroom. • Write down stories dictated by children that are related to a classroom theme or project. • Develop art and craft projects in which children can apply newly learned concepts. • Engage in inquiry projects related to the curricular theme. • Provide props related to the theme that may elicit theme-related vocabulary use.

Digital Download

urge educators to remember that teacher words and phrases are one of the main sources for giving children new knowledge. They stress giving explanations and examples:

> "When an animal goes to sleep for the winter, we say it is hibernating."

> Then, provide opportunities for children to practice their new language by saying "Do you remember what we call it when animals go to sleep for the winter? We call it hibernating." (p. 10)

The teacher prompts children's use of the words that the teacher provides. Most of the time, a teacher is careful to define new words immediately after using them. In number activities, number words are used in the presence of a corresponding number of objects. In movement activities, types of movement are discussed with quick demonstrations.

It is important to introduce new terms in a natural conversational tone rather than within the framework of an obvious lesson. Leading a

child or groups of children to new discoveries offers the teacher an opportunity to use specific and accurate terms and also makes children feel like partners in the discoveries. A theme on birds could include many terms and specific names that a teacher might need to research. Also, keep in mind that students need multiple, daily opportunities to talk about what they are learning, to confirm what they know, and to ask questions (Risko, 2011). In these conversations, a teacher can emphasize the importance and relevance of a child's comments and provide opportunities for children to explain their thinking. A teacher can provide time for children to elaborate on their ideas, to make connections to concepts, or to express further conclusions. Frequently, young preschoolers state and rethink their misconceptions or reasons for their thinking during discussions and sometimes teach their peers what they know.

The preschool classroom's character has a lot of influence on young children's vocabulary development. Kucan (2012) suggests providing a verbal environment in which words are not only noticed and appreciated but also savored and celebrated. Since a small vocabulary affects later reading comprehension, and the young child's vocabulary growth is highly impacted by adult input, a teacher's vocabulary-promoting ability becomes important for a child's success.

Pandey (2012) suggests teachers can provide or elicit synonyms, illustrations, examples, and verbal definitions when a new vocabulary word is encountered in a learning context. When the new word "itty-bitty" is used in a song or cooking recipe activity, a teacher might say:

"Itty-bitty means tiny."

"Can you think of another word that means very little?"

"If I just put a few seeds in my hand that would be an itty-bitty pile of seeds."

"A mark made by a pen, like this, would be an itty-bitty mark."

"Itty-bitty means a very, very small amount in our recipe."

"Hold out your hand if you would like an itty-bitty pile of sand in your hand."

A teacher might also explore word parts in itty-bitty that rhyme or that it is a hyphenated word. Pandey notes vocabulary words enable children to learn more words and—through time—content. Words are powerful content capsules (p. 26).

6-4 The Teacher as a Facilitator

A teacher encourages conversation on any subject the child selects, is never too busy to talk and share interests and concerns, and listens with the intent to understand. Understanding the child's message makes the teacher's response more educationally valuable. Time is purposely planned for daily conversations with each child. When teachers talk about what they are doing, explain why particular results occur, and let children ask questions about procedures and results, children will have more exposure to and experience with extended forms of discourse. These private, personal, one-on-one encounters build the child's feelings of self-worth and open communications. Conversations can be initiated with morning greetings such as the following:

- "Alphonse, I've been waiting to talk to you."
- "Tell me about your visit to Chicago."
- "How is your puppy feeling today, Andrea?"
- "Those new blue tennis shoes will be good for running in the yard and for tiptoeing, too."

Educators are aware of the "reciprocal opportunity" that is always present in work with young children. Teachers try to really hear verbal communications and sense nonverbal messages. They give their undivided attention whenever possible, which shows interest in children's ideas and also rewards their efforts to use language and initiate social contact. A teacher can respond skillfully, first clarifying what the teacher thought she heard and then adding to the conversation and attempting to stimulate more verbal output, child discovery, some new feature or detail, or a different way of viewing what has captured the child's interest. Children's verbal expression of their thoughts, feelings, requests, or other intent is corrected only if it is socially unacceptable speech.

Teachers can emphasize the symbolic component of an activity ("These words that you see on the handles say hot and cold.") and help children identify problems or dilemmas by suggesting that children put their ideas into words ("Adam, you wanted to give your scissors to Evan but couldn't. What happened?") Teachers may need to raise their own awareness of their interactions with children, in other words, to rate themselves on their ability to expand children's verbal output and accuracy (Photo 6-5). Recording daily conversations and analyzing them at times is recommended—even experienced teachers periodically do so.

It is wise to be aware of and up-to-date on topics of special interest to preschoolers. Current popular toys, cartoon figures, community happenings, sports, recording artists, movies, and individual family events may often be the focus of young children's conversations. When a teacher has background knowledge, such as what current Disney characters are popular or familiar to her students, or which children have a new infant sibling at home, her responses when children discuss these items could be more pertinent and connected to the reality of enrolled children's lives. Sharapan (2012) mentions Fred Rogers (Mr. Rogers), a well-known and beloved children's television show host, who took advantage of everyday moments to talk out loud

Photo 6-5 Teachers' comments are based on their knowledge of individual children.

about what was happening around him. He would draw attention to features and details that might be missed and offered children his developmentally sensitive thoughts, questions, and observations.

Early childhood educators use a technique called **extension**. Building on a child's statement, the teacher adds information, factual data, or additional meaning, and prompts the child to elaborate. This can add vocabulary and clarify some aspect or concept encountered in the conversational interchange. The child's "It spilled" might be answered with "Yes, Quan's hand knocked the cup over. I think maybe there was a time when you spilled something, too."

Many teachers have used a conversational interaction technique called **closure**. It involves pausing, specifically, hesitating in the middle of a sentence or at sentence endings. It is a technique that prompts guessing by the child, and the teacher is willing to accept any guess. Most often, children's guesses are logical, but may not be what the teacher expected. Those children with a sense of the ridiculous may offer off-the-wall guesses equally acceptable to the teacher. It often promotes further dialogue. The teacher's saying "The sun disappeared behind a . . ." might elicit "hill," "mountain," "building," "tree," "cloud," or other possibilities from the child. The teacher's

saying "Coats are hung in the . . . by the front door" is an example of middle-of-the-sentence closure or a fill-in statement. Using closure within a familiar context, like a well known story or song ("And he blew the house. . .?") is fun, and gives the teacher a chance to say "Emma, you guessed the *word* that I left out was 'down.' Yes. It is the word." Teachers often also made lists of guessed words immediately so the children see the written word they guessed.

In looking at individual children, Covey (1989) reminds us of what we know in our hearts to be true, fair, and compassionate. Each child is to be valued for his identity as a person and for his unique individuality, separateness, and worth. Comparisons between children cloud our view. Traits teachers may see as negative can be fostered by the environment we offer and our own perceptions of correct student behavior. An educator's job, according to Covey, is to recognize potential, then coddle and inspire that potential to emerge at its own pace.

Waiting for a child's response is sometimes difficult for some teachers. When you wait, you give the child time to initiate or to get involved in an activity. You are, in effect, giving her this message: "You're in control—I know you can communicate, so you decide what you want to do or

---

extension — a teaching strategy in which an adult expands the child's information by adding new, additional, related information or meaning.

closure — a conversation technique that prompts children to verbally guess and complete or fill in a teacher's sentence. The teacher pauses or hesitates, which prompts the child to finish a teacher verbalization.

say. I'll give you all the time you need." Studies of adult-child interactions have shown that adults give children approximately one second in which to respond to a question. After one second, the adult repeats and rephrases the question or provides the answer. One second! Most children need much longer than one second to process the question and figure out their response.

Adult speech containing a relatively high proportion of statements or declaratives has been associated with accelerated language development in young children. Adult-child conversations tend to last longer if adults add new relevant information. If adults verbally accept and react to children's statements with "oh, really?" or "I see," when they are trying to grasp a child's meaning, additional conversation seems to be promoted.

When a teacher answers a child by showing interest, this rewards the child for speaking. Positive feelings are read internally as an automatic signal to continue to do what we are doing. Many experts suggest that teachers should guide and collaborate to promote children's independent problem solving in any given situation. Most often, teachers show their attention by listening to, looking at, smiling at, patting, or answering a child, or by acting thoughtfully to what a child has said or done.

Experienced teachers know that children often will silently look for teacher's attention and approval across a busy classroom when they have accomplished a task or a breakthrough. They search to see if the teacher noticed. A busy teacher might give a thumbs up or smile in response, if they can't offer words just then. The child by his behavior has indicated that he feels this is a teacher who cares about me.

Dangel and Durden (2010) urge educators to challenge children to think beyond the moment and analyze and conjecture. They suggest teachers use thoughtful questions and comments during teacher-child verbal exchanges that promote children's labeling, describing, or connecting the prior ideas and knowledge they possess to what is on hand or occurring during an activity. A teacher's questions might also prompt child hypotheses, imaginations, or opinions. All involve higher level thinking skills. Teachers trying to determine their questioning skills can test themselves using Figure 6-4.

Teachers often act as interpreters, especially with younger preschoolers. The child who says "Gimme dat" is answered with "You want the

Figure 6-4 Assess your questioning and responding abilities.

Answer the following using A = always, S = sometimes, N = need to work on this, or U = unable to determine.

1. Do I respond to child-initiated comments 100 percent of the time? _____
2. Do I keep to the child's topic and include it in my response? _____
3. Do I ask questions that prompt children to see or discover an aspect that they might not have perceived or discovered? _____
4. Am I aware of the favorite subjects and interests of individual children and ask questions along these lines? _____

   Are my questions appropriate in light of the children's development levels? _____
5. Do I often answer a child's comments using teacher echolalia?
   Child: "I went to the zoo."
   Teacher: "Oh, you went to the zoo."
   Or would my answer more likely be, "What animals did you see?" _____
6. Are my questions usually open ended? _____
7. Are my questions thought-inducing, or are they merely seeking correct answers? _____
8. Do I provide a specific response to children's questions? _____
9. Do my questions take place in the context of mutual trust and respect, based on my genuine friendliness, unconditional acceptance, warmth, empathy, and interest? _____
10. Do many of my questions seem to put a child "on-the-spot" or fluster a child? _____

red paint." Do not worry about faulty teacher interpretations! Most children will let teachers know when they have interpreted incorrectly by trying again. Then the teacher has the opportunity to say, "You wanted the blue paint, Taylor."

Consider the dialogue of the language-developing teacher below. Did the teacher's speech interactions accomplish the goal?

Goal #1: Use language slightly more complex than the child's.

Child: "Those are cookies."

Teacher: "Yes, they're called Gumdrop Mountains because they come to a point on the top."

Goal #2: Speak with young or limited-language children by referring to an action, object, person, and/or event that is currently happening.

Teacher: "You're climbing up the stairs."

Goal #3: Base your reactive conversation on the meaning the child intended. There are two ways to do this: (1) repetition ("Pet the dog" to child's "Pet dog"); (2) expansion (the child says, "play bath," and the teacher expands with, "You want to play with your toys in the bath tub").

Goal #4: Use recasting. (The child says, "You no get in," and the teacher responds, "No, I can't get in, can I?")

Goal #5: Use "I see," "Yes," or a similar expression to indicate you are listening.

Encouraging children to tell about happenings and how they feel is possible throughout the preschool day (Photo 6-6). A teacher may find it harder to interact verbally with quiet and shy children or the ones that rarely stay in one place or sit down, but they keep on trying.

Teachers shift to more mature or less mature speech as they converse with children of differing ages and abilities. They try to speak to each according to his level of understanding. They use shorter, less complex utterances and use more gestures and nonverbal signals with speakers trying to learn English. Whenever possible, it is professionally appropriate to interact in a way that displays a belief that all preschoolers are capable thinkers that are able to weigh complex ideas, and at times, use abstract reasoning as they strive to make sense of what happens around them.

The teacher who interacts in daily experiences can help improve the child's ability to see relationships. Although there is current disagreement as to the teacher's ability to promote cognitive growth (the act or process of knowing), attention can be focused and help provided by answering and asking questions. Often, a teacher can help children see clear links between material already learned and new material. Words teachers provide are paired with the child's mental images that have

Photo 6-6 Bending or kneeling puts adults at an appropriate level to engage in intimate conversation.

© 2015 Cengage Learning®

come through the senses. Language aids memory because words attached to mental images help the child retrieve stored information. Intellectually valuable experiences often involve the teacher as active participant in tasks with the child.

Pica (2007) urges teachers to combine concepts and words with active physical movement and/or involvement. She believes young children still need to experience concepts physically, when possible, to fully understand them. Her book, *Jumping into Literacy,* abounds with early learning activities that promote language and literacy through music and movement. DAP

The teacher facilitates by supplying words to fit situations. It should be remembered that a new word often needs to be repeated in a subtle way. It has been said that at least three repetitions of a new word are needed for adults to master the word; young children need more. In some cases, when a new word is very salient and the child is highly motivated, a child may acquire the word after a single, brief exposure. This is called *fast mapping,* and children also more readily learn new words that are conceptually similar to words they already know (Wasik, 2006). Repeated exposure to a new word in the same and other meaningful contexts is still recommended in most situations. An example of a teacher reinforcing vocabulary and conceptual learning is presented in Figure 6-5. The teacher is conducting a summary review that includes newly introduced words after a cooking activity. She has asked the group to reenact (pantomime) their cooking experience as she speaks.

Walley, Metsala, and Garlock (2003) researched the ease with which children learn new words. They note that new words that are phonologically similar to a known word are also easier to acquire. If the child's vocabulary contains *hat,* *mat,* and *cat,* which contain similar morphemes, similar words may be learned readily.

Teachers often hear the child repeating a new word, trying to become familiar with it. To help children remember a new word, Bennett-Armistead, Duke, and Moses (2005) suggest making sure the words you say around the new word give clues to the word's meaning. For example, instead of saying "That is a fox," say "It is a furry animal called a fox. It looks like a small dog and has a big, fluffy tail." The best way to make a new word *real* to young children is to relate the new word to the child's own experiences and ideas.

There are times when a teacher chooses to supply information in answer to direct child questions. There is no easy way for the child to discover answers to questions such as "What's the name of today?" or "Why is that man using that funny stick with a cup on the end?" A precise, age-level answer is necessary; such as "Today is Monday, May 9" and (while demonstrating) "It's a tool, called a plunger. It pushes air and water down the drain and helps open the pipes so that the water in the sink will run out." As a provider of information, the teacher acts as a reference and resource person, providing the information a child desires. If the teacher does not wish to answer a question directly, she may encourage the child to ask the same question of someone else or help the child find out where the answer is available.

Figure 6-5 Teacher review narrative with pantomime actions.

"We gathered all the ingredients necessary to follow our bread recipe chart directions. We set the oven temperature at 350°. The flour, eggs, water, salt, yeast, sugar, milk, and butter were put on the table in our work area. We needed the yeast to make our bread texture fluffy. Then we lined up all the cooking utensils, pans, bowls, and a large, flat, breadboard. After washing our hands, each ingredient was added to our bowl. Each ingredient added something to the taste of our baked bread. We used measuring cups and measuring spoons and made sure the correct amount was level with the edge. We stirred and made dough. We kneaded the dough on the breadboard. We formed a loaf. Then we lifted it into the loaf pans and then I put them into the hot oven which said the temperature was 350°. The yeast in the bread recipe made it grow bigger and bigger. Because the recipe directions told us to leave the bread in the oven for 45 minutes I took the bread out using an oven mitt. We sat and ate large slices after spreading the soft, textured bread with butter. Yum Yum.

(Note: new vocabulary words are underlined.)

Child: "What's lunch?"

Adult: "Come on, we'll go ask the cook." *or* "Let's look at the menu. It lists all the food being served today. I'll read it to you."

Can teachers promote children's curiosity about words? By being aware that children sometimes ask about words they do not understand, educators can reward the child's interest with attention. Statements might include the following:

"You now have another word for car. It is the word automobile."

"I'm happy you asked what 'slick' means Josie."

"A new word in this book will be fun to say. The word is skedaddle and it means to move very quickly."

"When you hear a word that puzzles you, raise your hand. Ask about it, please."

"What a wonderful word that is!"

The teacher's reaction supplies children with feedback. The teacher is responsible for reinforcing the use of a new word and gently ensuring that the children have good attitudes about themselves as speakers.

Every day, the teacher can take advantage of unplanned things that happen to promote language and speech. Being able to make the most of an unexpected event is a valuable skill. Moving into a situation with skill and helping the child discover something and talk about it is part of promoting word growth (Photo 6-7).

6-4a Teachable Moments

You have probably run across the phrase "teachable moments" in your training and perhaps have become adept at using this strategy. It involves a four- to five-step process.

1. Observe a child or a child group's self-chosen actions and efforts.

2. Make a hypothesis about exactly what the children are pursuing, exploring, discovering, and playing with, and so on.

3. Make a teacher decision to intervene, act, provide, extend, or in some way offer an educational opportunity to further growth or knowledge related to the child-chosen agenda. This can be done in a number of ways, so this step often involves teacher contemplation.

4. Determine exactly what you will do or provide. Take action. Often, this can be as simple as asking a question such as, "You are putting small pieces of torn paper in Andy's cage. What do you think Andy is going to do with them?" or by silently providing wedge-shaped blocks to a group of children racing small cars down a ramp. Or perhaps you decide to let a child who has been watching the kitchen helper hand-whip eggs try the hand-whip himself.

5. As a final step, consider having the children tell, act out, communicate, dictate, or in some way represent what has been experienced, if this is appropriate.

A watchful teacher, who is working to promote early literacy skills may easily connect teachable moments to relevant opportunities involving literacy skills.

6-4b Time Constraints

Comments such as, "You finished," "That's yellow," "How colorful," "It's heavy," "I like that, too," or "A new shirt," may give attention, show acceptance, provide encouragement, and

Photo 6-7 Encouraging feuding children to express their feelings is a professional technique.

© 2015 Cengage Learning®

reinforce behavior. They feel like suitable and natural comments or responses, and they slip out almost unconsciously. In a busy classroom, they often are said in haste when the teacher may have no time for an extended conversation because she is supervising a group of children. In other words, the best a teacher can do, time permitting.

Consciously trying to be specific and expanding takes focus, effort, and quick thinking, but with practice, it can become second nature with teacher statements such as, "You pushed your chair in under the table," "In your drawing I see red and blue," "You helped your friend Alejandra by finding her book," "Those are shoes with lights," "Tell me more about your kitten," and "Returning your crayons to the box helps others find them." Teachers' specific and/or descriptive comments promote literacy.

6-4c Scaffolding

Scaffolding is a teaching technique that combines support with challenge. This includes responsive conversation, open-ended questions, and facilitation of the child's initiatives. Adults estimate the amount of necessary verbal support and provide challenging questions for child growth in any given situation. The idea is to promote the child's understanding and solutions. The adult attempts to build upon what a child already knows to help the child accomplish a task or may suggest breaking down the task into simpler components. As the child ages, his autonomous pursuit of knowledge will need less adult support. The author is reminded of the four-year-old who described the workings of a steam locomotive. His knowledge of trains and related terminology was way above that of other children his age and even his teacher. Someone in this child's life had supplied the type of "scaffolding" (support with challenge) that allowed the child to follow an interest in trains.

It is believed that children need experiences and educational opportunities with adults who carefully evaluate, think, and talk daily occurrences through. What specific teacher verbalizations and behaviors are suggested in scaffolding? They include comments that offer responsive and authentic conversation and facilitate child initiative. Educators ask open-ended questions. They prompt and promote language by modeling slightly more mature language forms. They help children express thoughts and feelings in words. An educator attempting to scaffold

- promotes longer, more precise child comments.
- invites divergent responses.
- offers specific word cues in statements and questions that help children grasp further information, for example, *what, who, why, because, so, and, next, but, except, if, when, before, after*, etc.
- provokes lively discussions and quests for knowing more about subjects that interest children.
- increases collaborative communication with adults and other children.

Scaffolding is not as easy as it first may appear to teachers. What is opportunity and challenge for one child may not be for the next. In scaffolding, teacher decision making is constant and complex. An educator using scaffolding believes understanding, discovery, and problem solving can be guided. Rather than always being dependent on adults for help, the child actually is moved toward becoming an independent thinker, advocates believe. Adults who accompany children at home or at school can use a scaffolding approach to talk through and plan activities as simple as setting the table, cleaning the sink, getting an art area ready for finger painting, or taking care of the needs of the school pet.

What is right or wrong becomes less important than the child's expression of his own conclusions. The child is encouraged to verbalize the "whys" of his thinking. For example, "Royal thinks the rabbit eats paper because he saw Floppy tearing paper into small pieces inside the cage."

Valuable teacher collaboration with children sustains the momentum of the search, actions, or exploration. Small group projects are often a natural part of children's block area play and can also be promoted in other aspects of daily play and activities. For example, a lemonade stand can be managed by a small group, or a present or card can be designed for a sick classmate at home and then completed and mailed by a small group of children.

6-5 Teacher as Balancer

A central task for the educator is to find a balance between helping a child consolidate new understanding and offering challenges that will promote growth. Some educators believe that there are two teaching styles—transmission and interpretation.

Transmission teaching is the traditional style, in which children's knowledge is thought to be acquired through the teacher talking, sharing books, and explaining classroom events and experiences. Interpretation teaching, on the other hand, is based on the understanding that children reinterpret information for themselves, and consequently, the teacher's role involves dialogues that support the children's efforts to verbalize their ideas and actual experiences.

One can easily see how easy it is to become a transmission teacher. It may have been modeled at some point in your own schooling. An interpretation teacher really listens and does not monopolize conversations by a display of what the teacher knows. Achieving balance between these two styles is the key. Educators both transmit and interpret.

In promoting developing language arts and literacy in early childhood, an interpretation style would not only help children talk about what they know but also would help them put ideas and impressions in print by offering to take dictation or by using some other form of expression. The teacher's role is to provide the occasions, resources, and enabling climate for the pursuit of individual meaning.

Teachers can be fun-filled and playful companions at times, exhibiting their love and enthusiasm for life and the child's company. This side of teachers comes naturally to some adults and less easily to others. Perhaps many of us remember adults from our own childhood years that were able to engage themselves in adult-child interactions that could be described as joyful playing or companionable give and take. Teachers also pay deliberate attention to their own actions and words in both classrooms and play areas, and notice how their own behavior helps children make connections, comparisons, contrasts, bridges to past experiences and prior knowledge, and discoveries. Why? Because an effective teacher realizes she can be adept at promoting higher level thinking skills.

6-5a Handling Interruptions

Young children rarely limit their questions or modify their responses to the teacher for the purpose of hiding their ignorance, as older children sometimes do. During conversations, most young children intent on answers will probe enthusiastically for what they want to know. Teachers actively promote guesses and appreciate

error making in an atmosphere of trust. They interact in conversations by focusing child attention, posing questions, discussing problems, suggesting alternatives, and providing information at the teachable moment.

Children often interrupt adults during planned activities. When an idea hits, they want to share it. Their interruptions can indicate genuine involvement and interest, or they can reflect a variety of unrelated thoughts and feelings.

Teachers usually acknowledge the interruption, accept it, and may calmly remind the one who interrupts that when one wants to speak during group activities, one should raise one's hand first. Other teachers believe preschoolers' enthusiasm to speak is natural and characteristic. These teachers believe asking children to raise their hands during group discussions is a practice best reserved for a later age. Interruptions give the teacher an opportunity to make a key decision that affects the flow of the activity. Will the interruption break the flow of what is going on, will it add to the discussion, or is it best discussed at a later time? The teacher may decide to defer a comment, or accept being sidetracked and briefly digress from the main subject, or develop the interruption into a full-blown teacher-group discussion. Examples follow:

Situation: The teacher is telling a flannel-board story about a squirrel preparing for winter by hiding nuts in a tree.

Child: "My cat climbs trees."

Teacher: "Michael, I've seen cats climb trees."

(a short acknowledgment)

Teacher: "Michael's cat climbs trees, and the squirrel is climbing the tree to hide the nuts he is storing away for winter."

(The teacher acknowledges, but refers listener back to the story line.)

Teacher: "Michael, you can tell me about your cat that climbs trees as soon as we finish our story."

(The teacher defers discussion until later.)

Because preschoolers are action-packed, they enjoy activities that include an opportunity to perform the action words they encounter in books, discussions, or daily happenings (Figure 6-6). Teachers can promote "acting out" words with their own behaviors. Some action words that are easily enacted include *pounce, stamp, sneak, slither, creep,* and *slide. Enormous, droopy, sleepy, tired,* and other descriptive words can be connected to real examples or visual reproductions.

Incorporating the children's ideas and suggestions into group conversations and giving children credit for their ideas make children aware of the importance of their expressed ideas such as

"Kimberly's idea was to . . ." and

"Angelo thinks we should . . ." or

"Christal suggests that we . . .".

6-5b Using Sequential Approaches to Instruction

Teachers need a clear understanding of how children learn words and concepts. Figure 6-7 includes guidelines for the teacher's words and actions to accompany the child's progress toward new learning. Sequential instruction can be described as teacher interactions that are explicit, intentional, and built on children's existing skills. One approach to teacher interaction during structured, planned, or incidental activities, described by Maria Montessori (1967b), is called three-stage interaction. It shows movement from the child's sensory exploration to showing understanding, and then to verbalizing the understanding. An example follows.

Figure 6-6 Sample teacher interaction verbalization.

Common Teacher Statement	Possible Consequences
"Tell me more."	expands
"Did you mean . . . ?"	clarifies
"Where did you see . . . ?" "Who said . . . ?" "When did the bike . . . ?"	specifying
"Whose name shall I write on . . . ?" "This belongs to . . . ?"	specifying possession
"Please tell Juan . . ." "Choose one person to help you."	conversing with others
"Can you show . . . ?"	provides information
"Tell me again . . ."	rephrase or repeat
"What would happen if . . . ?"	guessing or problem solving
"Thang thinks . . ." "Taylor says . . ."	valuing others' ideas
"What could we try . . . ?" "Where should we put . . . ?" "What's a good name for . . . ?"	problem solving creative thinking
"Who had the last turn to talk . . . ?"	turn taking
"Show me with your hands."	clarifies
"What will you need to . . . ?" "What will you do first . . . ?"	specifies
"Do you have a question for me?" "Did something happen that I didn't see?"	clarifies
"Did anyone hear a sound?"	listening skill
"Show me your hand when you want to tell us something."	turn taking

*This is not meant to be a complete or comprehensive listing. Each language exchange with children is a challenge and opportunity.

Figure 6-7 Language learning and teacher interaction.

Child Activity	Teacher Actions
• focuses on an object or activity	• Name the object, or offer a statement describing the actions or situation. (supplies words)
• manipulates and explores the object or situation using touch, taste, smell, sight, and sound organs	• Try to help the child connect this object or action to his past experience through simple conversation. (builds bridge between old and new)
• fits this into what he already knows; develops some understanding	• Help the child see details through simple statements or questions. (focus on identifying characteristics) • Use "Show me . . ." or "Give me . . ." prodding statements that call for a nonverbal response. (prompting) • Put child's action into words. (Example: "John touched the red ball.") (modeling) • Ask the child for a verbal response. "What is this called?" "What happened when . . . ?" (prompting)
• uses a new word or sentence that names, describes, classifies, or generalizes a feature or whole part of the object or action	• Give a response in words indicating the truth factor of the response. "Yes, that's a red ball" or "It has four legs like a horse, but it's called a cow." (corrective or reinforcing response) • Extend one-word answers to full simple sentence if needed. (modeling) • Suggest an exploration of another feature of the object or situation. (extend interest) • Ask a memory or review question. "What did we discover when . . ." (reinforcing and assessing)

Digital Download

Step 1: *Associating Sense Perception with Words.* A cut lemon is introduced, and the child is encouraged to taste it. As the child tastes, the adult says, "The lemon tastes sour," pairing the word sour with the sensory experience. Repetition of the verbal pairing strengthens the impression.

Step 2: *Probing Understanding.* A number of yellow fruits are cut and presented. "Find the ones that taste sour," the teacher suggests. The child shows by his actions his understanding or lack of it.

Step 3: *Expressing Understanding.* A child is presented with a cut lemon and grapefruit and asked, "How do they taste?" If the child is able to describe the fruit as sour, he has incorporated the word into his vocabulary and has some understanding of the concept.

When using the three-step approach, Montessori (1967b) suggests that if a child is uninterested, the adult should stop at that point. If a mistake is made, the adult remains silent. The mistake indicates only that the child is not ready to learn—not that he is unable to learn. This verbal approach may seem mechanical and ritualistic to some, yet it clearly illustrates the sequence in a child's progress from not knowing to knowing.

The following example of a variation of the Montessori three-step approach includes additional steps. In this teaching sequence, the child asks the teacher how to open the tailgate of a dump truck in the sandbox.

TEACHER INTENT:	TEACHER STATEMENTS:
1. Focus attention.	"Look at this little handle."
2. Create motivation, defined as creating a desire to want to do or want to know (note that in this situation this is not necessary because the child is interested).	"You want the tailgate to open." (Pointing)
3. Provide information.	"This handle turns and opens the tailgate." (Demonstrating)

| 4. Promote child's attempts or practice. | "Try to turn the handle." |
| 5. Give corrective information, feedback, or positive reinforcement. | "The handle needs to turn." "Try to push down as you turn it." (Showing how) Or, "You did it; the tailgate is open." |

Steps 1 through 5 are used in the following situation in which the teacher wants the child to know what is expected in the use of bathroom paper towels.

1. "Here's the towel dispenser. Do you see it?"

2. "You can do this by yourself. You may want to dry your hands after you wash them."

3. Demonstration: "First take one paper towel. Dry your hands. Then the towel goes into this wastebasket."

4. "You try it."

5. "That's it. Pull out one towel. Dry your hands. Put the towel in the wastebasket."

"Now you know where the dirty paper towels go. No one will have to pick up your used towel from the floor. You can do it without help now like some of your classmates."

Statements of this kind help the child learn both the task and the vocabulary. The ability to provide information that the child needs, without talking too much, is one of the skills required of a really excellent teacher. Most theorists believe that the successful completion of a task is a reward in itself. Others believe that an encouraging verbal pat on the back is in order.

The same dump truck scene detailed earlier could be handled using a discovery approach, instead of a teacher-directed sequence, with the following types of questions. "Did you see anyone else playing with this dump truck? Is there a button to push or a handle to turn that opens the tailgate? What happens if you try to open the tailgate with your hand?"

The goal of prompting in a child-adult conversation is to encourage the child to express ideas perhaps more precisely and/or specifically. It is used slightly differently with younger preschoolers, as shown in the following examples:

Young preschooler: "Cookie."

Adult: "You want a cookie?"

Child: "Dis cookie."

Adult: "You want this brown cookie?"

Older preschooler: "I want that cookie."

Adult: "You want one of these cookies. Which one of the cookies do you want? We have a chocolate cookie or a sugar cookie."

Child: "The chocolate one."

Can teachers really make a difference in the level and quality of children's language development? Very significant correlations have been found between both the frequency of informative staff talk, the frequency with which the staff answered the children, and the language comprehension scores of the children. Interaction does require teachers to "wonder out loud." They express their own curiosity while at the same time noticing each child's quest to find out what makes others tick and what the world is all about. How can teachers interact skillfully?

- Expand topics in which the child shows interest.

- Realize that children are likely to learn more when they are attentive and interested.

- Add depth to information on topics of interest.

- Answer and clarify children's questions.

- Help children sort out features of events, problems, and experiences, reducing confusion.

- Urge children to put what is newly learned or discovered into words.

- Cue children into routinely attending to times when the adult and child are learning and discovering together through discussion of daily events.

6-5c Dealing with Children's Past Experiences

A teacher encounters a wide range of children's perceptions concerning the way children think they should communicate with adults. A child's family or past child care arrangements may have taught the child to behave in a certain way. With this in mind, the teacher can almost envision what it means to be a conversationalist in a particular family or societal group. Some families expect children to interrupt; others expect respectful manners. Wild, excited gesturing and weaving body movements are characteristic of some children, whereas motionless, barely audible whispering is typical of others. Teachers working with newly arrived children from other cultures may see sharp contrasts in communication styles. Some children verbally seek help, whereas others find this extremely difficult. Some speak their feelings openly; others rarely express them. To promote child learning, a teacher needs to consider how she, their teacher, will interface to help each child understand that school may be very different than home.

Past child care experiences may have left their mark. A four-year-old child named Perry seemed to give one teacher insight into how speech can be dramatically affected by past undesirable child care arrangements. The following is that teacher's observations and conclusions:

> Perry sat quietly near the preschool's front door ignoring all play opportunities, and holding his blanket until his mom's return on his first day at school. He only spoke or looked up when teachers tried repeatedly to engage him in conversation and activities. He sat on adults' laps silently when they tried to comfort him, and ate food quickly and then returned to his waiting place near the door. The real Perry emerged a few weeks later as a talkative, socially vigorous child.
>
> Our verbal statements and actions concentrated on rebuilding trust with adults and other children; only later was language-developing interaction possible.

It can be difficult for a child to engage an adult in conversation, as was the case with Perry. Seeking the availability of a teacher or caregiver and ensuring one's right to her attention and reply often calls for persistence and ingenuity in a poor-quality child care situation. Perry may have long before given up trying, and decided it was best to "just stay out of the way."

In all roles, the teacher needs to maintain a balance. This means

- giving, but withholding when self-discovery is practical and possible.
- interacting, but not interfering with or dominating the child's train of thought or actions.
- giving support, but not hovering.
- talking, but not over talking.
- listening, but remaining responsive.
- providing many opportunities for the child to speak.
- being patient and understanding.

As is most often the case, when adults know the answer, many may find it difficult to be patient so children can figure out the answer for

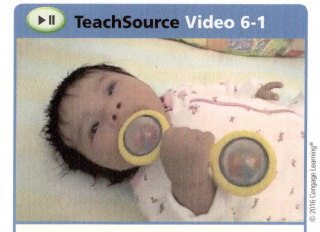

TeachSource Video 6-1

© 2016 Cengage Learning®

0–2 Years: Module for Infants and Toddlers

Skip past the first segment with the crying infant and focus on the three caregivers comparing their vocal comments to the child who is exploring one or more play objects.

1. Which of the caregivers is providing a running commentary on what the child is doing at particular moments?

2. Which caregiver names objects and seems to encourage exploration, but does not direct the child's attention to toy features? Would you recommend pointing out toy features to the child? Why or why not?

3. Which of the three caregivers seems to have more enthusiasm and involvement with her child? What makes you think so?

themselves. The teacher orally reflects and guards against being overly invasive and didactic. There is an old story about two preschool boys who discover a worm in the play yard.

First child:	"Boy it tickles! Look at him!" (He holds the worm up to be seen.)
Second child:	"Let's show it to teacher."
First child:	"No way—she'll want us to draw a picture of it and make us print 'worm'!"

Teachers thoughtfully screen their comments and conversation to ensure they are free of sexist or biased attitudes or stereotypes. If a teacher is talking about a stuffed teddy bear or the school's pet guinea pig (whose sex is yet to be discovered), use of the pronoun "it," rather than "he" or "she," is recommended.

Summary

6-1 List three roles of a teacher in early childhood language instruction.

The early childhood language teacher serves as a *model* of Standard English usage, is a *provider* of experiences, activities, and materials, is a *facilitator* who shares experiences and encourages and promotes word usage and conversation. A teacher is also an *observer* who supports problem solving, child discovery, and the expression of children's ideas and concerns. The teacher can be described as a *balancer* who guards against overly invasive and didactic approaches. Every day decisions are made that affect children's language learning opportunities.

6-2 Discuss ways teachers model positive language behaviors.

Teachers model Standard English and correct child errors in subtle ways. Their manner words, such as please and thank you are often copied by children. They also model dictionary use, listening skill, the use of gestures, good print form, and proper book care besides modeling positive attitudes toward reading, writing, listening, speaking and the enjoyment of the literacy-building activities. They continually model the functional usefulness of language in daily living.

6-3 State three reasons why teachers should use specific and detailed speech.

Specific, accurate, and detailed teacher talk builds children's vocabulary and increases a child's knowledge. The teacher offers words a little more advanced but related to the words the child already knows, and provides visual and physical examples of word meanings when possible. Specific words a teacher purposefully uses may be key words or root words found in early readers. This prepares and promotes initial reading success when reading instruction begins.

6-4 Describe how and why a teacher uses extension techniques to build child language.

A teacher using extension builds upon child statements to purposefully add information, factual data, meaning, and vocabulary, and to promote the child's further elaboration of his/her comment. This technique can clarify or personalize some aspect or concept associated with the child's topic. It creates a more remembered learning while the child is focused and interested.

6-5 Discuss two ways that a teacher acts as a balancer.

Balancing may include giving teacher information immediately or prompting child discovery, interacting rather than interfering, providing support without stopping the child's ingenuity to solve his own problems, being responsive rather than talking excessively, and being patient rather than in a hurry or pushy.

Additional Resources

Readings

Bloom, P. (2000). *How Children Learn the Meanings of Words*. Cambridge: MIT Press.

Burman, L. (2009). *Are You listening? Fostering Conversations that Help Young Children Learn*. St. Paul, MN: Redleaf Press.

Neuman, S., & Wright, T. S. (2013). *All About Words: Increasing Vocabulary in Common Core Classrooms*. Pre-K-2. New York: Teacher's College Press.

Helpful Websites

National Association for the Education of Young Children

http://www.naeyc.org

Provides articles, publications, and other information.

National Council for Social Studies

http://www.social-studies.org

Search for early childhood topics.

8 Children and Books

Objectives

After reading this chapter, you should be able to:

8-1 Describe the contents of children's books that existed before 1900.

8-2 Name four different categories of books for preschoolers.

8-3 Discuss criteria used to select read aloud books.

8-4 Discuss suggested techniques for reading a book to a group of children.

8-5 Describe an after-book reading discussion to promote child comprehension.

8-6 Name two reasons teacher- or child-authored books might be valuable additions to a classroom's book collection.

8-7 List three suggestions for features and furnishings of a book (library) center.

naeyc NAEYC Program Standards

2E08 Children have access to books and writing materials throughout the classroom.

2E04 Children have varied opportunities to read books in an engaging manner in groups or individualized settings at least twice a day in full-time programs.

2E04 Children have various opportunities and access to various types of books including storybooks, factual books, books with rhymes, alphabet books, and wordless books.

DAP Developmentally Appropriate Practice (DAP) Preschoolers

3H21 Teachers draw children's attention to print conventions.

3H22 To broaden children's knowledge and vocabulary, teachers use a variety of strategies, such as reading stories and informational books rich in new concepts, information, and vocabulary.

3H23 Teachers engage children with questions and comments to help them recall and comprehend what is happening in a story and make connections between the book and their own life experiences.

COMMON CORE Common Core State Standards for English Language Arts and Literacy

R.CCR.1 Read closely to determine what the text says explicitly and to make logical inferences from it, cite specific textual evidence when writing or speaking to support conclusions drawn from text.

R.CCR.2 Determine central ideas or themes of a text and analyze their development; summarize the key supporting details and ideas.

R.CCR.3 Analyze how and why individuals, events, and ideas develop and interact over the course of a text.

A Volunteer Reader

Mr. Mead, LaVon's grandfather, arrives in the four-year-old's classroom shortly after nap time and goes to the rocking chair. There is a small commotion in the book center as a few children dash for the reading shelf. A line of children clutching one book forms. The first in line peeks at Mr. Mead, who is reading a book and already has a child curled up on his lap, the child's face registering the intent of enjoying every minute. There is an air of magic and hopeful anticipation on the waiting children's faces. Mrs. Rex, the teacher, moves a few chairs in a row for the "waiters."

Questions to Ponder

1. One can hear Mr. Mead's laughter and a child's giggle. What would you like to know about Mr. Mead's reading technique?

2. What children's attitudes are being formed, and how might these affect their future academic success?

Picture books are an important beginning step on a child's path to literacy, as well as an excellent source of listening activities for the young child. Seeing, touching, and interacting with books is part of a good-quality program in early childhood education. Books play an important role in language development.

A child's first being-read-to experience can be thought of as his first curriculum. It is a curriculum rich in pleasant associations: a soft lap, a warm bath, and a snugly bed. This initial literature curriculum uses common words in uncommon ways, titillates the senses, nurtures curiosities, adds to the memory, and stretches the imagination. When handled with care, reading experiences at home and at school can create positive attitudes toward literature and can help motivate the child to learn to read. Attitudes toward literacy are most easily established early in life.

Many families read to their children; others do not. Mothers with no high school diplomas may read to their preschoolers less than a few times a month (Dionne, Mimeau, & Mathieu, 2014). Children from low-income families are often more dependent on school experiences for their literacy development than middle-class children. In fact, a teacher may offer some children their first contact with stories and books. Teacher and child can share the joy of this very pleasant experience. Many believe next to giving a child a hug, reading aloud is probably the longest-lasting experience that families can put into a child's life. Reading aloud is important for all of the reasons that talking to children is important—to inspire them, to guide them, to educate them, to bond with them, and to communicate feelings, hopes, and fears. In the beginning, the child is usually more interested in the reader than in the book or story.

Teachers know book-sharing time is an opportune time for teachers to help children build vocabulary, extend phonological awareness, and develop familiarity with literate forms (Photo 8-1). Reading books aloud to children exposes them to grammatical forms of written language and displays literate discourse rules in ways that conversation cannot. Discussions can encourage children to analyze the text, and these discussions can

Photo 8-1 Children often want to share with their teacher something they've found in a book.

have a powerful effect on the development of complex oral language, vocabulary, and story understanding—all critical abilities that young children will need when faced with later literacy tasks.

Early childhood teachers agree that book-sharing sessions are among their favorite times with children. Teachers introduce each new group of children to favorite books that never seem to lose their magic. There will be times when young children are rapt with enjoyment during picture-book readings and, at such times, the lucky reader will understand the power of literature and realize his responsibility as the sharer of a vast treasure. The value of offering thoughtfully selected books in a skilled way will be readily apparent.

What, exactly, do picture books offer young children? They open the door to literacy and create the opportunity to influence attitudes, broaden understanding, savor diversity, vicariously experience drama, expand the imagination, gain vocabulary and information, hear the rhythm of language and words, and enjoy the visual and aesthetic variety in illustrations. Another advantage is that young children learn to respond to the messages in children's stories that are told or read to them and in doing this they use the kind of language and thought processes that they will use in learning to read.

As you read through this chapter, other benefits of reading aloud to children will occur to you, and you will clarify your thoughts about the benefits you consider of primary and secondary importance. You will become acquainted with the cultural universals of story structure and form, which help us remember by providing meaningful frameworks. Stories make events memorable.

A special kind of language is found in books. Oral language differs from written language in important ways. Although many young children communicate well and have adequate vocabularies, they do not construct sentences in the same manner found in their picture books. Knowing the way books "talk" makes children better predictors of words they will discover in their early reading attempts.

Each child gets his own meaning from picture-book experiences. Books cannot be used as substitutes for the child's real-life experiences, interactions, and discoveries, because these are what help make books understandable. Books add another dimension and source of information and enjoyment to children's lives.

Careful consideration should be given to selecting books that are appropriate to the child's age and ability. Children younger than three (and many older than this age) enjoy physical closeness, the visual changes of illustrations, and the sound of the human voice reading text. The rhythms and poetry of picture books intrigue them. Experts point out that very young children's "syntactic dependence" is displayed by their obvious delight in recognized word order. The sounds of language in picture books may be far more important than the meanings conveyed to the very young child. Teachers of two- and three-year-olds may notice this by observing which books children select most often. Four-year-olds are more concerned with content and **characterization**, in addition to what they previously enjoyed in picture books. Fantasy, **realism**, human emotions, **nonfiction**, and books with a variety of other features attract and hold them.

8-1 History to Present Time—Children's Literature

The idea that children need or deserve entertainment and amusement is a relatively new development. Until the mid-eighteenth century, books for children instructed and aimed to improve young children, particularly their moral and spiritual natures.

Folktales were sung and told in primitive times, and stories of human experience were shared. Storytellers often attempted to reduce anxieties, satisfy human needs, fire the imagination, and increase human survival, among other aims. Orally passed down, tales appeared in most of the world's geographical locations and cultures. Much of today's **fiction** reflects elements of these old tales and traditional stories.

Early American children's literature was heavily influenced by English and Puritan beliefs and practices. Books that existed before William Caxton's development of printing in fifteenth-century England were hand-copied adult books that children happened to encounter in private wealthy households. Caxton translated *Aesop's Fables* (1484) from a French version and printed other adult books that literate English children found interesting. *Aesop's Fables* is considered the first printing of talking animal stories. Themes of other books in Victorian England included

---

characterization — the way an author presents a character by describing character verbalizations, actions, or thinking, or by what other characters say, think, or do about the character.

realism — presents experience without embellishment to convey life as it appears in a natural world limited by the senses and reason.

nonfiction — prose that explains, argues, or describes; usually factual.

fiction — imaginative narrative in any form of presentation that is designed to entertain, as distinguished from that which is designed primarily to explain, argue, or merely describe.

romances of chivalry and adventure, knights in shining armor, battles with giants, and rescues of lovely princesses and other victims of oppression.

Victorian families read to their children, and minstrels and troubadours were paid to sing narrative verses to the families of rich patrons. The English Puritans were dedicated to a revolution founded on the deep conviction that religious beliefs form the basis for the whole of human life. Writers such as Bunyan, author of *A Book for Boys and Girls* (1686), were intent on saving children's souls.

Chapbooks (paper booklets) appeared in England after 1641. Initially, they were intended for adults, but eventually they fell into children's hands. They included tiny woodcuts as decoration, and later woodcuts were used to illustrate the text. Salesmen (chapmen) traveled England selling these small, four-by-two and a half-inch editions to the less affluent. Chapbooks written to entertain and instruct children followed, as sales and popularity increased. Titles included *The Tragical Death of an Apple Pie* and *The History of Jack and the Giants*.

John Newbery and Thomas Boreman are recognized as the first publishers of children's books in England. Chapbooks, although predated, are considered booklets. Most of these newly printed books were instructional, but titles like *A Little Pretty Pocket-Book* (Newbery, 1744) were advertised as children's amusement books (Figure 8-1). In 1765, Newbery published *The Renowned History of Little Goody Two Shoes, Otherwise Called Mrs. Margery Two Shoes*. The book chronicles Goody's rise from poverty to wealth. Newbery prospered. Other publishers followed with their own juvenile editions, many with themes designed to help children reason and use moral judgment to select socially correct courses of action. Books used as school readers in early America contained subject matter of both a religious and a moral nature.

During the earliest years of our nation, many children had no schooling and could not read. Those few who could read often read works intended for adults, such as Jonathan Swift's *Gulliver's Travels* (1726). Reading was considered unimportant for children in agricultural society. Only the need for a literate workforce in the new industrialized society of the 1800s caused time to be set aside for children's education and more attention to be paid to books intended for children.

By the mid-1800s, adventure stories for older boys gained popularity with Mark Twain's *Adventures of Tom Sawyer*, published in 1876. Louisa May Alcott created *Little Women* in 1868 as a girl's volume. Toward the end of the nineteenth century,

Figure 8-1 Excerpts from *A Little Pretty Pocket-Book,* published by John Newbery, 1744.

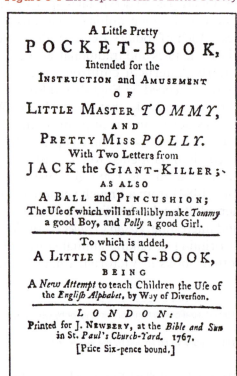

some picture books became artistic. English and French publishers produced colorful illustrations of charm, quality, and detail. The books of Randolph Caldecott, Maurice Boutet de Monvel, and Kate Greenway had captivating drawings that overshadowed the drab illustrations that were typically found in American picture books.

Although not intended or recommended for children, comic picture sequences, like those of A. B. Frost, appeared in American magazines from 1880 to 1890. Their humor was shared by families. Two American picture books resembling Frost's slapstick humor gained acceptance from American librarians: Gelett Burgess's *New Goops and How to Know Them* (Lippincott, 1928) and Palmer Cox's *Brownies* (1927).

E. Boyd Smith, an American, created illustrations for *The Story of Noah's Ark* (Houghton Mifflin, 1905), which are described as both artistic and humorous. The books Smith created delighted children and adults with colorful panoramic illustrations. Librarians speaking of Smith's illustrative work described it as honest, true, "better than any done by an American artist." The cost of full-color printing escalated, and illustrative color in picture books was not to reappear in the United States and become widely affordable until the later 1920s and 1930s. Little Golden Books became popular, and European books with colorful illustrative art were imported to the United States for those who could afford them.

Lynch-Brown and Tomlinson (1998) believe the establishment of book awards improved American picture books.

> By the 1920s a class of professional writers devoted solely or almost solely to writing literature for children—as opposed to moral reformers, teachers, and clerics as authors—produced a larger quantity and better variety and quality of children's books than had been seen to that point. This development was hastened by the establishment in 1922, under the auspices of the American Library Association, of the first of the great American children's book awards, the Newbery Medal. In 1938, with the establishment by ALA of the Caldecott Medal for illustration, more and better artists were encouraged to enter the field of children's books as well. For the remainder of the 20th century, book award programs were effectively used to create interest in children's books generally and to promote awareness of specific types of books. Competition for the most prestigious awards resulted in better, more original works. (p. 124)

American picture books for children began to reflect a worldview of children's literature. Colorful illustrations appeared in school readers. Stories for young children set in foreign countries were widely acclaimed during the 1930s. *Madeline* (Simon & Schuster, 1939) by Ludwig Bemelmans, is still found on most suggested early childhood reading lists.

The child-study movement and research at numerous universities and institutions during the late 1920s and 1930s led some well-known researchers to believe that young children's interests focused on "the-here-and-now." This was translated as home objects and environments, community settings, airplanes, trains, local workers and professionals, and "everyday matters." Approved and recommended book lists guided parents' selection of preschool books as early as 1913.

It is thought that Russian information and "how-to" books of the 1940s and 1950s increased nonfiction picture-book production in the United States. Books concerning machines and how they worked, insects, and science concepts became abundant. Photographs were used along with illustrations.

The Cat in the Hat (1957), by Geisel (Dr. Seuss), celebrated its 50th anniversary in 2007. Beloved by a generation of now baby boomers and enjoyed by succeeding generations of children, it is believed to have been written and illustrated by Geisel to allay his worry that basal readers were not aiding children's learning to read and that they also featured idealized illustrations depicting overly courteous and unnaturally spotlessly clean boys and girls (Freeman, 2007).

Geisel is thought to have developed his story line by intentionally maximizing the repetition of easily read rhyming words. He secured a beginning reading word list from a primary grade teacher and then attempted to incorporate as many list words as possible into his creation. Freeman notes virtually everyone in the English-speaking world who learned to read in the last 55 years is familiar with *The Cat in the Hat*.

Some of the changes in picture-book publishing during the 1960s occurred because several individuals spotlighted the lack of African-Americans in story lines and illustrations. The civil rights movement affected the social consciousness of many teachers and families. Ezra Jack Keats (1969) brought a new perspective to picture book illustration with the publication of his *The Snowy Day*, which featured an African-American protagonist. His use of authentic multicultural characters and urban settings in illustrations was a merging of collage and paint (*Wall Street Journal*, 2012).

Only a few research surveys conducted in the 1970s and 1980s attempted to pinpoint the numbers of picture-book representations for Mexican-Americans, Asian-Americans, or Native Americans. It is reasonable to say they were minimal in number.

Although published multicultural literature for young children increased and became an important part of language arts education, cultural accuracy that helps young children gain a "true" sense of the culture depicted (a so-called insider's view) is a relatively recent development. This type of picture book is eagerly sought by most early childhood educators.

The current trend toward publishing more multicultural literature to compensate for the almost total absence of it as recently as 35 years ago will continue as schools become more diverse and society becomes more accepting of different voices and viewpoints.

Picture books dealing with the reality of young children's daily lives, their families, and living problems (such as stress, fear, moving, and appearance) began appearing in larger numbers in the 1970s and 1980s, broadening subject matter believed appropriate and of interest to children. These books, many classified as "therapeutic," often attempted to build self-esteem or help young children cope in difficult situations. Characters in picture books always had problems to be solved by creative thinking and self-insight, but these new stories dealt more frequently with life situations children could not change themselves.

Literacy concerns and the whole-language movement (1980s to 1990s) have dramatically increased educators' ideas of the importance of quality literature in early childhood curriculum. More and more activities are based on children's reactions to books and language arts activities offered by their teachers.

Creative technology, including e-books, has interactive features not previously possible. New digital products capture attention and attempt to teach and entertain preschoolers. Yet most young children still enjoy traditional read-alouds with the special people in their lives. Today's picture books have historical roots. Some have outlived the generation of children for whom they were produced and are classics of quality. It is those that you, as a teacher of young children, will endeavor to find and share along with the "classics of the future."

8-1a Present Time Book Selection for Your Classroom

Each teacher should develop a personal collection. Librarians and bookstore salespeople can offer valuable suggestions and advice. Judging quality means reading and viewing a picture book to find out whether it contains something memorable or valuable. For every good book you discover, you may wade through a stack that makes you wonder whether the authors have any experience at all with young children. Each book you select may have one or more of the following desirable and valuable features:

- character development (such as *Madeline* by Ludwig Bemelmans, the wolf in *Goldilocks and the Three Bears*, or *Beady Bear* by Don Freeman)
- color (*Little Blue and Yellow* by Leo Lionni)
- an example of human courage, cleverness, or grit (such as *Peter Rabbit*, created by Beatrix Potter)
- aesthetic appeal (*Rain Rain Rivers* by Uri Shulevitz)
- wordplay (*Tikki Tikki Tembo* by Arlene Mosel)
- listening pleasure (*Make Way for Ducklings* by Robert McCloskey)
- nonsense (*What Do You Do with a Kangaroo?* by Mercer Mayer)
- onomatopoeia (the naming of a thing or action by a vocal imitation of the sound associated with it, as in *buzz* and *hiss*)
- suspense (*Deep in the Forest* by Brinton Turkle)
- humor or wit (*Nothing Ever Happens on My Block* by Ellen Raskin)
- fantasy (*Where the Wild Things Are* by Maurice Sendak)
- surprise (*Harry the Dirty Dog* by Eugene Zion)
- repetition (*The Little Engine That Could* by Mabel Bragg)
- hope (*The Carrot Seed* by Ruth Krauss)
- charm (*George and Martha* by James Marshall)

- sensitivity (*The Tenth Good Thing about Barney* by Judith Viorst)
- realistic dialogue (*Can I Keep Him?* By Steven Kellogg)
- cultural insight (*On a Hot, Hot Day* by Nicki Weiss)
- action (*Caps for Sale* by Esphyr Slobodkina)
- predictability (*Brown Bear, Brown Bear, What Do You See?* by William Martin)

Of course, this is only a partial listing. A book can excel in many different ways. An outstanding feature of many good stories is that they can cause the reader or listener to smile with recognition and think, "life is like that" or "I've been there myself." This promotes a positive feeling of connectedness.

- The theme of respect for individual differences in Bill Peet's *Huge Harold*, the gentleness of Uri Shulevitz's *Dawn*, or the tenderness of Charlotte Zolotow's *My Grandson Lew* may fit your criteria of quality. Or you may prefer the runaway fantasy of Frank Asch's *Popcorn* and Tomie de Paola's *Strega Nona*.
- The panoramic scenes of Mitsumasa Anno's *Anno's Counting Book*, the patterns and contrasts in Ezra Jack Keats' *The Snowy Day*, or the fun of discovery in Janet and Allan Ahlberg's *Each Peach Pear Plum* might help a book become one of your favorites because of visual appeal.
- For humor and wit, you might choose Steven Kellogg's *There Was an Old Woman*, Leah Komaiko's *Annie Bananie*, Robert Kraus's *Leo the Late Bloomer*, James Marshall's *Yummers*, Mercer Mayer's *Frog, Where Are You?*, or a selection of others that may make you laugh. You might never forget the way you trip over your tongue while reading about Jack, Kack, Lack, Mack, Nack, Ouack, Pack, and Quack in Robert McCloskey's *Make Way for Ducklings* or Arlene Mosel's *Tikki Tikki Tembo*. If you enjoy surprise or an ending with a twist, you might be delighted by Brinton Turkle's *Deep in the Forest* or Jimmy Kennedy's *The Teddy Bears' Picnic*. The sound pleasure in Wanda Gág's *Millions of Cats* or the onomatopoeia in Mabel Bragg's *The Little Engine That Could* might make these books memorable.

You might relive your experience of city living in *Tell Me a Mitzi* by Lore Segal. Perhaps discovering the facts through the colorful, precise artwork in Ruth Heller's *Chickens Aren't the Only Ones* will attract you to the world of nonfiction. You may look for books to promote children's phonological awareness, like Bill Martin Jr. and John Archambault's *Chicka Chicka Boom Boom* or Cheryl Hudson's *Afro-Bets ABC Book*. Unforgettable characters like Leo Lionni's *Frederick*, Don Freeman's *Corduroy* and *Dandelion*, Eugene Zion's *Harry by the Sea*, or Ludwig Bemelmans's demure individualist *Madeline* may be counted among your friends as you search for quality. Jewels will stand out, and you will be anxious to share them with children.

You will be looking for fascinating, captivating books. Some captivate by presenting believable characters. Character-drawing is like a tremendous, complicated conjuring trick. Appealing to imagination and goodwill, diverting attention by sheer power of technique, the writer persuades us (for the period of reading and sometimes for long afterward) to accept the identity of certain people who exist between the covers of his book. Some picture books fascinate to the extent that worries are forgotten, and the child lives in the fantasy world of the story during its reading and beyond.

Speaking about a true literature-based curriculum, teachers need to watch for stories that "catch on," stories that fulfill some deep understanding of human intentions, or express a developmental concern, or arouse our curiosity: these are the stories that should lead a curriculum of hearing stories, knowing them, and—if they appeal—reliving them through writing, drama, or retelling.

You will want to choose classics so that from the very beginning, the child has a chance to appreciate literature. Not everyone will agree as to what is a modern-day classic. *Where the Wild Things Are*, by Maurice Sendak, continues to cause arguments among adults about whether it is truly a classic. Teachers observe that some adults don't like it very much, but nearly all children respond to it. Many people think that Sendak is very much attuned to kids' wavelengths.

Knowing about family lifestyles, home language, and community individuality aids book selection and planning. Some schools order 50 percent of their books in the children's home language. The relevance of a farm book is bound to be different for children who have grown up on a farm, yet the human universality depicted may make it an attractive choice for urban children.

8-1b Award-Winning Books

Each year, the Association for Library Services to Children (American Library Association) recognizes the artist it believes has produced "the most distinguished American picture book for children" with the Caldecott Medal and Honor awards. Early childhood educators look for these and other award-winning books. Other awards given to books include the following:

- Newbery Medals
- International Reading Association Children's Book Awards
- The Parent Choice Awards
- Coretta Scott King Awards
- National Jewish Book Awards
- Catholic Book Awards
- The Children's Africana Book Award
- The McElderry Picture Book Prize (awards books by previously unpublished authors)
- The Ezra Jack Keats New Writer Award
- newspaper awards
- magazine reviews and recognitions found in *Book Links* (American Library Association) and *Language Arts* (National Council of Teachers of English)
- local public library awards or recognitions

8-1c Illustrations

In many quality picture books, the story stands well by itself. The illustrations simply visualize what is written. In others, illustrations play a dominant role and are an integral part of the entire action. Educators scrutinize illustrations to judge the amount of story support they offer and their connection and relationship to the text (Gaffney, Ostrosky, & Hemmeter, 2008). In some instances more information is conveyed in illustrations than is present in the text. One such picture book, *Love You Forever*, by Robert Munsch (1986, 2011) and illustrated by Sheila McGraw, depicts a toddler about to flush his mother's watch down the toilet. This is stated in the text. What isn't stated is the toddler has also pulled toilet paper across the room, squeezed toothpaste from a tube, and spilled liquid and cotton balls on the bathroom floor. A teacher reading this book aloud has an opportunity discuss the toddler's actions and the mother's emotions and reactions to more fully understand the story.

Picture books can be defined as books that rely on a combination of illustrations and **narrative,** with both being integral to the complete work. Fortunately, many picture-book illustrations are created by highly talented individuals. Justice and Lankford (2002) point out that about 95 percent of children's visual attention during storybook sharing is focused on the book's illustrations.

Young children may or may not have grasped the idea that book illustrations are drawn, created, or photographed by real people. The following happened to a student teacher at Evergreen Valley College Child Development Center.

> During a book reading activity the student teacher displayed the cover of the book *The Wide-Mouthed Frog*, and then read the title, the author's name, and said "This book's pictures were drawn for us by Jonathan Lambert." One four-year-old girl queried "Was it the frog or a people?" The book's cover has a large colorful green frog illustration.

A wide range of artistic styles exists in picture-book illustration, including line drawings, woodcuts, water colors, collage, crayon, pastels, oil paint, and photography. The style of art can be representational, impressionistic, expressionistic, cartoon, abstract, stylized, surrealistic, or a style that defies categorization. The true artist is one who is able to enter the realm that his work evokes and move as freely there as if it were the kingdom of his birth. As a consequence, the artist can show us things that we would not have seen as mere visitors.

Zielinski & Zielinski (2006) point out what they and many practicing educators believe:

> We are in a golden era of children's picture book illustration. There has never been a period where the number of high quality children's book illustrators has been so plentiful. But without question, active today, the quantity of quality book illustrators is without parallel. (p. 6)

Illustrations help give words reality. For young children, illustrations promote visual literacy. Additional benefits follow.

---

narrative — in general, a story, actual or fictional, expressed orally or in writing.

- provision of pleasure
- nourishment of the imagination
- promotion of creative expression
- development of imagery
- presentation and exploration of various styles and forms for the communication of ideas
- awareness of the functions of languages
- acquisition of metalinguistic awareness (defined as a sense of what printed language is all about)

Picture-book illustrations are often familiar objects in lifelike settings, and publishers are careful to emphasize figures rather than backgrounds. In addition to the simple, true-to-life depictions preferred by young preschoolers, illustrations of pure fantasy and illustrations that contain more detail appeal to older preschoolers. **DAP** **naeyc**

Many possible teacher opportunities for child-book involvement occur during read-aloud activities. Among the interactive behaviors research has identified in read-aloud activities connected to both the book's illustrations and print are questioning, scaffolding dialogue and responses, offering praise or positive reinforcement, giving or extending information, clarifying information, restating information, directing discussion, sharing personal reactions, suggesting physical movement or repeating speech mentioned in the narrative, and relating concepts to life experiences. A teacher reading this list can

never again believe that read-aloud book times are the simplest, easiest time of the day, although they will probably remain one of the teacher's favorite times (Photo 8-2). Children will have spontaneous and unconscious responses to books, including thoughts that agree or disagree, and other feelings and attitudes. At times children's responses to read-alouds are unexpected, immediately voiced, and can make the act of reading to young children a delightful experience because the teacher shares the excitement, concentration, joy, and laughter.

After studying young children's responses to read-aloud picture books, McVicker (2007) identified a wide variety of uninhibited and spontaneous verbal and nonverbal reactions. As children savor joyful language, meet interesting characters, or encounter personally significant story lines, teachers see evidence of the book's impact and effect. Just as adults are eager to share an interesting book with others, young children share their reactions with their teachers and peers.

8-1d Format and Genre

A book's format is defined as its overall and general character, that is, the way the book is put together. Decisions concerning format by book publishers and author/illustrators include the size and shape of the cover and interior pages, paper quality, printing colors, typesetting, content of each page, and binding. A book's format can enhance its narrative, appeal, and subsequent enjoyment, or it can confuse, frustrate, and alienate the reader. A book can reflect a thoughtful attempt to create a classic volume of enduring worth and value or represent a sacrifice of quality for the sake of quick profit.

Genre, another way of categorizing books, concentrates on a book's content. Narrative is either poetry or prose. Prose can be further classified as fiction or nonfiction. The category of fiction includes excursions into sheer fantasy as well as more plausible stories about people or situations that could be, could have been, or might be. The latter group is classified as realistic fiction. Most educators are eager to learn more about new children's books and are already quite knowledgeable. Picking books for a specific child's interest and then selecting books to suit some unique classroom situation or event are ongoing teacher tasks.

Photo 8-2 Schools provide as many one-on-one readings as staff and time allow.

© 2015 Cengage Learning®

---

genre — a category used to classify literary works, usually by form, technique, or content.

8-1e If Only They Would Choose Books and Book-Related Activities

Many early childhood teachers are worried that busy, money-tight families do not have the time or resources to make books part of children's lives. Consequently, they are expending extra effort and attention to books and book-related activities. Early childhood educators have been alerted to the idea that preschoolers who are read to and who are interested in stories and books are more successful students in the beginning years of elementary school and in accomplishing reading. They monitor how many children select classroom book-related activities and library areas and also monitor the amount of time each child is so engaged (Photo 8-3).

Teacher planning and thoughtful analysis can increase child interest. Thinking of classroom schedules and book-reading times more critically can initiate change and creative and imaginative presentation of activities. Time spent reading to children can be viewed as only one part of a book's introduction. What precedes and what follows are equally important. Practitioners need to ask themselves the following: How is this book relevant to children's lives? What can I do to increase child involvement and interest? What will make children eager to be part of story times? How can I discover child thoughts about what has been read and then build in further experiences? What can follow this story time, and will children give me clues? In other words, how can this book become part of their lives and at the same time be highly enjoyed? After attempting to answer these and other teacher questions, one can see that simply reading to children may not be enough to reach a teacher's true goals. Teachers spend considerable time in the classroom library (book center) themselves. One teacher technique is to introduce a new book or other printed material every day. Teachers think seriously about book variety, availability, child comfort, and adequate lighting. They determine a plan to "sell" the books they introduce.

8-2 Reading A Variety of Books to Young Children for A Variety of Purposes

Because children can gain so much from books, the teacher's way of presenting them is very important. The primary goal of a read-aloud event is the construction of meaning that develops in the interactive process between adult and child and the development of children's positive attitudes toward the activity. Becoming this type of teacher requires the teacher to view children as active, individual learners. In previewing Tomie de Paola's picture book *Strega Nona* (1975) for a group reading, a teacher might think as follows:

Photo 8-3 This classroom has been able to promote child self-selection of books.

© 2015 Cengage Learning®

What past experiences has this group had with pasta?

What follow-up, extending activities could be planned?

What teacher questions would guide a discussion that probes children's feelings and ideas?

How can I make the "overflowing," "too much" concept a real experience?

The teacher's goal should be to lead each child to understand that books can be fun and interesting, can hold new experiences, and can be enjoyed alone or in the company of others (Photo 8-4).

Children who enjoy read-alouds usually seek out other books. Preschool teachers think of the preschool years as a critical period for children to become "addicted" to books, when urges are felt as irresistible and objects that gratify the urge are also experienced as irresistible. The educator who wishes to capture a young child needs to ensure that early and repeated gratification from book-reading times exists.

In a diverse society, offering multicultural and ethnically representative literature is a must for young children. Although age-recommended lists are available, most teachers actively pursue additional publications. Librarians, publishers, and children's bookstores are excellent resources. Anti-bias themes and sex-equity themes are also eagerly sought to ensure book models give young children every chance to value themselves as individuals.

Not every child in preschool is interested in books or sees them as something to enjoy. Although children cannot be forced to like books, they can acquire positive feelings for them. Some of the positive feelings depend on whether children feel successful and competent during reading time. This, in turn, depends on whether a bond of trust and a teacher-child caring relationship has been established and how skillfully the teacher acts and reacts and how well the book sessions are planned. The key is to draw reluctant children into the story by making story times so attractive and vital that children simply cannot bear to stay away.

An important additional goal in reading books to children is the presentation of knowledge. Books can acquaint the child with new words, ideas, facts, feelings, and happenings. These are experienced in a different form than spoken

Photo 8-4 Creating enjoyment and interest when sharing big books involves promoting the children's positive interest toward books.

conversation. In books, sentences are complete; in conversation, they may not be. Stories and illustrations follow a logical sequence in books.

Teachers ought to be concerned with whether the child comprehends what is read. To ensure comprehension, the books must offer significant content, something that relates to the child's everyday experience. Humor and fantasy, for example, are common in favorite picture books. Usually, these books are not merely frivolous. A closer reading will often reveal that they deal with universal human emotions or imaginations. Comprehension is aided by open discussion. Children should be free to ask questions that will help them connect the book's happenings to their own past experiences. The more outgoing and talkative children often clear up misunderstandings of the whole group when books are discussed. Those who work with young children often notice children's innate tendency to try to make sense and derive meaning from the happenings in their lives.

Teachers can show that books may also be used as resources. When a child wants to find out about certain things, teachers can refer to dictionaries, encyclopedias, computers, or books on specialized subjects. The teacher can model the use of books to find facts. When a child asks the teacher a question about some subject of special interest and the teacher says, "I don't know, but I know where we can find out," the teacher can demonstrate how books and other resources can be used for finding answers. The teacher tells where to look and follows through by showing the child how the information is found. The joy of discovery is shared, and this opens the door to seeking more answers.

Many children pick up reading knowledge and reading skills as they become more familiar with book features. They will see regularities and differences in the book's illustrations and text that will aid them in their eventual desire to break the code of reading. An early type of reading has been witnessed by all experienced early childhood teachers. It is called imitative reading, and is defined as the child's reading the story from pictures, and sometimes speaking remembered text. Certain techniques can be used to encourage imitative reading. Reading and rereading favorites and reliving enjoyed sections helps. Giving attention and listening is positive encouragement for the child. A teacher can expect to hear some creative deviation from the book's original text, but correcting isn't advised. Instead, suggest other ways to read the picture book such as reading what is happening in each illustration in sequence. Consider children's imitative reading to be a mini-milestone.

Some preschoolers may begin to understand that the teacher is not telling a story or just reading illustrations but instead the teacher is reading the print (marks) in the book from left to right. The print may first look like strange rows of marks. As knowledge of the marks expands, the child may learn that the marks are single or grouped alphabet letters forming words, and that those words have spaces between them. Eventually the idea that alphabet letters represent sounds may become clear and then children may realize that the reader (teacher/adult) knows these sounds and can therefore "read" and speak words aloud. Many preschoolers recognize single words in books, particularly those that have been read and reread to them often. Some preschoolers develop a small sight word vocabulary and a few become actual readers of simple text. Eventually children come to know that readers use different parts of the text—such as words, photographs and illustrations, graphs, visual images, and the context of reading—to discern meaning.

Educators encourage children to learn how to care for books and where and how they can be used. Attitudes about books as valuable personal possessions should be instilled during early childhood. A number of emerging behaviors and skills will be noticed as children become fond of books. Learning to read is a complex skill that depends on smaller skills, some of which children develop during story times and by browsing through books on their own.

8-2a Common Core State Standards (CCSS)

Early childhood educators have become masterful "multitaskers" during read alouds. They select high-quality fiction and informational picture books and try to instill a joy, and hopefully a love, of picture book experiences. But educators also recognize a skilled reader can at the same time further children's literacy growth skills. By using planned and thoughtful strategies before, during, and after readings, they can achieve additional instructional goals. *Common Core State Standards for English Language Arts* (CCSS) (2010) sets specific expectations for kindergarten children in the areas of phonological awareness, print awareness, phonics, vocabulary, and comprehension. This text provides information on using read alouds to address these key literacy skills at preschool level.

8-2b Using Literature to Aid Conflict-Resolution Skills and Problem Solving

Concerned with rising levels of violence in our society, early childhood teachers are attempting to use picture books and stories to help children identify and define problems, a first step in conflict resolution. Books can be a valuable tool. Illustrations and book text may help children learn the conflict-resolution skills of **visualization** and empathy by providing nonviolent resolution to story-line disputes, portraying different types of conflicts, and giving examples of peacemaking at work.

Should early childhood educators use literature to help young children deal with their emotions and develop positive character traits? Kara-Soteriou & Rose (2008) point out that some picture books can encourage children's formulation of right and wrong. Many picture books depict good and bad behavior, whether teachers decide to discuss these themes is up to the school.

8-2c Selecting Book Collections for a Particular Classroom's Goals and Needs

Teachers are responsible for selecting quality books that meet the school's stated goals; often, teachers are asked to select new books for the school's collection. Book selection is not an easy task for teachers. When choosing books, educators must give much thought to each book's content and its relevance to particular children (Figure 8-2). They must be sensitive to how children might personalize a story. Teachers keep in mind family situations, cultures, religions, and social biases when they select. Some books may fill the needs completely; others may only partially meet the goals of instruction. The local library offers the opportunity to borrow books that can help keep storytelling time fresh and interesting, and children's librarians can be valuable resources.

Even when careful thought has been put into selecting a book, one child may like a book that another child does not. Some stories appeal more to one group than to another. Stories that are enjoyed most often become old favorites. Children who know the story often look forward to a familiar part or character. Selected books should match the children's needs, and their changing interests. They need books that range from simple to more difficult. They need books that are relevant and reflect the social and cultural reality of their daily lives.

Professional books and journals abound with ideas concerning the types of books that children like best. Some writers believe that simple fairy-tale picture books with animal characters that possess lifelike characteristics are preferred. Others mention that certain children want "true" stories. Most writers agree the success of any book for young children depends on its presentation of basic human tasks, needs, and concerns based on children's perceptions, and at a level at which they can respond. Condescending books that trivialize their concerns and efforts and present easy answers to complex problems are discarded for meaningful ones. Books that have intergeneration representations need to have realistic and sensitive depictions free of stereotypes of the old, young, teenagers, or any other age group.

Many families and educators have concerns about the violent nature of some folk and **fairy tales**. Others believe that children already know the world can be a dangerous and sometimes cruel place. Many old stories involve justice— good things happening to people with good behavior and bad things happening to people with bad behavior. Individual teachers and staff groups may decide that some folk tales are too violent, gory, or inappropriate for the age or living circumstances of attending children. Each book needs examination. It is likely that, at times, staff opinions will differ.

Some beginning teachers worry about book characters such as talking bears and rabbits.

---

visualization — the process, or result, of mentally picturing objects or events that are normally experienced directly.

fairy tales — folk stories about real-life problems, usually with imaginary characters and magical events.

Figure 8-2 Form for analyzing children's books.

Name _____ Date _____
Name of Book _____
Author _____
Illustrator _____
Story Line _____
1. What is the book's message? _____
   _____
   _____

2. Does the theme build the child's self-image or self-esteem? How? _____
   _____
   _____
   _____

3. Are male and female or ethnic groups stereotyped? _____

4. Why do you consider this book quality literature? _____
   _____
   _____

Illustrations _____
1. Fantasy? True to life? _____
2. Do they add to the book's enjoyment? _____
   _____

General Considerations
Could you read this book enthusiastically? Why?
How could you involve children in the book (besides looking and listening)?
How could you "categorize" this book? (e.g., firefighter, alphabet book, concept development, emotions, and so on)
On a scale of 1–10 (1—little value to 10—of great value to the young child) rate this book. _____

Digital Download

Make-believe during preschool years is an ever-increasing play pursuit. Most educators are not concerned if bears talk if the message of their speech is something with which children can identify. But they reject other stories that may seem more realistic if the problems the characters face have little to do with children's emotional lives.

The clear-cut story lines in many folk and fairy tales have stood the test of time and are recommended for a teacher's first attempts at reading to preschoolers. Good literature has something of meaning to offer any reader of any age, although on different levels of comprehension and appreciation. Each child will interpret and react to each book from an individual point of view, based on his unique experience.

Early childhood educators should include books depicting people with disabilities so that children can understand and accept people with varying abilities. This group of individuals has been overlooked and inadequately presented in children's books. It is prudent to be on the lookout for this type of depiction of physical differences in picture books.

You will want to introduce books with excellent language usage, ones that enchant and create beautiful images using the best grammatical structure, vocabulary, and imaginative style—in other words, memorable quality books.

8-2d Selecting Books for Specific Purposes

One might select a particular picture book because it increases children's knowledge on a certain subject or topic or its text includes a number of content-related words. Carle's (1969), *The Very Hungry Caterpillar*, is an excellent example of this, for it offers the life cycle of a caterpillar with many scientific and accurate content words. Other picture books support a wide range of teaching goals such as alphabet letter recognition, letter-sound correspondence, mathematical concepts, rhyming, wordplay, challenging vocabulary, graphics, technical illustrations, and so on. Books can be full of examples of cause and effect, classification, sorting, similarities and differences, action and reaction, or can involve predicting consequences. All of these features can promote intellectual growth if discussed and understood. There can be multiple reasons for sharing a book, rather than just one outstanding feature.

8-2e Reading Different Kinds (Categories) of Books

Children's book publishing is a booming business. Many types of books are available, as illustrated in Figure 8-3, which lists various categories in the left column. The figure identifies the major genre classifications and formats of children's books used in preschool classrooms, but it excludes poetry, which is discussed in another chapter. Many books do not fit neatly into a single category; some books may fit into two or more categories.

A vast and surprising variety of novelty books are also in print: floating books for bath time; soft, huggable books for bedtime; pocket-sized books; jumbo board and easel books (Scholastic); lift-the-flap books; flipbooks (Little, Brown & Co.); books that glow in the dark; sing-a-story books (Bantam); potty-training books (Barron's); and even books within books.

Figure 8-3 Categories of children's books.

TYPES	FEATURES TEACHERS LIKE	FEATURES CHILDREN LIKE
Storybooks (picture books) • family and home • folktales and fables • fanciful stories • fairy tales • animal stories • others	sharing moments seeing children enthusiastic and attentive making characters' voices introducing human truths and imaginative adventures sharing favorites easy for child to identify with small creatures	imagination and fantasy identification with characters' humanness wish and need fulfillment adventure excitement action self-realization visual variety word pleasure
Nonfiction books (informational) also referred to as *content books*	expand individual and group interests develop "reading-to-know" attitudes encourage finding out together provide accurate facts contain scientific content	provide facts; allow for discovery of information and ideas discuss reality and how things work and function answer "why" and "how" supply new words and new meanings
Wordless books	promote child speech, creativity, and imagination	provide opportunity to supply their own words to tell the story promote discovery of meanings include color, action, and visual variety
Interaction books (books with active child participation built in)	keep children involved and attentive build listening for directions skills	provide for movement and group feeling promote individual creativity and expression appeal to senses have manipulatable features
Concept books (books with central concepts or themes that include specific and reinforcing examples)	promote categorization present opportunities to know about and develop concepts many examples	add to knowledge visually present abstractions

Figure 8-3 (*continued*)

TYPES	FEATURES TEACHERS LIKE	FEATURES CHILDREN LIKE
Predictable books (books with repetitions and reinforcement)	permit successful guessing build child's confidence promote ideas that books make sense	provide opportunity to read along are repetitive build feelings of competence
Reference books (picture dictionaries, encyclopedias, special subject books)	provide opportunity to look up questions with the child promote individualized learning	provide answers are used with teacher (shared time) are resources that answer their questions
Alphabet and word books (word books have name of object printed near or on top of object)	supply letters and word models pair words and objects are useful for child with avid interest in alphabet letters and words can include letter and word play	discover meanings and alphabet letters and words see names of what is illustrated
Novelty books (pop-ups, fold-outs, electronic books, stamp and pasting books, activity books, puzzle books, scratch-andsniff books, hidden objects in illustrations, talking books) *Paperback books and magazines* (*Golden Books, Humpty Dumpty Magazine*)	add sense-exploring variety stimulate creativity come in many different sizes and shapes motor involvement for child many include humor are inexpensive come in a wide variety many classics available	encourage exploring, touching, moving, feeling, smelling, painting, drawing, coloring, cutting, gluing, acting upon, listening to a mechanical voice, and getting instant feedback include activity pages
Teacher- and child-made books	reinforce class learnings build understanding of authorship allow creative expression record individual, group projects, field trips, parties promote child expression of concerns and ideas build child's self-esteem	allow child to see own name in print provide opportunity to share ideas with others are self-rewarding
Therapeutic books (books helping children cope with and understand things such as divorce, death, jealousy)	present life realistically offer positive solutions and insights present diverse family groups deal with life's hard-to-deal-with subjects	help children discuss real feelings
Seasonal and holiday books	accompany child interest may help child understand underlying reasons for celebration	build pleasant expectations add details
Books and audiovisual combinations (read-alongs)	add variety offer group and individual experiencing opportunities stimulate interest in books	project large illustrations can be enjoyed individually
Toddler books and board books (durable pages)	resist wear and tear	are easy to use (ease in page-turning)
Multicultural and cross-cultural books (culturally conscious books)	increase positive attitudes concerning diversity and similarity	introduce a variety of people
Oversized books (big books)	emphasize the realities in our society have extra large text and illustrations	are easy-to-see in groups have giant book characters

Oversized Books (Big Books). Big, giant, and jumbo (20-by-30 or 24-by-36 inches) are descriptors used to identify oversized books. Publishers are mass producing this size book because of their increased popularity with both early childhood educators and whole-language curriculum advocates. Because they are easily viewed by groups of children, oversized books have been added to teacher curriculum collections. New and classic titles abound. Because the text is large, it is not overlooked by young children. Found in soft and hard cover versions with brilliant-colored illustrations, some have accompanying CDs and small book editions. Teachers use chalkboard gutters or art easels as book holders. Enlarged texts (Big Books) allow groups of children to see and react to the printed page. Active participation and unison participation can be encouraged. Using a hand to underline words while reading, the teacher can focus attention on print and its directionality.

Alphabet Books. Singing and learning the "Alphabet Song" is often a child's first introduction to the alphabet, one that precedes and promotes an interest in alphabet books. For a further discussion of alphabet books and print awareness, see Chapter 14.

Nonfiction Books. Teachers may encounter and share nonfiction books that answer children's questions, are related to a curriculum theme, or serve another teaching purpose, such as providing pictorial information. Nonfiction books can teach concepts and terms associated with various topics, people, places, and things children may never encounter in real life. A book with a simplified explanation of how water comes out of a faucet serves as an example. Nonfiction (books) may be perceived as more appropriate for older grades, and a real revolution has occurred in recent years in the writing and production of nonfiction books for young children. Much of the knowledge of our society, and many other societies, is accumulated in our nonfiction text (Duke, 2007). Duke notes:

- Using nonfiction reference materials in the classroom allows children to see one important and common reason that people read.

- For some children, reading nonfiction reference materials may be an especially compelling reason to read.

- Reading nonfiction reference materials may help deepen concepts of print and genre knowledge.

- Reading nonfiction reference materials provides a forum for building computer literacy.

- Reading nonfiction for reference provides another tool for developing comprehension and world knowledge. (p. 13)

Early childhood educators' attitudes concerning fiction and nonfiction books are changing due to the academic standards being adopted in most states. Common Core State Standards (2010) clearly position reading as the centerpiece of learning (Neuman and Roskos, 2012). The standards promote a more prominent exposure to nonfiction (informational) books. Nonfiction picture books may contain interesting storylines, narrative text and considerable vocabulary that is important to understand presented concepts and information on specific topics or themes. This does not mean that fictional picture books are not as valuable as before, for they also convey ideas and concepts through story, besides offering literary and literacy elements (Fisher and Frey, 2013).

Pentimonti et al. (2010) use the term *informational genres* to refer to two distinct types of text: expository texts (nonfiction) and mixed texts. Mixed texts are hybrids that blur the lines between genre categories. They contain features typical of both narrative and **expository** genres (Donavan and Smolkin, 2002).

Additional benefits for sharing nonfiction books can include introducing *technical* vocabulary and mathematics and science concepts. Nonfiction books may better suit the needs and interests of attending boys and girls who want answers to real-world questions. Nonfiction picture book illustrations can often aid vocabulary development, especially if they accurately depict word meanings. Teachers may believe nonfiction will not hold children's attention. They may not know that many are related in cumulative story form, some are wordless, and others have rhythmic features or include poetry. Most cover interesting topics, pique curiosity, and offer a

---

expository — provides accurate verifiable information about the social or natural world.

Figure 8-4 Tips for selecting informational texts.

LANGUAGE

Does the material:
- use simple, straightforward vocabulary?
- include some specific scientific or technical terms?
- present special or technical terms or context?
- use short, direct sentences?

IDEAS AND ORGANIZATION

Does the material:
- present one idea at a time?
- provide specific and concrete information?
- show relationships among ideas that are explicit and simple (e.g., sequence, cause-effect, descriptions)?
- use short paragraphs that begin with a clear topic sentence followed by details?
- use bold titles and headings?

GRAPHICS AND FORMAT

Does the material use:
- illustrations and graphics to support and provide content?
- clear relationship between text and illustrations?
- illustrations that elaborate and clarify the written text?
- type size that is 14 point or larger?

Digital Download

closer look at the world. Figure 8-4 offers tips on selecting quality nonfiction titles.

Early childhood teachers who are rediscovering informational texts find they often lead to projects, specimen collections, producing simple graphs, mapmaking, child interviewing activities, child reporting activities, documenting and recording activities, and interesting classroom displays. Best of all a "let's find out about it together" search can make a school day more exciting and rewarding.

Teachers realize that photographs, realistic drawings, paintings, collages, and other images should be accurate because young readers attend most directly to illustrations. If informational books sacrifice this, reject them.

A nonfiction book may be one or more people's opinion rather than widely accepted fact. Elementary school teachers purposely offer conflicting readings to promote discussion and critical thinking. At the preschool level, critical analysis is more commonly promoted during oral discussions.

Given a choice of reading materials, young children are as likely to state a preference for informational picture books as for fictional ones. The effects of immersing young children in nonfiction picture books are not fully documented in research. Most practicing teachers know children readily use and consult them. Examples of classroom nonfiction books follow.

Falk, L. (2009). This is the way we go to school: A book about children around the world. New York: Scholastic.

Hatkoff, J., Hatkoff, I., & Hatkoff, C. (2009). Winter's tail: How one little dolphin learns to swim again. New York: Scholastic.

Taus-Bolstad, S. (2013). From wheat to bread. New York: Lerner.

Kirby, P. F. (2009). *What bluebirds do.* Honesdale, PA: Boyds Mills.

After conducting a study of informational picture book read-alouds in early childhood classrooms, Pentimonti et al. (2010) suggest educators take several steps to begin to integrate informational nonfiction books into daily read-alouds. The steps include selecting books relevant to standards and preparing for discussions on key points. Identifying words that need clarification is also recommended. Book follow up activities might be planned for learning centers.

A growing number of favorite books put to music, and favorite songs published as books, are available. An adult sings as pages are turned. Teachers can introduce this literary experience and encourage children to join in. The added advantage of visual representations helps induce the child to sing. The novelty of a teacher singing a book also offers a possible incentive for the child to select this type of book because of his familiarity with an already memorized and perhaps enjoyed song. Word recognition is sometimes readily accomplished. Popular books of this type include the following:

de Paola, T. (1984). *Mary had a little lamb.* New York: Holiday House.

Kovalski, M. (1987). *The wheels on the bus.* Boston: Little, Brown & Co.

McNalley, D. (1991). *In a cabin in a wood.* New York: Cobblehill/Dutton.

Books With Nonviolent Themes. A good number of educators are offering picture books whose story lines include conflict resolution. These can lead to group discussion. Because many stories involve a conflict to overcome, it is not difficult to find positive models of character's actions, words, and behaviors in picture books.

8-2f Reading Books to Boys

Studies by Zambo (2007) and other researchers suggest preschool boys may have already formed a gender stereotype, believing that books and reading are an activity thought to be primarily associated females. When reading instruction begins, boys have more reading problems, take longer to learn, express less enthusiasm for reading, and, generally speaking, don't perform as well as girls on all types of standardized reading tests. Many educators attribute these boy behaviors to two crucial elements: motivation and attitude (Boltz, 2007). Early childhood educators realize they may build a positive attitude toward books in boys in many ways. Some of the most common are to provide read alouds with lots of action, overlook boys fidgetiness at reading time due to a boy's high energy level, help boys maintain attentiveness, watch the length of sitting necessary, select book subjects of particular interest to males, suggest acting out words or story parts, and promoting boys' confidence that their ideas and their oral statements concerning the book's content are accepted and appreciated. The wise teacher obtains individual interest books for individual boys. Extra efforts to engage African-American boys is critically prudent to attempt to mitigate and change the undeniable achievement gap that separates some young black males and their peers in elementary school classrooms in reading ability and achievement.

8-2g Interactive Technology

Technology and young children's books have been combined by companies like LeapFrog, Fisher-Price, and Publications International. With a touch of the finger or a stylus, a young child can flip pages, hear any particular word pronounced, hear a book read by a clear voice, select the reader's pace, play games, hear word definitions, and take quizzes. Some models have light attachments and a microphone. Some teach phonics; encourage children to pronounce phonemes, words, and sentences; and prompt children to record their names, which are then put into stories. Some models focus on writing skills and enable children to trace alphabet letters, work mazes, or engage in dot-to-dot activities or handwriting exercises. Individual companies have developed over 70 children's book titles that use technology.

Families are lured by educative features, and some preschools are adding electronic books to their book collections. Prices vary, but they usually are not prohibitive for the average center.

The terms digital book and e-book are sometimes used interchangeably and considered to be the same thing, even though e-books are usually static while digital books have multimedia features such as sound or other elements. An original digital book is specifically created to be read on a digital device. Other digital books were first published books and then turned into digital formats. There is an increasing use of e-books. A good number of young children have experienced them. Preschool figures are yet unavailable. Quality has become an issue with educators as both self-published e-books and digital bookstores grow. Educators are beginning to recognize high-quality digital publishing companies and are using websites that conduct e-book and digital book reviews. They are also conducting their own research and designing screening procedures to gain knowledge and the ability to assist parents and families in digital and e-book selection for children.

Educators do know that besides print and graphics, e-books can include multimodal features, such as sounds, music, animation, and videos. E-books most often are read with minimal adult involvement. What is unknown is whether e-books support or impede child comprehension. A few researchers believe e-books' features can be alternately beneficial and problematic (Verhallen, Bus, dejong, 2006). Other researchers theorize multimedia features may support children's ability to make inferences about characters' actions and feelings; but multimedia overload may concurrently inhibit and tax children's working memory. Another unknown is whether a child e-book reader is game playing, listening, or actually reading the text and what percentage of the child's time is given to each activity. Although controversial and unsubstantiated, some researchers believe distracting information embedded in an e-book's text may divert the reader away from main or key ideas and book meaning by focusing the child on clever but unimportant story details.

8-3 Criteria for Read-Alouds

Consider the attention span, maturity, interests, personality, and age of children you are targeting when selecting books. Developing broad literary and artistic tastes is another important idea. The following is a series of questions a teacher could use when choosing a child's book to read aloud.

1. Could I read this book enthusiastically, really enjoying the story?

2. Are the contents of the book appropriate for the children with whom I work?
   a. Can the children relate some parts to their lives and past experiences?
   b. Can the children identify with one or more of the characters?

   Look at some children's classics, such as *Mother Goose.* Almost all of the stories have a well-defined character with which children share some common feature. Teachers find that different children identify with different characters—the wolf instead of one of the pigs in *The Three Little Pigs*, for example.

3. Does the book have directly quoted conversation?
   a. If it does, this can add interest; for example, "Are you my mother?" he said to the cow.

4. Will the child benefit from attitudes and models found in the book? Many books model behaviors that are unsuitable for the young child. Also, consider the following questions when analyzing a book for unfavorable racial stereotypes or sexism.

5. Who are the "doers" and "inactive observers"?

6. Are characters' achievements based on their own initiative, insights, or intelligence?

7. Who performs the brave and important deeds?

8. Are value and worth connected to skin color and economic resources?

9. Does language or setting ridicule or demean a specific group of individuals?
   a. Are individuals treated as such rather than as one of a group?
   b. Are ethnic groups or individuals treated as though everyone in that group has the same human talent, ability, food preference, and hairstyle, taste in clothing, or human weakness or characteristic?
   c. Do illustrations capture natural-looking ethnic variations?

10. Does this book broaden the cross-cultural element in the multicultural selection of books offered at my school?
    a. Is the book accurate and authentic in its portrayal of individuals and groups?

11. Was the book written with an understanding of preschool age-level characteristics?
    a. Is the text too long to sit through? Are there too many words?
    b. Are there enough colorful or action-packed pictures or illustrations to hold attention?
    c. Is the size of the book suitable for easy handling in groups or for individual viewing?
    d. Can the child participate in the story by speaking or making actions?
    e. Is the fairy tale or folktale too complex, symbolic, and confusing to have meaning?

12. Is the author's style enjoyable?
    a. Is the book written clearly with a vocabulary and sequence the children can understand?
    b. Are memorable words or phrases found in the book?
    c. Are repetitions of words, actions, rhymes, or story parts used? (Anticipated repetition is part of the young child's enjoyment of stories. Molly Bang's *Ten, Nine, Eight* contains this feature.)

13. Does the story develop and end with a satisfying climax of events?

14. Are there humorous parts and silly names? The young child's humor is often slapstick in nature (pie-in-the-face, all-fall-down type rather than play on words). The ridiculous and farfetched often tickle them. Tomie de Paola's *Pancakes for Breakfast* (Harcourt, Brace, Jovanovich) is a wordless book.

15. Does it have educational value? (See Photo 8-5.)
    a. Could you use it to expand knowledge in any special way? Maureen Roffey's

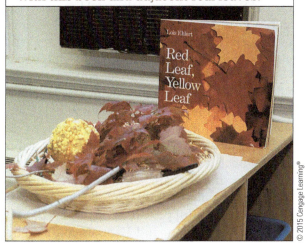

Photo 8-5 Color words are easily learned with this book and adjacent real leaves.

© 2015 Cengage Learning®

Home, Sweet Home (Coward) depicts animal living quarters in a delightful way.

b. Does it offer new vocabulary? Does it increase or broaden understanding? Masayuki Yabuuchi's *Animals Sleeping* (Philomel) is an example.

16. Do pictures (illustrations) explain and coordinate well with the text? Jane Miller's *Farm Counting Book* (Prentice Hall) has both of these features.

Some books meet most criteria of the established standards; others meet only a few. The age of attending children makes some criteria more important than others. Schools often select copies of accepted old classics. These titles are considered part of our cultural heritage, ones that most American preschoolers know and have experienced (Figure 8-5). Many classics have been handed down through the oral tradition of storytelling and can contain archaic words, such as *stile* and *sixpence*. *Green Eggs and Ham* by Dr. Seuss (Random House) is a recognized classic and is frequently mentioned in surveys of children's favorites. Most teachers try to offer the best in children's literature and a wide variety of book types

Anderson (2007) points out that much of children's literature is moralistic but may also contain excellent literature that is pleasurable to young children. If a book contains a moral or important human truth, look to see if it also shies away from an obvious, overdone attempt to teach.

8-3a Reading Aloud Culturally Conscious and Culturally Diverse Books

Multicultural literature can be defined as children's literature that represents any distinct cultural group through accurate portrayal and rich detail. Educators urge teachers to evaluate multicultural children's literature by examining both literary quality and cultural consciousness before reading them to groups. A different definition of multicultural literature states that

Figure 8-5 Stories, songs, rhymes, and poems considered classics for preschoolers.

A PARTIAL LISTING

"Ba, Ba, Black Sheep"	"Little Girl with a Curl"	"Row, Row, Row Your Boat"
Chicken Little	"Little Jack Horner"	"Silent Night"
"There Was a Crooked Man"	"Little Miss Muffet"	"Simple Simon"
Goldilocks and the Three Bears	*The Little Red Hen*	"Sing a Song of Sixpence"
"Here We Go Round the Mulberry Bush"	"Little Robin Redbreast"	"Take Me Out to the Ball Game"
"Hey Diddle, Diddle (the Cat and the Fiddle)"	"London Bridge Is Falling Down"	*The Three Bears*
	"Mary Had a Little Lamb"	*The Three Billy Goats Gruff*
"Hickory, Dickory, Dock"	"Mary, Mary, Quite Contrary"	"The Three Blind Mice"
"Humpty Dumpty"	"Old King Cole"	*The Three Little Pigs*
"Jack and Jill"	"Old Mother Hubbard"	"To Market, to Market"
Jack and the Beanstalk	"The Old Woman Who Lived in a Shoe"	"Twinkle, Twinkle, Little Star"
"Jack Be Nimble"	"Peter Piper"	*Ugly Duckling*
"Jack Sprat"	"Pop Goes the Weasel"	"You Are My Sunshine"
"Little Bo Peep"	"Ride a Cock Horse (Banbury Cross)"	
"Little Boy Blue"	"Rock-a-Bye Baby"	

multicultural literature is about some identifiable "other," a person or group, that differs in some way (e.g., racially, linguistically, ethnically, culturally) from the Caucasian-American cultural group. Publishers are beginning to create books depicting gay and lesbian families in loving relationships, such as *Molly's Family* (2004). When a center is selecting books, staff members will need to discuss whether books depicting gay and lesbian families fit into their book collection.

The question of authenticity or, more correctly, what constitutes an accurate portrayal of a culture, has plagued educators for years. Teachers try hard to present an authentic portrayal of cultural reality in the books they select. Multicultural books offer opportunities for children to learn to recognize similarities, value differences, and also respect common humanity. Children need literature that serves as a window into lives and experiences that are different from their own, and literature that serves as a mirror reflecting themselves and their cultural values, attitudes, and behaviors.

The books listed in the Additional Resources section at the end of this chapter include not only African-Americans, Asian-Americans, Hispanic Americans/Latinos, and Native Americans, but also subgroups of different and distinct groups under each heading. Other world groups are also included.

When offering multicultural and multiethnic books to young children, no attempt to give these books special status is suggested. Children's questions and comments that arise are discussed as all interesting books are discussed. These books are not shared only at certain times of year or for recognized celebrations but are included as regular, standard classroom fare.

Multicultural picture books may help a child from a diverse background by validating and affirming his life experiences as being part of a larger American culture (Oslick, 2013). This is especially true if a book mirrors and reflects similar looking living conditions, a family's cultural and ethnic characteristics, family structure, and community settings, in other words, the child's own circumstances. It also aids and promotes a child's development of a positive attitude toward books and book reading, especially if the story is enjoyed and the child identifies with a book's character who finds a solution to a recognizable life problem.

Hispanic children's literature does not refer to one culture but rather a conglomerate of Central and South American cultures. Hispanics have been poorly represented in children's literature until recently. Books that existed were often folktales or remembrances of an author's childhood.

In picture books classified as depicting the Asian culture, one may find Chinese, Japanese, Korean, Taiwanese, Laotian, Vietnamese, Cambodian, and Filipino cultural experiences depicted. Increasingly, published books about Asians deal with Asian assimilation into the American mainstream. One can find numerous books dealing with Asian folktales. Yet to be written are plentiful picture books from the Vietnamese, Cambodian, and Laotian cultures, but they are slowly appearing.

Books concerning Native Americans can be easier to locate. Most are folktales, but some deal with rituals, ceremony, everyday life, family joys, and problems. Books depicting Middle Eastern cultures are scarce. Again, the teacher needs to screen for stereotypical characteristics.

8-3b Bibliotherapy

Bibliotherapy, literally translated, means book therapy. Teachers, at times, may seek to help children with life problems, questions, fears, and pain. Some professionals believe that books can help children cope with emotional concerns. At some point during childhood, children may deal with rejection by friends, ambivalence toward a new baby, divorce, grief, or death, along with other strong emotions.

Fairy tales can reveal the existence of strife and calamity in a form that permits children to deal with these situations without trauma. These tales can be shared in a reassuring, supportive setting that provides a therapeutic experience. A small sampling of books considered to be therapeutic in nature follows.

Gershator, P. (2004). *The babysitter sings.* New York: Henry Holt. (Separation.)

Le Tord, B. (1987). *My Grandma Leonie.* New York: Bradbury Press. (Death.)

Mayer, M. (1968). *There's a nightmare in my closet.* New York: Dial. (Fear.)

Parr, T. (2001). *It's okay to be different.* Boston: Little Brown. (Rejection.)

Viorst, J. (1973). *The tenth good thing about Barney.* New York: Atheneum. (Death of a pet.)

8-4 Teacher Skills, Techniques, and Strategies When Reading

naeyc DAP

Teachers read books in both indoor and outdoor settings, to one child or to many. Koralek (2007) suggests that teachers look beyond the library corner as the only place to display, share, and read books with young children. Books can be linked to all areas of the curriculum, she feels. Her recommendations include carrying books outdoors, placing them near discovery tables, and displaying them alongside dress-up clothes. Other suggested areas are block areas, housekeeping areas, window seats where natural outdoor settings can be viewed, theme and display areas, and room settings where counting or number concepts are explored. Other room areas with comfortable seating should not be overlooked.

Mem Fox (2001) reveals the gift and opportunity teachers (and all adults) have when they participate in the act of reading aloud to young children.

> Engaging in this kind of conspiracy with children is perhaps the greatest benefit of reading aloud to them. As we share the words and pictures, the ideas and viewpoints, the rhythms and rhymes, the pain and comfort, and the hopes and fears and big issues of life that we encounter together in the pages of a book, we connect together in the pages of a book, we connect through minds and hearts with our children and bond closely in a secret society associated with books we have shared. The fire of literacy is created by the emotional sparks between a child, a book, and the person reading. It isn't achieved by the book alone, or by the adult who is reading aloud—it's the relationship winding between all three, bringing them together in easy harmony. (p. 10)

Teachers need to assess their ability to make books and book-reading times exciting and personally relevant and rewarding to each young child. In successful classrooms, observable child behaviors include eager attendance at book-reading times, joyous participation, active dialogue, and self-selected investigation and time spent in the classroom library.

How the teacher achieves this is critical. Most of us have seen well-meaning adults use reading techniques that are questionable and defeat the adult's purpose in reading. Your goals should include making reading aloud times an activity of intrinsic interest to the children, adding to children's comprehension of the world, and stimulating children's imagination. Some educators encourage the storybook reader to make comments and ask questions during the reading experience to increase child comprehension. Others believe maintaining the flow and tempo of the story to be paramount so that the story's literary quality remains intact. The first story readers might query factual details, child opinions, or during the reading ask children to infer, label, evaluate, summarize, elaborate, and predict. They might also make comments that point out, explain, or build bridges to children's experiences during story reading. While others, following the second method would instead save teacher comments and questions for an after-story discussion. A beginning teacher can attempt to ascertain if either approach is at work at their center. Or perhaps both approaches are used or the center has its own unique approach to reading aloud.

The burden of making reading interesting falls on the teacher. A teacher must also strive to make the book's content relevant to each child. This means relating and connecting story elements to children's lives and their past experiences whenever possible. This can be likened to building a bridge to the world of books—a bridge that children will be eager to cross because books are pleasurable and emotionally satisfying. Building these positive attitudes takes skill. A step-by-step outline is helpful in conducting group story times.

Step 1: *Think about the age, interests, and special interests of the child group and consider the selection criteria mentioned in this chapter.* If you are required to write a lesson plan for sharing a particular book, identify possible unfamiliar vocabulary and what child comprehension goals you are planning to achieve. Read the book to yourself enough times to develop a feeling for characters and the story line. Practice dialogue so that it will roll smoothly. For example, you might not be able to read *The House That Jack Built* unless you have practiced the incremental refrain. In other words, analyze, select, practice, and prepare.

Step 2: *Arrange a setting with the children's and teacher's comfort in mind.* The illustrations should be at children's eye level, and the teacher should face the audience as she speaks. A setting should provide comfortable seating while the book is being read. Some teachers prefer small chairs for both children and teachers; others prefer rug areas. Avoid traffic paths and noise interruptions by finding a quiet spot in the classroom. Cutting down visual distractions may mean using room dividers, curtains, or furniture arrangements.

Preschoolers who are read to in small groups make greater language gains than when they are read to in larger groups. Some classrooms use "instant replays" of storybook readings when adult supervision affects group size.

Step 3: *Make a motivational introductory statement.* The statement should create a desire to listen or encourage listening: "There's a boy in this book who wants to give his mother a birthday present"; "Monkeys can be funny, and they are funny in this book"; "Have you ever wondered where animals go at night to sleep?"; "On the last page of this book is a picture of a friendly monster." Then briefly introduce the author and illustrator.

Anderson (2007) suggests starting by showing the book's cover or first illustration and asking the group to predict book content using questions such as "What do you think might happen in this book?" Serafini (2012) challenges the wisdom of overusing this kind of book beginning and suggests using an alternate strategy, such as asking both what the children notice on the cover, and what they know about it before asking for prediction. This elicits a focus upon what is at hand as much as what is coming next.

Step 4: *Hold the book to either your left or right side or beneath the bottom centerfold.* With your hand in place, make both sides of the page visible. Keep the book at the children's eye level.

Step 5: *Begin reading.* Try to glance at the sentences and turn to meet the children's eyes as often as possible so that your voice goes to the children. Also watch for children's body reactions, including facial expressions, and try to ascertain whether children are engaged and understanding or have quizzical looks. Speak clearly with adequate volume, using a rate of speed that enables the children to both look at illustrations and hear what you are reading. Enjoy the story with the children by being enthusiastic. Dramatize and emphasize key parts of the story, but not to the degree that the children are watching you and not the book. Change your voice to suit the characters, if you feel comfortable doing so. A good story will hold attention and often stimulate comments or questions. Savor it and deliver each word. Try not to rush unless it adds to the drama in places.

Step 6: *Answer and discuss questions approvingly, and if necessary or prudent increase child interaction by guessing about or labeling character actions.* If you feel that interruptions are decreasing the enjoyment for other children, ask a child to wait until the end when you will be glad to discuss it. Then do it. If, on the other hand, most of the group is interested, take the time to discuss an idea, but be careful to resist the temptation of making a lengthy comment that will disrupt the story. Sometimes, children suck their thumbs or act sleepy during reading times. They seem to connect books with bedtime; many parents read to their children at this time. By watching closely while reading, you will be able to tell whether you still have the children's attention. You can sometimes draw a child back to the book with a direct question like, "Debbie, can you see the cat's tail?" or by increasing your animation or varying voice volume. Wondering out loud about what might happen next may help. For help in promoting child comprehension and analysis, read An Approach to Promote Comprehension that appears later in this chapter.

Step 7: You may want to ask a number of previously planned questions that deal with the book's story problem or probe the comprehension of main book elements. Creating questions that help clarify what the children newly understand about the story and how this relates to their lives and experiences is helpful. Open ended questions are okay when your goal is to encourage children to share their ideas and oral opinions. Keep questions spontaneous and natural—avoiding testing questions. Questions can clear up ideas, encourage use of vocabulary words, and pinpoint parts that were especially enjoyed. "Does anyone have a question about the fire truck?"

If you have initially asked for story predictions, this is the time to follow up with "Was your prediction about what was going to happen in this book correct?"

You will have to decide whether to read more than one book at one time. It helps remember how long the group of children can sit before getting restless. Story times should end on an enthusiastic note, with the children looking forward to another story. Some books may end on such a satisfying or thoughtful note that discussion clearly is not appropriate; a short pause of silence seems more in order. Other times, there may be a barrage of child comments and lively discussion.

Many children's comments incorporate the story into their own personal vision of things and indicate that the text has meaning for them. Personal meanings are confirmed, extended, and refined as children share their interpretations with others. The focus in after-book discussions is on meaning, and the goal is to "make sense of the text." If one wished to ascertain whether comprehension of certain story elements was achieved, one might ask about problems faced by the main characters, problem-solving solutions attempted, feelings characters displayed, or some other probe that refers to the main content of the book.

Judging oneself on the ability to capture and hold children's attention during group reading times is critical. Many factors can account for children's attention wandering, so analyze what can or did interfere with classroom focus. Factors to consider include group size, seating comfort, temperature, the way the light shines on the book, the child who cannot sit next to a friend without talking or touching, and so on, and, of course, the teacher's presentation skills. One teacher who hated distractions created a sign that read, "Story time; please wait to enter our room." The book itself may also need closer scrutiny.

Your personality will no doubt permeate your individual reading-aloud style. There is no exact right way (Fox, 2001). Become aware of your facial and body language, especially your expressiveness, your vocal variety, and animation at times. Hopefully, children will sense it is an especially enjoyable and looked-forward-to time as special for you as you wish it to be for them.

Teachers should examine daily programs to ensure that children have time to pursue favorite books and new selections (Photo 8-6). It is ridiculous to motivate then not allow self-selection or time for children to spend looking at and examining introduced books page by page at their own pace.

Additional Book-Reading Tips

- Check to make sure all of the children have a clear view of the book before beginning.

- Watch for combinations of children sitting side-by-side that may cause either child to be distracted. Rearrange seating before starting.

- Pause a short while to allow children to focus at the start.

- If one child seems to be unable to concentrate, a teacher can quietly suggest an alternative activity to the child. Clear understanding of alternatives or lack of them needs to be established with the entire staff.

- If one points to or makes references to print on a page occasionally, children will take notice, make more comments about print, and ask questions about it more frequently (Ezell & Justice, 2000).

Photo 8-6 There should be plenty of time to enjoy books with a friend.

- Moving a distracted child closer to the book, or onto a teacher's lap, sometimes works to improve attention.

- When an outside distraction occurs, recapture attention and make a transitional statement leading back to the story: "We all heard that loud noise. There's a different noise made by the steam shovel in our story. Listen and you'll hear the steam shovel's noise."

- Personalize books when appropriate: "Have you lost something and not been able to find it?"

- Shedd and Duke (2008) recommend teacher picture book reading discussions should go beyond the classroom and relate a book's feature to past or future happenings, if possible.

- Skip ahead in books, when the book can obviously not maintain interest, by quickly reading pictures and concluding the experience. It is a good idea to have a backup selection close by.

- Children often want to handle a book just read. Make a quick waiting list for all who wish to go over the book by themselves.

- Plan reading sessions at relaxed rather than rushed or hectic times of day.

- Handle books gently and carefully.

- At times when a new word with multiple syllables appears, repeat it, emphasizing syllables. Clap word syllables such as *festival* (fes-ti-val) and *interpreter* (in-ter-pret-er). This technique is primarily used with children nearing kindergarten age.

- Lower or raise your voice and quicken or slow your pace as appropriate to the text. Lengthen your dramatic pauses, and let your listeners savor the words and ideas.

- Introduce vocabulary words associated with the book sharing experience—*cover, title, author, illustrator, front, first page, beginning, print, middle, ending, turn, words, pictures, last page, ending, back cover.*

- Read a book a child has brought to school before you read it aloud to children. Share suitable "parts" only if necessary.

- Handle a child comment such as, "I've heard it before," with a recognizing comment such as, "Don't tell how it ends" or "See if you see something different this time."

- Savor new words as you introduce them. Think of them as words that are new friends entering the child's repertoire.

- Support and accept children's ideas without correcting or challenging.

- Unusual and fun-to-say words can be pronounced a few times for emphasis and either defined or looked up in the dictionary with children.

- Encourage children to talk about illustrations.

- Suggest children act out action verbs.

- Discuss what feeling illustrations arouse.

- After a book is familiar to children, reread it pausing and asking periodically, "What happens next?" Or "Then Beady Bear ___?" At the end ask, "Who knows how our story started?" "Then what happened?" Discuss making an event map together with children.

8-4a Clarifying the Act of Reading With Children

Teachers who want to enhance children's understanding of a book can elicit children's ideas about what might happen in a new book by examining its cover or interior illustrations. They might also focus on print (little marks in a row) or the title page, or the authors' or illustrators' names, or the first word in the story and where that word is found on the page, or the last word in the book, or the book's back cover. They can encourage children to "read" a book by using cover to cover illustrations.

Many teachers are more interested in building a love of books during preschool years than talking about book characteristics. But others believe that they are able to add to children's knowledge of books without diminishing children's enjoyment. What may preschoolers know about books?

- They contain stories and information.
- They can be read by adults and older children.
- A book has an author, and maybe an illustrator.
- The name of an author is usually printed on the book cover.
- Books have a front and back cover and first page.
- Adults read a page starting at the top left and read horizontally across the line of words.
- The last word on a page is usually printed on the right bottom corner.
- There are spaces between words.

- Words are made of alphabet letters.
- Letters are printed in capitals and small letters.

This is not a complete listing. Some children may know much more, including letter sounds, punctuation marks, and other print features.

8-4b Finger-Point Reading and Hand Underlining

Teachers often wonder if using a flat hand to underline words being read is appropriate. It is, but it depends upon the circumstances and the teacher. With chart reading or big book reading, one hand can easily do so because of print size. With most picture books, hand underlining would be awkward, block large portions of illustrations, and may distract the listeners.

Finger point reading is an accepted practice and is another technique to focus attention to the separate identity of words in a sentence while reading. Richgels (2013) suggests it is just one of a number of strategies used in reading and writing instruction. With both techniques it becomes a matter of teacher preference. There is meager research to confirm its value but some individual teachers have a strong conviction that it works.

8-4c Paraphrasing Stories

Paraphrasing means putting an author's text into one's own words, and this is done when some teachers realize the book or some other factor is interfering with children's ability to maintain attention. It brings the book to a speedy conclusion. By tampering with the text, the teacher may interfere with a book's intent, message, and style. Many professionals find this objectionable and urge teachers to read stories exactly as they are written, taking no liberties, respecting the author's original text. Other educators feel that when a book does not hold the interest of its audience, it should be saved for another time and place, perhaps another group. Some teachers believe that maintaining children's interest and preserving children's positive attitudes about books supersedes objections to occasional paraphrasing.

8-4d Targeting Words for Vocabulary Development and Building Participation

A recommended technique used to promote vocabulary development during book-sharing is referred to as targeting. The teacher attempts to ask open-ended questions during a book's re-reading, which allows the teacher to determine unfamiliar vocabulary words and then explain them. Explicit explanations are deemed best. Later, purposeful teacher use of the unfamiliar (target) words during daily or weekly activities takes place, therefore providing additional child exposure and deeper word understanding. To do this the teacher needs to guess which words her class may not know beforehand by scanning the book(s) to be shared.

When a picture book is identified as having the ability to reinforce or aid children's comprehension of theme-related concepts, teachers can decide which vocabulary words are salient to children's understanding. These then can be given particular teacher attention and emphasis during reading while teacher watches children's faces to assess their level of understanding. Teacher conversations in follow up activities can purposely include these vocabulary words to again connect, reinforce, and prompt child usage.

Words fit into a conceptual framework that surrounds any given topic selected for instruction or discussion. For example, if the topic is transportation, a conceptual framework includes the major concepts and realities of the topic. In the case of transportation, a short listing of some of these follows.

- People and **machines** may **transport** things from one **place** to another.
- There are many ways to do so. They are called **modes** of **transportation**.
- Forces of nature can **move** objects also.
- There can be different advantages and disadvantages for using one mode of transportation compared to another.
- People may own **vehicles**; machines or **tools** that help them transport things.

Often identified concepts of a topic can become goals for instruction and one can identify a set of vocabulary words used in any discussion of the topic. These are called set, key, or topic words. Identifying a listing of major concepts and realities of a topic can help a teacher identify significant set vocabulary words. They are the bold words above, but remember this was but a short example.

Children love to be part of the telling of a story. Good teachers plan for child participation when choosing stories to read. Often, books are read for the first time, and then immediately re-read, with the teacher promoting as much participation as possible. Some books hold children spellbound and usually take many readings before the teacher feels that it is the right time for active involvement other than listening. Listening skills are encouraged when children contribute to read-aloud sessions and become active, participating listeners. Three-year-olds take awhile to settle into appropriate and expected story-time behaviors. A young group may heartily enjoy the physical participation opportunities that a teacher plans ahead of time. This is possible if she has recognized portions of the about-to-be-read picture book where children can chime in, make movements or sounds, or in other ways mirror or duplicate something in the story.

Nonfiction books may not provide many opportunities for child involvement. Examining them closely may give the teacher ideas for children's active participation. Many of the benefits young children derive from adult-child readings come through adult reading strategies such as prompting responses, modeling responses for them to copy, asking children to relate responses to real experiences, asking questions, and offering positive reinforcement for children's participation.

The following is a list of additional ways to promote child participation and active listening.

- Invite children to speak a familiar character's dialogue or book sounds. This is easily done in repeated sequences: "I don't care," said Pierre.
- Pantomime actions: "Let's knock on the door."
- Use closure: "The cup fell on the . . ." (floor). When using closure, if children end the statement differently, try saying "It could have fallen on the rug, but the cup in the story fell on the floor."
- Predict outcomes: "Do you think Hector will open the box?"
- Ask opinions: "What's your favorite pie?"
- Recall previous story parts: "What did Mr. Bear say to Petra?"

- Probe related experiences: "Emil, isn't your dog's name Clifford?"
- Dramatize enjoyed parts or wholes.

Younger preschoolers, as a rule, find sitting without active motor and/or verbal involvement more demanding than older children.

8-4e Sharing Your Thoughts

A strategy suggested by Dori (2007) for use with preschoolers and kindergartners involves thinking aloud during read-alouds and during other teaching moments.

> When teachers think aloud, they stop whatever is going on and signal in some way (for example, I point to my head) that their next words will describe thoughts that normally are not spoken aloud. Then they talk through their thought processes. (p. 101)

And Dori describes the results:

> It's easy to see the effectiveness of think-alouds, because the children's voices begin to chime in as they add their own ideas to the adult's thinking. (p. 103)

Two teaching goals promoted by using this strategy are (1) encouraging children's self-initiated active thinking and (2) encouraging metacognition, the act of thinking about one's own thinking. At kindergarten level, it also helps create thoughtful readers.

8-4f A Read-Aloud Approach Designed to Promote Child Comprehension

McGee and Schickedanz (2010), after reviewing research on the value of reading aloud to children age three to six years, conclude studies suggest that merely reading books aloud is not sufficient for accelerating children's oral vocabulary development and listening comprehension. It is the *way* books are shared that matters. Teacher's conversation during read-alouds can enhance understanding when her comments include predictions or connect story happenings or prompt children's engagement in analytical thinking. This is considered crucial to child comprehension. It can also be done by modeling thinking aloud during a reading or asking thoughtful questions. Other teacher strategies that increase the value of reading books aloud are teacher comments that promote preschoolers retelling or dramatizing stories. Many reading experts feel that reading aloud in a way that engages children in dialogue is essential to building comprehension and expressive language.

Comprehension is defined as the process of deriving meaning from text and includes the objects, settings, events, interactions, and speech integral to the story. It involves understanding the connections and relationships among sets of people, actions, words, and ideas. In this discussion, it pertains to children's making sense of the storybook's narrative and/or illustrations. This is accomplished when children gain knowledge through gathering and remembering data and using it to make inferences and conjectures that make "sense" to them.

Educators believe the comprehension of stories is a progressive process beginning in preschool and continuing through life as one encounters stories of increasing depth and complexity. Children's early comments when being read to can seem somewhat unrelated to the book's narrative, but as they age comments are connected in some fashion. Then children grasp and talk about some story specifics and details and move on to relate them to past experiences. At this point, some children develop the ability to create their own narratives, and their stories resemble some of the features they've learned about in storybooks.

McGee and Schickedanz (2010) have identified four suggested *preparatory* teacher actions (techniques) to help build a stronger understanding of a to-be-read book. These are planning a book introduction, using planned vocabulary support techniques, identifying possible teacher analytical comments and questions, and planning an after reading "why" question. This is a systematic approach that also includes attention to vocabulary development that is—words that are critical to the story and are needed to analyze the story problem and/or character's motivation and traits. These words are defined succinctly during the read-aloud.

To try these comprehension building techniques, let's look at preparing to read a picture book titled *Best Best Friends*.* First, one would need to read the book and clarify what features of book or story problem one wants to help

children infer in order to better comprehend the story and understand what human characteristics are involved. A brief synopsis of the book follows.

Mary and Clare are best friends. But watching her best friend in a frilly pink dress receive special attention and treatment at preschool, including a pink-saturated birthday party, Clare is angry and envious. When the snack time party is over Clare has had enough. "Yellow is prettier than plain old pink," she declares, and before long both children are yelling at each other. Mary loudly screams, "YOU ARE NOT MY FRIEND!" and stalks off. After a cooling off period and nap time, all ends happily with the girls making up and becoming best friends again.

A planned book introduction of this book to a child audience might be "In this book Clare is having an unhappy day at school. She has some strong feelings and says some angry words to her best friend. Let's find out why." From this introduction you suspect the teacher feels this story and illustrations can generate a subsequent discussion leading perhaps to an in-depth comprehension of either jealousy, unfairness, feeling special, or anger and its relationship to children's lives. Before actually reading the book, the teacher is certainly going to prepare a definition of which feeling or feelings are certain to enter the planned discussion and examine which other book words are necessary to understand character feelings. She will also check which illustrations visually depict these feelings. At this point the teacher might develop a simplified and age appropriate definition of jealous such as "Jealous is how you feel when you want something someone has but you don't have. You may think that is not fair and you're unhappy." Then identifying possible analytical comments and questions comes next and might include the following.

"Does Clare look unhappy or upset?"
"Can you tell if all the children are enjoying the party?"
"I think Mary is feeling special."
"What might be making Clare feel jealous?"
"Has there been a time when you felt special?"
"I feel it is unfair when everyone else is eating a cookie, and I don't have one, do you?"
"Do you think Clare really means what she is saying when she says, 'You are not my friend.'?"

*Chodos-Irvine, M. (2006). *Best Best Friends*, New York: Harcourt.

"Have you been angry with one of your friends?"

"Have you felt left out when others don't pay attention to you?"

"Why do you think this book ended happily with Mary and Clare best friends again?"

"Does pink really look 'old'?"

Of course, many other thought-provoking questions are possible. When using this approach, one would preplan an ending "why" question or questions. It could be some of the ones that follow or others that might be more thought-provoking or age appropriate for a particular group of children. "Why did Clare feel jealous?" "Why did Mary forgive her?" "Why do people say things they don't mean sometimes?" "Was feeling jealous a good way to feel or could Clare have handled this situation in a better way?" "Why do best friends like each other but at times have angry feelings?"

What can a teacher do when children display some misconceptions during an after story conversation? (1) She can help children reconsider their initial misinterpretation by explaining and providing further information about the story or text; (2) help a child by prompting the use of the child's background knowledge; (3) by rereading or referring to relevant text passages, (4) by using teacher modeling of her own reasoning; and (5) by supporting the child's attempt to reason things out himself. These strategies have the potential to increase storybook comprehension and vocabulary, and to develop skills for early reading success.

Preschool teachers choosing to increase child comprehension during read-alouds would keep in mind the developmentally appropriateness of these strategies. And also, they would think about whether they could execute all of their preplanned actions, questions, and targeted vocabulary, and still be able to remain a spontaneous and enthusiastic companion enjoying the act of reading aloud.

Teachers without aides and/or volunteers in their classroom may never have undivided time to share books with individual children. One-on-one readings can be the most beneficial and literacy-developing times of all. The dialogue and the personalized attention exceed what is possible in group readings. In large groups, some children are reluctant to speak and consequently receive less appreciation and feedback. (Small groups are recommended.)

Busy families tend to rely on schools to offer books. Many centers have been clever in promoting home reading. Bulletin boards, lending arrangements, and mandating family classroom volunteering are among the most common tactics.

It is not the simple "I-read-you-listen" type of adult-child interaction with books that really counts. It is the wide-ranging verbal dialogue the adult permits and encourages that gives children their best opportunity to construct a full knowledge of how people use books. Schools consequently include and share reading techniques in their communications with parents.

Teachers plan times to be in the classroom's book center, book corner, library, or book-reading area (whatever it is called). A teacher's presence models interest and allows for individual child readings, questions, and interactions other than at planned group book times.

8-4g Rereading Stories

It never ceases to amaze teachers and families when preschoolers beg to hear a book read over and over. Beginning teachers take this statement to mean that they have done a good job, and even veteran teachers confess it still feels good. A teacher who can read the same book over and over again with believable enthusiasm, as if it were his first delighted reading, has admirable technique and dedication. Children often ask to have stories reread because, by knowing what comes next, they feel competent, or they simply want to stretch out what is enjoyable. The decisions that teachers make about fulfilling the request depend on many factors, including class schedules and children's lack of capacity to sit through a second reading (despite their expressed desire to hear it). It is suggested that books be reread often and that teacher statements such as, "I'd like to read it again, but . . ." are followed by statements such as, "After lunch, I'll be under the tree in the yard, if you want to hear the story again."

Requests to "read it again" arise as a natural developmental demand of high significance and an integral part of book exposure. The child's behavior alerts adults to which books hold and preoccupy them. Teachers can think of the behavior as children selecting their own course of study. Multiple copies of favorite books and fresh, new books that extend individual children's "course of study" are provided by alert teachers.

A curious response may occur when the same storybooks are read and reread to four-year-olds. Children may be able to make more detailed comments centering on characters, events, titles, story themes, settings, and the book's language with rereading. Experienced teachers have noticed that as children understand particular aspects of stories (gained through numerous rereadings), they shift focus and attend to additional story dimensions overlooked in initial readings.

Early childhood educators with any experience have met children who want to "read" to teachers or peers. Teachers often smile, hypothesizing that the child is using rote memory, but often find that the child is telling his own version of the story. Researchers suggest this indicates a child has displayed a deep understanding and response to the story's meaning.

Teachers decide to introduce books with objects or other visuals for a number of reasons. A chef's hat worn by a teacher certainly gets attention and may motivate a group to hear more about the chef in the picture book. A head of lettuce or horseshoe may clarify some feature of a story. The possibilities are almost limitless. With theme or unit approaches to instruction, a picture book may expand or elaborate a field of study or topic that has already been introduced. If so, some new feature mentioned in a book may be emphasized by using a visual.

When the teacher wears an article of clothing, such as the hat mentioned previously, it may help him get into character. Because children like to act out story lines or scenes, items that help promote this activity can be introduced at the end of the story. Previewing a picture book may make it easier to find an object or person who could add to the storytelling experience.

8-5 After-Reading Discussions and Activities

How soon after a story is read should discussion, which promotes comprehension of stories, take place? Some educators believe it is obvious that a discussion might ruin the afterglow that occurs after certain books are shared. Teachers are sometimes understandably reluctant to mar the magic of the moment.

The teacher's role during storybook readings is to act as a "mediator" who assists children in two ways: (1) by helping them learn to take knowledge they had gained outside of book-reading experience and use this knowledge to understand the text and (2) by helping them apply the meanings and messages gained from books to their own lives.

What can early childhood teachers expect when children make comments or have questions after book reading? Ezell and Justice (2000) suggest that book illustrations or book concepts account for approximately 95 percent of children's comments during shared readings. Children's questions about meaning can be less common, and their questions about alphabet letters, words, or letter sounds are infrequent, as are questions concerning the author, illustrator, title, or book's format.

The teacher's focus in asking questions in an after-book discussion may not be to check children's knowledge but rather to learn from the child, build comprehension, and promote oral dialogue. A preschool teacher's story-reading discussions can be described as negotiated, unfocused interactions in which teachers become aware of the "sense making" children express. The process depends on what children say about their confusions and interpretations and what they understand, together with the teacher's response to the meaning the group seemed to make of the story.

Early childhood teachers could at times consider asking questions that draw attention to major elements of characterization and plot and the moral or deeper implications of a story, if appropriate, as was discussed previously. The solution that some teachers favor rather than a planned and systematic approach is to wait until children seem eager to comment, discuss, and perhaps disagree, and only then act as a guide to further comprehension. All present are given the opportunity to respond or add comments and cite personal experiences. Teachers using after-book discussions believe book content, word meanings, and ideas are best remembered if talked about.

Some centers designate a time after a story is read as "story time talk time." It is described as a time when children's ideas may be recorded by the teacher on a "language chart" made of chart paper or large sized paper. This activity gives importance to children's ideas. Writing the children's names by their contributions affords additional status. Children's art related to the book can be appended. Other book follow up activities can include making a basket collection of inexpensive small plastic (or other material) figures of story characters, animals, houses, story objects, and so on, to go along with a book. These are so popular one teacher made home-sewn story dolls for the school basket collection.

Discussions can promote print knowledge and include the idea that books are held in a certain way, and pages are turned from front to back. They learn about beginnings and endings of stories, about title pages, authors, and illustrators. They discover that teachers and other adults read print rather than pictures. Children also acquire concepts about print directionality—in English, print is read from left to right and top to bottom—as well as concepts about letters and words—words are made up of letters and are marked by spaces on either side.

Photo 8-7 Many books for children have a train theme.

8-5a Story or Book Dramatization

Some early childhood educators encourage child dramatization of favorite picture books and stories. Young children's recollection of literal story details and their comprehension of story features are enhanced if enactment takes place. Planning for book enactment means teachers start with simple short stories and display various props, objects, costumes, and so forth, to serve as motivator and "get-into-character" aids. In previewing picture books or oral stories for story times, teachers become accustomed to looking for material with repeated words, sentences, or actions. These are the books or story parts that are easy to learn. In the telling of *the three little pigs*, most children will join in after just a few readings with "then I'll huff, and I'll puff, and I'll blow your house down!"

8-5b Picture Books as the Basis for Theme Instruction

Some early childhood centers experiment with using picture books as the basis for theme program planning (Photo 8-7). Under this approach to program planning, instruction branches out from the concepts and vocabulary present in the book. Usually, the meaning of the story is emphasized, and a number of different directions of study and activities that are in some way connected to the book are conducted.

The classroom setting can be transformed into the cabbage patch that Peter Rabbit was so fond of exploring. Activities such as counting buttons on jackets, singing songs about rabbits or gardens, taking field trips to vegetable gardens, and engaging in science experiences in vegetable growing are a few examples of associated activities. A "Stuffed Toy Animal Day" when children bring their own favorite to class might follow the reading of Frank Asch's picture book *Popcorn*. The book *Fast Food* by Freymann and Effers could initiate a study of restaurants. Memorable experiences connected to classic books can aid literacy development, and an increasing number of early childhood centers are using this approach.

8-5c From Books to Flannel (Felt) Boards and Beyond

Teachers find that a number of books can be made into flannel board stories relatively easily; Chapter 11 is devoted to these activities. Some books that are particular favorites have been adapted for flannel board presentation, such as

- *The Very Hungry Caterpillar* by Eric Carle
- *The Carrot Seed* by Ruth Krauss
- *Johnny and His Drum* by Maggie Duff
- *My Five Senses* by Aliki
- *Brown Bear, Brown Bear, What Do You See?* by William Martin

Teachers have attempted to advertise particular books in creative ways. Enlarged book characters might be displayed, or displays of the book of the week or book of the day may be placed in a special spot in a classroom. An attending child's family member may be a special story-time book reader. During a morning greeting to children, a teacher might say, "I have a new book in my lap. See the cover," so she can create excitement for story time.

A visit to the local library is often planned for preschoolers. Librarian-presented story hours often result in the children's awareness of the library as a resource. Selecting and checking out one's choice can be an exciting and important milestone. Most early childhood centers also do their best to encourage this family-child activity. Many libraries have well-developed collections and enthusiastic and creative children's librarians who plan a number of activities to promote literacy. Along with books, you may find computers, language-development computer programs, CDs, DVDs, book and electronic media combinations, children's encyclopedias, foreign language editions, pamphlet collections, puzzles, and other language-related materials.

Finding out more about the authors of children's books can help provide teachers with added insights and background data. One goal of language arts instruction should be to alert children to the idea that books are created by real people. Most children find a photograph of an author or illustrator interesting, as well as stories concerning an author's childhood or reasons for writing a particular picture book.

Becoming more familiar with authors such as Margaret Wise Brown, often called the "Laureate of the Nursery," helps a reader appreciate the simplicity, directness, humor, and the sense of the importance of life that are found in her writings. Identifying and researching the authors of your children's classroom favorites is a good idea and prompts discussion of authors' individuality.

Websites that give information about children's book authors and illustrators are helpful, and librarians can guide you to books with autobiographical and biographical information.

Some early childhood centers set up author displays, celebrate author/illustrator birthdays, and encourage guest authors and illustrators. Letters or emails to authors might be written with child input.

8-6 Child- and Teacher-Authored Books

Books authored by children or their teachers have many values. They

- promote interest in the classroom book collection.
- help children see connections between spoken and written words.
- contain material based on child and teacher interests.
- personalize book reading.
- prompt self-expression.
- stimulate creativity.
- build feelings of competence and self-worth.

Hostetler (2000) describes child-authored books in her classroom.

> The children in my class who are four and five years old love to dictate text and illustrate the pictures for our handmade books. These books become treasures. The first book the children usually write is about our field trip to the farm. (p. 34)

She suggests creating a group-produced classroom book in which each child has a page. The teacher suggests a focal point subject, such as something the children would like to have in their pocket or some family-related topic. Another idea is to ask older four-year-olds who will be going to kindergarten soon to help make a book for children coming into their four-year-olds' classroom. The book will give the new children advice about the good things that might happen at preschool, tips on how to play with others, and so on. Many teachers make an alphabet book as an ongoing class project. When too many "A" pages are collected, a separate "A" book is developed.

Ray and Glover extended the invitation to make books (picture books) to a group of preschoolers and the experience led to their authored book for teachers in *Already Ready* (2008). They developed a profound respect for the capacity of children to thoughtfully compose and create.

Teachers involved in their study and project made time, space, and materials available for "bookmaking." When child reticence or tentativeness happened after a child was offered a bookmaking opportunity, teachers explained it was an okay feeling. They stressed that three- and four-year-olds weren't expected to know everything about drawing or writing words. Instead, children were urged to do the best they could. Children were supported and came to see themselves as writers.

If a child-authored book is one of the school's books, the book corner becomes a place where the child's accomplishment is exhibited. Teachers can alert the entire group to new book titles as the books arrive and make a point to describe them before they are put on the shelves.

Child-made books require teacher preparation and help. A variety of book shapes and sizes add interest and motivation (Figure 8-6). But size should be large enough to accommodate children's degree of small muscle control. Covers made of wallpaper or contact paper over cardboard are durable. The pages of the books combine child art and child-dictated words, usually on lined print script paper, or print is enlarged with computer help. Staples, rings, yarn (string), or brads can bind pages together (Figure 8-7). Child dictation is taken word for word with no or little teacher editing.

Figure 8-6 Book shapes.

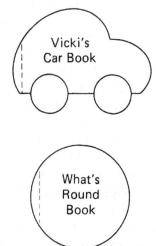

Figure 8-7 One way to bind pages.

BOOKBINDING

1.
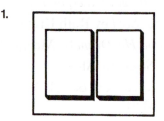

2.
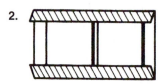

3.
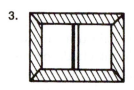

4.
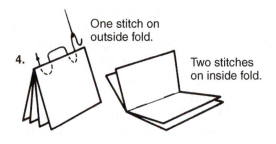

One stitch on outside fold.

Two stitches on inside fold.

5.

Masking tape with adhesive facing cover boards.

The following book, dictated by a four-year-old, illustrates one child's authorship.

THE WINDOW

Page 1: Once upon a time the little girl was looking out the window.

Page 2: Child's art.

Page 3: And the flowers were showing.

Page 4: Child's art.

Page 5: And the water was flushing down and she did not know it.

Page 6: Child's art.

Teacher-authored books can share a teacher's creativity and individuality. Favorite themes and enjoyed experiences can be repeatedly relived. Books containing pets' names are popular. Photographs of familiar school, neighborhood, or family settings are great conversation stimulators. Field trips and special occasions can be captured in book form.

Some educators suggest using what they call caption books with young children. Their caption books carefully place the print at the top left of the page; include photographs that give clues to the print message on the same page; and use short, meaningful sentences that repeat on succeeding pages. These writers also suggest teacher-made books that record nature walks, seasonal events, and holiday celebrations. Urging children to illustrate their favorite stories with their own art is recommended.

8-7 Book Areas and Centers

Classrooms with inviting book storage areas beckon curious browsers. Teachers have become exceptionally clever at devising eye-catching, comfortable, well-lighted, inviting, visually stimulating book-browsing classroom areas. If an educator is trying to attract children to the book collection or book display area, thought and effort may be necessary to sell the "look-at-books" activity. Use your creativity and use what is at hand, whether it is a sunny interior wall, a tabletop, an old bookcase, or an unused corner. Thematic and seasonal displays, potted plants, spotlights, and lamps have been used to lure children. Displays in or near the book center can broadcast, lure, shout, reach out, and grab the eyes and ears of passersby, forcing them to stop and pay attention.

Books should be at the child's eye level with book front covers in sight. Book-jacket wall displays and life-size book characters (drawings made by using overhead projectors to increase size, then tracing on large sheets of paper) have their own appeal. Comfort and color attract. Softly textured rugs and pillows, comfortable seating, and sprawling spaces prolong time spent

► ‖ **TeachSource Video 8-1**

© 2016 Cengage Learning®

Parent Involvement in School Culture: A Literacy Project

1. Linda Schwerty, a literacy specialist, is conducting a parent meeting. Parents are invited to publish a four-page book for their children's elementary school. If a similar project was undertaken at an early childhood center, how might it be planned?

2. Would you suggest using parent or child illustrations or photographs or another strategy?

3. How would you explain to parents interested in a book making project what features in a self-created picture book might capture attention and delight preschoolers? Would it be a good idea if the books became part of the classroom library? Would you add a photograph of both parent and child to the book's inside cover?

in book areas. Low round tables and plump pillows used as seating can also be inviting. Quiet, private spaces that are shielded from outside distractions and sounds and that have good lighting increase the child's ability to stay focused. Hideaways where friends can escape together and experience a book that has captured their attention are ideal.

Guidelines that outline the rules and responsibilities of book handling can be developed by the school. Rules should be designed to encourage children to return books to shelves, turn pages carefully, and respect the quietness of the area. Well-defined boundaries of library centers help books stay put. Teachers should promote the idea that using the area is a privilege and should monitor book centers frequently when younger preschoolers, who may have had little past experience with book collections and libraries, enter the area.

Rotating books by removing and storing some books from time to time and providing a different, previously stored set of books will make the area more interesting. Some centers categorize and store related books together and label them with a sign, identified picture, or drawing (such as animals, trains, things that are blue, and so on). Library books supplement the school's collection and may have special classroom-handling rules. Seasonal and holiday books are provided when possible. Paperbacks round out some collections, and multiple copies are considered for younger preschoolers' classrooms. Constant book repair is necessary in most classrooms because of heavy use. A classroom "Book Hospital" box reflects teachers' concern and esteem for books.

Teachers should browse in book centers, modeling both interest and enthusiasm when time and supervision duties permit. It is sad to think of curious children wandering into the book area, selecting a book, trying to grasp meaning from illustrations, wondering how teachers find a story within, and giving up after studying the book closely. Many teachers set up a system so that the story (or nonfiction) can be heard by using an "I-want-to-know-about-this-book" box. Children's name cards are adjacent. The child can select his book, slip his card inside, and place the card in the box. Younger children can find a name card with their picture and do the same. This system works well only if the staff finds the time to share the child-chosen book.

8-7a Group Settings

Most classrooms have areas suitable for picture-book reading in groups, besides areas for individual, self-selected browsing and places where children can be in the company of a few others. If these areas are not available, staff members can create them. The reading area should be comfortable and well lit and as far removed from interruptions and distractions as possible. Generally, lighting that comes from behind the children is preferred. Intense, bright light coming from behind the book can make it hard to see. During group readings, one center put a floor lamp in the reading area and dimmed the overhead lights. This setup worked well to cut distractions and focus the group on the reading. Another teacher brought a large packing case into the classroom with a light inside, added comfortable pillows, made a door, and called it the "Reading Box." A large, horseshoe-shaped floor pillow can increase child comfort. Many centers use small carpet sample squares for comfort and to outline individual space.

The number of children in groups is an important consideration; as the size of the group increases, intimacy, the child's ease of viewing, and the teacher's ability to be physically close to and respond to each child decreases (Photo 8-8). The ideal group size for story time ranges from five to 10 children. Unfortunately, staffing ratios may mandate a much larger group size. Some early childhood centers do "instant replays"—they have many small reading groups in succession, rather than large group reading sessions.

Most centers have developed rules about what behavior is expected from the child, whether the child chooses either to come or not come to a book-reading time, and whether a child can leave before the book's end. If the staff decides to give children a choice, usually the rule is stated thusly, "You need to find a quiet activity inside our classroom until story time is over."

By setting an example and making clear statements about handling books, the teacher can help children form good book-care habits. However, with time and use, even the sturdiest books will show wear. Teachers should be quick to show their sadness when a favorite book is torn, crayoned, or used as a building block. Some classrooms have signs reading "Books Are Friends—Handle with Care" or "Books are for looking, talking about, and sharing." Teachers need to verbally appreciate children who turn pages gently and return books to shelves or storage areas.

8-7b Resources for Finding Reading Materials

Many children's book stores carry popular new and older titles, but they are disappearing as online ordering becomes preferred. At teacher

Photo 8-8 Group size is an important consideration.

© 2015 Cengage Learning®

supply houses and school supply stores, a wide selection is often stocked, sometimes at discount prices. Teachers can contact children's book publishers for free catalogs with listings of new titles and summaries of contents or can find this information online.

Book clubs offer monthly selections of a wide variety of titles. These clubs usually reward schools with free books and teacher gifts that include posters and teaching visuals. Enough order forms for each child's parents are sent on a monthly basis. This offers parents an easy way to order books for their children by having school personnel send and receive orders.

Since 1919, the Children's Book Council has sponsored National Children's Book Week to promote reading and encourage children's enjoyment of books. A Digital Toolkit that aids teachers is often included on the Children's Book Week website. In addition, preschools that have overnight and weekend book-borrowing privileges promote book use and home enjoyment of books. The Additional Resources section at the chapter's end provides a list of books that are young children's favorites. You can help children learn the value of reading, first by falling in love with picture books yourself and then by developing your repertoire for sharing that enjoyment with children.

Summary

8-1   Describe the contents of children's books that existed before 1900.

Early books were printed to promote and improve children's moral and spiritual natures. Early American children's literature reflected English and Puritan messages. European fables contained animal stories and a few fables. In Victorian England, literature for children dealt with kings, knights, princesses, and oppressed victims.

8-2   Name four different categories of books for preschoolers.

Fiction and nonfiction are major book categories. Other book types include folk and fairy tales, poetry books, novelty books, oversized books, story songs, wordless books, concept books, predictable books, resource and reference books, alphabet books, therapeutic books, seasonal books, antibias themed books, infant and toddler books, board books, and multicultural books. Many preschool books fit into more than one category.

8-3   Discuss criteria used to select read aloud books

Many different criteria are considered when selecting read aloud books. Book features such as: is quality, has redeeming social value, contains specific child interests, offers multicultural and ethnically appropriate content, has significant and accurate content knowledge, matches children's everyday experiences, contains elements of familiarity, offers humor and fantasy, deals with universal human emotions, has desirable illustrations, includes interesting characters, may all be considered when selecting. A teacher might select a particular book for a particular teaching purpose or because the teacher can read it with enthusiasm.

8-4 Discuss suggested techniques or strategies for reading a book to a group of children.

The teacher begins with a book appropriate to classroom's particular children, and their age and interests. Instructional goals are considered. Then she arranges for comfortable seating and starts with a motivational introduction. The book is displayed so that whole pages are visible and at eye level. When reading the teacher makes eye contact, watches for feedback, speaks clearly, uses adequate volume, paces herself, and allows for children's proper hearing and ability to see. During the reading words or passages may be emphasized, key parts may be pointed out, and the teacher continually ascertains if she is holding children's attention and focus. The teacher acknowledges and discusses child remarks and questions and makes pertinent remarks moving along so as not to lose the thread of the storyline for children. If child interaction with the book is appropriate, it takes place. She makes time for ending discussion and clears up ideas, if necessary, and gives children the time to personalize what they have seen and heard.

8-5 Describe an after-book reading discussion to promote child comprehension.

Teacher behavior includes probing and asking questions that involve promoting children's deriving meaning from book features integral to the basic story. This promotes thinking about and understanding connections and relationships between people, actions, words, and ideas. Teachers help children make sense of the story by promoting knowledge and gathering, finding, or pointing out stated material in the text. She helps children remember data used to make inferences and conjectures.

8-6 Name two reasons teacher- or child-authored books might be valuable additions to a classroom book collection.

Books authored by children and their teachers can accomplish many goals, including enhancing child interest in books authored by someone he/she knows, and giving status to authorship. Authored books may contain material of mutual and familiar interest. It personalizes books, prompts going to the book collection library area, and can build a child author's confidence and feelings of self-worth. It also promotes child motivation and authorship, promotes an interest in bookmaking, allows for child creativity and expression. Authored books may contain concept knowledge and include material that forwards teaching goals.

8-7 List three suggestions for features and furnishings of a book (library) center.

A teacher, when creating an inviting book or library center, starts with considering comfortable seating, lighting, heating, and eye-catching features. The center will need adequate eye-level storage. Thematic related or seasonal displays may be added. Books are rotated from time to time as necessary and kept in good condition. Teachers develop necessary guidelines or rules concerning book handling and center use. A well-defined center with boundaries is a good idea and can be accomplished by furniture placement. The teacher becomes a resource person in book centers at times and models an interest in books. Personal individual space for children to read by themselves can be a plus feature.

Additional Resources

Children's Big Books

Crowley, J. (1986). *Mrs. Wishy Washy*. Bothell, WA: Wright Group. (Humorous.)

Hoberman, M. A. (1986). *A House Is a House for Me*. Ontario: Scholastic-TAB (Rhythm and rhyme.)

O'Donnell, E. L. (1995). *I Can't Get My Turtle to Move*. New York: Harcourt Brace School Publishers. (Predictive, colorful, and a drama enactment opportunity.)

Trumbauer, L. (1998). *Sink or Float?* Delran, NJ: Newbridge Educational Publishing. (Nonfiction, color photo illustrations.)

Tullet, H. (2007). *Juego De Colores*. Barcelona: Kokinos. (Colorful, interactive, and in Spanish.)

Multiethnic and Multicultural Children's Books

Ashley, B. (1991). *Cleversticks*. New York: Crown. (Multiracial class with Chinese-American child who questions his capabilities.)

Bruchac, J., & Ross, G. (1995). *The Story of the Milky Way*. New York: Dial Books. (Presents a Cherokee legend with colorful illustrations.)

Buchanan, K. (1994). *This House Is Made of Mud/Esta Casa Está Hecha De Lodo*. Flagstaff, AZ: Northland. (In both Spanish and English, poetic language about a home made of mud.)

Cave, K. (2003). *One Child, One Seed: A South African Counting Book*. New York: Henry Holt.

Chen, C. (2007). *On My Way to Buy Eggs*. New York: Kane/Miller. (Asian tale with an everyday problem that a child solves.)

Dale, P. (1987). *Bet You Can't*. Philadelphia: Lippincott. (African-American brother and sister clean room at bedtime.)

Garden, N. (2004). *Molly's Family*. New York: Farrar, Straus, and Giroux. (Nontraditional family.)

Garza, C. L. (2005). *Family Pictures*. San Francisco: Children's Book Press. (Multicultural families.)

Greenspun, A. A. (1991). *Daddies*. New York: Philomel. (Photographs of dads and children of diverse cultures.)

Hale, I. (1992). *How I Found a Friend*. New York: Viking. (Interracial friendship.)

Hamanka, S. (1994). *All the Colors of the Earth*. New York: Morrow Junior Books. (An exuberant, lovingly illustrated book celebrating the beauty of diverse people.)

Hoffman, M. (1987). *Nancy No-Size*. New York: Oxford University Press. (A middle child's self-concept in an urban African-American family is examined.)

Hutchins, P. (1993). *My Best Friend*. New York: Greenwillow. (Friendship between African-American children.)

Keats, E. J. (1964). *Whistle for Willie*. New York: Viking Press. (A well-known classic featuring an African-American child.)

Keller, H. (1995). *Horace*. New York: Mulberry. (About a spotted leopard who feels out of place in his adopted family of striped tigers.)

Kleven, E. (1996). *Hooray, a Pinata*. New York: Dutton. (A diverse way to celebrate birthdays and other special days.)

Machado, A. M. (1996). *Nina Bonita*. New York: Kane/Miller. (A fanciful story about a rabbit and a dark-skinned Brazilian girl.)

Marcellino, F. (1996). *The Story of Little Baboji*. New York: Harper Collins/Michael di Capua. (An authentic tale set in India.)

Morris, A. (1992). *Tools*. New York: Lothrop, Lee and Shepard Books. (Around the world encountering tool use.)

Perez, A. I. (2000). *My Very Own Room*. San Francisco: Children's Book Press. (A dream for private space.)

Pinkwater, D. M. (1997). *The Big Orange Splot*. New York: Hastings House. (Showcases diversity and pressures to conform.)

Roe, E. (1991). *Con Mi Hermano/With My Brother*. New York: Bradbury Press. (A loving relationship between Mexican-American brothers.)

Rosen, M. (1996). *This Is Our House*. Cambridge, MA: Candlewick Press. (Opens discussion concerning exclusion.)

Russo, M. (1992). *Alex Is My Friend*. New York: Greenwillow. (Child's disability handled with feeling.)

Samton, S. W. (1991). *Jenny's Journey*. New York: Viking Penguin. (Interracial friendship.)

Schaefer, C. L. (1996). *The Squiggle*. New York: Crown. (Asian child delights in imaginative play.)

Spinelli, E., & Iwai, M. (2000). *Night Shift Daddy*. New York: Hyperion Books. (Ethnic family relationships.)

Waters, K., & Slovenz-Low, M. (1990). *Lion Dancer: Ernie Wan's Chinese New Year*. New York: Scholastic. (Color photographs capture a Chinese New Year celebration in New York.)

Williams, V. B. (1990). *"More More More," Said the Baby*. New York: Greenwillow. (Love and life with multiethnic families with babies. Caldecott Honor winner.)

Zalben, J. (1988). *Beni's First Chanukah*. New York: Henry Holt. (Family traditions are experienced by a small child.)

Volumes Listing Multiethnic and Multicultural Children's Books

Bhattacharyya, R. (2010). *The Castle in the Classroom: Story As a Springboard for Early Literacy*. Portland, M. E.: Stenhouse.

Jenkins, E. C., & Austin, M. C. (1987). *Literature for Children About Asians and Asian Americans*. New York: Greenwood Press.

National Black Child Development Institute. (1995). *Young Children and African American Literature*. Washington, DC: National Association for the Education of Young Children.

Rand, D., Parker, T., & Foster, S. (1998). *Black Books Galore! Guide to Great African American Children's Books*. New York: John Wiley and Sons.

Schon, I. (1978). *Books in Spanish for Children and Adults: An Annotated Guide*. Metuchen, NJ: Scarecrow Press.

Favorite Children's Books

Aylesworth, J. (2003). *Goldilocks and the Three Bears*. New York: Scholastic. (An inquisitive child encounters problems; repetitive dialogue; a classic tale.)

Brown, M. W. (1938, 1965). *The Dead Bird*. New York: Young Scott Books. (Deals tenderly with the death of a bird.)

Carle, E. (1984). *The Very Hungry Caterpillar*. New York: Penguin-Putnam. (The hungry caterpillar eats through the pictures and emerges as a butterfly on the last page.)

Chorao, K. (1977). *Lester's Overnight*. New York: E. P. Dutton. (Family humor about a child's overnight plans and his teddy bear.)

Ets, M. H. (1955). *Play with Me*. New York: Viking Press. (A lesson to learn on the nature of animals.)

Flack, M. (1932). *Ask Mr. Bear*. New York: Macmillan. (The search for just the right birthday present for a loved one.)

Freeman, D. (1954). *Beady Bear*. New York: Viking Press. (Meet Beady and his courage, independence, and frailty.)

Freeman, D. (1968). *Corduroy*. New York: Viking Press. (The department store teddy who longs for love.)

Freymann, S., & Elffers, J. (2006). *Fast Food*. New York: Arthur A. Levine. (Contemporary life.)

Gag, W. (1928). *Millions of Cats*. New York: Coward-McCann. (Word pleasure and magic—a favorite with both teachers and children.)

Greene, R. G. (2003). *At Grandma's*. New York: Henry Holt. (Grandma's house can be a special place.)

Guilfoile, E. (1957). *Nobody Listens to Andrew*. New York: Scholastic Book Services. (An "adults-often-ignore-what-children-say" theme.)

Hazen, B. S. (1974). *The Gorilla Did It*. New York: Atheneum Press. (A mother's patience with a fantasizing child. Humorous.)

Henkes, K. (2005). *Chrysanthemum*. New York: Scholastic (A new classic.)

Hoban, R. (1964). *A Baby Sister for Frances*. New York: Harper and Row. (Frances, "so human," deals with the new arrival.)

Hutchins, P. (1968). *Rosie's Walk*. New York: Macmillan. (A fox is outsmarted.)

Hutchins, P. (1971). *Changes, Changes*. New York: Macmillan. (Illustrations of block constructions tell a wordless story of the infinite changes in forms.)

Hutchins, P. (1976). *Goodnight Owl!* New York: Macmillan. (Riddled with repetitive dialogue; a delightful tale of bedtime.)

Jenkins, S., & Page, R. (2003). *What Do You Do With a Tail Like This?* Boston: Houghton Mifflin. (Humor.)

Keats, E. J. (1967). *Peter's Chair.* New York: Harper and Row. (A delightful tale of family life.)

Kennedy, J. (1987). *The Teddy Bears' Picnic.* New York: Peter Bedrick Books. (A delight for the child who has his own teddy bear.)

Kraus, R. (1973). *Leo the Late Bloomer.* New York: Dutton. (Wonderful color illustrations and a theme that emphasizes individual development.)

Krauss, R. (1945). *The Carrot Seed.* New York: Harper and Row. (The stick-to-it-tiveness of a child's faith makes this story charming.)

Leonni, L. (1949). *Little Blue and Little Yellow.* New York: Astor-Honor. (A classic. Collages of torn paper introduce children to surprising color transformations, blended with a story of friendship.)

McCloskey, R. (1948). *Blueberries for Sal.* New York: Viking Press. (The young of the two species meet.)

Mosel, A. (1968). *Tiki Tiki Tembo.* New York: Holt, Rinehart and Winston. (A folktale that tickles the tongue in its telling. Repetitive.)

Potter, B. (1987). *Peter Rabbit's ABC.* Bergenfield, NJ: Frederick Warne. (Clever alphabet letter presentation.)

Provensen, A. (2003). *A Day in the Life of Murphy.* New York: Holiday House. (A memorable animal story for children who own pets.)

Raskin, E. (1975). *Nothing Ever Happens on My Block.* New York: Atheneum Press. (The child discovers a multitude of happenings in illustrations.)

Scott, A. H. (1972). *On Mother's Lap.* New York: McGraw-Hill. (There's no place like mother's lap!)

Segal, L. (1970). *Tell Me a Mitzi.* New York: Farrar. (New York City life.)

Shulevitz, U. (1969). *Rain Rain Rivers.* New York: Farrar, Straus and Giroux. (Illustrative fine art.)

Slobodkina, E. (1947). *Caps for Sale.* New York: William R. Scott. (A tale of a peddler, some monkeys, and their monkey business. Word play and gentle humor.)

Stevens, J. (1987). *The Town Mouse and the Country Mouse.* New York: Holiday House. (One's own house is best.)

Stone, J. (1971). *The Monster at the End of This Book.* Racine, WI: Western Publishing Co. (Suspense and surprise.)

Viorst, J. (1971). *The Tenth Good Thing About Barney.* New York: Atheneum. (Loss of family pet and positive remembrances.)

Viorst, J. (1976). *Alexander and the Terrible, Horrible, No Good, Very Bad Day.* New York: Atheneum Press. (Everyone relates to the "everything-can-go-wrong" theme.)

Zion, G. (1956). *Harry the Dirty Dog.* New York: Harper and Row. (Poor lost Harry gets so dirty his family does not recognize him.)

Finding Recommended and Award-Winning Books

American Library Association. (2003). *The Newbery and Caldecott Awards: A Guide to Medal and Honor Books.* Chicago: Author.

Deeds, S. (2001). *The New Books Kids Like.* Chicago: American Library Association.

Gillespie, J. T. (2002). *Best Books for Children: Preschool Through Grade 6.* New Providence, NJ: R. R. Bowker.

Children's Books Cited in This Chapter

Ahlberg, J., & Ahlberg, A. (1979). *Each Peach Pear Plum: An "I Spy" Story.* New York: Viking Press.

Aliki. (1962). *My Five Senses.* New York: Crowell.

Anno, M. (1975). *Anno's Counting Book.* New York: Crowell.

Asch, F. (1979). *Popcorn: A Frank Asch Bear Story.* New York: Parents Magazine Press.

Bragg, M. C. (1930). *The Little Engine That Could.* New York: Platt & Munk.

Chodos-Irvine, M. (2008). *Best, Best Friends.* New York: Harcourt.

de Paola, T. (1978). *Pancakes for Breakfast.* New York: Harcourt Brace Jovanovich.

Duff, M. K. (1972). *Johnny and His Drum.* New York: H. Z. Walck.

Gág, W. (1928). *Millions of Cats.* New York: Coward-McCann.

Garden, N. (2004). *Molly's Family.* New York: Farrar, Straus and Giroux.

Heller, R. (1981). *Chickens Aren't the Only Ones.* New York: Grosset & Dunlap.

Hudson, C. W. (1987). *Afro-Bets ABC Book.* Orange, NJ: Just Us Books.

Keats, E. J. (1962). *The Snowy Day.* New York: Viking Press.

Kellogg, S. (1971). *Can I Keep Him?* New York: Dial Press.

Kennedy, J. (1987). *The Teddy Bears' Picnic.* New York: Bedrick Books.

Komaiko, L. (1987). *Annie Bananie.* New York: Harper and Row.

Marshall, J. (1972). *George and Martha.* Boston: Houghton Mifflin.

Martin, B., & Carle, E. (1970). *Brown Bear, Brown Bear, What Do You See?* New York: Holt, Rinehart and Winston.

Martin, B., Jr., & Archambault, J. (1989). *Chicka Chicka Boom Boom.* New York: Simon & Schuster.

Mayer, M. (1974). *What Do You Do With a Kangaroo?* New York: Four Winds Press.

McCloskey, R. (1941). *Make Way for Ducklings.* New York: Viking Press.

Miller, J. (1983). *Farm Counting Book.* Englewood Cliffs, NJ: Prentice Hall.

Munsch, R. (1986, 2011). *Love You Forever.* New York: Firefly books.

Peet, B. (1961). *Huge Harold.* Boston: Houghton Mifflin.

Roffey, M. (1983). *Home Sweet Home.* New York: Coward-McCann.

Sendak, M. (1963). *Where the Wild Things Are.* New York: Harper and Row.

Turkle, B. (1976). *Deep in the Forest.* New York: Dutton.

Yabuuchi, M. (1983). *Animals Sleeping.* New York: Philomel Books.

Zolotow, C. (1974). *My Grandson Lew.* New York: Harper and Row.

Readings

Anderson, N. A. (2007). *What Should I Read Aloud? A Guide to 200 Best Selling Picture Books.* Newark, DE: International Reading Association.

Bang, M. (2000). *Picture This: How Picture Books Work.* New York: Chronicle.

Jalongo, M. R. (2009). *Learning to Listen, Listening to Learn.* Washington, DC: National Association for the Education of Young Children.

Keifer, B. Z., & Tyson, C. A. (2010). *Charlotte Huck's Children's Literature.* New York: McGraw-Hill.

Schon, I. (2001, March). Los ninos y los libros: Noteworthy books in Spanish for the very young. *Young Children, 56*(2), 94–95.

Temple, C. A., Martinez, M., & Yokota, J. (2010). *Children's Books in Children's Hands.* Boston: Allyn and Bacon.

Mantzicopoulos P., & Patrick, H. (2010). The seesaw is the machine that goes up and down: Young children's narrative responses to science-related informational text. *Early Education and Development: 21*(3): 412–444.

Trelease, J. (1995.2008). *The Read-Aloud Handbook.* New York: Viking-Penguin.

Helpful Websites

Miami University

http://dlp.lib.miamioh.edu

Contains information concerning 5000 abstracts of picture books for preschool through grade 3.

American Library Association

http://www.ala.org

Publications and awards of interest to teachers.

International Reading Association

http://www.reading.org

Download Children's Choices or IRA Choices reading lists.

Parents Magazine

http://parents.com

Search for best books by age.

9 Storytelling

Objectives

After reading this chapter, you should be able to:

9.1 Describe how storytelling can help language growth.

9.2 Identify three suggested story selection criteria.

9.3 Discuss types of stories commonly used for preschool storytelling.

9.4 List reasons to practice stories before telling.

9.5 Describe two teaching aids that might be used in a storytelling activity.

9.6 Describe the value of promoting child dictation stories.

naeyc NAEYC Program Standards

3G14 Teachers demonstrate their knowledge of content and developmental areas by creating experiences that engage children in purposeful and meaning learning related to key curriculum concepts.

3G01 Teachers have and use a variety of teaching strategies that include a broad range of approaches and responses.

2E04 Children have varied opportunities to retell and reenact events in storybooks.

DAP Developmentally Appropriate Practice (DAP)

3M1 Teachers give children daily opportunities for creative expression and aesthetic appreciation.

3M5 Teachers do not provide a model that they expect children to copy. However, they demonstrate new techniques or uses of materials to expand children's options.

3H7 Teachers help children use communication and language as tools for thinking and learning.

COMMON CORE Common Core State Standards for English Language Arts and Literacy

W.CCR.9 Draw evidence from literary or informational texts to support analysis, reflection, and research.

W.CCR.3 Write narratives to develop real or imagined experiences or events using effective techniques, well-chosen details, and well-structured event sequences.

Hey! Godzilla!

A tree in our yard was perfect for climbing, with a smooth trunk and a thick layer of tan bark underneath. I watched as Fenton climbed up and out on a limb. He was hanging on the limb with both hands, feet dangling a foot or so above the ground. He seemed unable to let go and unable to swing his legs back up on the limb. As I walked closer to help him, he yelled, "Godzilla help me." Other boys, closer than I, grabbed his legs. He let go, knocking them down with him. They rolled on the ground unhurt. Then Pierre jumped up and said, "My turn," and he headed up the tree.

Questions to Ponder

1. Could you create a short story with a beginning, middle, and end about a boy stuck in a tree?

2. How would you describe this tree to give listeners a vivid mental image?

Storytelling is a medium that an early childhood teacher can develop and use to increase a child's enjoyment of language. When good stories are told by a skilled storyteller, the child listens intently; mental images may be formed.

Storytelling enables teachers to share their life experiences and create and tell stories in their own way. It is a teacher's gift of time and imagination. Your style of storytelling will be individual and unique, and you will be free to improvise. Beginning teachers do not worry that their version of a favorite story differs from others.

Storytelling can be defined as the seemingly easy, spontaneous, intimate sharing of a narrative with one or many persons. The storyteller relates, pictures, imagines, builds what happens, and crafts characters, all of which is manifested through the storyteller's voice and body. Storytelling is the act that essentially makes humans human. It defines us as a species. We are shaped by the stories we hear. In storytelling, children leave the "here and now" and go beyond what is seen and at hand. They experience the symbolic potential of language with words themselves, the main source of meaning independent of the time and place they are spoken. Children

create imaginative scenarios quickly and easily in everyday play situations.

Early childhood teachers recognize the importance of storytelling in a full language arts curriculum. Good stories that are well told have fascinated young listeners since ancient times. Storytelling is a form of expressive artistry, and storytelling remains one of the oldest and most effective art forms. The oral story, be it aesthetic or pedagogical, has great value. It seems to be a part of the human personality to use it and want it. The art of the storyteller is an important, valuable ingredient in the lives of children.

America is rediscovering the magic of storytelling. Storytelling festivals are now held throughout the United States. There's also a National Storytelling Festival, which is a three-day storytelling celebration in Jonesborough, Tennessee. Regional, intergenerational, multicultural, and multiethnic story themes delight audiences.

In many cultures, oral stories have passed on the customs, accumulated wisdom, traditions, songs, and legends. Storytelling is as old as language itself. Storytellers in the ancient world often traveled from village to village enlightening and entertaining. They gained status as "the keepers" of the groups' treasured oral history and unwritten stories.

How could one describe skilled storytellers? They are gloriously alive, live close to the heart of things, have known solitude and silence, and have felt deeply. They have come to know the power of the spoken word. They can remember incredible details about a good story that interests them. Preschool teachers may know silence only at nap times, but they indeed live close to the heart of young children's forming character, personality, and growing intellect. When books or pictures are not used to tell a story, teachers tell a story with their face, gestures, words, and voice. The child pictures the story in her mind as the plot unfolds.

9-1 Storytelling and Literacy

The promotion of oral literacy is an important consideration for preschool program planners. Oral literacy involves a shared background and knowledge of orally told stories plus a level of competence. Being able to tell a story well depends on a number of factors, including observation of techniques. Natural storytellers, if they exist, are overshadowed by storytellers who have practiced the art. Some adult job hunters find telling a story is a requested part of their job interview and is used to assess intelligence, communication ability, and literacy.

Preschools are sure to offer picture-book readings, but storytelling may be neglected. Some teachers shy away from the activity for a variety of reasons, including not feeling like they can hold their child audience's attention. Teachers can increase their own storytelling skills by observing practiced storytellers, taking classes, or engaging in self-study (Photo 9-1). The best suggestion for a teacher wishing to develop her storytelling skills is to start by relating short, significant happenings from daily life. Keep it lively. Four-year-olds make a better audience for the beginning storyteller than do younger children.

As children observe and listen to the teacher's storytelling, they notice common elements, including beginnings, middles, and story endings. They discover some stories vary little between tellers. They imitate techniques using hand and body gesturing, facial expression, and vocal variation; they speak in character **dialogue,** and they may even copy dramatic pause. They also may attempt to make their audience laugh or add suspense to their stories.

Acredolo and Goodwyn (2000) suggest how young children begin to get "the idea of story":

> . . . They hear important people in their lives talking about the past: "Remember what we did today? We went to the zoo! And do you remember what animals we saw?" What's more it's clear that these people are especially pleased when the children themselves also remember. The implication is clear. Adults literally teach their children about beginnings, middles, and endings by structuring their own narratives in an organized way: "Remember we saw the flamingos when we first went though the gate? And then we went into the snake house and we got scared." (p. 16)

Sharing oral stories and verbally putting daily happenings into words can be cherished for what they are—the building blocks of thinking and imagining, describing, creating, expressing ideas, and later achieving writing and reading skill. Gallas (2003) suggests that not only is the storyteller absorbed in thought during the storytelling experience, but the audience is as well.

> Over the years as I have watched successive classes create stories for sharing time, I have seen that the storytelling child does one kind of imaginative, synthesizing work that takes skill and thought. The listening children, however, do another kind of imaginative, synthesizing work in order to become part of the story. That work is personal, social, and intellectual. (p. 176)

Educators try daily to really engage children in talk and to celebrate its occurrence. Forget quiet classrooms; strive for talk-filled rooms balanced with quiet times! Children attempt to make sense of the stories they hear and try to fit

Photo 9-1 Watching a skilled storyteller may increase teacher skill.

© 2015 Cengage Learning®

---

dialogue — a conversation between two or more persons or between a person and something else.

them into their lives. Stories can give meaning to events by making connections between them and the real world. The content of stories can have a lasting effect on children.

One benefit that is fostered by teacher storytelling is child story making. Other possible child competencies and understandings promoted by storytelling experiences include developing a sense of oral power and group inclusion. A child may understand he has personal stories to tell and becomes curious about others' stories. His sense of drama grows and storytelling may heighten his awareness of phonetic and phonemic elements in words. He may get the idea that gestures can enhance storytelling by influencing audience moods and feelings and also help clarify ideas. If exposed to multicultural stories, he may more fully realize cultural similarities and differences.

Much research encourages teachers to promote each child's oral development and the dictation of child-created stories and subsequent dramatization. The teacher then reads the child's work to child groups. Besides the obvious benefits of the speaking and writing involvement in this activity, it is based on child-relevant material. Experts believe that this kind of activity primes children's inner feelings and thinking processes for change and growth, and increases self-awareness and awareness of self in relation to others. All in all, it is a powerful language arts approach.

Gainsley (2003) describes a teacher dictation activity that took place before a firehouse field trip. Children were asked what they might see. The teacher made a list that was checked off during the trip. Later the teacher and the children discussed the things they saw that were on the list, along with other things children observed and recalled. The same approach could be used before, during, and after a storytelling experience. If the teacher said, "I've a story about a beach called Surfer's Cove. What do you think might be talked about in a story about a surfer's beach?" Other teacher dictation ideas cited by Gainsley were creating grocery lists, creating new verses for songs, and writing letters and cards.

9-1a Telling Stories Without Books

Chapter 8 described the merits and uses of picture books with young children. Storytelling without books has its own unique set of enjoyed language pleasures. Storytelling is direct, intimate conversation. The well-told story's power to hold children spellbound is widely recognized. It is the intimate, personal quality of storytelling as well as the power of the story itself that accomplishes these minor miracles. Yet in order to work this spell, a story must be learned, remembered, and so delightfully told that it catches and holds the attention of the most inveterate wrigglers.

Teachers observe children's reactions as they tell a story. A quizzical look on a child's face can help the teacher know when to clarify or rephrase for understanding. A teacher's voice can increase the story's drama in parts when children are deeply absorbed.

Many educators have noted how quickly and easily ideas and new words are grasped through storytelling (Photo 9-2). This is an additional benefit. Stories are told to acquaint young children with this enjoyable oral language art. Obvious moralizing or attempts to teach facts by using stories usually turn children away.

Storytelling may occur at almost any time during the course of the day, inside or outside. No books or props are necessary, but use of them may focus attention and add to the child's enjoyment. Teachers are free to relate stories in their own words and manner. Children show by their actions what parts of the story are of high interest. The storyteller can increase children's enjoyment by emphasizing these features.

9-1b Storytelling Goals

A teacher seeks to become a skilled storyteller so that she can model storytelling skill while providing another avenue to the development of oral competence. Another goal is to acquire a repertoire of stories that offer children a variety of experiences. The teacher's goals also include:

- increasing children's enjoyment of oral language.
- making young children familiar with oral storytelling.
- encouraging children's storytelling and authorship.
- increasing children's vocabulary.
- increasing children's confidence as speakers.
- increasing children's awareness of story sequence and structure.

Photo 9-2 A story about a singer prompts children to use cylinder blocks.

- increasing children's story comprehension and higher level thinking skills.
- promoting oral skill, use, and expression of ideas.

Mathias (2006) would add these goals:

- helping children gain listening skills.
- extending young children's knowledge of facts and fantasy.
- stimulating listener's imagination.
- creating an appetite for words.
- introducing audience experiences.

Storytelling is a wonderful way to promote understanding of audience behaviors and performer behaviors. Teachers experience rewarding feelings when their technique and story combine to produce audience enjoyment and pleasure. Child storytellers gain tremendous insights into the performing arts, their own abilities, and the power of orally related stories. Most reading experts agree that oral competence enhances ease in learning to read and promotes understanding of what is read.

Thoughtful writers have questioned the wisdom of always exposing children to illustrations at story time. By not allowing children to develop mental images, they believe we have possibly distracted children from attaining personal meaning. On the other hand, discussing what children see in a photograph or drawing and conjecturing with them about what is happening, the details they notice, the feelings that they or the person pictured might be having, and what might happen next can be both a visual literacy experience and a motivational strategy to encourage child storytelling. There are benefits children can accrue from both "with visuals" and "without visuals" literacy experiences.

9-1c Using Picture Books for Storytelling

At times, a picture book is the source for storytelling. The teacher later introduces the book and makes it available in the classroom's book center for individual follow-up. Used this way, storytelling motivates interest in books. Many picture books, however, do not lend themselves to storytelling form because illustrations are such an integral part of the experience (Photo 9-3). Books that have been successfully used as the basis for storytelling can be handled in unique ways. An experienced teacher using professional presentation skills in a storytelling experience using *Caps for Sale* by Esphyr Slobodkina would make it an audience participation story and would shake a fist at the monkeys. The audience, with only the slightest encouragement, might shake its fists at the peddler.

The following books are recommended for teacher storytelling:

Asbjornsen, P. C. (1972). *The three billy goats gruff.* New York: Harcourt, Brace, Jovanovich.

Fleming, D. (2006). *The cow who clucked.* New York: Henry Holt.

Galdone, P. (1961). *The old woman and her pig.* New York: McGraw-Hill.

Martin. D. (2006). *All for pie, pie for all.* Cambridge, MA: Candlewick Press.

During and After Storytelling Discussion.

Storybook discussions can aid children's narrative abilities. Justice and Pence (2006) urge teachers to help children master narrative skills and to use literate language. Literate language, as they define it, is a specific type of language that is highly precise and is necessary when little context is available—such as telling about an incident or happening in the past without a visual. Justice and Pence suggest that the following discussion activities are aligned to the objectives that characterize important early achievement in narrative knowledge.

1. to discuss the sequence of events in a story

2. to discuss what happens to characters in a story

3. to discuss the location or setting of a story

4. to discuss reported speech used by characters in a story

5. to identify the high point of a story (pp. 72–73)

9-1d Multicultural Story Resources

An increasing number of multicultural picture books are in print as publishers strive to react to America's changing and diverse school populations. The following are suggested as storytelling sources.

Escardo, M. (2006). *The three little pigs/Los tres cerditos.* San Francisco: Chronicle Books.

Hudson, C. (1999). *Glo goes shopping.* East Orange, NJ: Just Us Books.

Rylant, C. (2007). *Alligator boy.* New York: Harcourt.

Rocco, J. (2007). *Wolf! Wolf!* New York: Hyperion.

Tsubakiyama, M. (1999). *Mei-Mei loves the morning.* Morton Grove, IL: Albert Whitman & Co.

An increasing number of classrooms promote acting out stories after they are read. Immediately following this acting experience, children are urged to create their own stories. These can be taped and later written by adults. These child stories can also be enacted with the story's author or teacher selecting her actors or with actor volunteers.

9-1e Other Story Sources

Story ideas can be found in collections, anthologies, resource books, children's magazines, films, or story recordings. A story idea can also be self-created. Teachers shouldn't overlook nonfiction books, nursery rhymes, poetry, story songs, or stories created by other teachers or their families (Soderman, Clevenger, Kent, 2013). A teacher-created story can fill a void. In any group of young children there are special interests and problems. Stories can expand interest and give children more information on a subject. Problems can possibly be solved by the stories and conversations that take place.

New teachers may not yet have confidence in their storytelling abilities, so learning some basic techniques for selecting, creating, and telling stories can help build confidence. This, together with the experience gained by presenting the stories to children, should convince the teacher that storytelling is enjoyable for preschoolers and rewarding to the teacher.

Teachers telling children personal stories about their lives actually "model" storytelling. They also let children know that their actions and words are the stuff of stories too. Gestures, facial expressions, body language, and variety in tone of voice are observed. This type of storytelling is a natural part of social interaction. With young children, short anecdotes and humorous life incidents work well. "News of the Day Time" is often included in daily schedules.

Many stories can be introduced through song. Some may know of the delightful folk story song that begins "A fox went out on a chilly night" and tells of the animal's adventures. These types of songs may include opportunities for children's oral, physical, and creative expression or for child involvement in the storytelling. A creative teacher can use story songs to complement, extend, and reinforce a multitude of classroom activities. Vocabulary meanings are often more apparent to children when learned in the context of a story song.

Simple, quick definitions by teachers are offered in a conversational tone. Imagine the fun involved in a story song about the saga of a lump of dough becoming a loaf of bread: ". . . and they pushed and pulled me. Oh, how they pushed and pulled" or "It's warm in here. I'm getting hot. Look at me. I'm growing and turning golden brown."

9-2 Story Selection

The selection of a story is as important as the selection of a book because stories seem to have individual personalities. Searching for a story that appeals to the teller and that can be eagerly shared is well worth the time. A few well-chosen and well-prepared stories suiting the individual teacher almost always ensure a successful experience for all. The following selection criteria are commonly used.

1. Age-Level Appropriateness

Is the story told in simple, easily understood words? Is it familiar in light of the child's life experiences? Is it frightening? Can the child profit from traits of the characters?

2. Plot

Does the setting create a stage for what is to come? Is there action? Is there something of interest to resolve? Does the story begin with some action or event? Does it build to a climax with some suspense? Does it have a timely, satisfying conclusion? Are characters introduced as they appear?

The stories you will be searching for will have one central **plot**; a secondary plot may confuse children. Action-packed stories where one event successfully builds to another hold audience attention.

3. Style

Does the story use repetition, rhyme, or silly words? Does it have a surprise ending? Does it include directly quoted conversations or child involvement with speaking or movements? Does the mood help the plot develop?

4. Values

Are the values and models presented appropriate for today's children? Screen for ethnic, cultural, and gender stereotypes that would lead you to exclude the story or discuss the issue with children.

---

plot — the structure of the action of a story.

5. Memorable Characters

Look for a small number of colorful characters who are distinct entities in contrast to the main character and each other. One should be able to identify and recognize character traits.

6. Sensory and Visual Images

The visual and sensory images evoked by stories add interest. For example, phrases like "gingerbread cookies, warm and golden" rather than "cookie" and the "velvet soft fur" rather than "fur" create different mental images. Taste, smell, sight, sound, and tactile descriptions create richness and depth.

7. Additional Selection Criteria

Elements that make stories strong candidates for young children include stories with an economy of words, a polished quality, and tales with a universal truth, suspense, or surprise.

8. Themes and Story Structure

Many well-known and loved stories concern a problem that is insightfully solved by the main character. They begin by introducing a setting and characters and have a body of events that moves the story forward to a quick, satisfying conclusion. The story line is strong, clear, and logical. One category of stories described as cautionary seems to have been designed to keep children safe by teaching a truth or moral, consequently helping children make wise decisions. Tales can be selected based upon their versatility and the perceived needs of an individual child or a particular group of children.

> Storytellers are the direct medium between the story and the audience, able to change pace, alter or explain a difficult point, dramatize or play down an event, according to the needs of those listening. (Mathias, 2006, p. 9)

Teachers intent on increasing the vocabulary have the opportunity to introduce, emphasize, define, and weave in specific words of their choice into stories. **DAP**

9. Storyteller Enthusiasm

Is the story well liked by the teller? Does the teller feel comfortable with it? Is it a story the teller will be eager to share?

Finding a story you love may make it easier for the child to enjoy the story you tell. The easiest door to open for a child is one that leads to something you love yourself. All good teachers know this. And all good teachers know the ultimate reward: the marvelous moment when the spark you are breathing bursts into a flame that henceforth will burn brightly on its own (Photo 9-4).

Photo 9-4 A classroom prop can introduce a teacher's story.

© 2016 Cengage Learning®

MacDonald (1996) advises:

> Just jump in. Storytelling is like swimming. You can't do it by sitting on the bank. You have to jump in and start dog paddling. You take a story that you love and think would be fun to tell, and you just start telling it. You keep on doing it until you get good at it. It's that simple, but you've got to start. You'll never do it sitting on the bank. (p. 13)

9-3 Types of Stories

Some stories, particularly folktales and fairy tales, have been polished to near perfection through generations of use. Classic tales and folktales may contain dated words and phrases, but these might be important story parts that add to the story's charm. In retelling the story to young children, a brief explanation of these types of terms may be necessary. A **fable** is a simple story in which animals frequently point out lessons (morals), which are contained in the fable's last line.

Many great stories, called **participation stories**, have opportunities for active child involvement and the use of props. Props, such as pictures, costumes, and other objects, may spark and hold interest. An old cowboy hat worn by the teacher during the telling of a Western tale may add to the mood and can later be worn by children in play or during a child's attempt at storytelling.

Repetitive phrases or word rhythms are used in all types of stories, and chanting or singing may be necessary in the telling. If these aren't present, the teacher can create them and add them. Some tales, such as the adventures of Anansi, a spider of African origin, have a rhythm and cadence found in no other stories. Anansi stories, researchers believe, exist today because of an African oral storytelling tradition.

Stories of children of color are a natural part of the curriculum. Teachers should try to avoid the tendency to just look for stories in their own cultural and ethnic background. The right story, regardless of the characters' ethnicity, will fit emotionally, intellectually, and physically.

9-3a Story Ideas

Almost any life adventure or happening and any classroom-inspired story works well when it has a touch of drama. Don't be afraid to tell stories other teachers find unsuccessful, and borrow their good ones, too!

Classic Tales

Goldilocks and the Three Bears

Little Red Riding Hood

The Three Little Pigs

The Billy Goats Gruff

The Little Red Hen

The Gingerbread Boy

From Aesop's Fables

The Lion and the Mouse

The Hare and the Tortoise

The Ant and the Grasshopper

Traditional Stories

Hans Christian Andersen, *Ugly Duckling*

Arlene Mosel, *Tikki Tikki Tembo*

Florence Heide, *Sebastian*

Beatrix Potter, *Tale of Peter Rabbit*

It is wise for beginning teachers to not waste their time on material that does not inspire them to feel, "I can't wait to tell this!" You are sure to find such stories if you look.

9-4 Practice and Preparation

When a teacher has selected a story, a few careful readings are in order. Try to determine the story's main message and meaning. Next, look closely at the introduction that describes the setting and characters. Study Figure 9-1 and analyze how the selected story fits this pattern. The initial setting besides describing location and characters often sets up a problem or dilemma. The story can be outlined on a four-by-six-inch (or larger) cue card to jog your memory during practice sessions (Figure 9-2). Memorizing beginning and ending lines and interior chants or songs is suggested. Once the story rolls out effortlessly, the storyteller fine-tunes it by practicing

---

fable — a short tale in prose or verse that teaches a moral, usually with talking animals or inanimate objects as main characters.

participation stories — stories with some feature children can enact through physical movements, verbal expression, or both.

Figure 9-1 Common and classic story pattern form.

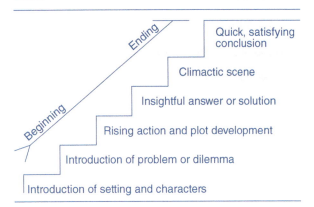

dialogue, and identifying pauses, gesturing, and facial expressions. Particular attention should be given to the rising action in the story's body so that one event builds on another until a quick, satisfying conclusion is reached.

In many cultural rituals, an air of magic, soft flickering embers, were part of the storytelling experience. African storytellers would begin, "A story, a story, let it come, let it go." Ritual can mean entering a particular "distraction-free" classroom area, lighting a candle, wearing a special teacher hat, dimming the lights, saying a chant, or engaging in a special finger play that

Figure 9-2 Cue and file card example.

Intro. "Once upon a time, there were four little rabbits, Flopsy, Mopsy, Cottontail, and Peter. They lived with their mother in a sand-bank, underneath the root of a very big fir tree."
Theme. Mind your mother.
Problem. Peter disobeys and goes into McGregor's garden.
Rising action.
Peter squeezes under garden gate and eats a lot.
McGregor sees him.
McGregor chases him, and he loses a shoe.
Peter gets caught in a gooseberry net and loses his jacket.
Peter hides in the tool shed in a can full of water.
Peter sneezes, almost gets caught, but jumps out a window.
Peter cries and sees cat (another danger).
Peter makes a dash for the gate and gets free.
Peter gets home without clothes and shoes, goes to sleep, and misses dinner. Mother serves him tea.
Ending lines.
"But Flopsy, Mopsy, and Cottontail had bread and milk and blackberries for supper. And that's the end of the Tale of Peter Rabbit!"

settles and brings anticipation. One clever teacher created a story sack and reached inside and slowly raised her hand to her mouth before beginning. Another teacher found only short, action-packed stories containing many move-the-body features appealed to his group of three-year-olds.

Use the following steps in preparing a story: The first step is to divide the story into units of action. As you read the story, you will notice that most divide into an easily definable series of actions, scenes, or episodes; these can be summarized in brief form, and then the sequence can be learned. The second task is to identify those sections that do need to be memorized verbatim. This may include some words, some repeated phrases, or perhaps some larger sections. A discerning storyteller learns verbatim these repeated sections, because the repetition encourages children to join in as the teller recites the lines. As you tell a story, your eyes might be constantly roaming the group, touching every face and drawing each listener back into the story over and over again. Many stories come to life and grab attention; you will notice changes in the children's behavior.

Select a setting with few distractions where everyone can hear and seating is comfortable. Do not begin until listeners are ready. Be at a level to maintain eye contact and prepare an introduction that piques children's interest. Use a prop, or tell something about the story's source or author, or discuss a related event, or ask a question to focus attention (Photo 9-5). Your opening phrase is your bridge between the world of ordinary conversation and the world of the story, and this crossing is best when both magical and deliberate.

9-4a Additional Techniques

The following storytelling techniques and tips should be kept in mind.

- Guard against sounding mechanical. Tell the story in your own personal way.
- Develop story sequence pictures. These can be mental images.
- Practice before a mirror or with another staff member.
- Use gestures.
- Maintain eye contact by scanning the group during the telling; watch for children's interest or restlessness.

Photo 9-5 Using pictures or photos to introduce the setting in your story is sometimes successful.

- The teacher should pace the storytelling by going faster during exciting or fast-action parts and slower in serious parts. Adventure stories may feature the unknown or unexpected and include elements of excitement and surprise.

- Use a clear, firm voice. Try changing voice volume and tone to fit the story; in some parts of the story a whisper may be most effective. Change your voice to fit the characters when they speak, if you feel comfortable doing so.

- Learn to lengthen or shorten a story for maximum effect and involvement of the audience (Mathias, 2006).

- Interrupt the story if necessary to explain some item, event, or action that does not seem clear to the audience.

- Don't worry about retelling a story exactly as before, but stick to the sequence of story events.

- Involve the children often, especially with repetitions, rhymes or actions, silly words, or appropriate questions, if the story lends itself to this.

- Sit close to the group; make sure all are comfortable before beginning.

- Include teacher's and children's names and familiar places in the community.

- Start by telling little personal stories about your family, pets, and daily happenings, if you are a novice; move on to simple stories with lots of repetition.

- Seek out talented storytellers in your community to observe your storytelling or to appear as guest storytellers in your classroom.

- Become very familiar with any pronunciations, including proper names and foreign or unfamiliar terms in stories.

- Use dramatic pauses to build suspense, after an exclamation, or to facilitate transitions between story events.

- Try to communicate characters' attitudes and motivations.

- Consider the flavor and language of the particular tradition from which the story comes.

- Let the story unfold as you picture scenes in your mind.

- Slow down. Some tales are best shared when spoken at half of normal conversation speed.

- Move your body with your story.

A storyteller who sees that children are losing interest in a story is free to make changes in it, based on intuition and knowledge of the group. Others would disagree with changing well-known, classic tales, but they do advise changing one's style, pace, or voice volume to draw listeners back to the story. It is important to remember that even the best storytellers have an occasional flop. If the storyteller is not able to draw the children back to the story, the story may be ended very quickly and tried at a later time, using a revised version.

9-4b Teacher-Created Stories

Many teachers find that they have a talent for creating stories and find that a popular character in one story can have further adventures in the next. Remember that "bad guys" in stories are enjoyed as much as "good guys." Whenever a teacher cannot find a story that seems tailor-made for a particular group of children, she can create one. Take care that themes do not always revolve around "mother knows best" episodes, and watch for sexism and stereotypes when creating a story.

9-4c Telling Stories for an Educational Purpose

If the story includes an important concept, *content* needs to be creatively conceived and made interesting. It can be made interesting by relating it to children's lives. *Motivation* is enhanced when children identify with some story element. Interactive storytelling, where children have some part in the telling, engages unmotivated learners.

Timing involves telling a story in a progression from beginning, to middle, to end. Pacing, at the right speed, holds attention. **Semiotics** considers cultural and cognitive differences. A story set in an imaginary preschool classroom similar to the children's own classroom and the inclusion of familiar words like block area or bicycle path will help children connect.

The writings of Vivian Paley (1990, 1994) are full of examples of purposeful educative storytelling, and show how one dedicated teacher used storytelling to change and enhance children's lives in and out of school.

9-4d Child-Created and Child Dictated Stories

Storytelling is probably the first situation in which the child must sustain a **monologue** without the support of a conversational partner. It is a complex cognitive endeavor that involves a kind of "story sense" and "story grammar." To be coherent, a child's story needs to be more than an unrelated series of events, as is often the case with beginning child storytellers. Teachers should realize that for some preschoolers, including those from low-income homes and minority backgrounds, personal storytelling may be their area of strength and giftedness.

As children are exposed to stories told and stories read, they construct their own ideas about the linguistic features of narrative storytelling. They use their stories as a way of expressing certain emotionally important themes that preoccupy them and of symbolically managing or resolving these underlying themes.

Many educators believe that despite our best efforts, we just do not reach young children on the inside, where they hide their stories. They think that teachers fail, at times, to consider children's individual and developmental histories—in other words, who they are and how they think. Watching children's dramatic play, teachers will see stories "acted out" rather than told. They will be spontaneous, creative, natural, and seemingly much easier and enjoyable than the act of child storytelling. Teachers can appreciate child actors in dramatic play situations, for they create their own script, improvise, and develop characters in the roles they have chosen or been assigned. At times, dramatic play may seem a series of unrelated events, but surprisingly, the teacher will witness many logically flowing scenarios, such as stories in action or preschool "soaps."

Encouraging child authorship and child storytelling goes hand-in-hand with teacher storytelling. It is an excellent way to develop fluency and elaborated language. Children's sense of "I am a story creator" is often incorporated into their self-concept. This helps children form the skills an author needs. It is a good idea to offer activities in which pictures or props are used as motivators. Children's attempts are not edited or criticized but simply accepted. Logic should not be questioned, nor should the sequence of events be corrected. Each story is special. Teachers can think of child-dictated stories as print-awareness activities. Young children may have had limited experiences with adults printing their ideas (Photo 9-6). Child story dictation presents another use of print—a personal important use. Beginning writers do not write because they have something they want to say; they write in order to discover what they have to say, just as they played with blocks and discovered what they could create. This is why dictation is so valuable to the young storyteller. Subtly and, over time,

---

monologue — literally "speaking alone."

Photo 9-6 The teacher explains that Tray has dictated a short story to accompany his artwork.

© 2015 Cengage Learning®

dictation helps teach the child-author that a written story is merely an oral story put into print.

If recorded or dictated, the story should be taken verbatim. Discussions that allow the children to tell what they liked best about a story can alert children to desirable story features. Egg timers may be useful if rambling, long-winded children leave little time for others. Asking for child volunteers to retell stories to other children works in some programs; an announcement may be made that Mark or Susie will be sitting in the storyteller's chair after snack. Teachers tactfully remind children before the volunteer starts her story that questions or comments will be saved until the story is over. An adjacent box of storytelling props may help a child get into character. If the teacher has told *Goldilocks and the Three Bears* using three stuffed bears, a yellow-haired doll, three doll beds, and three dollhouse chairs, chances are children will want to use the same props for their own telling of the story.

Clipboards can be used to list the stories that are created throughout the day. The creation of stories is given status, and sharing these stories is a daily occurrence. Sharing takes place with the child's permission, and the child chooses whether she or the teacher will present the story to the group.

Children's first storytelling attempts often lack sequence, have unclear plots, ramble, and involve long, disconnected events; as children mature and are exposed to stories and books, authorship improves. The goal is not to produce child storytellers but to encourage a love for and positive attitudes toward oral storytelling. The development of child storytelling seems to follow a sequence beginning with children's use of language to create a special or private world. This is believed to be a forerunner to the child's use of language to create a world of make-believe. It leads to the gradual acquisition of the specific conventions that constitute a sense of story. Jones (2011) points out that children's imaginative play involves making conscious choices. She proposes that when a child is engaged in mastering play skills, either constructive or dramatic, the child is practicing storytelling by recreating a plot, motive, character, and setting. As children mature, their stories increase in length and complexity. Children gradually acquire greater control over the events in their stories, moving from a loose collection of related and unrelated events to a tightly structured narrative that links a set of events to each other and to a common theme.

Children's Artworks and Storytelling. When a class conversation focuses upon a child's piece of art that depicts a real life event, the child usually becomes an eager translator and communicator. Not only is verbal fluency involved, but also child emotion. Many times higher-level thinking skills become apparent. Each individual child's story can offer new insights and the joy of realizing others have the same emotions.

9-4e Working on Comprehension

One important goal in formal reading instruction is promoting children's story comprehension. Another goal is to help children organize and understand the ideas, events, and feelings the story produced. Children get practice in using logic when they think about story sequence, cause and effect, emotions felt, fantasy versus reality, incongruities, and other story elements. After-story discussion led by the teacher might focus on

- making a visual graph of some story element (whether the monkeys ate grapes, bananas, melons, etc.).
- asking if anyone has a question about the story.
- listing on a chart what information about alligators was present.
- asking if someone heard a new word or name.
- asking about story noises or actions.
- discussing how children might change something a character did.
- having the children make up a different way to end the story.
- discussing how the children might have solved a problem in the story.
- asking the children if they could show the story in pictures and what would come first and last.
- making a story map showing the travels of a story character.
- asking the children's opinion of a story character's behavior as being good or bad—and why,
- asking about a character's possible emotions during story events.

Teachers wanting to use a storytelling activity to promote children's story comprehension, vocabulary, and analytic ability; and higher level thinking skills can use the same steps used with read alouds discussed in Chapter 8. This preplanned approach includes analyzing the story to be told for its story content, character development, and identifying the vocabulary words necessary for children's deeper level of understanding. A preplanned story introduction is then created offering a mini-overview to whet children's motivation to listen. It might include a prediction of what might happen. Key vocabulary word definitions are then considered and also the teacher questions and comments that aid understanding. The last teacher planning task involves a story question after the story ends that aids additional comprehension.

9-5 Teaching Aids

Encourage young children to tell a story while using pictures, photographs, or other visuals supplied by the teacher. Visuals stimulate both creative thinking and visual literacy skills. What is so interesting to teachers is the diverseness of stories a group of children may relate from the same visual images. Picture files are useful in many language arts activities and are well worth the time spent collecting, mounting, and protecting them with clear contact paper.

Story sequence cards are popular teaching aids. These are made for children's viewing and use rather than teacher practice cards. Children can see that stories progress from a beginning to an end, with events, actions, and happenings occurring in a sequence. Children can use them for storytelling and retelling by lining or propping them up in sequence to "picture read." Cards can be made from two picture books, teacher tracings, or photo copies pasted on cardboard, with or without adjoining print. Examine Figure 9-3, which displays picture sequence cards for a story found at the chapter's end called *It Was My Idea*. Elster (2008) notes:

> Storytelling through a sequence of pictures without words is an old and varied genre, appearing on church walls and American Indian Winter Counts (Native American tribal chronicles painted on animal skins), and in wordless comic strips. (p. 25)

One teacher offered storytelling using a clothesline activity. A new story scene was added to the clothesline each day until the story was complete. Children were asked to suggest and decide what might happen next after teacher pinned up each new scene. Only limited teacher

---

story — an imaginative tale with a plot, characters, and setting.

story map — a timeline showing an ordered sequence of events.

Figure 9-3 Story sequence cards.

Two snow geese flying   Geese by lake   Turtle

Geese with turtle
flying together   Farmer   Turtle falling
into haystack

art ability was necessary, for the children readily accepted her drawings. The teacher added a short printscript story sentence on each new scene after a group discussion took place.

9-6 Successful Dictation and Special Concerns

COMMON CORE

Teachers act in the dual role of scribe and facilitator when taking dictation of a child's story. Asking questions to clarify and help the child express ideas is deemed appropriate. Younger children seem to run out of steam after 10 minutes or more of storytelling, and some are done in less than two minutes.

Statements that help children start dictating stories follow.

- "Tell me the words you want me to write down on the paper."

- "Do you have a story to tell?"

"Let's write down what you said about your new puppy."

During dictation a teacher may guide a child toward developing the sequence of a story or help the child find the story's beginning and end. When working with a child who is more advanced, the teacher might encourage the child's use of dialogue or the child's development

of descriptive language. The decisions children make mentally during dictation are complex. The child may pause, start, and stop, all of which reflect the child's attention to the task at hand.

Preschool classrooms that announce that the teacher or volunteers are available and start a waiting list for a child-dictated storytelling time find that children accept and look forward to the opportunity. The success of the dictation activity may rely on the promise of dramatization. Linking dictation to children's opportunity to jointly act out before peers what the children have written is believed to be the key (Figure 9-4). Young children's interest in a concrete representation of their stories (the drama or action) coincides with young children's emotional need to establish their individual identity within the group.

Teachers experienced in recording dictated stories frequently find differences in boys' and girls' tales. Boys' stories are far less likely than girls' to have either a stable cast of characters or a well-articulated plot. Their action-packed themes are often not developed in a realistic progression of events. Girls' stories usually maintain a more sequential storyline and depict events in family life. Boys' stories focus on generating adventure and excitement. Boys' main characters are often big, powerful, frightening, wild, scary, and violent while girls may create animals that are soft, cute, and cuddly. Bathroom-type stories

Figure 9-4 Example of a child's story dramatization.

Teacher:	Alexandra's story goes like this: (Paraphrasing) "The lady knocked on the door. Her dog was big and fluffly. The lady said, "Do you want to buy my cookies?" The girl in the house told the lady "yes" if the lady could sing a song that would make her dog bark. She did. They had cookies and lemonade under the tree in the yard."
Teacher:	(to Alexandra) Who do you choose to be the lady with the dog and the cookies? (Alexandra chooses Dana.)
Teacher:	Dana will you be the lady? (Dana nods "yes.")
Teacher:	Alexandra choose your dog. (Alexandra chooses Patrick.)
Teacher:	Patrick can you be a dog that barks? (Patrick says, "Okay.")
Teacher:	Now we need a girl in the house. Who do you choose Alexandra? ("Maria," she answers.)
Teacher:	Maria would you play the girl in Alexandra's story? (Maria nods "yes.")
Teacher:	Dana, Patrick, and Maria, please come up here in front. Everyone else can move to where they can see and sit down. Alexandra's play is going to start. (Children move and sit.)
Teacher:	Dana and Patrick, let's start with you moving to the door of Maria's house. "The lady knocked on the door." "Do you want to buy my cookies?"
Teacher:	"I will if you sing a song and your dog barks."
Teacher:	Dana if you don't know a song to sing you can just sing la, la, la. "The dog barks." The teacher and the children finish the play sequence. Maria improvises giving Dana coins.
Teacher:	Good acting. Dana really sang a song. Patrick, what a good job of pretending to be a dog. You walked like a dog. Maria that was a good idea—giving money for cookies. A class discussion follows. Children decide to ask Alexandra if the story can be "acted" again.

or gory stories appear at times in child dictation and should be censored if inappropriate.

9-6a Early Writing Skill and Teacher Dictation

Should early childhood educators help children with *relating skills*? Relating skills would include the ability to speak and later write ideas clearly. To do so when dictating a story, the child needs some beginning idea of story structure: what comes first, next, etc. If they are giving a report of something experienced, they need some idea of a sequence of happenings. If they are providing directions that help someone accomplish a task, they will need to have some sequence of actions in mind. If they are dictating a note or message, children will need to identify what facts or information they want the receiver to know.

Early childhood teachers use picture-book readings, storytelling, flannel board stories, story songs, poetry, and other literary activities to provide young children with opportunities to acquire an understanding of story structure. They point out story sequence in picture-book discussions. Many other preschool activities deal with a sequence of time, actions, and steps needed to complete a task. Teachers gently promote children's clarification of ideas by accepting statements and children's ideas and their opinions. When a teacher makes comments such as "Jacob thinks we should have snack after recess" or "Ethan wants to know if the hamster has been fed," the teacher is restating what she thinks a child has said and this let's the child know she has been either understood or misunderstood. It gives the child the opportunity to correct and try again to express herself more clearly.

What early childhood teacher actions, strategies, and techniques encourage children's dictation of stories and other types of written communication? Some suggestions follow.

- Don't pressure the child to dictate. This is a child-choice activity.
- Encourage children to dictate their ideas concerning a real and present happening such as how they made a drawing or block structure, or how a problem was solved, or how a project was completed. They can also be encouraged to relate an important experience or happening or a message they want to send, or to dictate a sign for a dramatic play area, and so on.

- Listen raptly at the child's eye level.
- Probe for intent.
- Help the child articulate what she is trying to communicate.
- Help the child begin if necessary.
- Recap by reading what the child has already contributed after dictation starts.
- Give a short teacher example, when prudent.
- Talk about what you are doing as you take dictation.
- Date the child's work, and encourage creation of a title, if the child wishes.
- Compliment what story structures or features you can.
- Comment on descriptive word use that adds clarity and interest.
- Suggest that the child may want a visual to accompany her words—such as a drawing, etc.
- Post the child's work and/or encourage the child share the writing with others. (Teachers can read

Figure 9-5 Teacher dictation statements.

1. Probing for intent:
- "Those are scary words—monster, ghost, and devil. You are trying to tell a scary story, is that right?"
- "Your kitten's fur is soft and you are saying you like to feel the soft fur."
- "In your story something is going to happen to this very small mouse and you have used the words *little* and *tiny* to describe the mouse."

2. Commending children's efforts:
- "You've decided on an interesting title for your story. It tells me your story will be about a cat."
- "Your message begins with telling your mom something you want her to know. Is there something else you want to tell her?"
- "That's a good start. Now I know you are in a park when your story begins."
- "You've said three words—see, here they are."

3. Getting the ball rolling:
- "Lots of stories start with 'Once upon a time.' "
- "Is your story about a zoo, and airplane, a clown, or something else?"
- "Your first word is . . ."
- "Your story is about . . ."

4. Providing a short story or another writing example:
- "I wrote a story about how I locked myself out of my car yesterday."
- "I wrote a story about my horse, Captain, and how he jumped over a high fence."
- "When I write a note, I think about the important things I want the person to know."
- "Sometimes just one word in a sign says what I want others to know, like 'danger' or 'hot.' "

5. Talking about what you are doing as you are doing it:
- "I'm listening to hear your words."
- "I'm starting in the left-hand corner."
- "I'm printing the word _____."
- "It starts with a 'B.' "
- "That word has two syllables: 'door' and 'way.' "
- "Joseph is his name, so I printed a capital (big) 'J.' "

6. Giving compliments:
- "You told me three things about your dog. That's neat, because now I know more about him." (content)
- "Your story had a beginning, a middle part, and an end. All good stories have those, too." (appropriate story sequence)
- "You talked until you were finished and didn't stop to play—good going." (staying focused)
- "I liked that word you used. The word was *gigantic*. It's a big word that describes large objects like elephants, skyscrapers, and monster trucks." (vocabulary)

7. Commenting on the use of descriptive words:
- "You used the word *spotted* to tell me how your dog looks. That tells me he looks different from my dog."
- "When you said your favorite cookie was chocolate chip, I knew exactly what kind of cookie it was."
- "Your description of the snow floating to the ground told me it was a certain kind of snow."
- "When you said you ran very fast, I knew you were in a hurry."

and talk about the child's dictation, after asking the child if she wishes the teacher to do so.)

- Develop a classroom writing file where children's dictation is kept and explain that all will go home at the end of the week unless the child wants it to go home sooner.

Figure 9-5 gives examples of additional teacher statements that relate to the dictation suggestions in the above list.

9-6b Reaching Reluctant Storytellers

Educators may be faced with some young children who seem unable to initiate stories or who are reluctant interactive audience members. Reaching these children can be a challenge. Telling one's own story involves an element of risk. Becoming comfortable speaking before a group may be difficult for some children in light of their innate nature, home culture, or past experience. A classroom alive with "story," dramatization, and performance may slowly reach these children, as the fun, excitement, and "social connectedness" of storytelling become part of their classroom lives. Most child groups have a number of enthusiastic story presenters, who are learning which of their presenter skills or created story parts are enjoyed by their audience. These are willing and eager models.

Some children feel comfortable using active body movements and dance, and it has become integral to their storytelling style. The early childhood educator who introduces storytelling discovers that wild fantasy and vivid imagination are alive and well in most young children.

Limited-English Children. Pantomimes of eating dinner, going to bed, dressing, washing one's face and brushing teeth, opening a door with a key, rocking a baby to sleep, and other activities intrigue limited-English speakers. Pantomimes can include words in English and other languages enacted by children and adults. Props are sometimes useful. Guessing is half the fun. Using pantomimes can introduce and enhance the world of storytelling.

9-6c A Cut-and-Tell Story

Clever teachers have created cut-and-tell stories that readily capture children's attention, but these take practice so that a teacher's cutting

while telling does not dim the story line. A surprise at the story's ending usually delights. While telling these stories, the teacher cuts a paper shape relating to the story line. *The Boy in the Boat*, an example, follows.

Preparation

Step 1: Fold a piece of 9-by-12-inch (or larger) paper in half.

Step 2: Fold top corners of the folded side down toward the middle.

Step 3: Fold single sheet up over triangles.

Step 4: Turn over and fold single sheet up.

Those who know how to fold a sailor's hat will recognize the pattern. Tell the story with scissors handy.

Once there was a boy (or girl) who wanted to be a sailor. He had a sailor's hat. (Show hat shape.) And he had a boat. (Turn the hat so it becomes a boat.) One day he climbed in his boat and floated to the middle of a big lake. It was very hot, for the sun was bright. He took off his shirt and pants and threw them into the water. He had a swimming suit on under his clothes, and he felt much cooler. His boat hit a large rock and the front of his boat fell off. (Cut off front of boat.)

Then a giant fish took a bite out of the bottom of the boat. (Cut off the bottom.) It is best to use the scissors here. Cut a bite shape (half circle).

The back of the boat came off when a big bird flew down and sat on it. (Cut off the back of the boat.)

The boy didn't have but a little boat left and water was reaching his toes, so he jumped overboard and swam to the shore. He watched his boat sink. Then he saw something white floating toward him. What do you think it could be? (Unfold what's left of the boat.)

His shirt! (Using large newspaper sheets works also.)

9-6d Parents, Volunteers, and Community Storytellers

It is surprising how many family members, volunteers, and community elementary school-aged children, high school students, and adults will rise

Dear Parents/Guardians,

This letter is written to you to encourage you to tell personal and created stories to your children. The benefits of your storytelling are multiple. Every parent, family member, and grandparent can be a vast treasure chest of stories about real-life adventures. Families are unique resources and may possess knowledge of family heritage, stories of past family happenings, and contain family viewpoints. These stories will be lost if adults don't recall and share them.

You've probably already told a few stories to your children. Maybe you prefer to tell stories in a quiet private place or at a certain time of day. Building anticipation is a great idea. Opportunities present themselves frequently such as on car trips, and during waiting times. These are part of daily life. The more frequently you are with children the more opportunities present themselves.

If you can remember family stories told to you as a child, or stories told by your teachers or others, you probably remember how fascinating and appealing the stories were, and how they led you to ask for more and eventually to reading books. Some of us were very fortunate to have had a beloved storyteller in our childhood, and carry pleasant memories of the mental pictures that were conjured up.

It won't really take a lot of energy or effort because most of your stories are already in your head. Every story you tell makes you a better teller, that is, if you monitor the reaction you see in your listener's behavior. If you like to ham it up, you may have the makings of a great storyteller. If you don't that's fine because every storyteller has his own style and just being yourself, being natural, works very well.

Most storytellers take into account the age and interests of their child listeners and modify stories to fit. The goal is to make the experience enjoyable, pleasant, and stop before the child's ability to focus is exhausted. It's best to stop with the child still eagerly hear more, than to fall into the trap of overdoing it!

Sincerely,

Your Child's Teachers

Digital Download

to the occasion when asked to tell fictional stories or stories concerning significant life experiences. Grandparents and other seniors might relate stories from their own unique childhoods and backgrounds. Stories about contemporary happenings are also valuable. Many of these stories might involve a rich array of multicultural and multigenerational themes and offer wisdom accumulated through many years of living. Stories might also be told in the authentic language of the storyteller. Many individuals and groups work hard to preserve cultural and ethnic stories and techniques.

Many cities have storytelling clubs and associations. One well-known resource is the National Storytelling Association. Be sure to provide visiting storytellers guidelines regarding story suitability, time length, child seating arrangements, and fielding children's questions (Figure 9-6).

It Was My Idea

One winter two snow geese were on their way south flying high in the sky. They looked down and saw a beautiful lake. They were tired and hungry, so they landed together, splashing across the sparkling water. There were seeds and bugs everywhere, and they ate their fill. A talkative turtle poked his head up from the water, and talked, and talked, and talked. "We'll get no rest here," said one goose to the other. The turtle overheard, and said, "I want to see the world. Take me with you. Will you? Will you? Will you?" The geese laughed. "Now, how can we take you with us?" they said. "I'll get a stick. If you both hold it in your beaks, I can clamp down in the middle with my strong snapping mouth," explained the turtle. "It won't work turtle, you couldn't stop talking that long," laughed a goose. The turtle talked, and talked, and talked. Finally, the geese said, "Yes," just to shut him up. The three took off together with turtle biting the stick and hanging between them. Soon they flew over a farm. A farmer in the field looked up. He had never seen such a sight. He called to his wife, "Look at those clever birds, aren't they smart?" Turtle called back as he fell from the sky, "It was my idea." Turtle was very lucky to fall into a giant haystack. He was happy and ready to start a new adventure on the farm.

(This is a "bare bones" version of this tale. The author suggests you embellish it by adding descriptive words and developing further characterization. Invoke color and use sounds. Add details suiting your own personal style.)

9-1 Describe how storytelling can help language growth.

Through storytelling, children begin to realize the power and potential of the words they speak. Storytelling adds new words to their vocabulary and promotes their oral speech development and output. Children's listening behavior sharpens after hearing a number of stories. This adds to their recognition of common story elements and structure: beginnings, middles, and endings. Understanding how a speaker's gestures, facial expressions, body positions, and movements communicate meaning is also experienced. Storytelling offers children the opportunity to use words creatively and mentally form images that combine words and actions. Cultural traditions and classic themes are often presented through storytelling. This promotes additional cultural literacy understandings. Storytelling can prompt children's authorship, increase self-confidence, and improve their precision in their expression of ideas.

9-2 Identify three suggested story selection criteria.

Recommendations for the selection of a story to be told by a beginning teacher include:

- Choose stories that appeal to the teacher.
- Judge stories' age level appropriateness.
- Decide if children can relate to the story in light of their past life experiences.
- Judge if the story has a valuable or redeeming feature that adds to the children's knowledge and lives.
- Decide if the story transmits appropriate values.
- Decide if the story is too frightening.
- Choose a story that is well plotted and clear.
- Choose action-packed stories that involve the children in some physical or oral way.
- Successful stories often use repetition, rhyme, silliness, directly quoted conversation, and end in an engaging or satisfactory way.

- Cultural stories that include traditions and stories with classic themes can lead to additional literacy understandings.
- Choose stories that promote child authorship, self-confidence, and more precise vocabulary.

9-3 Discuss types of stories commonly used for preschool storytelling.

The variety of story types is large. Classic tales and folktales have been enjoyed by generations of young children. Some fables can be told. A story that invites child participation or uses props adds to child enjoyment and language learning. Repetitive phrases, chanting, or singing increase child pleasure. Cultural stories enlarge the child's base of experience and can increase vocabulary. Stories with a touch of drama are suitable and often sought. Teacher-created stories can be used for a specific teaching objective.

9-4 List reasons to practice stories before telling.

Practice first involves determining a story's meaning and message so that a teacher's actions and speech are appropriate and reflect intentions. A story's setting introduces a story's particular location and characters. When a story is understood and practiced, the teacher is able to prepare the child audience to begin to grasp what might follow and take place. This sets the stage for learning. Preparing cue cards helps the teacher remain confident and relaxed in her telling and also be better able to watch the children's reactions instead of concentrating on her own words and actions. Cards can display opening and ending lines when prepared beforehand. Teaching aids enhance the storytelling experience because they can jog the teacher's memory for details and dialogue. Gestures will better reflect story happenings when they are well in mind through both practice and preparation. With a story well prepared, the teller remembers a series of sequential scenes. As the story unfolds, the teacher can better gauge what pace, pause, or volume is necessary. When prepared, the teacher can choose the best possible classroom telling site suiting the story.

9-5 Describe two teaching aids that might be used in a storytelling activity.

Teaching aids are visuals that enhance the storytelling experience for they connect words and actions to representations. Pictures, photographs, picture files, story sequence cards and teacher drawings were mentioned. Objects and other items that are mentioned in the story can also be used.

9-6 Describe the value of promoting child dictation stories.

Children engaged in telling a story dictated to their teacher can come to understand stories have sequential happenings, dialogue, and descriptive language. They mentally make complex decisions about what words best relate their intentions. Story structure becomes clearer. Their story may lead to its enactment and increase their individual identity and confidence within their peer group. Children can gain the realization that their words are powerful and can entertain and elicit different audience reactions. Child dictation also benefits early print (writing) skill development.

Additional Resources

Readings

Bennett, T. (2013). *The Power of Storytelling: The Art of Influential Communication.* American Fork, UT: Sound Concepts, Inc.

Buvala, K.B. (2012). *How to Be a Storyteller.* Tolleson, AZ: Creation Company Consultants.

Cooper, P. M. (2009). *The Classrooms All Children Need: Lessons in Teaching from Vivian Paley.* Chicago, IL: The University of Chicago Press.

Christie, I., Raines, S., & Waites, W. (2000). *Tell It Again 2.* Beltsville, MD: Gryphon House.

Gottschail, J. (2012). *The Story Telling Animal: How Stories Make Us Human.* New York: Houghton Mifflin Harcourt Publishing Company.

Hamilton, M., & Weiss, M. (1996). *Stories in My Pocket: Tales Kids Can Tell.* Golden, CO: Fulcrum Publishing.

Simmons, A. (2001, 2006). *The Story Factor.* New York: Basic Books.

Vierra, J., & Gorbachev, V. (2002). *Silly and Sillier: Read-Aloud Tales from Around the World.* New York: Random House.

Helpful Websites

National Storytelling Network

www.storynet.org

Offers teacher storytelling resources.

The Internet Public Library

http://www.ipl.org

Includes some story text. Click "For Kids," then Story Hour.

Reading Is Fundamental

http://www.rifnet.org

Reviews storytelling history and benefits.

10 Poetry

Objectives

After reading this chapter, you should be able to:

10-1 Discuss what learning objectives poetry activities may promote.

10-2 Describe poetry selection criteria for preschoolers.

10-3 List three teacher techniques that improve poetry presentation.

10-4 Name two good sources for children's poetry.

naeyc NAEYC Program Standards

2E06 Children are helped to recognize and produce words that have the same beginning or ending sounds.

2E06 Children are encouraged to play with sounds of language, including syllables, word families, and phonemes using rhymes.

2E04 Children have varied opportunities to access books with rhymes.

DAP Developmentally Appropriate Practice (DAP) Preschoolers

3H12 Teachers introduce engaging oral language experiences that include rhyming and alliteration.

3H12 Teachers encourage children to add their own verses and variations.

2D1 Teachers consistently plan learning experiences that children find highly interesting, engaging, and comfortable.

2.3 Use a wide range of texts including poetry.

COMMON CORE Common Core State Standards, K-3

SL.CCR. 2 Integrate and evaluate information presented in diverse media and formats including visually, quantitatively, and orally.

Freckles

I notice Yolanda staring at my arm one day. She was new and had moved here from Arizona. She asked, "What are those?" It was summer, and my freckles really stood out. "They are called freckles," I said. She answered, "Have you tried to get them off?" I replied, "I tried buttermilk one time because someone told me buttermilk would make them go away. But it didn't work." She thought about that for a moment and said, "Have you tried soap and water?" I laughed, and told her that soap and water did not work either. Later that day, Yolanda walked by saying, "Sprinkles, speckles, freckles," while smiling up at me. "That's a rhyme, Yolanda," I answered.

Questions to Ponder

1. What do you think about Yolanda's logic?

2. Would freckles or Yolanda's created rhyme be something to talk about with children at a sharing time?

3. Were the teacher's verbal responses appropriate?

Children's poetry is an enjoyable vehicle for developing listening skills and oral language. Activities that involve poetry hold many opportunities to promote the association between pleasure and words. Poetry has a condensed quality that makes every word important. It prompts imagery through its sensory descriptions and can introduce enchanting rhyming tales. Nonsense verse appeals to the preschoolers' appreciation for slapstick.

The repetitive format of rhymes makes them "memorable." Expectancies are set up and gloriously materialize. Children's desire to hear more is intensified. The language of rhyme becomes easily remembered; it can become part of a child's linguistic and intellectual resources for life. **naeyc DAP**

Photo 10-1 Poetry can hold a child's attention.

© 2015 Cengage Learning®

Poetry is a perfect test for what language can do; it is full of wordplay. Poets have always used language in special ways, and in poetry, we have a vehicle for looking at the use of words; that is, the choosing of the one special word that fits perfectly. We need to share with children words that "taste good"—that tickle the tongue, tease the ear, create images in the mind's eye, delight us with their trickery, and amuse us with their puzzles and complexities.

Appropriate children's poetry is plentiful and varied. In addition to fast action and mood building, there is the joy of the rhythm of the words in many **poems**. Some rhythms in classic rhymes are so strong that they can motivate children to move their bodies or clap. The nursery rhymes "Jack and Jill," "Twinkle, Twinkle, Little Star," and "The Little Turtle" are good examples. Rhythm encourages children to join in orally, experiment with language, and listen to the rhythmic sounds. Some poems appeal to the emotions; others, to the intellect (Photo 10-1).

A preschool child with beginning literacy might be described as a child familiar with Mother Goose rhymes and other contemporary and classic poems, and one who knows that rhyming words sound alike. Three-year-olds delight in silly and playful poetry.

---

poems — metrical forms of composition in which word images are selected and expressed to create powerful, often beautiful, impressions in the listener and/or enjoyable rhythmic responses in young children.

10-1 Learning Opportunities

Poetry provides an opportunity for a child to learn new vocabulary, ideas, and attitudes and to experience life through the eyes of the poet. To remember how many days there are in a month, many people still recite a simple poem learned as a child. If you are asked to say the alphabet, the classic ABC song of childhood may come to mind. If you are a child trying to remember how to turn a water faucet on one might recite, "Left is hot, right is not."

Poetry has form and order. It is dependable, which makes it easy to learn. Simple rhymes are picked up quickly, as most families know from their children's ability to remember television jingles. Children in early-childhood centers enjoy the accomplishment of memorizing short **verses**. They may ask to share the poems they have learned with the teacher, just as they ask to sing songs they know (which are often poems set to music).

The teacher provides encouragement, attention, and positive comments to the child who responds to poetry. As with picture book reading, storytelling, and other language activities, the goal of the teacher in regard to poetry is to offer children pleasure and enjoyment of the language arts while expanding their knowledge and interest.

Poetry, then, is used for a variety of reasons, including the following.

- familiarizing and exposing children to classic and contemporary poetry that is considered part of our literary heritage
- training children to hearing sounds
- providing enjoyment through the use of poems with silly words and humor
- stimulating children's imaginations
- increasing vocabulary and knowledge
- building self-worth and self-confidence
- encouraging an understanding of rhyming
- alerting children to rimes (word families) is a productive way to explore an element of phonics (Rasinki & Zimmerman, 2013).

McNair (2012) points out that hearing and becoming familiar with poetry benefits children. Poetry often includes new vocabulary exposure. It increases attention and focus on language and wordplay, and offers insights about self, others, and the world in general. Literacy experts, such as Temple et al. (2010), suggest poetry encourages children's celebration of what is clear, precise, beautiful, artful, and true in our language.

10-1a Poetry and Early Reading Ability

Poems, rhymes, and chants acquaint young children with language in repeated pleasant patterns and with catchy rhythms, such as "The Grand Old Duke of York." Drop the words in this rhyming chant. Use da-Da, da-Da, da-Da, etc., and see how easy it is to isolate and sense the accented words and syllables. Pointing out rhyming words helps teach a child that different words share some of the same sounds.

Experts believe children's ability to discriminate, create rhyming words, and sense the rhythm of words is closely related to early reading ability. Playing sound-based word games with rhyming features help prepare children for ease in early reading (Dehaene, 2009). Educators agree that a great deal of evidence indicates that both early awareness of rhyme and nursery rhyme knowledge facilitate literacy acquisition. It is a significant predictor of later progress in reading and spelling. A relationship exists between early rhyme awareness and later phonological skills.

Nursery rhyme knowledge is a strong predictor of word attack and word identification skills when children begin early reading. The connection between rhyme awareness and the child's subsequent acquisition of literacy-related skill demonstrates that a developmental pathway to reading involves rhyme. Repetition of consonant sounds in the lyrics of **nursery rhymes** like "cock-a-doodle-doo, dee-doodle-dee doodle-dee doodle-dee-doo" certainly demonstrates rhyme and **alliteration.**

Children develop skill in identifying rhyme at an early age. The relationship between rime units

---

verses — lines of a poem or poetry without imaginative or conceptual power.

nursery rhymes — folk sayings with rhyming words for very young children

alliteration — repetition of beginning consonant sounds.

and words that rhyme is obvious: words that rhyme share the same rime unit. Refer back to the discussion of phonemic awareness and rimes in Chapter 7. Children's knowledge of nursery rhymes is believed to be predictive of their success in spelling two to three years later.

10-2 Selection

Poetry introduces children to characters with fun-to-say names such as:

- "Jonathan Bing" by Beatrice Curtis Brown.
- "Mrs. Peck Pigeon" by Eleanor Farjeon.
- "Godfrey Gordon Gustavos Gore" by William Rands.

The characters can live in familiar and farfetched settings, such as.

- under the toadstool, from "The Elf and the Dormouse" by Oliver Herford.
- the animal store, from "The Animal Store" by Rachel Field.
- in a little crooked house, from *Mother Goose*.

And they have various adventures and difficulties.

- "The kids are ten feet tall," from "Grown-Up-Down Town" by Bobbi Katz
- "Christopher Robin had wheezles and sneezles," from "Sneezles" by A. A. Milne
- "Listen, my children, this must be stopped," from "The Grasshoppers" by Dorothy Aldis

Teachers select poetry that they can present eagerly and that they believe children will like. Delight in words is a natural outcome when the poem suits the audience. Teachers look for poems of quality and merit. Three elements exist in good poetry: (1) distinguished **diction**, (2) carefully chosen words and phrases with rich sensory and associated meanings, and (3) significant content. Much of classic poetry has a song quality and a melody of its own. Poetry can say something to children, titillate them, recall happy occasions or events, or encourage them to explore.

Teachers have found traditional eighteenth-century nursery rhymes are still popular with today's children. Favorite rhymes with strong four-beat **couplets** ("Humpty Dumpty" and others) were repeated with the teacher exaggerating the beat (as children do). This technique held group interest. Categories of verse popular with most preschoolers have one or more of the following characteristics:

- simple story line ("Jack Be Nimble").
- simple story line with finger play ("This Little Piggy").
- story in song with repeated chorus ("London Bridge").
- verse/story with nonsense words ("Hey, Diddle, Diddle").
- descriptions of daily actions ("Little Jack Horner").
- choral reading in which youngsters could join in with rhymed words ("To Market, to Market").

No child should miss the fun, wit, and wisdom of Mother Goose. Literacy, in part, depends on a child's exposure to cultural tradition. Mother Goose is an American tradition with origins in Europe. Make a list of Mother Goose characters. You will be surprised at how many you remember.

Practicing teachers recommend the following poetry selection criteria. Begin with poems that are sure to please. Select poems that have strong rhythm and rhyme. Find poems that play with sound or are humorous. And, look for content that is familiar to children's lives and experience. Once children have been bitten by the poetry bug, focus on rhythm and rhyme, and explore how various poets use sound devices such as alliteration or onomatopoeia.

10-2a Types of Poetry

There are several types of poetry:

- lyric melodic is descriptive poetry that often has a song quality.
- narrative poetry tells a story or describes an event or happening.
- limerick is a poem with five lines of verse set in a specific rhyming pattern that is usually humorous.
- free verse poetry does not rhyme.
- nonsense poetry is often ridiculous and whimsical (Figure 10-1).

---

diction — clarity of speech; enunciation.

couplets — stanzas of two rhyming lines.

Figure 10-1 A whimsical poem.

"What's did you do?"   said the shoe.

"I sat on the hog,"   answered the dog.

"Is he dead?"   asked the bread.

"That is not funny!"   said the bunny.

"Is that a hat?"   said the cat.

"No, it is not,"   replied the clock.

"Well, what is it then?"   asked the hen.

"Stop. This poem is too silly!"   said Uncle Willy.

10-2b Poetry Elements

A particular poem's rhythm is influenced by sounds, stress, pitch, and accented and unaccented syllables. Manipulation of one or all of these features creates a particular idea, feeling, or message. Some rhythms are regular; others are not. The enjoyable quality of the Mother Goose rhymes stems from their strong rhythm and cadence. In poetry, authors use rhythm to emphasize words or phrases, consequently capturing children's immediate focus. Exciting, dramatic rhythms and relaxed, soothing rhythms can be included in the same poem. Poetry's rhythm is capable of making children feel that they are actively participating, rather than merely listening.

Children's literature is full of rhyming words and rhyming names (Photo 10-2). Poetic rhyme can occur within sentences or at line endings. Children often rhyme spontaneously, during play. Nonsense rhymes have given joy to generations of children; sayings like stomper-chomper, icky-sticky, and Dan, Dan, elephant man, can spread immediately among children.

Alliteration (defined as the occurrence of two or more words having the same initial sounds, **assonance**, or vowel sounds) is often used in poetry. All types of repetition are characteristic of children's poetry. Visual images are stimulated

Photo 10-2 Children often recognize rhyming words in their favorite digital and print books.

© 2016 Cengage Learning®

---

assonance — the repetition of words of identical or similar vowel sounds followed by different consonant sounds.

by the poet's use of sensory words and **figurative language** (nonliteral meanings). A poet may provide a new way of looking at things by comparing previously unconnected objects or events. **Similes** (direct comparisons between two things that have something in common but are essentially different) or **metaphors** (implied comparisons between two things that have something in common but are essentially different) are often found in poetry. Giving human characteristics and emotions to inanimate objects and animals **(personification)** is also commonplace, and talking dishes, trains, birds, bears, and pancakes are plentiful in children's poems.

The format of printed poetry (type size and style, page layout, punctuation, and capitalization) has been used to heighten enjoyment and highlight the subject matter. One can find poems printed in the shape of a tree or in a long, narrow column of single words.

10-3 Teacher Techniques

If a poem is read or recited in a conversational manner, rather than in a singsong fashion, the rhyme is subtle and enjoyable. Singsong reading and recitation may become tiresome and difficult to understand. Teachers know that reciting from memory requires practice, so the poems they memorize are a few favorites. However, memorization can create a mechanical quality, as the teacher focuses on remembering rather than enjoyment.

Often, poetry is shared through teacher readings from lap cards. A poem should be read smoothly without uncalled-for hesitation. This means the teacher has to prepare by reading the poem enough times for it to roll off the tongue with ease, savoring the words in the telling.

The enjoyment of poetry, like other types of literature, can be increased by an enthusiastic adult. Careful reading of poetry is necessary because of poetry's compactness, and tendency to make every word count. When encouraging children to join in and speak favorite poetry lines, sensitive handling is in order. A teacher can suggest, "Let's say it together" or "Join me in saying this poem if you like." A child should not be

singled out or asked to recite without volunteering. Some gregarious children will want to share poems they have learned. A number of repetitions of a favorite verse may be needed before it is totally remembered. Children usually start with a few words or phrases.

Giving careful attention to both pitch and stress is important. Another important element when reading poetry aloud is juncture, where one makes the breaks in the poem. Your awareness of juncture will make or break your presentation. The natural tendency is to break at the end of the printed line, which may lead to artificial segmenting, not intended by the poet. Look at Figure 10-2. Read the first two lines as one sentence without pausing at the word *tree*. Now, read the poem stopping at each line's end and you'll see what artificial segmenting means.

A technique that works well for a change of pace is to use music without lyrics but with a strong repeated beat as a backdrop for poems or

Figure 10-2 A rhyming chart.

I am a pine tree
growing on a hill.
I can stand so very,
very still. All at
once the wind
begins to blow.
I bend to and fro,
to and fro, to and fro.

---

figurative language — language enriched by word images and figures of speech.

similes — comparisons of two things that are unlike, usually using the words *like* or *as*. Example: "Love is like a red, red rose."

metaphors — figures of speech in which a comparison is implied by analogy but is not stated.

personification — a metaphorical figure of speech in which animals, ideas, things, etc., are represented as having human qualities.

teacher-created rhymed lines. The result is chant-like or rap-like and promotes children's joining in and at times also clapping. Being playful with rhyme is another strategy that can draw attention to the sounds in rhyming words. Teacher might say, "Let's say it again with an 's' sound and make it *'Swinkle, swinkle, little star.'*" Or try something fun like *"Pondon Pridge is Palling Pown."*

Poetry charts displayed on a stand next to the teacher are a helpful device for capturing attention and freeing a teacher's eyes to meet those of the children. When reading from a chart, quickly glance at a line and then turn so that the words are transmitted to the children. The school poetry chart referred to earlier (Figure 10-2) contains print and illustration. For Figure 10-3, children were encouraged to think of a poem that a book might say about book care and handling. The teacher printed the child-dictated poems and identified them with the authors' names.

Preschool children sometimes create rhymes during play. The teacher can jot them down for

Figure 10-3 If books could talk, what would they say?

A POETRY CHART

Be gentle	Sticky hands
Turn pages slow	Make a mess
I don't want to	When I'm clean
Rip you know!	I look my best.
by Ashad	by Carla
I fall apart	My printed words
In the rain	Will make you laugh
Pages crinkle	This book's about
It's a pain!	A funny giraffe.
by Ling	by Hensie
If after you hold me	Don't walk away
You put me back	I'm lonely today
Others will find me	Look at me
On the book rack.	Before you play.
by Rena	by Lori
Inside my cover	When you hold me
A story hides	In your hands
Pick me up	And turn my pages
And look inside.	I feel grand.
by Juan	by Omar
If you've never	I'm not safe
Been to the zoo	On the floor
Animals inside	Where feet kick
Might frighten you.	And make me sore.
by Sierra	by Bradford

display or to be taken home by the children. A child's "Amber, pamber, big fat bamber," was of great interest to other children. The teacher who recorded it shared it at group time as a rhyme created by a playmate.

Poems dictated by children should be recorded verbatim, with no editing or teacher suggestions. Each creation is regarded as special. Lionni's *Frederick*, a wonderful picture book, helps children understand rhyming. This book's last two lines read:

"But Frederick," they said, "you are a poet!"

Frederick blushed, took a bow, and said shyly, "I know it."

10-3a Ways to Introduce Children to Poetry

- Posting poems in conspicuous places may help create interest, particularly if pictures or illustrations are placed adjacent to the poems.

- A poetry tree, made by placing a smooth tree limb in plaster of Paris, can have paper leaves with poems on the back that can be selected at group times.

- A poem of the day (or week) bulletin board has worked well in some classrooms.

- The Academy of American Poets sponsors a *Poem in Your Pocket Day* and encourages teachers to share their pocketed poems in celebration of poetry.

- Pictures and flannel boards can be used in poetry presentation to interest and help children focus on words. Other props or costumes that relate to the poem (such as a teddy bear or police officer's hat) will gain attention. Some of the best collections of poems have no pictures; others have an illustration for each poem.

- A poem can be enjoyed indoors or outdoors, or between activities as a "fill-in" when the teacher or children are waiting.

- Mounting cut magazine pictures and trying to think up words that rhyme with what is pictured is a rhyming activity many teachers favor. Teachers can hold up a picture and say, "Here's a toy. Let's give it to a . . . "

Nursery songs emphasize rhyme, rhythm, alliteration, and playful enjoyment. Classic nursery and preschool songs are listed in Figure 10-4.

Figure 10-4 Nursery songs—old and new classics.

OLD CLASSICS

"Here We Go 'Round The Mulberry Bush"

"London Bridge Is Falling Down"

"Rock-a-Bye Baby"

"Row, Row, Row Your Boat"

"Sing a Song of Sixpence"

"Three Blind Mice"

"Twinkle, Twinkle Little Star"

"I'm a Little Teapot"

"Pop Goes the Weasel"

NEW CLASSICS

"You Are My Sunshine"

"Take Me out to the Ball Game"

"Blue-Tailed Fly"

10-4 Sources

A fine line divides finger plays, body and movement games, chants, songs, and poems. All can involve rhyme and rhythm. Poems presented later in this chapter are primarily the type that children would merely listen to as they were being recited, although many do contain opportunities for child participation. Many fine picture books contain rhymed verse and can enhance a center's poetry program. Collections, anthologies, and books of children's poetry are available at the public library, bookstores, online booksellers, and school supply stores, as well as in children's and teachers' magazines.

Teachers also can create poetry from their own experiences. The following suggestions for authoring poems for young children help the teacher-poet by pointing out the special features found in older classics and quality contemporary poetry.

- Include mental images in every line.
- Use strong rhythms that bring out an urge to chant, move, or sing.
- Use frequent rhyming.
- Use action verbs often.
- Make each line an independent thought.
- Change the rhythm.
- Use words that are within the children's level of understanding.

- Use themes and subjects that are familiar to the young child.

Teacher-created poems promote child-created poems.

Many teachers search for ethnic poems that allow them to offer multicultural variety. No one cultural group has a corner on imagination, creativity, poetic quality, or philosophic outlook. Each has made important contributions to the total culture of the country and the world.

Recalling the poems and verses of one's own childhood may lead a teacher to research poems by a particular poet. Remembering appealing poetry elements may also help a teacher find poetry that may delight today's young child. Poetry collections are cited in the Additional Resources section at the end of this chapter.

10-4a Suggested Poems

The poems that follow are examples of the type that appeal to young children.

If I Were an Apple

If I were an apple

And grew on a tree,

I think I'd drop down

On a nice boy like me.

I wouldn't stay there

Giving nobody joy;

I'd fall down at once

And say, "Eat me, my boy!"

Old Rhyme

Animal Crackers

Animal crackers, and cocoa to drink,

That is the finest of suppers, I think;

When I'm grown up and can have what I please

I think I shall always insist upon these.

What do you choose when you're offered a treat?

When Mother says, "What would you like best to eat?"

Is it waffles and syrup, or cinnamon toast?

It's cocoa and animals that I love the most!

The kitchen's the coziest place that I know:

The kettle is singing, the stove is aglow,

And there in the twilight, how jolly to see

The cocoa and animals waiting for me.

Daddy and Mother dine later in state,

With Mary to cook for them, Susan to wait;

But they don't have nearly as much fun as I

Who eat in the kitchen with Nurse standing by:

Having cocoa and animals once more for tea!

"Animal Crackers," © 1917, 1945 by Christopher Morley. From *Chimneysmoke* by Christopher Morley. Reprinted by permission of Harper and Row Publishers, Inc.

One Stormy Night

Two little kittens,

One stormy night

Began to quarrel,

And then to fight.

One had a mouse,

The other had none;

And that's the way

The quarrel begun.

"I'll have that mouse,"

Said the bigger cat.

"You'll have that mouse?

We'll see about that!"

"I will have that mouse,"

Said the eldest son.

"You shan't have the mouse,"

Said the little one.

The old woman seized

Her sweeping broom,

And swept both kittens

Right out of the room.

The ground was covered

With frost and snow,

And the two little kittens

Had nowhere to go.

They lay and shivered

On a mat at the door,

While the old woman

Was sweeping the floor.

And then they crept in

As quiet as mice,

All wet with the snow,

And as cold as ice.

And found it much better

That stormy night,

To lie by the fire,

Than to quarrel and fight.

Traditional

Whisky Frisky

Whisky frisky,

Hipperty hop,

Up he goes

To the tree top!

Whirly, twirly,

Round and round,

Down he scampers

To the ground.

Furly, curly,

What a tail,

Tall as a feather,

Broad as a sail.

Where's his supper?

In the shell.

Snappy, cracky,

Out it fell.

Anonymous

To Market

To market, to market,

To buy a fat pig,

Home again, home again,

Jiggety jig.

To market, to market,

To buy a fat hog,

Home again, home again,

Jiggety jog.

To market, to market,

To buy a plum bun,

Home again, home again,

Market is done.

Mother Goose

Secrets

Can you keep a secret?

I don't suppose you can,

You mustn't laugh or giggle

While I tickle your hand.

Anonymous

Oliver Twist

Oliver-Oliver-Oliver Twist

Bet you a penny you can't do this:

Number one—touch your tongue

Number two—touch your shoe

Number three—touch your knee

Number four—touch the floor

Number five—take a dive

Number six—wiggle your hips

Number seven—say number eleven

Number eight—bang the gate

Number nine—walk the line

Number ten—start again.

Traditional

Raindrops

"Splash," said a raindrop

As it fell upon my hat;

"Splash," said another

As it trickled down my back.

"You are very rude," I said

As I looked up to the sky;

Then another raindrop splashed

Right into my eye!

Anonymous

Pretending

I'd like to be a jumping jack

And jump out from a box!

I'd like to be a rocking horse

And rock and rock and rock.

I'd like to be a spinning top

And twirl around and round.

I'd like to be a rubber ball

And bounce way up and down.

I'd like to be a big fast train

Whose wheels fly round and round.

I'd like to be a pony small

And trot along the ground.

I'd like to be so many things

A growly, scowly bear.

But really I'm a little child

Who sits upon a chair.

Anonymous

Slow Turtle, Fast Rabbit

Turtle and Rabbit went walking each day.

They moved along in the funniest way.

Turtle talked s-l-o-w-l-y but he listened well.

Rabbit hopped fast and had much to tell.

He hopped in circles around turtle slow.

He talked and talked about all he did know.

Rabbit, of course, knew of every disaster

And he spoke out in spurts like a TV forecaster.

"Molefellinahole." "Roosterflewintoapole."

Words shot out of his mouth like an arrow in flight.

Turtle, a good listener, understood them all right.

Turtle answered, "T-o-o b-a-d t-h-a-t i-s s-o s-a-d."

Rabbit went on to relate,

"Snakeateawholecakegottastomachache."

"Bearlosthercub."

"Antwasswallowedbyabigyellowbug."

Turtle said, "N-o h-a-p-p-y n-e-w-s t-o-d-a-y?"

"OhsureIknowsomething," he did say.

"Skunkfellinthewellandhelosthissmell!"

J.M.M.

The Island of a Million Trees

I took my ship and put out to sea

Sailing to the Island of a Million Trees.

Lucky Duck flew on the deck

There was Happy Me, and Lucky Duck sailing free.

To Million Tree Island we sailed our ship.

Neal the Seal asked to join our trip.

The ship was big so we said, "yes."

Happy Me, Lucky Duck, Neal the Seal, our new guest.

The wind did blow and along we flew

Sailing, playing, eating lunch, too.

We heard a meow from a floating raft

And rescued a kitty named Sweet Little Taff.

*There was Happy Me, Lucky Duck, Neal the Seal, and Sweet
    Little Taff.*

Sailing free to the Island of a Million Trees.

We drifted east and drifted west.

A storm stirred the waves, we could not rest.

A voice cried out from the gray fog

And over the side climbed Sailor Bob.

There was Happy Me, Lucky Duck, Neal the Seal,

Sweet Little Taff and Sailor Bob.

Off to the Island of a Million Trees.

Off in the distance we spotted land

With a million trees and mile of sand.

Closer and closer our boat did go.

Hands on the oars we started to row.

There was Happy Me, Lucky Duck, Neal the Seal,

Sweet Little Taff, and Sailor Bob.

Stepping onto the Island of a Million Trees.

Danielle Tracy

Harry T. Bear Learns To Rhyme

Harry T. Bear says he can rhyme.

"Harry," I say. "Rhyme the word game."

He says, "Game rhymes with door."

I say, "Game rhymes with name."

"Give me a better word," says he.

"Well then try to rhyme the word bug."

Harry T. says, "Bug rhymes with bear."

"They start with the 'B' sound that's true

But Harry T. no rhyme is there."

He smiles and says, "Rhymes I can do!

Bug rhymes with rug, jug and mug, too."

"Harry T. you've got it hurray!"

That was the start of a very bad day

He could only talk in rhyme you see

His awful rhymes were bothering me.

When I said, "It's time to eat."

He said, "Meat, feet, sweet, tweet and seat."

I said, "I am going to bed."

He said, "Dead, lead and read."

"Stop please." I said "This is hurting my head!"

"But I can say rhymes anytime"

"Enough already," I then cried.

"Please take your rhymes and go outside."

Away he went out the door

My head ached I wanted no more.

As Harry T. Bear walked out of sight

I heard him say light, kite and bite.

Then his voice disappeared into the night.

He'll be back on my bed when I awake

I hope he has no other rhymes to make.

Danielle Tracy

Harry T. Bear Says He Can Read

At night Harry says "Is it time?"

He puts on pajamas when I put on mine

Harry T. Bear hides books in my bed

Under the pillow where I lay my head.

"See," Harry T. says "Black marks

In a straight row

Are alphabet letters

Making words that I know!"

Harry says, "I CAN read books

But you read them best"

He sits and looks

While I read his requests.

Harry picks books 'bout caves and honey,

Or silver fish swimming in streams.

I like books that are funny,

Or have birthday parties with chocolate ice cream.

Together we sit all snuggled tight.

I read the pictures by the lamp's golden light.

Harry T. Bear says, "Please read it again."

But I fall asleep before the book's end.

That's when Harry T. Bear says he reads to me.

Danielle Tracy

Permission granted by Danielle Tracy, 2008.

I Bought Me a Rooster

I bought me a rooster and the rooster pleased me.

I fed my rooster on the bayberry tree,

My little rooster goes cock-a-doodle-doo, dee-doodle-dee
   doodle dee doodle dee doo!

I bought me a cat and the cat pleased me.

I fed my cat on the bayberry tree,

My little cat goes meow, meow, meow.

My little rooster goes cock-a-doodle-doo, dee-doodle-dee
   doodle dee doodle dee doo!

I bought me a dog and the dog pleased me.

I fed my dog on the bayberry tree,

My little dog goes bark, bark, bark.

My little cat goes meow, meow, meow.

My little rooster goes cock-a-doodle-doo, dee-doodle-dee
   doodle dee doodle dee doo!

Traditional

Note: This is a cumulative poem that takes teacher practice; additional verses
include as many animals as you wish.

The Chickens

Said the first little chicken,

With a queer little squirm,

"I wish I could find

A fat little worm!"

Said the next little chicken,

With an odd little shrug:

"I wish I could find

A fat little bug!"

Said the third little chicken

With a small sign of grief:

"I wish I could find

A green little leaf!"

Said the fourth little chicken,

With a faint little moan:

"I wish I could find

A wee gravel stone!"

"Now see here!" said the mother,

From the green garden patch,

"If you want any breakfast,

Just come here and scratch!"

Anonymous

Talking Animals

"Meow," says cat.

"Bow-wow," says dog.

"Oink," says pig.

"Croak," says frog.

Hen says, "Cluck."

Lamb says, "Ba."

Cow says, "Moo."

and babies "Wah."

Lion says, "Roar."

Mouse says, "Squeak."

Snake says, "Ssssis."

Chick says, "Peep."

Pig says, "Squeal."

Owl says, "Hoot who."

Toad says, "Ree deep."

Cuckoo says, "Cuckoo."

Donkey says, "Hee Haw."

Horse says, "Neigh Neigh."

Turkey says, "Gobble."

And we all say, "HOORAY!"

J. M. M.

Note: Last line can also read, "And we say 'Happy Birthday!'"

Here Comes the Bus

Lights flashing, gravel crunching, the big yellow door
    swings open swooshing the air.

Big kids make faces in the windows and the driver smiles
    down the stairs.

When I climb in that bus I'm a big kid too

With my snack in my backpack and my new shiny shoes.

I'll wave to mom and kiss the glass. Today I'll be a
    kindergartner—at last.

I'll make new friends and run and play. There are things to
    do like blocks and clay.

I'm going to learn to draw and write, and spell and make
    my numbers right.

Mom says to share, be kind and good for the teacher has
    rules to tell.

I'll sit or stand like teacher says and listen for the bell.

Since I'm five, I know a lot like alphabet letters, left, right,
    and stop.

I can print my name and say colors, too. I'm a big kinder-
    gartner and that is new.

J. M. M.

Over in the Meadow

Over in the meadow, in the sand in the sun,

Lived an old mother frog and her little froggie one.

"Croak!" said the mother; "I croak," said the one,

So they croaked and were glad in the sand in the sun.

Over in the meadow in a pond so blue

Lived an old mother duck and her little ducks two.

"Quack!" said the mother; "We quack," said the two,

So they quacked and were glad in the pond so blue.

Over in the meadow, in a hole in a tree,

Lived an old mother robin and her little birds three.

"Chirp!" said the mother; "We chirp," said the three,

So they chirped and were glad in the hole in a tree.

Over in the meadow, on a rock by the shore,

Lived an old mother snake and her little snakes four.

"Hiss!" said the mother; "We hiss," said the four,

So they hissed and were glad on a rock by the shore.

Over in the meadow, in a big beehive,

Lived an old mother bee and her little bees five.

"Buzz!" said the mother; "We buzz," said the five,

So they buzzed and were glad in the big beehive.

Little Boy Blue

Little Boy Blue,

Come, blow your horn!

The sheep's in the meadow,

The cow's in the corn.

Where's the little boy

That looks after the sheep? Under the haystack, fast asleep!

Traditional

The Cat and the Fiddle

Hey, diddle, diddle!

The cat and the fiddle,

The cow jumped over the moon;

The little dog laughed

To see such sport,

And the dish ran away

With the spoon.

Mother Goose

The Little Girl with the Curl

There was a little girl

Who had a little curl

Right in the middle of her forehead;

When she was good

She was very, very good,

And when she was bad she was horrid.

Mother Goose

Summary

10-1 Discuss what learning objectives poetry activities may promote.

Early childhood language learning objectives attempted with poetry sharing can include connecting literature with pleasure and interest in words and the way words sound. Both listening skill and oral language development are encouraged. Children can gain a sense of poetry's rhythm, predictability, and patterns. Poetry introduces children to cultural classics and increases children's common literary heritage. Phonological sound play is a pre-reading activity, and the power of words to provoke emotions may be better understood. Vocabulary development often happens and poetry memorization can increase child self-confidence.

10-2 Describe poetry selection criteria for preschoolers.

Poetry selection criteria can include selecting poetry that a teacher can read with enthusiasm, content quality and value is assessed, diction is judged, strong rhythmic content is appropriate, variety in poetic verse can be a plus, and content that relates to young children's lives is sought.

10-3 List three teacher techniques that improve poetry presentation.

Teacher techniques when presenting poetry include reading in a conversational manner, memorizing but a few favorites while avoiding mechanical presentation, using lap cards, preparing by practicing beforehand, reading with enthusiasm, suggesting children join in, adjusting pitch and stress to suit words and phrases, considering juncture (natural breaks), drawing child attention to rhyming words, and reading from poetry charts.

10-4 Name two good sources for children's poetry.

Sources for poetry suggestions in the text were books of children's poetry collections and/or anthologies, public and professional libraries, bookstores, online booksellers, school supply stores, and children's or professional teachers' journals or magazines. Self-authored poems were encouraged.

Additional Resources

Readings

Cole, B. (1990). *The Silly Book*. New York: Doubleday.

Crews, N. (2004). *The Neighborhood Mother Goose*. New York: Harper Collins.

Elliott, D. (2010). *In the Wild*. Cambridge, MA: Candlewick.

Rovetch, L. (2001). *Ook the Book and Other Silly Rhymes*. San Francisco: Chronicle Books.

Yolen, J., & Peters, A. F. (2010). *Switching on the Moon: A Very First Book of Bedtime Poems*. Cambridge, MA: Candlewick.

Yolen, J., & Peters, A. F. (2007). *Here's a Little Poem: A Very First Book of Poetry*. Cambridge, MA: Candlewick.

To find multicultural poetry for young children using an Internet search, use the key words *Multicultural Poetry, African-American Children's Poetry, Hispanic Children's Poetry*, and so on.

Read-Aloud Rhyming Picture Books

Christelow, E. (1998). *Five Little Monkeys Jumping on the Bed*. Boston: Houghton Mifflin.

Collins, H. (2003). *Little Miss Muffet*. Toronto: Kids Can Press.

Guarino, D. (1997). *Is Your Mama a Llama?* New York: Scholastic.

Lansky, B. (2004). *Mary Had a Little Jam*. New York: Meadowbrook Press.

Miranda, A. (1997). *To Market, to Market*. San Diego: Harcourt.

Mosel, A. (1988). *Tikki Tikki Tembo*. New York: Henry Holt.

Shannon, G. (2006) *Busy in the Garden*. New York: Greenwillow

Seuss, Dr. (1960). *One Fish, Two Fish, Red Fish, Blue Fish*. New York: Random House.

Stead, P. C. (2010). *A Sick Day for Amos McGee*. New York: Roaring Book Press.

Poetry Collections

Brown, M. (1985). *Hand Rhymes*. New York: E. P. Dutton.

Brown, M. (1998). *Party Rhymes*. New York: Dutton.

Ghigna, C. (1995). *Riddle Rhymes*. New York: Hyperion.

Kennedy, C. (2005). *A Family of Poems. My Favorite Poetry for Children*. New York: Hyperion.

Moore, H. H. (1997). *A Poem a Day*. New York: Scholastic.

Prelusky, J. (2000). *It's Raining Pigs and Noodles*. New York: Greenwillow Books.

Roemer, H. (2004). *Come to My Party and Other Shape Poems*. New York: Henry Holt.

Schlein, M. (1997). *Sleep Safe, Little Whale*. New York: Greenwillow.

Trapani, I. (1997). *I'm a Little Teapot*. Watertown, MA: Charlesbridge Publishing.

Helpful Websites

The Academy of American Poets

http://www.poets.org

Select "For Educators" link.

Poetry Foundation

http://poetryfoundation.org

Articles about poetry for teachers.

14 Print—Early Knowledge and Emerging Interest

Objectives

After reading this chapter, you should be able to:

14-1 Discuss young children's print awareness and child behaviors that reflect it.

14-2 Outline the probable sequence of events occurring before a child prints a first recognizable alphabet letter.

14-3 Name two goals of print instruction in preschool.

14-4 Discuss drawing experiences' relationship to prewriting instruction.

14-5 Describe five ways that a classroom can promote alphabet awareness.

14-6 Print both the lowercase and uppercase printscript alphabet without using a guide.

14-7 Name four kinds of instructional charts.

naeyc NAEYC Program Standards

2E05 Children have multiple and varied activities to write.

2E06 Children are helped to identify letters and the sounds they represent.

2E03 Children have opportunities to become familiar with print.

2E03 Teaching staff help children recognize print and connect it to spoken words.

DAP Developmentally Appropriate Practice (DAP) Preschoolers

3H19 Teachers create a print-rich environment in which lots of print not only is present, but is also used in ways that show print's many purposes.

3H14 Teachers plan activities that give children a motivation to engage in writing.

3H20 Teachers draw attention to letters and their sounds and use various strategies to help children grasp the alphabetic principle and relate print to spoken language.

COMMON CORE Common Core State Standards, K-3

W.CCR.4 Produce clear and coherent writing in which the development, organization, and style are appropriate to the task, audience, and purpose.

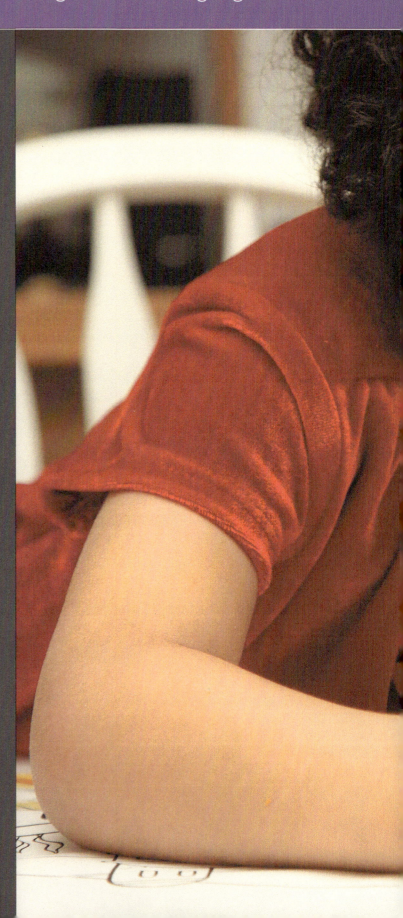

Questions to Ponder

1. What does this vignette tell you about Ong and Cheney?
2. Could the teacher turn this dramatic play into some kind of additional print-awareness learning?
3. What type of teacher-supplied materials could have added depth to the boys' play and print knowledge?

14-1 Printing in Preschool

Preschool teachers ask themselves two pertinent questions concerning print and teaching children to write in printscript:

1. Is it appropriate to offer lessons (activities) that teach print letter recognition and formation at this age?
2. How is instruction in printscript undertaken?

Resolving these questions is made easier by this chapter's discussion.

Current ideas about the child's development of **writing** (printing) skill have undergone a major change. Preschool children are seen as writers. Older ideas promoted the idea that teaching children to print and read should not be undertaken until children are in kindergarten or first grade. It was believed that at that stage children are mature enough or possess the readiness skills that would make these tasks much easier. Writing and reading skills were thought to be different from listening and speaking skills. Speech was accomplished without direct or formal teaching over a long period, beginning in infancy. Educators have revised their thoughts. **naeyc** **DAP**

The concept of early literacy suggests that the foundations of literacy develop from a child's early experiences with print before the onset of formal reading instruction. Educators take children's writing seriously, and they listen for their intended message and support writing development. They are aware early writing is one of the best predictors of children's successful reading (National Early Literacy Panel, 2008).

Symbol making is the essence of what it means to be human. Young children often talk about what they have done, constructed, and drawn, and they "read" meaning into their creations, a meaning they wish to communicate to others. Through talk with others, children invest their marks with meaning. Giving attention to children's work prompts children to translate their work's meaning to the interested adults. It is believed that this type of speech in children paves the way for their eventual use of written forms.

At some point, children gain the insight that print is categorically different from other kinds of visual patterns in their environment, and eventually they learn that print symbolizes spoken language and can be produced by anyone. Children also begin to realize that print holds information. Educators urge teachers to help children see that print holds ideas, observations, stories, and plans.

A review of current research with preschoolers shows that adult–child shared book reading, which stimulates verbal interaction, can enhance language (especially vocabulary) development and knowledge about concepts of print. In addition, activities that direct young children's attention to the sound structure within spoken words, and to the relationships between print and speech, can facilitate learning to read with greater ease.

Preschool children already know something about the world of print from their environment.

---

writing — the ability to use print to communicate with others.

Most children form primitive hypotheses about letters, words, and messages, both printed and handwritten. An estimated 40 percent of children entering kindergarten have a basic familiarity with print. It is a widely held view that learning to read and write will be easier for the child who has had rich home and preschool literacy experiences than for the child who has had little or limited literacy opportunities.

Much of young children's writing is a kind of exploratory play, common in the developmental beginnings of all symbolic media. **Print awareness** and beginning printing skill, and reading awareness and beginning reading skills are now viewed as developing at younger ages, simultaneously with children's growing understanding of a number of other symbol systems. Print awareness describes the child's sensitivity to the presence and use of print in the world around her. When supported by an educative environment, young children compose connected written discourse using emergent forms long before they hold conventional ideas about writing. Children's scribbling, drawing-used-as-writing, nonphonetic strings of letters, and invented spellings are now accepted and honored as reflecting underlying understandings about writing.

The clues have been there for some time. Early childhood educators have always had children that asked questions and displayed early attempts and interest in printing. Preschool children can respond to and learn about visual features of print, know some letters, write some words, make up pretend writings such as letters to people, and dictate stories they want written before they have begun to consider how the words they say may be coded into print, and in particular how the sounds of speech are coded in print. Through informal daily literacy events and adult–child interactions (such as making useful signs), children learn the many purposes and the power of print in their lives and in those of adults. Adults expect children to talk before they read, but they may not have noticed that children are interested in writing before they can read.

Alphabet letters appear in three- and four-year-olds' drawings. Young children go through the motions of reading books, and some have a keen interest in numbers and measurement. This supports the idea that children are attempting to make sense out of what they encounter and are expanding their understandings of symbol systems on a number of fronts (Photo 14-1). However, children do not leap from illiteracy to an understanding that our writing system is alphabetic. They may have hypothesized many conclusions, and they may have tried writing with a variety of their own inventions after puzzling over the relationship between print and speech.

Professional practice promotes teachers' supporting, welcoming, and recognizing children's efforts and accepting children's correct and incorrect conclusions about printing, just as they accepted and supported incorrect or incomplete speech and welcomed it. Teachers are encouraged to have faith in children's ability to discover and develop their own writing theories and symbol systems, as they did when they taught themselves to speak. This takes place in a print-rich environment with responsive adults. Some educators worry about providing too many literacy-focused activities, materials, and

Photo 14-1 Teachers promote interest by showing interest in children's printing attempts.

© 2016 Cengage Learning®

---

print awareness — in early literacy, the child's growing recognition of the conventions and characteristics of a written language. It includes recognition of directionality in reading (left to right and top to bottom), that print forms words corresponding to speech, and that spaces separate words and other features.

furnishings in classrooms, fearing that they may displace other toys and other curricula. This may turn children's play into literacy work.

Teachers must be willing to introduce, demonstrate, and discuss print's relationship and use it in daily activities to pique child interest. Optimal developmental opportunities can be missed in the very best equipped and print-prolific classroom environments. An environment conducive to a child's development of print awareness is a place where print is important and where interactions with print are a source of social and intellectual pleasure for individual children and the people who surround them. Preschoolers who observe and interact within a print-rich environment with sensitive, responsive teachers may discover that print is different from other kinds of visual marks and patterns, and it appears on all kinds of surfaces and objects in different locations (Photo 14-2). They may also notice adults read print materials aloud and silently. With further experience, children often conclude that print symbolizes oral language and holds information.

When preschoolers are read to frequently, they learn

- where one starts reading on a page.
- that reading moves from left to right.
- that at the end of a line, the reader returns to the left margin.
- that pages in a book are in a sequence usually starting with page 1.
- that there is a difference between letter, word, and sentence.

- that there are spaces between words.
- that there are marks, called punctuation marks, that have different names and meanings.
- that there are uppercase (big) and lowercase (little) letters.

Preschoolers will also discover a number of other print-related concepts. For example, they also may become aware that written language functions to label, communicate, remind, request, record, and create.

A child will not learn the name of the letter *B*, the sound of the letter *B*, or how to print it, simply by being with adults or by being with an adult who likes to read. Children learn these critical concepts because adults take the time and effort to teach them in an exciting, engaging, and understanding manner. Figure 14-1 is an example of a teaching assistant's approach.

Writing awareness and beginning writing attempts make more sense to children who have experienced an integrated language arts instructional approach. The areas of speaking, listening, reading, and writing are interrelated. The child's ability to see how these areas fit together is commonly mentioned in school goals. Adults in classrooms communicate with others daily—both orally and in written form. Written communication offers daily opportunities for teachers to point out print's usefulness.

Increased focus on children's early reading success in the United States has provided additional impetus for researching early writing and reading relationships. An increasing number

Photo 14-2 Print is at eye level and saturates this classroom area.

© 2015 Cengage Learning®

Figure 14-1 A teaching assistant helps a child print the word *Daddy*.

Child 1:	(three-year-old): I'm writing a letter to my daddy. How do you write "Daddy"?
Teacher:	Well, let's think about that. /d/, /d/, /d/. What letter do you think we might use to write /d/?
Child 2*:	[five-year-old]: D!
Teacher:	Yes. We do use D, but let's let Ana (fictitious) think about it. She's the one who is writing the word. If she needs help, I'll tell you and then you can tell me what your idea is.
Child 2:	OK.
Child 1*:	I can't make a D.
Child 2:	I can. I will show you. (*Gets up from his chair and puts his arm down next to the child's paper, indicating that he is ready to demonstrate.*)
Teacher:	Well, actually, wait just a minute. I'll grab the chart. (*Reaches toward an alphabet letter chart that is hanging from a book on the side of the paper display shelf in the writing center.*)
Child 2:	But I know how. I can show her.
Teacher:	I know that you know how, but Ana might like to know how you learned it, and she might like to know that this chart can show us how, so we'll just take a quick look at it, and, Allen (fictitious), get another piece of paper. Let's not do our demonstration on Ana's paper. She'll write her own *D* after we show her how.
Child 2:	(*Draws a straight, vertical line, very deliberately on his paper.*)
Child 1:	(*Watches Child 2 with eyes wide and bright.*)
Teacher:	Ok, that's just great. Now, Ana, you make that part of the D on your paper. Where was it you thought you wanted to write "Daddy"?
Child 1:	(*Points to the middle of her paper.*)
Teacher:	Ok, you want it down here in the middle. OK, start a little over here (*gesturing to the left side of the paper, across from where the child had pointed*) so that you will have enough room for all of the letters we'll need to write "Daddy."
Child 1:	(*Moves to the spot indicated by the teacher's finger and draws a pretty good straight, vertical line.*) Now what?
Teacher:	Well, now, there's a curved line that comes out like this (*uses index finger to trace curved line in the D on the chart*), and then it goes back in to touch the line down here. Allen is going to show you how to do that on the *D* he is making on his paper.
Child 2:	(*Draws the curved line very carefully to complete the* D.)
Teacher:	OK, now you can add that curved line to finish your *D*. Start right up here at the top of the vertical line you have already drawn, and then move your marker out this way and then gradually down to touch the line down here (*uses finger to trace the path*).
Child 1:	(*Draws curved line.*) Now what?
Teacher:	Well, let's see. *D* /ae/, /ae/, Daddy. That's a really hard sound to know how to write.
Child 2:	No it isn't. My name starts with that sound.
Teacher:	That's right, it does, and you know what's really funny? Ana's name also starts with that sound, and the sound in her name is spelled with the same letter as the sound in your name. What a coincidence! (*Said as if she had just noticed this herself and thought that it was a remarkable discovery.*)
Child 2:	*A*!
Child 1:	*A*?
Teacher	Yes, *A*. Just as in (*says both names, one after the other, isolating the first vowel phoneme in each name before saying the rest of it.*)
Child 1:	I know how to write *A*! (*Proceeds to do it.*) Now, what is next?
Teacher:	Da /d/, /d/ . . .
Child 1:	D?
Teacher:	Yes, there are two of them.

Figure 14-1 *(countinued)*

Child 1:	I already did one.
Teacher:	Well, I mean there are two more in the middle.
Child 1:	(*Writes the two* D's.)
Teacher:	(*Offers verbal guidance to support recall of lines needed and their direction.*)
Child 1:	OK. Now what?
Teacher:	Daddy, Dadd /e/.
Child 1:	E! (*Child begins to position her marker to begin making an* E.)
Teacher:	Well, the sound is /i/, but we write it with the letter Y. Let me show you one on the chart. (*Same process as was used before is used to instruct Child 1 on making Y and then to help Child 1 to make one of her own.*) OK, that says "Daddy." (*Underlines it with her finger.*) Did you want to write something else?
Child 1:	No, I'm finished.

of experts believe children establish early ideas about printing (writing) that serve as a basis for early printing and reading attempts. Some children can print a word (or many words) the first day they enter kindergarten, and a good number of children come to school believing that they can write. Their first attempts to print concentrate on messages rather than perfection. Generations of children have been asked to learn the letters of the alphabet, sound and symbol correspondences, and a vocabulary of sight words before they learned to write or read. If the same were true of learning to speak, children would be asked to wait until all letter sounds were perfected at age seven or eight before attempting to speak. Early-on children begin to understand that reading means getting meaning from print, and they become increasingly aware of the different functions and uses of written language. Enri (2002) suggests there are four phases children traverse in learning to read words—prealphabetic, partial alphabetic, full alphabetic, and consolidated alphabetic. These phases combine to form a process that involves first using a whole word strategy that doesn't involve letter-sound connections. Children sight read known words and guess at others using picture (contextual) clues. As they become phonologically aware, they start using a partial decoding approach. Developing further they employ a full decoding strategy. According to Enri, they enter the consolidated phase in which they read words by grouping rimes, syllables, and morphemes together.

Based on the notion that the child constructs from within, piecing together from life experiences the rules of oral language, educators believe that if children are given time and supportive assistance, they can crack the writing and reading code by noticing regularities and incongruence, thus creating their own unique rules. Children progress at their own speed, doing what is important to them and what they see others doing. Without formal instruction, children experiment with and explore the various facets of the writing process. They decorate letters and invent their own symbols—sometimes reverting to their own inventions even after they are well into distinguishing and reproducing different, recognizable alphabet letters. Some children expect others to know what they have written, regardless of their coding system.

Evidence indicates that children have extensive knowledge of some aspects of written language. A few children may have developed both phonological awareness and phonemic awareness. Researchers report that roughly 15 percent of three- and four-year-old children can identify words that begin with a particular phoneme and about 25 percent can reliably identify rhyming words. Tests designed to measure print awareness have been found to predict future reading achievement.

The concept of writing readiness began with some important figures from the past that influenced the directions that early childhood education has taken. It became popular to talk about writing readiness as being that time when an average group of children acquired the capacity, skills, and knowledge to permit the group to accomplish the task. Figure 14-2 compares traditional, readiness, and "natural" instructional approaches. It would be difficult to find an early childhood center that does not use some elements of each of the three approaches in the instructional program.

Figure 14-2 Comparisons of instructional approaches in printing.

Traditional Approach

- providing play materials and free time
- supplying art materials, paper, writing tools, alphabet toys and games, chalkboard
- reading picture books
- planning program that excludes instruction in naming or forming alphabet letters
- providing incidental and spontaneous teaching about print

Readiness Approach

- providing writing materials and models
- planning program with introduction to tracing, naming alphabet letters, and naming shapes
- reading picture books
- providing a language arts classroom center
- channeling interested children into print and alphabet activities by offering supportive assistance

Natural Approach

- providing writing and reading materials and models
- planning program that emphasizes print in daily life
- promoting dramatic play themes that involve print, such as grocery store, restaurant, newspaper carrier, print shop, and office
- creating a writing center for the classroom
- supplying alphabet toys and models
- answering questions and supporting children's efforts
- making connections between reading and writing and speaking
- reading picture books

14-1a Starting from a Different Place

At about 16 to 20 months, some toddlers become interested in scribbling. One sees them grasp a drawing or marking tool in their fist and use it in sweeping, whole-arm motions to make marks. Motions can be vigorous, rhythmic, scrubbing, and repetitive and may include sharp stabs at the paper, which tears because of the pressure applied. Adults can wisely provide sturdy, large pieces of paper taped down onto a surface that can take the punishment. Large flattened brown grocery bags work well.

Scribbling involves decision making. It coincides with young children's emerging sense of autonomy. Children make decisions about line, color, and the placement of marks on the paper. They also use and gain control over the tools of their home and classroom—crayons, markers, pencils, paper and so on—if it is regarded as a valued activity.

Past opportunity may have dramatically molded the individual child's literacy behaviors and language competency. Teachers hope to expand language competencies that exist and introduce children to new activities and opportunities. Much of young children's writing is exploratory. Through personally motivated and personally directed trial and error—a necessary condition of their literacy development—children try out various aspects of the writing process. They sometimes interact and collaborate with peers who are more literate (Photo 14-3). Competent others provide help and eventually children function without supportive assistance.

Photo 14-3 Teachers promote both individual and collaborative printing activities.

© 2015 Cengage Learning®

▶❙ **TeachSource Video 14-1**

© 2016 Cengage Learning®

Preschool: Communication through Language and Literacy Activities

1. Is the printscript displayed in the classroom functional and does it have a purpose for being there?

2. Do you think the classroom is well supplied with equipment that is useful for children's writing development? If yes, identify some of these items. If no, what do you think is missing?

3. Name some of the activities that promoted writing development.

14-1b Teaching Writing Tool Grip

Although somewhat controversial, some early childhood programs provide instruction for three- and four-year-olds on how to grip a writing tool. These programs purposefully provide broken crayons (ones of a short length that glide well) and promote young children's use of a finger gripping motion rather than whole hand grasping. Children are shown what these programs believe is the most efficient and comfortable finger gripping position. It is believed that this type of grip allows the best control of the writing tool and aids eventual speed in writing (printing). Children who have already found their own unique grip are shown a second way that they can choose to adopt. Program plans include enjoyable activities that promote small motor control with a finger pinching action, such as picking up small objects. Instructions for the "right" tool grip are as follows: hold the writing tool between a bent thumb and a first finger (index) pointed at the tool's marking tip, with the tool resting on the middle finger; the ring and little finger should be bent

inward toward the palm. Some educators are less enthusiastic about this instructional approach for many reasons, including research that points out that about half of all three-year-olds have already mastered the grip. Other educators feel that child motivation and interest is paramount before grip instruction takes place.

Advocates counter by describing a writing fundamentals curriculum that is without pressure, game-like, and uses songs with clever rhythms to introduce concepts and terms. Each early childhood program will decide how, or if grip instruction or writing fundamentals instruction, will be included in its program. Family members frequently demonstrate their own writing grip to children, and educators usually initiate instruction with a child who exhibits awkwardness or frustration. A right-handed teacher may find that demonstrating a writing grip is difficult with a left-handed child because the paper is slanted in a different direction than for right-handed children. Teachers routinely tape or secure writing paper to tables or large surfaces so the paper won't slip away from early writers, or they may show how holding the paper with the other hand solves the problem.

14-2 Research and Fundamentals in Writing Development

COMMON CORE

In *Literacy Before Schooling* (1982), researchers Ferreiro and Teberosky revolutionized educators' thinking about young children's development of print knowledge and writing. Subsequent research in children's self-constructed knowledge of alphabet forms and printing has followed, using anthropological, psychological, and other investigative approaches. Ferreiro and Teberosky identified three developmentally ordered levels.

1. **First Level**

In this level, children

- search for criteria to distinguish between drawing and writing. Example: "What's this?" referring to their artwork.

- realize that straight and curved lines and dots are present but organized differently in print. Example: Rows and rows of curved figures, lines, and/or dots in art.

- reach the conclusion that print forms are arbitrary and ordered in a linear fashion.

380 SECTION FIVE : Writing and Reading: Natural Companions

- accept the letter shapes in their environment rather than inventing new ones. Example: Rows of one letter appear in linear fashion in art.

- recognize from literacy-rich environments written marks as "substitute objects" during their third year. Example: "What does this say, teacher?" or "This says 'Mary.' "

2. **Second Level**

In this level, children

- look for objective differences in printed strings.

- do not realize that there is a relationship between sound patterns and print.

3. **Third Level**

In this level, children

- accept that a given string of letters represents their name and look for a rational explanation of this phenomenon.

- may create a syllabic hypothesis.

- may print letter forms as syllables heard in a word. Example: I C (I see).

- may develop knowledge about particular syllables and what letters might represent such a syllable.

- may look for similar letters to write similar pieces of sound.

- begin to understand that printing uses alphabet letters that represent sounds; consequently, to understand print, one must know the sound patterns of words.

What conclusions of this landmark research may affect language arts program planning and early educators' interaction techniques? Certainly, teachers will note attending children's active attempts to understand print. They will realize that each child constructs her own ideas and revises these understandings as more print is noticed and experienced. The seemingly strange questions children ask or off-the-wall answers some children give in classroom discussions about print may now be seen as reflecting their inner thoughts at crucial points in their print development. As teachers view children's artwork, they will more readily see early print forms, and they will continue their attempts to provide literacy-rich, print-rich classroom environments.

Some preschoolers demonstrate that they know the names and shapes of alphabet letters. They may also know letters form words and represent sounds. They might have grasped the idea that spoken words can be written and then read. They may be able to express daily uses of written words. Why would a young child write or pretend to write? It is not an easy motor task. Is it simple imitation or is it done for adult reaction? Do children do so because there is an inner drive to know or become competent? Research has yet to answer these questions. Teachers conjecture reasons with each young child they meet who has beginning printing skills. The reasons why children pretend to write are not the most important thing; what matters more are teachers' reactions and their commitment to providing additional opportunities to nourish and expand what already exists.

14-2a Young Children's Progress

Baker and Schiffer (2007) suggest that learning to write begins as children gain familiarity with the alphabet, learn about writing instruments, and recognize simple words in everyday places, such as *STOP* on the familiar red street sign. At some point, children learn that written marks have meaning. Just as they sought the names of things, they now seek the names of these marks and, later, the meanings of marks. Because each child is an individual, this may or may not happen during the preschool years. One child may try to make letters or numbers. Another child may have little interest in or knowledge of written forms. Many children are somewhere between these two examples.

Preschool children may recognize environmental print words before they know the name of any alphabet letters. This is termed **sight reading**, and some preschool children may recognize most of the children's names in their group if nametags are used. Quite a few researchers believe a period of time exists when a young child conceives of a certain alphabet letter as representing a person or object (for example, all "B" words remind the child of her own name). At that point, the child may say, "'B,' that's my name." A child may not understand that the alphabet is a complete set of letters representing speech sounds used in writing, but rather, she may have a partial

---

sight reading — the ability to immediately recognize a word as a whole without sounding it out.

Figure 14-3 The alphabetic principle.

The child may:
- understand that letters have different shapes.
- identify some letters by name.
- notice some words start with the same letter.
- realize letters make sounds.
- match some sounds to letters correctly.
- possess a sight word vocabulary—usually her own and peer's names.
- realize alphabet letters are a special category of print.

and beginning view of the **alphabetic principle**. Figure 14-3 displays possible child understandings concerning the alphabetic principle.

Writing (printscript) is complex. Many subcomponents of the process need to be understood. Development may occur at different rates, with spurts and lags in different knowledge areas. Besides the visual learning of letter features and forms, the ability to manually form shapes, and knowing that writing involves a message, a writer must listen to the sounds of her inner speech and find matching letters representing those sounds. Because letter follows letter in printing, the child needs to make continuous intellectual choices and decisions.

Many events happen between the ages of three and five. Children begin to vary their marks and move from imitation to creation. They produce a mixture of real letters, mock letters, and innovative symbols. A few written messages are readable. These actions signal several new behaviors and child discoveries. They are attending to the fine features of writing, noting shapes and specific letters, and they are developing an early concept of sign—the realization that symbols stand for something. Some children also see that there is variation in written language. Children refine and enlarge these concepts by experimenting with writing. They draw, trace, copy, and even invent marks and letter forms of their own.

Print awareness is usually developed in the following sequence:

1. The child notices adults making marks with writing tools.

2. The child notices print in books and on signs. When this time comes, a child is increasingly aware of all the print in the world around her—street signs, food labels, newspaper headlines, printing on cartons, books, billboards, everything. He may try to read everything. Already having a good foundation in translating spoken words to print, he may move on and try printing. If help is provided when he asks for it, he progresses. It can be a very exciting time for him.

3. The child realizes that certain distinguishable marks make her name.

4. The child learns the names of some of the marks—usually the first letter of her name. While building a sizable store of words recognized on sight, children will begin to make finer and finer distinctions about print by using more and more visual cues. They begin to pay attention to individual letters, particularly the first ones in words.

The child's imitation of written forms usually develops in the following sequence:

1. The child's scribbles are more like print than artwork or pure exploration (Figure 14-4).

2. Linear scribbles are generally horizontal with possible repeated forms. Children's knowledge of linear directionality may have been displayed in play in which they lined up alphabet blocks, cut out letters and pasted them in a row, or put magnetic board letters in left-to-right rows (Figure 14-5).

3. Individual shapes are created, usually closed shapes displaying purposeful lines (Photo 14-4).

4. Letter-like forms are created.

5. Recognizable alphabet letters are printed and may be mirror images or turned on sides, upside down, or in an upright position (Figure 14-6).

6. Words or groupings of alphabet letters with spaces between are formed.

7. **Invented spelling** appears; this may include pictured items along with alphabet letters (Figure 14-7).

8. Correctly spelled words with spaces separating words are produced.

---

alphabetic principle — the awareness that spoken language can be analyzed as strings of separate words and that words, in turn, can be analyzed as sequences of syllables and phonemes within syllables.

invented spelling — the result of an attempt to spell a word whose spelling is not already known, based on a writer's knowledge of the spelling system and how it works.

Figure 14-4 Scribbles are sometimes print-like.

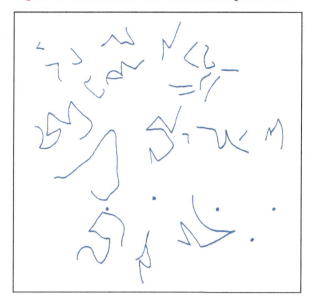

Figure 14-6 Recognizable alphabet letters.

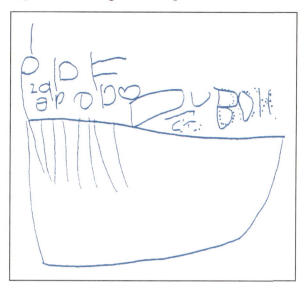

Figure 14-5 Linear scribbles.

Figure 14-7 Child read as "Blast off rocket to the moon."

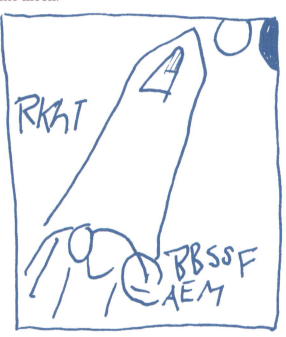

Photo 14-4 This boy has just made a closed-shape letter with purposeful lines.

14-2b Invented Spelling (Developmental Spelling)

Invented spelling is something children do naturally. It is a temporary phenomenon that is later replaced with conventional spelling. Until the mid to late 1980s, teachers gave young children the idea that until they learned to read, they needed to write only those words they had memorized or copied. Research has changed educational philosophy and methods. It suggests that children's literacy emerges during a span of several years. As young children slowly begin to understand what letters mean and how to string them together, some children will invent spelling. Often, the beginning consonant sound of a particular word is printed. A whole sequence might shortly appear and consist of single-letter words. The invented-spelling stage casts teachers in the role of detectives trying to ascertain meanings that the child may perceive as obvious.

In their early attempts to write, preschool children invent a system of spelling that follows logical and predictable rules before they learn the conventional forms. Vowels are commonly omitted in invented spellings. Words appear that may look like a foreign language—*dg* for dog, and *jragin* for dragon.

Identifiable stages in invented spelling are followed by some children and are given here for teacher reference.

1. Spelling awareness—alphabet letters represent words. Example: C (see), U (you).

2. Primitive spelling with no relationship between spelling and words—numbers and letters are differentiated. Example: tsOlf..DO.

3. Prephonetic spelling—initial and final consonants may become correct. Example: KT (cat), CD (candy), RT (write), WF (with).

4. Phonetic spelling—almost a perfect match between the symbols and sounds. Some vowels are used. Some sight words may be correctly spelled. Example: SUM (some), LIK (like), MI (my), ME (me).

5. Correct spelling.

Invented spelling serves as an important stage in the process of deciphering the sound–symbol system of written language. It is believed that at this point, phonics becomes important to children. Early on, the child selects letters in her inventive spelling that have some relationship to how the word is pronounced. Large items such as "elephants" may be written in huge letters and with more letters than small objects, because the child is operating under the misconception that bigger necessitates more letters. A perfectly logical conclusion! The names of letters may words (*u* for you) or parts of words. Young writers' invented spelling uses personal logic rather than or in conjunction with standard spelling, and the child's strategy of using a name of a letter has a frustrating side. There are only 26 alphabet letters but almost twice that many phonemes, or sound units. What do children do when they encounter a sound for which there is no ready letter–name match? They use a system of spelling logic based primarily on what they hear but also influenced by subconscious knowledge of the general rules of language usage and of how sounds are formed in the mouth when spoken.

What should an early childhood educator do when confronted with invented spelling in a child's work? Faith that children who are given help will evolve toward conventional spelling is needed. Invented spelling gives young writers early power over words. Professional writers do not worry about correct spelling on their first drafts and neither do inventive spellers.

Many primary teachers write out the standard spelling for words below a child's invented spelling. By doing so, teachers honor the original but provide further information so children can compare their spelling inventions with regular standard spellings. Inventive spellers who realize their spelling differs from text in books and the world around them may experience frustration and confusion. Teachers at this juncture may introduce phoneme spelling by "sounding out" words that they print.

Some educators recommend putting a small teacher translation on papers containing invented spelling. They record the child's intended message (or a translation of what the child has tried to write) using small letters on a remote corner of the page or on its back. This can be a satisfying arrangement if the child has no objection to the practice. It also gives the teacher the opportunity to observe and hear the child decode her message in her own words. In this way a family examining "take-home" papers can possibly understand the thought processes the child used to write the message and understand the child's great accomplishment. A family-teacher discussion is usually necessary for family to realize that beginning attempts are not immediately corrected. Teachers need to use these techniques carefully with older preschoolers, being mindful of the child's inventiveness and pride in her work. Many preschoolers object to teachers adding any marks on their papers.

When a child asks the teacher to write a specific word, the teacher has a chance to help the child with letter sounds (rather than letter names), saying *d-o-g* as she writes it. Time permitting, the teacher can add, "It starts with the alphabet letter d, like Dan, D-a-n."

14-3 Goals of Instruction

Providing experiences that match a child's interests and abilities is the goal of many early childhood centers. Most schools plan activities for those children who ask questions or seem ready and then proceed if the children are still interested. Others work with children on an individual basis. Yet others believe in providing a print-rich environment where the child will progress naturally with supportive adults who also model an interest in print and point out uses of print in daily activities. A fourth group of preschools identify a curriculum that includes emerging letter knowledge and print word recognition skills for their instruction program drawn from recognized standards, academic research, the findings of the National Early Literacy Panel (2008), or another professional group's recommendations. Most often these programs include phonemic and print awareness goals in their preschool program's goal statements. Specific proposed outcomes for a child attending their school are to be reached at the end of the year or another period of time and might look like the following. The child will

- Name most upper and lowercase alphabet letters in a fluent manner.
- Identify beginning letters in familiar words such as peer's names.
- Correctly match some sounds to letters.
- Identify words that rhyme.
- Create or remember a word that rhymes with a teacher's word.
- Stretch a three letter word and demonstrate he can hear the three sounds it contains.
- Clap syllables in one to three syllable words correctly.
- Substitute a new letter sound for a given word ending, therefore, creating a new word.
- Blend sounds in a few words.
- Print a number of recognizable alphabet letters using a printscript style that teacher has modeled.
- Dictate words for a teacher to print.
- Print in a lineal left to right direction.

- Make attempts to write a message.
- Use technology to print words when technology is available.
- Read a number of words by sight when requested.

Programs with at-risk students may design implicit and specific lessons that include selected alphabet and vocabulary instruction in common words that form the basis for successful early reading. Teachers plan activities involving authentic writing (printing), that is, writing done for the "real world" rather than for contrived school purposes. Research emphasizes that when planning printing activities, instruction should concentrate on using print in authentic activities that are meaningful and have a purpose and/or a reason in the child's daily life. An authentic written message may also involve a child's need or desire. It is possible to combine these approaches. A teacher might say, "Let's say the word you are trying to print very slowly, and stretch it out so we can hear its sounds."

As with other language abilities, goals include stimulating further interest and exploration. This should be done in such a way that the child is not confused by instruction that is either too advanced or boring. Most early childhood educators subscribe to the idea that teaching print concepts encountered during a read-aloud with a picture book should be kept to a minimum and used only when print in some way clarifies a main theme or feature in the book's format or story. Usually teachers concentrate primarily on children's understanding of a book's meaning and enjoyment.

As stated previously, an important goal concerning print awareness is relating writing to other language arts areas or other domains. It is almost impossible to not do so. Teachers are encouraged to consciously mention connections so that children will understand how writing fits in the whole of communicating. Figure 14-8 is a listing of both print and book awareness understandings that early childhood educators endeavor to promote before a child begins kindergarten.

Another important *teacher* goal would be having the ability to print every lowercase and uppercase alphabet letter in excellent form, so as to offer children the best model possible. A primary and overriding goal of early childhood educators involves basing their teacher–child

Figure 14-8 Print and book awareness goals.

Print and Book Awareness Goals

The child understands that:
- reading obtains information from books.
- writing communicates thoughts and ideas.
- print can carry messages.
- letters are different from numerals.
- book illustrations carry meaning.
- print can be read.
- books have authors who create books and their titles.
- print is read from left to right and top to bottom.
- alphabet letters in print can form words.
- alphabet letters have names.
- words are separated by spaces.
- spoken words can be written down.
- print has everyday functional uses (for example, shopping lists, messages, recipes, signs).
- one can follow print with one's eyes as it is read aloud.

interactions upon current research and best practices. Knowing that both young children's letter *name* knowledge and letter *sound* knowledge are recognized as important predictors of early reading competence, teachers work to promote each skill. Head Start centers are congressionally mandated to teach letter names to at-risk, low income children (U.S. Department of Health and Human Services, 2003). Research evidence points to the value of teaching letter names and sounds together. When children learn letter names it increases the possibility they know or will learn its sound. Most letter names include the phoneme the letter represents in the English language (Treiman & Kessler, 2003).

14-3a Coordination

Children's muscle control follows a timetable of its own. Control of a particular muscle depends on many factors—diet, exercise, inherited ability, and motivation, to name a few. A baby can control her neck and arms long before her legs. A child's muscle control grows in a head-to-toe fashion. Muscles closer to the center of the body can be controlled long before those of the hands and fingers. Large-muscle control comes before small-muscle control (Photo 14-5). Think of a toddler walking; the toddler's legs seem to swing from the hips. Just as each child starts walking and develops muscle control at different ages, so, too, does each child develop fine motor control, which influences her ability to control a writing tool. Under the right circumstances, fine motor skills can progress to very specific motor control at the fingertips. This is promoted by young children's access to developmentally appropriate activities and play materials that involve using the thumb and fingers and opposition or using pincher movements in play activities with tongs, tweezers, eyedroppers, or picking up small objects.

Photo 14-5 The small-muscle control Ria is using to trace a leaf will be needed when she begins to print.

© 2015 Cengage Learning®

Photo 14-6 This child displays her own unique finger-and-thumb grasp.

Precise writing is extremely difficult for some three- and four-year-olds, who grasp writing tools in their fists and guide them with movements started at the shoulder, elbow, or wrist. With the pivot and the writing tool point so far apart, children can't help but write large. Preschoolers' spatial skills are limited, and it can be difficult for them to construct and combine lines. Four-year-olds with more advanced fine motor skills can hold a pencil in a well-controlled finger and thumb grasp (Photo 14-6).

14-3b Cognitive Development

Mental growth, which allows a child to see similarities and differences in written symbols, comes before the ability to write. The child recognizes that a written mark is a shape made by the placement of lines. Seven prerequisite skill areas exist for handwriting. These are small-muscle development and coordination, eye-hand coordination, the ability to hold writing tools properly, the ability to form basic strokes (circles and straight lines), letter perception, an orientation to printed language—which includes a desire to write and communicate—including the child's enjoyment of writing her own name, and left-to-right understanding. A number of these skills deal with the child's cognitive development. Through past experiences, including child's play, ideas about print and writing have been formed.

14-3c Boys' Writing Development

Whitmire (2010), author of *Why Boys Fail*, urges educators to take particular care to help young boys verbalize and receive skilled adult verbal feedback. He believes some boys fail elementary and high school and avoid college for diverse reasons. Among these are their verbal and vocabulary skill development and their inability to express themselves. The largest gender gap involves boys' writing skills. Teachers, especially early childhood ones, need to find books of interest to young boys, which might include ridiculous or goofy ones. Listening and watching closely for boys' enjoyment and engagement during teacher-chosen readings is important. Minority and low-income boys seem to struggle the most with academics (Marklein, 2010). Zambo (2007) suggests boys may need special teacher attention and guidance. She recommends using stories and literacy activities to increase skills.

> Hearing stories about male characters acting responsibly improves a boy's vocabulary, helps him understand story structure, and, at the same time, teaches him how responsibility looks, sounds, and feels. (p. 12)

and

> Make sure the book has rich language and a substantive plot that will capture boys' attention and keep them interested. (p. 13)

14-4 Play, Drawing, and Other Influences

Print, signs, and writing imaginary messages often become part of a dramatic play sequence. During play, children may pretend to read and write words, poems, stories, and songs, and they may actually make a series of marks on paper. Play encourages children to act as if they are already competent in and able to control the activity under consideration. Through pretend play, they may feel that they are already readers and writers; at least a beginning move toward eventual literacy takes place. Children observe families using reading and writing in their daily lives. These activities are given status. Early childhood teachers can build on children's early attitudes by modeling, demonstrating, and providing dramatic play opportunities involving print, which promote collaborative peer printing.

14-4a Drawing Experience

A young child scribbles if given paper and a marking tool. As the child grows, the scribbles are controlled into lines that she places where desired (Figure 14-9). Gradually, the child begins to draw circles, then a face, later a full figure, and so on. Children draw their own symbols representing what they see around them. Educators urge teachers to examine one child's drawings over a few weeks' time; they may discover that the child is working on a basic plan. Perhaps a child makes the same pattern or schema again and again. It may seem as if the child has learned a plan of action for producing the pattern or schema. This gives the child enough control over pencil and paper to play with variations, which often leads to new discoveries. The length of time it takes this process to develop differs with each child.

A profound connection exists between experience and ability in drawing and interest in and ability to write (Photo 14-7). Drawings and paintings not only communicate children's thinking (when they reach the level of drawing that is representative of the environment), but

Photo 14-7 Nontoxic felt-tip pens (markers) are standard preschool materials.

© 2015 Cengage Learning®

also often display early attempts to create symbols. Some of these symbols may be recognized by adults, but others seem to be unique and represent the world in the child's own way. Children often want to talk about their work and create stories to accompany graphics.

Because alphabet letters are more abstract than representative drawing, most educators suggest that drawing precedes writing. One research study identified a characteristic that was common to almost all children in the study who read early and continued to hold their lead in reading achievement. The children in the study were described by their parents as "pencil-and-paper kids," whose starting point of curiosity about written language was an interest in scribbling and drawing.

Figure 14-9 Children start writing by scribbling and, when older, drawing symbols of the world around them.

14-4b Writing and Exposure to Books

naeyc DAP

Probably the most common experience that promotes a child's interest in print is hearing and seeing picture books read over and over. Through repeated exposure, the child comes to expect the text to be near or on the same page as the object depicted. Two- and three-year-olds think that pictures in a book tell the story; as they gain more experience, they notice that the reader reads the print, not the pictures. Memorized story lines lead to children's questions about print on book pages. Once a word is recognized in print, copying that word onto another piece of paper or manipulating magnetic alphabet letters to form the word is a natural outgrowth. This activity usually leads to parent attention and approval and further attempts. Scribblers, doodlers, drawers, and pencil-and-paper kids are all labels researchers have used to describe children who have an early interest in writing, and much of what they do has been promoted by seeing print in their favorite books.

Stages of print recognition are believed to exist, starting with a stage in which the text and the picture are not differentiated. Then children begin to expect that the text is a label for the picture. In a third stage, the text is expected to provide cues with which to confirm predictions based on the picture. Some important concepts that young children gradually understand concerning print are: print tells a story along with illustrations, and alphabet letters can be printed. Other concepts to learn are: words are clusters of letters, words have first and last letters, and they are found in upper- and lowercase. Spaces between words happen and punctuation marks have meaning are additional understandings.

Children may notice the left-to-right and top-to-bottom direction of printing and also the left-page-first directional feature. It is important to promote the idea that there are different purposes for print and text, and that it appears in different forms depending on its purpose. Road signs have large block print and may be colorful and reflective to alert pedestrians and drivers both day and night. This fact is an example of both purpose and form. There are other examples in classrooms, such as hot and cold written on water handles. Lists of print words, newspapers, dictionaries, and poetry usually look different from picture book text, whose purpose usually is to tell a story.

The acquisition of skills in writing and reading and the development of the attitude that books are enjoyable involve more than academic or technical learning. These skills flourish with a warm physical and emotional base with shared enjoyment and intimacy. Most experts believe that considerable support exists for the notion that oral language provides a base for learning to write. The importance of emotionally satisfying adult–child interactions in all areas of language arts cannot be overestimated.

14-4c Alphabet Books

Children's books in print before the twentieth century were mostly informational and moralistic. Alphabet books suited the then prevailing public view that a good children's book should promote learning rather than pleasure. Presently, library collections for young children include a variety of alphabet books. Although many are in print and some are classic favorites, new titles continually appear. It is said that almost every author of young children's literature yearns to develop a unique alphabet book. The following are some recommended titles:

Bunting, E. (2002). *Girls A to Z*. Honesdale, PA: Boyd Mills Press. (A girl-can-be-anything theme.)

Fleming, D. (2002). *Alphabet under construction*. New York: Henry Holt and Company. (Suits toddlers and preschoolers, with colorful and playful illustrations.)

Sierra, J. (2009). *The sleepy little alphabet: A bedtime story from Alphabet town*. New York: Alfred Knoff (Upper and lower case alphabet letters that rhyme.)

Wood, A. (2006). *Alphabet rescue*. New York: Blue Sky Press. (A creative and charming way to learn letters.)

Wordless books with printed signs in their illustrations are great for focusing young children's attention on print, alphabet letters, and their purpose in daily life. A side benefit is that it channels attention to the concept of word. Words consist of a string of letters with spaces between them and this can also be recognized. Teachers can easily finger point and identify individual letter names and sounds. When children are asking for alphabet letter names, and when alphabet letters are appearing in their art or writing, alphabet books can become favorites. Teachers notice that a first interest in alphabet letters often appears when the child sees her printed name and then notices similar letters in friends' names.

Ideas for ways to build alphabet books into further classroom activities follow: (1) paint on a giant alphabet letter shape; (2) hide an alphabet letter in a large drawing and have children search for it; (3) make a class alphabet book by outlining large alphabet letters on pages and encouraging interested individual children to decorate a letter; (4) create a "Who looked at this book today?" chart. Add children's names to the chart if they browsed the book; and (5) create a personalized alphabet book for each child or suggest this to families.

Full understanding of the alphabet requires children to understand four separate yet interconnected components (Bradley & Jones, 2010). Those components are (a) letter-shape knowledge or letter recognition, (b) letter-name knowledge, (c) letter-sound knowledge, and (d) letter-writing ability. Each component is described more specifically as follows.

(a) The ability to distinguish letters requires recognition of visual features, such as shape, orientation, and directionality and discerning key features presented in various sizes, fonts, cases, and handwriting styles.

(b) The realization that alphabet letters are symbols, each with a given name that can appear in both upper- and lowercase.

(c) The knowledge that letters represent different sounds, and sometimes multiple sounds, and

(d) The ability to form written alphabet letters. (p. 76)

Bradley and Jones (2010) point out as young children have opportunities to learn and develop fluent knowledge of the alphabet, their ability to read and write will likely be facilitated. When assessing a child's alphabet knowledge, each of the above components is important. These authors suggest children benefit most from alphabet books when teachers are explicit when presenting them.

14-5 Planning a Program for Print Awareness and Printing Skill

Program planning is often done on an individual basis, but standards have been initiated and used as a basis for program planning in an increasing number of child development centers. If group instruction takes place, it deals with general background information concerning print use during the school day and how it relates to children's lives, including print use in the home and community. A great deal of spontaneous and incidental teaching takes place. Teachers capitalize on children's questions concerning mail, packages, signs, and labels. In most preschool settings, print is a natural part of living, and it has many interesting features that children can discover and notice when teachers focus attention on print.

A supportive classroom environment allows children to design their own route to further knowledge about print. It is critical for children to have a literacy-rich, risk-free environment that includes time to invent, to play, and to experiment with written language for meaningful purposes in an authentic context while interacting with knowledgeable others. Such experiences allow children to work through questions and perplexities, and to build conceptualizations and understandings in ways meaningful to them. As children compare their inventions with the written language around them, particularly their names, they deepen their understandings of the complexities of our written language system.

A discussion is necessary here concerning the practice of asking the child to form alphabet letters and practice letter forms. The dangers in planning an individual or group experience of this nature are multiple. One has to consider whether a child has the physical and mental capacity to be successful and whether the child has an interest in doing the exercise or is simply trying to please adults.

The logical progression in learning about letters is to first learn letter names and then learn letter shapes, but this can be reversed when a child has an interest in making letter form in artwork. The child then has a solid mnemonic peg on which to hang the concept of "letter" as the concept is learned. Activities such as singing the alphabet song, reading alphabet books, and playing with alphabet magnets or puzzles help preschoolers learn letters. The uppercase letters are larger and research suggests that they are the easiest forms for preschoolers to reproduce. Preschools often present "big" and "little" letters together in the school's visual environment. It is the uppercase letters that most children recognize when they enter kindergarten. Preschool and kindergarten teachers also print children's names with an uppercase first letter followed by lowercase letters in printscript.

Teachers encourage children to print ("write") their own names on their artwork when they believe children have an interest in printing. Any attempt is recognized and given attention. These teachers may also say, "May I write your name on the back? With two names, one on the front and one on the back, we will find your work quickly when it's time to leave school." Teachers print names on the upper left corner of the children's work because that is the spot reading starts on any given page written in English. (It is hoped that the child and/or child's family has been asked before enrollment what name the child prefers to be called at school.)

Early writing instruction is not a new idea. Maria Montessori (1967a) (a well-known educator and designer of teaching materials) and numerous other teachers have offered instruction in writing (or printing) to preschoolers. Montessori encouraged the child's tracing of letter forms using the first two fingers of the hand as a prewriting exercise. She observed that this type of light touching seemed to help youngsters when writing tools were later given to them. Montessori (1967a) designed special alphabet letter cutouts as one of a number of prewriting aids. These cutouts were thought to help exercise and develop small muscles and create sight-touch sensations, fixing the forms in memory.

In seventeenth- and eighteenth-century England, a gingerbread method of teaching alphabet letters was developed. As a child correctly named a letter-shaped cookie or a word formed by cookies, she was allowed to eat it (or them). This is offered here to point out past educators' practices rather than to recommend. Brain learning advocates would advise giving children concrete (real) letter forms to touch and manipulate while naming them (Jensen, 2008).

One prekindergarten teacher's print awareness plan is described by Kissel (2008). Each day a writer's workshop took place after a read-aloud. The teacher crafted a follow-up mini lesson in which she made a drawing related to the storybook on a large paper to represent her "writing."

> As the year progressed, she included initial-letter word sounds next to some of the central themes of her writing. Near the end of the year, she added simple words that the children helped her sound out as she wrote. She always included a picture (teacher drawing). This evolution mirrored the writing of the children. She gently scaffolded their writing development, introducing print, when most of the children were ready. (p. 28)

Her teaching strategy, she believed, was based on the writings of Vygotsky (1976, 1980, 1986), and the idea that when she drew her pictures in front of the class she demonstrated the use of images and symbols to convey messages. Children were able during writing workshop times to confer with her and other children. She added words and short sentences to her drawings near the end of the school year.

Another early childhood educator designed a year-long writing awareness program for her class based upon the belief that preschoolers possess a seemingly endless supply of personal stories. She observed that they required varying levels of teacher and classroom support to enable them to put them down on paper (King, 2012). King's approach to acquaint preschoolers with writing (printing) entailed using a four component classroom instructional strategy: (1) she presented many lessons about writing; (2) she initiated a child-centered, open-ended classroom writing time; (3) she started a teacher–student conference time; and (4) she scheduled a child sharing his/her work time (p. 393). Her approach also promoted child journal writing in teacher-made individual child booklets in which a child could express a chosen story topic in a drawing or words or use it for writing alphabet letters, writing their name or common words, or using a combination of these.

14-5a Learning Print Conventions

The sub skills of print conventions may be learned in a number of ways, including through daily interactions and exchanges in a classroom. These sub skills follow in the left column below. In the right column are sample teacher comments. The teacher's goal is not only to inform, but also to pass on the information enough times for children to recall it or display their knowledge with an action or comment.

Front cover of a book	"Right here on the book's *front cover* it says..."
Back cover	"On this book's *back cover* we see..."
Author or authorship	"A lady named Mary Smith made up this story and we will find out..."

Illustrator	"The pictures in our book were painted by…"
Illustration	"I like to look at this *illustration* on page 3 because…"
Photographer	"The pictures in our picture book were taken with…"
Title or title page	"When I read a book's *title page* I find out…"
Alphabet letters	"Anna, your name starts with the letter 'a' and ends…"
Letter form	"To make the letter B you start with a straight line and…"
Symbols, symbolic representation	"The arrow pointing down tells us to push down…"
Directionality & top left progression	"The first word to read on this page…"
Sign directionality	"This sign has three words 'Park bikes here.'"
Left to right progression	"Pogo is the first word. I have my hand beneath it and the next…"
Last word on page	"I've run out of words to read on this page. The last *word* is…"
Lines on a page	"This is a paper with lines across it, if I write…"
Words are printed using alphabet letters	"You want a sign for the playhouse to say…"

14-5b How to Make the ABCs Developmentally Appropriate

In a print-rich classroom environment, children are bound to see alphabet letters as a natural part of their world and to develop curiosity about them. Teachers examine activities and take advantage of teachable moments. Educators realize alphabet knowledge prompts phonemic awareness. Teachers promote children's fluency in naming alphabet letters. Fluency can be defined as speed and accuracy. Children

fluent in alphabet letter names can recognize and correctly name alphabet letters without hesitation, thereby indicating that letter names have been well learned. The following are samples of alphabet-related activities.

- **Name of the Day.** One child's name is chosen and discussed at circle time. The first alphabet letter in the child's name is named and searched for in room displays.

- **Alphabet Letter Sorting Game.** A teacher-made box with slots under alphabet letters is provided, along with a deck of teacher-made alphabet cards. A child (or children) decide what card is slotted, and then the box is lifted and the cards retrieved for the next child. The box can be a large cardboard box upended with letters on the box and adjacent cut slots. This game needs a simple introduction and demonstration.

- **Alphabet Chart Game.** The teacher posts large alphabet letters on large paper around the room. Child volunteers choose how to get to one letter from the starting place to touch the letter and then how to get to the next. (Every child gets a turn.) The teacher may have to start by saying, "Let's tiptoe to the letter C" or "Who can think of a way to get to 'M'"?

- **Designing Game Activities.** When designing games, remember that in developmentally appropriate games everyone gets a turn, clear directions (rules) are introduced, everyone wins, competition is inappropriate, cooperation is promoted, praise or prizes are omitted, and creating musical games is possible. Movement games are wiggle reducers if they end on a cooling-down note. Games are designed to include or give a turn to every child who wants to play, and game parts are sturdy and well made to eliminate frustration.

Remember also that these games can promote listening skills and problem solving. It is recommended that alphabet letters be introduced. Most early childhood program staffs specifically designate exactly which letter form they will offer first and affirm alphabet letters named by children in either uppercase or lowercase. Teaching the sounds of alphabet letters is an instructional decision based on children's age, interest, and ability. Schools decide if it is developmentally appropriate and whether it is done only on a one-to-one basis.

14-5c Seeing and Hearing Patterns

Infants, toddlers, and preschoolers have an innate capability to see and hear patterns (Vergano, 2009). Vergano notes this is something psychologists doubted for decades. Learning research, he suggests, urges educators to discover patterns with young children during their play. Doing so may aid brain development and sharpen children's ability to recognize environmental patterns. Print recognition, during the preschool period, will involve this skill. Recognizing patterns in the environment such as a special friend knocking on the door in a specific rhythm sequence, or understanding there is a sequence of routines during the school day that repeat the next day, or recognizing a friend's name on artwork because of a sequence of certain alphabet letters are examples of this skill.

14-6 Environment and Materials

Children's access to drawing tools—magic markers, chalk, pencils, crayons, brushes—is important so that children can make their own marks. It is suggested that teachers create a place where children can comfortably use these tools. The following early childhood materials help the child use and gain control of small arm and finger muscles in preparation for writing—puzzles, pegboards, small blocks, construction toys, scissors, and eyedroppers.

Most early childhood centers plan activities in which the child puts together, arranges, or manipulates small pieces. These are sometimes called tabletop activities and are available for play throughout the day. A teacher can encourage the use of tabletop activities by having the pieces arranged invitingly on tables or resting on adjacent shelves. The following are examples of materials common in print-immersion classrooms.

- labels—pictures or photographs accompanied by corresponding words
- charts and lists—charts that convey directions, serve as learning resources (pictures and names of children in alphabetical order), organize the class (attendance roster or class calendar), show written language as a reminder (children's sign-up lists)
- materials and activities—various materials, including alphabet toys, puzzles, stamps, magnetic

letters, and games, along with clever teacher-made materials (Photo 14-8) or commercial furnishings, such as blocks, stuffed alphabet-shaped pillows, alphabet rugs, and wall hangings
- books and other resources—a variety of books and magazines, poetry, newspapers, computer software, picture dictionaries, riddle and novelty books, and other printed material

Early childhood centers create rooms that are full of symbols, letters, and numbers in clear view of the child. Room print should reflect teacher and child interests. Many toys have circles, squares, triangles, alphabet letters, and other common shapes. Recommended letter and symbol size for preschool playroom display is at least two to two and one-half inches in height or larger.

14-6a Labeling

Labeling activities revolve around the purpose and function of labels and signs in daily life. One educator created handheld signs for use during daily scheduled activities, such as clean-up,

Photo 14-8 Making charts that alert children to print's usefulness is a common teacher task.

© 2015 Cengage Learning®

Figure 14-10 Large printscript letters are used to label boxes.

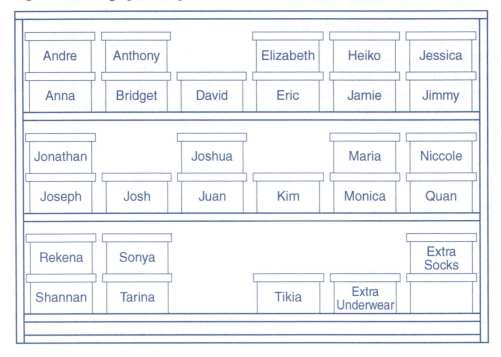

Andre	Anthony		Elizabeth	Heiko	Jessica
Anna	Bridget	David	Eric	Jamie	Jimmy
Jonathan		Joshua		Maria	Niccole
Joseph	Josh	Juan	Kim	Monica	Quan
Rekena	Sonya				Extra Socks
Shannan	Tarina		Tikia	Extra Underwear	

line-up, circle time, listening time, and washing hands. Each sign had printed words and a visual clue, such as a wastebasket for clean-up, an ear for listening time, and so on. In a classroom, many needs usually exist. A "Park bikes here" sign alerts bike riders to the proper storage area and may prevent yard accidents and be useful for a child looking for an available bike. A labeling activity initiated by a teacher to introduce the need for road signs and environmental signs can lead to an activity in which children decide the appropriate wording. Common classroom labeling includes the following: artwork, name tags, lockers and storage areas (Figure 14-10), belongings, common room objects, schoolroom areas, and place cards at eating times. Some educators believe labeling without a purpose is objectionable.

14-6b Display Areas

Display areas often include the following:

- magazine pictures with captions
- current interest displays, for example, "Rocks we found on our walk"
- bulletin boards and wall displays with words
- wall alphabet guides (Aa Bb . . .)
- charts
- child's work with explanations, such as "Josh's block tower" or "Penny's clay pancakes"
- folding table accordion display (Figure 14-11)
- signs for child activities, such as "store," "hospital," "wet paint," and "Tickets for Sale Here"

Figure 14-11 Folding table accordion.

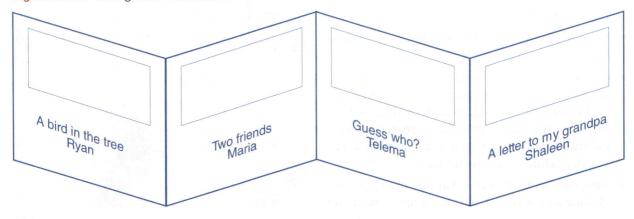

A bird in the tree
Ryan

Two friends
Maria

Guess who?
Telema

A letter to my grandpa
Shaleen

14-6c Message-Sending Aids

Classroom mailboxes, suggestion boxes, and message boards are motivational and useful. Writing short notes to children piques an interest about what is said. Large-sized stick-on notes are great for this purpose and can be attached to mirrors, plates, toys, and so on.

14-6d Writing Centers

Writing centers are planned, teacher-stocked areas where printing is promoted. A writing center can be a separate area of a room, or it can exist within a language arts center. Child comfort and proper lighting are essential, along with minimized distractions. Often, dividers or screens are used to reduce outside noise and activity. Supplies and storage areas are provided at children's fingertips so that children can help themselves. Teacher displays or bulletin board areas that motivate printing and have a listing of children's names can be close by. If water-based marking pens are provided, pens with distinct bright colors are preferred.

Through dialogue and exploration at a writing table or center, children are able to construct new ideas concerning print and meaning in a supportive mini-social setting. There should be a variety of paper and writing tools. Printing stamps and printing ink blocks, a hole punch, and brads are desirable. Old forms, catalogs, calendars, and computer paper may be inviting. Scratch paper (one side already used) or lined paper and crayons placed side-by-side invite use. Most local businesses or offices throw away enough scratch paper to supply a preschool center.

Colored or white chalk has an appeal of its own and can be used on paper, chalkboards, or cement. For variety, use brightly colored oil pastels or soft-lead pencils on paper. Most schools install a child-high chalkboard; table chalkboards are made quickly by using chalkboard paint obtained at hardware or paint stores and scrap wood pieces. Easels, unused wall areas, and backs of furniture can be made into chalkboards.

Computers capture interest. Shape books with blank pages and words to copy and trace appeal to some children, as do large rub-on letters or alphabet letter stickers (these can be made by teachers from press-on labels). Magnetic boards and magnetized letter sets are commonly mentioned as the favorite toy of children interested in alphabet letters and forming words.

Letters, words, and displays are placed for viewing on bulletin boards at children's eye level. Displays in writing centers often motivate and promote print. McNair (2007) suggests that young children are particularly fascinated by their own names. A name list or name cards can be used throughout the classroom.

14-6e First School Alphabets

In kindergarten or first grade, printing is done in printscript, sometimes called manuscript printing (Figure 14-12), or in a form called D'Nealian print (Figure 14-13). Centers should obtain guides from a local elementary school, because letter forms can vary from community to community.

Figure 14-12 Printscript alphabet.

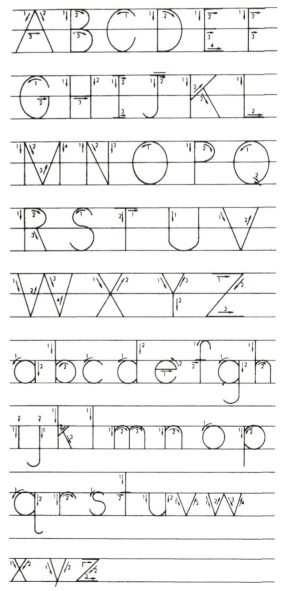

Figure 14-13 Samples of D'Nealian print and numerals.

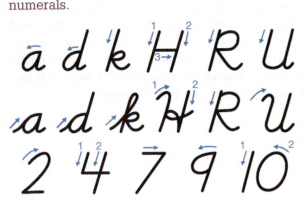

Teachers need to be familiar with printscript (or any other form used locally). It is easier for a child to learn the right way than to be retrained later. All printing seen by young children in a preschool usually will be either printscript, using both uppercase and lowercase letters, or D'Nealian style. Names, bulletin boards, and labels made by teachers should model correct forms. Printscript letters are formed with straight lines, circles, and parts of circles. In Figure 14-12, the small arrows and numerals show the direction to follow in forming the letters as well as the sequence of the lines.

The D'Nealian form, developed by teacher-principal Donald Neal Thurber and introduced in 1978, is popular because of its slant and continuous stroke features, which provide an easy transition to slant and stroke used in cursive writing introduced to children after second grade (Thurber, 1988). Cursive writing instruction in elementary school is disappearing (Bauerlein, 2013). He reports that common core state standards often neglect cursive writing instruction and promote keyboarding instruction.

Numbers in printed form are called numerals. Children may have used toys with numerals, such as block sets. Young children will probably hold up fingers to indicate their ages or to tell you they can count. They may start making number symbols before showing an interest in alphabet letters. Numeral forms (Figure 14-14) are also available from elementary schools. The numeral forms in one geographical area may also be slightly different from those of another town, city, or state.

14-6f Beginning Attempts

All children's attempts are recognized and appreciated by early childhood teachers as signs of the children's growing interest and ability. Figure 14-15 arranges alphabet letters in manuscript print from the easiest for children to manage and form to the most difficult. **Orthographic awareness** is the ability to notice and use critical features of the graphic symbols in written language. Children learn what makes a letter unique and that these features are often very finely drawn. The visual difference between the alphabet letters *n* and *m*, or *n* and *h*, are subtle, but many preschoolers have no difficulty. Educators realize that each child's knowledge is a very personal matter, with children finding their own ways of weaving understanding around a letter to help them remember it and reproduce it.

14-7 Planned Activities— Basic Understandings

Most planned activities in this language arts area, and most unplanned child–adult exchanges during the school day, involve basic understandings. Rules exist in this graphic art as they do in speech. Children form ideas about these rules. Print concerns the use of graphic symbols that represent sounds and sound combinations. Symbols combine and form words and sentences in a prescribed grammatical order. Alphabet letters are spaced and are in uppercase and lowercase form. They are written and read from left to

Figure 14-14 Printscript numerals.

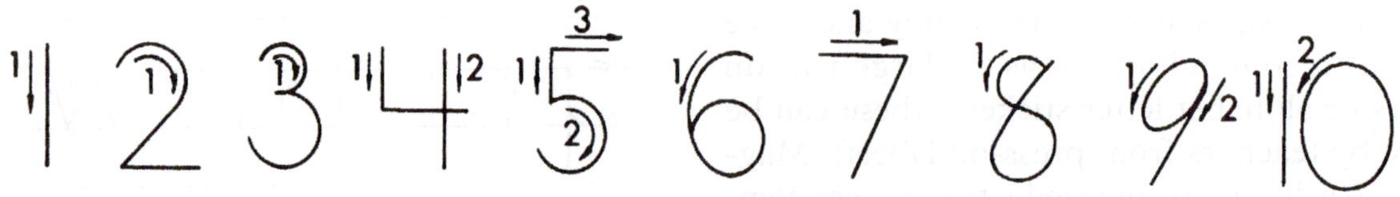

1 2 3 4 5 6 7 8 9 10

orthographic awareness — the ability to notice and use critical features of graphic symbols in written language.

1. l	14. V	27. Z	40. Y
2. o	15. c	28. t	41. d
3. L	16. x	29. B	42. R
4. O	17. T	30. Q	43. G
5. H	18. h	31. s	44. a
6. D	19. w	32. n	45. u
7. i	20. J	33. z	46. k
8. v	21. f	34. r	47. m
9. I	22. C	35. e	48. j
10. X	23. N	36. b	49. y
11. E	24. A	37. S	50. p
12. P	25. W	38. M	51. g
13. F	26. K	39. U	52. q

right across a page. Margins exist at beginnings and ends of lines and lines go from the top to bottom of pages. Punctuation marks end sentences, and indentations separate paragraphs. It is amazing how many rules of printing interested children discover on their own and with teacher help before they enter kindergarten.

Putting the children's names on their work is the most common daily use of printscript. The teacher asks the children whether they want their names on their work. Many young children feel their creations are their very own and may not want a name added. When a paper is lost because it has no name on it, children see the advantage of printing a name on belongings. All names are printed in the upper left corner of the paper, if possible, or on the back if the child requests. This is done to train the children to look at this spot as a preparation for reading and writing. Children's comments about their work can be jotted down at the bottom or on the back of their papers.

The teacher can be prepared to do this by having a dark crayon or felt-tip pen in a handy place or pocket. Dictation is written without major teacher editing or suggestions concerning the way it is said. The teacher can tell the child that the teacher will be writing down (printing) the child's ideas and then follow the child's word order as closely as possible. Some teachers prefer to print the statement, "Chou dictated these words to Mrs. Brownell on May 2, 2011," before or after the child's message. Most teachers would print the child's "mouses went in hole" as "mice went in the hole," which is minor editing. All child-dictated printing should be in printscript, using both uppercase and lowercase letters and proper punctuation.

When a child asks a teacher to print, the teacher stands behind the child and works over the child's shoulder (when possible). This allows the child to see the letters being formed in the correct position. If the teacher faces the child while printing, the child sees the letters upside down. Some teachers say the letter names as they print them. Letters or names written for the child should be large enough for the child to distinguish the different forms—more than one inch high. This may seem large to an adult (Figure 14-16).

Some schools encourage teachers to print examples on lined paper if a child says, "Make an *a*" or "Write my name." Others suggest that teachers blend letter sounds as they print words. Many centers expect teachers to respond to the child's request through conversation and by searching for letters on alphabet charts. This encourages the child to make her own copy before the teacher automatically prints it.

Teacher techniques often depend on the circumstances of a particular situation and knowledge of the individual child. One technique common to all centers is supportive assistance and voiced appreciation of children's efforts. Teachers can rejoice with a young child over approximations of intent in writing, just as we do with a toddler who makes an imprecise attempt to say a new word.

Children may show their printing attempts to the teacher or point out the names of letters they know. A positive statement to the child is appropriate: "Yes, that is an *a*" or "I can see an *a*, *t*, and *p*" (the teacher points to each) or

Figure 14-16 Letters should be large enough for the child to see easily.

"Marie, you did print the letters *a* and *t*." With these comments, the teacher encourages and recognizes the child's efforts. Often, the child may have the wrong name or form for a letter. The teacher can react by saying, "It looks like an alphabet letter. Let's go look at our wall alphabet and see which one" or may simply say, "Look. You made a *w*."

Encourage, welcome, and keep interest in print alive by providing attention. Children have many years ahead to perfect their skill; the most important thing at this early stage is that they are interested in the forms and are supplied with correct models and encouragement.

One technique is to have children who ask for letter forms trace over correct letter models or symbols. This can be done with crayons, felt-tip pens, or other writing tools. To explain the meaning of the word *trace*, the teacher gives the child a demonstration.

14-7a Environmental Print in Daily Life

A teacher of young children makes connections between print and daily classroom happenings. This is not difficult, but it does require teacher recognition and purposeful action. Print can be noticed starting with children's names and print on clothing, shoes, food, toys, and almost every object in the classroom, including light switches and faucet handles. Print is part of classroom life.

Children need to learn what print can do for them in satisfying personal needs. This makes print real. Children become aware of print by using it for real and meaningful purposes when they dictate and write stories, make signs for the block area, read names on a job chart, write messages, look for EXIT signs, follow recipes, have conversations and discussions, or listen to stories. Children may need teacher assistance in recognizing the usefulness of written messages. Many instances of sending or reading print messages are possible during a school day. For example, because print often protects one's safety, there are many opportunities to discuss and point out words that serve this function. Children's dramatic play offers many chances for teachers to support and suggest play actions and items that involve print use. See Figure 14-17.

Teachers look for functional use of print activities, such as:

- making necessary lists of children's names with children. Example: Teacher creates a waiting list.

- making holiday or special occasion cards.

- making group murals and labeling parts at a later date. Example: Teacher uses color words or children's ideas (Jane says, "This looks like a cat.").

- writing what-we-found-out activities. This can be done with many discovery experiences. Example: What floats, and what does not?

- classifying experiences. Example: "Shoes Are Different"—Teacher elicits from the group the kinds of shoes children see others wearing. It might be brown shoes, sandals, shoes with laces, and so on. Once these are listed across the top of the chart paper, children can choose under which headings their names should go.

- sharing the lunch or snack menu by discussing printed words on a chart or chalkboard.

- making classroom news announcements on a large sheet of paper posted at children's eye level. Examples follow: Enrico moved to a new apartment. Mrs. Quan is on a trip to Chicago.

Creating a large classroom journal will allow the teacher a daily or weekly opportunity to model writing a class-dictated sentence. The teacher can also talk aloud about her writing while using a large sheet of paper. The first step would be a joint discussion concerning what is to be written. The teacher can then "think aloud" as she writes, leveling her comments to the children's ability.

When working on the journal, the teacher may simply say, "We planted carrot seeds," and emphasize the number of words in the sentence by making three spaced lines. Or the teacher may say, "We will start by looking at the left side of the paper because the first word on a page is printed on the top left side of the page. We will put the first word of our sentence here." This can be repeated on other "journal days" before the teacher decides to think aloud about the names of the first letter in each word. No matter the journaling activity, the children will be watching their teacher form letters, use capital letters, form words, leave spaces between words, and end messages with a period. Depending on the class and its ability, the teacher may not think aloud about the sounds of the letters, but as journaling progresses she may choose to do so depending on the philosophy of the program.

Figure 14-17 Dramatic play themes and activities that promote print awareness and use.

Play Themes

Classroom Post Office
Suggested play items:
  stamps (many come with magazine advertisements), old letters, envelopes, boxes to wrap for mailing, scale, canceling stamp, tape, string, play money, mailbag, mailbox with slots, alphabet strips, writing table, felt-tip pens, counter, postal-employee shirts, posters from post office, stamp-collector sheets, wet sponge, teacher-made chart that lists children by street address and zip codes, box with all children's names on printed individual strips, mailboxes for each child

Taco Stand
Suggested play items:
  counter for customers, posted charts with prices and taco choices, play money, order pads, labeled baskets with colored paper taco items (including cheese, meat, lettuce, salsa, sour cream, avocado, shredded chicken, and onions), customer tables, trays, bell to ring for service, folded cards with numbers, receipt book for ordered tacos, plastic glasses and pitchers, cash register, napkins, tablecloth, plastic flowers in plastic vase, cook's jacket, waiter/waitress aprons, busperson suit and cleaning supplies, taped ethnic music, plastic utensils, soft pencils or felt-tip pens, line with clothespins to hang orders, paper plates
  A hamburger stand or pizza parlor are other possibilities.

Grocery Shopping
Suggested items:
  shopping-list paper, bookcase, pencils or felt-tip pens, chart with cut magazine pictures or labels from canned goods or vegetables labeled in print by teacher for children to copy if they desire, empty food cartons and cans, plastic food, shopping cart, purse and wallet, play money, brown bags, cash register on box, dress-up clothes for customers and store clerks

Print-Awareness Activities

Letter-Writing Classroom Center
  (for writing to relatives and friends)

Classroom Newspaper
  Make a class newspaper. Print children's dictated news or creative language after sharing a local paper with them. Child drawings on ditto master can be duplicated. Add teacher and parent news, poems, captions, drawings, and so forth. Some children may wish to print their own messages. These may range from scribble to recognizable forms and words.

T-Shirt Autograph Day
  Each parent is asked to bring an old T-shirt (any size) to school for T-shirt autograph day. Permanent felt markers are used by children under teacher supervision. (Washable markers can also be used, but teachers must iron or put T-shirts in a clothes dryer for 5 minutes on a hot setting.) T-shirt forms are necessary and can be made of cardboard. Material must be stretched over a form so marks can be added easily. It is a good idea to have children wear plastic paint aprons to protect clothing from permanent markers. Children are free to autograph shirts in any manner they please. A display of T-shirts with writing usually prompts some children to add letters to their own shirts. Most teachers own or can borrow T-shirts with writing.

(Teachers using journaling must know how each alphabet letter is to be formed. Go back to Figure 14-12 and notice the small numbered arrows.)

Daily journal sheets can be bound with large metal rings to make a class big book. Child art is often attached to the blank area under the sentence on each page. Large sheets are used so large teacher print is easily observed by a group of children. See the Activities section at the end of this chapter for more ideas related to classroom journaling.

14-7b Writing Table or Area

Many classrooms include a writing table or area for children's daily free-choice exploration. Stocked with different paper types, a variety of writing instruments, alphabet letter stencils, letter stamps, and letter model displays, this type of setup makes daily access available and inviting. However, just providing a writing center is not enough. Teachers need to be in it daily, as motivators and resources. Some writing areas have considerable use. In other classrooms, teachers spend little or no time there (Smith, 2001). Whether a writing center appeals to children, grabs children's attention, and is child-functional depends on the ingenuity of teachers.

Recognizing that children need time as well as opportunity, teachers notice that individual children involve themselves in classroom literacy events based on their maturity and interest. When a child senses a reason and develops a personal interest in writing or reading, she acts on her own timetable. There seems to exist in the child at this point a desire to do something her own way; the child wants to retain ownership of early literacy behaviors. The child who examines a classroom alphabet chart and then copies letter forms may choose to share her marks with other children and avoid the teacher. Another child the same age may prefer to consult the teacher. Other children may ask, "What's this say?" or "What's this called?" In all situations, teachers aim to preserve and promote each child's idea of competency as a writer or reader.

14-7c Left-Handed Children

Left-handedness or right-handedness occurs as the child's nervous system matures. Preschool teachers notice hand preferences when children use writing tools. Some children seem to switch between hands as though hand preference has not been established. Most left-handers use their right hands more often than right-handers use their left hands. Writing surfaces in preschools should accommodate all children, and both right-handed and left-handed scissors should be available. Teachers should accept hand preference without attempting to change or even point out a natural choice. Seating left-handed children at the ends of tables (when possible) during activities or making sure left-handers are not crowded against right-handers is a prudent course of action.

14-7d Lined Paper

Some children acquire the necessary motor control and can use lined, printed paper (Figure 14-18), so some programs provide it. Lines can easily be drawn on a chalkboard by the teacher. This provides a large working surface and an opportunity for children to make large-size letters.

Figure 14-18 Example of a five-year-old kindergartener's printing accompanying art.

14-7e Chart Ideas

Printscript can be added to playrooms by posting charts that have been made by the teacher. Charts can be designed to encourage the child's active involvement and contain words in a child's home language. Pockets, parts that move, or pieces that can be added or removed add extra interest. Charts made on heavy chart board or cardboard last longer. Clear contact paper can be used to seal the surface. Chart ideas include:

- experience charts (Figure 14-19).
- color or number charts.
- large clock with movable hands.
- chart showing the four seasons.
- picture story sequence charts.
- calendars.
- room task charts ("helpers chart").
- texture charts (for children to feel).
- poetry charts (Figure 14-20).
- recipe charts using step-by-step illustrations.
- classification or matching-concepts charts.
- birthday charts.
- height and weight charts.
- alphabet charts.
- rebus charts (Figure 14-21).

Many teachers make "key word" charts. Key words can be words inspired by a picture-book title, character, and so forth; words solicited from children; or words taken from some classroom event or happening. The chosen word is printed by the teacher at the top of a chart. The teacher then asks a small group, "When I say this word, what

Figure 14-19 Experience chart.

The Picnic

We had lunch in the park. We sat on the grass.

Figure 14-20 Poetry chart.

Mix a pancake
Stir a pancake
Pop it in a pan,
Fry the pancake,
Toss the pancake,
Catch it

If you   can!

Figure 14-21 Rebus chart.

do you think of?" or "Salt and pepper go together. We see them in shakers sitting on the kitchen table. What goes with [key word]?" or "Tree is the word at the top of our chart. What can we say about the trees in our play yard?" or some such leading question. Children's offered answers are put below the key word on the chart. This activity suits some older four-year-olds, especially those asking, "What does this say?" while pointing to text.

Charts of songs or rhymes in the native languages of attending children have been used successfully in many classrooms. Parent volunteer translators are often pleased to help put new or favorite classics into their native tongue. "*Uno, Dos, Tres Inditos*," a Spanish version of "Ten Little Indians," has been frequently enjoyed and learned quickly. A technique adopted in many schools involves using a color-code system when recording individual child contributions to a group-dictated chart. This enables a child to return to the chart and find her comments.

Think of all of the charts that can include a child's choice, vote, or decision! These charts are limitless. A child can indicate her individual selection under the diverse headings by making a mark, printing her name, using a rubber stamp and ink pad, or moving her printed name to a

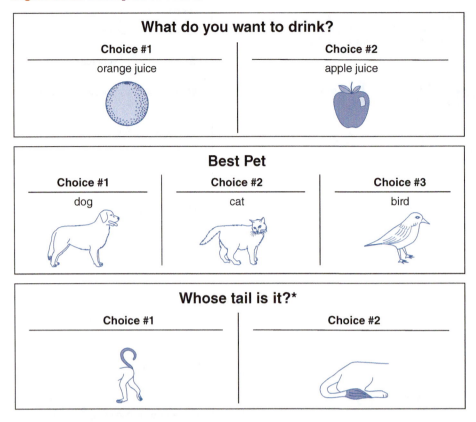

Figure 14-22 Examples of charts.

What do you want to drink?

Choice #1	Choice #2
orange juice	apple juice

Best Pet

Choice #1	Choice #2	Choice #3
dog	cat	bird

Whose tail is it?*

Choice #1	Choice #2

basket or pasting it onto the chart as shown in Figure 14-22. Child choices lead to discussions.

It is easy to see that placing pictures alongside print makes the task of choosing easier. Simple pictures are drawn by the teacher. This works well. The best charts relate to classroom themes or happenings. When making a chart, first draw sketches of the way words and pictures could be arranged. With a yardstick, lightly draw on guidelines with a pencil or use a chart liner (see Activities section). Then, add printscript words with a felt-tip pen or dark crayon. Magazines, old elementary school workbooks, old children's books, and photographs are good sources for pictures on charts. Brads or paper fasteners can be used for movable parts. Book pockets or heavy envelopes provide a storage place for items to be added later to the chart. The purpose of experience charts is to have children recognize that spoken words can be put in written form. Most centers keep large chart-making paper and felt-tip markers or thick black crayons in stock for chart making.

After an interesting activity, such as a field trip, visit by a special speaker, party, celebration, or cooking experience, the teacher can suggest that a story be written about the experience. A large sheet of paper or chart sheet is hung within the children's view, and the children dictate what happened. The teacher prints on the sheet, helping children sort out what happened first, next, and last. Figures 14-23 and 14-24 show examples of other word and picture charts.

Homemade chart stands can be made by teachers. Commercial chart holders, chart stands, chart rings, and wing clamps are sold at school-supply and hardware stores. Teachers using charts daily will attest to preferring commercially manufactured chart stands because of their mobility and stability. Commercially made letter patterns or teacher-made sets are useful devices that can be traced for teacher use in chart making, game making or for wall displays. Made of sturdy card stock or oak tag paper, they can be quickly and easily traced. See Figure 14 – 26 for sample letter patterns. A number of books called chart books, big books, or easel books are in print. These giant books are poster size and easily capture children's attention. The print stands out and cannot be missed. Creative teachers have produced their own versions with the help of overhead projectors that enlarge smaller artwork. Chart paper or poster board is used.

Figure 14-23 Rebus listening chart.

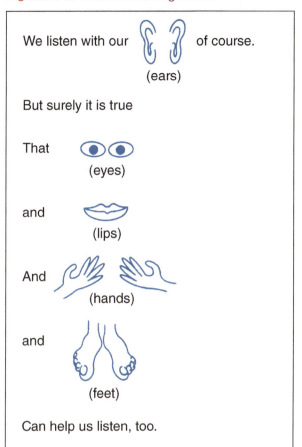

We listen with our 👂👂 of course.
(ears)

But surely it is true

That 👀
(eyes)

and 👄
(lips)

And 🖐🖐
(hands)

and 🦶🦶
(feet)

Can help us listen, too.

Figure 14-24 A chart using line drawings.

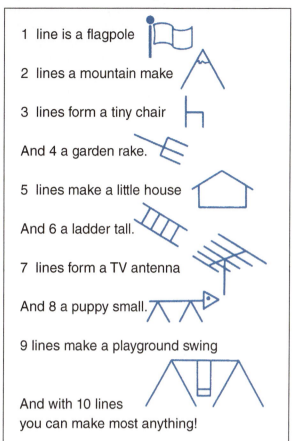

1 line is a flagpole

2 lines a mountain make

3 lines form a tiny chair

And 4 a garden rake.

5 lines make a little house

And 6 a ladder tall.

7 lines form a TV antenna

And 8 a puppy small.

9 lines make a playground swing

And with 10 lines
you can make most anything!

14-7f Generating Story Sentences

Story sentence activities are similar to chart activities. A child, or a small group of children, an author. After a classroom activity or experience, the teacher encourages generating a story (a written sentence). The activity is child-centered thereafter, with the teacher printing what the child or group suggests. The teacher can use a hand-wide space between words to emphasize the end of one word and spacing between words, and may talk about letters or letter sounds found at the beginning or end of children's names. It is not unusual for all children in a group of four-year-olds to recognize all of the names of other students in their class. Ideas and contributions from individual children are accepted, appreciated, and recognized by the teacher, and generated sentences are read and reread with the group. Long strips of chart paper or rolled paper can be used. Story sentences are posted at children's eye level.

14-7g Interactive and Scaffolded Writing

Interactive, or shared, **writing** times take place in many kindergartens and first-grade classrooms. They are described here to acquaint preschool practitioners with what lies ahead and what might be adapted, modified, or individualized for the few individual children who read (not memorize) simple text in picture books and write messages during their preschool years. Whether this strategy is adopted at a school where you are employed is the school's decision.

This kindergarten strategy is receiving an increased amount of use and attention from educators. Educators define interactive writing as an instructional context in which a teacher shares a pen—literally and figuratively—with a group of children as they collaboratively compose and construct a written message. Children participate

---

interactive writing — (1) an instructional strategy popular in American kindergartens; (2) a process involving a teacher who verbally stretches each word so that the child (children) can distinguish sounds and letters. This is also known as shared writing.

in every element of the writing process—deciding on a topic, thinking about the general scope and form of the writing, determining the specific text to write, and writing it word by word, letter by letter. Rereading, revising, and proofreading take place during and after the experience and usually lead to a child's (or children's) reading words, phrases, sentences, and the whole of what has been written.

Using the interactive writing process, a teacher focuses attention on letter sounds, names, forms, left-to-right and top-to-bottom progression, spaces between words, capitalization, punctuation, and spelling. Researchers believe interactive writing is an instructional strategy that works well for children of all linguistic backgrounds. Looking at a skilled kindergarten or first-grade child composing and constructing a message, one finds the child must think about and keep in mind the message, choose a first word, decide where to place it on the paper, consider what alphabet letter she knows makes the wanted sound, remember how the letter is formed, manually form it, decide if there are other sounds and other letters needed, know when the word ends, and know a space is needed before the next word. Immediately, an early childhood educator can see foundational understandings concerning writing must have been well learned.

Teachers who work individually with a child might define scaffolded writing as a process that involves supportive teacher assistance. Assistance by the teacher enables a child to do what she can't do by herself, but may be able to do if parts of the writing task are gradually handed over to the child. Bennett-Armistead, Duke, & Moses (2005) suggest that scaffolded writing consists of the following steps:

- Ask the child the message he would like to write. He may say something like "I played with my friend Matt yesterday."
- Repeat this message to the child.
- Draw one line for each word using a highlighter or ball point pen. Have the child write one "word" per line at the level that is most comfortable for the child.
- Read and reread the message together as necessary, as he writes, to help him remember the whole message. For instance, he may get

as far as "I played" and not remember what came after "played." At this point, you can remind him that he played with his friend Matt yesterday.

When scaffolded writing is attempted, teachers help children to sound out words and/or stretch out words to identify syllables and individual letter sounds.

14-7h Other Chart Ideas and Print Awareness Activities

1. Name-A-Part Chart

Enlarge a figure of a face, animal, house, car, bird, bike, or any familiar object that has parts or features children can name. (Draw freehand or use an overhead projector to enlarge a small drawing.) After introducing the chart, discuss and have the children identify what is pictured or a part of what is pictured. Make a printscript label or strip following children's suggestions. Children can glue strips or labels on the chart. Glue sticks work well, or children can apply glue to the back of the label or strip. Children sometimes creatively think up silly names, and that is part of the fun. At other times, they may discuss seriously what they believe are the correct labeling words. In a variation of this activity, the teacher draws an outline and parts are drawn as they are named by children.

2. Chart Liner Instructions

See Figure 14-25. Use Figure 14-26 for letter shapes if necessary.

3. A Word-a-Day Activity

Printing and defining just one word a day is a useful strategy for building vocabulary and promoting word recognition. Best if the word is drawn from the children at a group time, but teachers can add a word that might be encountered in the theme of study or for another purpose. A special display spot for word-of-the-day is recommended, and children can be asked when they might speak the word or how they might tell a short story using the word. Lots of activity possibilities exist.

Figure 14-25 Making a chart liner.

INSTRUCTIONS TO MAKE A CHART LINER

Cut a piece of Masonite® 12" by 36". Make 7 sawcuts 1½" apart, beginning and ending 1½" from either end. Then glue or nail 1½" square pieces of wood 12" long to each end.

Note: A teacher-made chart liner is a useful device that helps teachers make evenly spaced guidelines on charts that use lines of print. By placing the chart liner over chart paper, quick guidelines are accomplished by inserting a sharp pencil in sawcut slots.

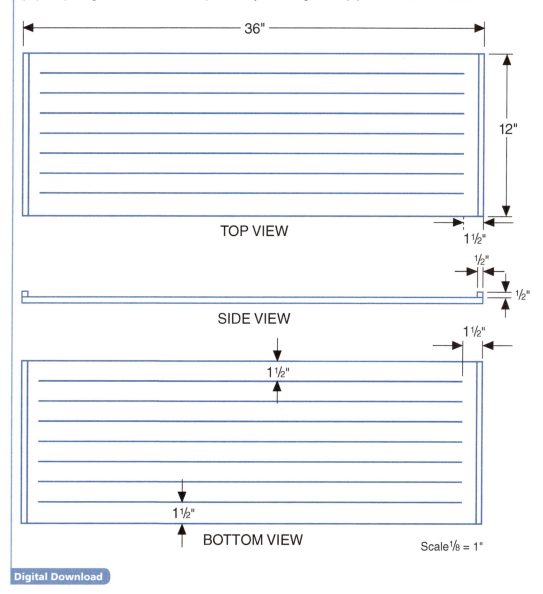

Scale ⅛ = 1"

4. Clay-On Patterns

These patterns can be used to enhance small, manipulative-muscle use and tracing skills. Materials needed include clay and 9 x 12-inch contact-covered cardboard sheets with patterns (Figure 14-27). The activity involves children making clay cylinders to form the patterns. The teacher demonstrates how to roll clay in cylinders and place them on patterns where clay can dry and later be painted.

Figure 14-26 Letter patterns.

A B C D E F
G H I J K L
M N O P Q
R S T U V
W X Y Z

Note: Letters will need to be enlarged for display in the classroom.

Figure 14-26 *(countinued)*

a b c d e f
g h i j k l
m n o p q
r s t u v
w x y z

Figure 14-27 Patterns.

5. Sticker Pictures

The children are shown the relationship between objects and words.

Materials:
stickers
paper strips
felt markers

Activity: The teacher has each child choose a sticker for her paper strip. The child names the sticker, and if the child desires, the teacher writes the name of the sticker on back of the strip. The children can then decorate the sticker strips.

6. Alphabet Eaters

Large-muscle use and visual discrimination are enhanced.

Materials:
cards with printscript
alphabet letters (small enough to be slipped into animal's mouth)
sturdy boxes on which animal heads and alphabet strips are glued (holes are cut in the opposite sides of boxes so that children can reach in for cards)

Activity: A child selects a card and "feeds" it to the animal that has a similar alphabet letter on the strip under its mouth (Figure 14-28).

7. Tracers

Tracers can be used over and over again. Waxy crayons or felt markers wipe off with a soft cloth. They can be used to help children recognize and discriminate among symbols and enhance small-muscle coordination.

Materials:
acetate or clear vinyl sheets
cardboard
scissors
strapping or masking tape
paper
felt-tip pen or marker

Construction Procedure: Attach acetate to cardboard, leaving one side open to form a pocket. Make letter or word guide sheets. Simple pictures can also be used (Figure 14-29).

Activity: A child or the teacher selects a sheet and slips it into the tracer pocket. A wax crayon or marker is used by the child to trace the guide sheet. A soft cloth erases the crayon or marker.

8. Rebus Stories

Teachers can use drawings or photographs to encourage child participation during storytelling time. At a crucial point in the story, the teacher pauses and holds up a picture, and the children guess the next word in the story. Teachers can name the picture and resume the story if the children have not guessed the

Figure 14-28 Alphabet "eaters" and cards.

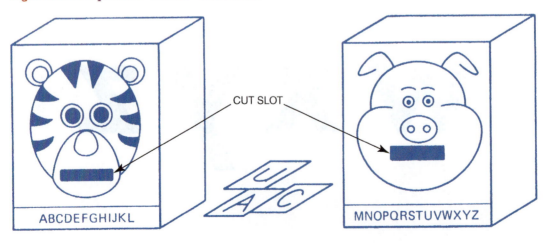

Figure 14-29 Tracers.

Open to slip in guide sheets

Back cardboard

Front acetate

Masking tape

Guides for tracing

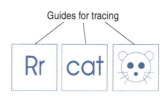

word. Any guess that is a close approximation is accepted; for example, "It is a truck, Josh, a fire truck." The rebus story in Figure 14-30 is an example of teacher authorship. Many additional teacher-created rebus stories are possible.

Figure 14-30 This rebus story, created by a teacher, uses computer-generated graphics

DUCK AND BEAR TAKE A TRIP

This is and this is his friend .

 cried one day and said, "Let's take a vacation!" had not

learned to fly.   "I get tired walking," said . "Let's ask

wise old how we can take a trip when a won't walk

and a can't fly."   Wise old  said, "That's not a problem.

Both of you can ride your to the airport.   Buy a ticket

Figure 14-30 *(countinued)*

and watch the [clock]. On an [airplane] [bear]

can sit down and [duck] doesn't have to know how to fly.

When the [airplane] lands, rent a [car].

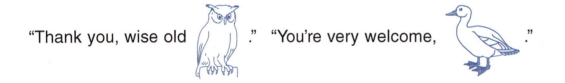

In a [car] [bear] can sit and [duck] can sit too."

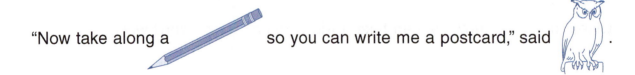

"Thank you, wise old [owl]." "You're very welcome, [duck]."

"Now take along a [pencil] so you can write me a postcard," said [owl].

Summary

14-1 Discuss young children's print awareness and child behaviors that reflect it.

Print awareness instruction is offered in programs that believe foundational knowledge about print can be acquired through early experiences during preschool years before formal reading and writing instruction begin. Early writing attempts are supported. Young children often talk about what they have done, created, constructed, or drawn by attaching meaning to their work. This behavior paves the way toward children's beginning understandings about written form and symbol use. Young children begin to grasp that print holds information and that it symbolizes spoken language. Children develop primitive hypotheses about print and explore making marks playfully.

14-2 Outline the probable sequence of events occurring before a child prints a first recognizable alphabet letter.

Research suggests the following sequence of events before a child makes a recognizable alphabet letter. The child:

- asks questions about artwork and/or marks being made.
- experiments with straight and curved lines.
- realizes forms are arbitrary and written in a linear fashion.
- concentrates on environmental shapes (forms) in drawings or art.
- searches for differences in a string or group of letters/marks.
- believes a string of letters or marks represents their own name.
- may display an understanding of syllables.
- may print syllables to represent a word or part of a word.
- may look for similar letters to write pieces of sounds.
- uses alphabet letters to represent sounds.

At some point in this continuum, especially when the child concentrates on the symbol shapes in the classroom, a recognizable alphabet letter may appear. A good number of preschoolers have learned to copy alphabet letters in their homes before they attend preschool through the efforts and direct instruction of a family member.

14-3 Name two goals of print instruction in preschool.

Preschool goals for print instruction include providing instruction that matches children's interests and ability. Being responsive to children's curiosity concerning print and providing a print-rich environment are important goals. Emphasizing the functional use of print in activities that are meaningful and have a purpose in the classroom is another prime goal. A school's curriculum and goal statements include promoting emerging skills, letter knowledge, and word recognition. Often curriculum goals are based upon reaching recognized professional standards for different preschool age levels. Goals can encompass acting on recognized child needs that relate to a child's success when eventually learning to read.

14-4 Discuss drawing experiences' relationship to prewriting instruction.

Teachers notice children's art (drawing) moves from scribbles to controlled lines, curves, and circles. Children begin to make their own symbols representing their world. Drawings seem to be based on a child's plan and often repeated patterns become apparent. Drawings expose children's thinking and recognizable symbol-like figures appear. Educators believe that drawing activities are prewriting experiences, a starting place. Engaging children in conversations about their work and providing supportive teacher comments can lead children to a greater understanding concerning their art as a form of communication. This may also prompt the children's realization that print is a form of communication, especially when teachers print words reflecting children's comments about their work.

14-5 Describe five ways that a classroom can promote alphabet awareness.

Many ways to promote alphabet awareness are possible. Alphabet book reading and follow-up activities are an example. Activities can also be designed around a child's interest in a particular letter, such as the first letter of his/her name, a daily happening with environmental print, especially on signs and labels, singing the alphabet song, playing with alphabet magnets, alphabet puzzles, or alphabet games, planning times and opportunities for child dictation, by creating room centers with writing areas and writing tools and materials, posting alphabet letter guides or charts in a classroom, through child experiences with sensory alphabet-shaped objects, an alphabet letter of the day activity, and through creating classrooms full of displayed words.

14-6 Print both the lowercase and uppercase printscript alphabet without using a guide.

To ascertain whether you were able to reach this goal it is necessary to obtain an alphabet letter guide for printscript lettering particular to your geographic (local) location or to use the one provided in this chapter. You will need to have letter forms memorized when you aid a child who wishes to use an alphabet letter in some way.

Testing yourself or asking a peer to check your printing when you immediately produce both uppercase and lowercase printscript without a guide is advised.

14-7   Name four kinds of instructional charts.

Classroom charts vary based upon need and instructional goals and plans. Charts mentioned in the text include: lunch charts, classifying charts, classroom announcement charts, alphabet charts, active involvement charts, experience charts, color charts, number charts, seasonal charts, story sequence charts, experience charts, calendars, helper charts, recipe charts, texture charts, concept charts, poetry charts, birthday charts, height and weight charts, rebus charts, keyword charts, multicultural charts, song charts, dictated charts, picture charts, and book charts.

Additional Resources

Readings

Barone, D., & Taylor, J. (2006). *Improving Students' Writing K-8.* Thousand Oaks, CA: Corwin Press.

Stacey, S. (2011). *The Unscripted Classroom: Emergent Curriculum in Action.* St. Paul, MN: Redleaf Press.

Temple, C., Nathan, R., & Temple, C. (2012). *The Beginnings of Writing.* Upper Saddle River, NJ: Pearson.

Children's Books with Writing Themes

Ahlberg, J., & Ahlberg, A. (1986). *The Jolly Postman.* Waltham, MA: Little, Brown & Co. (Letter writing.)

Barton, B. (2001). *My Car.* New York: Greenwillow. (Discusses road signs and other functional print.)

de Groat, D. (1996). *Roses Are Pink, Your Feet Really Stink.* New York: HarperCollins. (Writing or dictating Valentine rhymes.)

Alphabet Books

Catalanotto, P. (2002). *Matthew A. B. C.* New York: Atheneum. (A child's adventures.)

Marzollo, J. (2000). *I Spy Little Letters.* New York: Scholastic. (Finding letter shapes.)

Paul, A. (1999). *Everything to Spend the Night from A to Z.* New York: DK Publishing. (The overnight bag brought for an overnight stay with Grandpa yields A to Z objects.

Satin, A. S. (2004). *Mrs. McTats and Her House Full of Cats.* New York: Simon & Schuster. (Alphabet cats.)

Helpful Websites

National Association for the Education of Young Children

http://www.naeyc.org

Read NAEYC Position Statements link.

International Reading Association

www.reading.org

Search for position statements on early writing.

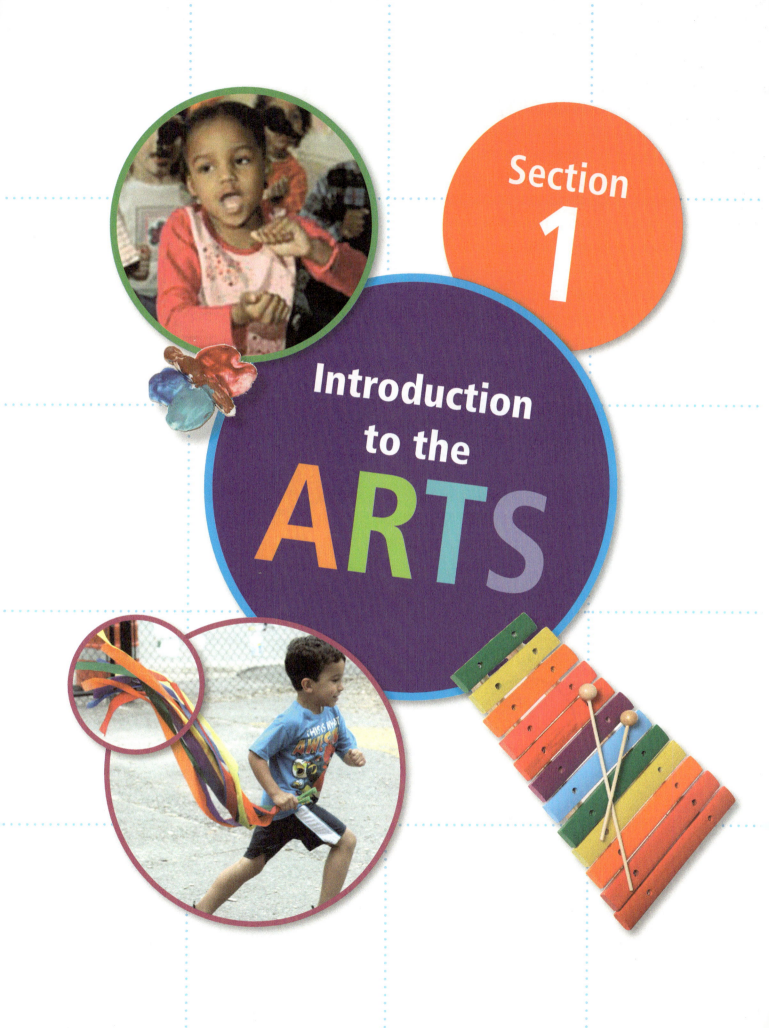

Section
1

Introduction
to the
ARTS

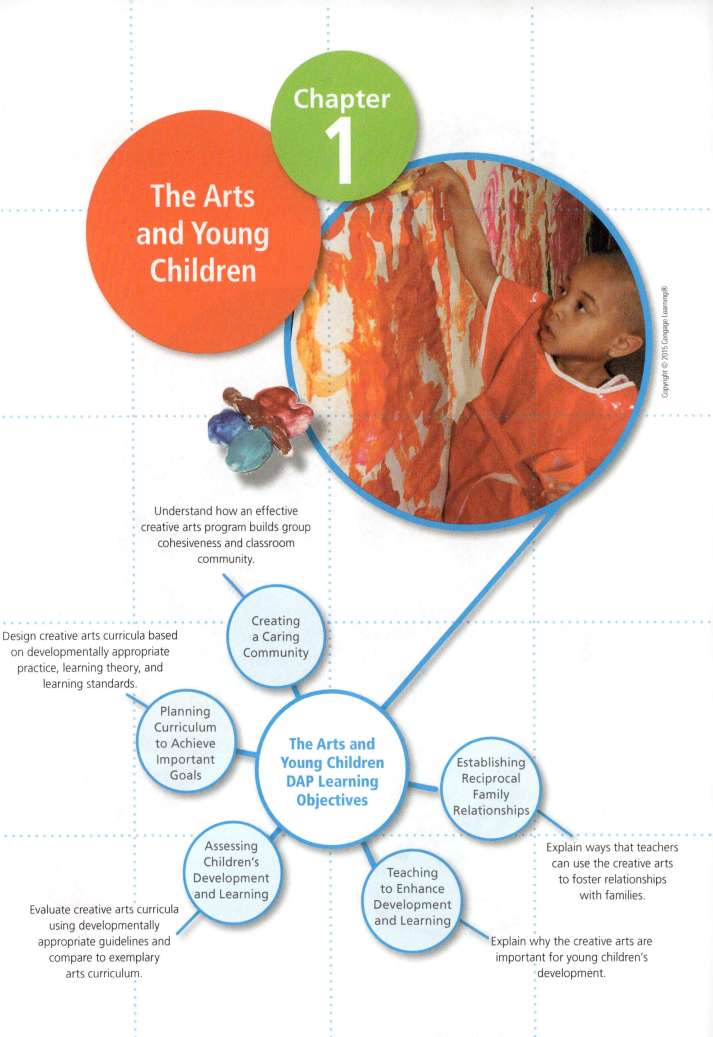

Chapter 1

The Arts and Young Children

Understand how an effective creative arts program builds group cohesiveness and classroom community.

Design creative arts curricula based on developmentally appropriate practice, learning theory, and learning standards.

Evaluate creative arts curricula using developmentally appropriate guidelines and compare to exemplary arts curriculum.

Explain ways that teachers can use the creative arts to foster relationships with families.

Explain why the creative arts are important for young children's development.

Creating a Caring Community

Planning Curriculum to Achieve Important Goals

The Arts and Young Children DAP Learning Objectives

Establishing Reciprocal Family Relationships

Assessing Children's Development and Learning

Teaching to Enhance Development and Learning

Young Artists Creating

Maria, age one, pulls her finger through a drop of spilled cereal and then licks her finger.

Steve, age two, hums a tune as he amuses himself during his bath by decorating the tub with handfuls of bubbly white soap foam.

Lorna, age four, splashes through a puddle and then with careful deliberation makes a pattern of wet footprints on the pavement. With every step she looks back to see her "trail."

Paul, age six, spends a busy day at the beach building sand mountains and decorating them with broken shells and beach pebbles. Other children join in his fun and watch excitedly as the surf slowly creeps up and then finally washes each mountain away.

Who Are the Young Artists?

Each of these children is a young artist, investigating elements of the arts—line, shape, color, texture, form, movement, melody, rhythm, and pattern. They are making the same artistic discoveries and decisions that all of us have made in our own lives. In doing so, they are repeating a process that has gone on as long as people have inhabited the earth. Like the circles, swirls, and lines on the walls of the caves and cliffs that were the canvasses of the earliest humans, the stone-smoothed satin black pot of a Pueblo potter, the intense sound of a jazz musician, and the flowing movement of a Chinese lotus dancer, the art of young children expresses their personal and cultural history. Their art reflects who they are at this moment in time.

Children from birth to age eight are busy discovering the nature of their world. They are not consciously artists in the way an adult is. They do not stop and say, "Now I am creating a piece of art." They are not creating a product—they are involved in a process!

They are at play. They enjoy manipulating the many materials that they find around them and expressing their creative power to change a piece of their world. In doing so they communicate their feelings and what they are learning. As they learn, they grow and develop.

In this process they gain control over their large and small muscles. Their skill in handling their bodies and artistic tools improves. Their repertoire of lines,

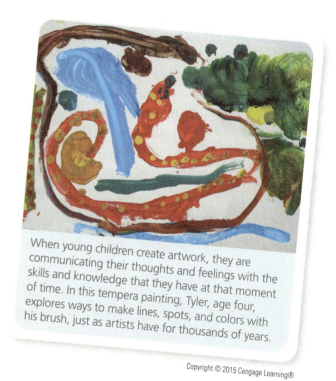

When young children create artwork, they are communicating their thoughts and feelings with the skills and knowledge that they have at that moment of time. In this tempera painting, Tyler, age four, explores ways to make lines, spots, and colors with his brush, just as artists have for thousands of years.

shapes, sounds, movements, and patterns expands. They repeat their successes over and over and learn to use artistic symbols that have meaning not just to themselves but also to others around them. By the time these young artists reach age eight, they already know a great deal about the world of creative expression.

But these growing artists are also still very young. They do not yet have skillful control over their bodies and the materials they use. They make messes. They sing out of tune and bump into things. They cry if they spill paint on their shoes.

Young children have short attention spans and are infinitely curious. They get distracted by a noise and run off, leaving their paintbrush in the middle of their picture. They do not always do things in an orderly sequence. Sometimes they glue their paper to the table. Sometimes they drop clay on the floor and unintentionally step on it when trying to pick it up. Anyone working with these children soon learns that great patience is needed.

But most importantly, each child is unique. As young as they are, they each bring to the creative arts experience their own personalities as well as their family and cultural heritage. Some are timid. Others are bold. Some have listened to many folktales and others have heard none. Some have been surrounded by music from birth, and others have rarely heard a tune. One child may have been taught not to get dirty and will not touch fingerpaint, while another child revels in being as messy as possible and smears paint up to the elbows. Children grow at their own pace, but through sensitive planning of creative arts experiences, each child can find his or her personal joy and growth through the arts.

> ### Did You Get It?
>
> **Young children from birth to age eight most resemble adult artists when they:**
>
> a. display a short attention span
>
> b. create a product
>
> c. play with materials
>
> d. make messes
>
> **Take the full quiz on CourseMate**

What Are the Creative Arts?

The arts exist in all societies and have been part of human existence since prehistoric times. Ellen Dissanayake (1995) points out that art creation is taking ordinary things and making them special. She argues that making art is part of being human—a normal behavior in which all people participate. Jessica Davis (2008) notes that as long as people have made tools

they have also made art. Through the creative manipulation of visual, auditory, dramatic, and spatial elements, the arts express the history, culture, and soul of the peoples of the world, both past and present.

A World Without the Arts

The arts are so much a part of our lives that we can recognize their existence only by imagining their absence. Envision our homes and clothing without patterns, textures, and colors; our books without stories; advertisements without pictures; a drive in the car without music; and our feet never dancing to the rhythm of a pop tune. Their purpose can be practical—as in the interior design of a home; communicative—as in an illustration or a television advertisement; or aesthetically and spiritually expressive—as in the swirling colors of a Van Gogh painting or the power of a Beethoven symphony.

In the same way, the creative arts are a part of every activity we offer children, through the clapped rhythms we use to catch their attention, in the box of blocks we give them to build with, and in the picture books we choose to read to them. The colors, textures, and forms of the toys we purchase, the pictures we hang on the walls, the patterns on our floors, and the sounds and rhythms they hear all form the artistic environment of the child. The arts surround us constantly. We can choose to ignore them, or we can select activities for children with an awareness of the role the arts play in our lives.

The Unique Arts

All of the arts incorporate creative problem solving, playfulness, and the expression of feelings and ideas. The term **the arts** encompasses all the different ways of doing this. In this text, the term **art form** is used to refer to the unique disciplines of creative movement or dance, drama, music, and visual art. However, these art forms should not be viewed as static, rigid categories. What makes them powerful is that they are expansive, and complementary, readily intermingled to create something new.

Creative Dance

Creative dance explores the movement and position of the body in space. Children involved in creative movement activities discover ways to physically control and coordinate the rhythmic movement of their bodies in a specific environment, alone and in cooperation with others. Specific information on creative dance and how to introduce young children to creative movement activities is provided in Chapter 11.

Drama

Drama is based on the presentation of ideas and actions through pantomime, improvisation, play acting, literature, and storytelling to create a visual and auditory performance. Dramatic activities and dramatic play engage children in verbal and physical communication through imitative role behavior, make believe, and social interaction with real and imaginary others. Chapter 12 presents many ways to interact with children through the dramatic arts and play.

Music

Music is organized sound. Music activities provide opportunities for children to learn how to control and respond to voices and instruments as they create rhythmic and melodic patterns through song and sound. Chapter 10 looks at ways to increase children's skill in listening to music, making music, and creating music.

Visual Arts

The **visual arts** draw on visual and tactile elements in order to communicate ideas and feelings. Children involved in visual arts activities use hand-eye coordination as they become skilled at manipulating materials and tools in symbolic ways. Two-dimensional and three-dimensional art activities for young children are provided in Chapter 9.

Did You Get It?

Creative dance, dramatic play, music, and visual art all share which feature?

a. colorfulness

b. playfulness

c. story structure

d. sound play

Take the full quiz on CourseMate

Why Should the Arts Be Taught to Young Children?

We need to teach the arts to young children, first of all, because the arts are an integral part of our lives as human beings. Second, and just as important, the arts help children grow and develop into learners who are stronger in the key developmental areas—intellectually, linguistically, physically, emotionally, perceptually, socially, and creatively.

The Arts Stimulate Intellectual Growth

Because the arts are multisensory and interactive, they are an ideal way to help young children develop **cognitively**. Infants are born ready to make sense of the world. From birth, their brains absorb and process sensory and spatial information. Billions of neural connections grow rapidly as the child interacts with the environment. The arts can play an important role in enhancing this process.

The arts enrich learning. Eric Jensen (2005, 2008) suggests the following ways to strengthen learning based on recent brain research.

1. **Provide multisensory, interactive activities.** Because the brain is capable of simultaneously processing information from many senses, we learn best when sensory, visual, and spatial information are combined. Providing hands-on arts activities stimulates the senses and makes learning more memorable.

2. **Create an enriched environment.** Young children, and infants in particular, constantly seek stimulation and are attracted to novelty—loud noises, sudden movements, bright colors, and unique textures. Unusual events call forth excitement and curiosity. Enriched learning environments have been found to have a positive effect on brain development, physically changing the brain. Animals provided with many toys, for example, develop more brain connections than animals in bare environments (Carey, 2002, p. 11). Hanging intriguing artworks on the wall for children to look at, singing a wide variety of songs, offering intriguing props for dramatic play, and providing

colorful, tactile art materials for them to explore are ways to enrich the learning environment and foster young children's brain development.

3. **Establish connections.** Searching for meaning is an innate process. The brain constantly examines incoming information, finding and creating patterns as it creates links to previous experiences. We help children learn when we draw on what they already know and present new information in integrated ways, such as when after a trip to the supermarket we set up a play store so that children can learn more about money through their dramatic play.

4. **Build on individual interests.** Every child is unique. A child's memories are constantly changing as new connections are made between past experience and incoming information. Making and talking about their creative work is a positive way for children to share what they know and like. Based on what they tell us, we can create a more personalized curriculum.

The arts help children develop logical thinking. To grow intellectually means to become skilled at finding patterns, organizing them logically, and using reasoning to solve problems.

For example, arts activities invite counting, sorting, and classifying. Through questioning, children involved in arts activities can become aware of numerical concepts. They can count the number of flowers they have drawn. They can graph the shapes in their collages and sort the leftover paper scraps by color. They can represent the rhythm of a song with symbols, or map the pattern in the steps in a dance.

Well-designed arts activities require children to make their own decisions and to order their behavior to accomplish a goal. Children who are busy creating develop skill in planning and sequencing. They learn that they must put glue on the paper before attaching the piece of yarn. They must dip the brush in the water to clean the paint off of it. They must beat the drum in a regular pattern if they want to follow the rhythm of the song. They must move their arms in a special way to imitate flapping wings. When they are done, they must put their artistic tools in the proper place so they will be ready to use again.

Arts activities provide children with experiences in identifying how properties change and in discovering

By participating in creative movement activities, these young children are not only increasing physical control over their bodies in space, but are also improving their health and well-being.

examples of cause and effect. Visual arts activities allow children to examine the properties of different substances—sticky glue, damp clay, shifting sand. Music activities let children play with changes in pitch, rhythm, and dynamics. Cause and effect are discovered when children explore how their fingers can change the shape of their play dough, or discover that spinning around makes them feel dizzy. Through discussion and questioning, we can help children formulate math and science concepts about these results.

The Arts Are a Child's First Language

Long before they can put their ideas into spoken and written words, children can demonstrate their concept of the world through the arts. It is through the creative exploration of their bodies, the materials and tools of the art form, and the environment that child artists begin to develop visual, auditory, kinesthetic, and graphic symbols with which to represent their thoughts.

Children's language abilities are enhanced through the arts in many ways.

1. **Listening.** All of the arts require children to attend carefully to directions in order to be successful.

2. **Communicating.** Children share their art creations in a variety of ways—some nonverbally, some through sound effects or movements, and others with intricate oral explanations and stories. This is an important part of language development—the prewriting stage.

3. **Vocabulary.** Children learn new words and develop fluency when describing arts materials, processes, their own work, and the works of others.

4. **Symbolically.** Between the ages of two and eight, children acquire the ability to make symbols and learn that these symbols can communicate to others. Children develop writing skills by creating a graphic symbol system to record their inner and outer observations. When children are asked to respond creatively in response to an experience, they are being challenged to communicate their ideas and thoughts in a symbolic mode. Responsive arts activities, such as imitating the movement of animals after a visit to the zoo and then talking or writing about it or keeping an illustrated journal, help them use this developing symbol system and refine the nature of their communication.

Special Needs

• ENGLISH LANGUAGE LEARNERS [ELLS] AND THE ARTS •

Because the arts are a nonverbal way to communicate feelings and ideas, arts activities are an ideal way to integrate non–English speaking children or those beginning to learn English into the community of the classroom. Directions for many arts activities can be given through modeling, physical clues, and hands-on demonstrations. Activities that are open-ended with no preconceived correct responses and that incorporate an element of play can allow ELLs to develop self-confidence and to gain acknowledgment from peers. For example, creative movement allows all children to express themselves nonverbally, so it provides an ideal communication tool for children who are nonnative speakers or who have trouble expressing themselves orally (Koff, 2000).

The Arts Improve Physical Well-Being

Physical activity promotes fitness and health. This is particularly important at a time when our children are becoming increasingly sedentary. A 2006–2007 study found that 20 percent of two-year-olds watch two or more hours of television a day, which can lead to childhood obesity and slowed development (Kent, Murphy & Stanton, 2010, p. 837; Louv, 2008, p. 7).

The arts are a motivating way to get children moving. Arts activities help children improve their ability to control large and small muscles and refine hand-eye coordination. An infant shaking a bell, a preschooler jumping up and down to music, and a first grader acting out a nursery rhyme are all learning to manage the way their bodies move.

Soft, pliable play dough and clay improve finger strength. Using brushes at an easel develops control of the arm and wrist. Large and small muscles are exercised and challenged through the manipulation of materials and tools when children stack blocks or tap a rhythm on a drum. Cutting a shape from paper or placing a leaf in a dab of glue requires the eye and hand to work together. Creative movement activities, such as imagining one's body as clay that can be made into different shapes, help the child relate physical movement and concepts. Listening to different types of music has been shown to slow down or speed up a person's heart rate and lower blood pressure (Using music, 2009).

The Arts Foster Emotional Well-Being

The arts have always been valued for the self-expression they can provide. However, their importance in emotional health goes far beyond this. Purposeful and playful physical movement, such as is found in arts activities, improves emotional well-being by causing the brain to release mood-altering chemicals, such as endorphins, which can heighten attention and provide a sense of well-being.

This is supported by current research on the effect of creative arts expression on healing. Heather Stuckey and Jeremy Noble (2010), in a summary of research done between 1995 and 2007, found a strong connection between each of the art forms and emotional well-being.

- **Music**—Music, which is the most researched of the arts, can control pain and restore emotional balance.

- **Visual Arts**—Visual art allows people to express feelings and thoughts that are difficult to put into words, such as grief, fear, and anxiety. Overall, creating visual art was found to be a positive activity that provided release from anxiety-producing situations, such as severe pain and health issues.

- **Creative Movement**—Creative movement not only improves physical condition but also improves self-awareness and body image.

- **Drama**—Theater training improves both long-term memory and feelings of self-confidence.

In all cases, participating in the arts reduced stress. Therefore, by providing a wide range of **open-ended**, developmentally appropriate arts activities, not only

do we set the stage for young children to express their feelings, but we also gift them with a lifelong way to relieve stress and a source of self-healing that will improve the quality of their lives.

The Arts Build Sensory Perception

The arts help children develop perceptually. Children learn through their senses. They absorb information from the world through touching, seeing, hearing, tasting, and smelling. This is how they acquire concepts about the nature of objects, actions, and events. Children learn better when teachers provide experiences that are sensually rich and varied, and that require children to use their perceptual abilities in many different ways. Children who have sung songs about, drawn pictures of, and acted out the metamorphosis of a butterfly will have a better understanding of the process than children who have only been told about the process.

The arts also enhance perceptive skills by teaching spatial concepts. Creative movement activities, for example, allow children to play with and use spatial concepts such as big/small, long/short, and under/over as they reach high or crawl along the floor. Visual arts activities let children explore the visual and tactile constructs of color, shape, pattern, form, and placement in space as they draw, paint, and play with modeling clay. Singing and playing instruments provide opportunities for children to develop their listening abilities as they investigate pitch, rhythm, and melody.

Most importantly, the arts, especially when integrated with experiences with nature, allow children to use all their senses to develop a sense of wonder and appreciation for the aesthetic qualities of the objects in our world. Chapter 4 presents activities that awaken children to the sensory landscape around them.

The Arts Create Community

Arts activities can help children develop socially by teaching them to take turns, to share space and materials with others, and to make positive choices in personal behavior. Arts activities often require children to work with others to accomplish a

The arts bring people together in ways that are enjoyable and fun. As these children learn to make music together, they are also learning how to listen to others and to work toward a common goal.

project or to produce a single, unified piece of art or a dramatic story.

Looking at artwork done by people different from oneself, taking a role in dramatic play, and experiencing unfamiliar styles of music are all ways to enhance children's understanding that each person has a different viewpoint and other individuals do not necessarily see things the same way they do. The arts provide the best entry point for developing media literacy (Nakamura et al., 2009). This is an essential skill for thinking critically in a society in which visual images, music, acting, and dance are frequently used in advertisements to entice us to make unnecessary purchases or propagandize one political point of view over another.

Across Cultures

Multiculturalism: What It Looks Like in the Arts

1. **Content Integration:** Information about diverse peoples and cultures are woven into the entire curriculum on a daily basis. *What this looks like:* Crayons and paints in shades of skin tones are available every day in the art center, not just for certain projects. Instruments from Asia and Africa are included in the bin of rhythm instruments, not just brought out on a special occasion.

2. **Knowledge Construction:** Diversity and cultural perspectives are valued and included. Prejudice and discrimination is recognized and addressed. *What this looks like:* A parent from Haiti visits the class and teaches a song she learned as a child. A Thanksgiving poster depicting Eastern Woodland Native Americans in Plains Indian headdresses is replaced with a more accurate image.

3. **Equity Pedagogy:** Teachers change the way they teach so that all students can understand and learn. *What this looks like:* Arts directions are given in a way that non–English speaking children can understand.

4. **Prejudice Reduction:** Teachers address prejudice when they see and hear it and actively celebrate diversity. *What this looks like:* In selecting art posters to share with the class, the teacher makes sure that many different cultures and types of people are represented.

See Chapters 5 and 7 for more ideas.

Sharing space and supplies, laughter and tears, and working on group projects with other young artists help children learn the power of cooperation and of empathy (Brouillette, 2010). Jessica Davis (2008) reminds us that the arts "excite and engage students, wakening attitudes to learning, including passion and joy, and the discovery 'I care.'" Chapter 5 presents many ways to foster community through the arts.

Studying the arts of other times, people, and cultures is another way the arts can draw us together as we learn to appreciate and understand the fabulous diversity of creative ideas as represented by unique art forms from around the world. In addition, sharing the arts from the cultures of students and their families is a respectful way to honor the diversity of our children. In Chapter 7 we will explore ways to present the art of others to young children.

Addressing bias and cultural differences. Our children come from different social and cultural backgrounds. Derman-Sparks and the A.B.C. Task Force (1989) encourage arts activities that help children accept racial and cultural differences and reject stereotypes. Selecting arts activities that show respect for their family backgrounds, home culture, and language can support children from diverse cultures and make families feel valued. Activities should reflect appreciation for different cultural beliefs, holiday customs, and family traditions, and they should develop a sense of community. Visual art materials should reflect the many colors of humanity; drama, music, and dance activities should reflect the stories, sounds, and rhythms of the world, as well as the local community; and artworks that decorate the walls should represent people from diverse backgrounds. Field trips and guest artists can provide access to culturally diverse musical, dance, and dramatic performances. Through seeing, touching, and talking about a wide variety of art forms selected from both their own culture and different cultures, children learn that the arts reflect the ideas and feelings of all people.

The Arts Nurture Creativity

The arts occupy the realm of the imagination. The unstructured quality of well-designed arts activities allows children to experiment with their voices, bodies, and familiar materials in new ways. They can use their own ideas and power to initiate and cause change and to produce original actions and combinations. Paint that drips, block towers that fall down, whistles that are hard to blow, and all of the other small difficulties arts activities present challenge children to find their own solutions to emerging problems.

Torrance (1970) defined creativity as being able to see a problem, form ideas about it, and then communicate the results. When children are engaged in the arts, they are creating something new and unique; in doing so, they are being creative. As Chapter 2 will illustrate, creativity is not something that can be taught but, instead, is something that must be nurtured.

Did You Get It?

Which of the following is true of the relationship between the arts and child development?

a. Children first develop their understanding of the world through spoken and written words.

b. The arts have no developmental effect on children before the age of two years, when they can understand arts concepts.

c. Arts activities develop those areas of a child's brain that are not concerned with logic and cognition.

d. The arts allow children to develop socially.

Take the full quiz on CourseMate

How Do the Creative Arts Help Children Learn?

Young children do not have a set goal in mind as they begin to create artistically, any more than they start the day with the goal of learning ten new words. They are caught up in the process of responding to and playing with the stimuli around them, such as the way paint drips, the way clay stretches and bends, and the way another child hums a tune.

As teachers, we can see children growing and developing through the arts activities we design. We can watch the changes in behavior that come with increasing experience in the arts—from the first tentative brush strokes of the two-year-old to the tuneful singing of the mature eight-year-old. However, it is also necessary that children grow in ways that will make them more successful in their interactions with the world.

The nature of an early childhood arts curriculum is determined by our philosophy of how children learn. Visits to most preschools, child care centers, and primary school programs will reveal children drawing, painting, singing, and dancing. However, what the children are actually doing as they draw, paint, sing, and dance will vary widely depending on what the adults in charge believe young children are capable of doing, what they think is the correct way to teach them, and how they interpret the role of the arts in education.

To strengthen our philosophy and establish our goals, we need to examine learning theories, contemporary viewpoints, current research, and successful approaches to the arts in the education of children. These ideas will provide direction in the creation of a successful and meaningful arts curriculum for young children.

Piaget and Constructivism

In the early 1920s Jean Piaget, a Swiss biologist, began studying children's responses to problems he designed. Based on his now-classic research, Piaget (1959) described how children develop their knowledge of the world. His findings have become the basis of the constructivist approach to early childhood education and include the following beliefs about how children learn:

- Children are active learners. They are curious and actively seek out information that helps them make sense of the world around them.

- Children construct knowledge based on their experiences. Because each child has different experiences, the understandings and misunderstandings acquired are unique to each child and are continually changing as the child has new experiences.

- Experience is essential for cognitive development. Children need to physically interact with the people and objects around them.

- Thoughts become more complex as children have more experiences. Although Piaget proposed that cognitive development was age dependent, many researchers today have modified his age categories and believe that complexity of thought follows gradual trends and may vary in different contexts and content areas (Ormrod, 2003).

TeachSource Video Case 1.1

0-2 Years: Piaget's Sensorimotor Stage

Watch the *0–2 Years: Piaget's Sensori-Motor Stage*. Do you think young children think the same way as adults? How does Piaget explain how children think and learn?

Watch on CourseMate

Theory in practice. Constructivism views children as self-motivated learners who are responsible for their own learning. Open-ended arts activities that offer many creative possibilities and choices are ideal for this purpose. Logical thought is developed by asking children to explain why they chose their particular creative solutions.

Vygotsky's Sociocultural Perspective and Social Cognitive Theory

Research on children's thinking in the 1920s and 1930s by Lev Vygotsky (1978) emphasized the importance of peers and adults in children's cognitive development. Vygotsky proposed that one way children construct their knowledge is based on past and present social interactions. His major points were the following:

- Complex thought begins through communication with adults and more knowledgeable peers. Watching and interacting with the people around them helps children internalize the thought processes, concepts, and beliefs common to their culture.

- Although children need to experience things personally and make discoveries on their own, they can also learn from the experiences of others.

- Children can perform at a higher cognitive level when guided by an adult or a more competent peer. Vygotsky defined the **actual developmental level** as what the child can do independently, and the **potential developmental level** as what the child can do with assistance.

- According to Vygotsky, most learning occurs when children are challenged to perform closer to their potential developmental level in what has come to be known as the **zone of proximal development**. It is when they are asked to perform tasks that require communication with more skilled individuals that children experience maximum cognitive growth.

- Vygotsky also thought that young children developed symbolic thought through play. Make-believe and dramatic play allow children to represent ideas using substitute objects (for example, pretending that a bowl placed upside down on their head is a hat) and so help children develop the ability to think abstractly.

Social cognitive theory emphasizes the role of modeling and imitation in children's learning. The well-known psychologist Albert Bandura (1973) found, for example, that children who watched a doll being treated aggressively repeated the behavior when alone with the doll.

However, for a child to learn from a role model, four factors need to occur.

1. **Attention:** The child needs to watch the role model perform the behavior.

2. **Motivation:** The child must want to imitate the role model. Bandura found children were more likely to imitate those they liked or respected, or who were considered attractive or powerful (Bandura, 1989).

3. **Remembering:** The child needs to understand and recall what the role model did.

4. **Reproduction:** The child must repeat the behavior enough times to improve in skill.

Theory in practice. These theories help us see children as members of a social community in which adults as role models are an important source of information about the nature of the arts. As teachers we

TeachSource Video Case 1.2

5-11 Years: Lev Vygotsky, the Zone of Proximal Development, and Scaffolding

Watch the video *5–11 Years: Lev Vygotsky and the Zone of Proximal Development and Scaffolding.* How do Piaget's and Vygotsky's approaches compare? What are some ways you can determine when a child is ready to learn something new?

Watch on CourseMate

1. **Linguistic:** The ability to manipulate the oral and written symbols of language

2. **Logical-Mathematical:** The ability to manipulate numerical patterns and concepts in logical ways

3. **Spatial:** The ability to visualize the configuration of objects in both two- and three-dimensional space

4. **Musical:** The ability to manipulate rhythm and sound

5. **Bodily-Kinesthetic:** The ability to use the body to solve problems or to make things

6. **Interpersonal:** The ability to understand and work with others

7. **Intrapersonal:** The ability to understand oneself

can model for children how artists think and behave. This is because the arts lend themselves to what is characterized as the "apprenticeship model" (Gardner, 1993). In an apprenticeship, the child learns not only how to do the task but also how experts think about the task. We can model artistic methods while thinking out loud about the process. We can make well-timed suggestions that guide the child to the next level of understanding, and we can ask children to explain what they are doing so that they make the learning their own. In addition, we can provide models of what the arts can be by introducing children to wonderful artists from all times and cultures. Doing these things will not only help children grow cognitively but will also nurture their ability to think and act as artists.

Multiple Intelligence Theory

Based on cognitive research, Howard Gardner (1983, 1991) has proposed that there are at least eight intellectual capabilities, or **intelligences.** These intelligences represent biological and psychological potentials within each individual. Everyone has capabilities in each intelligence, with special strengths in one or more of them. Gardner has identified these intelligences as follows:

Open-ended arts activities have no preconceived end result. Instead, they invite exploration of materials and concepts or pose a problem that can be solved in multiple ways. Playing with puppets allows children to express their ideas and feelings in a wide variety of ways as they engage in imaginative dramatic play. Will this dinosaur be angry and bite or will he be friendly? This child can create his own dinosaur story while developing his oral language skills.

8. **Naturalistic-Environmental:** The ability to sense and make use of the characteristics of the natural world

Traditional educational practice has focused mainly on strengths in the linguistic and logical-mathematical domains. Multiple intelligences (MI) theory provides a framework upon which teachers can build a more educationally balanced program—one that better meets the needs of children with talents in other areas. The arts as a learning and symbolic tool is particularly valuable not only because it embraces the talents often overlooked in education, but also because it crosses and links all of the intelligences.

It is important to note that Gardner (1993) does not believe that there is a separate artistic intelligence. Instead, each of the eight intelligences can be used for either artistic or nonartistic purposes. How an intelligence is expressed will depend on a variety of factors, including personal choice and cultural environment. Linguistic intelligence, for example, can be used to scribble an appointment on a calendar or to compose a short story. Spatial intelligence can be used to create a sculpture or to read a map. Conversely, to create a painting, a visual artist must draw not only on visual-spatial intelligence in order to visualize the artistic elements in the work, but also on bodily-kinesthetic intelligence in order to control the brush and logical-mathematical intelligence in order to plan the sequence in which the paint will be applied.

Theory in practice. MI theory broadens our view of children's abilities and potentials into a multidimensional view of intelligence. It means that we need to honor the special abilities of every child by creating an early childhood curriculum that includes many opportunities to use all of the intelligences in artistic ways.

Not every activity will engage all of the intelligences, but when activities are chosen that incorporate many of the intelligences, children can learn in whatever way best fits their intellectual strengths or learning style. In this book, Gardner's intelligences have been interrelated with the physical, linguistic, social, emotional, creative, and intellectual growth areas in order to create models of such balanced arts activities.

For an example of an MI curriculum planning web with correlated objectives, see The MI Planning Web on CourseMate.

Did You Get It?

Ms. Fanelli, a preschool teacher, believes in the constructivist approach to learning. Accordingly, she will most likely

a. allow children to physically interact with objects and people around them.

b. evaluate a child's ability to create an original melody by comparing the child's work to that of his peers.

c. develop arts activities that require the children to follow step-by-step directions.

d. view children as requiring constant supervision and direction in arts activities.

Take the full quiz on CourseMate

What Does a Well-Designed Arts Curriculum Look Like?

The Task Force on Children's Learning and the Arts: Birth to Age 8 (1998) has laid out three curriculum strands for arts-based curricula. These incorporate the need for artistic skills and judgments, while at the same time allowing for creative self-expression and cultural understanding. These strands are as follows:

➤ Children must be active participants in the arts process. They should create, participate, perform, and respond to carefully selected arts activities that reflect their culture and background experience.

➤ Arts activities must be domain based, relevant, and integrated. Arts activities should allow every child to be successful and reflect children's daily life experiences. The arts should be fully integrated into the rest of the curriculum and help children make connections with what they are learning. At the same time, these activities should build artistic skill and competence in the particular art form being used. Verbal and graphic expressive, reflective, and evaluative responses to arts activities can provide the opportunity to build literacy and intellectual skills.

➤ The learning environment must nurture the arts. Adequate quality materials, space, and time should be provided with the needs and abilities of the children foremost. Adult engagement should

Integrating the Arts

WHAT IS ARTS INTEGRATION?

According to the Kennedy Center Artsedge (http://artsedge.kennedy-center.org) arts integration means that children develop understanding of a concept and demonstrate that new knowledge through an art form. Integrated arts curricula creatively connect language, math, social studies, or science concepts together with one or more art forms so that the learning objectives in both areas are met.

Integrated arts curriculum design will be examined more deeply in Chapter 8.

share in and support children in their artistic explorations and reflect input from current research in the field and artists, arts specialists, early childhood teachers, parents, caregivers, and other community resources.

Developmentally Appropriate Practice and the Arts

The National Association for the Education of Young Children (NAEYC) has similar recommendations (Copple & Bredekamp, 2009). A developmentally appropriate curriculum provides daily opportunities for creative exploration and aesthetic appreciation in all of the arts forms using a wide range of materials from a variety of cultures. These activities are integrated into the children's total learning experiences and, while introducing arts vocabulary and concepts, and should have an open-ended design that has joy as its central purpose.

The Reggio Emilia Approach to Arts Education

These principles are well illustrated by the preprimary program of the municipality of Reggio Emilia, Italy. In this program, the arts are highly valued. Each school has an *atelierista*, or art educator, who works directly with the teachers in designing the program. In addition, each school has a beautiful art room where supplies are arranged by color. This attention to aesthetic qualities carries over to the

school itself, which is decorated with children's artwork that has been carefully mounted. Light, mirrors, and color produce wonderful spaces in which children can play and create. In the Reggio Emilia program, the arts are used as an important method of recording the observations, ideas, and memories of experiences in which the children have participated. The *atelierista* offers suggestions as the children work. The children also share their art with other children. Unlike in the United States, where arts experiences are often used as fillers and artwork is usually sent home at the end of each day, in Reggio Emilia, children are asked to return to their artistic works to reconsider, discuss and critique, and then to rework, or repeat their responsive arts activities.

The Reggio Emilia program is an example of **emergent curriculum.** Elizabeth Jones and John Nimmo (1994) describe this approach to teaching young children as one in which teachers are sensitive to the needs and interests of the children and then build on these through the provision of wonderful learning experiences. The teacher and children are coplayers sharing ideas and choices together in a curriculum that is open-ended and constantly adjusting to new ideas and needs. This does not mean that the teacher has no control over the

Creativity is nourished when children are allowed the freedom to express their unique ideas in an accepting environment that values the arts as a form of communication and self-expression. Jason, age four, has painted his own idea of a cat.

curriculum. Rather the guiding adult is more like a stage director, the one who "sets the stage, times the acts, and keeps the basic drama together" (1994, p. 5). In such a curriculum, the arts can play a major role as is seen in the work done by children in the Reggio Emilia schools.

The Project Approach

Another example of emergent curriculum in action is the Project Approach, as exemplified by the work of Lillian Katz and Sylvia Chard (2000). This approach identifies and investigates a topic based on child interest, and then the arts are incorporated as a rich, vital way to express learning will be examined more deeply in Chapter 8.

Goals for Learning

What do children need to learn about the arts? This is a key question in designing an effective arts curriculum for young children. According to Lillian Katz and Sylvia Chard (2000), there are four main categories of learning goals.

Knowledge. Knowledge includes the vocabulary and concepts we want our children to hear and use. In early childhood arts, this means that we must make sure that children will be learning to talk about and identify the elements of each art form, as well as the materials and methods belonging to each. We then want children to be able to apply what they have learned in their artistic performances and creations as well as in their responses to the artwork of others.

Young children construct this kind of knowledge from direct experiences and interactions with more expert peers and adults. It happens when we ask children to tell how they made a particular color in their paintings or when they learn a song from a friend. The knowledge to be imparted can be expressed in the vocabulary words selected, the concepts being applied, and the questions children will be asked as they are involved in arts activities. In the Exploring the Arts section of this book, examples of these are found under the "What to Say" heading.

Dispositions. Dispositions are the ways we behave as learners and performers. Examples of dispositions include being intellectually curious, using

the creative process, thinking logically, and being generous and helpful. Another way to view dispositions is to think of them as preferred ways of thinking and behaving. We can think and make decisions, as would a creative musician, an inquiring artist, or an observant poet. Dispositions are nurtured instead of being taught directly. They develop best in carefully designed open-ended learning environments that allow creative exploration, provide safe risk taking, and foster creative problem solving.

Many different dispositions can be developed in the creation of art. First and foremost is the disposition to think and to act like a creative artist, musician, dancer, or actor. For example, a young child playing a drum may say, "Look, I am a drummer like in the band. You can march to the beat of my drum." This is nourished through open-ended arts activities using real art skills, materials, and tools presented by a teacher who is passionate about the arts and who verbally and visually models what these artists do. At the same time, thoughtful statements and questions can promote intellectual curiosity, and careful organization of the activity can promote cooperative behavior and nurture the growth of a caring and socially aware individual.

Feelings. Feelings describe how children receive, respond to, and value what they are learning and are reflected in the emotional state of the child. Positive feelings about the arts, or any other subject area, develop in an arts program that makes children feel safe; when activities are challenging but possible; when mistakes are seen as positive ways to grow; and where accomplishments are enthusiastically acknowledged.

Children come to value the arts when we prepare a curriculum that provides activities that share with them a sense of wonder and awaken them to the aesthetic qualities of the world in which they live, and encourages them to respond positively to the art of others. In such an arts program, teachers and peers respond to artistic endeavors with heartfelt, thoughtful comments, and provide open-ended arts activities that allow children to express their unique personal feelings and ideas. Most importantly, a well-planned arts program allows all children to feel successful as artists, thereby enabling them to see themselves as competent individuals.

Skills. Skills are the observable behaviors used in arts creation, such as cutting out shapes with a scissors or shaping clay into a ball. Although some skills are learned spontaneously, most develop through practice. If we want our children to be able to use paint skillfully, for example, then we need to give them lots of opportunities to explore paint. In addition, skills from the different growth areas can be practiced through the arts. For example, intentionally having two children use the same glue bottle provides them with an opportunity to practice sharing. Talking about how it feels to move like a drop of water allows children to develop their oral language skills. In fact, well-planned arts activities usually address skill development in all of the growth areas.

National Core Standards for Arts Education

Another way of looking at what children need to learn about the arts is to examine standards for arts education. Standards provide us with a definition of what a good arts education is and provide a structure on which to build a successful arts program. Based on the specific concepts and skills identified in the standards, we can make sure that young children are introduced to a breadth of rich arts experiences through the curriculum units and activity plans we write. In conjunction with forming teaching objectives, the content standards for visual arts, music, dance, and dramatics are provided in Chapters 9 through 12.

The 2013 National Core Arts Standards (National Coalition for Core Arts Standards, 2013) address what competencies children from kindergarten to high school should have in the arts in order to become adults who understand, value, and enjoy the arts.

The 2013 Core Arts Standards are based on the following definition of artistic literacy, which recognizes the importance of the arts in our society:

> Artistic literacy is the knowledge and understanding required to participate authentically in the arts. Fluency in the language(s) of the arts is the ability to create, perform/produce/present, respond, and connect through symbolic and metaphoric forms that are unique to the arts. It is embodied in specific philosophical foundations and lifelong goals that enable an artistically literate person to transfer arts knowledge, skills, and capacities to other subjects, settings, and contexts. (p. 13)

To address this goal of artistic literacy for all students the standards delineate expectations in the following areas of competency in the arts:

1. **Creating:** Conceiving and developing new artistic ideas and work.

2. **Performing** (dance, music, theatre), **Producing** (media arts), and **Presenting** (visual arts): Although the various arts disciplines have chosen different words to represent this artistic process, they are clustered here as essentially parallel. This area of competency refers to the physical interaction with the materials, concepts, and techniques of the arts forms as well as the sharing of that process with others.

3. **Responding:** Interacting with and reflecting on artistic work and performances to develop understanding.

4. **Connecting:** Relating artistic ideas and work with personal meaning and contextual knowledge.

The 2013 Core Arts Standards also establish benchmarks starting at the end of second grade that assess the artistic literacy of the children. Early childhood arts education as described in this text will be key in making sure our children reach these high levels of artistic understanding. In addition, because the arts are a vehicle for learning in all areas of knowledge, the arts standards are linked to the National Common Core State Standards in English Language Arts and Mathematics.

Similar arts standards for the education of younger children have been developed by many states.

Photo Story

Oceans Integrated Arts Unit

Engaging in dramatic play with sea toys develops creative storytelling skills and at the same time allows a science-related investigation of buoyancy.

Observing and caring for live fish provides inspiration for arts production and performance while developing an understanding of aquatic life. The fish in the children's artworks sprout fins and gills.

Sorting seashells develops sensory and aesthetic perception as well as logical mathematical reasoning skills.

"Rainbow fish" Carved Styrofoam and sponge prints— Emma, Makenzie, Jason, and Jack ages seven and eight

"Shark attack" by Ben age seven

"Fish mobiles" Cut paper—Cynthia, Jake, and David ages seven and eight

For more information on arts standards and to see a sample of state arts standards, visit, *Learning Standards Resources* on CourseMate.

Did You Get It?

According to the Task Force on Children's Learning and the Arts: Birth to Age 8, the developmentally appropriate practice for arts education for young children should include

a. daily opportunities for active, creative exploration and aesthetic appreciation.

b. regular offerings of simple arts activities.

c. only materials that are familiar to the children.

d. step-by-step guidance of children as they participate in arts activities.

Take the full quiz on CourseMate

What Is the Teacher's Role in Creative Arts Education?

In an early childhood program that values the arts, music, dance, dramatics, and visual arts activities are inseparable from the total curriculum. It all seems so effortless. There is a rhythm and flow to a well-planned program that creates the sense that this is what will naturally happen if the children are just told to have fun with a lot of interesting materials. Nothing could be farther from the truth.

Behind that successful program is superb planning by teachers who have knowledge about how children think, learn, and respond to stimuli in their environment. These teachers practice **intentional teaching**. This means that they have a strong knowledge of how children develop in the arts and have practiced ahead of time what they will say and do to encourage young artists so that when that **teachable moment** arises—and it will if open-ended materials and experiences are provided—everything comes together in a moment of wonder and understanding.

We can be those teachers. We can learn what to say about arts production, presentation, and performance, how to say it, and when it is best left unsaid. We can know when to interact and when to wait and watch.

We will seek to be judged not on the children's products but on their growth. We can continually learn and grow along with our young artists from the first contact to the last. We can constantly improve the curriculum we offer, assessing each activity and noting how the children show growth in relation to the goals we have set for them. The result is an arts curriculum of our own creation, both meaningful and thoughtful.

As teachers, we do not need to be professional musicians, dancers, artists, or actors to be effective teachers of the arts. Rather we need to design an art curriculum made up of activities that nurture young artists.

In the end, the teacher is the most important part of the arts curriculum. Teachers are like gardeners, providing the "fertile ground"—the enriched arts curriculum—that gives children a start in thinking and working as artists. As the children grow in skill and confidence, it is our planning, enthusiasm, and encouragement that will allow the child's creativity to flower. It is the purpose of this text to help you become this teacher.

Did You Get It?

Intentional teaching means

a. using an idea found on the Internet.

b. using knowledge of children's artistic development to plan arts activities.

c. using materials that have one specific use.

d. ignoring the teachable moment.

Take the full quiz on CourseMate

Conclusion: The Well-Designed Arts Program

The stage has now been set for developing a rich and meaningful arts program for children. Children are natural artists, in the sense that they play creatively with the elements of the arts that they find in their surroundings. But those surroundings must be provided, determined by a philosophy of what child art is, and what it means. We need to consider why children should do certain arts activities, which ones should be selected, how they should be delivered, and what environment is most conducive to their performance.

This chapter has closely examined why the arts need to be taught. We have learned how the arts help children grow socially, emotionally, physically, intellectually, and linguistically. The following chapters will consider:

1. **How:** We will see how the delivery of arts activities affects what children learn, as well as how the way the child learns affects what activities will be successful.

2. **Where:** We will learn how to design the environment in which child artists will work.

3. **What:** We will investigate the appropriate selection and efficient delivery of arts concepts and skills.

It is the educator's role to nurture the artist within every young child. Although the focus will always be on guiding the artistic development of the child, in doing so the artist within the adult will also be rekindled. Adults and children must become part of the artistic continuum that stretches from our distant human past into the future. To guide young children as they grow through the arts is a deeply rewarding experience.

For additional information about the importance of the arts, arts organizations, and arts standards, see *Online Resources* on CourseMate.

Teaching In Action

An Integrated Arts Curriculum

The arts are integrated into the curriculum through emergent curriculum.

It is a warm spring day, and sunlight streams through the windows of the large bright room. Photographs of fish and sea creatures decorate one wall. Children's books about the sea are on display on the bookshelf. The teacher has already read several books about the sea to the children and talked to the children about experiences they have had during visits to the beach. Seashells, starfish, fishnets, floats, and other sea-related objects are placed around the room. It is easy to tell that the children have been learning about the ocean. In the center of the room an adult and several children, ages three and four, are hard at work painting a refrigerator box in which round windows and two doors have been cut. They are using yellow poster paint and large paintbrushes. Newspapers cover the floor. One child is painting broad strokes of color across the box, while the other child presses the brush down again and again, making rectangular stamp marks in one small section. In the background, a recording of the Beatles' classic "Yellow Submarine" can be heard.

Children develop socially by working on a group project.

The teacher enthusiastically responds to the artistic elements in the child's work with positive feedback.

While the painters work away on their submarine, other children are playing at the water table, experimenting with a variety of objects in different sizes, colors, and shapes that either sink or float. At an easel, a four-year-old has filled his paper with waving lines using mixtures of blue, green, and yellow paint. The teacher stops to help the painter at the easel remove his smock. "Look at all the blue-greens and turquoises you have made," she tells him, pointing to examples of those colors.

(continued)

Teaching In Action (continued)

Arts activities are open-ended. Children choose to use the art supplies in their own creative way.

At a round table, three children have taken premade paper tubes from the supply shelf and are decorating them with paper, yarn, glue, and crayons. One child asks the teacher to attach a piece of blue cellophane to the end of his "scope." A second child puts her tube up to her nose. "I'm a swordfish. This is my sword. I have a beautiful sword," she tells another girl as she makes a roaring sound through the tube. A three-year-old is exploring what happens when he glues a piece of yarn on the tube and then pulls it off. In another corner, two boys are engaged in noisy, animated play with trucks and blocks. At the computer, a four-year-old is making a multicolored line travel a wiggly path over the screen.

Visual images from diverse sources enrich the children's experience.

At the game table, two children are matching pictures. The cards have been made from prints of paintings, sculptures, and crafts from many cultures that illustrate subjects about the sea. These have been cut out of museum catalogs, glued to card stock, and laminated. On the wall behind them is a poster-size print of one of the artworks. One child finds a card that matches the poster and walks over and compares the two pictures. "They're the same, but this one is littler," he notes, holding the picture card up to the print.

Visitors provide common experiences that lead to integrated learning.

Suddenly everyone stops working. A special visitor has arrived! A father of one of the children brings in two plastic buckets, and all the children circle round. In the tubs are saltwater creatures borrowed from the pet store where he works. The children closely observe a sea urchin, an anemone, and a sea snake. One child looks at the sea urchin through his cellophane-covered tube. "It changes color," he states with wonder. He shares his tube with the others so they can see the change too.

Arts and language activities are unified.

When the visitor leaves, some children head off to a table where crayons, markers, and stapled paper booklets are set out. "I'm writing a story about a sea snake and an 'anoome,'" says one five-year-old girl. She draws a long wiggly line on one page. "Here he is very sad." Then she draws a purple circle. "This is his friend, the 'anoome.' Now he is happy!" When she finishes her book, she "reads" it to her teacher, inventing a long, detailed story to go with her pictures. "You made your anemone the same color as the one Sam's father brought to show us," the teacher says. The girl beams with pride and skips off to read her book to her friend.

Children explore sensory experiences.

A three-year-old has settled in with a lump of play dough. He rolls out a long "worm." "Look—I can make it wiggle like a sea snake," he says, as he twists and turns the play dough. Some children take cardboard tubes to decorate. They want to put cellophane on theirs so they can have their own "scopes." Several other children have taken colored paper, markers, and scissors. They talk quietly together as they invent new sea creatures.

"Mine has tentacles like the sea urchin."

"I'm going to give mine a big mouth and teeth," says another. They cut out their creatures and take them to the teacher.

(continued)

Teaching In Action

Children initiate and choose what they want displayed.

"Let's put a string on them and hang them up so they can swim in our sea," says one. The teacher hangs their creatures inside a large glass aquarium that has been decorated with sand and shells on the bottom. They join other paper sea creatures, made by other children, which are already afloat on the air currents.

Meanwhile, several other children have moved into the submarine. They are busy arranging blankets and pillows.

"I think it is softer this way," says Peter. Sam lies down and tries it out. He curls up and sucks his thumb.

"I think we should have a yellow blanket in the yellow submarine," says Sue, bringing in a piece of yellow cloth from the dress-up box. Other children look in through the portholes and make faces at their friends.

Creative movement grows out of the children's dramatic play, and, combined with music, provides a smooth transition to story time.

"We will be the fish swimming around the submarine!" they tell them. The teacher observes the children's play and puts on Saint-Saens's *The Swan*. The music matches the children's actions as they move around the box inventing fish sounds and motions. The teacher joins the dancers and invites the children in the box to come out and swim in the sea with them. Sue swirls the yellow cloth behind her. "This is my tail," she sings.

Children have made plans and look forward to the next day.

"Story time!" says the teacher. "Let's swim to the rug." The dancing children and those working about the room move to the rug and settle around the teacher, who reads the story *The Rainbow Fish* by Marcus Pfister. The children gather round the aquarium and look at their floating sea creatures.

"We need a rainbow fish," says one boy.

"Let's make lots of rainbow fish tomorrow," joins in another.

"I will find some shiny rainbow paper for you," says the teacher. Full of excitement about the next day, the children help put away the materials they have used and then get ready to leave.

Reflection Page

Why the Arts?

All of the following have been suggested as important reasons children should be taught the arts. Think carefully about each item and then rank each by its importance. Write a number in front of each, with 1 being the highest rank and 9 being the lowest. Based on your ranking, write a statement that explains why you feel the arts are essential for young children.

_____   The arts are part of being human.

_____   The arts stimulate brain development.

_____   The arts promote early literacy.

_____   The arts improve physical health.

_____   The arts promote emotional well-being.

_____   The arts create community.

_____   The arts foster cognitive growth.

_____   The arts nurture creativity.

_____

_____

_____

_____

_____

_____

_____

_____

_____

_____

_____

Reflection Page

How to Have a Successful Observation

Observing children involved in arts activities is an invaluable way to learn how children react to various kinds of arts experiences. As an observer, you are free of the pressure of performing and can devote your attention to the small details that busy, overworked caregivers often miss.

The following checklist will help you and the participants in the program you are visiting have a pleasant and rewarding experience.

Before the Visit

- Call for an appointment and get permission to visit.

- Write down the names of the people you speak to on the phone and those of the teachers whose children you will be observing.

- If you intend to use a camera or camcorder, make sure you have all the necessary permissions. In many programs, parents must be asked to sign a release form before you can photograph. Some schools may already have these on file.

- Prepare a form on which to record your observations.

On the Day of the Visit

- Arrive on time and introduce yourself to the teachers. If possible, have them introduce you to the children. If asked, give a simple explanation for your visit, such as, "My name is _____. I can't wait to see what you are doing today."

- Observe and record carefully. Do not bother the teachers. They are there to work with the children, not you.

- When it is time for you to leave, do not disturb the children or the teachers.

After the Observation

- As soon as possible, review your notes and add any special details that you remember. Some people find it helpful to make an audiotape recording while the experience is still fresh in their minds.

- Write a note of thanks to everyone with whom you had contact. A special handmade card for the children is always welcome.

Reflection Page

Observation: The Arts and the Child

The purpose of this observation is to observe young children in a typical learning situation. The observation will focus on the artistic behavior of the children in a group educational situation. This observation may be done in an organized school or a child care setting that services children between the ages of one and eight. The observation should last 40 minutes to 1 hour.

Date of observation: _____   Length of observation: _____

Ages of children: _____   Group size: _____

Observation

1. Which arts activities (creative dance, music, dramatic play, and visual arts) are the children involved in?

    _____

    _____

    _____

2. What are the adults doing?

    _____

    _____

    _____

3. How are arts activities made available to the children?

    _____

    _____

    _____

4. How did the children participate in these arts activities? (Examples: tried once, then left; engaged in nonverbal or verbal interaction with children and/or adults; worked alone; length of time at activity)

    _____

    _____

    _____

Reflection Page

Analysis: The Arts and the Child

Based on your observation, write a response to these questions:

1. How do the arts activities relate to the learning theories and arts standards discussed in this chapter?

_____
_____
_____
_____

2. Which artistic dispositions for children were being met, and which ones were not? Why?

_____
_____
_____
_____

3. What do you think are the guiding principles of the arts curriculum in this program?

_____
_____
_____
_____

Digital Download Download from CourseMate

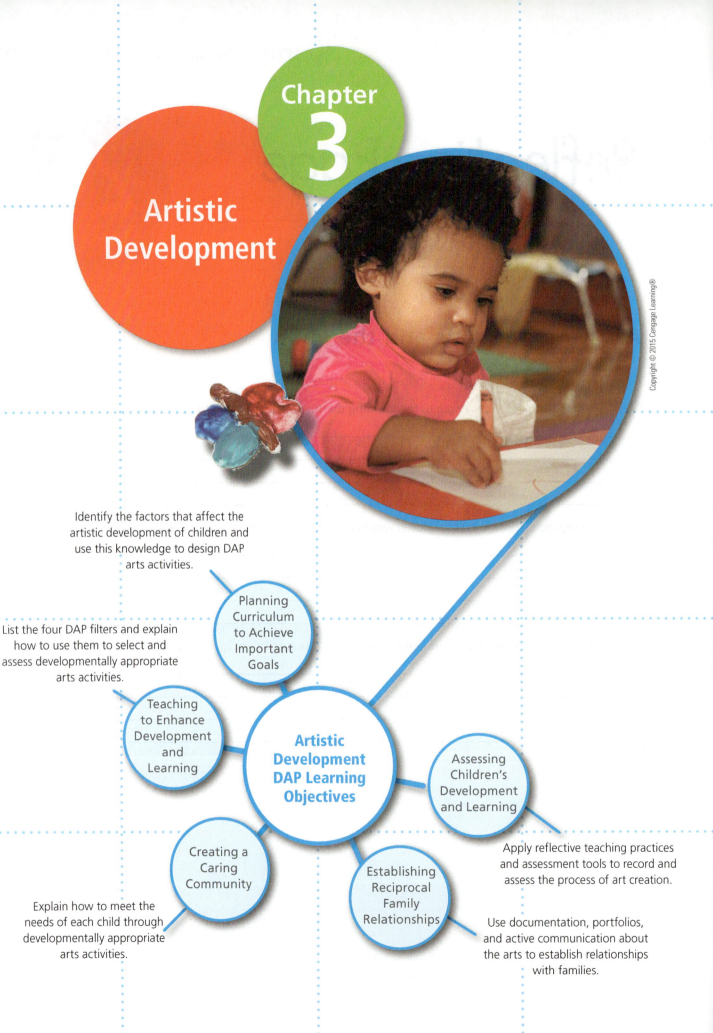

Chapter 3

Artistic Development

Identify the factors that affect the artistic development of children and use this knowledge to design DAP arts activities.

List the four DAP filters and explain how to use them to select and assess developmentally appropriate arts activities.

Explain how to meet the needs of each child through developmentally appropriate arts activities.

Apply reflective teaching practices and assessment tools to record and assess the process of art creation.

Use documentation, portfolios, and active communication about the arts to establish relationships with families.

Artistic Development DAP Learning Objectives

- Planning Curriculum to Achieve Important Goals
- Teaching to Enhance Development and Learning
- Assessing Children's Development and Learning
- Creating a Caring Community
- Establishing Reciprocal Family Relationships

Young Artists Creating

Andy picks up a crayon and grasps it tightly in his fist. He slowly approaches the large white paper before him. Arm held stiffly, he rubs the crayon on the paper. Lifting the crayon, he looks at the smudge he has left behind. With his other hand he touches it, rubs it, and looks at his fingers. The mark is still there. He bends over and sniffs it with his nose. Cautiously, Andy looks up. Is this all right? Can he do this? But no one is stopping him. He returns to the paper. With broad strokes, Andy makes his first true marks on the world. Broad sweeps of color up and down, back and forth. Again and again, on paper after paper, at the beginning of his second year of life, he draws. . . .

How Do Children Develop in the Arts?

It begins with a line, a sound, a movement—an action that reflects the child's physical control over the body. The infant is at the beginning of a long and complex process, which in the eighth year of life will end with a mastery of arts skills that is remarkably expressive and controlled. Young children do not know that this is where their explorations in the arts will lead; they only know the moment—this pleasurable and exciting moment in which they have acted and produced a result.

All of us were once infants, unable to move on our own. Step by step, we learned to crawl and then to walk. At first, we walked unsteadily, clasping a guiding hand. Soon we could take baby steps on our own, and in no time at all we could run and dance.

In the same way, each child grows artistically. Although no newborn is a musician, dancer, actor, or painter at birth, inside every infant is the potential to grow into one. When the time is right, children start their artistic journey, tentatively making small marks upon the world. Their marks enlarge and change from wavy scribbles to enclosed shapes to symbols that encompass their experience. Their gurgling sounds coalesce, become organized, develop rhythm and pitch, and become song. Their random movements become coordinated, and patterned into a fluid dance. This pattern of increasing competence repeats itself in every young child, everywhere in the world mediated by the unique cultural background and personal life events they experience.

Development in the arts begins in infancy. This infant shows her responsiveness to music and rhythms.

The Arts and Developmentally Appropriate Practice: DAP

Developmentally appropriate practice (DAP) is based on the idea that teachers need to know how young children typically develop, what variations may occur in this development, and then be able to adjust their teaching to reach each individual child (Copple & Bredekamp, 2009). To do this we must ask ourselves the following three questions, which are the basis of developmentally appropriate practice and which will help us select the best arts activities for our children:

1. What is known about child development and learning? This knowledge helps us identify the child's expected developmental level by directing

us to look at the child's similarity to others of the same age. This is called **normative development.**

2. What is known about each child's individual development? This knowledge will help us discover what makes each child uniquely different from others the same age so we can better meet that child's needs.

3. What is known about the social and cultural context in which children live? This knowledge helps us better understand the communication style, cultural beliefs and attitudes, strengths, and desires of both the child and the child's family.

What Is Known About Child Development in the Arts?

According to the National Association for the Education of Young Children's Position Statement on Developmentally Appropriate Practice (Copple & Bredekamp, 2009, pp. 1–31), being knowledgeable about **normative development,** or what children are generally like at various ages, allows teachers to make initial decisions about which activities and experiences will be safe, but challenging, for young children.

The normative age divisions used in this text follow those of Copple and Bredekamp (2009). They are intended to provide general guidelines from which appropriate arts activities may be selected.

Infant. In this text, **infant** is used to refer to children from birth to 18 months. Infants have the following characteristics:

- Explore first with mouth and later with eyes and limbs
- Use movements, gestures, and vocalizations to communicate
- Have very limited self-regulatory skills and require constant supervision
- Show development of physical control from the head down and from the center of body out to the limbs
- Are strongly attached to caregivers and respond best in one-on-one settings
- Have short memories and attention spans
- Can learn to respond to simple commands

Toddler. Throughout this text, **toddler** is used to refer to children between the ages of 18 months and 3 years who may exhibit the following characteristics:

- Need to explore with all their senses and may still put objects in their mouth
- Have limited self-regulatory skills and require close supervision
- Engage in parallel play
- Show developing control over large muscles in the arms and legs
- Have short attention spans, usually less than 10 minutes, and need simple materials to explore
- Need to repeat actions
- Say names of objects and understand more words than they can say
- Are developing a sense of self

Three- to five-year-olds or preschoolers. Most children of this age display the following characteristics:

- Show increasing self-control and can work side by side in small groups
- Usually will not put inappropriate items in mouth
- Show developing control over wrists, hands, and fingers
- Have an increasing attention span and can work independently for 10 minutes or more at a time

Five- to six-year-olds or kindergartners. Most children in this age range display the following behaviors:

- Show increasing control over wrists and hands and exhibit a more mature grip on drawing tools
- Can concentrate for a period of time, 30 minutes or more, on a self-selected arts activity
- Can work together in small groups of three to six on common projects and are able to share some supplies
- May dictate or be able to write stories with invented spelling
- Can follow a three-step direction

🎵 Can classify objects and make predictions

🎵 Can use words to describe the qualities of objects—color, size, and shape—and begin to sort them by those qualities

Six- to eight-year-olds or primary age. Most children in this age range show the following behaviors:

🎵 Hold drawing tools with a mature grip

🎵 Concentrate for an hour or more on a self-selected arts activity and return to an ongoing arts project over a period of several days

🎵 Initiate, participate, and assume roles in cooperative group arts activities

🎵 Begin to read and write stories with the majority using conventional spelling by the end of the eighth year

🎵 Understand that objects can share one or more qualities and can use this knowledge to make predictions and comparisons and to draw conclusions

Children's Development in the Arts

Much of the artistic performance of young children is determined by their physical development. This is particularly true in the early years. However, as children get older, what they have learned influences their artistic performance as well. As children develop language skills and knowledge about the arts, their artistic performance and works become more complex. In this chapter we will look at how physical growth and experience affect artistic behavior in general. Chapters 9 to 12 look at the specific influences of development in the four art forms.

The Role of Physical Development in Children's Artistic Performance

Although each of the art forms requires different skills, all of them are influenced by how children develop physically. This is particularly true in the early years. An infant who can sit but not walk will not be able to dance independently.

In young children the development of physical control over the body is usually sequential and predictable. For example, children usually sit up before they walk. This sequence is illustrated in Table 3-1.

Children develop from the head down and from the center of the body out (Cherry, Godwin, & Staples, 1989, p. 53). Infants turn their heads toward sounds and may show preferences for certain types of music. By age one, arm and leg movement shows developing control. They can now grasp musical instruments, crayons, and markers tightly in their fists and make whole arm movements, up and down, back and forth. They can also lift and drop their arms, stabbing and punching the paper with gusto and verbal expression, or beating a drum with wild enthusiasm. This period has been called by some researchers that of the "random or uncontrolled scribble" (Lowenfeld & Brittain, 1987). Watching infants drawing, it does seem at times that their scribbles have a mind of their own, careening off the edges of the paper and onto the table or floor. Listening to them shaking a tambourine, it might seem like they move to the beat of a different drummer. But there is also thoughtful deliberation. Watch the child at play in the arts, pausing in mid-line or mid-tap to express delight. The arm and hand may not yet be under control, but a mind is growing there!

By preschool age, many children can create original dance movements based on the dances they have seen adults doing.

TABLE 3–1	Sequence of Physical Development in Young Children			
Age	Arms	Head and Torso	Legs	Whole Body
At birth	Random movements	Need support	Random movements	
Infants *Newborn to 6 months*	Put hands in mouth Reach and grasp objects Bring object to mouth	Turn head Lift head Sit with support	Put feet in mouth Reach and kick objects with feet	Roll over
Infants *6 months to 1 year*	Pick up objects Drop objects Pass objects from hand to hand	Sit alone Roll	Can bear weight on legs Stand Walk holding on	Cross midline Crawl/creep Imitate actions Move whole body to music
Toddlers *1 to 2 years*	Throw objects Push and pull	Bend to pick up something	Walk "toddling" Kick object Run	Creep up stairs Climb up but may have trouble getting down Move mainly arms and legs to music
2 to 3 years	Catch large objects Throw underhand		Walk forward and backward Walk up steps Run with open stride Jump up and down Balance on one foot briefly	Climb up and down using alternating feet and hands
Preschoolers *3 to 4 years*	Throw overhand Bounce ball	Do somersault	Walk heel toe Balance on one foot Walk on a straight line Climb steps using alternative feet Jump over something Can do a standing broad jump Tip toe	Ride a tricycle Swing May have difficulty judging space and direction Switch quickly from one motion to another
Kindergarteners *5 to 6 years*	Hand dominance established		Hop on one foot Walk on balance beam Skip a little Skate	Smooth muscle action Coordinate movements with others
Primary Ages 6 to 8 years	Catch/throw small ball Know left from right Can dribble a ball		Skip on either foot Skip rope Walk forward/backward on balance beam	Remember dance steps Follow complex directions

Note: As in all the arts, physical development is strongly influenced by experience. This chart is intended only as a general guideline to what skills might be mastered in terms of age. However, the basic sequence of skill acquisition will pertain to most children.

One- to three-year-olds. Between the ages of one and three, children begin to have more control over their elbows. This increasing physical control is reflected in the child's ability to clap, wiggle, and sway in rhythm to music.

Sweeping arcs are created as children move their arms independently. Lines on paper now have curved edges. They loop and swirl across the paper exuberantly.

With continued physical maturation, toddlers develop control over their wrists and feet. Older toddlers can "dance" by bouncing, bending knees, walking on tiptoe, and swinging arms. They begin to match their movements with the beat. This is also when children start to learn their first tunes, clapping games, and finger plays. When they play, they may hum or sing made-up songs.

Now they can also control the line that issues from their drawing tools. They can start and stop at will and lift the crayon and place it down again close to where they want it. Scribbles begin to be joined into lopsided geometric figures. Control over the fingers is also slowly developing. The tight fist may be replaced by a looser grip, although some children may still have no particular hand preference.

As children persist in repeating motions and creating the resulting lines, figures, sounds, and motions, they develop skill and control, but something else is also happening. One day the child will look at the lines, the mess of scribbles, or stop in the middle of babbling or halt in mid-step and say: "Look at my doggie," or "I made a bear story," or "I sing a happy song," or "I am dancing salsa." And although 10 minutes later the child may give a totally different name to the scribble, the story, the song, or the dance—still unrecognizable to us—those actions have developed meaning for that child. This development is tremendously exciting. We can "see" and "hear" the child

thinking. Table 3-2 shows a normative view of artistic development in children from birth to age 8.

The Role of Cognitive Development in Artistic Performance

The arts have often been used as ways to investigate cognitive development in preliterate children.

Gardner Model of Cognitive Development. Howard Gardner has led the way in investigating the cognitive aspects of early childhood artistic development. In general, Gardner (1991) supports Piaget's idea (1959) that sensory learning dominates the first 18 months of life, and that this is followed by a symbolic period during the preschool years, in which children master the symbolic forms of language, number, and the arts. According to his theory of multiple intelligences, Gardner proposes that cognitive development takes place in waves rather than stages, with burgeoning knowledge developing within a specific intelligence and then overflowing into other intelligences.

TABLE 3–2	Development in the Arts			
Age Group*	**Language/Dramatics**	**Music**	**Visual Art**	**Movement**
Infancy to age 1	Respond to sound Identify different voices Make meaningful sounds Imitate voices Laugh, smile Make faces and show emotions in response to stimuli	Pay attention to music Respond to loud/soft Rock & bounce to music Imitate musical sounds	Random scribbles Use whole body Look at objects and pictures	Grasp and hold objects Move arms & legs Start & stop Match actions to needs Crawl, sit, stand, climb Cross midline Hand-eye, eye-hand coordination Walk with help
Ages 1 to 3	Use words and simple sentences Name objects Make believe conversations Scribble writing Imaginary play	Listen to music Identify types of sounds Make up own songs 5 note range Cannot match pitch or keep time Explore instruments' sounds	Basic scribbles Placement patterns Aggregates begin — suns, mandalas, people Action symbols Use whole arm Fist grip Identify items in pictures	Pound & roll play dough Walk, run, jump, hop Go up stairs with help Push & pull Throw
Ages 3 to 4	Recognize letters, some words Invent, retell stories Use invented spelling Take on a role in pretend play Act out invented stories with props	Sing simple songs 5 to 8 note range Begin to keep time Begin to match pitch Play simple instruments in group	Recognizable images Spatial relationships Begin to use wrist Finger grip matures Identifies, matches art by style	Catch & throw with both hands Climb stairs one foot at time Walk heel toe Balance on beam Ride tricycle, swing Match movements to rhythms

TABLE 3–2	Development in the Arts *(continued)*			
Ages 5 to 6	Read words and sentences Identify types of books Write story from picture Begin to use conventional spelling and writing process Enjoy jokes, riddles	Sing in tune in a group Identify pitches Add lower notes to range Identify changes in music Keep time Read simple notation Can begin piano, violin, etc.	Cultural symbols Add ground line and sky line Balanced placement Numerical concepts Tell stories through art Recognize styles of art	Make balls from clay Catch & throw large & small balls Climb stairs without support Skip. Jump rope Balance well Ride bicycle Coordinate movements with others
Ages 7 to 8	Read independently Write using most conventions Perform short simple plays	Hear harmony Sing rounds & 2 parts Keep time accurately Read music Play parts on instruments	Repeat established symbols but start to strive for realistic images Control over materials improves	Play group sports Learn dance steps

The first wave. Gardner believes that sometime between the ages of 18 months and two years, children become capable of using symbols to communicate their knowledge that events consist of objects and actions. Although language oriented, this symbolic realization "spills" into other intellectual domains. At this point, if asked to draw a truck, the child scribbles with the marker while making truck sounds.

The second wave. At about age three, a second wave called topographical mapping occurs. Now the child can express the spatial relationships of real objects, such as showing two adjoining circles and identifying the top one as a head.

The third wave. Around age four, the child begins to use numerical relationships (digital mapping). For example, children may draw four human figures to represent four people in their family, or count the beats as they tap on a drum.

The fourth wave. The most educationally important event occurs sometime during the fifth, sixth, or seventh year, when children begin to invent their own notational systems. Children now draw pictures using graphic symbols of their own invention, for such purposes as to remember experiences or to "list" belongings. They may invent ways to record the notes in a song. Gardner, although he points out the influence of seeing adults using notational systems, feels that there is an innate human propensity to create such systems.

Table 3–3 summarizes the relationship between cognitive growth and how it is expressed in children's artistic performance.

Did You Get It?

Mia teaches a preschool class of three and four-year-olds. Which of the following arts activities will be most suitable for the children in her class?

a. work in groups of ten to create a skit for Parents' Day

b. sing a round

c. fill out activity sheets for an hour

d. sing songs in a 5 to 8 note range

Take the full quiz on CourseMate

What Is Known About Each Child's Individual Development?

As anyone who has ever worked with young children can verify, artistic development in individual children does not follow the nice, neat patterns laid out in textbooks and on normative charts. Although developmental tables such as 3-1, 3-2, and 3-3 can provide useful guides in understanding what might be expected at various ages, they do not present the whole picture. Children are dynamic and ever changing. The second question we must ask as we design a developmentally appropriate arts curriculum is: What are the unique abilities of this individual child at this time and place?

DAP reminds us that children have unique strengths, needs, and interests.

TABLE 3–3	The Arts and Cognitive Growth, based on Gardner (1991)	
Age	**Cognitive Understanding**	**Arts Production**
Causal Relationships 1 ½ – 2 years	Discovers the relationships between object and event.	Bangs a drum to make a sound. Draws a cat by scribbling and meowing at same time. Makes a funny face and causes someone to laugh.
Spatial relationships 2-3 years	Discovers spatial relationships	Can place whole body or a body part in relation to an object or another person. Draws a person by putting a small circle (head) on top of a larger one (body).
Numerical relationships 3-5 years	Represents numerical concepts	Counts taps on a drum using fingers. Draws a dog with four legs, two eyes, one nose, two ears, and one mouth. Places dishes on the table in the housekeeping center equal to the number of children playing.
Notational Relationships 5-7 years	Invents or learns meaningful symbols of the culture	Makes marks or uses music notes to create an original melody. Draws a picture of his or her family and labels them – "mom," "dad," or by name. Puts on a Spiderman mask and acts like the superhero.

These may be due to maturational differences, developmental delays, physical challenges, or exceptional gifts. Development does not proceed in lockstep fashion, but rather in growth and spurts.

Physical Factors

Physical development happens at varying rates in different children. There may be periods of fast growth followed by periods of slower growth.

Sometimes a new ability will suddenly appear. At other times it will take the child months of trial and error before the behavior is exhibited. We see this in the variation that occurs in children learning to walk. Some stand up one day and take off at a run. Others take a step, fall down, crawl some more, and then try again over and over.

Growth patterns are strongly influenced by heredity, nutrition, and exercise. Poorly nourished children will exhibit delayed growth and physical coordination. For example, 40 percent of children in Head Start programs have been found to have delays in motor skill development (Woodward & Yun, 2001). Children who have the space, time, and encouragement to explore large areas physically, such as through creative movement activities, will be better coordinated and have stronger muscles.

Some children have physical challenges such as vision and hearing impairments or trouble controlling their bodies. Others may overreact or underreact to sensory stimuli. Some children may have had negative early experiences that have a delayed impact on language and personality development.

These children need special consideration in planning arts activities so they can enjoy the arts and participate fully in them. In fact, for many children with special needs, the arts can provide an alternate and meaningfully rich way to communicate with others.

"A flower." These twelve pictures, done by the same five-year-old, show how skill and familiarity with media affect how the resulting artwork looks. The pencil and crayon drawings are far more controlled and flower-like than the cut paper, yarn, and collage pictures.

Did You Get It?

In Mrs. Brown's kindergarten class, most of the five-year-olds can skip during creative movement activities. However, three of the five-year-old children cannot. This lack of ability to skip reflects

a. poor teaching on the teacher's part.

b. wearing the wrong shoes.

c. skipping not being part of their cultural heritage.

d. normal physical differences in growth.

Take the full quiz on CourseMate

What Is Known About the Social, Emotional, and Cultural Context In Which Children Live?

Children also differ in the life experiences to which they have been exposed. Lillian Katz and Sylvia Chard (2000) call this the "dynamic dimension of development." An examination of the emotional, social, and cultural context in which young artists function reveals that there are many important ways in which variations in maturation, educational experiences, and other environmental factors influence young artists.

Emotional Factors

A child's emotional state will greatly influence how the child performs in the arts.

Traumatic events. A child who has just experienced a disturbing event may use the arts as a way to express and release deep emotions. Tornados, earthquakes, accidents, family stressors, and death often elicit scribbling, stabbing at the paper, splashing of paint, and banging on drums from people of all ages. Because the arts can serve as an emotional release, we need to bring sensitivity to our artistic interactions with children. With understanding and encouragement, we can allow children to work through these deep feelings. Joe Frost (2005) found that work, play, and the arts were significant ways to heal children who were affected by Hurricane Katrina. (See Chapter 5 for specific ways to address children's special needs through the arts.)

Social pressures. Teachers also need to understand how their own actions and those of a child's family can influence how a child feels about the arts. Children who are pressured to make their arts performance match an adult "ideal," or are frustrated by an arts material or skill that is beyond their physical ability to master, may develop feelings of failure. Such feelings may cause reluctance to participate in future arts activities.

Rejection. Similarly, children who feel that their arts performance is rejected or unacceptable also retreat from arts activities. That is why it is equally important that teachers show their acceptance of the child's work and teach families how to encourage their young artists.

Environmental Factors

Young children may not see the world in the same way adults do, but they are influenced by the pictures they see, the kinds of objects that surround them, and the artistic reactions of their guiding adults to these things.

The role of culture. Children's development in the arts is strongly influenced by the culture in which they grow up. McFee and Degge (1981, p. 334) cite studies that indicate that children from cultures with particular stylistic ways of drawing will learn to draw in that style.

Children who have seen examples of a variety of art forms and are taught to value them are more likely to incorporate elements from these examples into their own creative works. Dennis (1966) found that children raised in environments with plentiful visual imagery, surrounded by many drawings of people, had higher scores on the Goodenough-Harris Draw-A-Person Test (Harris & Goodenough, 1963). Exposure to a wide variety of interesting musical styles challenges children to invent new songs or refine existing ones.

The role of exposure. Adults determine which artistic behaviors and skills are acceptable for children to learn. They set the limits on what is a creative arts performance and what is not. Smearing finger paint on paper is encouraged; smearing cereal on the wall is not. Are egg cartons an art material? Should we use food products in art? Is banging spoons on fine china making music? The adults' definition of what is and is not an arts activity will be transmitted to the child.

The home culture also influences the type of music, art, dance, and storytelling styles the child has experienced. Being aware of the types of music,

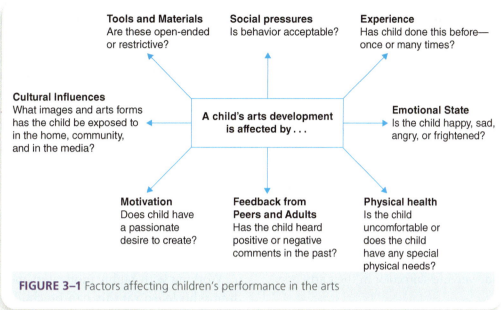

FIGURE 3–1 Factors affecting children's performance in the arts

dance, stories, and visual art valued by a child's family and including them in the arts program shows sensitivity and empowers the child.

The Effect of Experience

Adults also determine how much experience children have with an art form. The more opportunities children have to use arts media, methods, and tools the more comfortable and skilled they will become in the creative arts. All individuals, regardless of their age, need to spend time exploring and revisiting a medium before they can use it expressively.

Importance of practice. For example, if young children have many opportunities to draw, they will usually show their highest level of symbol development in their drawings. The same child may produce much less "competent" looking artwork if asked to use an unfamiliar material. Children will quickly revert to scribbles in their first finger painting or watercolor. Repetition and practice are the keys to improving skills at any level. Even adults with excellent fine motor control find themselves scribbling the first time they try to draw freehand using a computer mouse or trackpad.

Importance of role models. Children are influenced by the people around them. They are more likely to be interested in creating art if other people around them are as well, and if arts are readily available and highly valued. Young children may make drawings in mud and hum made-up tunes on their own, but they are not going to choose formal

Across Cultures

Language Acquistion And The Arts

Children who speak a language other than English go through sequential stages of language acquisition as they learn English:

1. **Nonverbal:** children listen to and study the patterns they hear.
2. **Rehearsal:** children repeat to themselves silently or by mouthing what they have heard in during activities
3. **Formulaic:** children respond with a single word, such as "yellow" instead of "that is yellow," or imitative phrase such as "sit here."

During these stages it may appear that the child is nonverbal or not learning English, when in fact the child understands much more than he or she can say. Gregory Cheatham and Yeonsum Ro (2010) suggest using intentional teaching in pretend play and storytelling as a way to help the early-stage English Language Learner's language transition. For example, teachers can:

- Suggest the child watch and, when comfortable, participate in pretend play.
- Respond to the child's nonverbal gestures and facial expressions and use of native language with an English response.
- When the child communicates with peers in any way, respond positively.
- As language facility develops, encourage the child to tell simple stories about him or herself.

drawing, singing, or dramatic activities unless parents and teachers have offered such opportunities to them.

Importance of real experiences. In the same way, the more opportunities a child has had to participate in real experiences, the richer and more meaningful their arts performance will become. A child who has seen a real chicken will more likely be able to imitate how it behaves in creative movement activities and draw it in more detail than a child who has not. Those who grow up in places where most houses have flat roofs draw house symbols that have flat roofs. Children who have seen that people come in many colors, whether in their community or in pictures, and are comfortable with that fact are more likely to include varying skin color in their artworks.

Giftedness

Young gifted children are those that exhibit an exceptional level of skill or the potential to learn rapidly in one area of the arts. Such high ability is often due to family values and education, inner motivation, or advanced physical development.

Early exposure to the arts has been shown to accelerate artistic development. In homes where one or more of the arts are highly valued, children are introduced at earlier ages to more complex experiences and skills. For example, all infants are born wired for music, but infants who are sung to and exposed to musical instruments at early ages begin musical expression earlier and are better able to match pitch than children raised in a nonmusical environment, whose only exposure to music is via television and recorded music (Kelly & Smith, 1987). A 2003 research study found that three-year-old children who have more music in their homes had increased auditory sensitivity (Shahin, Roberts, & Trainor, 2003). An enriched music environment for toddlers produced increased voice production (Gruhn, 2002). A study by Christo Pantev found that the younger a child learned the piano, the larger the area of the brain that responds to music (1998).

Another factor that causes some children to excel in one of the arts is motivation. Some children develop a passion for one particular art form. One child may spend hours drawing every day. Another may sing and invent songs. Many children have rich fantasy lives

and make up and act out stories. These children, on their own, put in many more hours practicing their chosen art than their peers and so have advanced artistic skills.

Gifted children, due to variable physical growth, may also exhibit earlier fine motor control. For example, one child might draw realistic-looking faces while most peers are still scribbling. Another child can finger a tune on a violin before others the same age can. Such exceptional abilities are quickly noticed and praised. However, it is important to remember that some children, particularly boys whose fine motor control develops slower than that of girls, cannot express their artistic gifts until later ages when physical development catches up with their creative potential.

Working with highly motivated and skilled children who learn rapidly can be challenging. They spend less time exploring and practicing with a material or technique and are ready to move on to responsive activities before their peers are. Open-ended arts activities that welcome many levels of responses are a good way to meet the needs of these gifted children.

Did You Get It?

Why is it important to include the styles of art, dance, music, and storytelling that reflect the home cultures of the children?

a. It shows sensitivity and empowers young children.

b. It makes the arts easier for young children to learn.

c. It increases creativity.

d. It's a good way to help children heal from traumatic events.

Take the full quiz on CourseMate

How Do We Make Sense of Children's Artistic Development?

Incorporating these physical, social, and environmental factors, Kindler and Darras (1994; Kindler, 1997) have proposed a model of artistic development that presents artistic production as a two-fold process, as depicted in Table 3-4. One part of the

TABLE 3–4	Multimedia Modes of Artistic Production, Based on Kindler and Darras (1994)				
Child	**Mode 1**	**Mode 2**	**Mode 3**	**Mode 4**	**Mode 5**
Drama: Says...	Random sounds	Words	Matches sound and action	Naming	Story in cultural style
Visual art: Draws...	Random marks	Shapes	Action symbols	Object symbols	Pictures in cultural style (understandable without verbalization)
Creative dance: Moves...	Random movements	Conscious control	Self-imitation	Repetition	Imitation of cultural style of dance
Music: Makes...	Random sounds	Controlled sounds	Rhythmic sounds	Melody	Song in cultural style
ADULT	Media exploration	Simple doodles	Complex doodles	Shorthand symbols (e.g., stick figures)	Detailed, recognizable symbols in style of culture

process is comprised of biologically propelled physical and cognitive growth. The other is the social and cultural learning, including formal teaching, to which the child is exposed. In this model, individuals do not lose their earlier approaches to arts production but incorporate them or return to them as needed throughout their lives.

Based on the physical, cognitive, and environmental factors affecting an individual child, there is a range of artistic behaviors that child might exhibit. In this model, rather than specific ages or levels, artistic production is organized by modes of behavior. During his or her lifetime, an individual may function in one or more of these modes in varying contexts. For example, upon meeting an unfamiliar medium, most children and adults will operate in the exploratory mode, making random movements as they try to assess the nature of the material. Once they have learned to control a material, they will attempt detailed, graphic, and symbolic expression.

The symbolic communication model shows how a child's arts performance can be viewed a multimedia blend of graphic, verbal, and kinesthetic communication that reveals the child's thought processes, rather than a lockstep process of growth.

Did You Get It?

According to the two-fold process in the model of artistic development proposed by Kindler and Darras,

a. individuals lose their early approaches to arts production and can't return to them at a later stage.

b. rather than specific ages or levels, artistic production is organized by modes of behavior.

c. social factors do not play a role in determining artistic development.

d. biological factors do not play a role in determining artistic development.

Take the full quiz on CourseMate

How Do We Select the Best DAP Arts Activities?

Looking at all the factors affecting a child artist is essential to planning an arts activity or, in fact, any learning activity for that child and assessing the resulting performance. While normative growth charts give us some idea of what to expect from a group of toddlers or primary age children, we should never assume that if a child is a certain age, or is offered the same arts activities as another, we will be able to predict exactly what that child will do with them. But when we understand the range of possible responses, recognize individual difference as normal, and know our children as unique beings with their own histories and passions, we will better choose activities for them.

The growth of young children, from exploring scribblers and babblers to symbol-creating artists, musicians, dancers, and actors, is an amazing journey. This is what makes teaching the arts to children so exciting. Every day is full of fresh, new creative arts performances for their teachers to enjoy.

Four DAP Filters for Selecting Arts Activities

Based on what we know about how children develop in the arts, we must consider four things in selecting appropriate arts activities for our students.

1. **We must have realistic expectations.** Developmental stage models and an understanding of the factors affecting individual development enhance our understanding of why children's arts performance looks the way it does. But it should not limit our expectations or make us hesitate to try a certain activity. Among young children, we should expect a range of behaviors, from simple exploration based on their level of physical control to complex expressions of their ideas. Within an age cohort, the creative arts produced by children will vary widely, depending on the children's cultural and social experiences and their familiarity with the art form. For example, it is not at all unusual within a group of four-year-olds to witness some children scribbling, some using a limited number of symbolic forms, and some drawing complex graphic symbols. We must accept the scribblers' and babblers' artistic performances as just as valid and important as the more adult-pleasing recognizable pictures, songs, and stories, and select open-ended activities that allow all participants to be creative and personally successful.

2. **We must value children's art production as a developmental process, not as a product.** It is essential to find ways of recording and presenting not just the final product or performance, but the whole process of creation. Anyone who has watched and participated in a child's arts activity knows that the final product may be a letdown. Young dancers may trip and hesitate as they attempt to glide around the stage. Beginning singers may sound out of tune. Arts activities needs to be accompanied by a record of what the children said, the stages the works passed through, and how the children moved as they worked. This is a challenge for a busy, overworked teacher, but it is not impossible.

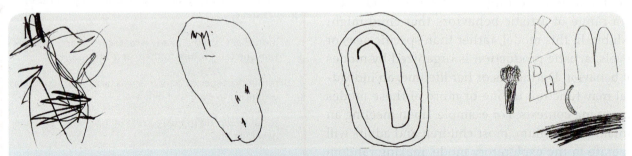

Within an age group, children working in all of the of the artistic modes can be found. (1) Exploration. Marker—Andrew, age three; (2) Initial shapes. Crayon—Kelsey, age three; (3) Action symbol. Marker—Ross, age three; (4) Story symbols. Pencil—Michelle, age three.

3. **We must understand better what the child is thinking.** Knowing the physical, social, cultural, and emotional factors affecting a child helps us better understand and accept the young artist's behavior and resulting creative work. For example, a smiling child banging and stabbing the paper with a crayon is probably not being aggressive, but more likely exploring the possibilities of the crayon. A child doing the same thing, but whose dog has just died, is probably expressing grief.

4. **We must select activities that are suitable for particular children.** Because there will always be a range of abilities in any group, the arts activities that teachers select must be open-ended and allow every child to be challenged. There must always be room for exploration as well as revisitation and responsive work.

Did You Get It?

Which of the following is good advice for a teacher designing developmentally appropriate practice (DAP) arts activities for children?

a. A normative growth chart can be used to predict exactly what a child of a certain age will do with the art materials provided.

b. Children within an age cohort will create very similar art displaying a standard set of skills.

c. Children's art must be valued for the final product created, and not the process involved.

d. Developmental stages should not limit our expectations or make us hesitate to try a certain activity.

Take the full quiz on CourseMate

How Do We Assess Children's Growth in the Arts?

There are many purposes to assessment. States and governments want to know that schools are doing an effective job at educating children. Standardized tests set the same standard for everyone to meet and pay less attention to factors affecting individual performance. Reflective teachers, on the other hand, want to know that they have chosen the best learning activities for their group of children and that each individual child is benefitting.

The preceding four DAP filters listed help us choose the way we examine children and their artistic performances. In choosing our assessment methods we must be sure we have realistic expectations for each child, record process rather than evaluate the product, elicit what the child is thinking, and evaluate whether the activity we chose was appropriate for the particular child. When we practice reflective teaching, ongoing assessment is incorporated into every activity we teach.

Setting Realistic Expectations

In order to set realistic expectations we need to know each child well. In the beginning we must rely on information given to us by the child's family and on our own careful observations of the child as the child interacts with arts materials and experiences.

Observing children and watching what they do is an essential component of good teaching. Teachers can learn many things from how children behave and react artistically.

Observing the individual. Individual behavior patterns can give us information about the following growth areas:

1. **Physical:** The child's physical control of materials, methods, and skills

2. **Social:** The child's ability to work alone, with adults, and with peers in arts activities

3. **Emotional:** The child's preferences, comfort level with arts materials, and reactions to the art of others as expressed in arts activities

4. **Perceptual:** The child's visual, spatial, and sensory perception skills

5. **Symbolic language:** The child's approach to understanding and creating ways to communicate through the arts

6. **Cognitive understanding:** The child's ability to express arts concepts and vocabulary through movement, sound, visual elements, play, and oral language

Observing group dynamics. No child functions alone. We must also place the child in the context of the group. Children learn as much from interacting with their peers as they do from adults. Every group

One of the best ways to observe children's growth and behavior is by carefully watching how they behave and react in different situations.

▶❚❚ **TeachSource Video Case 3.1**

Progress Monitoring: Using Transitional Time in an Early Childhood Classroom

Watch the video *Progress Monitoring Using Transition Time*. Can you think of ways to design a similar system to use with arts activities?

Watch on CourseMate

has a unique dynamic, and no two groups react in the same way to the arts activities that teachers offer. Observations of the behavior of groups of children can help us see each child more broadly. Group behavior patterns can provide the following information:

- The suitability of the arts experience for the particular group

- The interests of the group

- The role of the child within the group

Using Observation Tools

To be useful, these observations need to be made regularly and carefully recorded. Two ways to do this are checklists and anecdotal notes.

Checklists. A well-designed checklist can be a powerful tool. Watching a child moving to music and recording the way the child moves her arms and legs provides information that can be used to choose a more challenging piece of music for the next movement activity. Over time the checklists can show each child's growth, difficulties, and preferences in the arts.

Checklists strategically placed around the children's environment can provide a convenient way to record

behaviors. Make a list of the children's names and then hang it at the easels, near the blocks, near the listening center, and so on. Use Velcro® to attach a pencil near each list. Develop a simple symbol for the behaviors being observed, such as the initial letters or a shape. Throughout the day, mark the lists with symbols to indicate that a child is in a particular area and what behavior is being observed. Done on a regular basis, these checklists provide a better picture of the child's daily behavior, attitudes, and skill development than memory alone.

Anecdotal records. Although more time consuming than checklists, writing down an objective description of a child's interaction with an arts material or a story, and his or her level of expressiveness, can provide rich detail. Anecdotal records provide an ongoing picture of the child's behavior at set times in specific settings. They can be made at the time of the observation or soon after the event. To be useful, the record should document the setting of the event (including the time), the children involved, and any other related information. Anecdotes should be objective, recording only observed behaviors and direct quotes of the children, not the teacher's opinion about the reason for that behavior.

Index cards labeled with each child's name can be carried around in a pocket for a ready way to record quick observations. Labeling the cards with names means no child is missed. Some teachers are more comfortable using clipboards or notebooks with one page divided into sections for each child. Another method is to write on large, self-stick labels, which can then be peeled off and attached to the child's folder.

For examples of arts checklists and anecdotal notes, see Examples of Checklists and Anecdotal Records for the Arts on CourseMate.

Using intentional objectives to focus observations. One way to focus observations is to think about the objectives you have set for the child, make sure the activity provides opportunity for that objective to occur, and note what that will look or sound like. For example, if your objective is that Michelle, who has difficulty taking turns, will wait for her turn to play the drum, then your assessment part of the objective might be written: "I will know this is happening when I see Michelle standing next to the drum using the strategy I taught her of listening to and moving to the rhythm without touching the drum." Stating objectives this way fosters intentional teaching.

More information on writing intentional objectives will be found in Appendix B.

Recording the Process

Recording children's creative behavior provides another way to observe their approach to the arts. Today we have a great array of options for dynamic recording of children's creative ventures—running records, photography, video and audio recording, portfolios, and interactive digital devices and media. With the ease of digital media, children can even make their own recordings of their work.

Running records. Running records are longer observations that document everything a child does for a set number of minutes (such as a 20-minute period) written down by an objective observer. Although running records are most often used in analyzing reading skills, this type of close observation is very useful for analyzing social behaviors in the arts such as interaction in the dramatic play center or tracking cognitive or language skills during art activities.

Using photographs. Anyone working with children should always have a camera close at hand. If the camera is convenient to use and nearby, then it is more likely to be picked up at opportune moments during the activity rather than used just to record the finished work or a group pose. The camera does not have to be a fancy one, but it should be simple and foolproof to operate. Digital cameras, smartphones, and tablets are ideal for this purpose. Through photos, videos, and digital media, we can capture the excitement and passion of the child along with making a record of the child's performance for future assessment.

1. Photographs and videos of block structures, sculptures, and other three-dimensional projects in construction can be displayed long after the originals are gone.

2. Photo albums of children creating in the arts can be made into class books and kept in the book corner. Audio recordings can be placed in the listening and music centers.

3. Photographs, audio recordings, and videos of children working can be saved in their portfolios, and on class documentation and panels as a visual way to remember how something was done and as a way to emphasize the value of process over product.

4. Photographs of class members, families, friends, and visitors, as well as the children's homes and family events, can be used in portrait lessons and family studies.

5. Photographs of familiar objects shown from unusual viewpoints can challenge children's visual perception.

6. Photographs can be used to record arts activities, setups, and child interactions for teachers to use for reflection on their teaching methods.

7. Digital photos can be saved to a flash drive, CD, or DVD for more compact storage or uploaded into digital photo storybooks, into flipbook software, into PowerPoint presentations, on family pages of school websites, and into teaching materials for interactive whiteboards.

For more information on creating and using digital portfolios, selecting software platforms, and helpful online resources, see Digital Portfolios on CourseMate.

For successful photographs, use the following guidelines:

- Try to physically get down to the children's level when taking photographs so that the pictures do not all reflect an adult's perspective.

- If using flash, check the distance from the subject to avoid washed-out pictures.

- Do not shoot against a bright background, such as a window.

Videotaping. The availability of camcorders and the video function on digital cameras has made it possible to truly record the multimedia process of arts performances. It can be used to create a time-based record of a child's artistic growth. At regular intervals, record the child dancing, singing, playing an instrument, and creating an artwork. Videos can also be made to record group projects, as part of portfolios, and as a way to assess teaching style.

Obtaining releases. Before taking any photographs or making a video, it is essential to obtain a signed release from all families. Many institutions have parents fill out such forms upon enrollment. However, if special use is going to be made of the pictures, such as a public display in an exhibit or at a workshop presentation, then a more specific release should be obtained.

If a family refuses to sign a release, then that request must be respected. When shooting photographs and videos, be careful to avoid taking pictures of children without releases, except when shot from the back.

For an example of a release, see Sample Model Release on CourseMate.

Portfolios

A **portfolio** is a collection of the child's work and related materials made over a period of time. Each child should have either a physical or digital arts folder in which a record of their arts process and development is stored either in the form of the actual artworks and photographs of performances, or, if the equipment is available, in a digitized format. Find a list of what to put in an arts portfolio here.

For ideas of what to include in a child's arts portfolio, see Suggested Content for an Arts Potfolio on CourseMate.

Constructing a folder portfolio. A short-term portfolio can be made from a very large piece of paper

folded in half, or from two sheets taped together. If it will be used for only a short time, then this will suffice. If the folder will be used over a long period, such as a year or two, then it can be made sturdier by using clear packing tape to protect the edges or it can be made from two corrugated cardboard pieces taped together along one side to form a hinge. The portfolio must be as large as the largest paper used by an individual child. For ease of use, color-code or mark the folders with special symbols as well as names so children and parents can quickly locate their own folders. Find directions for making a portfolio here.

For directions on making a folder portfolio, see Making a Folder Portfolio on CourseMate.

CDs, DVDs, and audiotapes that record music, dance, and dramatic activities can be stored separately in shallow gift boxes or trays labeled with each child's name. These boxes can be sent home for the family's enjoyment on a regular basis.

One of the reasons educators hesitate to initiate portfolios is the problem of storing them while still retaining easy access. A pile of large floppy papers is unsightly and heavy. It becomes almost impossible to remove folders on the bottom without handling all of the folders stacked above. One solution is the

Classroom Technology

CHILDREN AND CAMERAS

Including children's participation in recording events using digital photography allows children to create their own documentation record. Bonnie Blagojevic and Karen Thomas (2009) found that young children could learn how to independently take photographs in ways that enhanced their language development while providing insights into how children viewed activities. After children learned how the camera worked, they asked the children what their favorite activities were. After listing their choices, they brainstormed what photos could be taken to show those favorites. The children's photographs were uploaded on to the class computer as a slideshow the children could watch. Then the children picked one photo for a classbook "Our Favorite Things" and dictated an explanation to accompany it. The book was put out for children to read and copies were sent home to families. Families completed a questionnaire and comment sheet as a way to involve the families and to provide feedback.

Photography is a great way to record the artistic process. Allow children to get into the act by letting them film their own work and their peers using inexpensive cameras.

commercially made, vertical, divided storage boxes that are used to store art prints (see Appendix C).

Digital portfolios. Saving children's work in digital format solves many of the aforementioned problems. The arts, in particular, lend themselves to this method. Digital photos and video clips of an individual child and of whole group performances can be kept in a folder on the computer and, at the end of a set time period, saved to a flash drive, CD, or DVD to send home to the family.

However, digital portfolios do have some disadvantages.

1. Not all families have access to a computer. In this case, a physical portfolio of actual artworks and photographs is a better choice.

2. Upkeep is more time consuming for the teacher, who must download and save the work to all the different children's folders.

3. It is the adult's task to manipulate the data on the computer, and unless special effort is taken, the children become less involved in the care and organization of their work.

4. In terms of visual art works, having the children look at a photo of their artwork on a computer screen is not the same as being able to touch the real work and experience its true texture, color, and size.

Combined digital and physical portfolios. To create the most effective and useful arts portfolio, digital recordings of music, dance, and dramatic activities recorded on a CD or DVD can be combined with a folder containing actual pieces of children's visual artworks.

Selecting work for the portfolio. Having a portfolio does not mean that every piece of artwork, every song sung, every creative movement, and every story acted out needs to be recorded and saved. Once children have been introduced to the idea of making a portfolio, they should be asked on a regular basis if they wish to put their artwork or a recording of their performance into the portfolio. If artwork is three dimensional, ask if they would like a photograph taken for the portfolio. The teacher can also select pieces for the folder. Children are more willing to part with their work if they know the reason why. For example, "This painting shows how you have learned to make orange and brown. Shall we put it in your portfolio? Would you like me to write anything about it to go with it?"

Preparing work for the portfolio. Artwork and photographs placed in a folder portfolio do not have to be mounted but should not be wrinkled or folded if possible. Each piece should be labeled with name, date, and any comments by the child. Camcorders and digital cameras can be set so the date is automatically included. Files are also dated when they are downloaded to a computer. When taking photographs and videos, be sure to include the child in order to make identification of the work or performance not only easier but more personal. This will help children feel more ownership of their work.

Timeline for collecting work. The portfolio should represent a natural timeline, such as one session, 3 months, or a half year. The time period should be long enough to show growth, but not so long that the collection becomes unwieldy. At the end of the time period, the work should be ordered by date to highlight the child's growth or changing interests. If the program is long term, extending over a year or more, then a few pieces from older portfolios can be selected to begin a new one.

Before sending the portfolio home, carry out a self-reflection interview as a culminating activity. This process helps children learn how to assess their own progress.

If using a physical portfolio, always send the entire folder home, and create a new one to use for the next time period. This provides families with a unified presentation of the artwork rather than a hodgepodge of papers, and keeps these simply constructed folders from becoming dog-eared. It is also beneficial for children to reestablish ownership of the portfolio concept through the creation and decoration of a new folder on a regular basis.

Eliciting Thinking

Whether in digital or folder format, the portfolio system allows arts experiences to be richer and deeper in many ways. Both formats allow the child, the teacher, and the family to look through the portfolio individually and/or together as a way to review past progress.

Sharing a portfolio with a child also provides an opportune moment to start a conversation that helps us know the child better while teaching self-reflective and self-evaluative skills in a non-threatening environment.

Physical portfolios. The physical portfolio may contain visual artworks, child-created books, illustrated stories, audiotapes, and photographs of the child. These can be examined and discussed as a way of eliciting self-reflection and deeper thinking on the part of the child. For example:

- After looking at a piece of artwork, the child might decide to add to it, such as using chalk over a painting or painting over a crayon drawing or they may add onto a story or be inspired to revisit or try something new.

- Together the teacher and child can collect, categorize, and make work logs, booklets, or a documentation panel showing growth in skill or knowledge or variations on a theme.

- Together the teacher and child might deliberate and select from a range of work what to put on display. A multimedia one-person show might feature chosen artworks, stories, photographs, and an audio recording playing the child singing.

Digital portfolios. Digital media expands these possibilities even more. Once photographs and video clips are stored on the computer, they can be used in a variety of formats.

- Together the teacher and child might decide what they wish to share with the family, the class, or the public. Digitized photos and video clips can be inserted into slide shows and PowerPoint-type presentations as well as newsletters, class web pages, and blogs. Children could have their own blogs or webpages viewable only to their family. Video with child narration can be edited using a simple video editor such as Windows Live Movie Maker, then uploaded to a video-sharing site such as YouTube or Vimeo, and made visible only to family members. Children's work and videos can be made into PDFs or page-turning books that can be viewed on many tablets and e-readers. Digitized photos can be printed out and used in a variety of creative ways such as in collages, class quilts, class books, cards, bookmarks, and identifying labels.

- Digitized photos, audio, and video clips can be saved on CDs, DVDs, and flash drives, and then viewed or listened to on the computer by the child as an activity choice.

- Digitized photos and video clips can be inserted into dictated stories and autobiographies written on the computer.

Eliciting child-reflection. Conduct portfolio sessions at intervals to assess changes in attitude to arts activities and to help determine what arts activities will interest the child.

Some questions to ask find out how the child feels about participating in the arts include:

- What is your favorite arts activity?

- What do you like best about creating _____ (stories, paintings, dances, songs, puppet shows, etc.)?

- What is your favorite _____ (artwork, dance, music, song, story, thing to pretend, etc.)?

- Who is your favorite _____ (artist, composer, dancer, actor, story writer, etc.)?

- What is your favorite book about the arts?

- Do you _____ (sing, dance, draw, play and instrument, use playdough, etc.) at home? Tell me about it.

Other questions can elicit information about the child's knowledge of arts concepts and techniques. For example:

- How did you do this?

- What is made from?

- What did you use to _____ (do this, make this sound, act this out, etc.)?

- What were you thinking when you ___ (made, wrote, danced, sang, acted, etc.) this?

- Do you remember how you solved this problem?

- Who did you work with?

- Where did the idea come from?

As we share the portfolio together, we can also encourage self-reflection by asking:

- Which shows something new you learned?

- Which one _____ (took the longest time, was the hardest, was the most fun, etc.)?

- Do you want to add a story or comments?

- Is there anything you want to add or remove from the portfolio? Why?

Did You Get It?

Lisa has decided to use anecdotal records to record how her students perform in dramatic play activities. Which of the following should she avoid when using this type of record?

a. noting down only observed behaviors of the children

b. noting down her opinions of the reasons for their behavior

c. noting down only direct quotes from the children

d. noting down details such as the setting of the event

Take the full quiz on CourseMate

How Can We Share the Arts with Families?

Families have a very different relationship with their children than do teachers and other caregivers. Children look to their families for exclusive attention and

ultimate acceptance as capable people. When children share their creative work with a family member and say, "Look what I made!" they want more than a tepid "That's nice" or an ordinary "Good work." Most importantly, they definitely do not want criticism from this all-important person whom they wish to please. Children really want to know that their families have taken the time to acknowledge their efforts and joy.

Unfortunately, families are far less equipped to give the deep response that children are seeking than are teachers and other trained caregivers. Where the educator sees exploration and creative experimentation, the families may see only what they think is a visible (and perhaps an uncomplimentary) reflection on the quality of their children and their family.

Ways to Help Families Appreciate their Children's Arts Process

It is the teacher's job to educate families about their children's artistic development. Remember, unless teachers make an effort to record children's creative arts process and educate family members, parents will make judgments based only on what they see—their children's products. To address this try to

- Provide many opportunities for families to review portfolios.

- When talking to families about their children's arts activities, emphasize process and growth rather than the project, and then help family members see this in the artwork. Checklists and anecdotal records will prove invaluable in remembering the specific actions of the children. Instead of saying, "Mary made a painting today," say, "Mary used paint today and learned how to make pink. See the pink spots in her painting." Instead of saying, "Arturo sang a song," say, "Arturo explored the chimes in the music center and invented his own melody and words. He sang his song to the whole group at circle time."

- Schedule "Arts Happenings" and workshops throughout the year at which families and children are invited to create together. This is a good time for group projects, such as murals and rhythm bands, in which everyone can participate. Watching

Reflective teachers work closely with parents, soliciting their opinions and feedback to better understand the child's home culture and provide the best creative experiences for each child.

families interact also gives teachers a better idea of their attitude toward their children's artwork.

- Attach simple, prepared descriptions of arts processes to work being sent home.

- Send home letters or, better yet, institute a regular newsletter that describes the children's arts activities along with other class activities, in terms of process and growth.

- Prepare an attractive booklet, illustrated with children's drawings, that briefly explains the goals of the arts program, what children learn through the arts, and what kinds of arts experiences will be offered.

- Send home suggestions for setting up a simple visual art center in the home. It should not be project based but rather provide a few basic open-ended art supplies that are always available, such as crayons, markers, paper, glue, scissors, and a modeling material such as playdough that children can use in their own ways. Help families by suggesting ways that they can contain messes,

such as by setting up a small area as an art studio, providing an "art table," or, if space is limited, designating a plastic tray as the art spot.

- Describe how to make simple homemade musical instruments, and send home copies of the songs the child has learned so the family can sing them together.

- Make up take-home bags containing a story and simple puppets so the child can dramatize the story for the family.

- Use a home arts survey to find out the artistic background and experience of individual children.

Ways to Help Families Understand Artistic Development

Families often do not have other children's work with which to compare their children's, and so they cannot tell if what their children bring home is appropriate or not. Teachers need to help families understand the process of artistic development and have them come to understand that exploration in which no final product results is a natural part of every child's artistic performance no matter what the child's age. It is the teacher's job to assure families that their children are performing in ways that are to be expected. There are a variety of ways to do this.

- Display many examples of creative work of all kinds, by children of all ages, either in the public areas where parents congregate, or through exhibits and open houses.

- Hold family workshops in which examples of child art and portfolios from unknown children are shared and concerns about the arts are discussed.

- Send to families, on a regular basis, arts notes detailing what children have accomplished in a specific project.

- Families gain a better appreciation for the creative process if they participate in workshops that allow them to draw, paint, sing, dance, play with puppets, and participate in arts activities similar to those of the children.

Teacher to Family

Sample Arts Note (Attach to Portfolios Going Home)

Dear Family Members,

This portfolio presents your child's learning in the arts over the last month. Take time to enjoy the portfolio with your child. Here are some things to talk about:

Visual Art: This month we made paintings, drawings and collages in the art studio. Here are the three she chose for the portfolio.

- The painting shows all the new colors your child can mix. Ask her to tell you what colors she used to make them.
- The collage is made from the beautiful things we collected on out nature walk. Ask her to tell you where she found them and why she chose them.
- The drawing was made of a bridge she built in the block center. Ask her how strong it was.

Music: At the music center we explored making original melodies using the chimes. Here is your child's melody written in colors. Listen to the tape of her playing it and ask her to show you how to follow along on her written melody.

Dramatic Play & Creative Movement: After our nature walk, we studied many different animals that we saw. Then we all imagined living in the woods. Here are photographs of our "Animals in the Woods" creative movement activity. Ask your child what animal she pretended to be.

Your child's teacher,

For more information on digital portfolios, see *Digital Portfolios* on CourseMate

Digital Download   Download from CourseMate

Did You Get It?

Isabella teaches first grade. When families ask questions about their children's creative work, Isabella should

a. rave about a particular project which the child did exceptionally well.

b. explain how their child's work compares to normative development in the arts.

c. explain how their child's work compares to that of others in the class.

d. show them their child's portfolio and discuss the process the child went through to create the works.

Take the full quiz on CourseMate

How Can We Practice Reflective Teaching?

Probably the most important assessment we can do is of ourselves. Without self-assessment, teachers cannot grow and improve. Teaching is not a static profession with only one right way to get the job done. The most exciting educators are those who constantly tinker with their programs, try new methods, and are willing to take risks. We need to reflect on our teaching to discover what is working and what is not. This is called **reflective teaching.** When we use reflective teaching practices we do not repeat the same activities day after day and year after year. Instead, we observe, monitor, discover, modify, and experiment in the moment and over time in order to make the best match between our children and our teaching strategies (Carter et al., 2010).

Reflective teaching calls upon us to:

1. Examine our reactions to our children and their behaviors.

2. Observe our children closely in all learning settings.

3. Document what we see and hear.

4. Make time to study our notes and photos.

5. Share thoughts about our observations and ideas with the children, co-workers, and families.

6. Ask for insights from the children, co-workers, and families.

7. Change the environment and materials in order to facilitate new opportunities for play and learning.

Documenting for Reflection

Because self-reflection is done for ourselves, it is tempting for us to skip this crucial activity when we are exhausted from a busy day with energetic and challenging youngsters. Preplanned, easy-to-use documentation methods make it more likely that we will take the time to assess the arts activities we deliver. The following methods are suggested as ways to accomplish this task. Each provides a different viewpoint; when used in combination, they give an overall view of how we are doing.

Checklists. Checklists can be designed to quickly survey almost any area of the program. They provide objective information on the frequency of particular behaviors and areas that may require attention. Checklists do not work if they are buried on a desk or in folders. They need to be strategically placed where they can be seen daily and acted upon.

Feedback from the children. It is important to ask children for their response to the activities. This can be done in conversation or through graphing favorites, or through using the arts as communication by having children mime or draw or act out the activity they enjoyed the most.

The checklists and anecdotal records that have been suggested for assessing the children can also be used for program assessment. These checklists reveal which activities attract interest and which are ignored. They document how many children choose to work in certain areas, how long they stay there, how much they interact, and what skills they are exhibiting. They also capture our interaction with the children and provide a picture of what we have said.

For a variety of ways to self-assess, see Examples of Reflective Assessments on CourseMate.

Feedback from others. The people we work with, especially colleagues working in similar settings are another important source of feedback. For example, Will Parnell (2012) observed co-teachers working at Reggio-inspired preschools benefitted from practicing reflective thinking with each other on a regular basis. Conversation with parents provides another point of view and can point to ways to increase communication with the home.

Reflective teaching journal. A reflective journal provides a place for teachers to record their inner feelings about their work. Journaling has been found to be a positive way to develop reflective practice (Mortari, 2012). Teachers need to set aside a time, such as when the children are resting, to write a few reflective sentences on how they personally feel about what has been happening as the children participate in arts activities. One way to approach this task is to respond to these sentence starters:

This week I felt competent when . . .
This week I felt frustrated when . . .
This week I felt exhilarated when . . .
This week I had a problem with . . .
This week I discovered . . .

"Terrific me" folder. Place a file folder labeled "TM" in a strategic place. Whenever you receive complimentary notes from parents, children, or others, place them in this folder. Also include copies of materials from workshops attended or given, extra work done, notes about major accomplishments, and any other positive materials and activities. It is human nature to remember the negatives. Reviewing the materials in this folder will provide not only an uplifting experience but also a more rounded view of one's accomplishments.

Personal arts notebook or portfolio. Create a binder or portfolio, much like the ones you keep for the children, in which to keep all of the documents you generate while formulating the arts aspect of your program. This serves as a tangible memory of the form and nature of the program. Keep copies of plans, anecdotal records, photos, checklists, and notes on what went well and what actions were taken to deal with difficult or unusual situations. Keep copies of all letters sent home to families. Looking back over this material will be invaluable in making better plans the next time.

Reflection-in-Action

Donald Shöen (1983) noted that effective teachers observed and acted in the process of teaching. He called this reflection-in-action. In the beginning, practicing reflective teaching while in the process of dealing with active enthusiastic children may seem daunting. However, Deb Curtis and Margie Carter (2010) suggest using a "reflective lens" or set of questions to ask yourself at first after an activity or day is

Photo Story

A Responsive Drawing Activity

A Visit to the Playground

The children in this kindergarten class made a special visit to their playground. Together with their teacher they looked carefully at the different shapes and forms, and noticed the spaces as well. Then they came back inside and drew pictures to record their experience. Even though they are all the same age, their artwork reflects their different interests and fine motor skills.

"My friends and I like to ride the swings." Marker—Brittany, age five

Carmela is sharing and playing safely. Marker—Carmela, age five

"I like to run and jump all over the playground." Marker—Joe, age five

over, and then, as the questions become integral to your thinking, during the activity itself.

- How do I feel as I observe the children?
- What shows me that the children are learning?
- What are the children thinking and feeling?
- How are materials or environment working?
- What is the influence of family culture and background?
- Are desired learning objectives being met?
- How can I strengthen this to better meet my goals and values?

For ways to use a reflective lens, see *Examples of Reflective Assessments* on CourseMate.

Did You Get It?

Which of the following is a characteristic of reflective teaching?

a. repeating the same arts activities day after day for consistency

b. asking for insights from children, parents, and teachers

c. designing arts activities with minimal experimentation

d. assessing the creative work of all children based on a common criteria

Take the full quiz on CourseMate

Conclusion: The Child Artist

Artistic development models provide educators with a general overview of children and the arts. But we must remember that actual artistic development of each individual child is a combination of the biological maturation patterns of the body and brain, mediated by social and cultural factors and experiences.

Creative arts for the child is more than the simple manipulation of materials at an art table or putting on a funny hat in the dress-up corner. It is a developmental process. Children's artistic growth is not the step-by-step process so carefully described by the early researchers. It is a multifaceted way for children to develop in the arts through new methods of expression and communication. This process can best be shared through the use of cameras, camcorders, and portfolios. It is our challenge as reflective teachers to continuously recreate the environment, to redesign the activities, and to rearrange the environment so that we nurture this multimedia event in every child.

For additional information on young children's development in the arts, and assessment, see Chapter 3 *Online Resources* on CourseMate.

Teaching In Action

Open-Ended Arts Activity: Learning About Us

Today was the first day of school. As my first graders entered the classroom, I greeted each one and handed them a piece of paper. "Draw me a picture that tells us something about you." I asked them. At the tables I had set out markers, crayons, and pencils. Soon they were all busy working. Some drew pictures of themselves and their families. Some drew their favorite things. Some drew their houses. I made a picture about me, too.

When they finished, I asked them to join me on the rug with their pictures. We went around the circle and introduced ourselves. We each showed our picture as we talked. Next I read

them the book *Everyone is Bob* by T. A. H. Markou (2010). We talked about how boring it would be if we were all the same like the Bobs in the book. How would we know who was who?

Then I wrote "Same" and "Different" on the top of the chart tablet, and we listed things that were the same and things that were different about us. It was amazing. By the end of the first forty minutes of school we all knew so much about each other and appreciated our differences. It was a great way to start the year.

Hillary Clark, First Grade Teacher

Reflection Page

Factors Affecting Your Artistic Work

A number of factors affect one's artistic development. Looking back to your own childhood, fill in this graphic organizer with those things you feel most influenced your development in the arts.

Available Tools and Materials	Social Pressures	Arts Experiences
Cultural Influences	My Artistic Development	Emotional State
Motivation	Feedback from Family, Teachers, and Peers	Physical Health

Reflection
How do you think these factors will affect the way you teach the arts?

_____

_____

_____

_____

Reflection Page

Looking at Children's Artistic Development

Using Gardner's and Kindler and Darras's models of artistic growth, reflect on the artistic development of the children described in the following examples and suggest an appropriate follow-up arts activity.

A child holds the paintbrush in his fist and moves it up and down, making large bold lines.

_____
_____
_____
_____

A child taps a spoon on the table in time to a song on the radio.

_____
_____
_____
_____

A child draws a detailed picture of her house that includes a ground line and skyline and writes a description below it.

_____
_____
_____
_____

A child puts on a funny hat, makes a face, and says, "I'm a clown. I can make you laugh."

_____
_____
_____
_____

Reflection Page

Documenting Artistic Behavior

Choose one of the following open-ended arts activities and imagine you are teaching it.

- Carpet squares cut into the basic shapes—circles, rectangles, squares, and triangles—are placed on the carpet to make a path. Toddlers are invited to follow the path and say the name of the shape when they step on it. Then they are encouraged to build new paths by moving the shapes around.

- First graders have been asked to collect things that are special to them and arrange them inside a shoebox to make a still-life story about themselves. Each child tells his or her own story orally to a partner.

- After a trip to the zoo, preschoolers decide to turn the dramatic play area into a zoo. Some are building pens with blocks and putting the stuffed animals in them. Some are building a birdhouse, like the aviary they saw, out of a refrigerator box. Some are drawing pictures of birds.

1. Write an intentional objective for each of the developmental areas for your chosen activity.

   Intentional Objective format: The child will be able to . . .

   (socially, emotionally, physically, intellectually, linguistically, perceptually, creatively)
   _____

   I will know this is happening when _____

2. Design a checklist for these objectives.

3. Write three self-reflective questions about the activity using the reflective lens.

Reflection Page

Observation: Observing Children and the Arts

1. Plan an arts exploration or practice activity suitable for an infant or toddler.

2. Obtain permission to work with one infant or toddler, either at home or in a child care setting.

3. Set up your activity and observe the infant or toddler at work. Take anecdotal notes. If possible, take photos or videotape the activity (get permission first).

_____

Age of child:
Setup of materials:
Length of time of observation:

_____

1. What did the child do first?

_____

2. What did the child say?

_____

3. How did the child interact physically? (For example, describe position of arms and hands, grip, any other body parts involved.)

_____

4. How long did the child work? (Measure periods of concentration. If child stopped, why? How did the child let you know he or she was finished?)

_____

5. Describe the process the child went through. (What did the child do first? What was repeated? What was surprising? Did you make any changes while working?)

_____

6. Reflect on how you would transform the activity to improve or expand upon it.

Chapter

4

Awakening the Senses

Know why it is important to foster sensory perception in young children.

Practice intentional teaching through sensory-rich interactions with children.

Planning Curriculum to Achieve Important Goals

Teaching to Enhance Development and Learning

Sensory Perception and the Arts DAP Learning Objectives

Assessing Children's Development and Learning

Assess children's perceptual develop perceptually and select appropriate activities to meet their needs.

Creating a Caring Community

Establishing Reciprocal Family Relationships

Plan safe sensory–perceptual arts activities that respect individual children's approaches to learning.

Work with families to select sensory activities that respect their culture and beliefs and personal knowledge of their child.

Web based on the NAEYC Developmentally Appropriate Practice (Copple & Bredekamp, 2009).

Young Artists Creating

"The sand is singing," says Byron as he pours sand into his pail with a soft whir. Mariah looks at her teacher through a tube. "I made you round," she says. Aleko lies down on the grass and says quietly, "I smell the grass growing."

What Is Sensory Perception?

It is through **sensory perception** that we learn about the world. Tastes, smells, textures, sounds, and sights, most often in combination, stimulate our sensory organs which convert them to neural impulses and send them to our brain for processing. Our eyes, nose, mouth, ears and skin are considered **exteroceptors** because they process external stimuli. The world is a noisy, whirling, colorful place full of sounds that tickle our ears, textures that twitch our fingers, odors that assault our noses, tastes that tempt our tongues and images that dazzle our eyes.

Our Senses

Each of our senses is uniquely designed to make sense of the multisensory sensory bath we live in and play a major role in arts education.

Visual perception. Discriminating lines, colors, shapes, movement, and dimension is the main function of **visual perception.** Called "visual thinking" by influential psychologist Rudolf Arnheim (1969) this is a cognitive process, as is all sensory perception, that takes images perceived physically by our eyes and gives them meaning. It is the key component that makes visual art possible.

Auditory perception. **Auditory perception** is sensitivity to sounds and noises. It is a key skill in musical development. Learning to discriminate meaningful sounds from the distracting noise that surrounds us is key to developing the ability to focus and attend.

Olfactory perception. **Olfactory perception** is using our sense of smell to identify odors. Although the sense of smell is often less valued than the other senses, it is a very powerful one. Smell stimuli travel directly to the limbic system of the brain, which primarily supports emotions and long-term memories.

Sensory perception is developed by presenting intriguing objects and using rich language to describe how they look, smell, and feel.

A whiff of a familiar odor from the past such as the scent of school glue can make adults feel like they are in kindergarten again. Opening a box of new crayons can bring to mind a drawing made at age five.

Smell is the first sense to develop, present before birth. Pleasant smells are preferred from early on. Infants smile at the scent of bananas and frown at the stink of rotten eggs. They play more with vanilla scented toys (Biel, 2011). A research study by Schifferstein and Desmet (2007) found that when the olfactory sense is blocked, activities are less pleasant, less predictable, and less emotionally engaging. Experiences relating to smell may be more subtle, often in the background of other activities, but drawing attention to the associated odors or adding pleasant smells will make them more engaging and memorable.

Gustatory perception. Taste is often the forgotten sense in arts education, particularly because teachers must be concerned that children not ingest hazardous art materials and so discourage oral

To develop visual perception, invite children to look at familiar things in new ways.

Special Needs

• SENSORY INTEGRATION •

Sensory integration refers to how we process information from our senses. All the sensations our body is feeling work together to help us understand and control our behavior and responses to stimuli. Children who have **sensory integration dysfunction (SID)** may be overly sensitive or under-reactive to touch, movement, sights, and sounds. Children exhibiting any of these characteristics may react strongly to arts activities by exhibiting fear, yelling, tantrums, or refusal to participate. These children need slow, careful exposure to many sensory activities with calm guidance from a facilitating adult. Many of the sensory and arts elements activities in this chapter provide gentle introductions to arts experiences.

exploration. However, we can emphasize the aesthetic qualities of food as it is served and eaten at snack time and meals. We can create taste centers where tasting is allowed. Dramatic play provides another place where tastes can be imagined and acted out.

Tactile Perception. The entire surface of the human body is sensitive to pressure and temperature, as well as to the textural qualities of the matter that makes up the world. This is **tactile perception.** Young children rely heavily on hands-on exploration to acquire knowledge about the characteristics of individual materials and objects and to develop an understanding of how things are spatially arranged and move.

In Montessori sensorial work the tactile sense is broken down into its components: **thermic**—sense of temperature, **baric**—sense of weight or pressure, and **stereognostic**—sensing three-dimensional form by touch alone. In sensorial tasks children order different temperatures of water, differently weighted cylinders, and identify objects hidden in a bag by touch alone.

Touch is not located only in our fingers. Our entire skin is a tactile sense organ. The environment and activities offered to young children should provide continuous opportunities to touch and explore with more than their hands. They can walk on textured surfaces with bare feet, and rub materials against their cheeks and down their bare arms and legs.

Sensory Perception Development

Every day researchers learn more about the amazing abilities of infants who are born with sensory systems functioning and ready to be refined through interaction with their environment.

The first months. Weeks before birth, the unborn child hears sounds and smells the amniotic fluid. Within hours of birth newborns recognize their mother's voice and her unique scent (Winberg & Porter, 1998). While their visual acuity and depth perception are weaker than an adult's, and their eyes still wander, babies in their first days have a sense of size and shape, prefer their mother's face over others, and complex shapes over simple ones (Bornstein, Arterberry, & Mash, 2011). Infants at this stage rely on adults to provide the necessary sensory stimulation that will allow them to grow and refine their reactions.

The sitting child. By age four to five months, infants can see a shape inside another, recognize turning three-dimensional forms, and know when one object passes in front of another. They move their heads at first, and then, their bodies toward a sound, can match pitch, and discriminate between rhythmic and non-rhythmic music.

Infants are born ready to learn through their senses in interactions with others. When interacting with an infant it is important to touch and talk and make expressive faces.

By age six to seven months, vision is well developed. Two-dimensional and three-dimensional features, such as shading, relative size, texture gradients, and linear perspective, are used by infants to locate objects around them. Infants at this stage are ready for supervised introductions to many different sensory stimuli.

Meaning makers. Not only are babies attracted to sensory stimuli, they also quickly attach meaning to what they perceive. They don't just hear, they listen. They don't just see, but examine. They don't just touch, they reach out or pull away. While newborns prefer faces over shapes, by age five months infants recognize and differentiate between emotional expressions showing anger, fear, happiness, and surprise. By ten months they are attuned to the sounds in their native language, and prefer familiar melodies to unfamiliar ones, and harmonious ones to dissonant ones (Sigelman & Shaffer, 2009, p.155).

Making meaning of what is perceived and knowing how to react develops and becomes refined through the growing child's daily interaction with the people, objects, and experiences in the environment (Cermak, 2009). As the child grows, sensory clues trigger memories based on past physical, social-emotional, and cultural experiences. For example, a toddler sees a brown square. It feels slightly waxy and smells like chocolate, and since the child knows she liked chocolate when she tasted it before, she decides to eat it. The kindergartner at the easel examines turquoise paint, notices its color and fluidity, compares it to a memory of a family trip to the sea, and flicks it on the painting. A second grader hears the teacher sing a folk melody, remembers the pattern and tempo of the notes, and sings along. Sensory perception has set the stage for learning.

Did You Get It?

Discriminating lines, colors, shapes, movement, and dimension is the main function of _____.

a. visual perception

b. auditory perception

c. olfactory perception

d. gustatory perception

Take the full quiz on CourseMate

Why Is Sensory Perception Important?

Sensory perception experiences are essential for functioning successfully in society. In fact, we rely so heavily on the intake of information through our senses that when deprived of all sensory input for as little as fifteen minutes, adults begin to lose their sense of reality (Mason & Brady, 2009).

The Effects of Sensory Deprivation

Infancy, in particular, is a critical time for developing sensory perception. When babies are deprived of one type of sensory information, because of a physical issue such as limited vision, hearing loss, or sensitivity to touch, their future growth is affected. Visual

Being held in the lap provides security as an infant explores the sensory stimulus of a crayon.

deprivation in the first seven weeks of life results in impaired recognition of faces (Johnson & Mareschal, 2001). Hearing loss not corrected before six months affects the child's ability to classify and understand distinct sounds, hindering language development. Infants who are under-responsive to tactile stimuli show increased social and communication impairments as they mature (Foss-Ferg, Heacock & Cascio, 2012).

Development can also be affected by a lack of sensory stimulation. Adopted children who experienced sensory deprivation in infancy react adversely to sensory stimuli even twelve years later (Wilbarger et al., 2010). Infants who receive infrequent touching from their mothers eat less and show slower physical growth (Polan & Ward, 1994). Preschoolers with below normal response to sensory stimuli, such as is found in some types of autism, are less able to understand the emotional state of other people (Chasiotis et al., 2006).

Building Deep Meaning

In addition, young children in this technological age spend less time outside, and are more likely to be sedentary in front of television and computer screens which, while visually compelling, do not provide the physical experience of manipulating real objects in three-dimensional space (Anderson & Hanson, 2010). Television viewing also affects parent–child interactions, vital to effective sensory processing. When adult-oriented television programs play in the background, parents become distracted and interactions with their children playing nearby reduce in quantity and quality (Kirkorian et al., 2009).

As this research shows, sensory perceptual deficits in early childhood often lead to physical, behavioral, and social difficulties, while exposure to television and technology reduces hands-on sensory experiences for many young children.

In addition, when the brain receives too much random, distracting, or general information, the child's brain creates superficial memories rather than deep ones (Caine & Caine, 1994). Surface memory might tell a child that the object in front of him is a round ball. Deep meaning is built up over repeated exposures in an emotionally positive context and tells the child: "This is my ball, the one I play with my brother. It is round and red and has words on it and a scratch on one side and it bounces when I drop it. When I rub it on my face it is bumpy and smells like the bottom of my sneaker. I love playing with my ball." As such, providing rich, meaningful sensory perception activities is a critical component of children's total development.

The Role of Sensory Perception Arts Activities

Bombarded constantly by sensory stimuli, children cannot pay attention to all of them. Starting at birth, the brain filters the information coming from the senses, discarding some and attending to others. (Merikle, Smilek, & Eastwood, 2001). In order to build deep meaning, the child needs to use **selective attention,** the underlying skill required for effective learning in all developmental areas.

Selective attention requires that the child choose the most important or compelling stimulus, focus on it, discover its meaning, and then react. For example, an infant hears a voice singing a pitch. Ignoring the rub of clothing against its skin, the colors on the wallpaper, the smell of the baby powder under its neck,

Natural objects, such as leaves, allow children to use their tactile perception as they touch the leaf, their visual perception as they examine its shape, their auditory perception as they hear the sound it makes as they crumble it, the their olfactory perception as they smell the damp woodsy odor.

Open-ended arts activities allow children to use their senses as they work with colors, textures, shapes, and patterns. Collage by Jon, age four.

Objectives for Sensory Perception Arts Activities

Although all arts activities involve using the senses, specific activities can be selected that enhance and challenge particular sensory modes, foster the development of selective focus, build discrimination skills, and remedy sensory deficits. At the same time these activities can address growth in all the development areas by creating an enriched learning environment that encourages verbal communication, cognitive processing, and motor development.

Through sensory perception arts activities, children develop:

- **Physically**—*by learning to control bodily movements in the presence of sensory stimuli.* **Kinesthetic awareness** grows as the child reacts to sensory experiences. Neck and torso strengthen and cross-body coordination increases as the child turns towards, searches for, and moves toward sounds and music. Hand movements come to match visual inputs during reaching and grasping arts materials. Finger control develops as the child touches the materials of the visual arts and explores their surfaces. Eyes improve in focusing as they examine visual images and track moving objects during dance and dramatic play.

and the trace of milk in its mouth, a baby makes a sound imitating that note.

Ann Lewin-Benham (2010), taking into account the growing body of research on sensory processing and the development of the brain in infants, suggests that experiences with sensory materials be started much earlier with babies than previously thought, and that the arts are an ideal way to develop sustained attention. Sights, sounds, textures, tastes, and smells form the basis of the creative arts and provide an ideal way to entice even the youngest infants to engage and focus in sustained ways.

Socially and Emotionally—*by interacting with peers and adults as they participate in sensory arts activities.* Through interaction with peers and adults, children learn to imitate and model the behavior that is acceptable in their community and culture. They learn to recognize faces and emotional expressions. The smells and tastes of the child's home and culture become familiar and recognized. Through words, touch, and active participation they come to recognize and understand the objects in their environment.

Cognitively—*by attaching meaning to their sensory experiences to understand how the world works.* Arts experiences draw on the senses to improve concentration and memory, provide opportunities for classification and sequencing, and teach cause and effect.

Linguistically—*by providing opportunities to use sound to communicate with and understand others.* Children learn to pick out important sounds from the environment and to ignore distracting sounds as they listen to singing and music. They learn to control sound to communicate needs and emotions when imitating and responding to the sounds of others engaged in arts activities.

Creatively—*by engaging curiosity and risk-taking while developing sustained attention and problem-solving.* When presented with open-ended sensory arts activities, children through control of their own actions can explore, focus on, change, and test the sensory properties of a wide variety of objects, materials, sounds, tastes, smells, and spatial elements.

How Should Sensory Perception Activities Be Selected?

Sensory arts activities should be selected based on children's developmental levels and previous arts experiences, while keeping in mind any specific strengths or sensory processing needs of individual children.

Well-designed activities provide multiple opportunities, both novel and repeated, which allow children to perfect their responses to different stimuli, develop memory, create meaning, and build a descriptive vocabulary. While every arts activity addresses all the aforementioned developmental areas, when presenting a sensory perceptual activity the teacher intentionally frames the sensory aspects. This is done by:

Selecting a sensory-rich experience.

Alerting the children to the experience.

An unbreakable mirror is an example of an open-ended sensory stimulus suitable for infants. The child can change the visual image by changing facial expression and body position, and by moving closer and further away, or by crawling on it.

> ### Did You Get It?
>
> **A child's ability to tell stories will most likely be affected by sensory deprivation in infancy related to_____.**
>
> **a.** visual perception
>
> **b.** tactile perception
>
> **c.** olfactory perception
>
> **d.** auditory perception
>
> **Take the full quiz on CourseMate**

Making Plans

ONE-ON-ONE ACTIVITY PLAN:
INTRODUCING A SQUISHY BAG – A SENSORY ACTIVITY

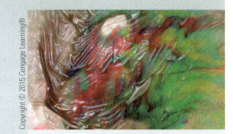

A squishy bag filled with cornstarch fingerpaint and food coloring provides an open-ended visual and tactile experience for infants.

WHO?   Group composition age(s): Older infant or toddler

WHEN?   Time frame: 5 to 15 minutes

WHY?   Objectives: Child will develop

- physically, by using the large muscles of the arm and the small muscles of the hand. I will see this happening when the child manipulates the squishy bag. (Bodily-Kinesthetic)

- socially, by interacting with a caring adult. I will see this happening when the child makes eye contact and makes verbal and nonverbal gestures. (Interpersonal)

- emotionally, by developing self-confidence from being allowed to handle the squishy bag. I will see this happening when the child doesn't hesitate to touch the bag. (Intrapersonal)

- perceptually, by visually exploring how colors change as different tactile pressures are applied and by learning that pliant forms change shape. I will see this happening when the child looks at and touches the bag. (Spatial)

- language skills, by verbalizing how the bag feels and looks, and by learning new words for color and shape. I will hear this happening as the child makes verbal responses to my use of these words.(Linguistic)

- cognitively, by observing cause and effect as their manipulation changes the color and nature of the form. I will know this is happening when the child makes the bag change and makes some verbal or non-verbal gesture in response. (Logical-Mathematical)

- arts skill and knowledge, by learning about color, a basic element of visual art, and by developing selective focus and tactile skill in handling a new material. I will see this happening when the child looks when I point my finger and say the name of the colors. (Content Standard 1 & 2)

WHERE?   Setup: Child in a high chair or on an adult's lap at the table. A sealed squishy bag is taped to the high chair tray or table.

WHAT?   Materials: Squishy bag: make one cup of cornstarch finger paint and add two colors that mix well together. (See Appendix D.) Seal bag and cover seal with duck tape. Tape the bag to the table or high chair tray using package sealing tape or masking tape.

HOW?   Procedure:
Wow Warm-Up: Sit with the child and show the child the squishy bag.

What to Do: Model how to poke it and pat it accompanied by enthusiastic words and expressions. Let the child see it, touch it, pat it, and poke it.

What to Say: Use this activity to talk about the tactile qualities of the squishy bag. In an excited voice, use words such as *soft, squishy, pat, poke, push, pull, sticky, press, squash*, and *flatten*. Sensory experiences are a wonderful time to chant or sing with toddlers. Make up some chants to accompany this wonderful activity. For example, chant something like this: *Pat, poke, press that. That's the way we make it flat.*

Transition Out: Let the child spend as much time as he or she wishes exploring the nature of the material. When done, store in a safe place to use again.

WHAT
LEARNED?   Assessment: does child respond positively to the squishy bag? Does child have sufficient hand strength to change the shape of the material? Does child repeat and use the descriptive terms modeled by the adult?

NEXT?   Repeat the experience with different colors to mix and try different sizes of bags. Follow up with finger painting.

For more examples of sensory activity plans for various ages, see *Sensory Activity Plans* on Coursemate.

🌀 Allowing a choice of interaction with the stimulus.

🌀 Actively engaging both verbally and nonverbally about the sensory qualities of the experience.

🌀 And as in all good teaching: observing, assessing, adjusting, repeating, and scaffolding as needed based on the children's reaction to the stimulus.

Selecting Open-Ended Sensory Materials, Objects, and Experiences

Although we tend to think of objects and materials first, sensory stimuli should not be limited to physical objects. Light, shadows, clouds, wind, a visit to a bakery, or a walk in the rain all are full of sensory stimuli. In the same way, while visual and auditory stimuli are more common in children's activities, taste, smell, and touch are powerful senses that can be tapped to motivate and inspire children.

Sensory activities can be designed to help children focus on input from one sense. This type of activity develops important discrimination and classifying skills. However, it is impossible to eliminate the input from all senses. For example, although Montessori sensorial work favors isolating the sensory element to encourage children to order and classify by smaller and smaller increments, children are still receiving input from their sense of touch and their sense of hearing as they observe and then organize, visual materials such as matching pegs with holes, building a graduated block tower, or classifying leaves. Auditory work which asks children to listen closely and match tones or order pitches, also involves feeling the texture and form of the wooden sound cylinders and seeing the colors of the tone bells. Gustatory tasks focus on identifying bitter, sweet, salty, and sour tastes but include the sound and feel of squeezing eye droppers of the solutions into a spoon and sensing the weight and temperature of the spoon in their mouths. Activities that activate multiple senses also enhance children's cognitive understanding and cement memories. An intentional teacher, for instance, might draw attention to the colors of fruits and their relationship to their tastes by asking questions such as "Do all green fruits taste the same?" Educators in the Reggio Emilia schools purposely mix contrasting

sensory experiences to create **synesthetic experiences** that combine visual and tactile, or auditory and shape elements (Lewin-Benham, 2010).

Selecting motivating sensory stimuli requires us to become of aware of our own surroundings, to look at things in new ways, and imagine how our particular children will react to them. While there are many commercial toys that attempt to attract children's attention, found materials and objects made by the teacher will often prove more engaging and are more readily adapted to match children's interests and needs.

A repetitive noise or hard plastic, primary-colored toys decorated with cartoon pictures cannot compete with the intricacies and textures of a veined leaf, a tub filled with soapy water and rainbow-hued bubbles, or the varying quality and expression of the human voice.

Criteria for selection. The core of a sensory arts activity is the chosen stimulus or set of stimuli which can be an object, a material, or an event. A carefully chosen stimulus will elicit the sustained attention basic to all learning.

Sand is an open-ended multisensory stimulus that invites active engagement and develops visual, tactile, and auditory sensory perception.

➤ The most important criterion in choosing the stimulus is that it allow open-ended exploration. This means that it should have integral complexity with multiple ways to view it, compare it, change it and use it, such as a mirror which can be viewed from various distances and positions while wearing different expressions, or paper which can be wrinkled, folded, crushed, colored, wet, torn, and cut. Translucent and transparent materials, noise makers, food, and living things make ideal sensory stimuli as they react to children's actions in unexpected ways.

➤ It should allow the child to respond and interact with it in a physical and multisensory way. In our technological world, hands-on experiences are essential. A sturdy basket the child can touch and fill with objects is a better choice for activating the senses than a picture of a basket on a television, on an interactive whiteboard, or on a computer screen.

➤ It should introduce novel elements into the child's experience. This could be something the child has not had contact with before, such as a set of Iroquois ankle bells on a suede strap tied to an infant's ankle or something familiar presented in a new way such, as bubble wrap for toddlers to dance on.

➤ The idea for the stimulus should grow from careful observation of children's needs, desires, and input. For example, after noticing that an infant is beginning to reach out and grasp, provide a sensory stimulus, such as a bell, that the child can hold and shake. If after reading a book about fish, a child wonders if the fish in the book looks like a real fish, it is time to bring a goldfish bowl into the classroom. Pebbles collected by children from the playground can become sensory stimuli as they wash them and watch them change colors as they dry.

➤ A well-chosen stimulus will provide opportunities for multiple uses as the child grows and develops sensory perceptual skills. Repetition develops memory and skill. A bell shaken by an infant's grasping hand can become the bell rung by a toddler to accompany a song, can become part of a set of bells in a preschool comparative sound center, and then, can become part of the musical bells used by primary students to compose an original melody.

For more examples of sensory stimuli, see *Examples of Sensory Stimuli* on CourseMate.

Safety Considerations. Select materials with safety in mind, especially with younger children who still put objects in their mouths. Objects shorter than two inches in length and one inch in diameter should not be used by children under the age of three. Materials that are dusty and can be inhaled should be avoided with all children. Seek input from parents about known allergies.

At all times, children should be supervised based on their developmental level and behavioral patterns. A focused teacher in a one-on-one situation can

Teacher to Family

Sample Letter to Families: Child Safety Information

Dear Family,

All of the arts materials used in our program have been carefully selected to be safe for young children. Some children, however, have special sensitivities. To help us select the safest arts materials for your child, please answer the following questions:

1. Is your child allergic to anything?   yes   no
If yes, please list:
2. Does your child have any respiratory
   problems?   yes   no
If yes, please explain:

3. Is your skin sensitive to anything?   yes   no
If yes, please list:
4. Are there any arts materials that your
   child should not use?   yes   no
Please list and explain.
Thank you for taking the time to complete this form. Together we can make sure that your child will have a safe and fun time creating art.

Your child's teacher,

Digital Download   Download from CourseMate

offer objects that would not be safe left alone with the child, such as a pinecone or sealed plastic bag of colored hair gel or paint. These challenging materials offer the opportunity to teach even infants safe behaviors. When infants go to put inappropriate things in their mouths, make a yucky face and say "No mouth." If they persist, replace with a material that can be safely explored orally and say "This is nicer to chew." More safety tips can be found in Appendix A.

Introducing Sensory Activities

Once a stimulus is selected, the next task is to alert the children and attract their focus to it, despite all the other sensory distractions vying for their attention. Pointing, modeling, and imitation accompanied by enthusiastic language draw attention and work for all ages, but are especially important for infants and young toddlers.

- **Pointing** helps them train their eyes on the selected stimulus and develop sustained attention. Even young infants will follow a pointing arm with their eyes.

- **Open-ended modeling** demonstrates one or more ways to react and increase skill and interest. Shaking a rattle to show infants that it makes noise increases the likelihood they will try shaking it.

- **Imitation** of the children's reactions tells them they have done something noteworthy.

- **Verbal and nonverbal feedback** that is enthusiastic and encouraging, and is rich in descriptive words builds vocabulary, provides emotional satisfaction, teaches social communication skills, and gives cognitive feedback.

Wonderful Object of Wonder. For toddlers and older children, the sensory stimulus should be a **WOW**—a Wonderful Object of Wonder—introduced with questions and wonderings by the teacher. The WOW can be anything that excites the senses and expands the curiosity and experience of the children: a stained-glass window, a bird feather found on the playground, wood blocks in a wooden bowl, or a rhythm tapped on an African drum.

In a sensory arts activity, the children's interaction with the WOW is the focal point. However, a WOW can also be used to elicit wonderment and curiosity when it is the starting point or warm-up in any arts or

Handmade instruments from around the world invite children to touch and explore. They are a good example of the types of sensory stimuli that can be used as Wonderful Objects of Wonder, or WOWs.

other curriculum area activity. See Appendix B for more ideas on the role of WOWs indesigning activity plans.

Guided discovery. Preschoolers and older children who have already had many sensory experiences can be alerted through a carefully orchestrated unveiling process. In guided discovery the object or even a center is wrapped or hidden from view to elicit curiosity and create opportunities for children to ask questions and to make predictions based on clues revealed through hints, observations, or a gradual uncovering. See Appendix B for using Guided Discovery in activity planning in general.

Did You Get It?

Alex is a new teacher of toddlers. He seeks the advice of Linda, a senior teacher at the school, on ideas about selecting a good stimulus for a sensory arts activity. Which of the following should Linda recommend to Alex?

a. The stimulus should clearly indicate to the child what needs to be done with it.

b. The stimulus should allow the child to respond and interact with it in a physical way.

c. The stimulus should be presented on a computer screen or tablet.

d. The stimulus should be specific to one sensory organ, and should not demand multi-sensory uses.

Take the full quiz on CourseMate

How Should Sensory Perception Activities Be Presented?

How sensory activities are presented will depend on the development of the child and the organization of the space.

Ways to Present to Infants

For infants not yet sitting up or children with physical or sensory issues, cuddling them against the body or holding them on a lap can provide security when introducing something new. As they become accustomed to sensory activities, vary their perspective by placing them on their backs or positioning them to sit facing outward. Be careful about moving objects rapidly toward the face as this can trigger a defensive response. Start slowly with all actions and add energy as the child shows active attention.

Based on careful observation of the way the baby reacts, change and adapt the activity until the baby shows boredom by losing interest, at which time, a new activity maybe started or a rest period given. This type of intimate reciprocal arts activity requires the complete one-on-one attention of the teacher, who provides a constant patter of vocally dramatic description delivered with enthusiasm. For safety, be sure to remove sensory objects and materials from the child's reach when teacher–child interaction is over.

Infants who are sitting up and those who are beginning to turn over, creep, and crawl can be placed on the floor and have the sensory stimulus placed at a distance to encourage them to reach for and move toward it, adding emotional satisfaction to the experience when the child is successful. Placing older infants in pairs encourages increased imitation and can motivate a reticent child. Expand the activities and add challenge by using a larger space and more movements and objects. Include things that roll, bounce, make noise, and change shape when the child moves them, such as long or wide cardboard or plastic tubes, paper bags with noise makers inside, or foam balls and blocks. Strip a crawling infant to her diaper, dip her hands in wet paint, and let her crawl under supervision on a large sheet of paper.

Visual activities. If an infant stares at a particular location, observe what is attracting its attention, and then see what happens if a new object or material is placed in that space. Try mirrors, blinking lights, and glittery materials. Move beyond commercial mobiles, and make your own with interchangeable pieces to provide ever-changing novelty. Tracking can be fostered by moving the objects in a constant direction. Spatial depth can be developed by moving the object or material closer or farther away. Building on infants' attraction to faces, move materials that reflect light in different ways, such as paper or velvet in front of your face. To change focus, alternate the baby's position. For example, rest the infant against your body so that the infant faces forward and hold objects out front and to either side so that the child must focus on it against a distracting background.

Make visually interesting items by filling plastic containers and bags with liquids, such as food coloring, water and oil, and small objects, such as pebbles, buttons, or glitter, sealed well with tape or hot glue.

Auditory activities. If an infant makes a sound or movement, imitate it. If the baby imitates you, repeat, and elaborate by changing it in some way. Sing songs and recite rhymes accompanied by exaggerated verbal and facial expressions. Look for sound makers that infants can hold comfortably like bells, rattles, and things to tap together. Make your own shakers by filling containers, both opaque and transparent, with different materials and sealing well. As the baby handles these objects describe the sounds and motions the child is making.

Tactile activities. Touching materials and objects encourages infants to coordinate eyes and hands and

Across Cultures

Using Food in Arts Activities

In selecting food items to use in sensory and other arts activities, be sensitive to family traditions and beliefs concerning foods. In some cultures, certain foods, such as rice, are highly valued and not considered suitable for children to play with. Others may feel that with so many hungry people in our country and all over the world, it is inappropriate to have children play in a sensory bin filled with food items like cereal, macaroni, or beans that will be thrown away when the activity is over.

Special Needs

• ADJUSTING FOR SPECIAL NEEDS •

Not all children respond in the same way to sensory stimuli. Some children may need special attention during sensory arts activities.

- **Limited vision.** Stroke from the palm out to the finger tips to increase tactile sensitivity. Use larger objects and sound makers and place within vision range if any. If the child can see some color, use that color. Provide clues that use other senses such applying a particular scent to mark personal toys. Increase tactile, auditory, and movement-based activities. For infants, allow more exploration with the mouth by providing objects that invite sucking. Look for things that vibrate and make noise like drums and rainsticks. Create Treasure Baskets from shallow containers in which everyday objects are grouped. However, minimize ubiquitous plastics in favor of ones that vary in weight and temperature such as fabric, metal, rubber, stone, and wood.

- **Hearing loss.** Emphasize visual and tactile sensory stimuli. Choose objects that reflect and emit light or catch the eye by moving. Make exaggerated visual expressions as you describe the objects. Try mirror, light tables, and sensory bins.

- **Tactile defensiveness.** Some sensory activities that help children become more accustomed to touch sensations include: painting with soap foam and pudding, playing in sand, finding hidden objects in rice or beans, squeezing out white glue, using play dough and clay, and drawing on squishy bags.

- **Distractibility.** Take a box and attach interesting sensory items to the inside. Position the child just inside the opening so that she can see and touch the objects.

- **Oversensitivity.** Lights, tastes, smells, touch, or sounds may cause some children to retreat or panic. These children need a slow, gentle introduction to the experience. Explore using soothing music and massage to calm.

- **Undersensitivity.** Other children may show no reaction to a sensory stimulus or be distracted and unable to focus. These children may need stronger stimuli such as allspice instead of vanilla.

A teacher draws toddlers' attention to the sensory qualities of the materials in a sensory bin filled with water, plastic strips, and pumpkins.

feet. Textures stimulate the skin. Look for materials that make sounds when the baby crunches them or that have unique textures such as aluminum foil and different types of papers and cloth. Laminate colorful paper shapes and natural objects such as leaves and flowers for the infant to handle. Lightly brush objects and materials across the baby's skin, hands, feet, and face.

Olfactory and gustatory activities. Accompanied by enthusiastic words, model smelling or tasting a food item and make a surprised or pleased face. Then present the item to the child. Hold pleasant smelling foods, candles, soap, and flowers to the baby's nose or touch the baby's lips with a piece of orange, banana, applesauce, or other pleasant infant-appropriate food.

Ways to Present to Older Children

For toddlers and older children who have more physical control and increased sensory discrimination skills, complexity can be added through the addition of more objects, materials, and events.

Sharing. Children can interact in pairs and small groups as they explore sensory items. Present a unique item to touch, feel, and look at during circle time or during a small group time. Then place it on the observation table, in the drawing center, or another selected location. For example, show a beautiful geode to the group, and have the children pass it around describing what they see and how it feels. Then show them where there are more in a basket for them to explore. Groups are also ideal for listening to auditory stimuli.

Sensory bins, baskets, and tables. Containers such as baskets, wooden bowls, dish tubs, and clear plastic storage bins can hold smaller sensory objects or liquids for exploration. Built to contain messy materials, large sand-and-water tables allow a group of children to explore at the same time and can hold many more things besides water or sand, such as hay, shredded paper, and goop made from cornstarch and water.

For more examples of sensory activities, see Sensory Perception Arts Activities on CourseMate.

Observation table or display. Place an unfamiliar object or an arrangement of objects from nature on a small child-height table. If possible, use materials the children have collected and grouped themselves. Add descriptive materials such as photographs of where they come from, identifying labels, and for older children, appropriate observation tools such as magnifiers and tweezers. Make a comment about it to draw attention and encourage the children to look and touch.

"Look, we have a beautiful conch shell from Florida! How do you think it feels?"

"Can you guess what is in the sensory table today? What does it look like?"

Learning centers. Many sensory experiences lend themselves to learning centers. Small attractively arranged samples of fruits or vegetables or different kinds of bread can be offered at a tasting center. Small boxes or containers containing different materials can be placed at a sound center where children can try to match the sounds or put them in order from softest to loudest.

Sources of Inspiration. Both Reggio Emilia and Montessori programs place a great emphasis on sensory learning. In the Reggio Emilia program, sensory stimuli range from shadows to bird feeders to walking in a crowd (Edwards, Gandini, & Forman, 2011). Many early childhood programs in the United States have documented the ways sensory learning is incorporated into their programs. *In the Spirit of the Studio* (Gandini et al., 2005), *Infants and Toddlers at Work* (Lewin-Benham, 2010), and *Learning Together with Young Children* (Curtis & Carter, 2008) all give examples of effective materials and objects, such as using egg beaters in soapy water, arranging translucent glass beads on mirrors, and making patterns of furry cloth of different types.

An observation table with living things, such as these chicks, provides a wonderful multisensory experience that draws children's attention and wonder.

Copyright © 2015 Cengage Learning®

Did You Get It?

Florence, a kindergarten teacher, selects a piece of bubble wrap as a stimulus for a sensory arts activity. Her next task is to

a. initiate interaction between the child and the stimulus.

b. alert the child about the stimulus he is about to experience.

c. explain about the sensory qualities involved in the experience.

d. observe and assess the child as he responds to the stimulus.

Take the full quiz on CourseMate

How Do We Create Sensory Interactions?

The presentation of a sensory stimulus alone is not a complete activity. Planned, intentional interaction between the child and the adult is an essential component. Sensory-rich interactions are made up of a combination of words, actions, and expressiveness that show wonder about and value of sensory qualities and respond to the actions and words of the child.

Open-Ended Questioning and Wondering

As we have seen in Chapter 2, questioning is one way to elicit children's ideas. When carefully worded so that there is no one right answer, an enthusiastic question can be a useful way to involve a child with a sensory stimulus. To ensure open-endedness, model the wonder of young children and try starting with "why" or "I wonder" instead of "what." Invite comparisons using the word "how" rather than "which."

Why is this paper sparkling?

I wonder how this stone got so round?

How is the outside of this peach different from the inside?

Building a Sensory-Rich Vocabulary

A sensory element exists in every activity in which children are involved. Instead of seeing blocks, see shapes and forms; instead of glue, notice stickiness. Listen and learn from children. Young children do not hesitate to invite us to "feel this" or "smell that," and we must do the same with them. Find a sensory element, and express it with language rich in adjectives, similes, and metaphors.

"Look at how the light is shining on your wet paint!"

"Oh, the sand is so cool and damp today!"

"The yellow paint smells like a field of flowers."

"Our tiger teeth fingers are crunching the paper. Crunch. Crunch."

Use textural adjectives to describe the tactile quality of materials such as silky, soft, smooth, squishy, damp, metallic, bumpy, wet, and rough. Refer to the temperature of the materials: "Oh, this finger paint feels cold!" or "The play dough is warm from your hand." Make them aware of the pressure they are using: "You pressed down with your feet on the floor when you marched," "You banged hard on the drum," or "Your puppet touched me very lightly."

Encourage children to make tactile observations of these items by asking questions such as the following:

"Is it cold to your touch?"

"Are there places you can put your fingers?"

"How does it feel on the bottom?"

Classroom Technology

PLAYING WITH LIGHT

Young children are fascinated by light. Overhead projectors and interactive white boards are two ways to provide open-ended sensory exploration of light as children move in the cast light. Here are some ideas to get you thinking:

On the overhead:

- Explore shining the light on a wall or curtains for shadow play.
- Look for transparent and translucent materials such as cellophane, used theater gels, and plastic wrappings to change the color of the light and the shadows.
- Investigate how a glass tray of water on the overhead can be gently stirred to create the effect of light shining underwater or to create rippled patterns.

Interactive whiteboard:

- Project patterns, colors, and shapes using a presentation software such as PowerPoint. Set the show up to change slides at varying intervals and add music if desired.
- Project photographs that set a scene such as a jungle or fire.
- Project children's own drawings and paintings.

Having children trace their shadows on a wall helps them develop their visual perception and increases their understanding of light and shadow.

Compare scents to other natural smells, such as:

"The paste smells so fresh and clean!"

"This play dough smells like pine needles."

Describe the visual and textural appearance of different foods, such as the rich pink and green of watermelon, the segmented circle shape of a sliced orange, and the bumpy surface of a chocolate-chip cookie.

Did You Get It?

Which of the following is an open-ended question?

a. "What shape did you make with the crayons?"

b. "Which drum sounds louder?"

c. "Did you try mixing yellow and blue to make green?"

d. "Why do you think the puppet is sad?"

Take the full quiz on CourseMate

What Are the Elements of the Arts?

Another source of sensory language is found in the distinctive sensory-based vocabulary of each of the art forms. Visual art is made up of the visual and tactile elements of lines, colors, shapes, forms, patterns, and textures. Music is composed of the auditory elements of beats, pitch, rhythm, dynamics, harmony, tempo, timbre, and texture. Creative movement incorporates visual tracking and baric perception within the elements of space, distance, direction, flow, effort, and connection. More detail about those elements specific to each of the arts is found in Chapters 9, 10, 11, and 12.

As children pursue arts activities, lavish the young artists with comments based on the arts elements that add sensory qualities to their efforts.

Line

A **line** can be a mark made by a tool moving across a surface. It may be curved or straight or zigzag or wiggly. Lines can be thick or thin or long or short and are used by artists to make shapes and symbols and by writers to form letters, words, and numbers. Lines can show movement and direction—horizontal, vertical, or diagonal. Most importantly, lines are the mainstay of children's earliest drawings and will continue to remain an important element in all of their art.

Lines are present in visual artwork in all media, but we can also see lines in the positioning of the body in creative dance, in group movements, and in the order of notes in a melody. In nature, lines are the edges, contours, paths, and grooves in natural objects. Line activities are designed to increase children's abilities to look for and focus upon linear elements in their environment.

Searching for lines is one way to develop sustained attention against distracting backgrounds. Find straight lines dividing the tiles on the floor, curved lines hanging from the electric poles, and zigzag lines in the cracks of a frozen puddle. Make up challenges and games that have children step on lines and walk along lines. Line up one behind the other, and make a line of people that moves, wiggles, and sways as they walk in an open space or around furniture.

Music also has a linear element. Play a simple melody and have children follow the melody by drawing a line in the air with their fingers, or give them paint and let them paint lines as they follow along with the music.

Read some of the many children's books that feature lines, and then put out blank booklets for the children to draw their own "line" stories. Study the different lines that make up the letters of the alphabet. Design new ways to write the letters using a variety of lines.

Color

Teaching the colors has long been a basic of early childhood education. However, color perception is an extremely complex process about which we learn more and more each year.

Infants can see color at birth. In fact, they are born with a fascination for colors, particularly reds (Franklin, Bevis, & Ling, 2010). Infants physically process color with the right sides of their brains. As toddlers acquire language, color perception transfers to the left side (Franklin et al., 2008). In addition, people vary in how they see individual colors. A particular pink may look more orange to one viewer, more bluish to another.

Integrating the Arts

Using the senses is an important way to activate learning in all subject areas. Wonderful Objects of Wonder attract and hold children's attention and make learning math, science, social studies, or language arts more meaningful.

Instead of counting circles on a paper, provide beautiful beach pebbles or seashells to count. In science, instead of looking at pictures of fish in a book, buy a whole fish at the supermarket to observe, sketch, then make Japanese-inspired gyotaki fish prints.* If the children are studying the rainforest, visit a zoo or pet store to see parrots, frogs, and lizards and a nursery to see tropical plants. When reading a book, look for a real object that relates to the story. It could be a hat, or a food item, something that the character uses, or a sensory object that serves as the starting point for a story.

*To make a gyotaki print, brush water-based printing ink over the surface of the fish. Use thin paper such as rice paper, tissue, or newsprint. Press against the inked fish.

Because not everyone sees colors in exactly the same way, color activities often need to be adjusted. Children who have limited vision or are **color blind,** for example, need to be identified so that they do not feel uncomfortable during color activities and games.

Approximately 6 percent of people have some form of color blindness. Color blindness is more common in boys than girls. Approximately 7 to 10 percent of men in the United States are color blind to reds and greens. Other color combinations, such as blue and yellow, are much more rare. Those color blind for red and green can often differentiate the colors when side by side, but not when the color is viewed alone.

Therefore, children who are color blind often have difficulty with color-related activities. These children quickly learn to try to hide their color discrimination difficulties, especially if they are laughed at by other children when using a color the wrong way, such as drawing a purple tree. Often adults mistakenly think the child does not know the colors yet and will try to force the child to learn them, so it is important to identify color blindness as early as possible. The Ishihara color test, which shows pictures made up of dots of different colors, is an example of a test for identifying color blindness that can be used.

Other children may have limited vision, which makes color identification difficult. Once a color identification problem is identified, try using scented crayons and markers and adding scents, such as vanilla and lemon extract to paints. It also helps to place the colors in the same order at the easel and to line up the markers and crayons in the same color order. When doing color games and activities, have these children work with the colors they can identify.

Color perception is also influenced by the cultural and emotional context in which we learn those colors (Dedrick, 1996; Juricevic, 2010). For example, in some cultures black is associated with mourning, in others, white is. This means that we need to be sensitive to young children's specific cultural backgrounds and experiences.

To develop color discrimination, take time every day to enthusiastically notice the wide range of colors in the children's environment. For example, comment on the colors of the clothing children are wearing; the color of the grass, leaves, and sky when playing outside; and the colors of the fruits and vegetables in their snacks.

Note that there are many varieties of each color and use descriptive or comparative words to identify a variation of a color. For example, "Your sweater is as green as the leaves on our tree," and "Today the sky

Teacher Tip

SCENTED MARKERS

Water-based scented markers have pleasant non-toxic odors and can be useful with children who have limited vision in helping them identify colors and for some scent activities. However, caution is advised in using these on a regular basis. Some disadvantages to consider are:

- The scents are similar to candy. For example black smells like licorice, and some children may be tempted to taste them or insert them in their noses.

- The scents are very strong and the smell can be overwhelming in a classroom when several are being used at the same time.

- The scents may become overly identified with a certain color such as lemon with yellow and mint with green, limiting the development of a more discriminating sense of smell.

reminds me of the color of a robin's egg," and "The leaves on that tree are a deeper green than on this one." Point out differences among **hues** in the same color family. Show how colors can vary in **intensity, tone,** and **value.**

Colors get mixed intentionally or unintentionally when painting and printing. Mixing new colors gives the child a sense of power and provides an opportunity for color identification. Finger painting with two or three colors is a very tactile way to combine colors, as is mixing several colors of playdough together.

Providing a preselected palette of colors helps children focus on specific color mixtures. Introduce the **primary colors** of red, yellow, and blue and let children discover how these three colors make the **secondary colors** of orange, purple, and green. Show how adding white makes a **tint**—a lighter version of the color and adding black makes a **shade,** a darker version of the color.

For more ways to mix colors using the color wheel, see Guide to Mixing Colors on CourseMate.

Shape

Everything has a shape. A **shape** is a two-dimensional area or image that has defined edges or borders. A two-dimensional shape has height and width and may be geometric, organic, symbolic, or free form. Many shapes have names based on their properties.

- Geometric shapes follow mathematical principles, such as polygons, squares, rectangles, circles, and triangles.

- Organic shapes come from nature, as in the shape of a leaf or butterfly.

- Symbolic shapes have a special meaning, such as that of letters or numbers or musical notes.

- Free-form shapes are invented shapes that follow no rules.

Each of the four categories of shapes may contain some shapes that are **symmetrical.** If a straight line is drawn through the center of a shape, it will be exactly the same on both sides. Squares, butterflies, the letter "A," and hearts are all symmetrical shapes. All of these shapes will be found in children's artwork, books, and in the classroom environment.

Looking through a tinted view finder adds complexity to how things are perceived, challenging the sensory perception of children as they explore the relationship of color and light.

To help children focus on the qualities of shapes, play games that involve finding specific shapes. Search the room and outside areas for types of shapes. Go on circle, rectangle, and triangle hunts. Hide shapes around the room for children to find.

Develop vocabulary by talking about the qualities of these shapes including and expanding beyond the simple names of heart, square and so on. Present sensory objects that have unusual shapes both symmetrical and non-symmetrical, such as leaves, flowers, and rocks that challenge description. With infants and toddlers, use colorful laminated shapes to make complex shape designs. Differentiate between the edge of the shape and the inside of the shape. Older children can use pattern blocks and tangrams. Take them apart and put them together into new shapes. Make mosaic-like designs by gluing small shapes onto colorful backgrounds.

Pattern and Rhythm

A **pattern** occurs when anything is repeated several times. Patterns and rhythms occur naturally, as in the designs on a leopard's skin and the chirping of crickets, or can be invented by artists, dancers, and musicians. In the visual arts, a patterned design may be made from repeated shapes, lines, and colors. Musical patterns occur when the same note sequence or rhythm is repeated. **Rhythm** is a time-based pattern. Creative dance is built on the repetition of body movements that create patterns and rhythms. Patterns are important not only in the arts; being able to find and understand patterns is also the basis of language and mathematical understanding.

Encourage children to find examples of pattern and rhythm in the environment. Find the shapes, lines, and colors in patterns on clothing, furnishings, and on nature objects. Physically create patterns to develop memory and meaning. Have children line up in ways that make patterns such as alternating tall and short or those wearing light colors and those wearing dark.

Show surprise and wonder as you comment on patterns in the art they are creating, the music they listen to, and the objects in their environment. Look for natural patterns like the scales on a pine cone and the spots on a Dalmatian. Help children see that a pattern is made up of smaller elements by providing materials that can be arranged in multiple patterns such as color tiles and cloth squares. Provide surprising objects such as books, markers, and shoes and challenge children to arrange them in pattern. Hands-on ordering of objects into patterns is a calming activity. It is also is important for developing connections in the brain. Children who self-generate knowledge through their own actions show better understanding of verbs and objects than those who only observe (James & Swain, 2011).

Explore patterns in dance and music. Read a poem or dance rhythmically, moving different body parts in repetitious ways, and follow the pattern by clapping or playing rhythm instruments. Listen for patterns in the words, melody, and rhythm in musical works. Clap and count the beats in a favorite song. Chart the patterns and rhythms using colors or shapes. For a responsive integrated music and visual arts activity, suggest that children record the song's pattern or create a new one by drawing invented symbols.

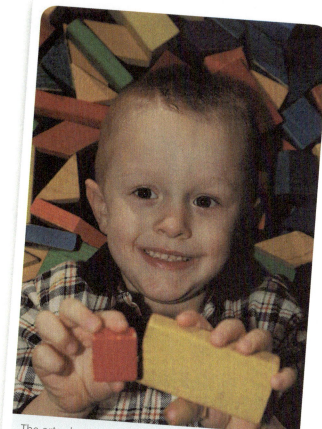

The arts elements are found in the clothes children wear and the toys they play with. We can find lines, shapes, colors, textures, forms, patterns, and spaces wherever we look.

Texture

Texture is the way something feels to the touch. Surfaces can be hard or soft, rough or smooth, or bumpy or jagged. Texture is found in all artwork and is an especially important element in collage and modeling activities. Texture plays a role in dramatic play as children dress up in costumes that can feel soft, rough, slippery, and so on against their skin.

We can both feel texture using tactile sensory perception and we can also see texture using visual sensory perception. Help children focus on the tactile qualities of their environment by inviting them to compare the textures of different items in the classroom or in the arts materials. To help develop focus, smooth the tips of an infant's fingers before inviting them to touch. Have older children rub their fingers together before touching a texture. Montessori programs prepare children for tactile discrimination

Providing contrasting textures for collages encourages children to compare and contrast the way the different tactile materials look and behave as they cut them and glue them down.

activities by having them dip their fingertips in warm water and blotting them dry before starting tactile discrimination tasks.

There are many open-ended tactile arts materials that allow children to create their own textures. They can fold and crumple paper, add different amounts of sand to paint, and press natural objects into pliant play dough and clay.

Feet can also explore textures. Check for safety and then allow children to walk on grass, gravel, sand, and cement. Dip into paint and make footprints. Collect carpet squares for children to arrange into textured areas to walk and dance on.

Many children do not have a rich vocabulary to describe the things they touch. Use words that describe textures as the children play and eat their snacks. Compare textures to things they have experienced, such as, "Oh, that's as wet as a rain puddle" or "This feels as soft as Alicia's bunny."

Form

Form is the three-dimensional quality of objects. Forms have height, width, and depth, such as found in spheres, pyramids, cubes, cylinders, and rectangular solids. Childhood physical handling and examination of many forms allow us as adults to recognize the nature of forms just by looking at them.

Forms are complex. They are not always the same on the back or on the bottom as they appear from the front. Point out examples of forms as part of other activities. Ask, "What form is your cup? What form is this block?" Use the correct geometrical term whenever possible, but also include comparisons to familiar objects to enhance understanding, such as, "Look, this rain stick is a cylinder just like our cylinder block, but much longer and fatter. Feel how round it is. See how far around your fingers can go around it. Let's get the block and feel the difference."

Active participation is essential in discovering three-dimensional qualities especially to counteract too much screen time. Block play and clay modeling activities are excellent ways for children to explore

Getting inside three-dimensional forms and crawling through them on the playground is a wonderful opportunity to learn about form and space. Follow up by asking the children questions about the sensory qualities of form and space.

and to create their own original complex forms and to invent their own way to describe them. Construction activities and papier-mâché also involve building in three dimensions. Develop stereognostic sensory perception skills by placing known objects in a touch bag or box for the child to feel and identify.

Creative movement activities allow children to discover the flexible form of their bodies. Encourage them to stretch and bend, to curl up, and lay down to change the forms of their bodies. Older children can create more complex body forms by working together with a partner to make cubes, spheres, and rectangular solids.

Space

Artists do not just see shapes and forms; they also see the **space** that surrounds them. This may be the empty space of the paper, the open spaces in a sculpture, or the silent rests in a musical composition. Space is an absence of elements that provides a quiet focus in the midst of color, form, texture, line, and pattern. Young children discover space when they look through a tube and see the view contained in a circle, peer through a hole poked in play dough, or clap at the moment when everyone else has stopped.

Because space is the absence of something, it is often invisible. Children need guidance in discovering the role of space in artistic creation. Bend arms and legs to touch the body and point out the openings they encompass. Hold hands with a partner and make bigger spaces. Show how the silent moments in a song (rests) are like holes or spaces. Construct clay sculptures and block structures that are full of holes. Use different objects, such as sticks and geometric-shaped cookie cutters, to form spaces you can see through in the clay. Explore how many and how big holes can be before the structure collapses. Make comments such as, "You have left a rectangular space in the middle of your painting," "You have made round spaces in your play dough. Can you see through them?," "Listen for the silent part in this song," and "Should you leave a big space between the blocks or a small one?"

Movement

Although **movement** is obvious in creative dance, all the arts are founded on movement. Visual art makes viewers track their eyes across the surface of the work. Dramatic works and stories move from introduction to climax. Music follows a similar sequence. Movement occupies space, takes time, and requires energy.

- *Space*—Movement can follow paths through space that are high, low, horizontal, vertical, and diagonal. They can consume the space or take very little.

- *Time*—Movement has speed and duration. It can range from slow to fast, brief to infinite. It can be rhythmic or arrhythmic.

- *Energy*—Movement can be fluid or sharp. It can flow gently like the melody of a lullaby or be as jerky as a puppet on a string. In the arts, energy most often comes from our bodies whether we are leaping across the room, wiggling a puppet on our finger, acting out a story, or dragging a marker across a piece of paper.

Because movement is so much a part of all the arts, it will be found in every arts activity. When talking about arts activities, try to describe the movement you are seeing. "You put a lot of energy into that high jump," "You are drawing a horizontal line across your page," "You are moving slowly just like the character in the story." Ask questions that help children discover the movements they are making. "Would a mouse make small movements or large ones?," "How is the music moving fast or slow?," and "Are you putting a lot of energy into your brush strokes?"

For more examples of arts elements activities, see *Arts Element Activities* on CourseMate.

Did You Get It?

Which of the following is a primary color?

a. green

b. yellow

c. purple

d. orange

Take the full quiz on CourseMate

How Can We Use Children's Literature?

Children's books are another way to engage children in sensory perception activities and develop focus and sustained attention. Almost any children's book can be used for a line or shape or color hunt. Name a shape that is used in one of the illustrations, and then ask the children to look for it as they listen to the story.

Look for other elements as well. Share stories about sounds, and tastes or that are filled with pictures with patterns, such as the books of Patricia Polacco. Introduce them to books that incorporate texture. Toddlers will enjoy any of the books available that contain actual textures to touch, such as the DK Publishing series *Baby Touch and Feel*. Older children can identify the different textures in the collages that illustrate many children's books such as Eric Carle's *The Grouchy Lady Bug* and then make collages of their own.

For more books incorporating sensory elements and related activities, see *The Annotated List of Children's Books* on CourseMate.

Making Books

Perhaps one of the best ways to incorporate books and sensory learning is to make your own book or have the children make books of their own. Individual or class books can be made that encourage children to use multiple senses.

A big book is the perfect size to read to a group of small children. The large pictures can be easily seen by everyone. However, you will not find big books on every topic you may need, nor will the books exactly fit your chosen activities. The ideal solution is to use your creativity and make your own incorporating hands on materials. Here are some examples to get you thinking.

Book on color. For example, in a book on color, feature a different color on each page. For each color, have children cut out a variety of shapes from different kinds of paper in that color. Write the color names in crayon and marker in that color. At the back of the book, attach an envelope containing shapes in each color. Invite the children to find the correct page for the "lost" shapes.

Book on pattern. For a book on pattern, use handprints, gadget or sponge prints made by the children to illustrate one or more of the following concepts:

- All patterns are made of repeated shapes.
- Some patterns are made from one repeated shape.
- Some patterns are made with two repeated shapes.
- Some patterns are made with three or more repeated shapes.
- Some patterns are made in only one color.
- Some patterns have lots of colors.
- Some patterns are made of different-sized shapes.

Use yarn to attach samples of the gadget objects used to make the prints to the book. Invite children to match them to the patterns, or if using handprints, have them match their hands.

Book on line. For a book on lines, have children use marker, crayon, or paint to draw different kinds of lines on each page. Some lines to include are straight, curved, zigzag, jagged, thick, and thin. Try to have each line be a continuation of the one on the previous page. On the last page, put all of the different lines together in a wild line "party." Invite children to follow the lines with their fingers.

Book on sound. Create a book of sound clues. Have children draw things that make sounds on each page and label each "How does _____ sound?" Read

Children's books show children how sensory and artistic elements can be applied to tell a story.

the book by making the appropriate sounds. Or for a more hands-on experience, attach sound makers to each page using ribbon or yarn. (See Reflection Page 15 for more big book topics.)

Conclusion:
The Sensitive Teacher

The sensory perception activities presented in this chapter may seem different from more "traditional" arts activities for young children. Some of them may cross into other curriculum areas; others do not use the expected materials. Nevertheless, these explorations, which start with the newborn child, form the basis of how children learn about their world.

It is our job to create an environment that welcomes exploration, is full of wonderful open-ended experiences, allows children to gain pleasure as they

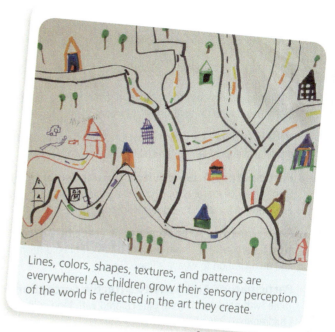

Lines, colors, shapes, textures, and patterns are everywhere! As children grow their sensory perception of the world is reflected in the art they create.

Copyright © 2015 Cengage Learning®

use their senses, and rewards children for using their natural learning style.

We must bring excitement and enthusiasm to the classroom daily. We must be open to the sensory wonders that surround us—the pattern of the raindrops on the windowpane, the rainbow in the spilled oil in a puddle, the warm fur of a kitten—and share these with children. If we visualize ourselves as enthusiastic nurturers of young artists' sensory development then the objects, materials, and experiences we provide will make every day special for a young child.

For additional information about sensory learning and the elements of the arts visit, see *Chapter 4 Online Resources* on CourseMate.

Teaching In Action

SAMPLE PLANS FOR A CELEBRATORY PRESENTATION

FESTIVAL OF LINES: A SENSORY CELEBRATION FOR TODDLERS AND THEIR FAMILIES

Location: The playground

Time: 2:00 to 4:00 P.M.

Welcome Table: Program and map; painted or paper streamer lines for visitors to follow to the different activities.

Art Display (visual perception): Children's drawings and paintings with associated dictation.

Photography Display (visual perception): Photographs of children involved in the activities.

Interactive Arts Display (visual and tactile perception): Children's paintings with a set of brushes hung

(continued)

Teaching In Action *(continued)*

on string. Participants are invited to match and trace the lines in the painting with the brush that created them.

Video (visual perception): Creative movement and music activities featuring the children are shown.

Participatory Arts Activity 1 (visual perception): Large sheet of mural paper, baskets of colorful markers, and an invitation to add some original lines.

Participatory Arts Activity 2 (tactile perception): Partner loom is set up with a basket of colorful yarn and an invitation to weave a line.

Participatory Arts Activity 3 (tactile perception): Table with paper and white glue colored with food coloring. Children make glue lines.

Participatory Arts Activity 4 (visual perception and math integration): Children's paintings are interspersed with bold graphics showing different kinds of lines. Participants are asked to find the total number of each kind of line visible in the paintings. A box and coupons are provided for the guesses. At the end of the celebration, names will be drawn to receive door prizes.

Puppet Show: The show put on by parents with help from the children features a simple tale about a magic string, based on the book *Billy and the Magic String* (Karnovsky, 1995).

Demonstration 1 (visual and tactile perception): A handspinner demonstrates how wool is turned into yarn. She gives pieces of yarn to participants to use on a partner loom.

Demonstration 2 (visual and tactile): Basket weaver creates willow baskets, surrounded by a display of photographs showing examples of lines in nature. Families and children can arrange willow branches in a pattern on a large sheet of paper.

Demonstration 3 (auditory): Washtub instrument and cardboard and rubber band "guitars." Families and children can try making different tones by changing length of strings.

Measurement Table (visual perception and math integration): Volunteers measure a length of string that is the height of each participant and tape it to a graph.

Musical Entertainment (auditory perception): Harp player and/or string players.

Dance (visual-spatial perception): A parent volunteer teaches families line dancing.

Refreshments (gustatory and olfactory perception): Foods that resemble lines (pretzel sticks, liquorice sticks, breadsticks, carrot sticks and curls, spaghetti).

Reflection Page

Reviewing Sensory Perception

Define each of the sensory perception areas and give an example of an open-ended activity that will develop skill in that area.

Visual perception	Gustatory perception
Auditory perception	Olfactory perception
Tactile Perception	Thermic perception
Baric perception	Stereognostic perception

Reflection Page

Selecting Sensory Objects, Materials, and Experiences

Choose a place such as your home, backyard, a park, or a store. Make a list of things that have interesting sensory qualities. Next to each item, record what sense or senses it will stimulate. Think of how you would introduce the item to young children and write down one or two things you would say to alert the child to its sensory qualities.

Sensory Item	Sense Stimulated	Rich Verbal Interaction

Review your list. Which ones are suitable for infants, toddlers, preschoolers, or primary children? Choose one item and write a two-part sensory perceptual objective for it. (See Appendix B for directions.)

Sensory perceptually—the child will . . .

_____

_____

_____

_____

I will know this is happening when I observe the child . . .

_____

_____

_____

_____

_____

_____

_____

Reflection Page

Designing A Big Book That Entices the Senses

A big book is the perfect size to read to a group of small children. The large pictures can be easily seen by everyone. However, you will not find big books on every topic you may need, nor will the books exactly fit the needs of your children. The ideal solution is to use your creativity and make your own or with older children have them make them.

Guidelines for Creating a Big Book that Entices the Senses

1. Select one of the senses.

2. Limit the book to five or six one-sided pages.

3. Use just a few words.

4. Illustrations should be made using materials that spark the senses.

5. Illustrations should be large, bold, and simple. Avoid cute, stereotypical, or cartoon-like drawings. Better yet have the children help make the pictures.

6. Plan the book so the children can interact with it. For example, include pockets that contain hidden shapes or holes to look through.

7. Make the pages from heavy oak tag, poster board, or corrugated cardboard. Join the pages with metal, loose-leaf rings.

Suggested Subjects for Your Big Book

Colors	Sounds Around Us	Things We Taste
Patterns	Textures	Smells We Like
Shapes	Things to Look At	Things to Touch

Reflection Page

Observation: A Sensory Experience

Choose one of the senses, and design a sensory experience for children. Present the activity to two or three children, and record what the children do.

Date of observation: _____   **Length of observation:** _____

Ages of children: _____   **Size of group:** _____

1. Describe the sensory stimulus and what you said.

   _____

   _____

   _____

2. What is the first thing the children do? How long do the children investigate the activity?

   _____

   _____

   _____

3. What do the children say?

   _____

   _____

   _____

4. Analysis: Using the information in this chapter and what you learned from the observation, defend the inclusion of sensory arts activities in an early childhood setting.

   _____

   _____

   _____

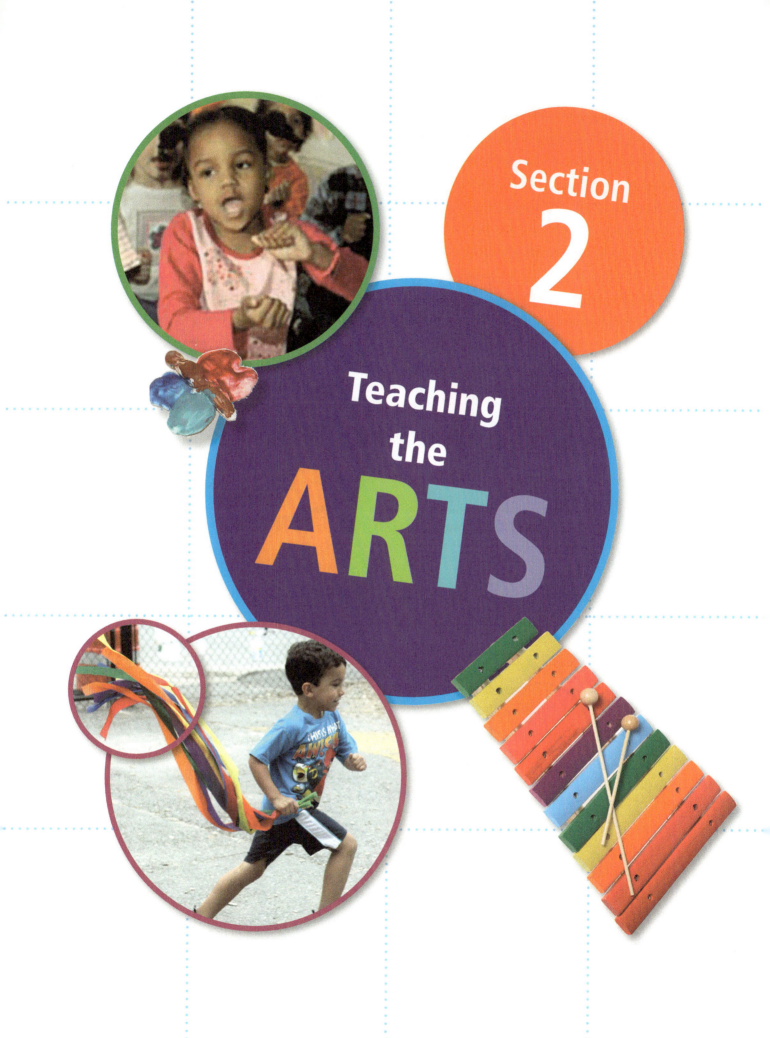

Section

2

Teaching the ARTS

Chapter

5

Coming Together Through the Arts

Copyright © 2015 Cengage Learning®

Select arts activities that develop children's abilities to work with others in joyful classroom communities.

Plan arts activities that develop social-emotional skills.

Creating a Caring Community

Planning Curriculum to Achieve Important Goals

Coming Together Through the Arts DAP Learning Objectives

Establishing Reciprocal Family Relationships

Assessing Children's Development and Learning

Teaching to Enhance Development and Learning

Evaluate the social-emotional developmental needs of all children.

Explain ways to use the arts to form reciprocal relationships.

Identify ways to develop cooperative behavior, nurture cultural respect, and address special needs.

Young Artists Creating

"Your monkey has really long legs."

"So does yours."

"That's because he's trying to climb up this tree."

"My person is up in the air. He's jumping. You need long legs to do that."

"Yep. My monkey is going to jump when he gets to the top of the tree."

"Oops, the paint is dripping."

"Hurry. Catch it before it runs over Sari's picture."

"Sari will be mad if the paint drips on her dog."

"You are working hard on your paintings for our mural," says the teacher. "I see that you have used two different sizes of brushes."

"Yes, I used Mandie's little brush to paint the buttons, and she used my big brush to paint the long, long legs."

"See," says the teacher, "When we share things, we have more choices of things to use in our art."

How Can Young Artists Work Together?

Some of the most joyful arts experiences children can have are those in which they work in a group to create something great together—a mural, a box robot, a musical revue, or an original dance. Working together for a common purpose forges children into a group. It becomes "our mural," "our robot," "our songs," or "our dance." It is not surprising that so many of the "class-building activities" of cooperative learning programs are based in the arts. It is easy to incorporate the ideas and skill levels of each individual into an arts activity. Using themes and providing opportunities for arts projects are other ways to foster social-emotional development and promote group bonding.

Developing Social-Emotional Skills

Social-emotional skills are the basis of rich, rewarding human relationships and an important focus in the early childhood classroom. Research with preschool children indicates that strong social-emotional learning profiles are associated with high social and academic performance ratings (Denham et al., 2012). For example, preschoolers with a high level of social-emotional control have been shown to have higher academic performance in first grade (Neubauer et al., 2012; Walker & Henderson, 2012).

Social-emotional skills include:

- **Confidence.** Being able to recognize our emotions, to understand how emotions affect our thoughts and actions, and to perceive ourselves in positive and realistic ways. Children's beliefs about themselves are influenced by their positive and negative experiences with the adults around them, and the way their culture, social class, religion, and gender are treated (Schiller, 2009).

- **Self-control.** Being able to control our feelings and actions so we can focus full attention on a task, particularly in stressful situations. Self-regulation is strongly associated with adjustment to school, cognitive competence, and positive classroom behavior (Allan & Lonegan, 2011; Garner & Waajid, 2012; Neuenschwander et al., 2012).

- **Empathy.** The ability to recognize and identify with the feelings of others, to trust others, and to

The arts provide time and space for children to learn to work with each other in joyful ways.

Copyright © 2015 Cengage Learning®

find joy in engaging with them. We are all born with the capacity for empathy. Infants show sensitivity to others at birth, crying in concern when another baby cries (Goleman, 2009), and the part of the brain that feels pain reacts when a child sees another in pain (Willis, 2012). But like creativity, empathy needs to be nourished. Children who have difficulty understanding and responding to the feelings of others are less stable emotionally and less popular (Panfile & Laible, 2012). Lack of empathy and not caring about others is strongly linked to bullying behaviors (Kokkinos & Kipritsi, 2012).

Cooperation. Being able to communicate our thoughts and feelings, to work well with others, and to manage social conflict in effective ways. Taking turns, sharing, and helping others are the keystones to better school adjustment and later success in the workplace.

The Arts and Social-Emotional Development

As children mature, their ability to control their behavior and interact effectively with others increases. However, not all children proceed at the same rate. Some children may struggle to focus and wait. Others may have difficulty recognizing the feelings of others and sharing. Children with physical disabilities or who have suffered trauma may lack the ability to communicate their own feelings or to interact effectively with others. Bullying, eating disorders, depression, delinquency, and other problems are associated with poor social-emotional skills often stemming from early childhood (Goleman, 2007, 2009).

Direct teaching of social-emotional skills by integrating them into daily teaching makes a difference

Teacher Tip

STAGES OF SOCIAL PLAY

Regardless of their age, children exhibit different levels of play depending not only on their social and cognitive development, but also on their previous experiences interacting with others. Observing how children play by themselves and with others can give us a better idea of their social skills.

Observing: The child watches others playing. This might be found in an infant who is not yet physically capable of joining in or in a child who is new to a group.

Solitary play: The child plays by him- or herself. The level of play can range from very simple, such as shaking a toy, to intense, focused imaginary play.

Parallel play: The child plays alongside another child, perhaps with very similar toys, but the children do not interact with each other. Parallel play usually begins around the ages of two to three years.

Cooperative play: Children play together first in pairs and then in larger groups. In cooperative play children develop language skills as they communicate ideas, needs, and desires. They develop social skills as they learn to share, come to agreement, and take group action. Cooperative play usually appears around the ages of three to four years.

Organized play: The ability to participate in games that have rules and winners, such as board games and sports, occurs slowly. It begins to develop around the ages of six to seven, but is most fully developed in eight- and nine-year-olds.

(Willis & Schiller, 2011). The arts provide a fertile ground for doing so because of the natural way they fit into children's play. When activities are creative and open-ended they allow safe risk taking, provide opportunities to express feelings and strengthen self-confidence. Depending on the age of the child and the type of play the child is involved in, there are many ways we can foster social-emotional development through the arts.

Infants. Babies begin life totally self-centered. For example, infants know when they are hungry and demand to be fed regardless of the time of day or night. But as infants mature they slowly become aware that they are separate individuals and show increasing awareness of other people around them. Newborn infants, for example, have been shown to look longer at faces with eyes open than closed, as well as at those with a direct gaze as opposed to those looking toward the side (Bower, 2002). Starting at two to three weeks, infants imitate adult facial expressions and hand movements with increasing sophistication (Bower, 2003). Most of the play of infants is **solitary play** or **observing** the play of others.

Erik Erikson (1963), in his classic analysis of children's social-emotional development, characterizes this period as one in which infants learn to trust other people. With attentive loving care from their caregivers, they will come to see other people as important companions and resources as they explore their world. It is not surprising, therefore, that the arts play a vital role in developing infants' social skills. Singing and moving together, looking at pictures in a book, and engaging in pretend play with a more knowledgeable peer or adult help infants learn how to explore and create joyfully in an atmosphere of trust.

Toddlers. Children from about eighteen months to three years are, according to Erikson, in the stage of autonomy versus shame and doubt. Toddlers want to be independent and in control, but cling to their caregiver when faced with new stimuli. They may see a toy they want and nothing short of physical restraint will prevent them from grabbing it from another child, or they may hide behind an adult when the booming drums pass by in a parade.

Toddlers work best in situations where they can pursue their arts explorations under the watchful eyes of caregivers. Adults can promote social growth by providing activities in which toddlers can work alongside others but have their own materials and space. Setting up activities in which two toddlers or a toddler and an older child are painting at adjoining easels or are smashing playdough together helps toddlers learn that they can work in close proximity to other children. Toddlers often engage in **parallel play** in which they imitate the actions of a child sitting near them (Einon, 1985). Imitation is one of the ways that children learn skills and behaviors. Adults and other children serve as artistic role models for the young child. One child will begin to pound the clay, and another child will imitate the same action. One child will see another shaking a tambourine and will demand one, too.

Preschoolers. By the age of three, children are beginning to play together in **cooperative play.** They will take on roles in pretend play and will work together to build a tower. At this stage children can work together on all kinds of arts projects, from accompanying a song with handmade instruments to painting a mural. They become enraptured by the excitement of the collective moment and yet are interested in and "see" only the part they personally created. Group arts activities for these children, therefore, do not have the same meaning as those designed for older children and adults in which ideas are arrived at jointly and the project is viewed as a whole. Young preschoolers develop confidence by working on projects that do not have definite end goals but instead allow each child to play an individual part in the process.

Playing side by side and watching each other is one way infants learn social-emotional skills.

Kindergartners. When children gain the ability to value and differentiate their own products from those of others, their **cooperative play** becomes more complex. They can start to see that each contribution is a part of something larger—a whole—that is different from each small part but is still partially theirs. Teachers can tell when children reach this stage, because they start to notice the artwork of the other children and will comment, "That is my friend's painting," or "That is Cheri's," when referring to a piece of art they see. They use the terms "we did" instead of "I did" when referring to group projects like "We put on a puppet show" or "we're floating like astronauts." They can identify who created the different parts of a project or played different roles. When children reach this stage, they are ready for more cooperative group activities in which each child works on a designated part of the project, sharing supplies or space.

Primary age. By this age children are capable of planning ahead of time what will be needed to accomplish their goal and which part of the project they will work on. At the stage of **organized play** groups begin to set tasks, make schedules, and assign jobs to group members. However, they may still need adult guidance in learning how to incorporate the ideas of each member in a gracious way.

Primary students, who are busy learning about the broader world, enjoy working on long-term projects that involve a common idea, such as turning the classroom into a rainforest complete with a painted mural background, life-size painted animals and paper trees and bushes, accompanied by authentic Brazilian rhythms played on handmade instruments. They can perform parts in a play they have written, enjoy choral reading and group singing, learn folk dances together, and perform in small instrumental groups.

Did You Get It?

If you were to plan arts activities based on Erikson's analysis of social-emotional development, which of the following would you suggest for toddlers?

a. Ensure that toddlers work on artistic activities alone.

b. Make two toddlers sit together and share materials and space.

c. Expect toddlers to cooperate with other members of a group.

d. Have toddlers work individually in close proximity with others

Take the full quiz on CourseMate

How Do We Create a Positive Social-Emotional Climate Through the Arts?

As with creativity, social-emotional skills flourish in an environment where children feel self-confident, where they are relaxed, and where they feel secure. A positive social climate develops when children feel that their ideas and feelings are accepted and valued. Qualities such as verbal encouragement, modeling empathy, using emotionally expressive language, and showing emotional warmth to each child have been shown to increase confidence, self-control, empathy, and cooperativeness (Spivak & Farran, 2012).

We model acceptance by giving appropriate time, attention, and assistance to every child. The open-ended nature of the creative arts provides the perfect setting to do this. While engaged in arts activities, we can develop social-emotional skills by:

- Modeling self-control by remaining calm and showing patience in trying situations.

▶⏸ TeachSource Video Case 5.1

2–5 Years: Play in Early Childhood

Watch this video showing children at different stages of play. What arts activities would you select for them to foster social-emotional skills?

Watch on CourseMate

- Communicating confidence and empathy by using words like we, us, ours, caring, and sharing on a daily basis.

- Providing opportunities to practice self-control and cooperative skills by offering arts activities that inspire children to want to work together.

- Giving positive feedback when children show confidence, act kindly, wait patiently, and share.

- Asking reflective questions such as: Are the children working joyfully? Are they aware of each other's needs?

Using Positive Guidance to Promote Appropriate Behavior

Working together requires children to exert self-control. Groups of children involved in well-designed arts activities are usually so engrossed that behavioral issues do not play a large role. However, there will always be occasions when children overstep the boundaries of safety and propriety. Responding to inappropriate behavior during arts activities requires a gentle approach that addresses the behavior without restricting creativity nor crushing self-confidence. You can foster safe, creative behavior in three ways: **prevention, redirection,** and **removal.**

Prevention.

1. Offer only those activities, props, materials, and tools appropriate for the child's skill level.

2. Keep materials and tools not on the child's skill level out of reach and out of sight.

3. Provide each child with adequate space in which to work and move. Dangerous behavior often happens when children accidentally bump or push each other.

4. Provide sufficient supplies to prevent the children from grabbing for that one special item.

5. Closely supervise the children while they work, especially during initial explorations of new materials and tools.

6. Keep group sizes small until the children know how to work safely with a particular technique, material, or tool.

7. Keep arts supplies, musical instruments, and dramatic play materials orderly so that children do not have to dig or grab for what they want. Be sure there is sufficient open space for creative movement.

8. Model safe movement and handling of tools and supplies at all times.

Redirection.

1. If a child begins to act or to use something unsafely, gently restate the safe way to act or use it, and model the correct behavior, if necessary. For example, if the child puts playdough up to her mouth, say, "Playdough is not food, we use it to make art."

2. Older children can be asked to restate or read the rules or the directions given for the activity.

Integrating the Arts

COMMUNITY BUILDING THROUGH THE ARTS

Drama and movement activities can be used to help children get to know one another better and strengthen the class community. Here are some examples.

Name Game. Sit in a circle and have the children call out their names. Repeat having the children call out their names in a new way each time—using a different "voice," adding a movement, showing an emotion, or making a funny face.

Greeting Each Other. Provide two greeting words, such as *hi* and *bye*. Have the children move around and greet each other. Repeat, adding a movement or singing the greeting.

What Happened? Have the children sit in a circle. Ask the first child, "What did you do when _____?" adding an appropriate phrase, such as when you woke up, or when you met a new friend. That child then turns and asks the one sitting next to him or her the same question. Continue around the circle. When children are familiar with the game, try some fantasy phrases, such as "What did you do when your house started dancing?"

Watch Me. Stand so that everyone can see everyone else. The leader mimes a brief action, such as meeting someone and shaking hands. The whole group copies the action. The leader then points to another child to be the leader who mimes a new action. Vary the activity by adding a sound to go with the action or mime the next logical step.

For more group building activities, see *Community Building Arts Activities* **on CourseMate.**

With gentle guidance from the teacher, sharing space and materials can help children learn how to work together.

3. If two children want the same supply or tool, provide other similar ones or help them set up a fair way to share it.

Removal.

1. When a child's behavior is developmentally appropriate and not unsafe, but annoying to the other children, such as when a toddler draws on other children's papers, gently move the child to a place slightly away from the others but too far away to reach someone else's workspace. Put the move in a positive light by saying, "You will have more space to draw over here."

2. If a child persists in unsafe behavior, redirect her or him to another activity that is more appropriate for that behavior. For example, if a child is snapping the scissors open and closed, explain that the scissors are too sharp to be used that way, but that she can open and close the toy pliers. Remove the scissors, and replace with the pliers.

3. When it is obvious that the activity, tools, or materials are inappropriate for the developmental level of the children, redirect them to another interesting activity, and then remove those supplies. Just because a particular activity may be recommended for children of a certain age or has been successful for others does not mean that it will be perfect for these particular children. It is better to say that this is not working and end it, than to set up a potentially dangerous situation or one that will cause children to misbehave.

Did You Get It?

In which of the following cases is a teacher using a redirection strategy to foster a desired behavior in students?

a. Sara arranges for the toddlers in her class to work together in groups and share materials.

b. Manuel teaches his class an action song and has them mimic the actions.

c. Tyra sees Michelle grab a drumstick from the child next to her so she moves Michelle to a place on the rug away from the other children.

d. Leanna observes Carla scribbling on the table and records it on her behavior chart.

Take the full quiz on CourseMate

How Should Group Arts Activities Be Organized?

Although each child needs to explore the arts in a personally meaningful way, children also need to discover that the arts are not just for individual self-expression. This is best learned by participating in arts experiences as a member of a group. Open-ended creative arts group projects allow children at different ages and skill levels to work together to create something uniquely different from what they would create on their own. When carefully planned, we can participate in many of these activities alongside our children. Great satisfaction is felt when we are part of a successful group arts activity.

Group art activities directly address social-emotional learning. Working with others means children have to control their feelings as they share space, time, and materials with others who have different abilities and needs from their own. Children become more understanding of others' special needs and more appreciative of the creative ideas of those whose background and cultural experiences differ from their own.

Accomplishing this requires the creation of an integrated cohesive unit in which both children and teacher smoothly work together. The challenge of good teaching is to take a group of unique, ever-changing individuals with different levels of social-emotional skills and turn them into a caring community.

We set the stage for group arts activities that are fun, flexible, relaxed, and based on a shared experience when we

Make it fun. Include an element of fun when working together. Songs, laughter, and excitement should all be part of the experience.

Are flexible and open to innovation. It is the group experience that is important, not the finished product. Value spontaneity and be willing to change course. Avoid the trap of planning an end use for the cooperative project before it is started or having children practice lines of a play over and over for a formal performance.

Are facilitators. The teacher's role in a group arts project is to be the guide, not the director. Provide the location, the materials, the excitement, and the beginning of an idea; then let the participants take over. In many activities teachers can participate themselves! The result will be a true expression of each individual's creative moment as a part of that group, at that time, and in that place.

Reduce stress. Well-designed group arts activities can provide an excellent way to introduce children to working in a group. However, it is important that children be familiar with the art form and materials to be used in the project and that they have had practice experiences with them. A group activity is not the place to explore something for the first time, but instead provides an opportunity to take pride in using a skill and creating something that requires a level of comfort and control. It is also vital that these projects be designed as open-ended activities, so that every child can participate fully.

Provide a shared experience. For preschoolers and up, a collective activity needs to start out with everyone in the group sharing an experience (WOW). This common experience will combine the ideas and actions of each child into a unified whole. The experience should be one in which children participate directly, otherwise they will come to rely on stereotypes and teachers' examples rather than thinking on their own.

The shared experience forms the basis for planning and carrying out murals, creative dances, original songs and music, dramatic play centers, and group sculptures. For example, after a trip to the zoo, children share what they saw, and the teacher makes a class chart of their observations. That chart then becomes the source of ideas for what children will put in their re-creation of a zoo in their classroom.

The shared experience can be the following:

1. a field trip

2. an event that occurs, such as rain, snow, or a parade

3. observation of something real, such as nature objects, animals, machines, or a store

4. reading a story or poem together

5. a class project topic

Some examples of shared experiences and related arts activities include

- Walking in the rain and then making a drip paint mural

- Looking at tire tracks in the mud or snow and then dipping the wheels of toy cars and trucks in paint and rolling them over a big sheet of paper.

- Visiting a flower shop and then making a flower store dramatic play area

Encourage peer modeling. Because imitation is one way that children learn new skills, slightly more advanced peers provide better models for young children than adults, whose skills may be far greater than children need or are capable of imitating. Working together on a group arts project provides the perfect opportunity for children to learn from one another.

Organizing Group Arts Activities

Select activities that each individual, no matter his or her ability level, can participate in fairly equally.

Group size. Group size is a critical factor in determining if children will work together successfully. At the Reggio Emilia preprimary schools the teachers have found that different group sizes create different dynamics. For example, pairs of children engage in intense social and cognitive interactions. The addition of a third child can produce solidarity, but also conflict. Groups of four and five have other dynamics (Edwards, Gandini, & Forman, 2011). A general rule should be: the younger the children, the smaller the group.

Mixed age and ability groups. Groups that contain a range of ages actually offer one of the best settings in which to develop cooperative arts behaviors. The older children and adults can model respect for each other's work and at the same time supervise the more impulsive little ones.

1. Have members of the group take turns working in pairs or in groups of three. Pair a more expert peer with one who has less experience. The older members should help the younger ones find a place to work and materials to use.

2. In the visual arts allow the youngest group members to go first, because older members will be able to work around one another, whereas the young children may not "see" the work already there and may work on top of it. In the performance arts, the older ones should go first to provide role models for the younger ones.

Arts activities provide a way for groups of children to interact creatively. Using their imaginations, this group of kindergartners turn themselves into a rock band using blocks and rhythm instruments.

Examples of Group Arts Activities

Types of group arts activities are found in all the arts areas and are limited only by our imaginations. A few ideas are listed as follows. Find more in the Exploring Arts section of this book.

Drum circle. Starting with a shared experience such as rain drumming on the roof, the rumble of a train or traffic passing by, or the sound of their feet running on the pavement, give each child a hand drum or show them how they can make different drumming sounds by patting their upper arms, thighs, chests, or the floor. Sit in a circle and start tapping a rhythm. Go around the circle and have each child lead with a new rhythm. With practice this can be accomplished without a break in the drumming.

Group sculptures. When many hands contribute to an artwork, incredible energy results. Group sculptures make lively activities for mixed-age groups. Even the youngest child can be helped to place a part on a group sculpture. Group sculptures can be simple and immediate. For example, children on the playground can collect stones or sticks and arrange them into a design on the pavement. Wood scraps collected as part of a visit to a carpenter's shop or trip to a lumberyard can become an amazing structure.

Group sculptures can be built from any easily handled and joined three-dimensional material. Try boxes, paper bags stuffed with newspaper, chenille stems, straws, wooden blocks, corrugated cardboard, telephone wire, or Styrofoam packing material.

Just like all group arts activities, constructions need to grow out of a shared experience. For example, visit a sculpture garden, and then come back and build a class sculpture out of corrugated cardboard. If children are using straws or toothpicks in a counting activity, finish by having the children glue them together into a linear sculpture using a piece of Styrofoam for a base. Walk through the neighborhood and identify different buildings. Then build a model of the community using boxes or pieces of wood.

As children work, encourage them to consider how their part will go with the rest. Describe the work

Making Plans

OPEN-ENDED ACTIVITY FEELING FACES GROUP ACTIVITY

WHO?   Group composition age(s): Suitable for toddlers and up

WHEN?   Time frame: Depending on age, children will work from 20 minutes to several days.

WHY?   Objectives: Children will develop

- physically, by using the large muscles of the arm and the small muscles of the hand to manipulate the various art materials and the muscles of the face to make different expressions. (Bodily-Kinesthetic)
- socially, by interacting with a caring adult, and by sharing materials, space, and ideas with others. (Interpersonal)
- emotionally, by examining their own feelings and those of others in a pleasurable stress-free setting. (Intrapersonal)
- perceptually, by using their senses to observe and select materials for their faces and arranging the faces spatially on a background in concert with others. (Spatial)
- language skills, by using words they know and learning new ones to describe their emotions and those of others. (Linguistic)
- cognitively, by classifying facial features by emotional expression (Logical-Mathematical)
- arts awareness, by manipulating the elements of color and shape to create an expressive face. (Content Standard 1 & 2)

WHERE?   Setup: On a rug for a large group. At table for a small group. One-on-one for special needs.

WHAT?   Materials: Markers or crayons, colored papers in different skin colors (white paper plates can be used if children paint them skin tones first), yarn and white glue, large hand mirror(s) (unbreakable), a long sheet of kraft paper long enough for everyone to add at least one face. Chart paper. For extensions: Clippings of faces from magazines, tubes, or cardboard strips.

HOW?   Procedure:
WOW Warm-Up: Hold up a mirror and make faces in it. Explore and name different emotions. Let children take turns looking in mirrors and making faces. Ask: "How do our mouth, eyebrows, eyes, and nose look when we feel happy or sad?" and so on.

What to Do and Say: Name feelings that go with different expressions. Encourage children to mirror expressions as you talk about the feelings. For toddlers and up, build emotional literacy by starting a Ways I Feel list including not only pleasant feelings and angry ones, but also neutral feelings like calm, patient, and comfortable (Adams, 2011). For toddlers, provide face-shaped paper in skin tones and let them draw eyes, noses, and mouths. For older children, put out materials at the art center and invite children to create faces showing different feelings using the yarn for hair. When done have children sit together in a group with their faces and take turns gluing them to the long paper to create a mural about feelings. Make cartoon "word bubbles" and have children share what their face is saying.

Transition out: Look at the mural with the children. For younger children, ask them to name the different feelings they see. For older ones discuss places where you see large groups of people, such as at a sporting event, a parade, or a circus. Imagine where your "crowd of faces" might be. Ask: At those events does everybody all feel the same? If there is space, invite children to add more faces when they wish.

WHAT LEARNED?   Assessment: Can the children name more feelings after the activity? Do they change the mouths and eyes to show different feelings? When they see another child showing a feeling, can they identify it, and are they more empathetic? Do they use more words about feelings in their play? Do they share materials and space fairly? What feelings are expressed most easily? Which ones are left out? Which feelings were the most difficult to express? *Reflection:* Do I see any expressions of bias? What did the children learn from this activity? What activity should be offered next and why?

NEXT?   Extensions: **Stick puppets**: Encourage them to make more faces. They can add a cardboard stick or tube to a face and use their stick puppet to tell stories about feelings. **Literature connection:** Read stories that show children struggling with their feelings such as *When Sophie Gets Angry, Really Really Angry* by Molly Bangs (2004) or Jamie Lee Curtis' *Today I Feel Silly* (1998).

as it changes with each addition: "Look, it's getting taller." Respond positively to each child's contribution: "Your piece helps make it stronger."

Mosaics. Because a mosaic is a work of art made from small pieces glued to a cardboard or piece of wood to create a picture or shapes, it is eminently suitable for group arts projects with young children. A wide variety of objects can be used ranging from stones to leaves to cancelled stamps to Styrofoam packing peanuts. Collecting the objects and sorting them by color or shape can be the shared experience from which a mosaic can grow.

Murals. The word **mural,** although technically defined as a "wall painting," in literature on children's art, usually refers to a very large, two-dimensional piece of artwork created by a group of children. That is the definition used here. Murals are ideal group projects for children and adults of all ages. They can either be created on the spot in response to an exciting experience, or carefully planned in response to a field trip, study topic, or piece of literature.

Any number of children can contribute to a mural as long as the background is big enough. Do not hesitate to add to the background or to create several murals at the same time, if necessary. Murals enable children of different levels and abilities to work together successfully. One toddler can work with an older child or adult. Preschoolers can work in groups of three and four. Primary students can work in groups of four to six.

Quilts. Quilts are ideal for creating a sense of belonging and fit perfectly into teaching units about family and community. Show a finished quilt as the initial shared experience, and if possible, tell the story of how it came to be made. Read a book about quilts such as Anne Jonas' *The Quilt* (1984) or, for older children, Valerie Flournoy's *The Patchwork Quilt* (1985). Children's families can be asked to contribute a square of fabric or help decorate a square of muslin with crayon drawings or with fabric shapes attached with iron on facing. Sewn together the quilt can be used in the story corner or dramatic play areas to soften surroundings and provide comfort. Paper versions of quilts can also be made.

Shared experiences lay the groundwork for successful group activities. After reading the book *Where the Wild Things Are* by Maurice Sendak, a group of children aged four to seven created this mural, working together to paint a night sky background and then adding their own imaginative "wild things" which they drew, cut out, and glued to the background.

Rhythm Band. Following a shared experience such as watching a band in a parade or listening to recorded band music, create your own band. Making noise together is a wonderful opportunity for children to practice self-control and cooperation. After children choose their sound maker, teach them a simple hand signal for starting and stopping. Practice following the signals for starting and stopping together. Once they know how, have children take turns conducting the band. When everyone is playing together, try marching around the school.

For more ideas for group arts activities, *see Shared Experiences and Group Arts Activities* on CourseMate.

Teachers Working Together

Educators also benefit from working alongside their peers. Teaching is often seen as an individual affair. We need to meet often with our peers to share ideas and frustrations. Projects are easier to plan when there are two or three minds brainstorming. We need to involve parents as partners in our programs. Foot painting, creative dancing, and nature collages are easier to manage when there are extra hands. Everyone needs to come together in order to grow together. The program will be richer, and the young artists will show more growth.

CAPTURE THE PROCESS

When engaged in group art projects, remember to record the process. Digital cameras, smartphones, and tablets are exciting supplements to more hands-on methods.

- **Draw it:** Encourage children to make drawings showing the sequence of steps they went through. Clarissa Willis and Pam Schiller, for example, recommend developing self-confidence by asking a child who has succeeded at a challenging task draw a picture of the experience and put it on a wall labeled "I did it" (2011, p. 42).

- **Record it:** Take notes or record what children say during the process. For group-created visual artworks display or play a recording of the children's own words next to the finished piece. For music, drama, and creative dance, display photographs with their words as captions.

- **Capture it:** Take photographs and make video recordings as they work.

- **Reflect on it:** Record the children's description of what they did on an **experience chart,** in a documentation panel, or in e-story form or PowerPoint.

Did You Get It?

Which of the following would you use as a guideline for organizing a group activity?

a. The teacher should plan an end use for the cooperative project before initiating it.

b. The teacher's role should be to guide and not direct.

c. The teacher should not participate in group events.

d. A general rule should be the younger the children, the larger the group.

Take the full quiz on CourseMate

How Are Children with Special Needs Included in the Arts Program?

Because of the open-ended nature of well-designed arts activities, children with special needs can participate fully in most arts programs and group arts activities, often without many modifications. If necessary, changes can be made in the tools and environment to allow active participation. The other children also need to be encouraged to accept and support those with special needs.

Defining Special Needs

Children with special needs are a tremendously diverse group. Some have obvious disabilities, and others have disabilities that cannot be seen by the casual observer. The **Individuals with Disabilities Act** (Public Law 105–17) has identified ten categories of children who can receive special education services. These include children with learning disabilities, speech and language disabilities, mental retardation, emotional disturbance, multiple disabilities, autism, hearing disabilities, visual disabilities, orthopedic disabilities, and other health disabilities.

In addition, the law mandates that children with disabilities be educated in the least restrictive environment. As a result of this law, many children with disabilities will be found in regular educational settings (Heward, 2000). This has led to many inclusion programs for young children in which special provisions are made so that all children can achieve success.

Meeting Special Needs

Because children with special needs have unique developmental paths, inclusive early childhood programs need to focus on ways to help them become engaged in learning and in interacting socially with peers. Many of the techniques suggested for working with mixed ages and abilities will also help children with special needs be successful.

Select open-ended activities. Exploratory arts activities, which entice children with colors, textures, sounds, movements, and unexpected results, and which can be done alongside peers who are also exploring, can be vital to this process. Arts activities provide an opportunity for children to apply skills needed for further development. Grasping a marker or paintbrush prepares a child for holding a pencil for writing. Pushing and pulling playdough strengthens finger, hand, and arm muscles. Playing a xylophone improves hand-eye coordination.

Special Needs

• INCLUSIVE PRACTICE •

Inclusive practice asks us to look at how we can adapt the environment and the activities we offer so that diverse learners can participate to their full extent.

Diverse learners

- are not all the same; they have different needs and abilities
- have the same rights and responsibilities as other children
- are still part of the class even though their ways of performing and learning may be different

Inclusive arts activities

- are available and accessible to **all** students irrespective of class, gender, ethnicity, cultural background, or disability
- are adjusted to meet individual learning requirements
- match the materials and environment to the child's needs

Inclusive teaching

- is proactive, flexible, and reflective
- recognizes that students and teachers process, store, organize, and retrieve information in different ways
- takes into account a diversity of learning styles and learning preferences
- considers the way in which materials will be used
- considers the way in which materials are delivered
- focuses not on the disability, but on the effect the disability has on the student's ability to access, learn, and demonstrate knowledge and skills

Gentle assistance can help a child with special needs participate in arts activities. Here an adult helps a child clap along with a song.

Using the Arts to Facilitate Growth

Children with disabilities gain social-emotional, language, and cognitive skills more readily when these behaviors are part of play (Davis, Kilgo, & Gamel-McCormick, 1998). Because the arts share so many qualities with children's natural play, they provide a wonderful way to help children with special needs improve in these needed skills.

This is important because children with developmental delays need more time and practice to accomplish educational goals. Therefore, every minute that the child is in an educational setting must focus on the basic skills and behaviors that the child needs to develop and learn. Teachers can facilitate needed development by joining the child in an arts activity and using the time to focus on general instructional goals. For example, if the goal for a particular child is to learn to ask for things rather than pointing, then as part of a collage activity, the teacher may sit beside the child and place some intriguing collage materials to the far side in order to elicit a request from the child.

Research also indicates that when a child talks more, language skills improve (Hart & Risley, 1995). For children with speech delays and disabilities, the teacher may encourage verbalization by asking targeted questions about their creative work and by

Provide assistance. When a child needs additional help to be successful, try to provide it in a way that does not draw a lot of attention. Pairing a child with special needs with a knowledgeable child or adult, for example, who can either get the supplies or help the child move in a dance activity without constant teacher direction reduces the chance of the child being singled out.

Use role models. Because the child may need to approach the task differently from others, model the method or action in many different ways to the whole group.

Special Needs

• BEING THE MOST SUCCESSFUL •

Linda Mitchell (2004) suggests using the MOST (**M**aterials + **O**bjectives + **S**pace + **T**ime) strategies in planning arts activities for all children, including those with special needs.

M Choose materials carefully so that all children will be successful using them. Make modifications as needed to meet individual requirements.

O Build into the activity objectives taken from individual children's **Individualized Education Plan (IEP).**

S Change the classroom setting to provide the best use of space for every child. This may require designating certain areas for specific activities.

T Children with special needs may require more time to engage in and complete an activity.

responding to nonverbal child-initiated interactions by soliciting a verbal response. Talking about the child's creative process and work provides a non-threatening environment in which to do this.

Adjusting the Activity

The teacher may also need to do a task analysis and break down arts activities into small steps so the child can achieve success. These steps can then be modeled and verbalized for the child, either one by one or in a series based on the child's needs. For example, an exploratory printmaking activity might be broken down into several parts:

1. The child selects a printmaking tool from a tray containing several.
2. The child dips it into the chosen paint color.
3. The child presses the tool onto paper that is taped to the table.
4. The child puts the tool back into the tray.

The steps are then repeated until the print is completed. At each of these steps, the guiding adult should give verbal and visual cues. With each succeeding repetition, the adult can withdraw some of the support until the child can carry out the tasks independently. Another method to help develop social skills with children with autism in the context

of an arts activity is to set up a small dramatic play group of two or three children and provide the child script cards with clues in pictures and words for the child to say during the activity (Ganz & Flores, 2010). Cards might say: "Ask _____ for a turn" or "Ask _____ what he's doing." During the activity the teacher can prompt the child as necessary and slowly withdraw as the child uses the social skills more independently.

Getting Help

An important part of working with children with special needs is obtaining information and assistance from the child's family. Families play a major role in caring for the child, and they understand much about the child's needs and capabilities. They can share what interactions and modifications of the environment have been successful for them. In addition, an early intervention team or professionals with expertise in the child's area of need can also offer needed assistance.

The Role of Arts Therapy

All children find emotional release through the expressive nature of music, drama, dance, and arts activities, so it is not surprising that some children may use the arts to work through traumatic experiences. For example, a child who has experienced a natural disaster may draw pictures of houses and trees that are then scribbled over or "destroyed," as happened in the disaster. Gradually, such pictures decrease as the child comes to terms with the occurrence.

For some children, however, the release of otherwise unexpressed feelings and thoughts may require adult help. A child whose pet was killed in an accident may draw increasingly bloody pictures, indicating that the incident is still very disturbing and that there is a need to work through these deep feelings.

Gerald Oster and Patricia Crone (2004) identify several reasons why the arts are a useful way to engage children for therapeutic and psychological assessment purposes.

1. It is less threatening than verbally expressing deep emotions.

2. It provides a product that can be discussed in a variety of ways.

3. The act of creating allows the child to fantasize and try out solutions to problems.

However, it is dangerous for untrained observers to make judgments about a child's emotional state based on just one or a few pieces of artwork. The constant use of one color of paint may simply reflect what color was available or closest to the child. Research indicates that many young children often use paint colors in the order that they are arranged at the easel (Winner, 1982, p. 151). Pictures of family members may reflect attempts by children to control their world. The parents may be shown small and the child huge, a new baby may be left out, or divorce and remarriage may not be reflected at all in the child's "family" portrait. On the other hand, the arrangement of images may just indicate how well the child controls the art medium.

Our role as teachers should be to allow children to use the arts as a personal way to express their thoughts and emotions—a safe place to show their feelings and, incidentally, give adults a peek inside of an often otherwise private world. However, in the case of serious traumatic experiences, arts therapy may be recommended. Arts therapy is a distinct field of study that requires expertise in both art and psychology. The **music, art,** or **drama therapist** functions as an educator who modifies arts activities to

Special Needs

• USING MODELING MATERIALS FOR EMOTIONAL RELEASE •

The creation of modeled forms is often accompanied by children's enthusiastic destruction. Pliant modeling materials give children the power to control a small part of their environment. Clay and playdoughs are regularly used by children to release strong feelings in an acceptable way. Clay, unlike other children, bossy adults, or precious belongings, can be hit and smashed, slapped, pinched, and poked, and torn apart and put together again. Children who are having difficulty controlling their social behavior benefit from redirecting this behavior to the forgiving clay.

meet the emotional needs of troubled children. Qualified arts therapists work with a team of professionals to interpret the child's artwork, based on many observations and interactions. They then provide healing arts activities.

General Modifications for the Arts

All children with special needs are individually unique in terms of how they cope with arts materials and will require individualized adaptations. The following list provides some general ideas. Specific suggestions for each of the art forms will be found in the "Exploring the Arts" section of the book. See also Table 5-1.

TABLE 5–1	Examples of Ways to Adapt Arts Activities				
Activity	Disability	Material Modification	IEP Objectives	Setting Modification	Time
Painting	Physical	Use thick-handled brush wrapped in foam	Child will strengthen right arm	Paper will be hung on easel at wheelchair height	Activity will be during open-ended center time
Singing a song	Hearing disability	Add signing to song	Child will use sign language to communicate	Child will sit near teacher in circle	Repeat song several times, adding the signs
Creative dance	Visual disability	Have children hold hands and move in a circle	Child will hold head erect when walking	Circle will be marked on floor in brightly colored tape	Children will practice walking around the circle
Acting out story	Autism	Use familiar objects the child is comfortable with as props	Child will look at others when speaking	Use tape to mark where actors will stand	Before activity have child visit area and see where to stand

Meeting needs for muscular control.

1. Put trays across wheelchairs.

2. Provide wheelchair-height tables.

3. Make sure there is sufficient space for wheelchairs to join in creative dance activities.

4. Use pillows to position the child to better manipulate materials and participate in singing and musical activities.

5. Art tools such as crayons, markers, pencils, brushes, and pens, and musical instruments, such as drumsticks, rattles, bells, maracas, and triangles, can be wrapped in foam hair curlers to improve grip. Velcro pieces can be attached to a cotton glove and to the arts object.

6. Attach the drawing tool, paintbrush, or musical instrument to an arm, prosthesis, foot, or headgear. Some children without the use of their arms use their mouths. Drawing tools can be taped into cigarette holders, or a special holder can be made or purchased. Remember, children do not draw or make music with their hands, but with their minds.

7. To facilitate cutting, provide a rotary cutting wheel and a cutting mat instead of scissors.

8. Use no-spill paint containers and thickened paint. Choose brushes in a size that best matches the child's muscle control. Short, stubby brushes may work better than long-handled easel brushes. Foam brushes may make the paint easier to control.

Meeting visual needs.

1. Place a screen or textured surface under the paper to add texture to drawn lines.

2. Use a fabric tracing or marking wheel to create a raised line. Place pads of newspaper or rubber mats beneath lightweight paper.

3. Use scented crayons and markers; add scents to paint and glue.

4. Provide many tactile materials.

5. Place arts materials and props in the same locations every time, and attach tactile, identifying symbols on supply containers. For example, attach an actual piece of each collage material to collage storage bins. This will allow children to develop independence in obtaining their own supplies.

6. If the child has some vision, find out which colors are easiest to see, and provide many materials in those colors. For example, fluorescent colors and reflective safety tapes may appeal to some children. Mark bold lines on the floor to guide the child during movement and dramatic activities.

Behavioral and emotional needs.

1. Select activities that have few steps and instant results, such as modeling, painting, making sounds, and puppetry. Expect lots of exploration and physical expression of feelings.

2. For children who are easily distracted, provide work areas that allow plenty of space and that seem separate from the rest of the room.

3. Select and arrange arts supplies carefully to help limit distractions as well.

Other assistance.

1. Some children who have visual or motor difficulties may need hand-over-hand assistance. Place a hand over the student's to assist with such skills as dipping the paintbrush into the container and then onto the paper, or dipping a finger into paste and then applying it to the object to be glued.

2. Some children may need their base paper taped to the table to keep it from moving or wrinkling when they work.

3. Add picture clues and labels.

4. Use real objects to further understanding (i.e., a real apple as opposed to a picture of one).

5. Incorporate children's communication devices into the activity. For example, a child could play a sound on a communication board to accompany a song.

6. Use multiple delivery modes. Say the directions, show the directions in pictures and words, use sign language, and act out the directions.

Helping Other Children Accept Those with Special Needs

Although young children can be very accepting of individual differences, they may react in outspoken ways to things that are unfamiliar or strange. We need to be sensitive as we help children learn to live with all kinds of people.

1. Do not criticize children for expressing curiosity. When children notice and ask questions about disabilities and special equipment, answer matter-of-factly with a simple and accurate reply. It is important to be honest when answering. Use correct terminology whenever possible.

   Child: *"Why does Jared need a special holder for his crayons?"*

   Teacher: *"Jared uses a holder because he has trouble holding small objects tightly. Jared likes to draw like you do, but he has muscular dystrophy, so we figured out a way that he could do it."*

2. Do not deny differences, but help children see their shared similarities.

   Child: *"Maya just makes noises with the xylophone."*

   Teacher: *"Maya likes to make music, just like you do. She has learned how to do many things. Now she is learning how to play the xylophone. Would you like to play along on the drum with her?"*

3. Children need to become familiar with special equipment and devices but also need to learn to respect the equipment of a child with special needs. If possible, rent or borrow a variety of equipment for children to explore, but make it clear that they must respect the personal equipment of the child who must use it.

4. If children are comfortable doing so, have them explain how their special equipment helps them participate in the arts and why it is important to take care of it. If they cannot do this on their own, then have them demonstrate how the equipment is used while an adult explains.

5. Invite artists with disabilities to share their arts. Make sure they are prepared for the sometimes bold questions of children.

6. Reading books about children with special needs is another way to introduce and talk about how similarities and differences. For example, *Moses Goes to a Concert* by Issac Millman (1998) shows how children who are deaf can enjoy a concert.

Did You Get It?

Aki is a first grade teacher. A child in a wheelchair joins his class. Which of the following would you recommend to Aki?

a. Eliminate all creative movement activities.

b. Have the child leave the room during dance activities.

c. Move the furniture and push the child around the room during creative movement activities.

d. Have the child watch a video of creative movement activities.

Take the full quiz on CourseMate

How Can the Arts Be Used in Anti-Bias Activities?

Arts activities can be used to help children express their feelings about individual differences. They provide an opportunity for teachers to initiate a dialogue to correct mistaken beliefs and model respect and empathy for others.

In offering the arts to young children, teachers need to be sure that the choice of activities creates an environment in which children from all backgrounds feel comfortable and can be creative in their artwork. Children differ in their racial and ethnic backgrounds. Research shows that children begin to be aware of these individual differences by age two, and that between the ages of three and five they develop a sense of who they are and how they differ from others (Van Ausdale & Feagin, 2001). Before children can feel free to relax and express themselves in creative arts activities, they need to feel valued for who they are, not for how they look, talk, and behave. They need to be treated fairly and have their differences seen as strengths that enrich the learning of all of the children. The visual, physical, and tactile nature of the arts allows children, regardless of their differences, to explore and learn together. Children who speak different languages can learn by observing each other as they create with the arts. Because the arts are common to all cultures, it can be a vehicle through which cultural differences can be explored.

Creating an Arts Environment that Celebrates Differences

Teachers must take action to encourage the development of an **anti-bias** atmosphere among children. They need to consider the materials they choose to supply and the pictures they display. Activities should be provided that foster discussion and the elimination of the misconceptions that are the basis of many prejudicial beliefs held by young children. The arts can be used in a variety of ways to support an anti-bias curriculum.

Selecting anti-bias visual images and supplies. Children need to see and become familiar with people who look different from them. They also need to develop an authentic self-concept based on liking themselves without feeling superior to others (Derman-Sparks & Ramsey, 2006). Taking the following steps will help children do this:

1. Provide arts materials that reflect the wide range of natural skin tones. Paints, papers, playdough, and crayons in the entire range of skin colors need to be regularly available, along with the other colors.

2. Mirrors and photographs of themselves and their families should be available at all times for children to learn about themselves and each other.

3. Images of people who represent the racial and ethnic groups found in the community and in the larger society need to be displayed. There should be a balance in the images so that there is no token group. It is recommended that about half of the images should represent the background of the predominant group of children in the class. The remainder of the images should represent the rest of the diversity found in society (Derman-Sparks & the ABC Task Force, 1989).

4. When selecting visuals and posters, look for ones that show a range of people of different ages, genders, sizes, colors, and abilities. Display photos of people who are involved in activities that depict current life. Many prints are available that reflect this diversity, including those depicting arts from Haitian, African, African-American, Native American, Mexican, and Asian sources. (See Chapter 7 for suggestions and Appendix B for sources.)

5. Artworks, music, stories, and dances should represent artists of diverse backgrounds and time periods, including the present and counteract stereotypes. This is particularly important for Native Americans.

6. Illustrations in the books read to the children and available for them to use should also reflect society's diversity.

7. Stereotypical and inaccurate images should be removed from display in the room and used only in discussions of unfair representations of groups of people. Avoid so-called "multicultural" materials such as bulletin board kits and patterns that depict people from around the world wearing traditional clothing from the past. These materials leave children with the impression that, for example, all Native Americans wear leather and feathers, all Japanese wear kimonos, and all Africans wear dashikis.

Selecting anti-bias activities. Arts activities can be chosen that help children acquire inner strength, empathy, a strong sense of justice, and the power to take action in the face of bias. Louise Derman-Sparks and Patricia Ramsey note that there are four basic goals of anti-bias education.

1. Help children develop self-confidence and a positive group identity with their home culture and with that of our society.

2. Develop empathy for, and a feeling of, commonality with those who are different.

3. Assist children in developing an understanding of fairness and the knowledge that discrimination and exclusion hurts.

4. Nurture children's ability to stand up for themselves and others in the face of unfairness and prejudice.

Anti-Bias Arts Activities

Arts activities, because of their open-ended nature and emphasis on working together to accomplish a creative goal, are an ideal way to develop this inner strength. The following activities show how the arts can be used to address racial prejudice based on skin color.

Mixing my special color. Read a book about skin color, such as *All the Colors We Are* (Kissinger, 1994). Help children mix paint that matches the color of their skin. Place the paint in a container that closes tightly. Label the container with the child's name, and have the child give the color a beautiful name. Explain that whenever children want to paint a picture of themselves or their friends, they may use those special paint colors.

Valuing children's unique colors. Make sure skin-color paints are available at the easel. Then, when children use the paint color that is closest to their skin color, hair color, or eye color, make a comment about the beauty of that color and express its relationship to the children's coloring, such as: "You are painting with a beautiful almond brown (rich peach, soft beige, deep brown, etc.). It is the same color as your skin (hair, eyes)." Read the book *The Colors of Us* (Katz, 2002) in which different skin colors are given luscious names and then have children create their own names for their color skin.

Read a book that celebrates differences, such as Jenny Kostecki-Shaw's *Same, Same but Different* (2011) in which two pen pals—a boy from a village

in India and a boy from an American city find they have a lot in common. Collect a variety of paint-chip samples from a paint store. Have children sort them into groups. Then have them find the ones that match their hair, skin, and eye color. Make a graph or chart of the different range of colors in the group.

Washing up. This interaction can occur following any messy activity in which the children's hands get covered with an art material—such as finger painting, printing, clay work, or painting. When children are washing up at the sink, say, "What do you think might happen to the color of our skin when we wash the paint off? Look, it stays the same color. Our skin color doesn't come off, only the paint." Also, provide opportunities for children to wash dolls that have different skin colors.

Color awareness collages. Children need to learn to cherish all the colors skin can be. Transition into a skin color awareness activity by reading a book that celebrates the colors brown and black, such as *Beautiful Blackbird* (Bryan, 2003). Have the children find or make a list of all of the beautiful black or brown things that they know. Take a neighborhood or nature walk and look for brown or black things. Look at the many different colors skin can be. Put out the collage items, exclaiming over the beautiful color of each material.

Talking to Children about Differences

When arts materials that reflect skin differences, images of a variety of people, and anti-bias arts activities are introduced to young children, occasions will arise in which biased or unkind remarks will be made, and a response will be required by the teacher. A child may not want to handle black playdough because it is "ugly," or another may say, "My skin color paint is prettier than yours." Whether it is during an arts activity, or at any other time of the day, children's discriminating behavior must be addressed. Such comments, even by very young children, must not be ignored or excused, nor is the teacher's personal discomfort in dealing with difficult subjects a reason not to act. Reacting strongly to biased statements shows children how to act when they see unfairness. The following suggestions may help:

Talking about skin color differences and engaging in arts activities that celebrate similarities and differences develop self-confidence and empathy. Here a youngster makes a handprint in her skin color after reading the book *All the Colors That We Are* by Katie Kissinger.

1. Immediately address the child's negative response. A response to the aforementioned statements might be: "All colors are beautiful. Why do you say that?" If the comment is directed to another child, say: "That is a hurtful thing to say. Why do you say that?"

2. Help children figure out why they are uncomfortable. Identify why it was unfair or based on stereotypes.

3. Explain why such remarks are hurtful, and give examples of things the child might say or do instead.

How Do We Address Cultural Differences Through Arts Activity?

We build children's self-confidence and foster cooperation when we select culturally relevant arts activities that respect children's cultural, linguistic, religious, and ethnic diversity and create a sense of belonging. Faced with a group of young children we see, at first, unique individuals with temperaments, likes and dislikes, and a personal way of doing things in the classroom. But we must also come to see them as embedded in a family, a community, a culture, and a society, all of which will influence how they play, what language they speak, and how they will meld into the classroom community.

Culture, like creativity, has many definitions. In the broadest sense it is a group's way of thinking, acting, and responding based on a set of rules or beliefs

that make sense of the universe. We value children's cultures when we:

- Use the child's home language in daily interactions, and in bilingual storytelling and reading.

- Select arts activities and materials that reflect the child's home culture.

- Incorporate and welcome family and community members into the classroom as integral parts of the arts curriculum serving as cultural experts, resources of information, and as helpers who can mediate for the child in culturally relevant ways.

Respecting Family Culture and Beliefs

As teachers we bring our own backgrounds with us into our classrooms. However, the way we were raised may not match that of the children we teach. For example, although play is universal in every child's development, how it looks and what is considered normal and acceptable varies greatly from place to place and culture to culture (Kendall, 1996).

Environment. Home environment is one factor. Children who live in crowded apartments where it is not safe to go outside engage in different activities and have a different sense of movement in space then a child growing up on a farm with acres of woodland to explore. This will affect how children respond in creative movement activities such as when they are asked to pretend they are walking outside. Being sensitive to a child's home environment will help us frame our arts activities so that all children feel like they belong.

Socioeconomic background. Family economics also has an effect on a child's home culture. Some children grow up with access to many toys and electronic devices, and others have only a few and must create their own playthings from the things they find in their environment. They may be overwhelmed by an overabundance of materials and choices. For example, children who grow up in middle-class homes may be given excess adult clothing and shoes with which to play dress-up, whereas a child from a poor family is happy to have one pair of sneakers. A dress-up corner full of glitzy dresses and glittery shoes may overwhelm such a child. Adding dress-up garments mirroring familiar community occupations and ethnic groups may increase a child's sense of belonging.

Adult behavior. Children's art and dramatic play will reflect what they see around them in daily life and on television. Pretend play often mimics adult behavior. While children in hunting societies pretend to hunt, children in the inner city act out gang fights and dodging bullets as they walk to school. Children imitate the action heroes they see in television cartoons. When children act out violent stories in their pretend play, we need to think about why they are doing this and mediate their play with cultural sensitivity rather than punishment or disapproval.

Gender expectations. Cultural expectations about gender often determine appropriate play for boys and for girls. Boys are expected to play with trucks and guns while girls are expected to play with dolls and housekeeping. Gender, race, and physical characteristics should not determine what roles children play in a story, or how they are expected to move in a dance. If children object to a child taking a certain role, share a book such as *Amazing Grace* (Hoffman, 1991) in which an African-American girl plays the role of Peter Pan in the school play. Some children may come from homes with only a mother or only a father, or two fathers or two mothers, or homes in which the father stays home and the mother works. Room must be made to welcome all children's families.

In carrying out arts activities, teachers have to consciously stay alert to their own biases. Research has shown, for example, that teachers often react differently to boys than they do to girls (Sadker & Sadker, 1995).

Teacher Tip

THE POWER OF CHILDREN'S LITERATURE

Children need to see themselves and others in the books we read to them. Reading books that depict children with similar life experiences develops self-confidence (Brimson, 2009). The book *The Two Mrs. Gibsons* by Toyomi Igus (2001) celebrates love and caring in a family of mixed heritage. Stories about children who are both the same and different from them develops understanding and empathy (Koster, 2005). A story such as *Yo Yes* by Chris Rashka (1993) or *The Other Side* (2001) by Jacqueline Woodson show children ways to make friends with children who are different from them. *Lucy's Picture* by Nicola Moon (1993) in which a little girl creates a touchable collage for her grandfather helps children understand blindness.

For an annotated list of books that address diversity, see *Books that Make a Difference* on CourseMate.

Communicating with Families

In order to better understand our child artists, we need to know about their families and their families need to

Teacher to Family

Communicating with parents is critical in establishing reciprocal relationships. Because creative arts experiences have the potential to be positives in children's lives, they provide an important resource upon which to build relationships with parents and welcome them into the school community. To do this effectively both one way and two-way forms of communication need to be pursued.

One-way methods:

Newsletters highlighting the arts, letters home about arts activities, art notes, school-to-home notebooks about adjustments and successes in the arts, class websites featuring the arts, videos of activities, and portfolios and projects sent home.

Two-way methods:

Phone calls and e-mails celebrating creative works, learning "bags" such as an arts bag with a feedback journal, conferences that include the arts as a major component of the child's accomplishments, home visits to talk about the child and interests in the arts, art-home surveys, informal arts shows and performances, invitations to participate in children's projects and fieldtrips, parent visits to share about culture, work, and family arts, parents helping in the classroom with arts projects, parent workshops to explore the arts, and parent-child arts workshops.

understand and contribute to our knowledge. To establish two-way communication with families:

1. Make families feel welcome in the classroom and invite their participation. Arts activities provide a wonderful opportunity to involve parents.

2. Avoid presenting yourself as someone who knows all the answers. Ask questions about parents' goals and hopes for their children. Work together to find solutions to problems.

3. Communicate regularly. Newsletters and arts notes home can share successes in the arts. Set up opportunities for parents to respond in creative ways that take into account the harried lives many of us live.

4. Respect parents' feelings about their child and their culture. Remember if there is a disagreement, the goal is not for you to win and the parent to lose, but rather to find a middle ground in which to find agreement and make the best decision for the child.

Using a Multicultural Lens

All members of the classroom community should feel welcome in our classrooms. We need to foster children's pride in their own cultural identity but also develop curiosity, enjoyment, and empathy for others' cultural similarities and differences. Derman Sparks and the ABC Task Force (1989) suggest the following as the basis of a multicultural curriculum.

- **Include everyone.** When selecting culturally based activities, build on the cultural backgrounds of the individual children in the class and their families first.

- **Avoid stereotyping a child or a culture.** Not all Mexican-Americans speak Spanish. Not all Indians wear saris. Make references to differences specific to a particular child. Say: "This is what Keena's family does when they visit her grandparents at Thanksgiving." and invite her family to share photographs and stories about their customs rather than saying: "Everyone eats turkey at Thanksgiving." Emphasize similarities as well as differences.

- **Avoid singling out a "minority" child.** Make learning about all children and their similarities and differences the focus. Encourage children to draw pictures of their families and the things they do. Make a class book about the families of children and the staff members. If different languages are spoken, make a class book illustrating some common words in each language.

- **Bring cultural diversity into the classroom every day.** Go beyond a few pictures on the wall. Take walks around the communities the children come from many times. Make class books about the community to be kept in the classroom library. Have families and children share artifacts that reflect their family life such as musical instruments, special bowls and utensils, and the tools they use in their work. Add items to the dramatic play area that reflect their home culture. If a child's parent works in construction, add a hard hat and gloves. If a parent is a nurse, add a lab coat and a stethoscope. If a family prepares rice, add a bamboo steamer and rice bowls.

Food and Arts

A controversial issue in art for young children is the use of food and food products in art activities. People have strong feelings on both sides of this issue.

Using food in art activities. Those who believe it is all right to use food items often give the following reasons:

- Many traditional art materials, such as egg tempera, play dough, and white glue, are made from food products.

- It is easier to determine the ingredients in food products than in commercial art materials so they are safer, especially if the child puts it in her mouth.

- Food items are readily available at the supermarket.

- Children can appreciate the aesthetic qualities of the foods such as when they make a print using an apple half.

- Children are motivated by food and have a lot of fun doing these activities such as when they are told they can lick their hands after finger painting with pudding.

Avoiding food in arts activities. On the other hand there are many reasons why food items should not be used in art activities:

- Many children are severely allergic to food items such as milk, wheat, soy, eggs, and nuts.

- Most traditional art materials, such as crayons, chalk, and paper, are not food based.

- Safe art materials for children are widely marketed in department stores, drug stores, and through catalogs.

- Children become confused when told they can eat one art material and not another.

Using a multicultural lens. When making a decision on an art activity that calls for food we must consider all of the above plus the cultural message we are sending the children and their families. We need to ask ourselves:

- **Does this use of food respect our families' cultural beliefs?** Some ethnic groups are offended if food they highly value is used for play and not shown respect. For example, some families of Asian heritage may object to the use of rice in sensory play.

- **Does this use of food respect the fact that people are hungry?** Making a necklace out of macaroni or cereal might not bother well-fed middle-class parents and their children, but may distress those who struggle daily to put food on the table. Many children come to school hungry or see hungry people every day on the street.

- **Does this use of food create needless waste?** Food is expensive and should be valued. We tell children not to waste their food. Making prints with apples or bananas or potatoes is a common art activity. But what do children learn when they see all that food thrown into the wastebasket afterward? There are many other things that can be used for printmaking besides foods. Or if there is a specific reason for the activity, consider ways to lessen the waste, such as if the goal is to show the beautiful design inside an apple, use only one apple instead of every child having a half with which to print.

- **Does this use of food teach children healthy eating habits?** Parents may have specific ideas about what they want their children to eat. Giving children candy and sugary cereal to use in art projects highlights these foods in positive ways. Edible playdoughs and finger paints entice children to taste all playdoughs and paints.

For alternatives to use instead of food items, see *Substitutions for Food in Arts Activities* on CourseMate.

The Role of Holidays

In many early childhood programs, holidays are often a major focus for arts activities. Arts activity books abound with exciting new ways to create holiday art and decorations and perform festive songs and dances. Holidays are fun; they involve rituals, they build a sense of solidarity, and they are part of a society's cultural life. However, it is easy to trivialize a culture when it only makes a once a year appearance in the form of stereotyped art projects, songs, dances, and plays. To develop deeper understanding of different cultures, we need to do the following:

Celebrate everyone. Not all holidays are celebrated in the same way by everyone. The holidays of all children in the group must be presented with

Instead of using three perfect circles, snowmen can be made in various ways that allow children to express their own creativity as this snowman by Joseph, age four, demonstrates.

equal emphasis. One holiday should not receive more time and attention than another. Look to parents to provide thoughts, information, and resources on respectful ways of sharing their holidays.

Celebrate year round. We need to be sure that a culture is not presented only in the context of a holiday. Presenting artwork and activities that relate to different cultures throughout the year rather than just in the context of a holiday helps prevent children from associating the arts of that culture with only the holiday. For example, Native American arts and culture should be displayed and discussed in many arts contexts—when making masks, working with beads, creating with clay, learning to spin and weave, and examining baskets—not just at Thanksgiving.

Avoid stereotypes. One of the hardest things to avoid when dealing with holiday-related arts activities is the stereotypical images related to holidays. These images limit children's creativity and visual imaginations, often do not reflect their home cultures, and undermine their artistic self-confidence as they quickly learn that they cannot replicate the perfection of a commercially made holiday symbol.

The perfect Christmas-tree shape, for example, is impossible for young children to make successfully without resorting to patterns or step-by-step copying, and the image becomes so ingrained that many upper-level arts teachers find that they have to take their students on nature walks just to prove that all pine trees are not symmetrical, and that they can be represented in many other ways in their art. Hearts, egg shapes, bunnies, turkeys, and pumpkins all become bland, perfect symbols instead of reflecting the infinite variety of their actual forms.

It is hard to avoid these symbols because they permeate the markets and media of this society. However, we need to consider carefully which images we want to surround the children in our care. Teachers can take the following actions to expand children's artistic imaginations and fight the prevailing stereotypes.

1. In visual arts provide geometric shapes that children can make into their own creative ideas instead of holiday-related shapes that limit what they can do. Let children draw their own versions of Christmas trees, turkeys, pumpkins, hearts, and other holiday shapes, instead of giving them teacher-prepared paper shapes, holiday cutouts, coloring pages, foam shapes, or stickers.

2. At the playdough and clay center, instead of holiday-shaped cookie cutters, use simple geometric shapes from which children can build their own versions of these symbols if they wish.

3. Provide a range of color choices of materials, not just those of the prevailing holiday.

4. Instead of displaying stereotypical holiday images, provide aesthetic experiences with a collection of pumpkins, piles of pine boughs, a display of turkey feathers, a basket of eggs, or a cage of real rabbits, so the children use their senses to see and touch and discover similarities and differences on their own.

5. Introduce songs and dances from different cultures throughout the year not just at holiday time.

Did You Get It?

Which of the following should be avoided when creating an atmosphere of respect for all cultures in class?

a. displaying images of racial and ethnic groups not represented in the class

b. selecting images that show a range of people of different ages, genders, sizes, colors, and abilities

c. displaying artworks, music, stories, and dances representing artists of diverse backgrounds and time periods

d. using the children's home languages in daily interactions

Take the full quiz on CourseMate

Conclusion: Caring For Each Other

Group arts projects can take many forms. From painting a mural to acting out a story, working with others gives children a chance to interact with the arts in a way that is different from individual artistic pursuits. There must be a common vocabulary. "Should we put aqua paint on the fish?" There must be collaboration. "Should this character be a pigeon or an eagle?" And there must be cooperation. "I'll hold the drum for you, and then you can hold it for me."

Photo Story

We All Have Feelings

What makes us angry? What makes us happy? What makes us sad? To start off the year, first graders explored their feelings through these questions using pantomime, drawing, painting to music, reading books, and journaling.

"Feeling sick." John Pencil—age seven

"Feeling happy." By Leah Pastel—age five

"Feeling angry." By Marti, Marker—age six

Documentation Panel for First Grade We All Have Feelings Integrated Arts Unit

The result is more than the sum of its parts. Group arts activities turn "me" into "we" and unite individuals.

Group arts activities can also be used to help children express thoughts and feelings that are hard to put into words. Teachers need to be sensitive to the personal needs and beliefs of their students. Children can and should talk about the differences among them, but actually painting with different skin tones, learning each other's personal likes and cultural backgrounds, and working on the same arts projects with those who are different help children form tangible links. The arts activities that we choose can broaden children's perspectives in ways that will make them more successful participants in a multicultural society.

This chapter has offered ideas that challenge the educator to address sometimes controversial issues.

Overheard comments could be ignored. Black and brown playdough could be avoided, because it makes some children uncomfortable or makes them act silly. Teachers could focus on the more readily available "old masters" instead of looking for the harder-to-locate artwork of African-Americans, Latinos, and those of other cultures. Teachers could give in to the pressure to make commercialized holiday "art," or they can make the other choice, the one that takes a little more effort and haul in ten imperfect pumpkins or take a trip to the turkey farm. They can make a commitment to do what is best for the children, knowing that change happens not all at once but a little bit every day.

For additional information on teaching children to work cooperatively, address bias, and use a multicultural lens, see *Chapter 5 Online Resources* on CourseMate.

Teaching In Action

Spaceship Command Center: A Box Project

The following excerpts from a teacher's journal show how the project approach and a flexible approach to room planning was used in a prekindergarten class to correlate children's interests in space with the arts, science, and language studies.

Week 1

Day 1: The idea: Mike, Bobby, and Jeff arrived all excited. It seems there was a show about space on TV last night. At meeting, all they wanted to do was talk about the spaceship. At blocks, they built a launch pad and used cardboard tubes as rockets.

Day 2: Discovering the depth of interest: Today I decided to read Ezra Jack Keats's *Regards to the Man in the Moon* (1981). Then I asked: "What do you think we would need for a trip into space?" What ideas! I couldn't write them down fast enough on the chart. Toby said she has a cousin who went to NASA Space Camp. I wonder if she could come for a visit? I must get in touch. I noticed that many of the paintings and drawings were about space today.

Day 3: What do we already know? Today I asked: "What do we know about space?" I made a huge web of children's ideas. I can see they have heard about stars, planets, and the sun, but not much else. There was a discussion about aliens and Star Wars. I must find some factual books about space. Not surprisingly, everyone was building a launch pad today at blocks!

Day 4: Building on the interest: I found out about a space exhibit at the discovery center. I called and arranged for a visit the end of next week. That gives me time to plan the bussing and the parent volunteers. We will use this time to read more about space and make a list of questions. I put a sheet up labeled "Our questions about space" in the meeting area. I put up a big poster of the solar system. Then I pretended I was the sun and the children were the planets, and they had a grand time circling around me to the music of "The Planets" by Gustav Holst. I will try to read another two pages and do a movement activity each day at morning meeting.

Day 5: Small groups begin: At small group time, I started off by having my group of children look at a picture of the space shuttle and then figure out what the different parts were. I wasn't surprised when Mike, Bobby, and Jeff asked if they could build a spaceship. Everyone started to call out ideas. I said, "Why don't we draw some pictures of our ideas?" Boy, did they work on those pictures! So much detail!

Carol [the aide] had her group looking at photographs of each of the planets and talking about the sizes, colors, and names. Some children in her group wanted to make a mural about space.

Week 2

Day 6: Group work continues: We found a huge roll of black paper. I hung it on the wall, and the children sat in front

(continued)

Teaching In Action (continued)

of it, and we tried to imagine the blackness of space. I gave them each a tube to look through and turned off the light. It was very effective. At group time we continued to work on sketches for the spaceship. We put out gold and silver tempera paint at the easel, and the children had a grand time painting stars and comets of all kinds to paste on the mural. The spaceship group made tons more sketches. Carol's group made planets.

Day 7: Finding direction: I read Gail Gibbons's *Stargazers* (1992, New York: Holiday House). I simplified the text a bit. Then I passed around a telescope for children to look through. They cut out and pasted their stars on the mural. They even made a Milky Way! I can't believe they had such patience to cut out even their little tiny stars. We had so many we even hung some from the ceiling. Then we sat in front of the mural and sang "Twinkle, Twinkle Little Star" and made wishes. Suddenly someone said, I think it was Jeff, "Why don't we make our spaceship in front of the mural so we will be heading into space . . . like we could have a big window. The captain and his mates could sit here and look out."

Day 8: Building begins: Toby's cousin couldn't come, but she sent in a videotape of the training. We watched it twice. The second time we looked for ideas for our spaceship. We added seat cushions and seatbelts to the parent wish list by the door. We decided to move a table in front of the mural, and I cut open a large cardboard box. The children drew big windows, and I cut them out. Then they painted it. Now I have taped it to the table, and it looks great! They have already set up three chairs and sit there counting down.

Day 9: Our trip—What did we learn? It was wonderful! The children were so well behaved. I could see that all of our preparations made a big difference. They had a space shuttle model the children could go inside. When we got back, the first thing they wanted to do was make the control panel like the one at the museum. But I got everyone together first, and we wrote down the answers on our question chart. Then I got out some boxes, and everyone helped paint them. It was a good release after being so controlled all morning at the museum.

Day 10: The command center: It's done! I can't believe the children had such a great idea. We put some low boxes on the table and the bigger ones on the floor around it. Catie had the idea of using bottle lids for the dials. I attached them with chenille stems so they turn. Then the best idea of all was Louie's. He said, "Why don't we put the computer here?" At the museum, there was a computer in the spaceship. So we did! Some parents even brought in cushions and belts for the chairs. We all took a turn sitting in the command seats. Wow! Next week I will put out paper bags with pre-cut openings so they can make helmets if they wish. But the funny thing was when my colleague, Joanne, poked her head in and said, "What book gave you that neat idea for a computer center?"

"It's not in a book," I said. "It grew in the children's imaginations."

Reflection Page

Exploring Ourselves

Knowing our feelings, beliefs, and cultural viewpoint allows us to better understand those of our children and our families. Self-awareness exercises help identify areas we need explore more so that we can be better teachers. Select one or more of the following activities and then reflect on what you learned about yourself and how it might affect your choice or presentation of arts activities.

1. Choose a popular fairy tale and rewrite it, changing the gender of the characters. Reread the story and think about how the change makes you feel.

2. Try to accomplish one of the following arts activities while experiencing one of the following handicaps:

   - Wearing a thick snow glove on your dominant hand, or, using your mouth or toes draw a detailed pencil drawing.

   - Wearing a heavy boot on one foot, dance a complete folkdance.

   - Wearing a blindfold or very dark glasses, make a colorful painting or crayon drawing.

   - Place your tongue against the back of your top teeth and sing a song.

3. Write a story about your childhood about how you learned about your ethnic, racial, and cultural identity. Which aspects were fun and which were unpleasant?

Reflection: How have your personal experiences affected the way you feel about people different from yourself?

_____

_____

_____

_____

Reflection Page

Shared Experiences

Think of one or more open-ended group arts activities that could be done in response to the following shared experiences.

Shared Experience	Activity Ideas
A sudden thunderstorm	
A trip to a shoe store	
Watching birds	
A zookeeper's visit	
Studying patterns	
Setting up a classroom fish tank	

Reflection Page

Dealing with Difficult Situations

Consider each of the following situations, and decide what you would say and do.

1. A parent picks up her son's painting and says, "Another painting all in black! Why don't you use some pretty colors when you paint?"

   _____

   _____

   _____

2. A little girl refuses to touch the brown playdough. "It's yucky!" she declares.

   _____

   _____

   _____

3. Michael, age five, draws only faces with blood coming out of their mouths.

   _____

   _____

   _____

4. An aide shows the children how to trace their hands to make turkeys.

   _____

   _____

   _____

5. A child with muscular dystrophy is having trouble holding her crayon.

   _____

   _____

   _____

   _____

Reflection Page

Observation: Bias in the Environment

Visit a school or childcare center when children are not present, and observe the following:

1. Are there crayons, paper, modeling clay, playdough, or paints available in a variety of skin colors?

   _____

   _____

2. Are there child-height mirrors?

   _____

   _____

3. Are there images or artworks that depict people of different racial and ethnic groups?

   _____

   _____

4. Are predominant groups represented by the majority of the images or artworks?

   _____

   _____

5. Is society's diversity represented by the images or artworks displayed?

   _____

   _____

6. Are books available that reflect society's diversity?

   _____

   _____

7. Are there any stereotypical or inaccurate images representing certain groups, such as Native Americans?

   _____

   _____

8. Are there any commercial or stereotypical holiday artworks on display?

   _____

   _____

Based on what you observed, would you judge this a bias-free environment for young children?

If yes, write a letter to the director telling him or her what you especially liked about what the program offers young children. (Optional: This letter may be mailed to the director, if desired.)

If no, make a plan of action that could be used to eliminate bias in the environment. Include cost, time frame, and personnel necessary to accomplish this task. Remember, change occurs bit by bit.

Digital Download Download from CourseMate

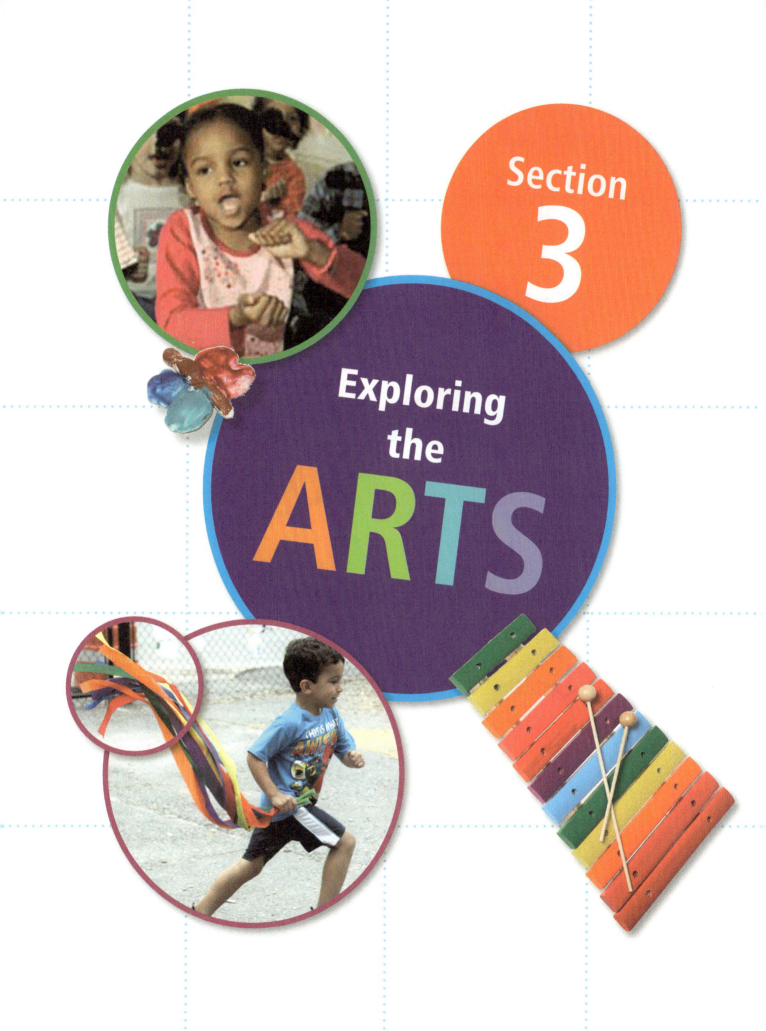

Section
3

Exploring the
ARTS

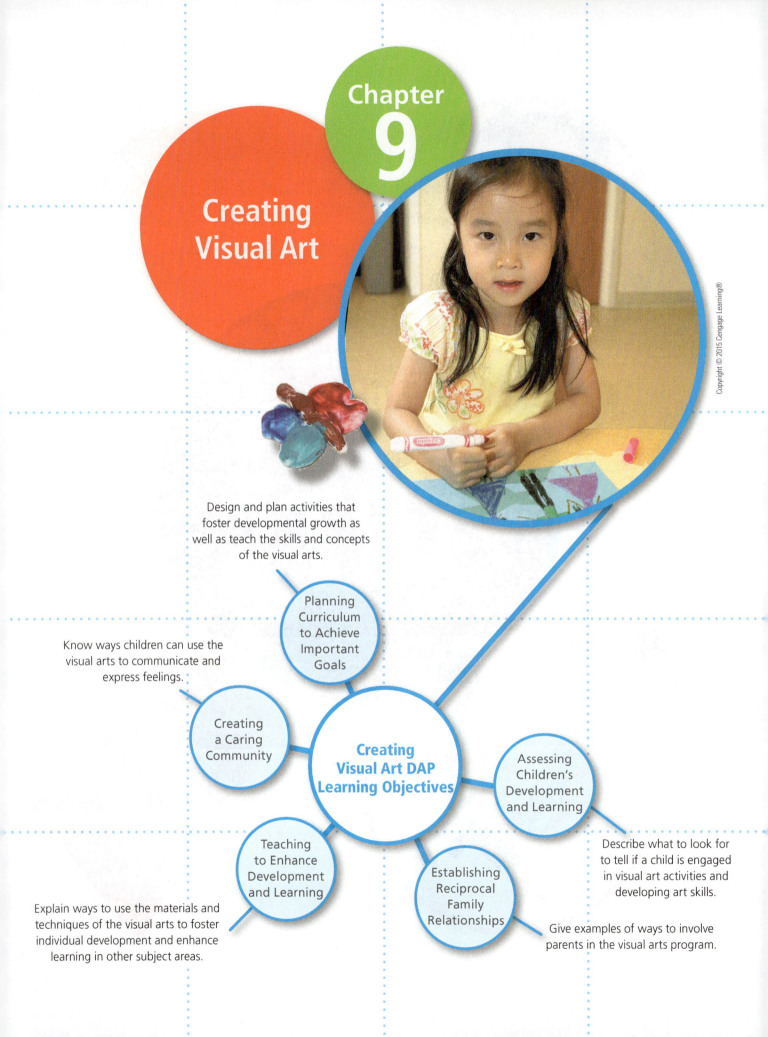

Chapter 9

Creating Visual Art

Design and plan activities that foster developmental growth as well as teach the skills and concepts of the visual arts.

Know ways children can use the visual arts to communicate and express feelings.

Planning Curriculum to Achieve Important Goals

Creating a Caring Community

Creating Visual Art DAP Learning Objectives

Assessing Children's Development and Learning

Teaching to Enhance Development and Learning

Establishing Reciprocal Family Relationships

Describe what to look for to tell if a child is engaged in visual art activities and developing art skills.

Explain ways to use the materials and techniques of the visual arts to foster individual development and enhance learning in other subject areas.

Give examples of ways to involve parents in the visual arts program.

Young Artists Creating

Benjamin, age one, draws a crooked line across his paper.

Alana, age three, dips her brush into yellow paint and then dabs it into the blue paint. "I made green," she says.

"Look I've made a nest," Manuelo, age five, says as he holds up his clay project.

Vanessa and Shakari, both age seven, dip newspaper into papier-mâché paste and wrap it around a cardboard box. "We're making a robot," they say.

What Are the Visual Arts?

The *visual arts* involve the creation of two- and three-dimensional images that communicate ideas and emotions. The traditional media for doing this includes drawing, painting, collage, printmaking, and sculpture, but in fact, visual art can be made from almost any material imaginable, ranging from natural fibers to industrial waste to computer screens. The key ingredient is the manipulation of the visual and tactile elements of line, shape, color, form, texture, pattern, and space. These elements are arranged by the artist into a composition, which combines the selected materials into a unified whole.

How Do the Visual Arts Help Children Grow?

Through the visual arts children will develop

- **Physically**—By using the large and small muscles of the arm and hand and eye-hand coordination to handle the different art media. (Bodily-Kinesthetic)

- **Socially**—By working alongside other children and sharing arts materials. (Interpersonal)

- **Emotionally**—By learning to enjoy the act of creating visual art and by developing self-confidence in their ability to control a part of their environment as they handle challenging tools and materials safely. (Intrapersonal)

- **Perceptually**—By exploring new ways to make graphic symbols in two- and three-dimensional

space, and by responding to the visual and textual effects they have created. (Spatial)

- **Language skills**—By learning a vocabulary of visual art words, and by learning how to communicate about their artwork and the work of others, orally, with graphic symbols, and, at the primary level, through writing. (Linguistic)

- **Cognitively**—By seeing that their creative actions and decisions can cause the effect of producing a visual image, and by developing the ability to compare and evaluate their own work and the work of others. (Logical-Mathematical)

- **Visual art concepts and skills**—By meeting the Common Core Standards for Visual Art.

Creating: Students will initiate making works of art and design by experimenting, imagining and identifying content.

- **PreKindergarten.** Engage in self-directed play with materials

- **Kindergarten.** Engage in imaginative play with materials

- **First Grade.** Engage in collaborative imaginative play with materials.

- **Second Grade.** Collaboratively brainstorm multiple approaches to a problem.

Presenting: Students will intentionally select and analyze their artwork and the work of others when deciding what artwork to present.

- **PreKindergarten.** Identify reasons for saving and displaying objects, artifacts and artwork

Drawing is one of the first visual arts experiences young children have. Matthew, age two, has used both broad strokes made with the whole arm and smaller marks made with wrist movements. He is in the scribble stage and learning to control the marks he makes. What drawing materials would you offer him?

Did You Get It?

John, a four-year-old, paints a picture using his imagination. He compares it with his friend's painting and notices they used the same color green. In which of the following ways are the visual arts helping John develop in this scenario?

a. emotionally

b. cognitively

c. physically

d. linguistically

Take the full quiz on CourseMate

🎵 **Kindergarten.** Select art objects for display and explain why they were chosen.

🎵 **First Grade.** Explain why some objects, artifacts, and artworks are valued over others.

🎵 **Second Grade.** Categorized artwork based on a theme or concept for an exhibit.

Responding: Students experience, analyze and interpret art and other aspects of the visual world.

🎵 **PreKindergarten.** Distinguish between images and real objects

🎵 **Kindergarten.** Describe what an image represents.

🎵 **First Grade.** Compare images that represent the same subject.

🎵 **Second Grade.** Categorize images based on expressive properties.

How Do Children Develop in Two-Dimensional Expression?

In the past 100 years, children's art has attracted the attention of many researchers. Some have collected samples of children's art and looked for patterns (Kellogg, 1969, 1979; Schaefer-Simmern, 1950, Sheridan, 2010). Others have tried to use it to measure intelligence (Cox, 1993; Goodenough, 1926; Harris & Goodenough, 1963). Many have used it to understand how children think (Gardner, 1991; Golomb, 1981; Winner, 1982; Hope, 2008). More recently, children's art has been used to assess emotional needs (Di Leo, 1970; Levick, 1986; Silver, 2002). Over the years, several models of artistic development have been created. These provide one perspective on the teaching of visual art to young children.

However, other research (Kindler, 1997; Wilson, Hurwitz, & Wilson, 1987) indicates that normative sequences do not always reflect the actual development of individual children, but rather visual arts development proceeds in stops and starts and is heavily influenced by a number of factors, including instruction.

Development in Two-Dimensional Expression

From the 1950s to the 1970s, Rhoda Kellogg (1969, 1979) collected over 1 million drawings done by children from the United States and other countries. These drawings provided the basis for her in-depth analysis of the patterns and forms found in children's art and represent a commitment to the collection of child art unparalleled in early art education research. Kellogg was one of the first to recognize that the scribbles of young children were an important part of the child's development, and that the marks made by young children the world over were more the same than they were different.

1. **Basic Scribbles.** Kellogg isolated twenty kinds of markings (Basic Scribbles) made by children age two and under. The Basic Scribbles consisted of all of the lines the children make, with or without the use of their eyes, whether using a crayon on paper, fingerpaint, or scratching the lines in the dirt. She saw these strokes as representative of the neural and muscular system of the child and forerunners of all of the strokes needed to make art and language symbols. Her descriptions of these Basic Scribbles were offered as a way to describe the art of the very young child.

2. **Placement Patterns.** In addition, Kellogg looked at how children under age two placed these scribbles on their paper. She felt that the Placement Patterns were the earliest evidence that the child was guiding the initial formation of shapes. She hypothesized that children react to the scribbles they make by seeing shapes in the drawing itself rather than trying to represent the shapes seen in the world around them, and that visual and

Mandalas, suns, and people. Marker—various children

motor pleasure was a motivating factor in causing children to scribble.

3. **Aggregates, Diagrams, and Combines.** Between ages two and three, Kellogg found that children began to draw shapes that they then combined into groups. She termed these groups aggregates, diagrams, and combines. At this stage, children move from unplanned scribbling to being able to remember and repeat shapes they have drawn previously. These shapes become the basis of all the symbols later found in children's drawings.

4. **Mandalas, Suns, and People.** Kellogg was most fascinated by the symbols that often emerged between ages three and four. She noted that the symbols seemed to follow a developmental sequence, and she felt that the mandalas and suns provided the stimuli for the child's first drawings of a person.

At the time Kellogg did her research, most adults considered child art a poor attempt to represent objects and persons in the child's environment and, therefore, worthless or in need of correction. Children were discouraged or even forbidden from scribbling and were encouraged to copy adult models. Kellogg felt that drawing was an expression of the growth of the child's physical and mental processes; it was the process of drawing that was important. She argued that children need plenty of time for free drawing and scribbling in order to develop the symbols that will later become the basis of all drawing and writing.

More recently, Susan Sheridan (2010) has looked at the scribbles and drawings of very young children as brain-building behavior that she characterizes as "one of the predetermined ways a child's brain naturally builds itself" (p. 9). She proposes six stages of scribbling and drawing.

1. **Early Scribbling.** Infants make only a few marks, usually lines and dots. They push and pull and stab at the paper without paying full attention to what they are doing.

2. **Middle Scribbling.** Most toddlers make more and more complex loops and circles.

3. **Mature Scribbling.** They continue to develop more complex patterns using loops and circles and place them in a more controlled manner.

4. **Early Drawing.** As they reach preschool age, children start naming the scribbles being made; this shows the beginning of representing the natural world and events.

5. **Middle Drawing.** Older preschooler and many kindergarteners show a mix of scribbling and the beginning of recognizable shapes and images, which vary from child to child and drawing to drawing. The child's explanations of the work produced become more verbally complex.

6. **Mature Drawing.** Mastered shapes and movements are combined in new ways to create meaningful and imaginative images during kindergarten and the primary years. They add marks that look like writing, which become words as they learn to write.

However, as we have seen, this development does not necessarily follow in this strict order or time schedule. For children with small motor difficulties this process may take longer. In some cases, children do not obtain sufficient fine motor control to represent their ideas the way they wish until well into the middle years. Outside influences also play a major role in children's graphic skills. The more opportunities children have to draw and use art materials as a way of expressing ideas and capturing visual images, the more skilled they will become.

Did You Get It?

Which of the following is true of Rhoda Kellogg's in-depth analysis of the patterns and forms found in children's art?

a. She hypothesized that visual and motor pleasure was a motivating factor in causing children to scribble.

b. She hypothesized that children under the age of two attempt to represent the shapes seen in the world around them through their art.

c. She concluded that children should be asked to avoid scribbling and should be encouraged to copy adult models instead.

d. She discovered that the marks made by young children from different parts of the world have nothing in common.

Take the full quiz on CourseMate

How Are Two-Dimensional Activities Designed?

Drawing, painting, collage, and other visual art media can be used by children of all ages, but children vary greatly in maturity level and ability to concentrate on a visual arts activity. The choice of an activity should be based, first of all, on each child's day-to-day behavior rather than on chronological age. In the Making Plans boxes, ages are given only as a guideline.

The presentation of the activity should always be adjusted to the developmental level and needs of the children.

One-on-One

For infants and young toddlers, who still put things in their mouths, the best way to introduce arts materials and tools is to work with just one child at a time. This allows the child to work under close supervision with a caring adult who can provide immediate positive feedback and share in the child's joyful creation.

Exploration Centers

Older toddlers and preschoolers will need to spend time discovering how the different art media work. This is the exploration stage. At this level visual art is best presented through art centers where arts materials are arranged in attractive and organized ways that invite independent use. Children should be able to freely choose from a variety of materials and explore on their own as part of their natural play.

Practice Activities

Once children are familiar with a material, they will need plenty of opportunity to revisit and practice. This is the revisitation stage. Art centers, stocked with beautifully displayed, familiar materials allow choice and continued exploration. Centers allow children to return again and again to familiar materials and tools. In addition, these materials will be at the ready for use in small group or class projects and integrated arts units.

Whether incorporated into the classroom or in a separate space such as the *atelier* in Reggio Emilia type programs, working at beautifully arranged centers should form the backbone of the visual art program from toddler to the primary grades.

Responsive Activities

Once they have gained sufficient fine motor control and arts skill, children will be able to focus and refine the ideas and feelings they are trying to communicate in their artwork. This is the responsive stage. Responsive activities are often based on common experiences shared by the whole class. In these cases, opportunities for the whole class to make paintings or work with clay at the same time make sense. Working together in this way allows children to see how each of them responds in different ways to the same stimuli. But whole class activities should never replace access to a well-supplied art center.

Vary the drawing experience by providing different sizes of paper, a variety of drawing materials, and demonstrating new ways to draw. Here children draw at an easel.

Did You Get It?

Martha works at a daycare center in Virginia. Which of the following points should she bear in mind while organizing visual art activities for the infants under her care?

a. She must allow the children to discover how different art media work on their own.

b. She must choose activities based on chronological age, rather than on each child's day-to-day behavior.

c. She must work with only one child at a time.

d. She must supervise the children's activities in groups.

Take the full quiz on CourseMate

The Drawing Experience

Drawing is the most basic of all the visual arts. It is usually the first art experience young children have and is the first step toward literacy.

Selecting Drawing Materials

Because many ways of drawing are simple and safe, drawing can be offered to even the youngest of children.

Crayons. Crayons have been the mainstay of early childhood drawing for many years. Their durability, relative safety, and ease of use will continue to keep them popular. The thick kindergarten size will prove most sturdy for grasping fists. However, other shapes and sizes can be slowly introduced over time. Breakage is to be expected, and removing the paper wrappers expands their creative possibilities. As the children gain better finger control, provide regular-sized crayons. Children can also be offered a much wider variety of colors. Fluorescent crayons, metallic crayons, and multicolored crayons will provide great enjoyment for children at this level. Two or three notches can be cut in the side of a large unwrapped crayon. Rubbed sideways on the paper, it will produce an interesting effect.

Markers. Unscented, water-based markers should be the backbone of the drawing program. The smooth, fluid nature of markers allows a level of detail not possible with other drawing materials. Markers are much loved by toddlers. Choose water-based, broad-tipped markers. They create broad sweeps of vibrant color with little pressure. Taking off and putting on the caps provides small muscle practice, although some youngsters may need help doing this for a while.

Pencils. Look for pencils with very soft leads, both regular and colored. Using pencils makes young children feel grown up and lets them draw finer lines than they can with the other materials. Children who have some control over drawing materials can also explore using charcoal pencils. The soft lines can be gently blurred with a tissue to create shading.

Chalk. Chalk is not suitable for infants because of the danger of inhaling the fine particles. If toddlers are able to keep their hands out of their mouths while working, thick sidewalk chalk used outside on the pavement will provide an interesting color and texture change from using crayons and markers. Avoid the use of chalk on paper or any other surface when working with toddlers. The dust created is hazardous to their health (see Appendix A).

For preschoolers, kindergarteners, and primary age children, regular white and colored blackboard chalk can be offered. To keep dust under control, moisten the paper with liquid starch, milk, water, or thinned white glue. Alternatively, the chalk can be dipped into the liquid and then used for drawing. To prevent inhalation of dust and toxic pigments, use only blackboard chalk, not artists' pastels.

Selecting Drawing Surfaces

Changing the drawing surface changes the way drawing materials work.

Paper. There are many ways to vary the paper offered to children. The size and shape of the paper will affect how the child uses it. Generally, the younger the child, the bigger the paper should be, because smaller paper requires more muscle control to stay within its borders. Newsprint and 50-lb. manila and 50-lb. white drawing paper should be provided for basic drawing activities. Paper can be cut into squares, rectangles, triangles, and circles. Use paper of different colors and textures as well.

Mural paper. Long, rolled paper can be hung on a wall, inside or outside, to create a "graffiti" mural. A large sheet can also be laid on the floor, and several children can draw together.

Other surfaces. For infants, zip closure plastic bags can be filled with hair gel colored with food coloring and taped closed. Infants can use their fingers to make marks. Older children will enjoy drawing on rocks, on the sides of cardboard boxes, and in sand and rice. With increasing fine motor skills, they can also work on materials with more confining shapes and sizes, such as strips of adding machine tape and sandpaper. Scrap pieces of wood that have been sanded on the edges make an interesting drawing surface. Small, decorated pieces may then be used in wood sculpture constructions.

Open-Ended Drawing Activities

Provide drawing explorations daily or as often as possible. For infants, provide playful one-on-one experiences.

As infants mature and gain experience, offer more choices of drawing materials and times and places to work. By preschool, children are usually familiar with drawing tools and beginning to develop control over where their lines go. Increased fine motor control allows older children to explore more responsive activities. Figure 9-1 provides a suggested way to introduce drawing as an open-ended activity over a period of five weeks.

Paper and drawing materials are enough to inspire most children. Add variety through small variations that increase choice and creative problem-solving opportunities. Here are some suggested drawing activities to try.

All one color. Offer a combination of markers, crayons, and pencils in the same color range, such as all reds or all blues. Then talk about dark and light, and dull and bright. Infant and up.

Contrasting colors. Use dark-colored paper with light-colored or metallic crayons. Infant and up.

Shaped paper. Paper can be cut into a variety of geometric shapes, but keep these large and simple. Squares; long, thin rectangles; and large triangles are easy to prepare. A paper cutter is invaluable when working with a large number of children. Infants and up.

Drawing everywhere. Put paper and crayons or markers in various places around the classroom, such as at the science center and block center. Encourage children to record what they see and do. Preschool and up.

Bookmaking. Booklets can be made either from 9-by-12-inch paper or in big book size from 12-by-18-inch sheets. Staple the paper together on either the long or the short side. Start with two pages. As the children develop their story-making skill, increase the number of pages. Tell the children that pages can be added if they need more to complete their story. Show the children how to fold back the pages so the booklet lies flat while they are drawing. Preschool and up.

Draw what you see. Set up a still-life arrangement of fruits or flowers or display a live animal. Put drawing materials nearby and invite children to sketch what they see. Preschool and up.

Drawing boards. Provide large clipboards with an attached pencil so children can sketch anywhere. Take these on field trips to record what they observe. Preschool and up.

For more open-ended drawing ideas, see *Open-Ended Drawing Activities for Young Children* on CourseMate.

WEEK 1: On the first day of class, sit on the rug and open a brand-new box of crayons. Have children name their favorite color. Ask: "How do we use crayons?" Talk about how, when, and where they can be used. Show children where crayons are kept. Have children model getting crayons from the supply area and going to a worktable, and then putting them away. Keep this brief—no more than five minutes. For the rest of the week, have white paper and crayons on the storage shelf. Encourage children to get them and draw. Monitor proper use. Save their drawings for the next lesson.

WEEK 2: Start the week by reviewing what the children did with the crayons. Sitting together on the rug, make up a song or movement about lines. Say, "Last week you learned how to get and use the crayons. Here are some drawings you made. What do you see? Do you see lines? What colors do you see?" Let the children respond.

"I will be putting different kinds of papers on the shelf this week. Do you think the crayons will work the same way on them?" Each day put out a different color or texture of paper. Encourage children to compare these to drawings on white paper. Save or photograph their drawings.

WEEK 3: Work with a different small group each day. Begin by looking at their drawings. Ask, "What was your favorite paper?" Then say, "Now you know how to get crayons and choose paper. Today I will show you our drawing boards. You can use the drawing board to draw anywhere in the room. You could draw a picture of your block tower. You could draw the fish. You could find a quiet place to draw an imaginary picture. This is how you get a board (demonstrate). Take a crayon container and find your very own drawing place. Draw a picture, and then put away the board and crayons. Gina, can you show us how to put the board and crayons away? Now let's have everyone try it. Find your special place to draw." During the week, encourage children to use the drawing boards.

WEEK 4: Start the week by introducing drawing outside. Say, "Today when we go outside, I will take the drawing boards and crayons. Maybe you will find a special place to draw outside." Continue to encourage children to draw inside and outside. By the end of the week, children should be able to get their own drawing supplies and find a place to draw. Now they will be able to do responsive drawings or keep journals as part of thematic units or during projects.

FIGURE 9-1 From Exploration to Responsive Drawing Activities in Five Weeks

Reading about Drawing

Read books about drawing or illustrated with drawings such as *The Ish* (Reynolds, 2004) or the classic *Harold and the Purple Crayon* (Johnson, 1998) and its sequels.

For more books featuring drawing, see *Books Celebrating Drawing* on CourseMate.

Looking at and Talking about Drawings

Expand children's ideas about drawing by sharing drawings by well-known artists. Select art prints that have subjects of interest such as the cave art of the Paleolithic or Picasso's drawings, to share with your group of young children. Encourage them to trace the drawn lines with their fingers.

As children become more familiar with artworks by others introduce art prints that illustrate more complex drawing techniques, such as the work of Albert Durer and M. C. Escher. Challenge children to figure out what drawing material the artists used and provide similar materials for them to try.

Questions to ask about their drawings and those of others:

- What lines do you see?
- Can you trace these lines?

Did You Get It?

Cathy works at a daycare center. She wants to organize some visual art activities for the toddlers in her care. Which of the following types of drawing materials should she let them handle?

a. multicolored inks

b. scented oil-based ink markers

c. fluorescent and multicolored crayons

d. regular white and colored chalk

Take the full quiz on CourseMate

🎨 Where do you think the artist start drawing?

🎨 What kinds of lines did the artist make?

🎨 Why do you think the artist choose this materials to draw with?

🎨 What story does this drawing tell?

The Painting Experience

There is nothing else quite like it. Long tapered brushes dip into liquid color that flows and falls with abandon across a white rectangle of paper. For a moment, the young artist is alone, focused on the interplay of mind and muscle, action and reaction. Painting provides the sensory link between the childish finger that plays in the spilled milk and the masterly hand that painted the Mona Lisa.

Before beginning a painting exploration with children, take a moment to make a tempera painting. Swirl and spread the paint, and concentrate on the way the brush responds to muscular commands and the visual result that is created. Feel the way the brush glides over the surface, and watch how the wet paint catches the light and glistens. Creating a painting is the perfect way to appreciate the importance of process over product to the young child, for whom painting is first and foremost a sensory experience.

For young children, painting is a sensory experience. Watching a young child paint and develop control over a medium that drips and smears is the perfect way to learn to appreciate process over product.

Selecting Paint

A variety of paints are available that are safe to use with young children. In addition to liquid tempera, other types of paint can be offered. Most of these will work better if used on a table rather than at the easel.

Fingerpaint. Commercial **fingerpaint** provides vibrant color in a smooth, easy-to-clean formula and should be the main fingerpaint used. For other fingerpaint explorations, after checking for allergies, try whipped soap flakes or liquid starch colored with a small amount of food coloring or tempera paint. Find recipes for various paints in Appendix D: Recipes.

Tempera blocks. This paint comes in dry cakes that fit in special trays. The children must wet the brush to dampen the cube for use. Choose the larger sizes in basic colors and fluorescents. Some adults like the fact that these do not spill. However, the colors and texture of the block paints are not as exciting as liquid tempera paints, so these should never be the only type of paint the children use but, rather, an interesting addition to the program.

Paint "markers." These small plastic containers have felt tips. Fill the container with tempera paint, and use like a marker. The stubby shape of the bottles fits well in little hands, and the paint flows out easily. Keep them tightly capped in a resealable plastic bag when not in use (see Appendix C: Supplies for paint marker sources).

Watercolors. The small size of the individual watercolors in a set, even in the larger half-pan size, makes them suitable only for preschool and primary age children with well-developed fine-motor control. Watercolors are also more likely to stain clothing than tempera paint. Before giving watercolors to the children to use, wet the color pans and let them sit a short time to soften the paints. Watercolors produce interesting effects when used on wet paper or on top of crayon drawings. Paper can be dampened with a sponge or paintbrush before painting.

Selecting Brushes

A multitude of commercial paintbrushes are available on the market. Always buy the best quality you can afford. A good brush that is regularly washed out will hold its point and last many years. Poor quality brushes lose their hair rapidly and do not come to a point. Brushes usually come numbered. The higher the number, the larger the brush. Offer children an assortment of brushes to choose from when painting.

Flats. These brushes are rectangular shaped and have a straight edge, instead of a point. They are good for painting in broad areas of color, edges, and for making thick even lines.

Rounds. These rounded brushes come to a point. These are good for detail work and painting thin lines and dots.

Easel brushes. These brushes have a long handle. They are best used when painting at the easel.

Bristle brush. A stiff brush made from hog hair.

Fine hairbrush. A pointed brush made from ox hair or in the more expensive ones, from sable.

Polyester or nylon. A brush made from synthetic material. These are usually very durable.

Stencil brush. This is a stubby round brush with very stiff hair.

Sumi. A soft-haired brush with a bamboo handle, traditionally used in Japanese painting. It works best in watercolor.

Selecting Surfaces for Painting

Although plain white paper provides an adequate surface for most types of paint, create exciting sensory experiences by providing a variety of surfaces for children to paint on.

Brown paper. Brown kraft paper (or a cut, flattened paper bag) provides an absorbent surface with a color that contrasts well with the lighter colors that are often lost on white paper. Try it with mixtures of pink, sky blue, yellow, and white paint. Try wrinkling the paper and then smoothing it again to create a bumpy texture that is fun to paint on, too.

Colored paper. Colored construction paper in dark colors also offers a good contrast for light-colored paints.

Commercial fingerpaint paper. This is heavy, with a smooth, shiny surface. Although relatively expensive, children should occasionally have the opportunity to fingerpaint on this paper. Freezer paper, shiny shelf paper, and other sturdy papers can also be used. Paper may be dampened with a wet sponge to make the paint spread more easily.

Fabric. Burlap or fabric glued to a cardboard base serves as a challenging texture for painting. This would be a good choice when exploring texture.

Paper products. Paper placemats, coffee filters, shelf paper, and thick paper toweling offer different textures for painting.

Wood and stone. The varying texture and absorbency of wood scraps and stones provide an interesting contrast to flat paper.

Other papers. Some papers are more difficult to paint on for young children. Tissue paper dissolves when it gets wet. Metallic papers and aluminum foil do not take water-based paint well; when dry the paint flakes off.

Paint Colors

Half of the wonder in the painting experience is using the glorious colors. Tempera paint gives the most painterly effects with luscious colors and a nice thickness. Fight the tendency to use paint right out of the bottle every time. Primary and secondary colors are wonderful, but children need to experience the nuances of color. Using a range of tones allows for more sensory comparisons to be made such as blueberry blue and watermelon pink. Add small amounts of white or black to the primaries to tone them down. Try other mixtures as well. Add yellow to green, purple to red, and green to blue and lighten and darken the resulting colors with white or a dab of black. Having toddlers and older children help mix up containers of new colors is a wonderful activity to engage children in learning new colors.

Store mixed colors in sealed containers such as margarine and yogurt cups. If paint needs to be stored longer, wrap the cups in a sealed plastic bag.

In addition to tempera paint you can make your own. Homemade paint recipes abound. Find a list of paint recipes to try in Appendix D.

Introducing Painting to Infants and Toddlers

Painting activities for infants need to be safe and carefully supervised but allow plenty of free exploration. The squishy bag activity described in Chapter 4 is one way to "paint" with infants. However, despite the cleanup to follow, don't be afraid to try tempera paint as well. It makes a wonderful sensory activity.

Exploration. Work one-on-one with infants and no more than two to three toddlers and be ready with clean up supplies. Strip infants down to their diapers. Have the child sit on your lap or in a high chair or for those who can sit and crawl place them on a large sheet of paper on the floor. Toddlers can sit at a low table.

Pour a small amount of paint in the middle of the paper. Model touching the paint and spreading it around. Allow the child to explore as you make enthusiastic descriptions and encouragements. If a baby tries to eat the paint or mouth a painted hand, gently redirect. If the infant is persistent, it is time to stop and have fun washing up. Repeat as often as possible offering more and different colors of paint each time.

Using a brush. Introduce the infant or toddler to using a brush by offering a short-handled brush with stiff bristles that can be grasped in a fist and scrubbed in the paint. Rounds work well for first experiences. Older infants and toddlers with more painting experience can explore other types of brushes. Other objects can also be used to spread the paint such as

plastic net pot scrubbers, sponges, new toothbrushes, bottle brushes, toilet brushes, and vegetable brushes. Look around and see what you can find.

Fill low-sided containers only high enough to color the bristle of the brush. For maximum sensory effect select clear containers so the infant can see the color. Commercial hummus containers or cut down deli containers work well.

Setting Up a Painting Center

A painting center for toddler, preschool, kindergarten, and primary classrooms can be set up as part of the general art center. It should have both a table and easel. Provide a ratio of one easel for every five children (i.e., if there are 20 children, have four easels set up), or a table on which four children can paint at one time. Side-by-side easels provide the most opportunity for the children to interact. Make sure the easel is low to the floor so the child can reach up to the top of the paper. Cover the table and easel surface with newspaper or other protective material. Kraft paper wrapped around and taped under the table provides a durable and smooth surface. To protect the floor put a piece of heavy plastic under the easels. Use spring-type clothespins to clip the paper to the easel. Provide a place for children to put wet work to dry. To attract children to the center, display clear containers of paint on open shelves and display children's paintings and works by famous artists.

Open-Ended Painting Activities

Remember that the process of painting is far more important that the final product. Here are some open-ended painting activities to try.

Special Needs

• DRAWING AND PAINTING MODIFICATIONS •

Visual: Children with limited vision should work on a tilted surface or easel so that their eyes are closer to the work surface. Choose the colors of crayons, markers, and paint that they can see best, and add sawdust or sand to the paint so they can feel their finished painting. Different scents can be added to the paint to help with color identification.

Physical: Some children with orthopedic handicaps work best if they can lie on the floor when painting. Tape paper to the floor or other work surface so that it does not move while they are working. Wrap foam around the handles of the brushes or drawing tools to make them easier to grip. Use wide, low-sided containers for the paint, such as cut-down margarine or frosting containers. If necessary, use tape to hold paint containers in place.

Accommodate children in wheelchairs by hanging the paper on the wall at a height that allows them to work comfortably. Provide plenty of room for them to extend their arms out full range. If necessary, attach a brush or marker to a dowel to extend the child's reach. Keep the paint thick, and make sure all children have ample working space, so if there are involuntary movements or lack of control, paint does not splatter on the paper or clothing of other children. (See Chapter 5 for more ways to meet special needs.)

Teacher Tip

PAINTING SMOCKS

A good smock that will cover most of the child can be made from a large adult's shirt that buttons up the front.

1. Cut the smock sleeves very short.
2. Put it on the child backwards, and fasten it together in the back with a spring clothespin.
3. Make sure the child's sleeves are pushed up above the elbows.

Icy paint. On a hot day add tempera paint to water in ice cube trays and freeze to make colorful ice cubes. If desired, insert a craft stick to serve as a handle or use popsicle molds. The child can move the ice cube around the paper to make colorful marks. Infant and up.

Water painting. Give children large brushes and buckets of water. Go outside and paint walls and pavement. Infant and up.

Table painting. Put fingerpaint on a smooth, washable tabletop or piece of Plexiglas and let children explore. To save artwork, place a piece of paper on top and press to capture the child's work. Infant and up.

Lots of colors. Once the child understands painting procedures, offer new colors. There is no rigid formula for selecting the colors. Let them self-select or mix their own. Infant and up.

Celebrate a color. Offer the featured color and related **tints** and **tones** at the paint set-up. On purple day, for example, help children mix up a range of purples, lavenders, and deep indigos. Infant and up.

Add textures to the paint. A variety of materials can be mixed into the liquid paint to give it a different feel. Infant and up.

1. The simple addition of a little more water makes a thinner paint and changes the sensory response of the brush as it moves across the paper.

2. Detergent, liquid starch, and corn syrup added to the paint will make it spread differently.

3. To make the paint thicker and textured, add sand, sawdust, cornmeal, flour, oatmeal, dry cereal, or soap flakes.

4. Salt added to the paint will produce a bubbly effect.

5. Salt and Epsom salts sprinkled on the paint produce a glittery effect.

Varied papers. In addition to the large newsprint, vary the painting surface by providing colored paper, cardboard, and smooth shelf paper. Cut the paper into a variety of large rectangles and squares, or occasionally into a triangle or circle.

Draw over paint. Encourage children to add more details to their dry paintings using marker and crayon. Toddler and up.

Explore other ways to apply paint. Paint can be applied with all of the following items: branches, pieces of cardboard, twigs, feathers, feathers, and more. Encourage children to be inventive in figuring out new ways to apply paint. Toddler and up.

For more ideas for painting activities, see Open-Ended Painting Activities for Young Children on CourseMate.

Reading about Painting

Read books about painting and those illustrated with paintings. For example, Tomi de Paola's *The Legend of the Indian Paintbrush* (1988) tells the story the flower "Indian Paint brush" and explains the role of painting in the lives of Plains Indians. This book relates well to painting activities using natural materials such as twigs and plants to apply paint. *The Art Box* (1998) by Gail Gibbons shows tools and materials used by artists for drawing and painting. Karen Beaumont's *I Ain't Gonna Paint No More!* (2005) features a little boy who loves to paint everything. The text is set to the bouncy tune of "It Ain't Gonna Rain No More."

For more books that celebrate painting, see Books Celebrating Painting on CourseMate.

Looking at and Talking about Paintings

Introduce children to colorful paintings with bold shapes such as the work of Wassily Kandinsky, Joan Miró, Georgia O'Keeffe, and Vincent Van Gogh. For preschool and up, use art prints and art cards to introduce different ways of painting. Select works that are noticeably different in style, such as a painting by Vermeer and one by Monet.

Compare art prints, art cards, or digital images of paintings done in different styles or techniques, such as a portrait by Rembrandt and one by Amedeo Modigliani. Then challenge children to make two paintings of the same subject using two different styles or techniques of their own invention.

Questions to ask about their paintings and those of others:

- What colors do you see?
- How do you think the painter mixed that color?
- What do you think the artist painted first?
- What kinds of paint strokes did the artist make?

Teacher to Family

Sample Letter to Families about Painting

Dear Family,

Painting is an important part of our art program, and the children will be painting almost every day. In order for your child to have a wonderful time painting, please dress him or her in clothing that is easy to wash. It is important that sleeves are pushed up above the elbows to prevent them from dragging in the paint.

Children will be wearing smocks when painting. However, accidents do happen. The water-based tempera paint we use will come out of most fabrics if it is washed in the following way:

Apply detergent to the spot and rub.

Wash normally.

If the spot still shows, repeat rubbing and washing.

Line dry. Do not put in the dryer until the spot is gone, as the heat will set the color.

It may take several washings to remove the stain completely.

Painting activities help your child grow in many ways, as he or she learns to control the paintbrushes and other painting tools. Please help your son or daughter enjoy painting without the worry of getting paint on clothing.

Your child's teacher,

Digital Download   Download from CourseMate

Did You Get It?

Daisy works for Redwood Care, a daycare center. She wants to introduce the toddlers at the center to painting. Which of the following should she offer the children?

a. provide each child with an inexpensive brush.

b. provide each child with a set of watercolors

c. provide the children with tempera paint blocks.

d. provide the children with liquid tempera in two or three colors.

Take the full quiz on CourseMate

What story does this painting tell?

Is this a **landscape, portrait, seascape,** or **still-life?**

The Collage Experience

Every art program for young children includes the art activity called "collage." Children are offered various papers, magazine pictures, and small objects to glue onto their pictures. Collage has become one of the most popular art forms for young children. It is also one of the most creative. Young children can arrange their bits and pieces of collage materials in a multitude of ways. Because we do not expect children to produce "realistic-looking" collages, we do not evaluate them in the same way as drawings. Children are extraordinarily free of restraints as they become immersed in the creative process of making a collage.

Every collage experience can be new and different. It is easy to vary the materials that are offered so that the children's motivation to explore and practice will remain high. Children will steadily develop more control over the paste and glue if they are given many opportunities to make collages. The challenge of applying paste to objects of different textures and forms will help develop their hand–eye coordination.

Selecting Pastes and Glues

Glue Sticks

Advantages—Large glue sticks are easy for young toddlers to use. Children can grasp them in one or two hands and easily rub the glue on the backing paper. Disappearing-color glue sticks help the child see where the glue has been put. Glue sticks work best for most paper and fabric.

Disadvantages—One major difficulty is that caps are difficult for young children to remove and put back on. Often the stick of glue is damaged in the process. This is a skill that needs to be taught and practiced. In addition, children often push up the stick more than needed and apply too much glue. Glue sticks do not work well for three-dimensional objects, so they are limited to only paper collage. Compared to bottled glue, they are also expensive.

Paste

*   **Advantages**—White paste or school paste has many advantages. It is easy to use because it is thick and does not run. Paste holds a variety of materials well. It can be placed on a piece of paper or in a plastic lid and applied with the fingers or a craft stick. It provides a wonderful tactile experience for young children.

*   **Disadvantages**—It has a tendency to crack and flake off when dry if applied too thickly.

White Glue (also called School Glue)

*   **Advantages**—This is a strong, durable adhesive that can be used to glue all kinds of objects. Choose only the type that indicates it washes out of clothing. White glue can be thinned with water and spread on a base to provide a pre-glued surface for collage. It will stay wet for 5 to 10 minutes. It easily cleans up with water, and is available in a wide variety of sizes and bottle designs. It dries clear. Squeezing the bottle helps children strengthen and improve control over their hands.

*   **Disadvantages**—The runny consistency makes this glue a little more difficult for young children to control. When applied heavily, it wrinkles the paper. Its major disadvantage is that it dries very slowly. Projects must be dried flat for at least 30 minutes before they can be handled. (Tacky or craft versions of this glue can be used in specific situations when instant adhesion is required, but it does not wash out of clothing.)

Gel Glue

*   **Advantages**—This glue is transparent and may be lightly colored. It dries clear, leaving a shiny mark on the paper. It is strong enough to hold a variety of lightweight- and medium-weight objects. It cleans up with water and does not stain

clothing. It is available in bottles similar to that of the white glue, as well as in roller and tube forms.

*   **Disadvantages**—This glue is runnier than white glue and is hard for children to control. When gluing fabric, for example, the glue quickly comes right through and wets the fingers. It dries slowly and wrinkles the paper.

Other adhesives. Many other pastes and glues are available on the market. Some of them are not safe for young children (see Appendix A). Others are difficult for the children to handle, such as the mucilage, cellulose, and wheat pastes, which are very sticky or runny. Glue pens and rollers are much more expensive (often three times the cost of white glue!) and work best with children who are skilled in handling drawing tools. Find recipes for homemade pastes in Appendix D.

Tape. Avoid masking tape and transparent tape. Even though tape is easy to use, it is neither a permanent nor an artistic way to hold arts materials together. Many times, once children become accustomed to using tape, they do not want to use the messier and more challenging paste and glue.

Selecting Collage Materials

Fascinating materials for collages can be found in nature, from around the house, and from craft activities. Look for interesting papers as well. Send a letter home to parents asking them to contribute found items to the collage center.

Selecting Cutting Tools

Select scissors that are lightweight and move easily at the pivot. They should be sharp enough to cut paper with very light pressure. They should have a blunt tip. Scissors are traditionally designed for use in the left or right hand, but many children's scissors are now on the market that can be used with either hand. Select ones that work with both left- and right-handed children, if possible. If separate left- and right-handed scissors are used, then color-code them so children know which they should select.

All-plastic, blunt-tipped scissors are a good choice for toddlers and younger preschoolers. These scissors will not cut hair, skin, or fabric. Older children can use pairs with lightweight stainless steel blades and plastic handles. They can also use the children's scissors that make decorative cuts. Other cutting tools include the following.

Training scissors. For toddlers or children with impaired finger dexterity, select training scissors that have blunt tips and spring-apart, plastic-coated handles.

Double-ring training scissors. These scissors have a pair of outer rings so that as the child holds the scissors, you can guide the actual cutting. They are most useful for children who have dexterity and strength but do not turn the wrist enough to hold the scissors vertically to the paper. This problem is usually manifested when the child tries to cut, but instead the paper folds. Usually the child needs to use them only once or twice. If there continues to be a problem, have the child try the training scissors.

Rotary hand cutter. This cutting tool, similar to ones used by quilters, is very sharp and must be used with close supervision. However, this may be the only way some children with special needs can cut. Look for ones designed for use by children that have a protective cover over the blade. Make sure the blade is covered and the handle is easy to grasp. It should have an automatically closing cover. It must be used with a cutting mat underneath at all times. This set-up will allow a child who can grip only with a fist to become quite proficient at cutting.

Teacher's scissors. Adults are always cutting many unusual items for collages. Invest in the best quality, all-purpose snips to be found. These usually have stainless steel blades, spring-apart blades, and a lock mechanism, which makes them safer to have around young children. They should be able to cut through heavy cardboard, all fabrics, carpet, leather, branches, pipe cleaners, wire, and more.

Dealing with Cutting Problems

Children face a variety of challenges when learning to use scissors.

- **Hesitancy**—If children have been forbidden to use scissors in the home, they may be hesitant to begin at first. Give them gentle encouragement to try the scissors.

- **Difficulty holding scissors**—Watch for children who are having difficulty holding the scissors

vertically to the paper. Check that they are using the thumb on top and opposing fingers on bottom to hold the scissors. If they are, gently guide their scissors into the correct position. It may help to hold the paper for them to practice the first few snips. The training scissors can be used to give them a start.

- **Difficulty controlling scissors**—Sometimes the scissors are too heavy or large for the child's hand. In this case, the scissors will tip or wobble unsteadily, and the child will not be able to cut paper. Light, plastic, appropriate-sized scissors should be made available to these children.

- **Hand position**—Some children may need help positioning the hand that is holding the paper. Make sure that they learn to keep their fingers out of the path of the scissors.

- **Paper bends**—One of the most frustrating things for a young child is when the paper bends instead of being cut. This often indicates that they are not exerting enough pressure as they close the scissors. If they keep trying to cut in the same spot, they will never succeed. Suggest that they try cutting in another place or using a different piece. Check that the child is holding the scissors in the correct position, as poor hand position often causes the paper to bend.

- **Wrong paper**—Paper that is either too thin or too thick is difficult for beginner cutters to use. Avoid tissue paper, thin gift wrap, and cardboard when children are still learning. White drawing paper and construction paper have the right amount of stiffness for first-time scissors users.

- **Weak grip**—Children who have difficulty using their fingers, hands, or wrists will find cutting with traditional scissors difficult. Scissors that are squeezed together between the thumb and all of the opposing fingers, and that open automatically with a spring, work well for some children. These are often called "snips." Try to select the lightest-weight pair with the bluntest point. Another option is the use of a rotary cutter.

Making a collage is the perfect way to practice using scissors.

Because there are no preconceived ideas about what a collage should look like, creating a collage is a very open-ended activity that allows unlimited choices. Joey, age three, has glued down precut paper and other materials in his own unique way.

Setting Up the Collage Center

The collage center can be part of a general art center or can stand alone. Provide a low table where the children can comfortably stand or sit. The tabletop should be bare and easy to wash. If the table must be covered, use an old shower curtain or a plastic tablecloth rather than newspaper, which can stick to the projects. A laminated sheet of construction paper also works well.

Because pasting and gluing with young children is a "messy" activity, and one that can be confused with food, it is important to set up a place where collages can be done away from food areas. This can be a special table that is near a water source. If working in a kitchen area, a large plastic tray or plastic tablecloth can be designated for collage activities, and pasting and gluing can be done only when that surface is set up.

As children gain skill, set up a permanent collage center with attractively displayed paper and objects grouped by texture and color, and set out on low shelving in shallow trays or clear plastic jars and bins.

Introducing Collage to Infants and Toddlers

Infants can participate in simple introductory collage activities such as these.

Paper shape play. Prepare infants and toddlers for future collage activities by cutting out a variety of colorful shapes from heavyweight tag board. If possible, laminate them or use foam. Together, play with the shapes on the high chair tray or table. Describe the shapes and arrange them in different ways. Let the child decide where to put them.

Tearing. As a precutting activity, give an older infant or toddler strips of easy-to-tear paper and let the child tear them into small pieces.

Paper balls. Show infants and toddlers how to squeeze small pieces of light-weight paper into balls. Drop balls onto sticky-side up contact paper or pre-glued paper.

Open-Ended Collage Activities

In the beginning, offer only a few types of materials at a time. Slowly, as the children grow in skill, introduce materials that are more difficult to cut, paste, or glue.

Counting collage. Have children select paper shapes from the collage offerings and paste to paper. Together, count the shapes used. Infant and up.

Photo collage. Print out digital photographs of family and familiar objects. Let children paste pictures onto a stiff paper or tag board background. Infant and up.

Picture collages. Preselect pages from magazines and cut them into simple shapes. Initial selections should focus on color, texture, or pattern rather than on objects. Be prepared for the children to paste them down with either side facing up. Toddler and up.

Cloth and yarns. Textiles make interesting additions to collages. Most young children cannot cut such materials, so precut them into simple shapes. In addition to fabric, offer ribbon pieces, rickrack, lace, thick yarns, and strings. Cut all of these linear items into short lengths, no longer than 6 inches, to make them easier for young children to handle. Toddler and up.

Mosaics. A **mosaic** is a picture made from small objects. Make mosaics from paper cut in 1-inch squares, or any small items, such as seeds, small pebbles, buttons, or tiles. Preschool and up.

Invent paste. Set up a center with flour, cornstarch, sugar, water, and milk and small cups for mixing. Provide measuring spoons and explore making a new recipe for paste. Preschool and up.

Go to CourseMate to find more ideas, see *Open-Ended Collage Activities.*

Teacher Tip

CHOOSING SAFE COLLAGE MATERIALS

Make sure objects offered for collage are safe for children under age three. Use the choke test to be sure (see Appendix A). Glitter and metallic confetti are also not recommended for young children. These items stick to children's hands and can be rubbed into the eyes. Lick-and-stick papers are not recommended. They give the children the impression that it is all right to put arts materials into their mouths.

For a list of suggested collage materials, see *Collage Materials* on CourseMate.

Reading about Collages

Numerous books are illustrated with collages. Ezra Jack Keats' classic Jennie's Hat (2003) shows a little girl who does not like her hat improving it by adding on all sorts of collaged objects. Lois Ehlert *Mole's Hill* (1998) is illustrated with paper collages inspired by the Woodland Indian tribes' beadwork and ribbon applique. Introduce older children to the collages of Henri Matisse using the book *Drawing with Scissors* by Jane O'Connor (2002). For more books focused on collage, see *Books Celebrating Collage* on CourseMate.

Looking at and Talking about Collages

The word collage comes from the French word for glue: *coller.* When doing collages share the work of Pablo Picasso. During his cubist period he added real items to his paintings. For example, while sharing Picasso's *Three Musicians,* have children look for the piece of real newspaper. Other artists who made collages include Georges Braque and Kurt Schwitters.

Questions to ask about their collages and those of others.

- What colors, shapes, and textures do you see?
- Which parts looked glued on?
- What materials can you identify?
- What story does this collage tell?

Did You Get It?

Jeremy has trouble cutting paper. Even though he has the dexterity and the strength, he does not turn his wrist enough to hold the scissors vertically to the paper. Consequently, the paper folds every time he tries to cut it. Which of the following types of cutting tools will allow Jeremy's teacher to guide him as he attempts to cut paper?

a. a rotary hand cutter

b. a pair of double-ring training scissors

c. a pair of training scissors

d. a pair of teacher's scissors

Take the full quiz on CourseMate

Making Plans

OPEN-ENDED ACTIVITY PLAN: LEAF COLLAGES

WHO?	Group composition age(s): Toddler and up
WHEN?	Time frame: 45 to 60 minutes on a fall day
WHY?	Objectives: Children will develop

- physically, children will develop fine motor skills, and gain control and strengthen hands and fingers. I will see this happening when they pick up and glue down leaves squeezing the right amount of glue out of the bottle. (Bodily-Kinesthetic)
- socially, children will develop social skills by participating in a group experience. I will see this happening when they walk in pairs on our trip outdoors and when they share their leaves. (Interpersonal)
- emotionally, children will develop self-confidence. I will see this happening when the leaves stay on their collage. (Intrapersonal)
- visual perception skills, children will develop skill at identifying leaf shapes. (Spatial)
- language, children will develop their vocabulary of descriptive words. I will hear this happening when they use color, texture, and sensory descriptions of the leaves. (Linguistic)
- cognitively, children will develop comparative, sequencing, and computation skills. I will see this happening when they compare, order, and count leaves. (Logical-Mathematical)
- art awareness, children will practice controlling the amount of glue they apply.

WHERE?	Setting: With assistants holding their hands, class will go outside under the big maple tree in the yard. Then they will return and use the leaves at the collage center.
WHAT?	Materials: Need a basket, leaves, paper, and glue (or contact paper with the backing peeled off).
HOW?	Procedure: Warm-Up (WOW): Take children outside on a fall day. Try to have one adult or older child paired with one or two children. Together, collect leaves.

What to Do: As children find leaves, help them name the colors and describe how beautiful they are. Put the leaves in an attractive basket. Inside, put the basket of leaves in the collage center and invite them to use them when they make a collage.

What to Say: As the children work at the center talk about the colors and shapes. Count them. Help children remember how it felt to collect them. Ask them why they chose the leaves they did. Describe the colors in exciting language, such as golden reds and brilliant yellows.

ASSESSMENT OF LEARNING	Transition Out: When all children have made a collage, read *Red Leaf Yellow Leaf* (Ehlert, 1991) or *Leaf Man* (Ehlert, 2005). Have children point out the leaves in the collage illustrations and see if they match any they found.

1. Can the children use descriptive terms for color, texture, and shape of leaves?
2. Can the children explain why they chose the leaves they used?
3. Can the children successfully glue the leaves to paper?
4. Are the children enthusiastic? Do they bring in different leaves for the center?

For more visual art activity plans, see *Sample Visual Arts Plans* on CourseMate.

The Printmaking Experience

Printmaking is any art form that involves making a copy of something. Some printing techniques can produce multiple prints, others only one copy **monoprint**. Printmaking can provide another way for young children to explore the sensory characteristics of objects. The children use their sense of touch as they handle the object and apply pressure to make the print. They can compare the stiffness of the object with the slippery wetness of the paint. The print provides a visual image of the texture, pattern, and shape of the object, and the stamping process often creates a rhythmic sound. Printmaking is also a very active art form that requires the children to move their arms with vigor and apply pressure sensitively.

Selecting Printmaking Materials

Printmaking requires three basic materials—paint, paper, and something with which to make a print.

Paint. Choose several colors of very thick tempera paint or fingerpaint. Make sure that the paint colors will not stain hands. White is always a safe choice, as are pastels that are mixed using white and a few drops of a color. If the paint is thin, thicken it with flour. Place a small amount of paint in each tray.

Trays. Put the paint in low-sided trays. Use Styrofoam or plastic food trays that have been sanitized (see Appendix A). Ensure that the sides are no higher than half an inch, or try paper plates.

Printing tools. For the first explorations, provide the children with large, easily grasped objects that they can dip in the paint, such as a variety of potato mashers or long, cardboard tubes. Place one tool in each tray. As children grow in skill, smaller objects can be added. Look for objects that make different shapes and patterns such as corks, cans, and spools for circles, blocks, erasers, and small boxes for rectangles, berry baskets, pinecones, and small wheeled toys for patterns.

Paper. Use paper in the 9-by-12-inch size range. Larger paper makes it difficult for the children to reach the trays and objects without leaning into their prints. Have plenty of extra paper so that children can make more than one print if they wish.

Drying rack. A cardboard box drying rack or other wet project storage unit placed near the printmakers will provide a quick place for the prints to dry while still supervising the children. With experience, the children can put their own prints away.

For plans for making a drying box, see Making a Print-drying Box on CourseMate.

The repetitive quality of printmaking provides the perfect opportunity for children to work together and allows children to explore how shapes can be put together in new ways to create patterns.

Setting Up a Printing Center

For initial printmaking explorations with infants, hold the child on your lap or use a high chair. For older children provide a low table that they can work at while standing. Children usually spend only a few minutes making prints and can do so standing up. This also enables them to reach the trays of paint and objects more easily. Cover the table with newspaper. Have all materials set out before inviting children to begin. Place the trays between the papers or down the middle of the table, depending on the size and shape of the table. Have smocks ready for the children to wear.

Limit the group to one or two toddlers or four older children. Once the children are familiar with the technique and can work more independently, the group size can be increased.

Once children are skilled at printing, consider merging the printmaking center with the painting center by putting the printmaking tools and plates with small amounts of paint near the easels and painting table. This will encourage more innovative work because children can add printed shapes to their paintings.

Introducing Printmaking to Infants and Toddlers

Handprints and footprints make a good introduction to the concept of making a print.

Water printing. Provide a tray of water and let the children make hand or foot prints outside on the pavement.

Sand prints. Press a hand or foot into the damp sand. Note: The print can be preserved by pouring plaster over it.

Open-Ended Printmaking Activities

Printmaking allows you to make multiple copies like a copy-machine. However, unlike a machine copy, each handmade print will be unique in its own way. Once children understand this concept they are ready to try making prints of all kinds.

Some printmaking activities involve stamping the image of some object over and over to make a pattern. This usually produces a one of a kind picture. Others involve making a master "plate" and then making multiple copies of it. The following activities provide ways to make a variety of prints.

Gadget prints. Gadget prints are made by dipping an object into paint and stamping it to make a mark. For infants and toddlers, provide large items that the child can easily grasp such as small plastic water bottles, spice jars, and potato mashers and use flat trays or paper plates of tempera paint. Older children can use smaller items like spools, bottle caps, and small blocks of wood or foam. Vary the printing tools, combining new ones with familiar ones. Infant and up.

Tire tracks. Dip the wheels of toy cars and trucks in tempera paint and drive around a piece of paper. Infant and up.

Sponge prints. Sponges make great printing tools. Cut the sponge into simple geometric shapes. Attach a clothespin to the top of the sponge shape, or, using craft glue, attach a spool "handle" to the sponge. Toddler and up.

Monoprints. Make a painting on paper or on a smooth washable tabletop. While still wet, place a piece of paper on top. Lift to see its print. Infant and up.

"Rubber" stamps. Commercial rubber stamps are too small for little hands to grasp, but larger ones are easy to make. Cut out simple geometric shapes—square, circle, triangle, rectangle, oval, and so on—from sticky-backed foam. Peel off the backing and affix these shapes to sanded wooden blocks. Toddler and up.

Splatter prints. Make a screen box by cutting an opening in a cardboard box and fastening a piece of screening over it. Tape edges well so that there are no rough places. Remove the bottom of the box. Place paper and washable or disposable objects, such as shells, plant stems, lacy doillies, and plastic spoons, under the screen box. Dip a toothbrush in tempera paint and rub across the screen. Remove objects carefully. Toddler and up.

String monoprint prints. Dip a piece of yarn or string in tempera paint. Drop the string onto a sheet of paper. Place another piece of paper on top and press. Remove to see the print. Toddler and up.

Rubbings. Place flat textured objects, such as pieces cut from plastic berry baskets, under a piece of paper and rub with the side of a peeled crayon to

Integrating the Arts

MAKING MATHEMATICAL CONNECTIONS TO THE COMMON CORE

Visual art activities can be used to reinforce mathematical concepts found in the Common Core Math Standards for K–2.

During drawing activities, children can draw and identify geometric shapes (2.G.A1).

During painting and modeling activities, children can use more, less, and equal as they mix two colors or different size pieces of clay together (K.CC.C6).

When printmaking, children can count orally each time they stamp a shape and add and subtract the numbers of shapes on their paper (K.CC.A.1; K.CC.B4a; 1.OA.A1; 2.OA. B2). They can name the shapes they make and identify their attributes (K.G.A.1-4). They can compare quantities and group and classify (K.CC.C6; 1.G.A1). They can make arrays and identify odd and even groups in patterns (2.OA. C3-4). They can use geometry terms to describe the shapes they make (1.G.A1). They can compose larger shapes using simpler ones (1.G.B6; 2.G.A2).

In fiber art activities children can measure out the length of the materials they will be using and sort by length (1.MD. A1 & 2; 2.MD.A1 &2)

capture the texture. Commercial textured rubbing plates are also available. Toddler and up.

Reading about Prints

Explore books that feature hand printed illustrations such as Bernard Waber's classic stories *"You Look Ridiculous" Said the Hippopotamus to the Rhinoceros* (1996) and *I Was All Thumbs* (1975), and the beloved *Swimmy* by Leo Lionni (1973).

Talking about Prints and Patterns

It is easy to find examples of printed materials. Wallpaper, upholstery, rugs, and clothing are often covered with printed designs that form patterns. Expand children's experiences by including examples from home cultures and other places in the world. Look for silkscreen prints by Native American artists of the Northwest coast such as Tim Paul, Bill Reid, Tony Hunt, and others. Also seek hand-printed fabric from India and Africa. Indian wood blocks used for printing cloth can sometimes be found in import stores. Questions to ask about their prints and those of others.

🐛 What colors, shapes, and patterns do you see?

🐛 Can we match the print to the object that made it? How is it the same or different?

🐛 How is this print the same or different from other prints?

🐛 What does this print make you think about?

For more ideas for printmaking activities, see Open-Ended Printmaking Activities on CourseMate.

Did You Get It?

Jenna wants her second grade students to explore patterns in math by making prints of repeated shapes. Which printmaking activity should she choose?

a. gadget prints

b. monoprints

c. string prints

d. rubbings

Take the full quiz on CourseMate

The Fiber Art Experience

Fiber art refers to any art form that involves the use of yarn, cloth, or the raw materials that are used to make them. Because fabric plays such an important role in everyday life in terms of clothing and furnishings, it is often seen as a functional object rather than an art form. Yet, even the simplest piece of clothing bears the mark of unnamed artists who determined the shape of its pieces, the drape of the fabric, and its texture and pattern.

Introducing fiber art to children helps them appreciate this often "hidden" and ancient art, which has found unique expression and form throughout time and across cultures. It is an excellent example of an art medium that can serve as a unifying theme for young children. Fiber activities can be used as part of the study of texture, line, and pattern.

In addition, fiber art activities give children experience with counting and the concepts of top and bottom, in and out, over and under, below and above, and in front and behind which are part of the Common Core Mathematics Standards for kindergarteners. Measuring length and using odds and evens are two other math skills that can be applied in the fiber arts and relate to the first- and second-grade math standards.

Weaving on a simple frame loom allows children to explore pattern and texture as they move in a rhythmical pattern.

Selecting Materials

Yarn and cloth form the basis of most fiber activities and are readily available. People who knit and sew will often donate leftover yarn and cloth to schools.

Yarn. Provide children with a wide range of yarns in different colors, thicknesses, and textures. Look for one- and two-ply yarns made from cotton, acrylic, and wool. Use the thicker yarns with very young children.

Cloth. Burlap is a sturdy, textured cloth that can be used as a base in stitchery and appliqué activities. Cross-stitch canvas is an open plastic grid that comes in different flexibilities that also provides a sturdy base for beginning stitchers. Unbleached muslin is an inexpensive cotton cloth that can be used to draw on and as a background for appliqué. Felt is easy to cut and handle. More elaborate cloth, such as satins and brocades, provides sensory stimulation. It can often be obtained in discarded sample books from upholstery and carpet stores.

Basketry materials. Commercial basket reed is a natural plant material that softens in water and stiffens when dry. It comes in a range of thicknesses. Willow branches collected from neighborhood trees make a good substitute but must be used green as they do not soften in water. Raffia is a strong grassy material that comes dyed in vivid colors.

Needles. Choose long 2- to 3-inch plastic needles with large holes for most stitchery activities that use burlap or large-hole cross-stitch as a base.

Open-Ended Fiber Activities

Remember that, for young children, process is more important than product; do not expect to see perfect baskets or pieces of cloth. Keep activities simple and exploratory and avoid craft kits that limit children's creativity.

Some fiber activities, for example, share many commonalities with collage. Once stitchery and appliqué have been introduced as an activity, yarn and cloth can easily be added to the collage center and cloth cut to size for backgrounds can be offered alongside paper. Other activities such as weaving baskets and fabrics are encouraged by providing a simple framework and allowing children to take turns weaving as they desire.

Integrating the Arts

WEAVING A DANCE

The patterned movements found in the weaving process lend themselves to integration with creative movement. Try some of these.

Threading the needle. Have children hold hands in a line. The first child is the needle and threads through the line, ducking under the uplifted arms. Still clasping hands, the others follow.

The Weaver. Sing the song "In and Out the Window." Have all the children but one stand in a circle holding hands. Children lift their arms as the child weaves in and out under their arms as the song is sung. Continue until all children have had a turn to be the "weaver."

The Star. Stand in a circle. Take a ball of yarn and hold on to the end. Toss the yarn to a child on the other side. That child holds on to the yarn near the ball and tosses it to another. Continue until all the children are holding onto the yarn. The resulting design will look like a multi-pointed star. With everyone holding on try different movements while singing a song like "Twinkle, Twinkle, Little Star." Raise and lower the star, come into the middle and move out and so on. This may take some practice to get it going but is very satisfying when successful.

The fiber arts encompass the following techniques suitable for young children to explore the following.

Cloth pictures. Appliqué is a design made by attaching pieces of cloth to a fabric background. Reverse applique is when a hole is cut in the top fabric so that the fabric underneath can show. To introduce young children to appliqué, provide precut cloth or felt pieces and a piece of felt or a felt board for the background. Have infants place the cloth pieces as they wish. The pieces will "stick" temporarily. Older children can use white glue to attach the cloth pieces on an individual piece of felt or cloth. Infants and up.

Stitchery. Pre-thread large plastic needles with doubled and knotted pieces of various colored yarn about 10–12 inches long. Children can help measure out the yarn to help develop measuring skills. Threaded needles can be poked into a piece of Styrofoam to keep the yarn from tangling. Depending on the age and experience of the children provide cross-stitch canvas, sanitized Styrofoam food trays, or burlap taped to an inexpensive picture frame or stretched in an embroidery hoop. A large piece of stretched burlap can be used for a group stitchery. Children can sit on either side and pass the needle back and forth to each other. When they have mastered the in-and-out pattern, give them buttons or beads with large holes to attach.

Model how to push the needle from the front to the back and from the back to the front. Then let them explore on their own. When they run out of yarn, cut off the needle and tape down the end on the back. Provide one-on-one supportive assistance for infants and toddlers. Preschool and up.

Handweaving. To weave children intertwine flexible materials such as yarns, ribbons, strips of fabric in an over-and-under pattern using some kind of frame or **loom** to hold them taut. Anything with regularly spaced openings can be used to weave fibers. Try berry baskets, old dish drainers, and chicken wire.

A simple loom can be made from a piece of cardboard with notches cut at each end. Wrap yarn around and then let the children weave in lengths of yarns and so on that are 2-3 inches longer than the width of the cardboard to create a fringe effect. These weavings can be left on the cardboard for display. A large piece of sturdy cardboard or a wood frame can be used for a group weaving. Preschool and up.

Basketry. Baskets are made by intertwining grasses, twigs, and other linear materials to form a container or rigid surface. For young children provide a framework by inserting 6- to 8-inch pieces of thick basket reed into holes punched into the outer edge of a plastic lid to form the basket's ribs. The bigger the lid the better. To help children discover the in-and-out pattern color or mark every other rib with a marker, but don't expect perfection. Children can help collect grasses and willow branches or use yarn, ribbon, and even wire to weave in and out. Preschool and up.

Quilting. Making fabric designs from joined pieces of fabric provides an opportunity for a group to work together. Each child can contribute a unique piece of cloth either from a selected fabric or one they have decorated with fabric crayons or even glued-on fabrics if the quilt is intended to be decorative. These pieces can then be sewn together, padded, and backed. Children can help poke threads through to be tied to hold the batting in place. Preschool and up.

Dyeing cloth and yarn. The safest way to dye cloth with young children is to use powdered drink mix with a small amount of water added. Food dyes can also be used but will be more expensive. For the cloth, use inexpensive white cotton such as muslin or old sheets. Wool yarn will take the color more vibrantly than cotton.

Natural plant materials are another source for dye stuffs. Try grape leaves, tomato leaves, onion skins, beets, and tea to start. If there are no nut allergies, walnut hulls make a very strong color. Natural materials need to be heated in water and boiled until the water takes on the color. Then dip the cloth in the stained hot water. The longer the material is exposed to the dye, the darker it will be.

None of these colors will be permanent in sunlight but will produce satisfying bright colors during the process. Children can apply the dye using a brush or by dipping in the dye. To **tie-dye** children can fold or pull fabric together and wrap rubber bands around. Wearing rubber gloves while using the dye teaches good safety practices. Kindergarten and up.

Reading about the Fiber Arts

Story cloths are traditional Hmong embroidered appliqués that tell people's life stories. The bilingual English-Hmong *Grandfather's Story Cloth* (Gerdner & Langford, 2008) tells the story of a young boy who helps his aging grandfather remember his past using a story cloth.

Huichol yarn paintings are made by pressing yarn closely together into soft wax to form textured shapes. *When Animals Were People* (Larsen, 2002) is a collection of bilingual English-Spanish Huichol folktales illustrated with yarn paintings. Children can make their own yarn paintings by pressing yarn onto the sticky side of contact paper or into wet glue spread on a sturdy paper.

M is for Mola (Striker, 2012) is a multi-lingual alphabet book (Chinese, English, French, Hebrew, Italian, Japanese, Kuna, Portuguese, Russian, Spanish, and Swedish). Each letter is accompanied by a photograph of a mola, an applique method used by the Kuna of Panama as part of their traditional dress.

For more books about the fiber arts, see *Books Celebrating Fiber Art* on CourseMate.

Looking at and Talking about the Fiber Arts

Talk about and look at the different articles of clothing that can be woven or knitted from yarn, such as sweaters, socks, and hats. Bring in examples of traditional clothing from different places in the world, and look for similarities and differences. Embroidery and handweaving are used in the traditional dress of many cultures such as Ukrainian, Greek, Chinese, and Indian. Have families share special articles of clothing or traditional fiber arts such as knitted items, crocheted and tatted lace, and quilts. Add interesting clothing items to the dress up area and encourage children to ask questions to ask about their fiber art and the art of others.

▶ What do you see?

▶ How does it feel?

▶ How do you think it was made?

▶ What does it remind you of?

Did You Get It?

After looking at needlework done by one of her student's parents, Anne wants to engage her kindergarten students in a stitchery activity in which the children will make designs on stretched burlap. While organizing the activity, Anne should choose _____.

a. very thin yarns

b. long 2–3 inch plastic needles

c. artificial permanent colors as dyes

d. metallic needles with small holes

Take the full quiz on CourseMate

The Digital Art Experience

Very sophisticated conversations about art happen not only at the art table but also between children working at the classroom computer. Computers and digital media have found their way into the hands of

Classroom Technology

SUMMARY OF THE NAEYC POSITION ON TECHNOLOGY AND INTERACTIVE MEDIA

1. Children are spending increasing hours using screen technology (includes television, computers, tablets, mobile phones, etc).

2. Worries about increasing passivity and obesity suggest that screen time should be limited. Recommendations suggest no more than 2 hours a day total for children between ages 2 and 5 with no more than 1 hour of that during school time. There should be no screen time for infants and toddlers.

3. Total screen time means using any and all digital devices both passive and interactive. It is up to educators to choose the most educative technology activities and to prevent misuse and over use of screen media.

4. It is important for educators to be digitally literate and have sufficient knowledge, skill, and understanding of child development to make wise choices in how screen technology is used with young children.

5. Some children may have little access to the latest technology at home. Integrating technology into early childhood programs is a step towards equity. Technology-handling skills, like book-handling skills, should be in place by age 5.

6. Developmentally appropriate practice should guide decisions about technology integration.

7. Technology activities need to be active and hands-on. They should be playful and involve co-viewing, problem solving, and critical thinking.

8. Technology should be used to enhance home-school relationships, provide those with special needs assistance so they can participate fully, and help dual language learners by providing access to the home language.

Find the complete Position Statement at http://www.naeyc.org/content/technology-and-young-children.

the very young, and they are providing an interactive medium unlike any other art form. Like collage, computer graphics provide an avenue of art exploration that challenges both child and teacher to accept new ways of thinking and working with the elements of art. This section will look at how the use of computers and other digital processes can enhance the visual art program offered to children.

Digital art is here to stay. It is fun and exciting to see one's art appear on the screen. However, care must be taken to limit viewing the screen for long hours. Recent research on the effect on the vision of children by the overuse of computers and hours spent indoors (Seppa, 2013; NAEYC, 2012) strongly suggest that computer exposure be limited.

The Computer as Art Medium

When the computer is viewed as an art medium rather than as a teaching tool, the logic of its inclusion in any art program involving children becomes apparent. A computer loaded with a simple graphic "paint" program is just another way to create lines and shapes. The monitor screen is the "paper," and the mouse is the tool for applying the lines and shapes and colors. The child manipulates colored light rather than pieces of paper, paintbrushes, or glue, but the artistic decisions are the same.

In this technologically sophisticated society, even very young children are familiar with computers. Being able to create their own "television" picture makes children feel independent and powerful. Properly selected and set up, computer art software provides a wonderful way to introduce children to the computer, beginning a pattern of comfort and success with this technology that will play such a large role in children's futures.

The computer provides the perfect place for an art conversation. An older computer loaded with an open-ended drawing program and with the keyboard placed on top is ideal for young artists.

The computer as art medium can be viewed as another component of the arts program, just like easels and collage centers. It is neither more nor less important than any of the other arts activities offered to children. Like the other arts activities, the computer allows children to play with the art elements in a creative way. Opportunities to work at the computer can be offered as one of the children's daily play choices.

Selecting Art Software

The computer **software** discussed in this section is of one type only. These are often called "paint," "**graphic**," or "drawing" programs and may come as part of the initial software on the computer; may be the graphic part of "works" programs that combine word processing, spreadsheets, and data processing, may be purchased in special versions designed just for children, or may be downloaded from the Internet. Because the specific software programs available change rapidly, use the following general guidelines for making sure the one selected will work well for young artists.

1. There should be a large workspace of white or black on which to draw.

2. The **cursor** should be large and easy to see.

3. The **menu** of color, shape, and line choices should be visible at all times, either at the side or top of the screen.

4. Menu choice boxes should be large, with logical symbols for line types, shapes, and fill options.

5. The program should have a limited number of menu options. Children do not need such things as multiple pages, graduated colors, and inversions.

6. Programs that load quickly are most convenient. If the only one available requires a complicated loading procedure, be sure to load the program before the children arrive. Turn the monitor off until it is time for the children to work.

7. The ability to save and print the children's pictures allows the children to review what they have done or to put on a computer art show.

8. Most importantly, the program should be open-ended. It should not have pre-drawn coloring-book-style pictures to color, nor should it involve the manipulation of shapes or pictures on an already drawn background. Just because the words *draw*, *paint*, *picture*, or *art* are in the title of a program does not mean it is a true art program. Always preview a program before offering it to children.

For suggested software and drawing programs, see *Digital Media Resources* on CourseMate.

Positioning the Computer

The computer should be located away from heavy traffic and in a "clean-hands" location. There must be an electrical outlet capable of handling the necessary power, preferably with a surge protector. Make sure the computer area will be visible from all parts of the room so that assistance can be offered when needed. Provide space so that two children can work together. It is a perfect way to develop collaborative skills.

Choosing Equipment

Consider the following equipment when setting up a computer art program.

Computers. Any computer that runs the appropriate software can be used. Many child-appropriate art programs can be put on older, lower-powered machines. If the right combination of a program and an older machine can be found, then that may allow one computer to be dedicated to art exploration alone.

Printers. A printer is a nice addition, as it provides a way to capture the children's work, but it is not essential. For young computer artists, just as in all of the other art forms, process is more important than product, and the printed versions of children's art are often pale imitations of the glowing images on the screen anyway. For many children, part of the fun seems to be making their pictures disappear when they are done.

Input devices. A **mouse** is the best way for young children to draw on the computer. A cordless mouse provides more freedom of movement. Try to put the keyboard out of the way so that the child can

focus on the mouse and the screen. On some computers, the **keyboard** can be placed on top of the monitor, or it can be removed and the mouse plugged in directly. If the keyboard is not removable, then it is essential to cover the keys with a protective skin. This will keep sand and other deleterious items out of the keyboard. The keyboard can also be covered with a cardboard box when children are using the mouse to draw. There are also graphic tablets that hook onto a computer like a mouse on which the child can draw freehand with a stylus using Adobe Illustrator. Another alternative is a touch-screen computer or an e-tablet, which lets children work directly on the screen with their fingers. Tablets should be fitted with a protective cover.

Open-Ended Digital Art Activities

Here are some ways to broaden the digital art experience.

Adding on. Have children take turns adding on to a picture. Preschool and up.

Animate a drawing. Using the free online drawing program SketchFu, at http://sketchfu.com/, children can draw a picture and then hit a button to see the picture redraw itself. Preschool and up.

Digital collage. Use prints of digital designs and photographs to make a collage or add them to a traditional collage. Preschool and up.

Making multiples. Children can be taught to insert their digital artworks into prepared layouts or templates created in a software program such as iWorks and Portfolio on an Apple computer, or Publisher, Word, or OpenOffice or Printshop on a PC to create cards, bookmarks, and calendars to share with families. Preschool and up.

Pattern design. Create simple and complex patterns using the shape and stamp feature of the software. Preschool and up.

Slide show. Children's digital pictures can be saved and incorporated into a show. Some art programs save groups of pictures with a "slide show" feature or in a presentation format such as PowerPoint, Kizoa, or Animato, or made into a flipping pages book using a program like FlipBook or made into a PDF file that can be viewed on some e-readers. Preschool and up.

How Are Three-Dimensional Activities Designed?

It is important for all children to have many opportunities to work in three dimensions. Infants can explore form by building with blocks and boxes, and through closely supervised one-on-one activities with play dough. By giving children the opportunity to explore a material that has many sides, that can be turned over and around and looked at from different points of view, teachers strengthen children's understanding of the spatial realm in which they exist. Three-dimensional art forms call upon different perceptual modes and different areas of skill development than do drawing, painting, and other two-dimensional activities.

The Modeling Experience

Modeling, or working with three-dimensional pliable materials, is one of the great joys of early childhood. Soft, smooth clays and playdough are just waiting to be squeezed and poked, to the great delight of the young artist.

When children draw or paint, there is a strong visual response to the marks they make on the paper. In working with modeling materials, although the visual element is still there, the children respond first to the tactile qualities of the forms as they create them. Young children working with play dough or clay will often manipulate the material vigorously while focusing their eyes on something else or staring off into space.

A great deal of talking and noisemaking goes on as children explore clay. Children working on drawings or paintings will perhaps make a comment or two while they work or add a special sound effect, but many at the clay table will pound, slap, and talk incessantly. Modeling materials will provide an opportunity for children to practice their social skills as they respond to each other's actions and exchange pieces of clay or tools.

Development in Three Dimensions

As in their two-dimensional work, children go through modeling modes that mirror their physical

Ben, age five, has made many pictures using the computer. His picture "House" was made using the online children's art program Tux Paint.

Mode	Child's Behavior
1. Initial Exploration	Manipulates material using all of the senses; uses large motions of arm and hand
2. Controlled Exploration	Begins to make basic forms— pancake, worm, and ball; uses palms and fingers
3. Named Forms	Gives names and labels to modeled forms; begins to use them in symbolic play; uses fingers for shaping
4. Symbolic Forms	Plans the forms that will be used; can attach forms; can pull a form out of a larger piece of modeling material; can use fingers to create small details

FIGURE 9–2 The Development of Modeled Form

and cognitive growth. The sorts of forms that children can produce are determined by the amount of control they have over their arms, wrists, hands, and fingers; by their mental ability to imagine a form and then produce it; and by their previous experiences with the material (see Figure 9-2).

Initial exploration. When first confronted with a modeling material, children often approach it with a caution that quickly turns to abandon. They push their fingers into it, pat it, pick it up and put it down, drop it, and squeeze it until it oozes out between their fingers. They may lick it and taste it, rub it on their faces, and stick it up to or into their noses for a good whiff. They will bang it with fists, peel it off their arms when it sticks, and throw it, if not stopped. There is no attempt to make the clay or dough into something but only a pure, multisensory exploration of this exciting material.

This purely exploratory behavior is seen in the youngest children, those between the ages of one and three, and it corresponds in some ways to scribbling in drawing. However, it is often seen in older children as well, especially as they first start to handle a new or an unfamiliar modeling material.

For toddlers, the behavior reflects their lack of small motor control, their reliance on large motor movements of the arm and hands, and their sensory approach to learning about their environment. For older children, this initial exploratory behavior reflects an attempt to understand the material's possibilities and limits. Even adult artists spend time working freely with a medium in order to assess its parameters before beginning to create a sculpture in earnest.

Controlled exploration. After the initial explorations of the modeling medium, children will begin to explore the clay or dough in a more systematic way. At this stage the children may flatten the clay into pancake-like forms using the palm of the hand. With their fingers, they may poke a series of indentations into the surface or pull off small pieces and flatten them. They may stick the pieces back together or create a stack of them. One of the first forms that they can make due to the increasing control over their hands is a long, thin cylinder created by rolling a piece of clay between the palms of their two hands.

In the fourth or fifth year, children discover they can form a sphere or ball by rolling the clay between the palms or between the table and one palm. This is a much more complex skill, as it requires the child to move the hand in a circular motion and is often preceded by much experimentation. Once the ball is perfected, it often becomes the object of manipulative play; it may be rolled across the table, or several may be lined up in a row.

For children who have had many opportunities to use clays, controlled exploration reflects their increasing control over hands and fingers. Older children and adults may also repeat these same manipulations as part of their preliminary explorations of modeling media.

Named forms. The difference between a named form and controlled exploration is not one of form or physical control. It relates instead to the cognitive development of the child. The long, thin cylinder becomes a "snake," the poked pancake becomes a "face," the clay balls become "snowballs." This naming of the modeled forms correlates to the naming of scribbled drawings and reflects the child's developing language skills and the growth of mental imagery.

The manipulative nature of modeling materials allows children at this stage of development to pursue symbolic play in a way that they cannot with two-dimensional art media. Young children "cook" playdough bits in the pots on a toy stove. They offer a "taco" to taste. They make mommy snakes and baby

As children become more skilled with modeling materials, they begin to make recognizable forms. Tina, age three, creates a simple person shape from her playdough.

Elizabeth, age six, has used playdough to create a flower.

snakes that hiss and wiggle around the room and then turn into bracelets wrapped around active wrists. They "bowl" with their clay balls.

Although the child's creations may take on a life of their own, they still are, largely, the result of unplanned manipulation. Once made, they are then "seen" to resemble or represent something. As in drawing, children will repeat these behaviors as they perfect the skills needed to create the basic forms of sphere and cylinder at will.

Three-dimensional symbols. In the final mode of modeling development, children are able to plan the forms that they will need to create an object. Instead of using the clay solely as a vehicle for sensory sensation and the release of feelings, the modeling material now becomes a means of self-expression for internal images. These images can be formed in several ways. Some are created by bending, flattening, or distorting one of the basic forms; for example, making a "nest" by poking a hole in a clay ball. Others are produced by joining simple or distorted basic forms, as when a child creates a person from a clay ball and four flattened cylinders. As with the graphic symbols of drawing, the children are not trying to create actual representations of these objects but rather the idea of the object. Once created, they assume a major role in the symbolic dramatic play of the child.

Airplanes fly and drop bombs; animals eat clay bits from the clay bowl; birds sit on eggs in the nest and then fly off to find clay worms.

Modeling Center Design

Like paste and glue, modeling materials are quite often tasted or eaten. Provide constant close supervision until children have learned not to eat the material. A low, smooth-topped table that is easily washed makes the best working surface. There should be plenty of space for each child. If the tabletop is not appropriate for modeling, or when working at home in a kitchen area, provide each child with a large tray to be used whenever he or she models or does other artwork. Pottery clay requires a different set-up because of the need to keep dust to a minimum (see Appendix A).

Selecting Modeling Materials

A range of pliable materials is available.

Playdough. The safest, most pliable modeling material for young children, especially infants and toddlers, is playdough. Use a commercial brand, or produce a homemade version. Many recipes are available in books on art for children, or consult Appendix D: Recipes.

For the child's initial exploration, the dough should be a nonfood color and have a nonfood scent. A homemade dough has the advantage of being able to be made without scent for the first few explorations. Use only one color of dough for the first experience so the child can concentrate on the tactile qualities of the materials. Provide each child with a baseball-size piece of the modeling dough. If the dough will be reused, offer separate, tightly lidded containers or resealable plastic bags, clearly labeled with each child's name. Preschoolers and primary-age children can be given several colors of playdough at a time, which they will mix with great enthusiasm. Try to pick colors that when combined form attractive new ones, such as red and yellow to make orange, or blue and yellow to make green.

To vary the experience, scents and textures can be added to the dough. Scents should not be food scents that will entice children to taste the dough. Lavander oil and baby powder are two possible scents to try. Sand and coffee grounds can be used to add texture.

Salt-flour dough.   Children can also mix their own playdough. A salt-flour dough is the easiest for children to use independently. Note: Salt may cause a burning sensation or irritate any small cuts or scrapes that children have on their hands. Check the children's hands first. If children complain about burning, let them wash their hands right away.

1. Work with a small group of three or four children that can be closely supervised.

2. Give each child a bowl, and help each child measure and pour one cup of flour and one-quarter cup of salt. Add one-quarter cup of warm water, and let them knead it together.

3. If the dough is too dry, add some drops of water. If it is too wet, add more flour.

4. Children can add liquid tempera, food coloring, or unsweetened powdered drink mix to the dough to color it.

Non-hardening clay.   This is an oil-based modeling material, also called *modeling clay*, that does not dry out when exposed to the air. It is more rigid than playdough and suitable for older children who have more developed finger strength. Non-hardening clay, like playdough, is suitable for individual or large group work. Modeling clay should not be ingested. It is not appropriate for children who still try to taste or eat modeling materials. It works best on a smooth, washable surface such as a plastic laminate tabletop, a plastic placemat or tray, or even a laminated piece of construction paper. Do not use it on newspaper, as it picks up the ink.

Pottery clay.   This is the real clay that comes from the earth and from which pottery is made. It has been used for thousands of years by people around the world. China dishes and stoneware mugs we use every day are made from it.

Purchase only talc-free, moist clay (see Appendix C for sources). Due to dust hazards avoid all powdered or dry clay mixes. Clay contains silica, alumina, and in clay contaminated with talc, asbestos, all of which can cause lung irritation. See Appendix A for specific risks.

Children should wear a smock or covering to keep dust off their clothing. Make sure they keep their hands away from their face to avoid inhaling the fine dust, and they should wash their hands well when done.

Figure one pound of moist clay per child. Store unused clay in double plastic bags that are tightly closed and placed inside a covered plastic can. When used clay is returned to the bag, add a half-cup of water per piece to replace evaporated moisture. Clay will keep a very long time this way. Dry clay can be soaked in water to make it soft again, or it can be baked in a **kiln** to preserve it forever.

For more information on using a kiln and firing pottery clay, see *Firing Pottery Clay* on CourseMate.

Here are some guidelines for working with pottery clay.

1. **Joining.** Two pieces of clay will not join and stay together when dry without special preparation: To join: apply **slip**—a watery clay mixture—to each piece. Press together. Smooth joint so it cannot be seen.

2. **Dampening.** The more the clay is handled, the more it dries out. Overly dry clay cracks and will not stay together. Small amounts of water should be added as needed. It takes a lot of experience

Special Needs

Children who have limited vision love the tactile nature of modeling materials. Provide a large tray with slightly raised sides for the child to work on—this will make it easier to find small pieces of the modeling material.

to know just how much water to add. Children will quickly learn that too much water reduces the clay to a mud pile. Use this experience to help children see cause and effect.

3. **Location.** Avoid using pottery clay in any multi-purpose room or where food is eaten. If possible, use pottery clay outdoors. Indoors, because the fine dust spreads easily, cleanup is very important. The clay-covered newspaper will need to be folded up slowly to not spread the dust. Inside there will be less mess if the children work standing at a table covered with several layers of newspaper.

4. **Clean up.** Wash all tools and wipe down all surfaces. Use buckets for the initial hand and tool rinsing so that the clay-filled water can be dumped outside on the ground where it will not clog the sink drain.

Modeling Activities for Infants

Because infants readily put things in their mouths, all modeling activities should be one-on-one and last as only as long as the infant is enthusiastically exploring the dough or clay. Begin with brief experiences with unscented homemade play dough or pottery clay.

For an infant, modeling experiences will be primarily sensory. Start when the child can sit securely upright in a high chair. Let the infant touch the dough or clay and move it around as you enthusiastically describe the tactile sensations and the child's actions. When the baby loses interest, remove it and offer it another day.

Over time, demonstrate poking the modeling material with fingers and pulling off bits and sticking them back together. To develop finger strength, avoid providing tools.

Open-Ended Modeling Activities

Once children are familiar with safe ways to use play-doughs and clays, the modeling activity can be varied in many ways. However, the basic sensory interaction between child and materials should always remain foremost. Too often we surround a child with all kinds of plastic tools, cookie cutters, and rolling pins. Modeling is not a cooking activity, nor is it solely for the creation of flat shapes.

The goal should be on as much direct contact between the hands and the material as possible in the formation of three-dimensional forms. As the children work, encourage this by reminding them to look at their sculptures from all sides and naming the forms they make using geometry terms that are similar, such as cone, cylinder, sphere, cube, and rectangular solid.

Impressions. Give the children objects with interesting textures to press into the dough or clay. Try berry baskets, plastic food trays, plastic forks, lids, bottle tops, potato mashers, keys, coins, and any other washable items. Compare the impressions with prints made from the same items. Toddler and up.

"Stick" sculptures. Use a lump of dough or clay as a base in which to insert materials such as sticks, toothpicks, pipe cleaners, cardboard strips, craft sticks, beads, buttons, drinking straws, and natural materials, such as pinecones, acorns, shells, dried grasses, and twigs. When the dough has dried, the objects will be securely fastened to the base. Toddler and up.

Play dough with color. Let the children color their own playdough by squeezing a drop or two of food coloring or liquid tempera paint onto uncolored, homemade dough and then mixing the color with their hands. Drink mix can also be used to color the dough. Preschool and up.

Geometric forms. Older children can use non-hardening modeling clay to make forms such as cubes (made by tapping a sphere on the table to create the sides) and slabs (flat, rectangular "pancakes"), which can be used in building structures. Kindergarten and up.

Pinch pots. Making a pinch pot starts by making a roundish ball. To form the pot push a finger or thumb into the center of the ball, and then pinch the dough or clay slowly between thumb and fingers widening the center and thinning the sides until the dough or clay has a bowl shape. Preschool and up.

Pottery clay provides a different sensory experience from playdough. The damp, firm texture helps develop finger strength.

Animal sculptures. Children love making animals from play dough, and modeling clay but often have difficulty making the legs and necks strong enough to support the body and head. Talk about how large animals need strong legs. Offer the idea of attaching the animal to a slab base or making it sitting or lying down. Kindergarten and up. .

For more ideas for working with pottery clay, see Pottery Clay Activities *on CourseMate.*

Reading about Modeling and Clay

Reading books about potters around the world who have worked with clay is a great way to help children feel a unity with others. There probably is no more beautiful children's book about clay than Bryd Baylor's class *When Clay Sings* (1972) a poetic ode to the glorious pottery of the American Southwest. *The Pot that Juan Built* (Anderson-Goebel, 2011) is a cumulative book about a clay pot being made by a Mexican potter. *Dave the Potter: Artist, Poet, Slave* (Hill, 2010) is the story of a gifted potter named Dave who lived 200 years ago in North Carolina, but whose pots are widely admired today.

For more books about modeling and clay, see Books about Modeling and Clay *on CourseMate.*

Looking at and Talking about Modeling and Clay

Introduce children to modeling by sharing a special handmade pottery bowl or dish. Use handmade pottery to serve snacks. Have a potter visit and demonstrate making a pot, or visit a potter's studio.

To encourage children to work in three dimensions, share the sculptures of Henry Moore. His gently rounded human forms are appealing to young children. Compare them to work by other sculptors. If possible, visit a sculpture in the neighborhood, and study and sketch it from different sides.

As contrast, display brightly colored Mexican figurines of roosters and other common animals. Talk about why artists might use color on some sculptures and not on others. *The Sweet and Sour Animal Book* (Hughes, 1997) features Langston Hughes' poetry illustrated with photographs of children's painted clay animals.

Questions to ask children about their modeling and claywork and about that of others include the following.

- How is it shaped?
- How do you think it was modeled?
- How does it look from the other side? From the top? From the bottom?
- What textures do you see or feel?
- Can you imagine modeling the shape with your hands?
- What does it tell you?

Did You Get It?

Which of the following is true of controlled exploration with regard to modeling?

a. It relates to the development of the child's intrapersonal skills.

b. It reflects the child's developing language skills.

c. It relates to the cognitive development of the child and the growth of mental imagery.

d. It reflects the child's increasing physical control over his hands and fingers.

Take the full quiz on CourseMate

The Constructed Sculpture Experience

All children are builders. They create environments. They are the architects of the spaces they inhabit, often creating complex arrangements of toys and furnishings indoors and shelters of sticks and grass outdoors.

Much has been written on the importance of block play for young children (Chalufour & Worth, 2004; Church & Miller, 1990; Gelfer, 1990). In this section, the focus will be on the artistic and creative learning that is developed in building structures with blocks and other materials.

Selecting Construction Materials

Blocks are often the first construction materials offered to children. Many different kinds are available from which to choose. Other construction materials can later be added to the block center or used on their own.

Blocks allow children to creatively investigate form and structure in open-ended ways. Provide a variety of building materials for children to choose from. Here a child uses sturdy architectural blocks.

Architectural blocks. These blocks are based on various architectural styles such as Greek, Roman, and Moorish.

Boxes. Empty cardboard boxes are an inexpensive way to provide both units to stack and spaces inside which to build. Jewelry or pudding mix boxes can be used to make miniature houses to be arranged in a model of the neighborhood or town. They can also be made into homes for tiny toys or special treasures, or glued together into unique, three-dimensional structures. Boxes can become homes for beloved stuffed toys. Shoe boxes and cereal, pasta, and oatmeal containers can also be made into houses, homes for treasures, and creatures of all kinds. Giant boxes are instantly appealing to young children, providing an immediate sense of privacy and drawing forth imaginative play. Painting larger boxes provides large motor movement for young children. Appliance boxes can be turned into spaceships or submarines.

Large blocks. Made of plastic, wood, cardboard, or foam, large blocks allow children to build structures they can sit on or go inside. They are excellent for dramatic play and for balancing towers. They provide a fun way to discover spatial relationships by building walls to peek over, through, and around.

Large cardboard pieces. Pieces of cardboard cut from the sides of boxes can be used to create walls, roofs, and ramps. They can also be fastened together using paper fasteners or chenille stems to make structures that are more elaborate and moveable.

Light table blocks. These are transparent plastic blocks that come in a variety of designs to be used on a light table or in combination with other blocks as windows and skylights.

Pattern blocks. These small, flat, colored blocks of wood or plastic demonstrate many mathematical relationships. They are excellent for developing ideas of symmetry and pattern, as well as for inventing creative designs.

Plastic blocks. Preschool-size interlocking blocks of different designs, such as Duplo® or bristle blocks, allow children to investigate other ways to support what they build.

Tree cookies. These are cross-cut slices from branches and logs of different sizes. They may or may not still have the bark on them and maybe sanded or finished with varnish. They can be mixed with regular blocks or used with stumpy cylinders made from thick branches.

Tubes. Long cardboard tubes from paper towels and gift wrap make a wonderful building material.

Unit blocks. These blocks are usually wooden and come in a variety of geometric and architectural forms. They represent mathematical concepts, such as two right triangles aligning to form a rectangle the same size as the rectangular unit block. This offers the children an excellent opportunity to investigate symmetry and geometric relationships.

Wood scraps. Collect small leftover pieces of wood from carpenters or lumberyards, and sand lightly. Children can stack, to glue, or nail together.

Setting Up a Construction Center Featuring Building Materials

The number of children who can be in a building area will be determined by their ages and the size of the area. Infants work best one-on-one with a caring adult. Two toddlers can work side by side if there are enough blocks and space. If there are only a few blocks in a small, enclosed area, then bumping and grabbing may result.

Preschoolers and primary-school children, who may become involved in cooperative building projects, often can work in larger groups, but attention must always be paid to each child having enough room to move around and get more blocks without knocking over someone else's structure. Use masking tape to mark off a distance from the shelves in which building is not allowed, so that children can get blocks off the shelves without knocking someone's structure down.

Other factors that affect the group size are the size of the blocks and the floor surface. A flat, low-pile carpet makes a good surface because it muffles the blocks when they fall. It is also more comfortable for the children to sit on while working. A smooth wood or tile floor, however, provides a slightly more stable base on which to work and allows smooth motion for wheeled vehicles. A well-designed block area should include both types of surfaces.

Block Safety

Like other supplies, blocks need to be arranged aesthetically and safely. Low shelves are essential. Blocks stored higher than the child's waist can fall and cause injuries. On the shelves, the blocks should not be stacked more than several high, and each type of block should have its own location. Create a label for each location by tracing the shape of the block on paper and then attaching it to the correct shelf. Put the heaviest blocks on the bottom. Use the top of the shelves for accessories stored in clear plastic bins.

Adding Drawing to the Building Center

Art materials can be added to the block area to increase the dramatic and architectural possibilities.

1. Paper, markers, and crayons for making maps, and drawing pictures of the buildings.

2. Blue paper and white pencils or crayons to make "blueprints."

3. Cardboard pieces, tubes, and scissors for the construction of roofs, signs, ramps, and more.

4. Fabric pieces to use for rugs and furnishings in houses.

5. Non-hardening clay to make people and animals.

6. Bottle caps and thread spools to add decorative patterns.

7. Aluminum foil to cover blocks for a sparkling effect.

Note: These materials should be slowly added to the block area, so that children have time to investigate the possibilities of each before being overwhelmed by too many choices.

Working with Papier-Mâché

Papier-mâché is a wonderfully sticky material that dries hard and is paintable. It is a good way to convert flimsy boxes into sturdy constructions, to join boxes together, or to cover rolled newspaper or cardboard tubes to make them solid.

Papier-mâché should be seen as a medium to be used when children have a specific construction problem or project in mind. For example, if children are frustrated because paint will not stick to the box they are painting, suggest papier-mâché. If some children want to build a box robot and the boxes will not stick together, suggest papier-mâché.

Piñatas are also made with papier-mâché. Read *Hooray! A Pinata iñata!* (Kleven, 1996) to introduce papier-mâché to young children. Colorfully illustrated with painted collages, a note at the end explains the Mexican custom of the piñata. To make a hollow form for a piñata cover a balloon with several layers of papier-mâché and pop the balloon when the papier-mâché is dry.

For the paste, use thinned white glue, plain flour and water, or one of the special papier-mâché pastes available. Do not use wallpaper paste, as it contains toxins. If using flour, be on the alert for gluten-sensitive children who may have severe allergic reactions.

Using papier-mâché requires children to follow a set of orderly steps and works best when children work in pairs or small cooperative groups. The papier-mâché process is simple.

1. Demonstrate how to dip a strip of paper into the paste, and then place it on the box or tray. Explain that it is like making your own tape.

2. Encourage children to keep their hands over their paste buckets, which should be set directly in front of them in order to catch drips.

3. Suggest that the children cover the box or item completely, so that nothing shows. One layer is usually sufficient for a first papier-mâché experience. In future experiences, children can be encouraged to put on more layers to make the base sturdier.

4. Place finished projects on a sheet of plastic to dry. They will stick to newspaper. Then place them near a heater or in the sun to speed drying time.

5. When the papier-mâché is dry, it can be painted or collaged.

Construction Activities for Infants and Toddlers

Safety is the first concern when building with infants. Provide soft blocks with no hard edges such as those made from foam or cardboard or use boxes, cardboard pieces, and cardboard tubes. If the infant is sitting or creeping, place the building materials around the child and encourage exploration.

Boxes are also perfect for toddlers. They are light and can be both stacked and filled. Large ones can be used to build mazes and tunnels. A refrigerator-size box makes a cozy house.

Open-Ended Construction Activities

Blocks and boxes introduce children to the world of architecture. It is natural for young children to build structures that mirror the buildings they inhabit and see around them. Encourage this connection by pointing out the relationships between the basic geometric forms and their architectural counterparts. Allow plenty of open-ended exploration with building materials for children of all ages. As they develop skill, try some of the following activities.

Pull-toy. Attaching a string turns a box into a vehicle in which stuffed toys can ride. Infant and up.

Special place. Art can be created inside of the box as well as outside. Color boxes with crayons and markers. Let children glue colored papers to the sides or paint the box using large paintbrushes. Toddler and up.

Houses. Boxes make perfect dream houses, houses for toys, and for pets. Spark children's interest by walking around the neighborhood looking at houses and displaying photographs of their homes. Provide wallpaper, fabric, and carpet for decorating the inside of their houses. Blocks of wood, foam, and small boxes can be used for furniture. Preschool and up.

A personal space. Plan a day for older children to each be given a small section of the room or playground in which to build her or his own private place using blocks, moveable furnishings, and other delineating materials to form the walls. Share the story *Roxaboxen* (McLerran, 1991) as the perfect complement to this activity. Kindergarten and up.

Add ons. Pieces of flat cardboard can be rested against boxes as ramps and roofs or attached onto boxes in various ways, such as with glue or tape. For a sturdy attachment or one that swings like a door, poke holes in the cardboard so that chenille stems can be passed through and twisted closed. Preschool and up.

Puppets. Use glue-soaked strips to cover a cereal-type box with papier-mâché. Leave one end open so that it fits over the child's hand. Paint on a face and add yarn hair. Preschool and up.

Masks. A cardboard or plastic tray can be used to make a mask-like shape. Cover the tray with two to three layers of papier-mâché strips. Let dry several days. When dry, the tray will fall away. Trim edge into shape for mask and cut out eyeholes. Finish by painting and adding yarn hair. Kindergarten and up.

Reading about Building

Construction activities provide the perfect opportunity to talk about architecture and three-dimensional design. *Architectural Colors* (Crosbie & Rosenthal, 1993) is one in a series of board books for toddlers and up. On one side there is the name of a color and on the other a building featuring that color. For older children *Architects make Zigzags* (Maddox, 1986) introduces different architectural features.

For an annotated list of books about construction and building, see *Books about Building* on CourseMate.

Looking at and Talking about Building

Start by looking at actual buildings and how they are made. Explore the school and the neighborhood and find cylindrical columns, triangular roofs, rectangular bricks, arches, and more. Note how doorways are created by placing a crosspiece over two vertical supports (post and lintel), and point out similar constructions in children's block buildings.

Next introduce the children to the artist's role as architect. Display a print of one of Frank Lloyd Wright's buildings. Tell the children about how he loved to build with blocks. Invite an architect or architecture student to come and share his or her sketches, plans, and models of buildings. Such a visit will inspire the children to draw "blueprints" of their own.

Inspire new ways of thinking about building by sharing the box assemblages of Duchamp and Nevelson, such as Nevelson's *Case with Five Balusters* (Take 5: Collage and Assemblage) and then giving children boxes they can use to design their own constructions.

Expand children's ideas about the possibilities of papier-mâché by sharing prints or actual papier-mâché artifacts, such as masks from Mexico.

Improve focus and develop language skills by asking open-ended questions. Questions to ask about their constructions and those of others include the following.

- What do you see?
- How is it different when you look from about viewpoint?
- What forms do you see?
- How are they the same or different from each other?

Did You Get It?

Why should young children play with blocks?

a. They improve their ability to see in two-dimensions.

b. They introduce the children to architectural concepts.

c. They have fun building with them.

d. They are used in all early childhood programs.

Take the full quiz on CourseMate

How Do We Share Children's Artwork with Families?

There are many ways to include families in the visual art activities of children. Invite them to visit the classroom any time and paint, draw, and paste alongside their child. Send home artworks and videos of their child at work using the materials of the visual arts and invite them to art workshops where they can learn more about the art of young children and can explore using art media on their own. Parents can also be enlisted to help make playdough and other homemade modeling materials and paint. Welcome home cultures by inviting parents to share artworks that are meaningful for them.

Conclusion:
The Power of The Visual Arts

Visual artists have been creating with paper, paint, clay, fiber, and more for thousands of years. Much of what is known about civilizations of the past has been bequeathed to us through the culture's visual artworks. Providing young children the opportunity to work with a wide variety of visual arts media in open-ended ways facilitates the growth of both the mind and hand. It is also a link to our past and our future. As teachers, we need to be sure that all children have the opportunity to explore new media, create graphic symbols, and develop technical skill.

For additional information on teaching the visual arts, see *Chapter 9 Online Resources* on CourseMate to young children visit our Web site at http://www.cengagebrain.com.

Teaching In Action

A Day with Clay: A Teacher's Notebook Entry

My friend Julian, who is an art student at the local college, came today and showed the children how he makes a clay pot. We set up a table out on the grass by the playground fence. We all gathered around and watched. Outside was perfect. It was very informal and open. The children would watch awhile, go play, and then wander back.

All the while Julian worked he kept describing how it felt. He said things such as, "This is bumpy; I must make it smoother." He also described what he was doing, as in, "I am pushing the clay with my fingers." He was so patient and answered all of the children's questions. He let them touch the clay and the pot he was making, too.

When Julian was done, he invited the children who were standing around him to make pots also. He gave them each a piece of clay and guided them in making it rounded and pushing a hole in the middle with their thumbs. When they were finished, a few others came over and made some pots. Several just wanted to pound the clay flat. Julian showed them how to press sticks and stones into the clay to make impressions. Some children decided to do that to their clay pots. He carved the child's name on each one and took all of the projects to fire in his kiln. He said he thought they would turn out fine. I had a bucket of water for the children to rinse their hands in, and then they went inside to wash up at the sink.

I took lots of photographs. I can't wait to get them back. Then we can make a class book about our Clay Day!

Reflection Page

The Elements of Art

In Chapter 4 we learned about the elements of art. For each of the elements listed below, give an example of a visual art activity you could do with children in the age groups indicated.

Element	Infant or Toddler	Preschool	Primary
Color			
Shape			
Texture			
Form			
Line			
Pattern			

Reflection Page

Planning an Art Center

Select an age group and visual art media. Explain how you will set up the center and introduce the children to it.

Age Group: _____   **Media:** _____

Where will the center be located?

_____

_____

What materials will be there?

_____

_____

How will these be aesthetically arranged?

_____

_____

How will you introduce the children to the new center?

_____

_____

What questions will you ask at this center to develop visual arts concepts and skills?

_____

_____

Reflection Page

Observation: Children Drawing

1. Plan a drawing exploration or practice activity suitable for an infant or child up to the age of eight.

2. Obtain permission to work with the child or children, either at home, at school, or in a childcare setting.

3. Set up your activity and observe the child or children at work. If possible, take photos or videotape the activity (get permission first). With the child's permission, save one or more of the drawings for your own collection.

_____

Age of child(ren):
Set-up of materials:
Length of time of observation:

1. What did the child(ren) do first?

_____

2. What did the child(ren) say?

_____

3. How did the child(ren) manipulate the drawing tool(s)? (For example, describe the position of the arm and hands, grip, and any other body parts involved.)

_____

_____

4. How long did the child(ren) work? (Measure periods of concentration. If the child stopped, why? How did the child(ren) let you know the drawing was finished?)

_____

_____

5. Describe the art produced. (What did the child(ren) draw first? How many drawings were made? What was repeated?)

_____

_____

_____

_____

Reflection Page

Observation: Children and Modeling

1. Plan a modeling exploration or practice activity suitable for a child between infancy and eight. Use a modeling material of your choice such as playdough or pottery clay.

2. Obtain permission to work with one child, either at home or in a school setting. If possible, take photos or videotape the activity (get permission first).

_____

_____

Age of child(ren):
Set-up of materials:
Length of time of observation:

1. What did the child do first?

_____

2. What did the child say?

_____

3. How did the child manipulate the modeling material? (For example, describe the position of the arm and hands, grip, and any other body parts involved.)

_____

4. How long did the child work? (Measure periods of concentration. If the child stopped, why? How did the child let you know he or she was finished?)

_____

5. Describe the art produced. (What did the child do first? What actions were repeated?)

_____

6. Reflection: Was the modeling material suitable for this child(ren)? Was the experience enjoyable?

_____

_____

Chapter 10

Making Music

Design and plan music activities that foster children's developmental growth as well as teach the skills and concepts of music.

Know ways to use music to soothe, to express feelings, and give children a sense of belonging.

Planning Curriculum to Achieve Important Goals

Creating a Caring Community

Making Music DAP Learning Objectives

Assessing Children's Development and Learning

Teaching to Enhance Development and Learning

Establishing Reciprocal Family Relationships

Explain a variety of approaches to teaching music using listening, music making, and singing to increase children's developmental growth in all areas.

Describe what to look for to tell if a child is engaged in music activities and developing music skills.

Give examples of ways to involve parents in the music program through sharing music of their musical heritage and their expertise.

Young Artists Creating

Xavier, age two, picks up a spoon and begins to tap on the high chair tray. "Let's make music," says his caregiver seizing the teachable moment. She claps her hands and nods her head keeping time with his taps. "Now let's count to the beat." she says. "One, two, three, four. One, two, three, four. Hear the rhythm?" Xavier says the numbers and taps harder. His whole body bounces up and down. The caregiver begins to hum the tune to *Row, Row, Row the Boat* as she claps. "Now let's sing Xavier's song," she says. "Tap, tap, tap the spoon. Xavier, tap the spoon. Tap. Tap. Tap. Tap. Xavier taps the spoon."

What Is Music?

Music is organized sound. One of the tasks of teaching music is to introduce children to the different ways in which music plays with and orders sound. Listening, rhythmic activities, singing, and playing instruments form the basis of creative music experiences, through which the elements of music—rhythm, timbre, dynamics, form, melody, and harmony—are organized into compositions that speak to our mind, our body, and our emotions.

The Elements of Music

We are all familiar with everyday sounds: the honk of a car horn, the clatter of dishes, children's voices on the playground. On their own these are not considered music. However, any ordinary sound can be turned into something musical. At its most basic music is made up of repeated beats. At its most complex, it is a **composition** of rhythm and **tempo,** dynamics and pitch, timbre and texture, and melody and harmony. These are the elements of music.

Rhythm. Rhythm is a time-based pattern that orders sound and makes it musical. A car horn pressed first short and then long repeated over and over creates a rhythm. Each honk on the horn is a **beat.** A rhythm can be varied by changing which beat has the strongest emphasis or **accent.** For example, a long horn blast followed by a short one would consist of a strong or down-beat and a weak or up-beat as in *one* two, *one* two, *one* two and so on. Repeated patterns of strong and weak beats create the **meter** of the rhythm. A waltz or polka meter, for example, is made up of one strong beat followed by two weak

beats—*one* two three, *one* two three. **Syncopation,** found in some genres of music such as jazz, is a deliberate change in where the regular stress is expected to come. For example, the stress might come on the weak beat as in one *two* three four or there might be a rest where a strong beat is expected.

Tempo. Tempo is the speed at which a rhythm or musical composition is played. It is usually indicated by a term written at the beginning of the piece. Largo, for example means slow. Allegro means lively and fast. Up-tempo or presto means very fast. Within a piece of music the tempo may change many times, or it may remain steady throughout.

Dynamics. Dynamics refers to changes in volume from loud to soft and to the accenting of certain tones in a rhythm or piece of music.

Pitch. Sound is created through vibration and is measured by the frequency of that oscillation. The lowest sounds most people hear are in the range of 20 Hz. The highest are about 20,000 Hz. The highness or lowness of a particular sound is referred to as its pitch. Many instruments have vibrating parts such as a drumhead on a bass drum, which produces a low pitch, or the strings on a violin, which can produce high pitches. Others such as tubas and clarinets make sound using a vibrating column of air.

Timbre. Timbre or **tone color** is the unique quality of a sound. It is how we can tell the sound of a car horn from that of a bird's song or identify the particular voice of a friend on the phone.

Melody. A **note** is a single sound or tone. Melodies are created by varying the pitches of notes and playing them in a sequence that may repeat. How the sequence is arranged and repeated creates the form or composition of the musical work. For example, a song might be composed of alternating verses and choruses. The American folksong *The Erie Canal* has this type of form.

Harmony. Accompanying the melody may be a sequence of tones that enriches it and makes the sounds blend. Harmony is often created by using a **chord**—several notes played together at the same time. Harmony creates what is called musical texture or a layer of sound that can be pleasant or dissonant to the ear.

Did You Get It?

Which of the following describes the rhythm of a piece of music?

a. a time-based pattern that orders sound and makes it musical

b. the speed at which a musical composition is played

c. changes in volume and the accenting of certain tones in a piece of music

d. the highness or lowness of a particular sound

Take the full quiz on CourseMate

How Do Children Develop Musically?

Musical development starts early. In fact, research suggests that the optimal time for auditory and musical perceptual development is the first year of life although it continues to be refined during the years up to age eight (Trainor & Corrigall, 2010).

Music Development in Infancy

Unborn babies' ability to hear sounds in the last trimester is believed to set the stage for future musical responsiveness (Parncutt, 2006). Before birth, fetuses can differentiate between a familiar song and a novel one (Abrams, et al., 1998). They also remember what they hear. Right after birth, babies show recognition of tunes heard repeatedly during pregnancy (Hepper, 1991; Wilkin, 1995).

Infants attend to music by turning their heads and making sounds and movements. They show a preference for music over other sounds. For example, infants will concentrate on a musical happening such as

a person clapping or singing despite distracting noises (Bahrick, Lickliter, & Flom, 2004). At two months, infants will turn toward musically pleasant sounds and away from dissonant ones (Weinberger, 2004). Infants in the first year also develop skill in recognizing contrasting pitches and pitch combinations, timbres, textures, and styles (Ilari & Polka, 2006; Krumhansl & Jusczyk, 1990; Trainor, Tsang, & Cheung, 2002). With exposure they can learn to recognize individual works such as folk songs, Mozart piano **sonatas,** and the music of Ravel and remember them weeks later (Ilari & Polka, 2006; Saffran, Loman, & Robertson, 2000; Trainor, Wu, & Tsang, 2004).

With innate attraction to and ample exposure to music, it does not take long for children to become familiar with their cultural musical heritage. Infants begin by matching facial expressions and the voice of the singer (Bahrick, Lickliter, & Flom, 2004). The rhythm and melodic quality of a mother's voice will keep a child's attention, the musicality of speech helping the child acquire language (Mithen, 2006). It is hypothesized that this is one reason adults in all cultures tend to talk to babies in singsong voices called **motherese** and to sing lullabies.

Music Development in Early Childhood

Music ability and skills continue to develop all through the early years, although as children age, experience, interest and hearing ability make a major

Infants are naturally musical, moving with delight to simple songs and rhythms.

difference in children's performance in the musical area. Toddlers continue to be as fascinated by music as they were as infants. They can repeat sounds, move to rhythms, and start to learn simple songs. During this period their vocal range expands rapidly as does their ability to perceive timbre and identify the sounds of different instruments.

By preschool, children begin to make up their own songs, hold a steady beat, and match body movements to it. Spontaneous music making is a characteristic of the preschool years. Children freely mix tunes and words of their own invention with familiar songs during solitary and group play (Whiteman, 2009).

By kindergarten, children can learn to match and classify sounds, can play singing and movement games, and can reproduce musical patterns. In this period they continue to develop pitch accuracy and an expanded vocal range so that by the start of first grade, 50 percent can sing a full **octave** with 10 percent reaching an octave-and-a-half

(Kreutzer, 2001; Wassum, 1979). They can now indicate changes in pitch by raising and lowering their hands and note a melody with rising and falling lines with dots for beats (Gromko, 2003).

In the primary grades, children improve in their ability to sing in tune and in large groups. Corresponding to their increasing skills in reading and writing, they can learn to read music and to notate melodies and compose original musical pieces. It is during this period that children should begin to learn to play an instrument. Adults who studied an instrument before the age of eight have more brain development in the corpus callosum then those who started formal lessons later (Schlaug, 1995).

Musical development seems to reach a plateau by the age nine (Stellaccio & McCarthy, 1999). This means that the music activities we present to young children are vitally important. The early years are when children learn to sing accurately, acquire their vocal range, and learn basic concepts about rhythm, pitch, and melody (see Table 10-1).

TABLE 10–1   Musical Development in Young Children

Age	Rhythm	Listening	Instrument	Song
Before birth	Surrounded by rhythm of mother's body	Respond differently to familiar and novel music	Hear music	Hear mother's voice
Infants Newborn to 6 months	Respond differently to different types of music	Turn toward sounds; Notice difference between melodies; Respond to loud and soft; Recognize and remember different complex musical pieces	Make sounds with objects such as rattles	Babble to musical stimulation; Babble on own with pitch and rhythmic pattern; Coo in open vowels
Infants 6 months to 1 year	Rock and bounce to music	React to music with sound and motion	Show interest in instruments	Respond to singing by vocalizing
Toddlers 1 to 3 years	Move feet with rhythm of music; Cannot keep time; Clap to music	Listen to music on radio and recordings; Identifies types of sounds; Show preferences for certain music; Matches sounds and objects	Seek objects to make sounds	Real singing begins; Tag on to the end of a song; Make up songs and chants; Sing on own with recurring pitch center and consistent tempo; Have a five-note range; Cannot match pitch

(continued)

TABLE 10–1	Musical Development in Young Children *(continued)*			
Age	**Rhythm**	**Listening**	**Instrument**	**Song**
Preschoolers 3 to 4 years	Begin to clap on beat Begin to echo clap Improvise complex rhythm Imitate simple rhythms	Can listen for longer periods while remaining quiet Can identify familiar songs Can talk about speed and volume of music Can identify musical phrases Can identify the source of a sound Can identify the sound of familiar instruments Can talk about what they hear using music vocabulary they have learned	Tap a beat on an instrument Interest in real instruments increases Play simple instruments in small group Play short melodies on tonal instruments Can improvise melodies Can invent original symbols to represent sounds	May sing along with familiar songs with increasing accuracy Can sing in different keys Have a five- to eight-note range Begin to match pitch and echo words in rhythm Spontaneously invents new songs as they play Can sing along with a group
Kindergarteners 5 to 6 years	Can march and clap at same time to music Keep time with music Improvise complex rhythm structure with a climax and conclusion	Identify change in music Recognize a familiar song played on an instrument without words Become active listener and can talk about music heard Can listen respectfully at concerts Can describe the elements and mood of musical pieces	Can tell sounds made by different instruments apart Play sequential and diatonic and chromatic tones on tonal instruments Can learn to read simple notation Focus on one instrument for extended time Can begin lessons on piano, violin, etc. Imitate a rhythm using a different instrument accurately	Make up own songs and write musical symbols Sing in clear tone taking breath at appropriate points Begin to know that a song's melody is fixed Sing in tune Whole steps easier to sing than half steps Descending patterns easier to sing than ascending ones Large intervals more difficult than close ones Most accurate in the A1D1 range (C1 is middle C) Add emotion through facial expression, pitch, dynamics, and tempo to voice
Primary ages 6 to 8 years	Keep time accurately	Can hear harmony Recognize familiar songs played in different contexts Can differentiate between music reflecting different styles and moods	Can learn to read music Play parts on instrument	Can sing familiar songs accurately and has a repertoire of memorized songs Sing more accurately as individual than with group Can reach higher notes Can sing rounds and two-part songs Know that melodies are fixed

Note: As in all the arts, musical development is strongly influenced by experience. This chart is intended only as a general guideline to what skills might be mastered in terms of age. However, the basic sequence of skill acquisition will pertain to most children.

How Does Music Help Children Grow?

Music has been part of human society since the dawn of culture over 30,000 years ago. It has the power to make us cry and to make us feel joy. Beyond pleasure, music positively affects brain development and health affecting development in the physical, social, cognitive, and language areas. When we share music with children, we provide another way to help them grow.

Music and the Brain

Music has the power to change the brain. Musicians who began their training before age six have hyper-development in some parts of their brains (Rauscher & Hinton, 2003). Even just fifteen months of formal music instruction at age six has been shown to cause growth in multiple areas of the brain (Hyde, et al, 2009; Schlaug et al., 2005). Babies who were exposed to a complex work by Ravel paid more attention to this longer, more difficult piece of music than they did to unfamiliar ones indicating growth in neural networks (Ilari, Polka, & Costa-Giomi, 2002).

Music has also been shown to enhance long-term memory (Wolfe & Horn, 1998). Long-term memory is always forming and reforming interconnections with the information being absorbed (Caine, Caine,

Interacting one-on-one with an adult is essential to music skill development.

McClintic & Klimec, 2008). Adding music to learning activities helps establish memories more quickly and firmly (Stuckey & Nobel, 2010). Many adults, for example, rely on the ABC song, learned during childhood, to assist in alphabetizing.

Music and Well-Being

Different types of music produce physiological changes in the listener (Krumhansl, 2002). Listening to music has been shown to lower levels of stress, affect the heart rate, and aid healing (Using Music to Tune the Heart, 2009; Nakahara et al., 2009). When premature babies were exposed to music daily, they grew faster and went home from the hospital earlier than those who were not (Sousa, 2001, p. 223).

Music and Developmental Growth

Music affects a child's total development. Through music activities children develop:

◆ **Physically**—By using the body to participate in and create music. Physical development occurs when children listen, sing, and move to music. Music stimulates and develops a child's auditory perception. Making music with hands and instruments foster the control and coordination of large and small body movements. Research has shown that musicians who play instruments have more ability to use both hands (Weinberger, 2004).

◆ **Socially**—By learning music skills with and from others. For thousands of years music has drawn groups together in song and performance. Young children learn about their culture as they sing traditional songs, and they develop cooperative skills as they work together to create a musical moment. At the same time, music ties together all humanity. All societies have tonal music and sing lullabies to their children (Wade, 2003).

◆ **Cognitively**—By developing the **auditory discrimination** and spatial relationship abilities of the brain. Music allows children to investigate sequencing, and cause and effect. Jensen (1998) notes that playing an instrument helps children discover patterns and develop organizational skills. Although simply listening to music seems to "prime" children's spatial thinking abilities, numerous studies have found a stronger correlation between spatial reasoning and early instruction in music, particularly as related to learning the piano or keyboard (Costa-Giomi, 1999; Graziano, Peterson, & Shaw, 1999; Hetland, 2000; Rauscher et al., 1997).

◆ **Language skills**—By talking about and listening to music. Speech and music draw on the same modalities. The fact that music perception skills have been found to predict reading success indicates that similar auditory processing is needed for both (Anvari et al., 2001). Oral language is developed as children compose their own rhythms and songs to express their ideas. Listening skills increase as children pay attention to the music they hear and play. Causal relationships have been found between music instruction and reading skill (Butzlaff, 2000). Music has also been found to help English language learners. Songs can help children learning a second language to gain skill in pronunciation, grammar, vocabulary, phrasing, and speed of delivery (Scripps, 2002).

◆ **Emotionally**—By using music to express and respond to feelings. Music provides another way for children to express their feelings. Listening to music can also soothe and help children focus better on other tasks (Hetland, 2000). A case study of students who were emotionally disturbed found that they wrote better and had an improved attitude when listening to music (Kariuki & Honeycut, 1998).

◆ **Music concepts and skills**—By meeting the National Common Core Music Standards.

Creating: Generate and select among multiple musical ideas relevant to a personal experience, interest, or specific purpose.

◆ **PreKindergarten.** With guidance, explore musical ideas (i.e. move, chant, sing) to use for a specific purpose.

◆ **Kindergarten.** With guidance, explore tonal and rhythmic patterns, and combine selected patterns to create musical ideas relating to a specific purpose or interest.

◆ **First Grade.** With support, improvise tonal and rhythmic patterns, and combine selected patterns to create musical ideas relating to a specific purpose, interest, or personal experience.

◆ **Second Grade.** Generate ideas for an original improvisation and/or composition, using free improvisation and varied sound sources, and select multiple ideas to develop that best relate to personal experience, interest, and specific purpose.

Performing: Select work(s) to present based on interest, knowledge, ability and context.

◆ **PreKindergarten.** With guidance, demonstrate (i.e. move, chant, sing) or say which musical selections they would like to perform

◆ **Kindergarten.** With support, demonstrate (i.e., play instruments) or say which musical selection they prefer to perform for a given purpose.

Special Needs

• PROVIDING ASSISTANCE TO CHILDREN WITH SPECIAL NEEDS •

Auditory Processing

- If the child has partial hearing, the use of earphones and preferential seating near the player may help. The child may also respond to low-pitched drums.
- Children with cochlear implants have poor pitch resolution, which limits recognition of melodies played on a piano or single instrument, although they have normal responses to rhythm. More complex musical pieces that contain multiple clues, such as voice and definitive patterns, are easier for them to recognize and enjoy (Vongpaisal, Trehub, Schellenberg, & Papsin, 2004).
- Percussion instruments are an ideal choice for children with limited hearing. Sprinkling rice or small stones on top of a drum allows the child not only to feel but also see the vibration.
- Children with no hearing respond best to rhythmic pieces, which they can feel through vibrations. If possible, let them touch the speaker as the music plays. Providing a visual element may also help. Media players on the computer often have wave visuals that can accompany the music. The 1995 movie *Mr. Holland's Opus* provides insight into how musical performances can be presented visually to the deaf using lights and visuals.

Physical Needs

- Children with motor issues may need help in order to grip an instrument and make a sound. Choose instruments that are easy to hold such as an open tambourine or can be rested on a table or tray such as a drum.
- If the child's muscle control is weak, select instruments that will make a large sound with little effort.
- If the child has limited movement, attach the instrument to the body part the child has the most control over or to a steady surface. Bells and shakers can be attached to arms, legs, or head with hook and loop tape. Triangles can be suspended from a stand or chair.

Assistive Technology

Using Assistive Technology to Make Music

When children cannot participate verbally or have trouble with motor control, they may need assistive technology in order to participate fully in music activities. One of the assistive tools that can be used very effectively to allow participation in music activities is a touch communication device that can be programmed with a message, words to a song, or music. This device can be a stand-alone specialized communication device, computer software on a computer provided with an extra-large keyboard, or software downloaded on a tablet. Children who use a sound board to communicate may contribute to a rhythm or song activity by pressing a key on the beat or they might use computer software that lets them press the right pitch, say a repeated word in the song, play a recording of the melody, or a recorded line from the chorus at the proper time.

 First Grade. Demonstrate or say which musical selection they prefer to perform for a given purpose (e.g., Open House, Grandparents Day).

 Second Grade. Demonstrate and explain which musical selection they prefer to perform for a given purpose

Responding. Support the choice of music for a specific purpose or situation.

 PreKindergarten. With guidance, demonstrate (i.e.., move, chant and/or sing) or say/indicate what musical selection(s) they prefer based on personal preference.

 Kindergarten. With support, demonstrate or say/indicate what musical selection(s) they prefer to experience or listen to for a given purpose.

 First Grade. Demonstrate (i.e., play instruments) or say/indicate what musical selection(s) they prefer to experience or listen to for a given or student-selected purpose.

 Second Grade. Demonstrate and explain what musical selection(s) they prefer to experience or listen to for a given or student-selected purpose.

How Are Music Activities Designed?

Musical activities can be organized in three ways: as individualized instruction, as open-ended, independent exploration, and in organized groups. An effective music program needs to incorporate all these approaches into the curriculum in order for children to develop fully as confident musical creators.

One-on-One Interactions

For infants and toddlers, in particular, but for all children as well, interacting one-on-one with an adult has been shown to be vitally important in acquiring musical competence. Children, for example, sing more accurately when singing individually than with a group (Goetz & Horii, 1989). Learning to play an instrument proceeds faster when the child receives intensive one-on-one lessons.

One-on-one musical interactions can occur throughout the education of young children. Singing to an infant or toddler while going about daily activities, such as dressing, diaper changing, putting on outerwear, eating lunch, walking places, and so on fit naturally into adult–child interactions. In preschool, kindergarten, and primary classrooms one-on-one echo singing and instrumental solos can be purposely planned into group activities.

Exploration Centers

Music centers allow children to explore sound, rhythm, and music in playful, creative, and open-ended ways.

A center for exploring sound can be problematic in a busy, noisy preschool and primary classroom. However, it is possible. To muffle the sound, include soft items such as a pile rug, pillows, and draped fabric. A sturdy table covered on three sides with heavy cloth and open in front makes a cozy "music house" in which to listen to music and explore making sounds, but still allows teacher supervision. Several types of music centers address different components of music education.

Conducting center. To the listening center add flashlights covered with different-colored cellophane that children can move in concert with the music while shining the light on the wall.

Composing center. Alongside instruments of varying kinds, provide a metal tray and magnet-backed notes, plain paper and markers, or paper with staves for older children so they can try their hand at composing.

Instruments. Provide handmade and commercial instruments to accompany the recorded music or to use in making up original songs. Make sure there is an assortment of percussive, drums, shakers, and so on, and melodic instruments, such as a xylophone or hand bells.

Listening center. Stock the center with a child-friendly CD/music player, or tape recorder, and earphones.

Sound discovery center. Set out materials that can be used to make sounds or musical instruments. For example, offer different plastic containers with easy-to-close lids and a variety of small objects, such as pebbles, jingle bells, and buttons that fit inside. Children can use these to make their own shakers to keep time to the recorded music or their own singing.

Responsive Group Activities

Music is mainly a social activity. Although individuals may play or sing for their own personal enjoyment, music is usually experienced as part of a group. However, the size and purpose of musical groups can vary.

Small group. Small groups of children can participate in listening, singing, and composing activities as part of projects and at centers. For example, primary students might compose a song to accompany a skit, or a group of preschoolers may sing a lullaby to the dolls in the housekeeping center.

Integrating the Arts

MAKING MATHEMATICAL CONNECTIONS TO THE COMMON CORE

Musical activities can be used to reinforce mathematical concepts found in the Common Core Math Standards for K–2.

Preschool

- Children learn one-to-one correspondence as they clap and tap a beat and sing counting songs.

Kindergarten

- They can count to 100 orally by ones and tens, recognize cardinality, and learn that the last number is the total beats as they count out the beat in a piece of music.
- They can count forward from a given number when starting in the middle of a line.
- They can write out the number of beats as one way to record the rhythm of a piece of music.
- They can answer questions about how many beats there are, add on beats, and take away beats.
- They classify patterns of beats and count the number of beats in the pattern.

First Grade

- Children can continue to count beats to amounts beyond 100.
- Children can solve simple additions and subtraction word problems that ask them to learn or invent a rhythmic sequence and then add or subtract beats or groups of beats from it.
- They can use the clock to time different rhythms, pieces of music, and songs.

Second Grade

- Children can count beats by 5s, 10s, and multiples of 100.
- Use addition to find the total number of beats in a song by adding the together the beats in each line.
- Children can count orally each time they tap out a beat.
- Children can use more, less, and equal as they compare groups of beats, two strings of notes, or two different lines in a song or set of songs.
- During rhythmic activities they can compare quantities and group and classify by beats.
- They can identify even groups in rhythmic patterns.

Did You Get It?

Which of the following would you recommend for developing the musical abilities of young children?

a. Have young children practice in groups, rather than individually, to help them sing accurately.

b. Ensure young children are taught how to play music formally, rather than having them experiment on their own.

c. Provide one-on-one rather than whole group activities to teach young children to sing accurately.

d. Ensure young children listen to simplified music, as they will not understand complex music.

Take the full quiz on CourseMate

Whole group. Many music activities lend themselves to whole group settings. Children can listen to music during a nap or snack. They can sing favorite songs together as part of group meetings as a way to build community. New songs can be taught to the whole group so everyone can sing along. A rhythm band in which everyone participates can show children what can be accomplished when every member works together.

Transitions. Music as a form of communication can be used to signal changes in activities, mood, and behavior. Playing calm music while children work and play can create a peaceful, relaxing environment and build a sense of community.

The Listening Experience

According to Shore and Strasser (2006), an effective music curriculum starts with a developmental series of listening activities. It should include a wide range of music, including complex music. This is based on the research that shows that early listening to complex music by infants leads to richer cognitive and language development.

Listening activities should include music from other times and cultures, as well as listening to natural sounds.

Selecting pieces for listening. Music intended solely for children is commonly part of most preschool and primary music programs. However, regardless of the children's ages musical selections should never be limited to only simplified pieces, because all children are capable of more sophisticated listening. Without exposure to complex music, not only in the Western classical tradition, but also that of other cultures, they will not develop the aesthetic awareness and close listening skills needed to truly appreciate and love music.

We cannot begin too early. The early years are critical in the formation of music appreciation. By eight-months an infant can tell the difference between two complex musical works. In doing so they respond more to the **scale** and the meter found in the music they have heard in their home environment (Hannon & Trainor, 2007; Hannon & Trehub, 2005; Lynch & Eilers; 1992; Soley & Hannon, 2010).

Music preferences continue to solidify throughout early childhood. However, research indicates that children up to the age of five are more willing to respond positively to unfamiliar styles than older children and adults (Flohr & Persellin, 2011; Kopiez & Lehmann, 2008). Therefore, the earlier children experience a variety of musical genres and styles the better.

Table 10-2 presents a sampling of music from many cultural traditions that will both appeal to young children while challenging their listening skills.

Listening Activities for Infants

Sensitivity to sound is one of the most highly developed senses in infants. Listening activities help them learn to focus attention and make sense of the many sounds in their environment.

Lullabies. Lullabies are a very special category of song. To soothe infants, play lullabies and rock them gently. The soothing songs help infants learn how to self-regulate and sooth themselves (Parlakian, 2010). Brahms, Handel, and Mozart all wrote wonderful lullabies. Traditional lullabies are available from all cultures. Alice Honig (2005) points out that it does not matter to infants in what language the lullaby is. Nevertheless, families will appreciate a caregiver's initiative in learning lullabies from the child's culture. Singing familiar songs will increase the infant's feeling of comfort and belonging. Try to memorize several

TABLE 10–2	Music for Listening and Study
Artist/Producer	**Title**
Puntamayo	*Acoustic Africa*
Benedictine Monks of Santo	*Chants*
Frederick Chopin	*Sonata No. 3 Op. 58*
Hamza El Din	*The Water Wheel*
Edward Grieg	*Peer Gynt*
Gustav Holst	*The Planets*
R. Carlos Nakai	*Dancing into Silence*
Inca Sun	*Peru: A Musical Journey*
Thelonious Monk	*My Funny Valentine*
Wolfgang Amadeus Mozart	*Symphony No. 39 in E Flat*
Modest Petrovich Mussorgsky	*Pictures at an Exhibition*
Michael Oldfield	*Tubular Bells 1 and 2*
Nikolai Andreyevich Rimsky- Korsakov	*Scheherazade*
Wayna Picchu	*Folk Music from Peru*
Igor Stravinsky	*Petrushka*
Vangelis	*Antarctica*

Note: These are just a few of a multitude of musical selections that can inspire young children.

Digital Download   Download from CourseMate

to sing often to the infant. Vary saying the words and humming the melody.

For a list of multicultural lullaby albums, see *Lullabies from Around thve World* on CourseMate.

Attention getters. Sing, hum, or play a lively song to get the baby's attention.

Clock. Place a loudly ticking clock near the infant.

Mobiles. For non-sitting infants, hang a mobile that makes soft sounds or plays a lullaby. For older infants, securely suspend noise makers that they can reach for and pull. For safety, supervise at all times.

Movements. Encourage a young infant to move along to a song you sing or to music you listen to, such as by bouncing and rocking the baby to the music.

Shakers. Shake a rattle, set of keys, bells, or play a musical instrument to attract attention. Move the shaker around so the baby follows it with eyes and head. With an older infant, play peek-a-boo with the noisemaker.

Listening to music can be an intensely personal experience. Having paper and drawing materials in the listening center offers children a way to communicate their feelings.

Copyright © 2015 Cengage Learning®

Singing. Make singing a daily occurrence. Make up little songs to accompany daily activities from eating to washing up. Vary the loudness of the song and the pitch of the notes sometimes singing higher and sometimes lower.

Listening Activities for Toddlers

Toddlers are becoming more aware of the sounds around them and can begin to identify the sources of many of them. They are also starting to develop preferences for certain music.

Sound walk. Take a walk outside in the neighborhood or in a park and notice the different sounds heard. Look for other places to visit that have interesting sounds, such as a kitchen, a factory, a pool, or beach.

High low. Choose a fun word or the child's name and repeat it over and over. Start low and get higher and higher in pitch. As the pitch gets higher, raise your arms over your head. As the sound gets lower, lower arms to your sides.

Identify sounds. Make a sound using an object, then hide it, and have the children try to guess what it is. When they are familiar with several, see if they can pick out one from the others only by listening.

Loud and soft. Explore ways to make sounds louder or softer. Cover and uncover ears. Whisper and yell. Turn the volume up and down on the player.

Listen to music. Play and sing many different kinds of musical pieces from all over the world. Continue to soothe the child with lullabies and gentle classical music. Play dance music for children to move to creatively.

Listening Activities for Preschoolers and Up

With their longer attention spans, preschool, kindergarten and primary children are much more sophisticated listeners. They can participate in individual and group activities that ask them to compare and contrast sounds and music recognizing the timbre of different instruments and identify instrumental versions of familiar songs. They can start to use the vocabulary of the music to describe what they hear and to share their ideas with others.

Primary students can also begin to write about their listening experiences. This, plus increasing knowledge in the different subject areas, allows activities to become more integrated into other areas of learning.

The following are some suggested activities.

Body sounds. Explore all the different sounds you can make with your body—rubbing hands; slapping chest, thighs, or floor; snapping fingers; clapping hands; tapping fingers; stamping feet; clicking teeth; popping cheeks; and so on. Then use these sounds to accompany music as they listen. Preschool and up.

Collect sounds. As new sounds are discovered, record them on a class chart. Preschool and up.

Find the sound. Have the children close their eyes while one child makes a sound somewhere in the classroom. See if they can identify from where the sound came. Try this game outside as well. Preschool and up.

Listen to relax. Provide quiet times when music is listened to solely for enjoyment and relaxation. For preschoolers this can be at naptime. For older children it can serve as a stress-reliever after recess. Preschool and up.

Silence. True listening takes focus. To help children develop auditory focus, make time on a regular basis for silence listening. Stop what you are doing and have everyone stop making noise, close their eyes, and listen. Then share what you heard. Preschool and up.

Sound scavenger hunt. Go on a scavenger hunt outdoors. Collect nature objects that can be used to make interesting sounds. Preschool and up.

Introduce new tunes. Slowly introduce new music styles so children have time to become accustomed to them, but keep coming back to tunes they already know to maintain recognition. Preschool and up.

Ordered sound. Fill small metal cans or film containers with different materials so there is a range from soft to loud. Seal containers shut so the children cannot open them. Let the children explore them at the sound center and think of different ways to group them. Encourage them to put them in order from softest to loudest. Make another set that has matched pairs and see if the children can match them up. Preschool and up.

Listen closely. Play a piece of music while the children close their eyes. have them raise their hands when they hear a preselected part, melody, or pattern, or when they hear a change in pitch, tempo, or dynamics. At first play a sample of what to listen for before beginning the activity. Later as the children get more accurate, try it without a sample. Kindergarten and up.

Classify sounds. Collect items and instruments that make interesting sounds. Group them by loudness, length of sound, timbre, and pitch. Preschool and up.

Invent sound machines. Using boxes, paper, sandpaper, tin foil, Styrofoam, cardboard, straws, and other similar materials, build machines that make an interesting sound. Preschool and up.

Discover musical forms. Introduce children to the many styles and forms of music. Listen to children's opera, country dances, symphonies, and jazz sessions. Develop understanding of these forms by comparing and contrasting what makes these types of music different from each other. Could you dance to an aria in an opera? Is it hard to sit still during a country dance or does it make your body want to move?

For a comprehensive list of musical forms, see *Musical Forms* on CourseMate.

Tell stories. Most popular music has **lyrics**. Children will be less familiar with instrumental pieces.

Help children listen more closely to instrumental pieces by telling a story about the music that makes it come alive and be memorable. For young children this could be a simple made-up story, such as "Can you hear the birds flying to their nests?" For older children tell stories about the composer, how and why he or she wrote it, and the instruments used to play it. Encourage children to make up their own stories by setting out puppets they can animate to the music or by providing writing materials in the listening center.

Reading about Music

Numerous children's books introduce composers and their work. Listen to instrumental pieces that tell a story through the music such as *Peter and the Wolf* by Sergei Prokofiev and *The Carnival of Animals* by Camille Saint-Saëns and then read the story. Re-listen to the work to gain deeper understanding of how music can set a **mood** and create character.

Other books introduce famous musicians and music genres such as Celenza's *Gershwin's Rhapsody in Blue* (2006) and Pinkney's *Duke Ellington: The Piano Prince* (2006). Accompany the book with recordings by the musician.

For an annotated list of books about musical genres and composers, see *Books about Music and Musicians* on CourseMate.

Talking about Music

Research shows that music elicits strong emotional and physical responses in the listener (Standley, 2008). Build on this emotional-physical connection by providing opportunities for intense listening to a musical piece before talking about it. Play the piece numerous times. Invite children to move their hands to the changes in pitch or dynamics, or tap and sway to the rhythms. Allow children to move in the way they best feel matches the music even if it differs from your ideas about the music. When we allow children to move in their own ways, we encourage creativity and foster active listening.

After they have had time to absorb the music through their bodies and make it their own, try asking some of these open-ended questions.

🎵 How did this music make you want to move?

🎵 How did this music make you feel?

🎵 Did you hear any changes in the music that made you move differently or feel differently?

🎵 What did the music remind you of? Or make you think of?

🎵 Did the music tell a story?

For more ideas for listening activities, see Listening Activities for Young Children on CourseMate.

Did You Get It?

When selecting pieces for children under the age of five to listen to, a teacher should _____.

a. have children listen to only simple music from other cultures

b. avoid music that is unfamiliar to the children

c. include complex music from a variety of cultural traditions

d. focus on music intended solely for children

Take the full quiz on CourseMate

The Rhythmic Experience

Rhythm is fundamental to life. Each of us carries our own natural rhythm in our heartbeat. Before birth babies respond the sound of their mother's heartbeat (Parncutt, 2006). After birth, infants

Rhythm instruments are ideal for young children. Playing together in a rhythm band teaches children to cooperate and helps them develop mathematical counting skills.

as young as two months notice rhythmic patterns and groupings (Ilari & Polka, 2006; Krumhansl & Jusczyk, 1990; Mithen, 2006). By seven months they can perceive variations in tempo and frequency (Trainor & Corrigall, 2010).

At around two-and-a half toddlers can hear a steady beat and will attempt to match their body movements to it (Provasi & Bobin-Begue, 2003). By preschool children are able to hold a beat and move to it, and by kindergarten most children can identify the rhythmic pattern in a piece of music and match changes in the tempo (Eerola, Luck, & Toiviainen, 2006; Trainor & Corrigall, 2010).

Designing Rhythmic Activities

Rhythmic activities should develop children's sense of rhythm through open-ended exploration that allows them to create their own rhythm instruments and rhythms. Rhythm activities are naturally engaging to young children and do not have to be complicated. They should involve the child in listening to rhythms and physically responding in some way. Variety can be introduced by using new ways to make sounds and sharing music with different rhythms.

In addition to planned engagements with rhythm we can also incorporate rhythm into daily activities. For example, carry around a small drum or tambourine, or simply clap, to catch and mirror the rhythms of the children at play. As children paint at the easel or jump on the playground, tap out a beat that matches their movement as you bring it to their attention:

🎵 "Listen. Can you hear the tapping beat of the brush?"

🎵 "Listen. Can you hear how fast your feet are stamping as you jump up and down?"

Another way to incorporate rhythm into daily events is to use echo clapping when you want the children's attention. Clap a rhythm and have everyone else clap the same rhythm back. This is an excellent way to get the focus of a group even when they are deeply involved in play.

Rhythmic chants can be used to transition from one activity to another. It is easy to invent your own. For example, when cleaning up chant something like "Clean up. Clean up. Everybody clean up," while

Teacher Tip

KEEP A STEADY BEAT

1. Signal the start of the song by tapping a steady beat on your thighs, a table, by clapping or by using a rhythm instrument.
2. Give any instructions as you keep tapping.
3. Give a start signal that matches the beat such as "One Two Ready to Go."
4. Sing the song emphasizing the word syllables that land on the beat.

Example:

Polly **put** the **ket**tle **on**

Polly **put** the **ket**tle **on**

Polly **put** the **ket**tle **on**

We'll **all** **have** **tea**

clapping a regular beat to the words. As children work they can join in and chant along.

To encourage growth, rhythm experiences should occur every day. Rhythm activities can be offered one-on-one, in exploration centers, and as whole group experiences. Here are some activities to try with infant and toddlers.

Rhythm Activities for Infants and Toddlers

Rhythm activities for this age focus on helping the child discover the rhythm and respond to it. Infants and toddlers benefit most when rhythm is explored one-on-one with a caring adult. Watching our faces and movements as we make rhythmic sounds and movements builds on the natural way infants learn. When we move the child's limbs or as we hold the child and move to a beat the child physically feels the rhythm and our enthusiasm is contagious as we model our own response to the rhythm. We can tell a child is engaged when they rock and bounce along with us.

Infants and toddlers also need opportunities to explore making rhythms on their own.

Introduce infants and toddlers to ways to create sound patterns by providing safe, simple objects for them to shake and tap, such as rattles, spoons, margarine containers, and wooden dowels. Instruments and

sound makers for infants and toddlers should meet the choke and poke test, i.e., be longer than 2 inches in length and 1 inch in diameter and have smooth, rounded ends on sticks and handles and be at least 1 inch in diameter. If needed, wrap handles in foam for added protection and ease of handling.

Use the following activities as inspiration for inventing your own.

Foot dance. Attach rattles or bells to an infant's ankles and encourage the child to kick as you sing or listen to music.

Exercising. Play a lively tune with a distinct beat. Move an infant's arms and legs in time to music. If the child is able to move on his or her own, model moving to the rhythm.

Rocking. Hold the child and rock back and forth in time to music or singing.

Name rhythm. Clap out the syllables of the child's name.

Nursery rhymes. Select a familiar nursery rhyme or poem and follow the rhythm clapping or using rhythm instruments. Listen for the accented beats.

Exploring Sound Centers

Set up a sound center where toddlers can explore the sound and rhythms they can make using simple objects they can tap or shake. A list of rhythm instruments follows the next section. Vary the activity by add to or changing the objects.

Preschoolers and older children can make their own sound makers independently if provided with some basic materials, such as containers to fill and tap on. Provide the center with a tape recorder so they can play back their rhythms, paper and markers so they can record their rhythms, or provide a CD player so they can shake, rattle, and tap to the music.

Whole Group Rhythm Bands

Rhythm sticks make a good introduction to whole group rhythm activities using sound makers starting in preschool. Try to have all the sticks the same color to keep children focused on the sound possibilities rather than who has their favorite color. An inexpensive substitute for commercial sticks is wooden spoons. Child-made shakers or margarine tub drums can also be used.

There are hundreds of different rhythm instruments. Look for instruments all kinds including those from other cultures to share with children. From left to right: maracas, hand drum, castanet, cacho shaker from Peru, sleigh bells, wood tone block.

No matter which sound maker is introduced first, provide plenty of space between each child and show them how to rest the sound maker on the ground in front of them or in their lap until the group is ready to play. Practice picking up the sound maker and putting it down. Teach the children a verbal or visual start and stop signal and practice it. When the children have the idea, put on a march or piece of music with a strong beat and have them tap along. Once they have mastered that, have them think of other ways to make sounds with the sticks or sound makers such as tapping them end to end or gently against their shoe. Play the piece again trying out some of the different ways the children have created.

Incorporate spatial and kinesthetic learning by having them play their instruments to one side or the other, across their bodies, above or below their heads, and using different body parts.

Vary the activity further by playing different kinds of music, tapping along to songs as you sing, and exploring other rhythm instruments like the ones described below. And don't forget to make photographs and videos and audio recordings of your band in action.

Selecting Rhythm Instruments

Rhythm instruments for young children are usually **percussion**-type instruments, although any instrument can be used to create a rhythm or steady beat. Percussion instruments create sound by being struck or shaken. Although many items found around the house can be used to provide rhythm experiences, a wide range of traditional and nontraditional rhythm instruments can be purchased reasonably. Others are easily made. However, do not rely solely on ones you can make; children need to experience real instruments as well as homemade ones.

Bells. All varieties of bells can be used, such as sleigh bells, cowbells, brass bells from India, and gongs. Jingle bells can be attached to elastic wristbands for children who have not yet developed fine motor control or attached to arms or legs to allow infants and toddlers to move their bodies in rhythm.

Claves. Made from thick polished sticks, one is held in the palm and the other used to tap it. Explore the sounds made by tapping different sizes and shapes of wood.

Cymbals. Children love the large sound they can make with cymbals. Child-size cymbals usually have handles and are designed to fit little hands. Louder cymbals can be made from old pan lids. Finger cymbals come from Asia and because of their small size and high pitch, are ideal for young children.

Drums. Drums come in all sizes and shapes ranging from the bass drum to the hand drum. Drums for children should be stable and make a good sound without too much effort. Bongos, tom toms, and the different African drums, such as a *doumbek* or *djembe*, add variety to drumming activities. Drums can also be made from margarine and larger plastic containers with lids, plastic and metal pails, steel pie plates and pots, and five-gallon clean plastic buckets. A quiet drum can be made by stretching a balloon over the top of a coffee can using lacing, elastic bands, or heavy tape to hold it in place. A community drum can be made by using rubber roofing scrap and attaching grommets. Stretch the rubber over a large 3-gallon water tub. Heavy-duty plastic water tubs, intended for farm animals, come in very large sizes and make pleasant-sounding drums when turned upside down.

Electronic drum machines are another way to explore rhythms. Built-in recoded rhythms and songs allow the child to match the beat or play along. Some of them will allow you to record what you play. However, they are expensive, and young children will have just as much fun with homemade drums that allow them to use their whole body.

Maracas. Originally made from a dried gourd with the seeds still inside, today they are often plastic. Similar shakers can be made from soda and water bottles filled with different materials, with the lids hot glued on. Preschoolers can fill plastic eggs and margarine-type containers with lids. Put out a selection of items from which to choose, such as sand, gravel, and marbles that make interesting sounds. Paper plates, filled with rice or beans, can be stapled together to make easy-to-use shakers.

Rainstick. Purchase a traditional one from an import store or make your own. Insert nails at regular intervals in a cardboard tube, fill with rice, and seal both ends well. Wrap the entire tube in sturdy tape so that nails cannot be removed.

Rhythm sticks. These are ubiquitous in children's rhythm bands because they are inexpensive and easy to use. They can be made from well-sanded wooden dowels or wooden spoons. Sometimes they are grooved and a different sound results when the sticks are rubbed up and down against each other.

Sand blocks. Two wooden blocks can be wrapped in sandpaper and rubbed together to create a soft scratching sound.

Strikers. Depending on the instrument, most percussion requires something with which to tap or hit. Drumsticks are usually too large and loud for children. Hard rubber mallets can be purchased for a softer tone. Soft-sounding mallets can also be made by attaching a tennis ball or rubber ball to the end of a heavy wooden dowel. Cut a hole in the ball, insert the handle, glue, and then wrap in duct tape or cloth so it is firmly attached.

Tambourines. A tambourine is a hoop with jingles set into the frame. Some tambourines have a skinhead; others are open. It is an easy instrument for young children to play because it can be either shaken, tapped, or both. Its pleasant sound makes it ideal for creating rhythms to accompany children's activities or for rhythmic transitions.

Tappers. A number of instruments make tapping sounds. Castanets are made of clamshell-shaped wood; although plastic ones may be more appropriate for children. They are held in the palm and clicked by opening and closing the hand. Spoons made of wood, plastic, and metal also make good tappers. The spoons, an American folk tradition, are played by holding two metal spoons back to back with one between the thumb and the index finger and the other between the index finger and the middle finger. Hold the palm of the other hand above the spoons and hit the spoons against the knee and the palm to create a clicking rhythm.

Tongue drum. The pitched tongue drum is made from hollowed wood and is of Aztec origin. It has wood "keys" that make different pitches when tapped.

Triangles. A favorite of young children because of its pleasing high pitch, the triangle is made of a bent piece of metal hung from a string and tapped with a metal stick. Explore the sound made by other metal objects, such as pie tins and old spoons. Suspend the pie tins and spoons from a string so they can vibrate.

Wood blocks. These are hollow pieces of wood that create a pleasant sound when tapped.

Rhythm Activities for Preschoolers and up

By preschool, children have a much better ability to respond on the beat. They can mirror back a rhythm and invent rhythms of their own. Children in kindergarten and older usually can keep time fairly accurately, especially if they have had many rhythmic experiences earlier. They can now play complex rhythms in group activities with small groups or an individual playing a contrasting part. They can start to compare and contrast rhythms, find the accented beat, and combine rhythms in new ways.

The following activities help children practice finding the rhythm, holding it, and matching changes in tempo and dynamics.

Bubbles. Blow bubbles. Ask each child to select one bubble to watch. When that bubble pops, they are to say "pop." Repeat, having them make different sounds when the bubble pops. Ask them to listen for any rhythms or patterns that they hear. Do the "pops" come faster as all the bubbles disappear? Follow up by creating a bubble song.

Body talk. Select a word of two or more syllables. Say the word and match its syllables by clapping or moving a body part, such as nodding the head, stamping the feet, waving the arms, clapping the thigh, and so forth. Try it using two or more words.

Clocks. Find a clock with a loud tick. Have the children say "tick tock" and keep time with claps or rhythm instruments. Follow up by introducing a **metronome,** a device that produces a regular beat that can be changed. Show how the tempo of the beat can be sped up and slowed down. Have child clap or move their rhythm instruments to the beat. Being able to maintain a regular beat correlates with greater achievement in the primary grades (Weikert, Schweinhaer & Larner, 1987).

Drum circle. Provide each child with a commercial or homemade drum. Ideally, there should be drums in an assortment of sizes, and hands should be used instead of drumsticks. Sit in a circle and have one child start a rhythm, which is picked up by everyone else. In turn, signal a different child to change the rhythm. The same thing can be done using other rhythm instruments as well.

Explore rhythm instruments. Provide plenty of time for the children to explore rhythm instruments on their own before starting any group activities. Introduce new instruments one at a time to the sound center. At the exploration level children will play around with the instruments making sounds, but no recognizable rhythm. As they gain mastery they will start tapping with a regular beat. At the response level they will play a rhythm as they sing a song to themselves. They will vary the rhythm by manipulating instruments or combining two or more in new ways.

Assess progress. To assess the ability of an individual child to remember and repeat a rhythm, clap a short rhythm for the child to clap back. Challenge children by making the rhythm longer.

Heartbeat. Have the children sit very still and silent, put their hands on their hearts, and feel their heartbeats. Have them tap the floor or their thigh, and shake an instrument with the other hand to match the rhythm. Investigate: Is the rhythm the same for everyone? Does the speed change if you jump up and down? Listen for the heart beat in popular songs. Preschool and up.

Name rhythms. Have the children clap out the syllables of their names. See whether children can identify a name just from hearing it clapped. Look for names with the same or similar rhythms. Preschool and up.

Rhythm pass along. Have children sit in a circle and hand out a variety of different instruments. Play or sing a familiar song and keep time. At intervals have the children pass their instruments to the person sitting next to them so everyone gets a chance to play

every instrument. Music activities like this encourage turn taking in a rewarding fashion. Preschool and up.

Reading and Writing Rhythm

Rhythm and poetry are a natural combination. Identification of syllables and understanding how regular beats supply rhythm to a poem or song are skills found in the Common Core Standards. Nursery rhymes are ideal for introducing rhythm and pattern at the preschool level. Have younger children clap or keep the beat using rhythm instruments as they chant "Baa Baa Black Sheep" or "Jack and Jill." Teach older children to write or act out original versions of the rhymes and then add their own rhythmic accompaniment.

Use nursery rhymes to help children learn about meter. Start by saying the rhyme together. Say it again accenting the main beat. This is the start of the **measure.** Next, tap the beat using rhythm instruments. Finally, decide whether the rhythm moves in 2's (strong| weak strong| weak) or 3s (strong weak weak |strong weak weak). Some nursery rhymes with a strong meter are "Humpty Dumpty," "Jack and Jill," and "Jack Be Nimble."

Explore rhyming poems with a strong beat such as the nature poetry of Aileen Fisher in *The Story Goes On* (2005) or Jack Prelustsky's *Read Aloud Poems for the Very Young* (1986) and *It's Raining Pigs and Noodles* (2000). There are also books like Chris Raschka's *Charlie Parker Played Be Bop* (1992) in which the simple text has a jazz rhythm or Matthew Gollub's *The Jazz Fly 2: The Jungle Pachanga* (2010) which introduces Spanish and Latin jazz.

For a list of annotated books with rhythmic text, see *Books with a Rollicking Rhythm* on CourseMate.

Explore writing rhythms by making a large copy of a simple poem and marking the beat with an agreed upon symbol. In the rhythm center have children create their own rhythms to go with a poem or rhyme and invite them to invent a way to write it down on paper using symbols so their friends can play it.

Another way to combine reading, writing, and rhythm is to have the children write stories on a specified topic such as animals or cars, or choose a story from a book. With a partner, add rhythms to parts of the story that reflect what is happening. For example, if a character is walking, then play a slow, even beat. If the character is running, play a quick, heavy rhythm. Invite them to share their stories.

Talking about Rhythm

Introduce the vocabulary of rhythm by explaining that the beat is like a road or track that keeps everybody together. Use the terms tempo, dynamics, upbeat, and downbeat and together invent hand signals or ways of moving to show changes in these. Play different rhythms using sound makers and have the children describe differences in them using these words. Move on to playing two different musical works and listening to the rhythm. Make a chart listing how the rhythms sound in different styles of music.

As children explore the rhythms they create and those they hear in musical works, use enthusiastic descriptions, lots of movement, and open-ended questioning.

- How does the beat make you feel like moving?

- Does the beat change in any way?

- What else have you heard that has a similar beat?

- What words would you use to describe how this beat sounds?

For more rhythmic activities to try, see Rhythmic Activities for Young Children on CourseMate.

Did You Get It?

Amanda wants to help her preschoolers develop a sense of rhythm. Which of the following activities will best help her achieve this?

a. Amanda should give the children simple percussion instruments to play with.

b. Amanda should play a complex piece of music and ask the children to identify the individual instruments.

c. Amanda should play a piece of music and ask the children to indicate changes in pitch by raising and lowering their hands.

d. Amanda should teach the children songs that they can sing in a group.

Take the full quiz on CourseMate

The Musical Instrument Experience

Rhythmic activities naturally grow into explorations of tonal musical instruments and melody. First experiences with musical instruments should allow children to explore the different sounds they can make.

One-On-One

Like percussion instruments, tonal instruments should be offered one-on-one at first. Many of them are delicate and need to be explored with supervision. Help children learn to identify the instruments by name. Ask them to describe the shape and sound of each.

Music Center

Follow up by expanding the sound center into a music center, and provide simple, durable instruments, both homemade and purchased. Make a recording of each instrument's sound, and place it in the music center so the children can explore timbre—the unique quality of the sound—by matching the mystery sound to its instrument.

A computer, MIDI keyboard, and music software can be added as well. As in visual art, an older computer dedicated solely to music exploration is a valuable addition to the arts program. Research has shown that using music software intended for children provides a playful way for them to explore timbre, pitch, and melody (Higgins & Campbell, 2010).

Whole Group

Expand the rhythm band to include tonal instruments or try creating a melody band of just bells or recorders playing simple tunes and those of the children's own composition. As children gain skill and confidence, stage impromptu parades and concerts. Add child-created tunes to a favorite story or poem. Always remember to keep these activities open-ended and flexible. Performances that require hours of rehearsal and create stress are inappropriate for young children and steal away the child's natural affinity for making music.

Selecting Musical Instruments

Although rhythm instruments are the most convenient and usually least expensive instruments for

Tonal instruments allow children to explore melody.

children, young children also need opportunities to explore tonality. Providing tonal instruments allows children to discover melody.

Bells.   Pitched bells can be a wonderful instrument for young children because they are similar to rhythm instruments and yet they can be used to play a melody. Hand bells are widely available and can be used with all ages. A double set of Montessori bells can also provide excellent training in learning to identify the different pitches.

Keyboard.   These instruments usually have keys to press. Those designed for infants and toddlers usually have just a few notes and colored keys. Search the Internet for "baby pianos" to find ones designed just for infants. On the traditional keyboard the white keys are in C major scale and the black keys are sharps and flats. The piano and electronic or MIDI keyboard can be used with very young children, even infants held in a lap, for a variety of music activities. They have the advantage of making it easy to name the notes and play harmony. If the keyboard has sufficient range, you can play along with the child either mirroring the same notes or playing chords. Music software that can be played with the MIDI keyboard can teach very young children about the music elements and how to begin to read and compose music. Other keyboard instruments include the accordion, harpsichord, clavichord, and organ.

Pitched percussion.   The xylophone and chimes are pitched instruments struck with mallets. Rubber and plastic mallets can be used to soften the sound in the classroom. Simple eight- and twelve-note xylophones allow children to compose and adapt simple melodies as well as explore rhythms. Other pitched percussion instruments include the bell lyre and the vibraphone. These are usually found in full orchestras. The thumb piano or kalimba is an African instrument that is easy for children to play. A simple chime can be made by placing nails on a piece of foam. Select a graduated set of nails in a range of sizes from 10 to 60 penny (2 to 6 inches). To play, tap the nails with a pencil.

Strings.   String instruments feature vibrating strings. Guitars and autoharps can be used to accompany children singing and to introduce playing simple melodies. Violin, viola, cello, bass, and harp are usually found in orchestras. Folk string instruments include the ukulele, dulcimers, banjo, zither, and mandolin.

Stringed instruments are found around the world. Each has a unique timbre that gives music from those cultures their characteristic sound. The *oud* is common in Arab countries. The *sitar* and *santoor* are from India. The *bouzouki* is from Greece and the *balalaika* from Russia.

Wind instruments.   These instruments are played by blowing air across or into the instrument.

Across Cultures

Instruments from Around the World

Display instruments from other cultures, such as Tibetan singing bowls; carved frog and cricket wood rasps from Indonesia; rain sticks and goat hoof chachas rattles from Bolivia; the telavi from Ghana; and woven shakers from Africa, Brazil, and India.

Find information on these and other instruments at https://www.worldmusicalinstruments.com/.

The pitch changes either by varying the amount and direction of the breath or by pressing down keys which change the length of air in the instrument. Woodwinds have keys, which release the air at different lengths down the tube of the instruments. Many woodwinds also have a reed, which vibrates when blown. In order of descending pitch, there is the fife, piccolo, flute, oboe, clarinet, saxophone, and bassoon. There are also many folk wind instruments, such as the bagpipe, harmonica, penny whistle, and recorder. Brass instruments are played by putting lips into a metal mouthpiece, such as the trumpet, trombone, French horn, and tuba. The sound is created by the vibration of the lips.

For health reasons, children need personal wind instruments. Because of this, wind instruments are rare in most preschools and general classrooms. Inexpensive penny whistles and plastic recorders are sometimes used in the primary grades. Children can make kazoos by rubber banding wax paper to the end of a cardboard tube.

Instrumental Activities for Infants

Because infants up to the age of one explore the world with all their senses instruments are particularly fascinating to them. Safety, of course, is the number-one issue and instruments offered to this age group should be sturdy with no sharp edges. Close supervision is vital and the best experience is one-on-one with the infant in the adult's lap.

Chime blocks. Commercial pitched chime blocks make a wonderful introduction to melodic instruments for the infant. If these cannot be found, similar blocks can be made by putting pitched bells inside small sturdy boxes, which are securely taped closed.

These should be used only with adult supervision. Make sure the bells being used pass the choke test.

Keyboard play. Play a melody on any keyboard instrument while holding the baby on your lap. Let the child "play" along, demonstrating how to press individual keys with a finger rather than banging with the whole hand.

Stringing along. Let the child pluck the strings of any stringed instrument. Be sure the instrument is secure—often you can wedge it between pillows and then hold the child on your lap. As the child plucks a string, finger some notes so different pitches result.

Chimes. For very young infants, hang baby-safe chimes where they can kick and bat them. Simple xylophones or chimes set in foam rubber are available for older infants. These should be used with close supervision.

Instrumental Activities for Toddlers

Toddlers are curious about everything, and instruments are no exception. They are still at the exploratory stage and are more likely to just want to make noise than to create actual melodies. However, the toddler's awareness of and attention to timbre makes tonal instruments very engaging to them.

Classroom Technology

MUSIC SOFTWARE

Music software for young children can be used to introduce them to timbre, pitch, provide ear training, and reading musical notation. Many programs also allow children to compose original musical pieces and hear them played back. They can add accompanying rhythms and harmonies.

Although many of the programs are recommended for toddlers and up, digital music making should never replace hands-on interactions with actual instruments. Children need to move their bodies to the beat and hear the changes in sound as it moves nearer and closer to them. Use musical software as an addition to all of the other wonderful music activities we can do with children.

Always preview software before offering it to children. Write simple directions using symbols to help little ones know what to do independently.

In selecting music software for children, look for the following:

1. Large, easy-to-click buttons.
2. Limited choices for beats and harmonies.
3. Ability to add a MIDI keyboard. Using a mouse or computer keys is an awkward way for little fingers to play notes.
4. A game-like atmosphere in which children can try again and again to solve puzzles or master a concept rather than drill and practice type activities.

For more information on music software, see *Music Software* on CourseMate

Provide toddlers daily opportunities for playful exploration of sturdy tonal instruments. There are numerous keyboard and chime type instruments made for this age group. Enthusiastic modeling during supportive one-on-one activities is an effective way to guide the child into discovering the melodic possibilities of the instrument. As they play they can learn the names of music instruments and how they look and sound. Older toddlers can also begin to experiment with musical timbres using computer software designed for them.

Exploring instruments. Create a music play area and provide sturdy toy instruments, such as chimes, xylophone, plastic guitar, hand bells, and a child-size piano or keyboard instrument as well as the more common rhythm instruments. Tape the child making music often.

Music mats. Large piano-like mats that children can walk on to make notes, let toddlers explore melody bodily.

Instrumental Activities for Preschoolers

By the time they enter preschool, children are able to handle instruments more carefully. They still like to explore and need plenty of sturdy instruments, such as those listed for infants and toddlers, but they can also be trusted to handle a guitar or piano with supervision. Preschoolers will freely compose original melodies and songs if given the opportunity to use melodic instruments. A music center for preschoolers should include, if possible, a piano or electric keyboard with a range of several octaves.

Instrument timbre match. Perform a melody on a familiar hidden instrument or play an audio recording and let them try to guess which instrument it is. Once they can do this regularly, try identifying the same instruments being played on recordings of music by famous composers or from other cultures.

Match the note. Place two xylophones or chimes on opposite sides of a screen. Have one child play a note and see whether another child can play the same note back. As children grow in skill, challenge them to match two or more notes up to an entire line of a familiar melody.

Name the note. This is the age when it is important for children to hear the names of the notes in association with playing the note. Provide many opportunities for children to say aloud or sing the note names such as when playing the xylophone, hand bells, or keyboard. For example, instead of saying the words to "Baa Baa Black Sheep" as they tap it out on the chimes sing the note names with the child. Label the notes on other tonal instruments too.

Melodic music center. Preschoolers can explore more varied instruments at a music center. In the beginning they will bang and run the mallet up and down the keyboard. They may snap strings and blow on homemade kazoos without making a tune. With experience and teacher support, they will begin to tap individual keys on the keyboard or hit individual keys on the chimes. Melody begins when the child plays random notes while humming or singing a familiar song and develops as the child begins to raise and lower the pitch to correspond with the song until it matches. Or the child may invent a melody and then sing along with it.

Instrumental Activities for Kindergarten

By the time they reach kindergarten, children have the hand–eye coordination to handle more complex

Teacher Tip

THE SUZUKI METHOD

Dr. Shin'ichi Suzuki believed that any preschool child could learn to play a musical instrument, usually the violin, but others as well, if the right environment was created. This environment consists of the following:

1. Beginning formal lessons between the age of three and five.
2. Teachers who are well trained in the method.
3. Learning by ear before learning to read music and all pieces memorized and reviewed regularly.
4. Playing the same piece together in a group.
5. Frequent public performance so children become accustomed to it.
6. The expectation that parents will attend lessons and supervise daily practice.

The Suzuki method has had much success in getting young children started on instruments, but it has also been criticized for requiring too much formal practice for such young children (Bradley, 2005).

Teacher Tip

READING MUSIC

Introduce older preschoolers, kindergarteners, and primary students to the staff and the names of the notes. The spaces are F, A, C, and E, easily remembered as "face." The lines are E, G, B, D, and F, for which there are several different mnemonic phrases, including "Every Good Boy Deserves Fudge." Once these are known, the whole keyboard makes sense because the white keys go from A to G and then repeat in the same pattern.

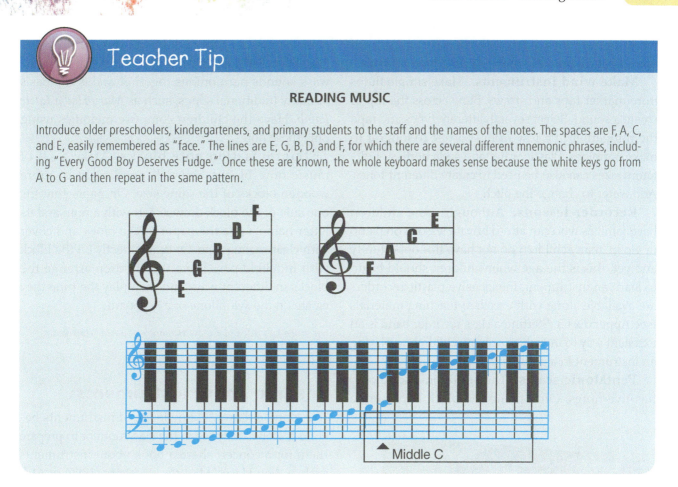

instruments, and can identify many instruments by sound. They can add harmonies to songs they improvise and, if given the opportunity, can start to read music.

Guess the instrument. Share a variety of instruments and hang up posters or photos of them. Play notes on the instruments so the children learn how each one sounds. When the children are familiar with them, hide the instrument and play it or play a recording and see whether children can identify it.

Name that tune. Make a list of songs children know. Play one of these familiar melodies on a keyboard, piano, xylophone, or guitar. See whether the children can select the song from the list. Vary the game by playing the tune on less familiar instruments, such as a thumb piano.

Playing with notes. Make large different-colored notes and a large staff labeled with the letter names of the notes. Put Velcro on the back of the notes and laminate the staff. Hang it in the music center so the children can explore composing a melody and then playing it on a xylophone labeled with the names of the notes. If the xylophone has color

keys and note labels, make sure the notes you make match in color as well.

Instrumental Activities for Primary Age

Primary-age students can identify familiar instruments by timbre. They can start to understand how instruments work. With instruction they are capable of reading music and playing the piano and violin on their own and in organized groups. Hand bells and recorders can also provide opportunities for group musical experiences. Although formal instruction on the larger string instruments—viola, cello, and bass—and the wind instruments does not usually begin until the end of the primary years, younger children will benefit from many opportunities to explore the basic instruments.

Make string instruments. Create a finger harp by wrapping rubber bands around a very sturdy piece of cardboard or wood. Make a guitar by cutting a hole in the top of a sturdy box and wrapping rubber bands around it. Explore how the sound box changes the dynamics of the rubber bands. Explore what happens with different thicknesses and sizes of rubber bands, and different sizes and types of boxes.

Make wind instruments. Make simple flutes from marker tops and straws. Blow across the top to create a sound. Select several different types and tape them together in a row from shortest to longest to make panpipes. Plastic water and soda bottles of different sizes can also be used to create different tones. Add water to change the pitch.

Recorder lessons. Although some children have families who can afford private lessons on piano or violin, many children do not have this opportunity and yet, this is the age when children should begin to learn an instrument. Inexpensive plastic recorders are available along with excellent teaching materials (see Appendix C). Starting a class recorder band is an excellent way to introduce primary children to playing an instrument in a group.

Pentatonic scales. The pentatonic scale only has five notes. On a piano the black keys form a pentatonic scale. On a xylophone it is the first, second, third, fifth, and sixth notes. This set of notes always sounds harmonious together and is the basis of many traditional songs, such as *Mary Had a Little Lamb.* Have the children compose melodies using only these notes.

Improvisation note blocks. Make a set of music note blocks. You will need eight or more wooden blocks of the same size. On paper that fits one side of the block draw a staff with a note and its letter name. Glue the paper to the block and cover with clear sealing tape. Or draw directly on the block with indelible pen. Have the children arrange the blocks in different ways and then play the tune they create on the xylophone or a keyboard.

For more activities using instruments, see *Activities with Tonal Instruments* on CourseMate.

Reading about Instruments

To expand children's knowledge of instruments beyond the ones they see in the classroom or to prepare them for a concert share a book about instruments such as Ann Hayes' *Meet the Orchestra* (1995) or *M is for Music* (Krull, 2003).

For an annotated list of books about musical instruments, see *Books about Musical Instruments* on CourseMate.

Reading and Writing Music

By preschool children are ready to start using written symbols to represent music. They become aware of notes and start to draw lines or dots in one-to-one correspondence to a musical piece (Gromko, 2003). To introduce reading music, give the children paper and crayons and then play a short simple melody. Challenge them to draw the melody on their papers. When they are done, compare the different symbols they invented. Tell them that all of these are great ideas. Then show them sheet music and explain that most composers use the same symbols so that other people can read and play the music.

After this experience, follow up with playful ways to interact with the **notation** of melody such as note card matching games or note reading software on the computer. Be sure to put paper and drawing materials at the listening center so they can write down the music they hear using their own symbols, and in the

Ask families if there are any members who play an instrument. An older sister who plays the clarinet makes an ideal role model to inspire young musicians.

music exploration center so the children can notate their original melodies.

For kindergarten and primary students, more formal instruction in composition can be started. Introduce them first to the vocabulary. Staff notation in which notes are indicated on a five-line staff is the most common system used today in writing music. The five parallel lines on which music notes are written is called the **staff.** The plural of staff is staves. A scale is a set of notes ordered by pitch.

For more about teaching children to read and write music, see *Steps to Music Literacy* on CourseMate.

Talking about Musical Instruments

Set the stage by providing many different experiences with instruments. For those instruments that the children cannot experience directly, try to provide opportunities for them to hear and see the instruments played. Sometimes older brothers or sisters, parents or local high school students will volunteer to come visit and demonstrate how the instrument is played. Contact the local high school band and orchestra teachers and arrange regular visits. Remind performers to play a very short piece and to share how the instrument is played with the children. If possible, see whether the children can touch the instrument or try it out under supervision. Do not allow the children to blow into a wind instrument, however, for sanitary reasons. Try to find local people who play unusual instruments or create digital music to come share as well.

Open-ended questions to ask about musical instruments.

- How does it sound?

- How does it sound different from _____? (Name another instrument)

- What other instrument(s) is it similar to?

- Does the instrument make a happy (sad, angry, sleepy, tired, etc.) sound?

- How does the sound of the instrument make you feel?

Making Plans

CENTER ACTIVITY: COMPOSING A MELODY

WHO?	**Group composition age(s):** Preschool, kindergarten, or primary
	Group size: Four at the center
WHEN?	**Time frame:** 10 to 20 minutes
WHY?	**Objectives:** Children will develop

- physically, by using their fine and gross motor control to play the instrument. I will know this is happening when I see the children holding the instruments and using them successfully to create tones. (Bodily-Kinesthetic)

- socially, by sharing ideas with others. I will hear this happening when they work together to make a melody. (Interpersonal)

- emotionally, by developing confidence in their ability to make music. I will see this happening when they smile and share their melodies (Intrapersonal)

- auditory perception skills, by listening for repeated melodic patterns. I will hear this happening when they repeat a pattern back to me and when they tell me they have repeated a pattern in their melody (Musical)

- language skills, by putting words to their melodies. I will hear this happening when they sing their melodies (Linguistic)

- cognitively, by comparing different melodies and making decisions about their own melody. I will see this happening when they listen to each other's melodies and devise a symbol system and record their own music. (Logical-Mathematical)

- music skill and knowledge, by improvising and performing an original melody. I will know this is happening when I see their finished composition and hear them play.

(continued)

Making Plans *(continued)*

WHERE?   **Set-Up:** At the music center. This area is in a corner of the room. It is carpeted and has instruments displayed on low shelves. On the walls are posters of musical instruments. Children should be familiar with the rhythm instruments at this center.

WHAT?   **Materials:** Child-size xylophone with colored keys labeled with their note names and soft rubber mallets on a low table. A child-friendly tape recorder is nearby. Crayons and paper.

HOW?   **Procedure:**

Warm-Up: Share the xylophone when the children are gathered on the rug. Tap out a short simple melody line of a familiar song like "Row, Row, Row Your Boat." Ask: Could you make up your own melody?

What to Do: Let the children explore the xylophone when they visit the music center. Visit the center regularly and demonstrate how to tap out a melody line while pointing out the key colors and names. Encourage the children to use crayons to write their melodies on paper in colored lines or dots labeled with the note names.

What to Say: Help the children listen closer. "Does your melody go up or down?" "How many notes do you hear in your friend's melody?" "Are those notes close or far apart? How do they sound different?" Encourage them to write down their melodies. "What color is the first note? What is its letter name?"

Transition Out: Collect the melodies the children write and staple them into a class music book. Keep the book in the center for all to use. Play some of the melodies at group time and have the children add words to them. Try joining some of the melodies together into a song.

ASSESSMENT   1. Are the children able to create original melodies?
OF LEARNING   2. Are the children able to record the melody using symbols?
   3. Can the children read their symbols and play their melodies?

For more sample music activity plans for all ages, see Open-Ended Music on CourseMate

---

Did You Get It?

Which of the following is a tonal instrument that allows children to discover melody?

a. drums

b. cymbals

c. keyboards

d. shakers

Take the full quiz on CourseMate

The Singing Experience

Children sing spontaneously from as early as age two. They often make up little tunes based on simple, repetitive words while playing. Singing daily helps develop self-confidence, expands vocal range, and helps draw a group of children together into a cohesive group.

Many adults, however, may feel uneasy singing aloud. Nevertheless, all teachers can teach children to enjoy singing. Although we may not like how our voices sound, that does not mean we cannot sing with children. As is true in all arts activities, our level of enthusiasm is far more important than having a trained voice. Children will be more involved in their own participation and learning a new song than in criticizing their teacher's voice.

To develop your confidence, always practice a song first. If possible, learn the song from a fellow teacher or friend. If that is not possible, sing along with a recording. Many children's songs are now available on the Web. The National Institute of Health Sciences has an extensive collection of children's songs, lyrics, and MIDI files. Many of the songs suggested in this chapter can be found on their Web site at http://www.niehs.nih.gov/kids/home.htm. Songs from around the world with both English lyrics and the lyrics in their original languages, plus videos of the songs being sung can be found at http://www.mamalisa.com/.

Selecting Songs

Choose songs that are short, easy to sing, have a steady beat, and lots of repetition. The pitches of the song should fall within their comfort range, which varies with age. Repetition of the whole song, rather than phrase-by-phrase teaching, seems to foster quicker acquisition of the song (Tarnowski & Leclerc, 1994). Body movements are effective in teaching songs, especially hand gestures indicating pitch and other characteristics of the music.

Children (and adults) usually learn the chorus of a song long before they know all the verses. For example, many people know the chorus to "Jingle Bells," but how many know more than one verse? Use the following guidelines when choosing a song to sing:

- **Infants**—Songs for infants are often very short with lots of repetition. Lullabies are soothing melodies with a slow beat. Teasing songs, such as "This Little Piggy Went to Market," allow adults to interact with the child physically through tickling, finger actions, and sound effects.

- **Toddlers**—Songs for toddlers should have a limited range. The majority of children will sing most comfortably from middle C to G. Middle C is the 24th white key from the left-hand side of the piano (see Teacher Tip: Reading Music). Nursery rhymes and folk songs are often in this range. To appeal to active toddlers, select songs that have interactive elements and movements that draw the child into the song and make it more memorable. Toddlers also love nonsense songs and songs that involve moving their bodies. Songs about feelings help them understand emotions better.

- **Preschool and kindergarten**—For preschoolers, look for songs that tell a story or have words strongly tied to the beat and melody. Many of these are traditional folk songs that have been passed down for generations. Preschoolers particularly like songs that are personal and relate to their everyday lives. Make up songs that feature their names, feelings, body parts, daily activities, and special occasions such as birthdays: Songs can also help them learn to count, spell, and learn other rote material (Wolfe & Hom, 1993; Wolfe & Stambaugh, 1993). Interactive elements and movement are still an important element

in songs for this age and help children remember the words better. Song games encourage children to practice singing and moving to the music.

- **Primary age**—As children get older their vocal range extends to as much as an **octave** above and below middle C. Songs for primary children should use this range because children will lose the high and low notes if they do not use them

Teacher Tip

ABSOLUTE PITCH

Absolute or perfect pitch is the ability to identify or sing a named note without reference to other notes. Those with this ability may be able to name all the notes in a chord and even identify the pitch of everyday sounds, such as a car horn. It is a cognitive process of memory that is much like identifying a color. It is believed that there is also a genetic component because children with autism, Well's syndrome, and savants have a much higher incidence of perfect pitch than people in general.

Some research has shown that absolute pitch is a combination of inborn ability and very early exposure to music during a critical period of development in which children between two and four are taught the names of musical tones (Chin, 2003). However, absolute pitch is not required to be a musician or composer. Although Mozart, Beethoven, and Liszt all had perfect pitch, Hayden, Ravel, and Wagner, for example, did not. Most trained musicians have relative pitch in which they can identify notes in comparison to others.

IMPLICATIONS FOR TEACHERS

Early childhood programs put great emphasis on teaching color names, but almost none on learning the names of the notes. Between the ages of two and four, try to expose children not only to the sound of notes, but also their names. This is done most easily with a piano or keyboard, but any tonal instrument can be used. If you do not know the names of the notes, refer to the piano illustration in this chapter, or use a child's xylophone on which the notes are labeled. Sit the child on one's lap, play a note, and sing its name. Also, play each note in a selected chord, such as C E G, as you sing the letter names. Encourage the child to sing the names, too. Such early exposure may not necessarily result in perfect pitch, but will certainly help in developing relative pitch.

regularly. As children learn more about the world, they enjoy learning the story behind the song. Songs in foreign languages fascinate them. They also enjoy songs from their favorite movies and from radio (see Table 10-2).

Chants. **Chants** are words spoken in rhythm with no or limited change in pitch. Often they are half spoken and half sung in a rhythmic, repetitive way. Sometimes a chant is performed on just one note and sometimes on two or more notes. Nursery rhymes, such as "Jack and Jill," and traditional **finger plays** such as "Pat-a-Cake," are good examples of this. Jump-rope rhymes are traditional chants. Some familiar ones are "Miss Mary Mack," "My Name is Alice," "Lady, Lady," and "Touch the Ground." For more fingerplays and jump rope rhymes, see *Finger Plays and Jump Rope Rhymes* on CourseMate. In addition, numerous books and Web sites list jump-rope rhymes.

Chants provide a bridge between early language development and singing and, as such, are very appropriate for infants and toddlers. Because of their simplicity, these are often the first "songs" children sing. Young children will also make up their own chants as they play. Chants are easy to invent on the spot. To help develop a child's singing voice an adult can chant a request to a child and the child can chant it back.

Invented songs. Music naturally engages children in learning. In particular, there is a strong link between literacy development and singing. Shelly Ringgenberg (2003) found that children learn vocabulary words better through a song than through conventional storytelling. She suggests that teachers take the melody and rhythm from familiar songs, such as "Mary Had a Little Lamb" or "Twinkle Twinkle Little Star," and add new words based either on a story in a book or that use the concepts or vocabulary being taught.

This type of song is also known as a "story song," "zipper song," or "piggyback song," and many examples can be found in books and on the Web. However, it is just as easy to invent our own to fit the needs of our own children. In addition, allowing children to participate in making up songs based on old favorites is a powerful way to begin a creative music community. Children, if allowed to contribute to the writing of the song will take ownership and pride in the song (Hildebrandt, 1998). Ringgenberg points out some other advantages as well:

Children sing better when you sing with them than when singing along with a recording.

- The melody will be familiar, making it quicker and easier to learn the song.

- Because you choose the content, speed, and length, the song can be tailored to fit the needs of the moment.

- It saves time that would be spent searching for an existing song that might fit.

- No materials are needed except voices and creativity.

Teaching a New Song

The best way to introduce a new song is spontaneously when it fits what is happening in the children's lives. Singing "Rain, Rain Go Away," for example, will be far more memorable when first heard on a day when rain has spoiled an outdoor playtime or event. Teach a lullaby when children are resting quietly. Introduce a silly song when they need cheering up. Tie songs into integrated units and projects. Sing songs to help chores get done faster.

Children learn a song first by hearing it, then by tagging on to an accented word or phrase, then by joining in on a repeated or patterned part like the chorus, and finally, they can sing it on their own (Wolf, 1994). There are many approaches to introducing a song. Using a combination of them is most effective, but remember, singing with children should always be fun and impromptu. Do not expect young children to learn all the words of a song. It is fine if they chime in on the chorus or on silly words or sounds, and let

Teacher Tip

SINGING WITH CHILDREN

Jan Wolf (1994) makes the following suggestions for singing successfully with children:

- Show expression on your face.
- Maintain eye contact with the children.
- Be enthusiastic.
- Signal when to begin, such as with a "Ready, go!"
- Really know the song. Practice it many times beforehand.
- Pictures and props will help the children (and you) remember the song better.
- Choose simple, repetitive songs that are easy to remember.

the teacher sing the verses. Do not expect or demand perfection. If the same song is practiced over and over, it will become boring or a chore to sing. If children become resistant to singing, or lack enthusiasm for a song, it is time to teach a new one.

Songs can be taught to one child, a small group, or a whole class depending on the age of the children and the situation. Children learn songs best from another person's singing rather than from a recording. This is because they are best at matching pitches in their own vocal range and you are free to match their pitch, whereas a recording is preset. Men may find that singing in falsetto may help children sing in better tune. Nevertheless, most young children only begin to sing in tune in the primary grades.

Here are some ways to introduce new songs:

Whole song method. Sing the song two or three times. Then sing it again and leave out a key word for the children to fill in or have the children join in the chorus or last line.

Call and response. Sing one line of the song and have the children sing it back to you.

Say it first. Sometimes it helps to say the words before or after singing the song to help the child understand the words better. We are all familiar with the child who thinks that "Oh say can you see" in the "Star Spangled Banner" is "Jose can you see?"

Write it out. For older children, write the words on large chart paper. For beginning readers use a combination of pictures and words. Point to the words as you sing the song.

Clap the rhythm. Particularly in songs with a strong beat, clapping or tapping the rhythm helps children feel where the words fit best.

Act it out. Many songs lend themselves to movement and dramatic performance. Adding movement helps children remember the words better, as do open-ended songs to which children can add their own words. For example, "Pop! Goes the Weasel" is easily acted out.

Substitute meaningful words. Making the song personal also makes it more memorable. The words can be varied by substituting a child's name, a familiar place, or a daily event. For example, instead of singing "Mary had a little lamb" sing "_____ (child's name) has a little _____ (substitute child's pet)."

Tell the story. Explain the song as a story, or for primary students, talk about the history of the song. For example, explain that the song "Yankee Doodle" was composed by British soldiers to make fun of the poorly dressed, uneducated Americans, who then adopted the song as their own.

Make it familiar. When introducing a new song, play it in the background for a while. This helps children feel more comfortable with it. However, children will not learn a song heard only in the background. There has to be active listening by the child. To learn a song, active involvement in the singing is needed.

Add signs. Sing the song accompanied by American Sign Language (ALS). The hand movements make the song easier to remember as well as introduce children to a way they can communicate with those who are deaf. Videos are available for learning how to sign familiar songs (see Appendix C).

Singing Activities for Infants

Singing activities for infants should build on their developing verbalization skills.

Sing along. Accompany the child's movements and activities by humming and singing familiar songs.

Match it. Sing along with infant vocalizations. If the child says, "Ba ba" sing "ba ba" back.

Move to it. Move the young infant's arms and legs to match the words of the song. Mirror moves for older infants who can sit and crawl.

Singing Activities for Toddlers

Toddlers are just beginning to sing. At this age children often make up little songs and melodies spontaneously. Nourish this inventiveness by being a responsive partner rather than a leader. Try to match what the child sings. Research shows this leads to a longer engagement in spontaneous song making and more inventiveness over time (Berger & Cooper, 2003; Tarnowski & Leclerc, 1995).

Singing activities for this age group should help them become familiar with the words and melodies of songs in a playful, risk-free atmosphere.

Move. Help active toddlers learn new songs by adding motions to accompany simple songs.

Body awareness. Foster body awareness by selecting songs that involve body parts such as "The Hokey Pokey" or the French Rhyme "Clic Clac Dans Les Maines (Clic Clap Clap Your Hands)."

Repeat, repeat. Choose songs that have repeated words, phrases, and rhymes. This helps toddlers' early literacy development as they hear phrasing and develop phonemic awareness. Try "Blue Bird Blue Bird,"

Teacher Tip

INVENTING A STORY SONG

Shelly Ringgenberg (2003) makes the following suggestions for creating an effective story song:

1. Make sure it is developmentally appropriate.
2. Use short, familiar melodies.
3. Choose a key that is comfortable for the children and you. If you are not sure, listen to the children sing and join in with them.
4. Keep it short and rhythmic to hold the children's attention and make it easier to learn.

Sample story song. To the tune of "Mary Had a Little Lamb"
This is how we make an A,
Make an A; make an A.
This is how we make an A,
Up, Down, Across.

(Note: On the last three words, act out making an A: Move fingers up and down to make the point of A. Then draw a finger across it.) Continue the song using other letters of the alphabet.

"Paw Paw Patch," or the chorus to "Pony Boy." Pause on repeated words and let the children fill in the words.

Cooperate together. Toddlers can begin to engage with others through musical interactions. They can each play an instrument and march in a parade. They can hold hands and circle while a short song is sung such as "Ring Around the Rosy."

Sing it. Instead of talking, sing to the child while involved in daily activities.

Keep a steady beat. The beat of a song is not the same as its rhythm. The rhythm is in the words and the accented syllable marks the beat. We can help toddlers to learn to hear a steady beat by playing songs and marking the beat.

Singing Activities for Preschoolers

Preschoolers are ready to learn to sing songs on their own and in groups. Design activities that help them remember the words and melodies and that encourage them to create their own songs.

Picture it. Use props or a flannel board to dramatize a song. Make a simple flannel board by gluing felt to a thick piece of cardboard. Make your own figures or let the children draw their own ideas on tag board and attach felt to the back.

Use puppets. A puppet makes an ideal companion with whom to sing. Use the call-and-response method, with the puppet echoing the song line along with the children. Encourage the children to sing to puppet friends by keeping the puppets at the music center.

Hands free. Tape yourself singing a song you want the children to learn as you accompany yourself on an instrument. Play the tape as you teach the song. This will leave you free to add gestures and movements.

Singing Activities for Kindergarteners

Singing to learn. Make letter, word, and number cards to accompany songs with repeated words, ABC, and number songs. Hold up the card at the appropriate time. Once the children are sure of the song let them hold up the cards.

Singing games. Play traditional and original singing games with the children. For kindergarten, keep the game simple, active, and noncompetitive. A good example is "The Farmer in the Dell." To play the game, sit or stand in a large circle. The child chosen to be the farmer walks around the circle and chooses the wife. The wife then chooses the animal named next and so on. The game ends when all children have been chosen. It is easy to change the subject of simple songs such as this and keep the game the same. Instead of a farmer, try a zookeeper, or a school bus driver. For example,

> *The keeper of the zoo*
> *The keeper of the zoo*
> *Heigh ho the derry oh*
> *The keeper of the zoo.*
> *Along comes a camel*
> *Along comes a camel*
> *Heigh ho the derry oh*
> *Along comes a camel.*

More singing games are found in Chapter 11.

Singing Activities for Primary Age

Primary age children can sing much more accurately in a group setting. Singing activities for this age group can begin to introduce part singing as a way of developing the ability to create harmonies.

Use cue cards. Chart the song using words and pictures, such as a rebus as a guide for more accurate group singing and to develop literacy. If singing a song in parts, have separate cards for each part.

Taking a part. Introduce part singing by having some of the children chant a simple phrase while the others sing the melody. For example, for the song "Hickory Dickory Dock" have half the children sing the song and the others chant "tick tock." It helps if the two groups sit with a space separating them.

Rounds. Start with very simple rounds based on the most familiar songs. "Row, Row, Row Your Boat" and "Frere Jacques" are commonly two of the first rounds children learn. Start with two groups and as children gain experience divide them into three and four groups.

For a list of songs to sing with children of all ages, see *Songs for Children* on CourseMate.

Teacher Tip

THE KODÁLY METHOD

Zoltan Kodály (1882–1967) was a Hungarian composer and educator. Kodály believed that every person was a musical being and that singing was the foundation of music education because the voice is the one instrument everyone has. His approach to teaching music has been widely adopted, particularly in public schools. The Kodály approach is founded on the following:

- Music instruction for children should focus first on the folksongs of the child's culture, followed by the works of great composers.
- Music training should be active, using folk dances, singing games, and moving to music.
- The goal of music education is music literacy—the ability to look at written music and hear it in one's head.
- Pitch, intervals, and harmony are taught using hand signals based on the sofège syllables (*do re me fa so la ti do*) that visually show the relationship of the notes. Using hand signals helps make learning to sing a more concrete experience.
- Instruction starts with *sol* and then adds *me* and *la*.
- Visit the Organization of American Kodály Educators Web site for more information: http://www.oake.org/.

Adding movement to songs helps children learn the song faster.

Reading about Singing

There are numerous books that use the words of familiar songs with attractive illustrations that can be shared with children of all ages. The song can be read in a normal voice and then sung if the children are familiar with the song. Many of these books come with CDs of the song.

Children can also be introduced to singing techniques through books like John Feierabend's *The Book of Pitch Exploration: Can You Sing This?* (2004). Other books tells stories about singing, such as *Opera Cat* (Weaver, 2002), *The Dog That Sang at the Opera* (Izen & West, 2004), or *When Marion Sang* (Ryan, 2002).

For a listing of these types of books, see *Books Based on Popular Songs* on CourseMate.

Observing and Talking about Singing

Lay the groundwork for talking about singing by giving children plenty of opportunities to sing themselves in different ways and to experience the singing of others. Children may be familiar with popular singers and groups featured on television and radio. Introduce them to different types of performing groups, such as choirs, barbershop quartets, and *a cappella* groups. Videos of singing performances and other children singing can be found on the web. But don't neglect the experience of viewing real performances. Take children to performances by local singing groups and school groups or have groups visit the program. Ask families to come in and share songs.

Center questions on children's own experiences of singing.

♪ Can you clap or move to the beat?

♪ How do the voices sound?

♪ Can you sing along?

♪ What pitches do you hear? Can you sing that high? That low?

♪ How does the song make you feel?

♪ What is another way this song could be sung?

Did You Get It?

Jenna is picking a song for her preschool class to sing as a group. Which of the following characteristics should she consider?

a. It should avoid repetition.

b. It should be long.

c. It should have a steady beat.

d. It should be a classical piece

Take the full quiz on CourseMate

How Do We Share Children's Music with Families?

There are many ways to include families in the musical activities of children. Invite them to visit the classroom any time and join in singing and playing in the band. Send home recordings and videos of their child making music, and invite them to musical instrument workshops where they build instruments for their child to use. For example, parents could work together to make large bucket drums or PVC pipe thunder drums and pipe organs instruments.

For information on building these, see *Making Instruments for Children* on CourseMate.

Did You Get It?

Jazlyn wants to include the families of her pre-schoolers in her music program. What is the best way for her to do this?

a. Invite them to come observe the class singing a special song.

b. Stage a musical production of Jack and the Beanstalk.

c. Invite them to come anytime and join the class rhythm band.

d. Send home a note telling them about the music program.

Take the full quiz on CourseMate

Conclusion: Becoming Musical

The goal of music experiences for young children is to develop each child into a musical person. A musical person is not a just a consumer of music, nor a professional musician. A musical person is someone who is tuneful, beatful, and artful. A tuneful person carries the melodies of wonderful songs in their head. A beatful person feels the beat of music of all kinds and the natural rhythms of the world around them. An artful person responds to the expressiveness of all music with all their body and soul.

We owe it to the children we teach to give them the gift of music. Music education must start before the child is born and be intensive through the early years. To do this we need to become comfortable ourselves in the world of music. We do not need to be virtuosos. However, we do need to become enthusiastic and confident. Teachers must also be learners. It is never too late to learn to play an instrument or take voice lessons.

For additional information on teaching music to young children, see *Chapter 10 Online Resources* on CourseMate.

Teaching In Action

A Literacy-Based Integrated Music Activity

"What do you think is in this box?" I ask my class of prekindergarteners.

"A dog!" Billy yells out, forgetting to raise his hand.

"No way. It's too small." Amy says, her large eyes fixed on the box.

"Can I shake it?" Hughie, my little scientist, asks.

I hand him the box.

"Hmmm. Sounds like there's lots of small things inside."

The box passes around the circle of children. Each holds it to his or her ear and gives it a shake.

"They don't bang like metal."

"It's a soft sound."

"I think it's not so many—maybe three or four things."

"I'll give you a hint," I say, after everyone has a chance to listen. "Today we are going to read the story *My Crayons Talk* by Patricia Hubbard."

"It's a box of crayons," everyone says at once. "Open it, Miss Giradi. Open it, please!"

With great majesty I unwrap the box, and show them the nine crayons inside. I hold each one up and the children call out the colors: red, blue, green, yellow, brown, orange, black, pink, and purple.

I read the book to the children, holding up the appropriate crayon when its color is named.

"Now we will read it again in a different way." I open up the plastic container that holds our rhythm instruments. Chloe claps her hands. "Oh, we're going to make music."

"That's right. We're going to make the colors talk. Let's decide which instrument reminds us of each color."

"Yellow goes with the bell, because it's yellow too." Latasha says.

I hand the bell to Latasha.

"I think the drum goes with black, because they are both loud," Billy says.

As each child makes a suggestion, I hand the instrument to them.

"We are going to need some yackity clackers too," I say. I hand out the claves and castanets to the rest of the children.

Now we are going to read the book again. This time when we say a color, if you have the instrument we chose, make a loud sound. When we get to the yackity clakity parts, everyone will play together."

Highly motivated and intently focused each child listens for her or his cue to play as we bring the words in the book to life through the rhythms of the children.

Reflection Page

Discovering One's Musical Heritage

What factors have influenced how you feel about music?

1. What are some family songs you learned as a child? Do they reflect any special ethnic or cultural influences?

    _____

    _____

    _____

2. Were any members of your family involved in music? What did they do?

    _____

    _____

    _____

3. Have you ever studied any instrument or had voice training?

    _____

    _____

    _____

4. What are some of your favorite pieces of music? How often do you listen to them?

    _____

    _____

    _____

5. What area of music would you like to learn more about?

    _____

    _____

    _____

Reflection Page

Selecting Appropriate Music Activities

Based on the information in this chapter, decide what would be the most appropriate age group (s) for each suggested music activity below and explain why.

1. Clap a rhythm and have the children echo it back to you.

    Age group: _____   Why? _____

2. Move a maraca around a child's head while shaking it.

    Age group: _____   Why? _____

3. Hide a familiar instrument behind a box. Challenge a child to guess which instrument it is.

    Age group: _____   Why? _____

4. Have the children write stories and then add rhythms and songs.

    Age group: _____   Why? _____

5. Have the children make up new words for a familiar song.

    Age group: _____   Why? _____

6. Play a musical work by Sebastian Bach while the child is relaxing.

    Age group: _____   Why? _____

7. Have the children invent their own way to write the melody of a song.

    Age group: _____   Why? _____

8. Sing songs in a limited range, such as nursery rhymes.

    Age group: _____   Why? _____

Reflection Page

Meeting Special Needs

How would you adjust these music activities to meet the special needs of each child?

Child	Activity	Adjustments that might be made
A child with a cochlear implant	Listening to music	
A child with some hearing loss	Playing rhythm instruments	
A child with total hearing loss	Having a musician visit the class	
A child with poor coordination	Playing a tonal instrument, such as the xylophone	
A child in a wheelchair	Playing rhythm instruments while marching around the room	

Reflection Page

Supporting Music Education for Young Children

Why is it important to teach musical skills and concepts in early childhood? Write a letter to the families of an early childhood program, explaining why music activities are part of the curriculum. Justify your reasons using research cited in this chapter.

_____

_____

_____

_____

_____

_____

_____

_____

_____

_____

_____

_____

_____

_____

_____

_____

_____

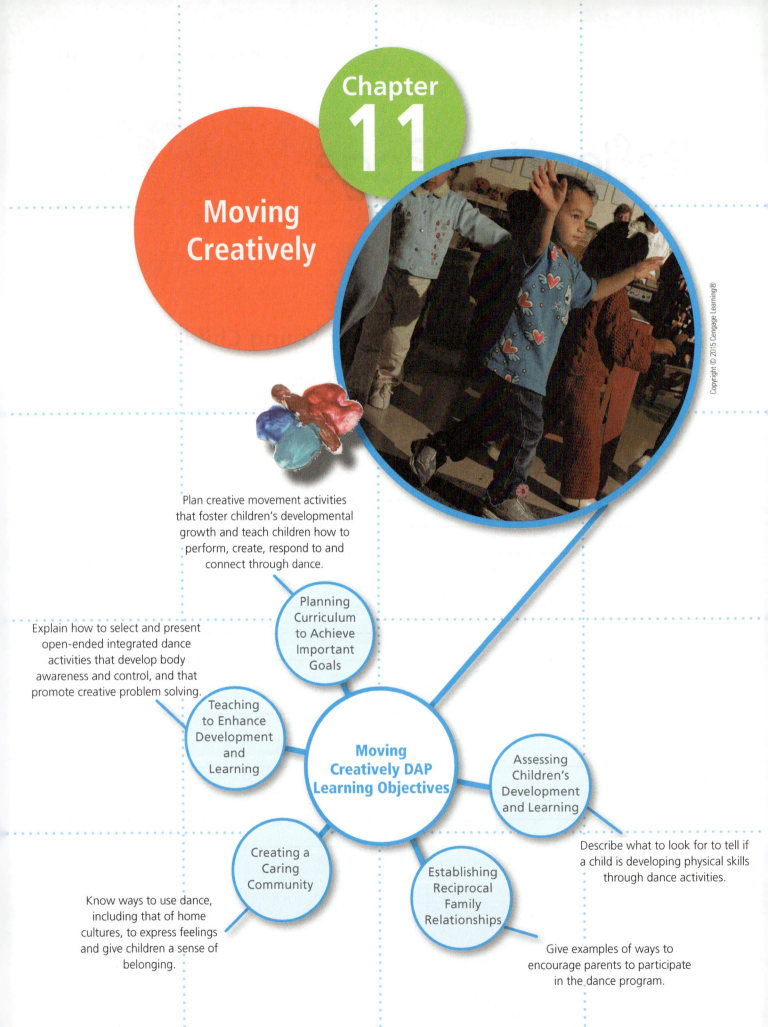

Chapter 11

Moving Creatively

Copyright © 2015 Cengage Learning®

Plan creative movement activities that foster children's developmental growth and teach children how to perform, create, respond to and connect through dance.

Explain how to select and present open-ended integrated dance activities that develop body awareness and control, and that promote creative problem solving.

Planning Curriculum to Achieve Important Goals

Teaching to Enhance Development and Learning

Moving Creatively DAP Learning Objectives

Assessing Children's Development and Learning

Creating a Caring Community

Establishing Reciprocal Family Relationships

Describe what to look for to tell if a child is developing physical skills through dance activities.

Know ways to use dance, including that of home cultures, to express feelings and give children a sense of belonging.

Give examples of ways to encourage parents to participate in the dance program.

Young Artists Creating

"Let's move like the sea turtles we saw at the aquarium," the teacher sings out. Some of the children lie down on the floor. Others get down on hands and knees. A few remain standing.

Kyle pulls in his arms and legs. "I'm inside my shell sleeping," he says.

Franco moves his head forward and back. "I'm looking for a fish to eat," he says.

Maura glides around the room as she swings her arms outward in large circles. "I'm swimming to shore to lay eggs," she explains. "Who's coming with me?"

"I'll swim with you," Taketa replies.

"Look at all the different ways our turtles are moving," the teacher exclaims with a smile.

What Is Creative Movement and Dance?

The ability to move is a function of three interacting bodily systems. First, our muscular and skeletal system provides support and a framework for action. This framework is guided by kinesthetic awareness—the system of sensors found in our muscles, joints, and tendons, which provides information on posture, equilibrium, and the effort required for a motion to occur. Both these systems are kept balanced by the vestibular sense located in the inner ear, which keeps track of the motion and position of the head relative to the rest of the body. All these parts work together to create the simple and complex actions that we perform unthinkingly each day of our lives.

Our capacity to move allows us to interact with the world and people around us. However, when these movements are organized into a work of bodily art we come to understand how marvelous our bodies are. Through carefully chosen creative movements, we can communicate feelings, tell stories, and become part of the music. We dance.

Creative movement and dance are inherently human and incredibly ancient. Paintings on pottery indicate that dance was as much a part of life in Neolithic times as it is today. Then as it is now, the creative movement of the body was tied to social and spiritual rituals. In the past these rituals were often related to everyday life and needs. The first dances probably imitated the movements of activities such as hunting, harvesting, and planting. Today we dance to feel part of a group, to make friends, and to release bodily tensions.

Is It Creative Movement or Dance?

The art form based on moving our bodies has been called both *creative movement* and *dance*. Usually in early childhood education, the term *creative movement* is used to emphasize the open-ended nature of movement activities that are developmentally appropriate for young children. Dance, on the other hand, more often refers to formalized styles of movement in which children are taught specific ways to move and particular dance positions and steps, such as ballet or the polka.

In truth, both aspects of movement are essential in the education of young children. All children need the opportunity to use the creative process in discovering their own original ways to move and in using their bodies to communicate their emotions and ideas. However, as they grow they also need to learn how to control their bodies and match their movements to rhythms, music, and the movements of others by participating in simple dances from our own and other cultures. For this reason the term **creative dance** can be used to encompass both these aspects of the movement arts.

Creative movement activities draw children together and create relationships.

The Core Processes of Creative Dance

The National Dance Educational Organization (NDEO) has identified four core processes integral to dance they call the inner core and which form the basis of the new Common Core Standards in the Arts for Dance (National Coalition for Core Arts Standards, 2013).

🎵 **Performing.** Although we usually think of performance as something done in front of an audience, in this definition performance is the actual physical movement that a dancer does. A dance performance can be done alone or with a group, and with or without an audience.

🎵 **Creating.** This is the invention of original movements by the dancer either through solving movement problems through improvisation or through choreographing movements to be performed alone or with others.

🎵 **Responding.** Responding is when we observe a dance performance and express our ideas about it. Reflections on a dance performance can take many forms ranging from talking and writing about it to creating a movement in response.

🎵 **Connecting.** Dance does not exist in a vacuum. It is an expression of ideas, viewpoints, and experiences. It is learned best when the physical, creative, and responsive processes are interconnected and taught together, and when creative dance is integrated into all areas of learning, culture, and life. Because dance develops the strength of and control over the body, it is also connected to healthful living.

The Elements of Creative Dance

The elements of dance describe a body in motion and so are not separate but simultaneous actions. The National Dance Educational Organization depicts the elements as a concentric circle with the person dancing at the core. See Figure 11-1.

In the center is the dancing self. Each individual is uniquely gifted with personal expression. As we move we express ourselves using the elements of dance. The physical elements are how we move in space. These are time, space, and energy. They are what create individual differences in a dancer's style, form, and expressive meaning. See Table 11-1.

🎵 **Time**—We can move our bodies slowly or quickly using varying speeds and duration.

🎵 **Space**—Space refers to how we position our bodies in the space that surrounds us. Our bodies can occupy different levels and be open or closed.

🎵 **Energy**—This is the effort we use as we move our bodies through distances in that space. Our body can move in a relaxed way or under tension. We can attack and release.

The physical performance of dancing is created in a context of personal and cultural influences which influences the aesthetic quality and meaning of the movements. This context consists of the following:

🎵 **Body**—The body is the tool we use to create dances. It is our muscles, bones, tendons, reflexes, and breath. It is the medium through which our ideas and feelings are expressed. Each body is unique in size, shape, and muscular control. This

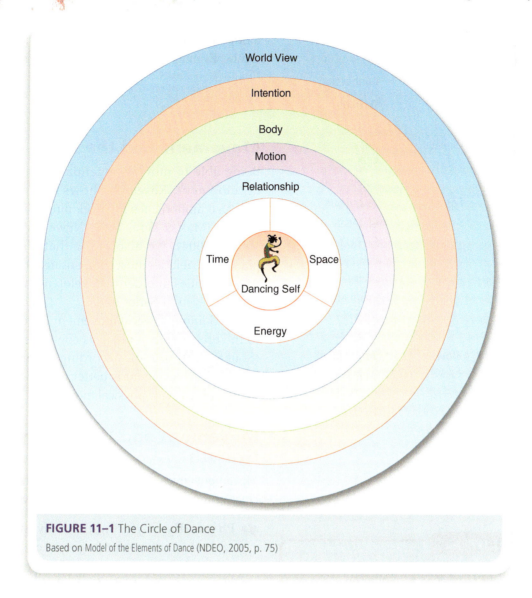

FIGURE 11–1 The Circle of Dance
Based on Model of the Elements of Dance (NDEO, 2005, p. 75)

makes dance "the most personal of all the arts" (Walter, 1942).

Motion—We use our bodies as an expressive art medium when we move. Creative dance is made up of motions, which consist of streams and pauses in a sequence. Locomotion means the movement moves from one place to another as when we leap, hop, and run. Nonlocomotion refers to those moves we can do standing in one place such as bending, twisting, and swinging. Movements can go in any direction, any distance, and be balanced or unbalanced, large or small.

Relationship—This refers to the way that the dance elements, the body, and motion are combined with each other to communicate the dancer's meaning.

Intention—This is the dancer's or choreographer's purpose for the dance. The performance of the dance fulfills its intention.

World view—Both dancer and the viewer bring unique personal and cultural experiences to the performance which determine what the dance communicates and how that message is received.

TABLE 11–1 Describing Movement

Space	Effort	Connection
Place	**Time**	**To body**
Size	Speed	Balanced
Distance	Duration	Unbalanced
		Stretched
		Compressed
Direction	**Force**	**To objects**
Forward/back	Attack	Close/far
Left/right	Tension	On top/underneath
Up/down	Release	Side-by-side
Clockwise/counter clockwise	Relax	Inside/outside
		In front/behind
		Around
		Through
Level	**Flow**	**To people**
High	Open	Partnered
Middle	Closed	Leading
Low	Rhythmic	Following
	Accented	Solo
Path	**Distance**	
Straight	Near/far	
Bent	Short/long	
Curved	Wide/Narrow	

Did You Get It?

What is the difference between creative movement and dance in early childhood curriculum?

a. There is no difference.

b. Dance is only done by trained dancers.

c. Dance is more formal and has set steps and positions.

d. Creative movement is only for children under the age of five.

Take the full quiz on CourseMate

How Does Creative Movement and Dance Help Children Grow?

Movement is basic to life. From birth children spend their waking moments in constant motion. The newborn waves arms and legs, the infant crawls, the toddler toddles, and the preschooler jumps, runs, and climbs. Even in the womb, the fetus swims and kicks.

For an overview of physical developmental milestones, see *Physical Milestones* on CourseMate.

Movement and the Brain

Being able to move is essential for normal brain development. Research shows that young children use motion cues in developing concepts about objects (Mak & Vera, 1999; Newell, Wallraven, & Huber, 2004). We also know that children with physical disabilities must compensate for their limited motor abilities in order to develop normally (Bebko, Burke, Craven, & Sarlo, 1992).

In addition, physical movement increases oxygen to the brain, which enhances cognitive functioning (Sousa, 2001, p. 230). According to Jensen (2005), academic achievement is better in schools that offer frequent breaks for physical movement.

Movement and Developmental Growth

Movement affects a child's total development. Through creative movement activities children develop

- **Physically**—By using the body to move with control in the performance of creative movement. Creative movement is a powerful form of exercise in which the body is strengthened and made fit. Introducing young children to creative dance teaches them a pleasurable way to stay fit and healthy. This is especially important because so many of us are prone to be inactive most of the time. A 2004 government survey found that 30 percent of Americans participated in no leisure-time activities and another 30 percent participated only minimally (National Center for Health Statistics, 2006). Moving through dance helps regulate weight, maintain glucose metabolism, and fosters heart health as well. Endorphins are released, which create a state of well-being. Dancing improves posture, balance, physical endurance, and flexibility.

- **Socially**—By learning how to move in concert with others. Creative movement group activities create social unity. Moving with others is an opportunity for children to experience the role of both leader and follower. Children learn how to communicate their ideas to others using only their bodies. Group dances instill collective discipline on the children and make cooperation physically visible as they focus on each other's roles in the performance and note each other's relative position in space to their own. Creative dance also provides the opportunity to learn about and experience culturally different ways of moving as children move creatively to music from other places and perform folk dances from other parts of the world.

Cognitively—By developing thinking and problem-solving skills. Sensorimotor learning has long been recognized as central to early cognitive development in young children (Piaget, 1959). More recently, the powerful relationship between movement and thinking has been supported by the evidence presented by Howard Gardner (1993) for a separate bodily-kinesthetic intelligence. Jay Seitz (2000) outlines two components of bodily thinking that support the deep connection between mind and body. First is the ability of the brain to order movement through motor logic. **Kinesthetic thinking** integrates cognitive, sensory, and emotional experiences, and then responds with the best physical action. Second is **kinesthetic memory,** also known as motor memory, which allows us to remember how to move in specific ways, such as dancing a waltz, by reconstructing the effort, position, and action needed to be successful, even if one has not waltzed in years. In addition, the close relationship between mind and body is shown in the ability to mentally rehearse a physical action through **mental imagery** so that without actual practice one can improve that physical skill.

Open-ended creative movement activities also provide the opportunity for children to use problem-solving skills as they match the movement of their body to the physical challenges being asked of them. For example, if children are asked to move as if they were a cloud, they must first think what a cloud is and how it moves and then decide how they might make their body imitate that movement. Next, they must actually perform that movement, and follow up immediately with self-assessment to see if they have accomplished their initial goal, and then make any needed correction. Because dance extends over time, this self-correcting feedback between mind and body can continue throughout a dance sequence in a way not always possible in music or fine art.

Spatial and mathematical concepts require children to be aware of their orientation to the environment and how objects behave in space. They need to have a physical understanding of distance, force, and time in order to figure out how objects around them move. This knowledge is obtained by physical investigation and body memory. Dance provides many opportunities for children to move in, around, under, and above the things in their environment cementing these important words in place.

Language skills—By using their bodies to communicate ideas and by a developing vocabulary related to mathematical and spatial concepts. Movement is an essential part of language and communication. Studies show that hand control and speech develop from the same neural systems as evidenced by the fact that gesture precedes speech in infants, and even toddlers will ignore a vocal command if it conflicts with a physical gesture (Seitz, 1989, p. 31). Gesture remains an important form of communication into adulthood. Creative movement activities provide an opportunity for children to explore gesture and body position as a way to express feelings and communicate ideas.

Emotionally—By improving self-confidence and allowing self-expression. Being in control of one's body and feeling fit are essential components of positive mental health. In adults physical fitness has been strongly linked with lower incidences of depression and reduced stress (Fox, 1999). Children who are overweight, clumsy, or uncoordinated are at a disadvantage in most sports activities. Creative dance, which welcomes all bodily responses, provides a safe, pleasurable way for all children, regardless of ability or fitness, to release inner emotions and feel successful.

- **Dance concepts and skills**—By meeting the National Core Dance Standards.

Connecting: Understand dance in relation to personal identity, values, and beliefs.

- **Prekindergarten.** Recognize a feeling in a dance. Identify an important movement in a dance done at home.

- **Kindergarten.** When watching or performing a dance, describe a feeling. Explain the importance of something observed.

- **First Grade.** Examine feelings and new perspectives evoked by observing, creating, or performing dance.

- **Second Grade.** Express or portray a personal experience and identify expressive movements. Describe or perform personally meaningful movements in a dance from one's own culture and explain how the movement is personally meaningful.

Creating: Imagine and generate movement using a variety of strategies

- **Prekindergarten.** Respond in movement to a variety of sensory stimuli with teacher guidance. Find a different way to do a basic movement.

- **Kindergarten.** Respond in movement to a variety of stimuli with teacher guidance. Find a different way to do a basic movement by changing at least one of the elements.

- **First Grade.** Explore and improvise movement ideas inspired by stimuli or observed dance in a teacher-guided experience. Explore basic movements by changing the elements.

- **Second Grade.** Explore and improvise movement ideas with awareness of space, time, and energy in a teacher-guided experience. Explore a teacher-directed movement problem and demonstrate a solution.

Performing: Develop and learn safe movement skills, techniques, and artistry through body-mind connections and practices.

- **Prekindergarten.** Explore and identify whole-body locomotor and non-locomotor movements with teacher guidance. Dance safely using identified isolated body parts.

- **Kindergarten.** Explore and identify a range of same-side and cross-body movement possibilities while safely dancing locomotor and non-locomotor movements with teacher guidance.

- **First Grade.** Explore and identify a range of dance movement possibilities to coordinate body parts and demonstrate safe whole-body locomotor and non-locomotor movements in many directions with cues from the teacher.

- **Second Grade.** Explore and identify a range of dance movement patterns that coordinate body parts and demonstrate whole body organization in locomotor movements while safely moving through space using a variety of pathways and levels, and non-locomotor movement patterns.

Responding: Perceive and understand artistic intent through sensory, personal, and cultural lenses.

- **Prekindergarten.** Identify a movement in a dance by repeating it. Identify a dance movement done by a family member and repeat it.

Teacher Tip

IS IT CREATIVE MOVEMENT?

Creative movement activities allow children to be creative and make kinesthetic decisions. In selecting activities, ask the following questions:

1. Are the children free to move all parts of their bodies within safe limits?
2. Can the children make their own decisions about how to move?
3. Can the children express their own ideas?
4. Can they do it without tedious practice?
5. Are there a multitude of acceptable movements and few or no incorrect ones?

- ❧ **Kindergarten.** Find a movement that repeats in a dance. Describe observed or performed dance movements from one's own culture that repeat.

- ❧ **First Grade.** Find a movement that repeats in a dance to make a pattern. Describe observed or performed dance movements from one's own culture that create a style of movement.

- ❧ **Second Grade.** Find movements in a dance that develop a pattern. Describe movements in a dance from one's own culture that is different from another style of dancing.

Did You Get It?

Infants and children with limitations on their motor control are best taught first through _____.

    a. exploration exercises

    b. group movement sequences

    c. many-to-one activities

    d. one-on-one activities

Take the full quiz on CourseMate

How Are Creative Movement Activities Designed?

Creative dance is concerned with the role of movement in artistic creation. Activities that support this differ from physical exercises and sports, which are also concerned with physical development. In creative movement activities children are asked to imitate and expand on everyday behaviors and actions using their bodies, sometimes with music and props, to create what Jay Seitz (1989) calls a "metaphorical twist" in which the body part is no longer itself but rather a representation of something else. For example, waves can be represented by gently undulating one's arms. Even formal dance has this aesthetic element to it. As the dancers move in choreographed motion, geometric and symbolic patterns are created.

Creative movement activities are best organized by the skill, attention, and experience level of the children.

One-on-One Activities

Creative movement is by its very nature a social activity and most movement activities for young children are usually done in a group setting. However, infants and children with limitations on their motor control are best taught first in one-on-one and then pair situations where they can practice and develop the skills needed for successful participation in a larger group. For example, while being held in one's lap, an infant's arms might be gently moved to a lullaby. An older child might play a game of hand mirrors with an adult where they sit or stand opposite each other and place hands palm to palm, while they take turns being the leader and moving the hands in different ways.

Exploration Exercises

Explorations are activities that allow children to explore the possibilities of how to move their bodies and to solve creative movement problems. These can be done one-on-one or with small or large groups of children. In the beginning, these may form the entire movement experience. Later on, they can be used as warm-up exercises for more complex movement experiences.

Group Movement Sequences

The richest creative movement experiences are those in which a whole group participates. Depending on the age of the children, these can range from having the whole group responding to the same open-ended prompts to elaborate story dances in which individuals and small groups play different roles. Movement sequences, such as those in Table 11-2, can be based on or include traditional and formal dance forms familiar to the group and are best when improvised or choreographed by the children themselves.

The Reflective Teacher's Role

Although children go through the same patterns of physical development, each child develops according to her or his unique timetable. For example, although most 4-year-olds can leap over an object 6 inches high, a child with physical delays or a child who has never done this before may have difficulty doing so. A child in a wheelchair will experience movement activities

TABLE 11–2	Creative Movement Starters
Here are some ideas to get the children moving. Ask them how would it feel to be a _____? How would it move?	
Cloud blowing	Parachute collapsing
Balloon floating	Plane flying
Bird peeking	Popcorn popping
Cat washing itself	Puppet collapsing
Butterfly fluttering	Snake wriggling
Detective sneaking	Snowflake floating
Egg hatching	Spider creeping
Gelatin wiggling	Turtle lumbering
Helicopter hovering	Water dripping
Ice cube melting	Wind-up toy running down
Leaf falling	Worms burrowing

differently from a child who has limited vision, but both will need to feel included in the activity.

In organizing creative movement activities, the teacher's role is to be a guide or a facilitator providing the framework, positive guidance, and cues that will inspire children to respond using their own creativity and imaginations in their own ways. Developmentally appropriate practice tells us we need to reflect on the needs, expectations, and physical abilities of each child and be prepared for wide variation in response before beginning.

Reflective questions to ask before beginning a creative movement activity include:

↝ How will each child be able to engage in this activity and will they want to?

↝ What can I do to prepare the environment so that every child feels less self-conscious and participates freely?

↝ What guidelines or limitations are needed so the activity is safe but not restrictive?

↝ What learning domains and skills can this activity address?

↝ What issues of family background, culture, or exposure to popular media might influence the children's participation and behavior?

↝ How is my background influencing the music and dance motions I am choosing?

Creating a Space for Creative Movement

Movement activities require a carefully prepared environment in which children have plenty of space to move boldly and freely. This requires careful structuring of the environment and the creation of safety guidelines.

Floor. For very young children who are not yet walking steadily, a carpeted area provides the best surface for movement activities. Once children can walk securely, a bare floor, preferably wood, provides more stability. However, if the surface or undersurface is cement, some kind of cushioned layer or carpet is essential. Movement activities can also be performed outside on the grass in good weather.

Children's shoes should match the surface on which they are dancing. Bare or stocking feet are best for carpeted or carefully prepared grass areas, but be sure nonslip soles are worn on smooth-surfaced floors such as in a gym.

Space requirements. Depending on the ages and sizes of the children more or less space will be needed. A general rule is that the children should be able to spread out their arms in any direction and still be an arm's length away from anyone else, a wall, or object.

Adding props helps children accentuate their movements.

Safety requirements. Furniture and objects along the edges of the movement area should be closely checked for sharp edges. For example, metal shelving can cut a child who slides into it. The corner of a bookcase can injure a child's eye. It may be helpful to outline the edge of the area with tape or paint so children know where to stop or the edge of the carpet can be the stopping point.

Creating cues. As anyone who has worked with young children knows, having a whole group of them in motion at one time can be harrying. Before starting any creative movement activities, it is necessary to have in place easily recognized cues or rituals for starting, stopping, listening, and resting. These signals should be ones you can do easily while dancing yourself, such as a voice command, clapping, or a particular tap on a small drum or tambourine.

No matter the method of cueing, use it consistently and take sufficient time to practice it. One of the goals of initial movement instruction should be to have the children internalize the cues. Ruth Charney (1992) suggests the following steps in teaching children to respond quickly and efficiently to attention signals:

1. First, explain why a cue is needed. "Sometimes we will need to stop dancing and listen so that I can give you new directions."

2. Sound the cue and then model the expected behavior as you explain it.

3. Sound the cue and have individual children model the behavior for the group.

4. Now have several children model the behavior for the group.

5. Last, have the whole group respond to the cue.

6. Repeat as many times as necessary until the whole group performs the task in the expected way.

7. At the start of future activities, always review the cues and have the children practice them as part of a warm-up.

8. If at any time the children do not respond to the cue as expected, take time to practice the behavior again.

Moving in Concert

Creative movement activities require both sharing space and moving in conjunction with others. Before beginning, set up simple, positively worded behavior rules that foster cooperative behavior and have children role-play what to do in situations such as bumping into another child. Keep the rules simple. It is generally recommended not to have more rules than the age of the child. A good rule for one-year-olds might be "Be safe." Then as children get older add, "Be a friend." "Be a listener." "Be a thinker."

Teacher Tip

LEARNING TO RELAX

To move creatively with young children the teacher needs to feel relaxed and calm. Try these relaxation exercises to get ready to move:

1. Wear loose clothing and sit in a comfortable chair.
2. Inhale through your nose and exhale through your mouth.
3. Inhale slowly, counting to four. Imagine the air flowing to all parts of your body.
4. Exhale, imagining the tension flowing out.
5. Next, as you breathe in, tense one muscle group. As you breathe out, relax.
6. Repeat often.

Did You Get It?

Which is the best way to introduce movement activities to infants?

a. Sit the infant in a high chair and move enthusiastically in front of them.

b. Sit the infant on your lap and move together to music.

c. Put the infant in the crib and play dance music.

d. Put three infants on a rug and play dance music.

Take the full quiz on CourseMate

The Creative Movement Experience

Creative dance may be done with or without music. It is an open-ended approach to moving the body that asks children to solve a problem while making independent choices. It differs from formal dance because it allows many possible responses. At its simplest, it asks children to explore the elements of dance or parts of their body as they develop physical and mental control. Complex creative movement activities let children create a sequence of movements with a beginning, middle, and end that express an idea or feeling.

Selecting Music for Creative Movement Activities

Movement activities are often accompanied by music. In selecting music, look first of all for pieces that make you feel like moving in different ways. The music should be mostly instrumental because lyrics can be distracting unless they relate directly to the movements being done. Symphonies can also be overpowering in their complexity. Short, carefully selected selections are often more effective. Solos and ensemble performances, for example, have a clear sound quality that makes moving to them easier. In addition, be sure to expose children to a range of musical styles, genres, and instruments from around the world because each evokes different emotions and ideas. For a list of suggestions for music to accompany creative movement, see *Music for Moving* on CourseMate.

Using Silence and Body Percussion

Movement activities do not need to be accompanied only by music. Sometimes it is best to begin with silence so that children can focus on the cues, your guiding questions, and their own movements. Next, try adding body percussion—clapping and tapping various body parts—or vocalizations—catchy sound effects such as pop, bing, and swoosh. Rhythmic poetry can also be used.

Adding Props

Props are anything held by the children while moving. Props take the focus off the child's own movements and allow the children to move more

Large group creative dance activities require an open space that allows children to move freely and safely.

freely and with more force. For this reason, they are particularly useful when working with children who are shy, self-conscious, or who have a physical disability. Props enlarge the child's movements and add fluidity. For example, although children can certainly imagine they are moving as if they were planting flowers, holding and manipulating long-stemmed artificial or real flowers will help the child better visualize the needed movements. Scarves and streamers entice children to imagine they are floating and flying as they move. For more suggestions for other props, see *Props for Moving* on CourseMate.

Props can also be used to literally tie a group together. Have young children hold on to a jump rope or scarf as they move. Hula hoops, boxes, carpet squares, and even bubble wrap can be placed on the floor to provide a spot for each child to move within. If using bubble wrap or carpet squares on a slippery floor, be sure to use double-sided tape to hold them in place.

Planning Creative Movement Activities

Creative movement activities work best when presented in a flexible format that allows the activity to adjust and change in response to the movements of the children. There should be plenty of opportunity for children to

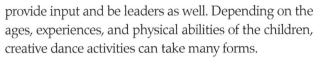

provide input and be leaders as well. Depending on the ages, experiences, and physical abilities of the children, creative dance activities can take many forms.

Assessing Proficiency. Creative movement activities should closely match children's physical development. Careful observation of a child's movements can provide important clues to the child's level of physical skill. Graham, Holt-Hale, and Parker (2001) have identified the following four levels:

- **Precontrol**—The same movement cannot be repeated in succession.

- **Control**—The same movement can be repeated somewhat consistently but cannot be combined with another movement or object.

- **Utilization**—The same movement can be repeated consistently and used in new situations and combinations.

- **Proficiency**—The movement is automatic and effortless and can be performed at the same time as other actions as well as modified to fit planned and unplanned situations.

Open-Ended Creative Movement Activities for Infants

Creative movement is a natural way to interact with infants who are still mainly sensorimotor learners. In general, most infants who do not have a physical or environmental disability develop bodily control from the head down and the center out. In the beginning, the newborn is all head, following objects with the eyes and turning the head toward sounds and objects with arms and legs moving randomly. For infants, initial movement activities focus on moving the head and then the whole body, followed by large arm and leg movements. We can build on this ability by moving together with the child, rocking the child, or moving arms and legs in rhythmic patterns or to music.

By six months infants have gained control over arms and hands and are developing spatial awareness, reaching out for objects and grasping them. In the next six months they develop torso control, learning to sit, crawl, and stand. Older infants who are crawling, creeping, and pulling themselves upright are learning how to move their bodies in space. By holding them

Special Needs

• INCLUDING CHILDREN WITH SPECIAL NEEDS •

Susan Koff (2000) points out that the power of creative movement is that it allows all children a way to express themselves nonverbally. Creative movement activities are easily adaptable to meet special needs through **inclusive** practices.

Physical limitations. For children with limited physical control or strength, alter the environment.

- Eliminate hazards, such as low objects that could trip children. Make sure there is room for wheelchairs and walkers to move in the same way as the rest of the children.
- Keep the environment consistent so that children come to know where furniture and objects are located.
- Reduce distances and heights that might be expected in the activity.
- Put low-pile or indoor/outdoor-type carpeting on the floor to cushion falls and prevent slippage.
- Use helpers, either peers or adults, to provide gentle support by holding a hand or shoulder or to push a child in a wheelchair.

Spatial awareness. For children having trouble maintaining their position in an open space, try moving in circles or along the edge of an area rug. Make lines and shapes using tape or paint on the floor for children to follow.

Visual disabilities. Have children hold on to a rope, ribbons, or scarves. If children have difficulty balancing their bodies, provide a bar or study table that they can hold onto as they move or alternatively, pair children up so that everyone, including the child with limited vision, has a buddy.

Deafness. Children who are deaf can participate fully in creative movement activities with minimal changes. Naomi Benari (1995) notes that having in place large, clear visual signals for starting and stopping are essential. She suggests a raised arm or drumstick. Take extra time to be sure children who are deaf understand what each sign means. Play games such as "Follow the Leader" or "Eyes on Me" which require the children to keep their eyes on the teacher as they move. Benari advises using music with a low, loud beat such as Caribbean and African music. Children can also hold on to a piano or kettledrum while moving.

The organization DanceAbility International (http://www.danceability.com/) provides information and examples for integrating everyone into dance activities.

For more suggestions for creating inclusive creative dance activities, see Inclusive Practices for Creative Dance *on CourseMate*

First counting. To develop knowledge of body parts and introduce one-on-one correspondence ask the child to move a certain number of body parts in a specified way using voice cues, such as "Wave one hand" or "Shake two feet." With young infants, gently help them respond.

Creeping and crawling. Creeping and crawling are essential to cross-lateral development which activates the brain and is important for future learning success (Hannaford, 2005). Put on some music, get down on the floor, and creep and crawl with the infant.

Open-Ended Creative Movement Activities for Toddlers

Energetic toddlers are always moving, walking forward and backward with the characteristic toddling gait that gives this age group its common identifier. As they develop confidence they discover they can jump and climb, but they may still have trouble balancing and coming to a stop after running or jumping. With their increasing independence of movement, toddlers may invent motions to go with music. They are also primed to imitate dances and moves they see being done by others. While holding hands, they can be led in simple group creative movements.

Tap into that energy with movement activities that let them jump and wiggle as they develop their physical skills.

Beginning balance. Develop balancing skills by placing a rope or strip of tape on the floor and have the children imagine it is a "tightrope" to walk across or jump over.

Beanbags. To develop balance and body awareness, have children try moving in different ways with a soft beanbag on the head, arm, shoulder, foot, and so on. Stay relaxed; part of the fun is having it fall off again and again.

Partner up. Hold the child's hands and have child put their feet on top of yours. Then move together in different ways. Try sliding, hopping, and wiggling to music with a beat.

Play pretend. Together, pretend to be some familiar thing that moves in interesting ways and invent movements to express it. For example, pretend to be birds flying, balls bouncing, and flowers growing. Remember that toddlers have very short attention spans so keep the directions to a sentence or

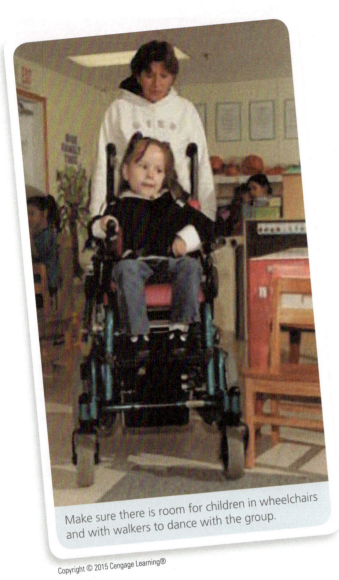
Make sure there is room for children in wheelchairs and with walkers to dance with the group.

with feet barely on the floor and moving to music or hugging them to our bodies and swirling to a song, children can begin their first partner dancing. On their own, they may bounce to musical rhythms while sitting or hanging on the railing of crib or playpen.

Try some of these basic movement activities as a way to engage infants in the wonder of dance.

Monkey see. To develop body awareness, make a movement and encourage the child to imitate you. If the child does not respond, imitate the motions the child is making. Say the name of the body part that is moving. This can be done with or without music in the background.

Rock together. To develop a sense of time, hold the child and move together in rhythm to music of different kinds.

Teacher Tip

PLANNING CREATIVE MOVEMENT ACTIVITIES

Component	Question to ask yourself
Exploration	How will you introduce the movements?
Free practice	What will the children do to practice?
Rhythmic accompaniment	What instruments, music, or body sounds will you add?
Movement control	What signals for start, stop, listen, and rest will you give?
Props	What can children use to emphasize or enrich the movement?
Extensions	What other themes or topics using these movements can you introduce?

two delivered with enthusiasm and accompanying motions. For example, say: "Look at those birds flying up there. Let's fly like birds to the tree," as you flap your arms up and down.

For more movement ideas for infants and toddlers, see Open-Ended Creative Movement for Infants and Toddlers *on CourseMate.*

Open-Ended Creative Movement Activities for Preschool and Kindergarten

With increasing control over their hands and feet and better balance, preschoolers can respond to suggestions that they move their arms, legs, or bodies in a particular way. They will continue to imitate the creative movements of others, but will also initiate original moves in a process of discovery and by recombining movements already mastered. Simple, safe props, such as small scarves and short ribbons, can be held and used to enhance the child's natural movements. With the increasing ability to pretend, children can move as if they were somebody or something else.

Physical growth is very rapid during this period. By kindergarten, children are beginning to have smooth control over their bodies. They can shift their weight from foot to foot, allowing them to skip and slide. They can coordinate their arms and legs and use their sense of balance to move on a balance beam and climb effectively. Following directions, they can move

in a series of patterns and can work together to learn repeated movements and simple folk dances. They can also use their new moves to invent dances of their own.

To introduce preschoolers and older children to creative dance movement activities, use guided explorations.

1. A guided exploration starts with an open-ended question. For example, it could start with pretending to be an animal. Say: How would it feel to be an animal? What animal would you be? How would it walk if it were tired? Hungry? Happy? Allow children to make their own decisions about how the movement should be expressed. Do not say, "Move like an elephant" which makes it sound like there is only one way elephants move. Instead, say, "How do you think an elephant would move?"

2. Then provide plenty of free practice time during which children work individually creating their movement. Take time to allow the children to share their movements by having them pair up and perform them for each other. This is quicker and less frightening than having each child perform before the whole group.

   (If it seems appropriate, consider adding a rhythmic accompaniment such as beating a drum or shaking a tambourine or related prop.)

3. Finally, if the children seem to be deeply involved, add some music that matches the movement.

4. Repeat similar guided movement explorations on a regular basis. For other suggestions for guided group movement explorations, see *Guided Creative Movement Explorations* on CourseMate.

Here are examples of guided creative dance activities to explore with preschoolers and kindergarteners.

Body shapes. To develop flexibility and imaginative movements while reinforcing geometric concepts, have the children try to make their bodies into different geometric shapes, such as a circle, a square, and a triangle. Have them start out working alone and then working with a partner. Once they are in position, have them hold still as you count together. Repeat this often and extend the count each time.

I can be the alphabet. To reinforce the letters of the alphabet and to develop critical thinking and problem-solving skills, have the children lay flat on the floor. Call out a letter of the alphabet and have them try to make their bodies into its shape. For some letters, such as M and W, suggest they work in pairs.

Balancing challenge. Continue to help children refine their sense of balance. Lay out a rope or piece of tape on the floor. Challenge the children to try to move in different ways while keeping one or both feet on the line, such as hopping, walking backwards, walking with eyes shut, and so on.

Worms. After looking at worms, snakes, snails, or other wiggly creatures, have the children hold their hands at their sides and wiggle around on the floor. Teach children to control the energy of their bodies by exploring the forces of tension and release as they pull in and stretch out. Have the children think of other wiggly things they could be. Add rhythmic music to develop their sense of time as they explore this way of moving.

Growing. Strengthen children's control over their movements by having them control the amount of energy they expend and the different levels at which they work. Have some children imagine they are seeds or baby animals curled up still, waiting to grow, and have the rest walk around pretending to water them or feed them. Each time they get nourished they should grow a tiny bit. Slowly tap a drum as they grow.

Floating. Have each child stand in a hula hoop or designated spot and imagine how a feather, balloon, winged seed, leaf, or other floating, falling object would move. Focus on moving from level to level smoothly with control. After they have explored their ideas, add clapping, drum beats, music, or props for practicing.

Tip tap. After the children have had time to explore the different levels with their bodies, have them practice moving from level to level by tapping a drum and calling out: up, middle, or down. Vary the speed of the taps, getting faster as they gain more control. Use the same method to practice other contrasting movements, such as turning left and right, forward and back, attacking and releasing, and so on.

More than one way. To foster creative problem solving and critical thinking, challenge children to come up with two or more different movements in response to a creative movement starter, such as "How do you think a small boat might move in a storm on the ocean?" Wait until all the children have completed their movement and then say: "Now show me another way that little boat might move."

Call and response. To refine children's vocabulary of dance, post the words to be practiced such as balance, level, path, and speed (see Table 11-1 for terms) on the wall or write them on cards. Have children take turns leading the group movements by giving verbal cues: "Change your level." "Balance on one foot." "Move in a curved path." "Move your arm fast." Have the performers repeat back the cue.

Dance makes me feel. To develop skill in observing and responding to dancing have children watch a dance performance by their peers, family member(s), guest artists, or a children's performance. If a live performance is impossible, children can watch a video of children or adults dancing. Afterward have the children describe what movements the dancers made and how the performance made them feel. Their responses can be oral, drawn, or shown in a creative movement.

Open-Ended Creative Movement Activities for Primary Age

Because creative movement is often neglected in the elementary school, children may need to start with simpler activities before trying the more complex ones suggested here. All the activities for preschool and kindergarten can also be used with primary children.

Remember to establish cues and behavioral guidelines at the start. Once in place, using movement to enhance learning is very effective.

The following integrated activities show ways to connect creativity and kinesthetic memory to learning facts and concepts in different subject areas.

On the Count (math). Reinforce counting or adding and subtracting skills by giving the children a number to count to or addition or subtraction problem and challenging them to count off that number or illustrate the problem using movements of their bodies. For example, given the number 10 a child might decide to stamp a foot 10 times or given the addition problem of 3 plus 4, the child might wave a hand 3 times and shake her or his head 4 times while counting up to 7.

Cycles (science). After studying one of the natural cycles, such as the water cycle, the rock cycle, the movement of the sun and moon, or the life cycle, have students work in teams to create a sequence of movements that illustrate it. Children can add props and music to enhance their performance. Remember to ask them to point out how they use the different dance elements in their creative movements.

Stories (reading). After reading a story, challenge the children to retell the story through creative dance movements using props and set to music of their choice.

Systems (science or social studies). Have individual or groups of students read and learn about one part of a system being studied, such as the solar system, a bee hive, a transportation system, a machine, the rainforest, and so on. After learning about the specified part, the students should create a creative movement sequence to represent that part. When everyone is ready, call each part in a logical order. Have each add their unique movements until the whole system is up and running.

For more creative dance activities for preschool, kindergarten, and primary age, see *Creative Dance Activities for Preschool and Up* on CourseMate.

Making Plans

OPEN-ENDED RESPONSIVE ACTIVITY PLAN
UNDER THE SEA

WHO? **Group composition age(s):** Primary age: 1st or 2nd grade

Group size: Whole class, 20 to 25

WHEN? **Time frame:** Three days, about an hour a day

WHY? **Objectives:** Children will develop

- physically, by moving their bodies with varying force in rhythmic ways. (Bodily-Kinesthetic)
- socially, by combining their ideas to create a unified presentation. (Interpersonal)
- emotionally, by developing self-confidence in their ability to communicate through movement. (Intrapersonal)
- spatial awareness skills, by learning how to locate their bodies in relation to one another. (Spatial)
- auditory awareness skills, by listening and moving in concert with the music. (Musical)
- language skills, by describing their ideas and how they used the element of force. (Linguistic)
- cognitively, by designing a sequence of movements to express an idea. (Logical-Mathematical)
- movement skills and knowledge, by creating an original creative dance sequence using the element of force, which communicates an idea.

WHERE? **Set-Up:** Large, open space in the classroom, outside, or in a gym

WHAT? **Materials:** A small glass fishbowl with a goldfish, an overhead projector, a clear glass pan, chart paper, and markers.

HOW? **Procedure:**

WOW Warm-Up: Set up a small fishbowl with a goldfish in it. Place it on the overhead projector. Have students observe the fish and describe how it moves. On chart paper write down their descriptions.

What to Do: *Day 1*—Following the fish observation, lead an open-ended guided movement activity: If you were a fish, how would you move? Before starting, review the start/stop/listen/rest signals. Have students stand in a large circle and remain in the circle as they move. After guiding them, play the musical selection *The Swan* from the *Carnival of Animals* by Camille Saint-Saëns as they swim around the room. After a few minutes, have the children sit on the rug and share how it felt to be a fish.

What to Say: Guiding questions: "How would you swim?" "How would you turn?" "How would you move if you were resting?" "How would you move if you were being chased by a predator?" "How would you eat your food?"

(continued)

Making Plans (continued)

What to Do: *Day 2*—On chart paper, write the heading "Effort" and the words "attack," "tension," "release," and "relax" below it. Have different students act out these different words with their bodies. Put students in groups of three or four and pass out books about sea life. Have students choose a fish or sea creature from the book and then as a group work out how that creature might move. Challenge them to include all four of the effort words in their movement. Allow about 10 minutes for them to explore different ways to move. Then have the group come together on the rug and have each group share the movement they created. Point out examples of tension and release, attack and relaxation.

What to Say: "When would a fish be relaxed?" "How does your body feel when you attack or when it is under tension?" "Does it feel similar or different?" "Does it feel good to release the tension from your body?"

What to Do: *Day 3*—Set up the overhead projector and place the glass dish on top with a small amount of water in it. Project it on a screen or bare wall. If possible, darken the room. Stir the water to create ripples on the wall. Have the groups from the day before get together and perform their movement in the ripples. Signal stop and listen and then discuss how they could all move together in a beautiful, safe way to create a sea scene. Play *The Swan* again as the class dances in and out of the ripples. Videotape the performance.

What to Say: Point out examples of the different forces. Give lots of positive feedback.

Transition Out: Give the stop and listen signal and have the students gather together to watch the video of themselves.

ASSESSMENT OF LEARNING
1. Can the students incorporate the different forces into their movements?
2. Do they include everybody's ideas in their movements?
3. Do they move in rhythm to the music?

For more examples of creative movement plans, see *Creative Dance Plans* on CourseMate.

Integrating the Arts

MOVING TRANSITIONS

Follow the leader. Form a line behind the designated leader. As the group walks to their destination try to match steps and arm motions with the leader.

Gathering on the rug. Move in slow motion or, in contrast, imagine being rockets blasting off and landing on the rug.

Leaving the rug. Take tiny steps or giant steps to the next activity.

Lining up. Form a train with the teacher or child leader as the engine.

Quiet moves. Tiptoe from place to place or imagine being a quiet animal like a bunny or mouse.

Rest time. Move slower and slower until you come to a complete stop at the resting place.

Did You Get It?

Rylee, a four-year-old, has trouble repeating the same movements in succession during dancing games. Which of the following levels of proficiency is she exhibiting?

a. Control

b. Precontrol

c. Utilization

d. Proficiency

Take the full quiz on CourseMate

The Creative Dance Experience

Dancing is moving to music in a repeated pattern or using formal positions. Knowing the steps to a dance allows us to easily move in concert with other people. However, for young children, learning to dance should not be for the purpose of public performance or learning perfect steps, but rather to learn how to better control their bodies, and thereby find joy in moving to the music with others.

Formal dancing instruction is not appropriate for young children. However, children can be introduced to styles of dance and then be allowed to incorporate these styles as they move in their own ways to the music. Select dance forms that have a few repetitious movements that closely match the words or accompanying music, such as those found in children's play songs and folk dances. Choose works that allow individual creative movements and do not require rigid conformity to prescribed dance steps or matching one's steps to those of another. For example, a Greek circle dance allows more freedom of movement than does a square dance.

Selecting Developmentally Appropriate Dances

Young children learn to dance much as they learn to sing a song. They begin by tagging on, repeating one or two of the main movements of the dance over and over. A child attempting to waltz may sway back and forth. Over time and with practice they will slowly add more parts to the dance until they have mastered the entire piece. Dances for the very young should consist of one to three basic movements that match the beat of the music and are open-ended enough that children can invent other ways for doing the dance for themselves. This turns what could be a lockstep performance into a creative arts activity.

A danceable song for young children has a strong beat with lots of repetition. In addition, some children's songs provide directions for how to move. An example of this type of song is "All Around the Kitchen" by Pete Seeger, in which the lyrics provide directions for the movements. There are many wonderful children's albums that feature danceable songs from around the world. For a list of some suggested songs, see *Music for Dancing* on CourseMate.

However, do not be afraid to invent ways of dancing to any favorite song or piece of music. Many songs have obvious places to insert a repeated motion. For example, Woody Guthrie's "Car Song" lends itself to driving motions. There should also be plenty of opportunity for children to make up their own dance moves to teach to others.

Open-Ended Creative Dance Experiences for Infants

Dance experiences for infants should focus on the joy of moving together with a caring adult.

Hug me. Name a body part and hug it in a repeated pattern. Say: "I hug my leg, leg, leg. I hug my head, head, head" and so on. For very young infants, hug their body part for them. Older infants can hug themselves or their caregiver. Change the words to hug other parts of the body or use a different action such as tap, kiss, and so on.

Bouncing. Place the infant on one's lap. Put on a catchy tune and bounce the infant gently up and down to the music, providing any needed head and back support. An older child can sit face-to-face holding your hands. Move the child up and down to the music. Say "up" and "down" as you move together. Then explore other ways to move together to the tune.

Dancing feet. Play a danceable song and hold the infant upright so that the child can wiggle and kick his or her feet to the music.

Dance Experiences for Toddlers

Toddlers with their newfound independence need open-ended dance experiences that let them join in as they wish.

Buddy dance. Have the toddler put his or her feet on your shoes as you move gently to a dance tune. Then let the toddler dance on his or her own.

Shake a leg. Put on a peppy instrumental piece of music and shake different body parts as you dance. Toddlers may have trouble moving each limb separately and keeping their balance. Make sure the floor is cushioned and all forms of movement are accepted.

March. Put on a John Phillip Sousa march and parade around the room. Add props and rhythm instruments.

Open-Ended Creative Dance Experiences for Preschoolers and Kindergarteners

With their better physical control and more fluid movements, three- to five-year-olds are ready to learn simple repetitive dances that they can use as springboards to inventing their own dances.

A sheet of bubble wrap adds sound effects to a child's movement while at the same time providing a designated spot in which to move.

Slow motion. To increase body control, take any dance the children are familiar with, such as "Head, Shoulders, Knees, and Toes," and do it in slow motion. Then do it as fast as you can.

Chain dance. Have the children join hands. Put on a tune with a regular beat. The leader starts the chain off by moving the free arm or leg in an interesting way as he or she leads the group around the room. The rest of the children then copy that movement. Have different children take turns being the leader, each of whom improvises a new dance movement.

Open-Ended Creative Dance Experiences for Primary Age

Children who can perform a sequence of movements are ready to learn and remember more formal dances. Even so, start with dance games and open-ended dances before trying fancy footwork. Use creative movement activities as warm-ups. Remember that the goal is feeling part of a group, not public performance.

Open-ended line dancing. Have the children line up one behind the other. Then have the leader improvise a pattern of changing movements. Play a drum or put on a piece of music and have everybody follow his or her lead. Give everybody a turn at being a leader. Next, try an improvised dance in which everyone holds hands and moves around in a circle.

Free waltzing. Play a waltz and have the students invent a dance step that matches the one-two-three beat. Try other types of dances.

Obstacle course dance. Create an obstacle course in a large space such as a gym or a grassy lawn. Include large fabric tubes to crawl through, small

A rope or tape on the floor helps children control their movements and guides those with special needs.

trampolines, a balance beam, ramp, and so on. Put mats down anywhere children are likely to tumble. Have the children improvise a dance step to a selected piece of music. When they have practiced enough, challenge them to do the obstacle course while dancing to the music. When done, discuss how they had to change the movement to get through the course.

Foot mat choreography. After the children have invented a dance step, give them a large sheet of paper and, working with a partner, have them trace their feet in the various positions, and then number the steps taken in order. Give the mat to another student to try. Does the mat dance match the original dance step?

Invent a dance. Have children practice choreography by having them work in a group to compose a dance. Have them record the dance by writing down a number of steps and the direction to move in, such as two steps forward, three steps back, four steps to the left. Challenge them to have the dancers end up in the same place they started. Let them try out their dances to different types of music.

Folk Dancing for Children

Folk dance refers to dances that are at least 100 years old and are not copyrighted. They are usually danced at informal gatherings and have as many versions as the people who dance them. In a folk dance, the dancers can stand in many formations: in a circle, a square, a spiral, a line, or two facing lines. Sometimes participants may dance in small groups of four, as paired partners, or as solo dancers. There may be a caller or leader who gives directions to the dancers such as in American square dancing.

Folk dancing teaches children how to move in a pattern while maintaining a constant rhythm. The predictability and rhythm of the movement and the accompanying song or music helps children learn the sequence of steps and practice counting.

The best way to introduce young children to this kind of dancing is to start with simple singing games in which the song cues the children how to move. Examples of these kinds of games include the well-known "Ring Around the Rosy" and "London Bridge Is Falling Down."

Follow this by introducing the concept of line dancing by having the students march to different dance tunes. When they seem comfortable with

Putting a CD player in the dress-up center encourages children to create their own dance moves.

the rhythm of a tune, have them form two lines and face each other when dancing. This naturally leads into circle dances. Finally, introduce four- and two-partner dances. For some developmentally appropriate dances for young children, see *Dances for Children* on CourseMate.

The Dance Steps

When selecting folk dances, look for ones that use basic movements. If you wish to try a dance and the moves are too complicated, don't be afraid to simplify them or even invent your own steps to a song or type of music. Here are some basic steps found in many folk dances from which to build original dance combinations:

- *Slide*—In this move one foot moves away from the other and then the other foot moves over to join it. You can slide in any direction and for any number of steps. This is best taught by standing with your back to the children.

Skip—This move is very hard to describe in words. Basically, you take a step, hop with a rocking motion on the back foot, then bring that foot forward so you can hop on the other. The hop is shorter than the move and uneven in feel. Skipping is one of the last large motor skills children develop, so be accepting of all children's attempts. Holding a child's hand and slowly skipping with him or her as the motion is rhythmically described is one way to help children improve their skipping.

Step-Hop—Although similar to a skip, the step-hop is evenly balanced. The step and hop are equal in timing. Once children can skip, play an even one-two beat on a drum or clap until they can match the beats.

Cross-Kick—The foot is kicked out and across the body with the toe pointing outward at a slight angle to the body. Other kicks include back and front. This step requires children to be able to balance on one foot. It helps to have children hold hands or lock elbows in the beginning.

Jumps—Some dances involve jumping in place or forward or back on both feet. The "Bunny Hop" is an example of a dance built on jumps.

Taps—The dancer taps toe or heel on the floor to make a tapping sound. This is the basis of tap dancing in which shoe soles have metal plates to emphasize the sound.

Dealing with Gender

Many traditional dances specify different roles and positions based on gender. However, there is no reason to follow these dictates. Instead of separating them into boys and girls, have children line up randomly or have them count off by twos.

Process Not Performance

For children, moving creatively through dance is the process of learning how to control their bodies in space as well as a delightful way of expressing themselves. As they whirl about the room with their peers, they do not need to worry about how they appear to others. However, expecting them to perform these same movements in front of an audience instantly changes the focus from process to product.

Anyone who has ever attended a dance recital for young children knows that children and teachers become nervous and stressed in such situations. As an

Across Cultures

Language Learning and Dance

Whether a child is an English language learner or a native English speaker, creative dance activities provide an ideal way to practice learning a new language. Many dance story and motion games tie repetition of words together with body movement. Research shows that we learn more when we are moving (Gardner, 1983; Dryden & Vos, 1997, Jensen, 2011).

To get started try the classic "Head, Shoulders, Knees and Toes." Mama Lisa's World (http://www.mamalisa.com/blog/head-shoulders-knees-and-toes-with-an-mp3-recording/) has versions of it in a multitude of languages. Other songs in different language versions can be found doing a search of the Internet.

alternative to staged performances for young children, consider having parents partner with their children, and together perform creative movement activities or learn simple dances in a workshop-type setting.

The best dance activities happen when we watch how children move and build on their ideas.

Reading about Dancing

One of the best ways to increase the attention span and develop attentive listening when reading aloud to young children is to encourage them to move in concert with the story. Almost any children's book can have movements added to it effectively with a little forethought. If there is a rabbit in the story, you can cue the children to make wiggly bunny ears every time they hear the word "rabbit." If the book is about going on a car trip, cue them to drive the car by turning the steering wheel every time you turn a page. In Bill Martin's *Brown Bear, Brown Bear, What Do You See?* (1995), the children can shade their eyes and turn their heads every time they here the cue words "What do you see?"

There are also many children's books about moving, dancing, and dancers from around the world that can be shared with children. *Spicy Hot Colors: Colores Picantes* (Shaham, 2004) interweaves nine colors and four dance steps with a jazzy bilingual text. *Lion Dancer: Ernie Wan's Chinese New Year* (Waters, 1991) is a photographic essay about a boy preparing for Chinese New Year and his role in the traditional Lion Dance.

For an annotated list of books featuring dance, see *Books that Celebrate Dance* on CourseMate.

Responding to Dance

All discussions about dancing should start with the body and its movements. Begin with naming the body parts and describing the different ways they can move. Have children describe their motions using their own descriptive language, as well as the vocabulary of the dance elements. Ask questions that make them think critically about their movement choices.

- Why did you choose to move in that way?

- What is another way you might have shown that tempo or feeling?

- How could you extend that movement?

- Is there a way to combine these ways of moving?

Provide opportunities for preschool through primary-age children to record their responses to dance activities in their journals or at the art center using pictures and words. For example, have children draw pictures of themselves dancing. This is a useful way to assess how children see themselves as dancers. Do they draw themselves alone or with others? Do they show themselves doing active motions or standing still?

Children also need to watch others dancing, not only their peers, but people of all kinds from all cultures. It is easy to bring the world's dance to the classroom using video and the Internet. Dance has long been available through television shows and movies. Early movies featured sweeping dance numbers, such as those of Busby Berkeley, and famous dancers such as Bill Bojangles Robinson, Fred Astaire, Ginger Rogers, Gene

Classroom Technology

DANCE AND THE USE OF MEDIA & TECHNOLOGY

In recent years, live dance performances have featured a wide range of electronic media ranging from projected images to sensors attached to dancers' bodies that signal changes in lighting and background as they move.

Some ways to incorporate technology into children's creative dance activities include:

- To create a changing background, use a computer and digital whiteboard to project photographs onto the children as they dance. Photographs can be selected to go with an integrated unit or be selected by the children. Set up the photographs to run as an automatic slide show with accompanying music.

- To create the effect of dancing with a digital partner, videotape the children dancing and then project the video on a digital whiteboard while the children dance with themselves either mirroring the moves or moving in response.

- Use Wii technology such as Just Dance Kids, which lets children follow the moves of children dancing on the screen.

- Use an overhead projector to project an image or array of colors on dancing children. Use colored cellophane, overhead transparency shapes, and other translucent materials to create designs or for an underwater effect put a clear glass or plastic tray of water on the overhead and make ripples.

For some examples of digital dance performances, see *Online Resources* on CourseMate.

Kelly, and Shirley Temple. Video excerpts of these old time dancers can be found on the Internet. Today millions of people regularly watch dance-focused reality televisions shows, such as *Dancing with the Stars*, and tune in to watch ice dancing in the Winter Olympics. Classical ballet has been featured in adult movies such as *Mao's Last Dancer*, *Center Stage*, and *White Nights*, and is also available on the Internet. Feature cartoonslike the Disney classic *Fantasia* also incorporate dancing. For many this is their only exposure to dance being performed, and for children, this is often their first introduction to watching dance. Viewing dance through electronic media is not the same as attending a live performance. However, research has shown that people who are exposed to dance through media are also more likely to attend live performances (Capristo, 2012).

Expand on what children are exposed to on television and in movies by showing videos and DVDs of dances from other places that they are less likely to see at home. Videos of folk dances and classical ballet performed by both professionals and children can be found on the Internet. Show short excerpts that relate to creative movement activities and integrated units.

For a listing of recorded materials available on the Internet, see *Online Resources* on CourseMate.

When watching a dance with children on television, computer monitor, or digital whiteboard, use the opportunity to create a setting much like one at a live performance. Have children sit facing the screen either on the floor or in rows of chairs and review audience etiquette. Encourage the children to clap at appropriate moments as preparation for attendance at actual live performances.

After viewing a performance by their peers, on a video, or at a live performance, have children draw a picture of what they saw in which they imagine they were part of the performance and include themselves in the picture. Alternatively, they can dictate or write a story about what they saw in which they are the main character.

Making Connections with Dance

Bring the dances of children's home cultures into the classroom by having families teach a favorite dance. Hold dance parties and festivals at which dances from many cultures are shared and enjoyed by families and the school community. Bring in dance groups from local

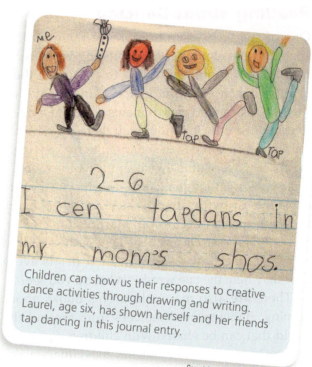

Children can show us their responses to creative dance activities through drawing and writing. Laurel, age six, has shown herself and her friends tap dancing in this journal entry.

dance schools and folk dancing groups to peform classic and folk dances. Provide opportunities for children to compare similarities and differences in the various dances they participate in and observe. Videography of the children dancing provides an excellent way to do this.

Primary children can research dance genres, famous classical ballets, and world culture dancing groups and traditions using the Internet or a teacher-prepared Web quest and then teach their peers about what they learned.

Connect dance to healthy living by emphasizing how dancing makes the body stronger and more flexible. Time how long children can hold a position, jump up and down, or measure how far they can stretch an arm or leg or touch the ground. Do a series of practice activities daily. Then retime and record the new time. Total the scores and make a class graph as a way to visually celebrate the class's improvement without singling out individuals.

Conclusion: Let's Dance!

The power of creative movement and dance is immense in terms of developing children's ability to think spatially. Yet, it is often the one art form that is missing from young children's educational experience. If children do movement activities, it is usually in the form of simple dance games with little input from the children themselves. Although "Head, Shoulders, Knees, and Toes" and "Ring Around the Rosy" are perfectly fine, simple movement activities for young children, they are not all that creative movement education can be. Creative movement and dance must allow children to think with their bodies. The teacher of creative dance must be willing to improvise along with the children. The best dance activities happen when the teacher watches what the children are doing and builds on their ideas, adding props, music, and enthusiasm as needed.

Remember too that dance happens in a fleeting moment. Unless it is caught on video, there is no record of it happening. There is no artwork to hang on the wall or tune to hum. Today with digital photography and videos, there are more opportunities than ever to capture the imagination of children as they discover the potential of their bodies to communicate ideas and express feelings.

For additional information on teaching creative dance to young children, see *Chapter 11 Online Resources* on CourseMate.

Teaching In Action

Open-Ended Creative Movement in Action

The Bridge: After visiting a bridge or learning about bridges, have children stand in two lines about 3 feet apart. Play a slow, gentle piece of music and ask children to slowly reach across to the child opposite and join hands to make a bridge. They can make their bridge at any height. As the music plays they should sway with their bodies. Now, have the children go under the bridges one at a time to get to the other end where they form a new bridge with a partner.

The Machine or Robot: Have each child think of a machine-like movement and a sound to go with it. Establish a start and stop signal and then have them practice their movement. Now ask everyone to touch someone else to become part of a giant machine or robot.

Dancing Dolls: Put out a variety of materials, such as paper, wood, metal, cloth, stuffing. Have children feel these and study how they move. Ask: "Which are rigid?" "Which are flexible?" Have children choose one of the materials and imagine how they would sound and move if their bodies were made out of it. Have them explore their creative moves and then share with others. To extend the activity, have two different materials join together and move in a new way reflecting that combination.

Dance Cards: On large paper or poster board, draw different kinds of lines, swirls, spirals, dashes, and dots in different sizes, weights, and directions, as in these examples.

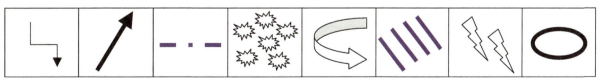

Hold up the cards and ask children to create a movement that relates to the image on the card. Repeat at different speeds and at different levels. Next, add music and move to the beat. For older children have them pair up and combine their two movements.

Reflection Page

The Elements of Dance

For each of the elements, give an example of an activity you could do with children that would reinforce the concept.

Movement

_____

_____

_____

Space

_____

_____

_____

Energy

_____

_____

_____

Time

_____

_____

_____

Body

_____

_____

_____

Reflection Page

Meeting Special Needs

Creative movement activities can be challenging for children with special needs. Adapt each of these activities to meet the needs of the child described.

Child	Activity	Adjustments that might be made
A child who walks with crutches	Pretending to fly like birds	
A child who has limited vision	Crawling like worms	
A child with total hearing loss	Moving around the room and crossing a "river" made from tape on the floor	
A child with Down syndrome	Working with a partner mirroring each other's actions	

Reflection Page

Selecting Appropriate Creative Movement and Dance Activities

Why are the following activities not appropriate for young children? Use what you know about children at different developmental ages to explain why they are not approriate.

1. Teaching toddlers to square dance.

   _____

   _____

   _____

2. Having preschoolers perform an elaborate ballet with many parts in front of their parents.

   _____

   _____

   _____

3. Presenting an activity to toddlers in which everyone has to move in exactly the same way, at the same time, over and over.

   _____

   _____

   _____

4. Putting on loud music and letting a group of preschoolers run all around the classroom.

   _____

   _____

   _____

Reflection Page

Observation: Children Moving Creatively

Observe a group of children involved in a creative movement or dance activity.

Date of observation: _____   Length of observation: _____

Ages of children: _____   Group Size: _____

1. Do the children have control over their movements as expected for their developmental age?

   _____

   _____

   _____

   _____

   _____

2. Which movements come easily for them? Which types of movements give them difficulty?

   _____

   _____

   _____

   _____

   _____

3. How do individual children express themselves through their movement choices?

   _____

   _____

   _____

   _____

   _____

4. How did the children participate in these dance activities? (Examples: tried once then left; engaged in nonverbal or verbal interaction with children and/or adults; worked alone; length of time at activity)

_____

_____

_____

_____

_____

5. What are the adults doing while the children dance?

_____

_____

_____

_____

_____

6. How are dance activities made available to the children?

_____

_____

_____

_____

_____

7. Suggest some other creative movement and dance activities that would be appropriate for this group of children.

_____

_____

_____

_____

_____

Digital Download   Download from CourseMate

Chapter 12

Nurturing the Imagination

Design and plan dramatic play activities that foster children's overall development as well as teach children the skills of the dramatic arts.

Explain ways to use open-ended dramatic activities to develop focus, self-regulation, creative problem-solving, literacy skills, and a sense of story.

Know ways to use dramatic play to help children express their feelings and develop social bonds with their playmates.

Planning Curriculum to Achieve Important Goals

Teaching to Enhance Development and Learning

Nurturing the Imagination DAP Learning Objectives

Creating a Caring Community

Establishing Reciprocal Family Relationships

Assessing Children's Development and Learning

Describe how to use dramatic play to assess children's social-emotional, physical, cognitive, and language skill growth.

Give examples of ways to involve parents in children's dramatic play activities.

Young Artists Creating

"The puppet I'm making is going to be a spaceman."

"So's mine!"

"Let's pretend they are going to the moon."

"Okay, but what can we use for a rocket ship?"

"How about the tall drum?"

"That'll work. Hey, we can even drum on it to make it sound like the rocket is taking off!"

What Are the Dramatic Arts?

Drama and theater are highly integrative art forms. Visual art, music, and creative movement can all be incorporated into dramatic performances whether they are elaborate movie productions or skits put on by children. In addition, problem solving, mental representation, communication skills, language usage, and storytelling play an essential role in the creation of a dramatic work. This means that the dramatic arts are a vital way to foster cognitive and literacy development in young children as well as offering a way to integrate learning across the disciplines.

The Core Processes of the Dramatic Arts

The Common Core Standards in the Arts for Theater has identified the following core processes integral to dramatic or theater arts (National Coalition for Core Arts Standards, 2013).

*   **Performing.** As in dance, performance in theater arts is defined as the actual physical participation in a dramatic experience. A dramatic performance can be done alone or with a group, and with or without an audience.

*   **Creating.** This is the invention of an original dramatic performance either through interpretation and problem solving while acting out a role or through creating original dramatizations and stories to be performed alone or with others.

For children, child-initiated play forms the basis of the dramatic arts curriculum. As they imitate the activities of the adults in their lives, they develop socially, emotionally, creatively, and intellectually.

*   **Responding.** Responding is observing a dramatic performance and expressing ideas about it. This can take many forms, ranging from talking and writing to creating a dramatic work in response.

*   **Connecting.** Participation in dramatic performances provides a safe, playful space in which to connect personal experiences and to express emotions. It affords a way to test out ideas and work out problems, and it can be a healing force in therapy for emotional and mental trauma (Casson, J., 2004).

What Are the Elements of the Dramatic Arts?

The elements of drama and dramatic play share much in common. First, to be successful as an actor a person must be able to imitate others. This requires proficiency in oral language and in controlling the body. The foundation for imitative behavior is established in early childhood as infants learn how to make themselves understood by parents, caregivers, and older children using gesture, words, and actions.

Second, actors also need to know how to use props, costumes, and settings as a way to enhance the meaning of their performance. Through play, the ten-month-old playing peek-a-boo with his father's hat, the toddler putting shoeboxes on her feet and pretending to skate, and the preschooler "cooking" a meal in the playhouse are all learning how to use parts of their environment for dramatic effect.

Third, theater productions are formed around an aesthetically organized and creative presentation of a message or story. The development of narrative skills is a key feature of children's dramatic play. The toddler pantomiming falling in a puddle, the preschooler playing with an imaginary friend, kindergarteners acting out the story of *Goldilocks and the Three Bears,* and second graders writing and producing their own playlets about life in the rainforest are learning the principles of story creation, structure, and self-expression.

The Elements of Drama

The ability to use the elements of story and those of drama develop rapidly in the early childhood years. By the age of five most children are capable of creating and performing complex stories, often sustaining them over an extended time period (see Table 12-1).

The elements of drama are the underlying components that add texture and uniqueness thereby bringing stories to life. They include:

- **Focus**—Successful performance in the dramatic arts requires self-regulation and concentration. Actors show focus when they maintain the attributes of a character throughout a performance. Audiences show focus when they mentally and emotionally center their attention on the dramatization they are watching. Children show focus when they assume roles in their pretend play scenarios that may last over several days.

- **Tension and contrast**—Tension is the creation of suspense, conflict, or rising action which carries the play scenario or story towards a conclusion. Contrast is what keeps dramatizations from being boring by creating tension. We watch action movies to see the battle between good versus evil. We respond viscerally when a quiet parting scene is followed by a noisy chase scene through busy

TABLE 12–1	Dramatic Elements in Children's Play
Dramatic Element	**Children's Natural Play**
Focus, timing, and rhythm	Watches, imitates, and repeats behaviors of the people around them. Takes on roles. Creates sequences of events with beginning, middle, and end.
Language and sound	Imitates vocalizations of people around them.
Rhythm and space	Imitates and invents movements in interaction with others.
Place and mood	Explores the characteristics of objects and how they are used to create a setting.
Symbol	Expresses ideas and feelings by inventing new uses for familiar objects. Creates pretend people, events, objects, and settings.

Digital Download   Download from CourseMate

city streets. The artful combination of tension and contrast is the backbone of effective narrative.

Timing—Timing refers to the manipulation of movements and gestures so that they best match the needs of the dramatic action.

Rhythm—Rhythm is built from tension, contrast, and timing to create the rise and fall of action and emotion in a drama. When we talk about fast-paced action or quiet romance we are describing the rhythm of the production.

Language and sound—An actor communicates ideas and concepts through gesture and words. A written script communicates the actions, movements, and vocalizations of the actors. In addition to voice, sound effects and music can also enhance the performance.

Mood—The combination of setting, movement, sound, and rhythm creates the overall effect or mood. A darkened theater, the sound of drumming rain, and an actor whose head is drooping create one kind of mood. Dorothy dancing down the yellow brick road in the *Wizard of Oz* sets another.

Place—This is the setting in which the story or play takes place. It can be communicated through the arrangement of actual objects and props or created in the imagination through the creative actions and words of the performers.

Space—The area around the performers forms the dramatic space and includes the different levels as in dance.

Did You Get It?

Which of the following elements of drama is responsible for the creation of suspense, conflict, or rising action which carries the story towards a conclusion?

a. timing

b. focus

c. tension

d. symbolization

Take the full quiz on CourseMate

Symbol—Symbolization, the use of one thing to stand for another, is a key element in the dramatic arts and in children's play.

What Is the Relationship Between the Dramatic Arts and Children's Play?

Historically, theatrical drama has been used most often to entertain an audience. We are all familiar with the plays of Shakespeare and the movie productions of Walt Disney. Both of these are examples of the dramatic arts. However, as we will see, the role of the dramatic arts is very different in the lives of young children.

The presentation of a theatrical production to an audience is the most formal form of the dramatic arts. This level of performance is not developmentally appropriate for children under the age of eight (Edwards, 1993). Requiring children to memorize lines and follow a director are skills beyond the ability of most young children. Instead, dramatic activities need to be built around children's own creative play.

For young children, creative dramatics mirrors their natural form of play. Both play and the dramatic arts are centered on

1. **Using the imagination and solving problems.** Infants play with objects, discovering their properties and uses. Toddlers imitate what they see other people doing. By the age of two most children have entered the world of imaginative and symbolic play in which objects and actions can represent other things (Hyson, Copple, & Jones, 2006). A wooden spoon becomes a magic wand and an old shawl a king's robe. The ability to make-believe and create stories is the main characteristic of play in young children.

2. **Developing a positive identity through self-expression.** Before actors can pretend to be someone else, they must first know who they are and what makes the character they want to be different so they can imagine how that character would move, talk, and react to disaster. In pretend play, children do the same thing as they try on

new roles and see how they fit. In doing so they learn more about themselves and others.

3. **Bonding socially with others.** Through play, children learn about their world and how to interact with the people around them. Like actors on a set, group play requires communication skills and the willingness to both lead and follow others to create a play scenario. They learn to respond to the pretend behaviors, improvisation, and fluid rule-making of their peers as they match their behaviors to the needs of the group.

The Power of Play

To understand children's ability to imagine and pretend we need to examine the research related to children's play. The basis of current understanding about children's play and the development of young children is the classic work of Jean Piaget (1962) and Lev Vygotsky (1976).

Piaget's Levels of Play

Piaget believed that play provided children with the opportunity to practice and make sense of new concepts solidifying what they learned through repetition. Piaget identified three levels of play:

1. **Practice play,** in which infants and toddlers at the sensorimotor level of development explore and interact with objects and people using repeated actions, such as when an infant repeatedly knocks an object off the highchair tray.

2. **Symbolic play,** which happens when preschool-age children imitate things they have seen, heard, or experienced. This can be observed when they enact make-believe scenarios such as playing house, taking care of their doll babies, and serving dinner, just like they see their families do.

3. **Game-based play, which occurs during the concrete operational** stage, when children's increasing ability to think logically allows them to enjoy games with preset rules, such as board games and organized sports, and to re-enact the narrative sequence of events in a story or movie they have seen.

Play and the Emergence of Abstract Thought

Vygotsky studied how children's play contributed to cognitive development. He thought that the object-focused play of infants at the sensorimotor or Piagetian practice level of play represented a stage of cognitive development in which the child was incapable of imaginative thought. The object and its meaning were so fused together in the child's mind that the child could not think of it without actually seeing it. He saw the emergence of the ability of children to make believe as the beginning of abstract thought. Vygotsky also believed that play promoted learning by providing children the opportunity to practice in a safe, accepting setting social behaviors they had not yet mastered. Later researchers have supported this idea. Jerome Bruner (1990, 1996) and Brian Sutton-Smith (1998) see play as the way children learn how to adapt and be flexible in meeting future challenges in their lives. Bruner has also posited that play helps children learn how to think in logical sequence as they create story narratives.

Play and Flexible Thinking

According to Brian Sutton-Smith, the adaptability fostered through play prepares children to face an unpredictable future as adults. As children pretend, they move in and out of roles assuming different viewpoints. One minute they might be a puppy begging for a bone, and the next, they are the veterinarian coming to heal the puppy's hurt paw. They also have to adjust to other children playing roles different from their normal selves. This ability to fluidly switch roles, point of view, and think metacognitively about their own thinking in relation to others' is important for later school success where to be successful students have to understand and coordinate their own views with those of their teachers and classmates (Bodrova & Leong, 2004).

Children's Play and the Brain

Current brain research tells us that a child engaged in open-ended play is developing vital brain connections. When children are active participants in play they perform complex movements such as matching their facial expression to a pretend emotion and make novel decisions, such as finding an object to symbolically represent another. This engagement develops the neural connections that form the foundation of future brain development. During play the neocortex or thinking center of the brain is activated as well as the amygdala or emotional center of the brain and the connection between the two centers are strengthened (Jensen, 2005; Johnson, Christie, & Wardle, 2005).

Engaging in play is fun. It reduces stress and facilitates learning. Stress has been shown to impair children's thinking (Jensen, 2005). As children play, the parts of the brain involved in creative thinking and problem solving are more engaged while their stress levels decrease. Children, for example, show fewer nervous habits such as nailbiting while engaged in active play (Johnson et al., 2005).

Did You Get It?

Jessica and her little brother, Mike, are sitting inside an old cardboard box, pretending to drive a car. Which level of Jean Piaget's levels of play does their behavior demonstrate?

a. symbolic play

b. practice play

c. game-based play

d. parallel play

Take the full quiz on CourseMate

How Do Children Grow Through the Dramatic Play?

Children at play are active, intrinsically motivated, and integrating everything they know into a new creative form. In the act of playing children develop longer attention spans and pursue interests more deeply. They develop creatively, socially, emotionally, and cognitively. Most importantly, they are having fun. Because dramatization calls on so many different abilities dramatic performance is a composite of social-emotional, physical, cognitive, and linguistic skills (see Table 12-2). Because of this the dramatic arts are an ideal way to develop skills in all these areas.

Through dramatic arts activities children develop

- **Physically**—By moving the body to characterize the movements of real and fantasy people, behaviors, and objects. We see this when children pretend they are driving a car or flying like Superman. The skills and concepts of creative dance are also closely connected to dramatization.

- **Socially**—By learning to make connections to others through facial and bodily behaviors, by trying out new roles, assuming viewpoints other than their own, and cooperating with others to create meaning and narrative. Dramatic play allows children to connect to their own culture and to imagine that of others. We see this when a group of children, after learning about Mexico, pretends they are going to the store to buy tortillas.

- **Cognitively**—By developing the ability to think logically in narrative sequences. Play lets children create and use symbolic thinking as they use one object or action to represent another. It is powerful because it allows children to repeat and analyze their behaviors. For example, a group of children, playing with puppets, may repeat their story several times, each time trying different ways for the puppets to act.

- **Language skills**—By using language to communicate ideas and feelings, and to tell stories. In playing a part, children can explore the control they have over their voices and ways of speaking. Guided participation by the teacher in children's dramatic play has been shown to increase language and literacy skills (Copple & Bredekamp, 2009, p. 14; Bromley, 1998). Organizing play around a theme with ample materials, space, and time helps children develop more elaborate narrative skills. Dramatic arts activities are often the same as early literacy activities. Children build a sense of story from hearing books read aloud, and from telling and acting out their own stories, and those of others. Dramatic play increases children's comprehension and helps them become aware of narrative elements (Vukelich, Christie, & Enz, 2012; Wanerman, 2010).

- **Emotionally**—By giving children a sense of power and control and by reducing stress. In dramatic play, children can take on the roles of the controlling adults in their lives, they can

TABLE 12–2 Sequence of Development in the Dramatic Arts

Age Group	Object	People	Language	Imagination	Narrative
Infants *newborn to 6 months*	Attracted to bright objects, mirrors, pictures, and rattles	Look at familiar faces	React to sounds Match vocalizing Babble Express feelings by crying, yelling, and cooing		
Infants 6 to 12 months	Enjoy large toys that move	Play peek-a-boo Mirror facial expressions Solitary play predominates	Communicate with gestures, first words Imitates voices and sounds Respond to name, gestures, and simple commands "Talk" to toys	Pretend familiar actions, such as sleeping, hiding, and talking on phone	Play is disconnected
Toddlers *1 to 3 years*	Like to play with real things, such as pots and pans	Rough and tumble play begins Solitary play leads into parallel play	Use words and simple sentences Name objects Speech grows from 25% to 75% understandable Respond to requests Talk to self Knows 100+ words	Imitate familiar actions and events with realistic toys that resemble the real objects, such as sweeping with a broom Imitate familiar actions of people around them and seen on TV, movies Have make-believe conversations	Story play has no definite structure or end
Preschoolers 4 to 5 years	Constructive play becomes most predominant, such as blocks and sand	Incorporate other children in play with increasing division of roles	Use voices to match character Speak in full sentences, slowly adding adjectives, prepositions, adverbs. Changes tone to match feelings Listen and make requests in response Talk about things happening elsewhere Use self-talk to control behavior Recite nursery rhymes Know 1000+ words	Play becomes more fictional Can imagine one object is something else Imaginary playmates Role-play imaginary characters	Retell invent, and act out stories Stories have rudimentary plots Invented stories incorporate ideas from stories they have heard

(continued)

TABLE 12–2	Sequence of Development in the Dramatic Arts *(continued)*				
Kindergarteners *5 to 6 years*	Object and constructive play becomes more orderly	Cooperative play in which there is a shared purpose	Talk about their play Tell stories Tell "jokes" Use past tense consistently Knows 10,000+ words	Fantasy play is more complex and fluid	Use invented spelling and drawing to tell a story
Primary Ages *6 to 8 years*	Construction becomes more complex Create objects to go with story or play Like games with rules	Enact roles from life, fiction, and media Assign roles in logical, fair ways	Increased control over voice and matching it to role Makes up stories Tells jokes, riddles, and verbal exaggerations Use mostly correct grammar Follow and give instructions Learn 10–15 words a day Knows 20,000+ words Evaluate dramatic performance	Can use very dissimilar objects to represent others Know difference between real and pretend Daydreaming replaces pretend play	Write invented stories from experience or picture Stories can have elaborate plots Create scripts for drama and puppet shows

Note: As in all the arts, dramatic arts development is strongly influenced by experience. This chart is intended only as a general guideline to what skills might be mastered in terms of age. However, the basic sequence of skill acquisition will pertain to most children.

determine what will happen in their play, and they can take risks as they try out new ways of behaving. Through dramatic play children develop independence and self-control. Increased time spent in dramatic play has been shown to correlate with the ability of children to control their behavior in circle time and clean up (Elias & Berk, 2002). Dramatic play allows children to learn how to deal with conflict and diversity and to delay gratification of immediate wants as they share materials, and incorporate the play schemes of others into their own or incorporate themselves into the play narratives of others (Bodrova & Leong, 2004).

↯ **Drama concepts and skills**—By meeting the National Common Core Theater Arts Standards.

National Standards in Theater

Based on the National Common Core Standards in Theater Arts, children should be able to do the following:

Connecting: Communicate how and why an awareness of relationships between drama processes, theatre experiences, and the world is used to make meaning of community, cultural, global, and/or historical contexts. Apply ideas, experiences, and elements from different art forms and other disciplines to DAP dramatic activities.

↯ **Prekindergarten.** With teacher guidance compare themselves and their experiences with those of characters in dramatic play and stories.

Kindergarten. With teacher guidance relate characters, stories, and conflict in dramatic play, process drama, and developmentally appropriate theatre experiences to their own lives.

First Grade. With teacher guidance connect their personal experiences with characters, stories, and conflict to their dramatic activities.

Second Grade. Identify and express in multiple ways how and why relationships are made between themselves and the world during participation in and observation of DAP dramatic activities.

Creating: Imagine, research, and explore through drama processes, play, and theatre experiences to discover diverse creative ideas.

Prekindergarten. Navigate, with prompting and support, transitions between imagination and reality within dramatic play and process drama occurring in relation to self and others in role and transformation of place and objects.

Kindergarten. Transition, with prompting and support, between imagination and reality; share original ideas for problem solving within dramatic activities.

First Grade. Work with peers to develop imagined worlds with characters, settings, and stories while problem solving in dramatic activities.

Second Grade. Explore and question, collaboratively and independently, ideas about imagined worlds, characters, and stories in process drama while problem solving with peers.

Performing: Communicate realized artistic ideas in a formal/informal presentation of drama processes or theatre experiences.

Prekindergarten. With teacher guidance, use voice, gestures, body position, and facial expressions to demonstrate basic role-play skills.

Kindergarten. With teacher guidance, use voice, body, and facial expressions with detail and variety to demonstrate basic role-play skills.

First Grade. Manipulate and sustain, with prompting and support, the voice, body, and face to communicate imagined worlds, characters, and emotions within extended process drama and work shared with peers.

Second Grade. Manipulate and sustain, collaboratively and individually, purposeful choices for voice, body, face, and/or design elements to communicate imagined worlds, characters, and emotions.

Responding: Analyze perspectives, articulate feelings, and critically evaluate on drama processes/theatre experiences using criteria such as aesthetics, preferences, beliefs, and contexts.

Prekindergarten. Recall with prompting and support, plots, preferences, and feelings about stories in DAP dramatic activities, and theatre performances.

Kindergarten. Recall and describe, with prompting and support, sequential plot, voluntarily shared preferences/feelings, and details about stories and experiences in DAP dramatic activities and theatre performances.

First Grade. Use verbal and non-verbal communication to explain plots, preferences, and feelings about stories and experiences in DAP dramatic activities and theatre performances.

Did You Get It?

Why is dramatic play important for developing cultural understanding?

a. Children get to go to other countries.

b. Children get to celebrate holidays from around the world.

c. Children learn another language.

d. Children get to imagine living in another culture.

Take the full quiz on CourseMate

Second Grade. Use verbal and non-verbal communication in groups and individually to discuss plots, preferences, and feelings prompted by stories and participation in DAP dramatic activities and theatre performances.

How Do We Address Special Needs?

Dramatic activities, because they involve movement and language, require many of the same adaptations as creative movement and dance so that all children can participate fully.

Children with auditory needs. For consistency, use the same visual start, stop, listen, and relax signals developed for creative movement and dance activities. Select activities that do not rely exclusively on language. Use picture cue cards for preschoolers and word cue cards for those who can read. Visually mark the area of the performance or play space.

Children with visual needs. Start by making sure the children know the location of the props and the boundaries of the area to be used. Survey the area with the child and handle the materials with them before beginning the activity. Give personal asides during dramatic play and performances that let the child know where to find things. Provide a buddy and plan activities for pairs.

Children with attention-deficit disorders. Children who have trouble focusing are easily distracted in dramatic play settings where there are many choices and materials. To help these children develop focus, partition off play areas with low dividers that allow visibility for adults but shield one play area from another at the children's eye level. Offer clear directions and simple oft-repeated rules using multiple modalities. Provide plenty of hands-on activities and offer new materials or suggested ideas when the child seems to lose focus. Participate in the play with the child anticipating the child's needs and modeling ways to interact with peers. Have on hand other activities that the child likes and can do independently for use when the child indicates she or he is ready to move on to something else.

Children with autism. Because these children have impaired communication and social skills, group play is especially challenging for them, and they often prefer solitary play. With peers they may miss social cues and not be able to follow the improvised narrative script of child-initiated pretend play. Teachers can help foster interpersonal skills by playing one-on-one with these children while modeling ways to interact with others. For example, the one-on-one Floortime Model has been shown to increase social, cognitive, symbolic, and creative behavior in children with autism (Greenspan & Weider, 1998). It utilizes five steps to help children learn how to interact with a playmate. These same steps can also be used to join in the play of all children, especially infants.

1. Observe the child playing and decide how to approach him/her.

2. Join the activity and match the child's emotional tone.

3. Follow the child's lead.

4. Expand on the child's activity by making a gentle suggestion, asking a question, or modeling an action.

5. When a child' responds to your expansion, "the circle of communication" is completed and the process is started over again from step 1.

To help a child with autism participate in group play establish rituals for entering and interacting with peers. Task cards can be used to cue appropriate behaviors. The Integrated Play Group Model is based on Vygotsky's model of learning from expert peers (Wolfberg & Schuler, 1993). Using this strategy, the child with autism is paired with several other children who serve as the play "experts." In the beginning the teacher sets up the play theme and materials and models for the peers how to include the child in their play. The group meets consistently on a regular basis. As the children learn how to interact with each other, the teacher slowly withdraws, becoming an encouraging onlooker, and lets the play evolve naturally.

Accepting differences. A large part of the dramatic arts is stretching the imagination. Challenge stereotypes by refusing to accept limiting responses. Gender differences, for example, are established as early as twelve months of age and many children

Did You Get It?

How can a teacher help children with hearing difficulties participate more fully in dramatic play with their peers?

a. Select activities that rely exclusively on language.

b. Use picture and word cue cards.

c. Provide a separate area for them to play in.

d. Let them watch close-captioned videos.

Take the full quiz on CourseMate

Through imagination, stories come to life. Dressing up as a firefighter allows a girl to act out being brave, rescuing people, and putting out a fire.

Copyright © 2015 Cengage Learning®

What Is the Teacher's Role in Children's Play?

Play is the natural activity of childhood. Children the world round, when left on their own, will find ways to make believe, as they have for generations, Yet, despite research showing the value of play, accountability and the need to master academic skills at a young age have come to be seen as more important than playtime for future success by both parents, school administrators, and politicians. Play is viewed as time wasted especially for children with disabilities or economic disadvantages (Snow, 2003; Zieger, Singer, & Bishop-Josef, 2006). More and more time spent in early childhood settings is devoted to direct instruction rather than open-ended play with the assumption that they will get their playtime at home. Unfortunately this is not true, since children are spending increasing time in front of televisions and computers rather than engaging in social bonding with playmates. Opportunity for child-initiated play is also hindered by the fear of many parents to let their children walk around their neighborhoods to play with others.

We can address this increasing lack of playtime by including time for children to play as part of classroom instruction. However, it is important that the play opportunities be designed for maximum developmental growth while not hindering the fluidity and creativity of children's natural ways of playing.

Research has shown that teachers assume a range of roles in interaction with children at play as illustrated in the continuum of teacher participation in

and parents have definite ideas about what toys are appropriate for boys and girls. In dramatic play, there is no reason that a girl cannot play the part of a boy or vice versa. Encourage exploration of many roles by calling the housekeeping center the dramatic play area instead, and including materials that will interest boys as well as girls, such as a tool chest, and by creating more open concept centers such as a bakery or restaurant where roles are less stereotypical.

One way to expand children's story narratives is to read stories that involve character reversals such as Robert Munsch's *Paper Bag Princess* (1992) in which a princess defeats the dragon and saves the knight or San Souci's *Cendrilla: A Caribbean Cinderella* (1998) in which Cinderella is a native of Martinique.

Uninvolved	Onlooker	Observer	Stage Manager	Co-Player	Mediator	Play Leader	Director
Teacher is busy with other things or talks to other adults.	Teacher watches in an encouraging way using positive feedback but does not interfere.	Teacher watches children for a specific purpose and may record the children's behavior or patterns of interaction. Observations are then used to inform future instruction.	Teacher observes the children's natural play and provides assistance with props, and setting but does not enter into play.	Teacher joins in children's play, taking a minor role and following the children's lead, modeling appropriate interaction strategies if needed.	Teacher serves as a conflict manager stepping in as necessary to teach children how to solve problems so that they can play happily and safely.	Teacher takes an active role in initiating the theme of the play and providing props and materials that enhance the children's learning in specific ways or refocus the children to extend the play.	Teacher stands on the sidelines and tells the children what to do or asks questions focused on academic goals that disrupt the play.

FIGURE 12-1 Continuum of Teacher Participation in Children's Play

children's play shown in Figure 12-1. At one end of the continuum is non-involvement in the children's play. Uninvolved teachers spend only two to six percent of their time engaging with children at play (Johnson, Christie, & Wardle, 2004). Instead, they spend the time doing work or talking to other adults. In such situations children's play is characterized by simplistic, repetitive narratives, and rough and tumble play, which is often based on characters and superheroes from television, films, and video games.

▶❚❚ **TeachSource Video Case 12.1**

School Age Cognitive Development

What role on the continuum has the teacher played in setting up this imaginative dramatic play activity?

What social, cognitive, and language skills are developed as the children play?

Watch on CourseMate

Joining children's pretend play as a co-player is a wonderful way to enhance language and social skills.

At the other end of the continuum, teachers assume a director's role and tell the children what to do and solve problems for them. This level of direction disrupts children's intrinsic motivation to play and often the activity is abandoned, creating the myth that young children have short attention spans. Elizabeth Jones and Gretchen Reynolds put it this way: "Teacher interruption of play for the purpose of teaching abstract concepts and discrete skills, contradicts everything we know about the learning process of young children" (2011, p. 15).

The roles in the center of the continuum are the ones that are correlated with the greatest growth in cognitive, language, and social-emotional skills. When teachers participated in children's play in effective ways such as these, children's play lasted longer and was more cognitively complex (Sylva, Roy & Painter, 1980; Howes & Smith, 1995). There was also more cooperation and increased amounts of literacy behaviors (Christie et al., 2003).

Did You Get It?

Andria, a preschool teacher, spends most of her time talking with her colleagues, and little time engaging with her students at play. What effect will her behavior have on her students' dramatic play?

a. Their play will be characterized by simplistic and repetitive narratives.

b. The children will lose their intrinsic motivation to play and will eventually abandon their activities.

c. The children will work together in a better fashion and show increased amounts of literacy behaviors.

d. Their play will last longer and will become more cognitively complex.

Take the full quiz on CourseMate

How Are Dramatic Arts Activities Designed?

In the classroom dramatic play can be used to help children develop their language skills, experience the creative process, consider the visual aesthetics of settings and costumes, and much more. These kinds of dramatics activities should be designed in open-ended ways that allow children to use their imaginations to re-create and express ideas and feelings.

Ideas for play activities can be child-initiated such as in informal play, teacher-initiated, such as using pantomime and improvisation to illustrate new words, or inspired by some special event, such as reading a new story and then acting it out.

Informal Dramatic Play

Informal dramatic play is characteristically spontaneous, growing out of the natural inclinations of the children. It is child-initiated, but can be supported by teachers when they enter into children's ongoing play and provide facilitation as a co-player, such as by joining a tea party and modeling the use of "please" and "thank you" as part of the play. Elaborating on children's pretend play scaffolds language usage and models positive ways to interact socially.

Facilitating with words. Close observation of children at play allows teachers to facilitate language skill development. For example, a caregiver might notice two toddlers playing with toy cars and making car sounds, but not using words. She might walk over to them and join in driving a car too, while asking them questions about where their cars are going to increase their use of oral language.

Facilitating with props. Teachers can also enrich play by showing children how to create their own props. An observant teacher functions as a stage manager when he notices that a group of kindergarteners has built thrones and are pretending they are kings and queens. He puts out some paper strips, scissors, glue, and sparkly paper and invites them to make their own crowns.

Social facilitation. The flexibility of dramatic play allows everyone to participate. Children, such as those with developmental delays or autism, may not know how to enter into group play situations. We need to be aware of potential social difficulties and be ready to step in. One way to do this is to model how to ask to join a playgroup. Another is to make suggestions that open up the play to more participants. If two children are imagining they are a shopper and a store clerk and another wants to join, the teacher could point out that there are usually many shoppers in a store. Another is to set up rules to make sure that play is fair. Vivian Paley (1992), for example, told her kindergarteners that they could not exclude other children from play, and then enforced the rule through storytelling and ongoing discussions with her students.

Open-Ended Play Centers

The teacher can also set the stage for informal dramatic play by creating play centers that build on children's natural interests and everyday experiences, such as a playhouse or a store. Other centers can help children learn about how things work or address concerns. For example, many children are fearful of doctor's visits. Creating a doctor's office in which to play can help children work out their fears. Lisa Miles (2009) following up the interests of her preschoolers after reading the *Little House* books by Laura Ingalls Wilder, built an old-fashioned general store stocked with baskets of yarn, ribbon, metal buckets and scoops, a scale, wooden crates, and jars of beans, buttons, and cinnamon sticks. She found that putting a piece of plywood on the floor provided the sound and feel of an old store.

For more center ideas, see *Open-Ended Dramatic Play Centers* on CourseMate.

Prop Boxes

Prop boxes are similar to play centers in providing children with starting points for child-initiated dramatic play. They have the advantage of being easy to store and ready to use at the opportune moment.

A prop box consists of a collection of objects that will spark children's imaginations. The items can all relate to the same main idea, such as a butterfly net, a wide-brimmed hat, magnifying glass, "cages" made from berry baskets, plastic caterpillars, and butterflies. Other prop boxes can be based on an experience. Prop boxes can include child-safe objects, books, tapes of relevant music, and suggestions for use. Label the box clearly when putting it away for storage so it is immediately ready to use another time.

Prop boxes can be used individually or with small groups of children and are particularly effective when using an emergent curriculum design and for the primary grades, where large play centers are less likely to be found. For example, a teacher might make up prop boxes to go with the children's literature used in the classroom as a way to provide opportunities to revisit the story through role-plays.

Prop boxes can also be used outdoors to spark children to take a new direction in their play and increase their experiences with language and literacy. Celeste Harvey (2010) found that when she provided prop boxes containing chalk, magnifiers, identification guides, and books on insects, children spent time observing lady bugs and drawing them on the sidewalk. Children became so excited they set themselves the task of finding a new bug every day.

For more suggestions for outdoor prop boxes, see *Outdoor Prop Boxes* on CourseMate.

Addressing Diversity

Diversity and bias can be addressed through dramatic play activities by the careful selection of materials.

Play centers. Play centers can include items that recognize cultural and ethnic differences. In selecting materials, make sure that all the cultural backgrounds of the children in the class are represented. Families are usually quite happy to help out with suggestions and donations of items. Once there is representation of all family backgrounds, expand the offerings to include items from ethnic groups and cultures not found in your classroom. These can become springboards for research and discussion.

Anti-bias props. In choosing culturally diverse props, look for different eating utensils, ethnic foods, unisex materials for different kinds of work, realistic clothing from other cultures, and props for different disabilities, such as wheelchairs, crutches, canes, hearing aids, leg braces, and dark glasses.

Selecting dolls. Dolls for pretend play should be selected to show the different skin tones of the wide range of groups found in the United States. There should also be fair representation of male and female dolls and those with disabilities.

Commercial dolls can be supplemented with "Persona Dolls" (Derman-Sparks & the ABC Task Force, 1989). These are handmade dolls or large puppets that are given specific characters through the telling of their life story by the teacher. Persona Dolls can be customized to represent children with disabilities, diverse ethnicities, or unique family experiences.

Having Persona Dolls in the class provides a way to bring up topics or feelings that would otherwise be difficult. Jan Pierce and Cheryl Johnson (2010) found that when they used Persona Dolls with their preschoolers to solve classroom problems, children identified with dolls with whom they shared similar characteristics. In addition, timid children spoke up more. Derman-Sparks recommends introducing the Persona Dolls that are most like the children in the

Teacher Tip

INTRODUCING PERSONA DOLLS

Persona Dolls teach inclusive social-emotional skills and foster self-regulation and problem-solving skills. They provide a safe, engaging way to address difficult issues. To introduce the dolls to children

1. Create a unique personality and background for the doll that shares similarities with one or more of the children in the class. Later introduce dolls that are very different.

2. Introduce the dolls to the children just as you would a new student in the class. Tell the dolls' age, family members, and what their likes and dislikes are.

3. Use your natural voice when speaking for the doll, not a puppetlike one.

4. Have the doll(s) participate in everyday activities such as circle time and during small groups, but do not put them in the housekeeping center. Show the children these dolls are special. Keep them in a place where children can see them and ask for them to play with them when they have a particular dramatic story in which the dolls play a role.

5. When a problem comes up in class, use the doll to rephrase the problem as one the doll is having and ask the children to help solve it.

Open-ended props, such as these foam cushions, increase children's engagement in dramatic play, and help children invent new places to imagine. Perhaps they will cross a mountain or stand on top of a tower.

class first. To allay first-day fears, for example, she suggests having three dolls talk about how they got to know each other, and how they felt when they said goodbye to their parents. If there is a child with a disability in the class, a Persona Doll with that disability can offer opportunities to talk in a more relaxed way about the child's special needs and equipment.

Adding diversity to prop boxes. Prop boxes also make ideal ways to integrate multicultural materials into children's play (Boutte, Van Scoy, & Hendley, 1996). For example, seeing an interest among several girls in playing with each other's hair, a teacher could take out the hair dressing prop box. In the box are not only the typical hairbrushes, combs, empty containers of shampoos, and barrettes, but also empty containers of hair products used by other cultural groups. In addition, there could be books about hair, such as *Cornrows* (Yarborough, 1997), *Hairs Pelitos* (Cisneros, 1994), and *I Love My Hair!* (Tarpley, 2001) as well as photographs of men and women from different races and cultures wearing a wide variety of wonderful hairstyles.

Developing the Imagination

Mental representation is at the core of all the arts. It is the ability to produce and act upon **sensory images** in one's mind. These images may involve one or more of the senses, such as visual, auditory, tactile, and olfactory. Although they are not real, these images activate the same parts of the brain as do actual sensory experiences (Kosslyn, Gainis, & Thompson, 2006). The mind is able to combine, remember, and re-create such images to produce new thoughts. This is the realm of fantasy and imagination, and is the basis of literature, which relies on our ability to create mental images as we hear and read stories.

Mental representation is used in the dramatic arts when authors visualize the characters and places in the stories and plays they write, and actors create mental images of the characters they are playing so they can become that person. In the visual arts artists plan their paintings in their minds before they begin.

Dancers mentally rehearse their performance before they step on stage. Musicians and composers hear the music in their mind as they read the notes on a page.

Benefits of creating mental images. Creating mental images has been shown to be effective in improving cognitive skills, maintaining energy levels, and strengthening concentration. In one research study, first- and third-grade students who created mental images before reading a story had higher levels of comprehension (Rushall & Lippman, 1997).

Using our imaginations is also an important way to relax. When we are creating mental images, we can escape from everyday life into a world of our own creation. We can daydream ourselves into a favorite place, or do something we can only do in our dreams, such as swim in the deep sea with a mermaid. The relaxation aspect of imagery has been used to help people reduce stress, fear, and pain. Imagery has been shown to help cancer patients feel less stressed during chemotherapy, and to relieve tension during childbirth (Mandle, Jacobs, & Arcari, et al., 1996).

The power of imagery to affect our physical state has been elegantly presented in the well-known work of Ellen Langer (1989). She points out that it is our mental perceptions that influence how we see and understand the world, and not just the external stimuli around us. Langer, in particular, emphases the powerful link between mind and body. She gives the examples of the professor who felt no pain from his severe arthritis when lecturing, and of patients who tolerated surgical pain better when they imagined their surgical wounds came from playing a football game or from an injury from a kitchen knife. There is also the proven ability of placebos to cure patients of disease.

Planning Guided Imagery Activities

With practice, mental images can become clearer and deeper. **Guided imagery** is one way to develop children's imaginations and get them ready for storytelling and other more active dramatic activities. It is most appropriate for children who have learned to fantasize and can remember what they have imagined, usually by the age of four or five. Start with simple visual imagery games and then proceed to more complex multisensory experiences.

Mind pictures. A good introductory activity is to have the children look at an interesting picture. It could be a photograph or famous artwork. Then have them close their eyes and describe the picture to you.

Memory pictures. Have the children close their eyes and imagine a place they have been. Then ask them to describe the place in words or make a drawing of it.

Imagining the familiar. After the children have become familiar with the classroom, have them lie on the floor or sit in a circle on a rug and close their eyes. Ask them to imagine they are walking around the room. Describe entering the room and some things you see as you walk around it, such as what is on the walls, on the desks, where the supplies are, and so on. Stop frequently and ask the children if you forgot anything. Accept all their additions to your description. Slowly let the children take over the description as you cue them to where you are standing. When you have made a complete circuit of the room, have the children open their eyes and see if anything was missed.

Trips of the imagination. To begin an imaginary trip, have the children sit or lie down and close their eyes. Cue them to relax by saying: "Wiggle your toes. Now let them relax." Repeat for each body part moving up until you reach the head. Next, say: "Today we will be traveling to . . ." or "We will be imagining we are. . . ." Then in a slow, quiet voice describe the trip or characteristics of what is being imagined. Use many descriptive words that describe the sounds, colors, odors, and tastes you encounter. Add more complexity as the children become skilled at creating mental images.

For an example of a script for a guided imagery experience, see Guided Imagery: A Peaceful Cave *on CourseMate.*

Expressing mental images. Guided imagery is a good way to introduce arts activities. Follow up imagery experiences with opportunities to create freely such as having an open studio time during which the children can choose to express what they imagined by writing a story, acting it out, drawing a picture, or composing a musical work.

Here are some ideas for guided imagery experiences. Imagine you are:

- A cloud floating over the earth. Describe the different things you can see—birds, planes, forests, rivers, and houses below.

- Water flowing down a stream. Describe how it joins a creek, then a river, and finally reaches the sea.

〰️ Traveling to another planet. Describe the blackness of space, the huge size of the planets as you get near to them, the stars, and the comets swooshing past.

〰️ Traveling to a distant place. Describe all the different ways to travel. Start in a car, get on a train, then take off in an airplane, land, sail on a ship, and finally take local transportation depending on the place, such as a donkey or camel.

Did You Get It?

Which is an example of guided imagery?

a. Delia helps children put on dress up clothes and imagine they are community workers.

b. Nyah asks her students to look at an interesting picture, close their eyes, and then describe the picture to her.

c. Margaret gives her students a prop box filled with child-safe objects for imaginary play.

d. Deborah draws a picture on the board and asks her students to copy the picture into their notebooks and color it.

Take the full quiz on CourseMate

The Pantomime Experience

Pantomime is acting out an idea without using words, although it may include sound effects. This type of dramatic play can be child-initiated or teacher-guided and occurs when children are given cues either by the teacher as in guided pantomime, or are influenced by what has been taught, such as dramatizing a book the class read, or reenacting an event from history. One advantage of teacher-guided or **process drama** activities is that they help children explore ideas they might not think of otherwise and provide opportunity to practice dramatic arts skills. Participating in simple pantomimes prepares children for the more complex activities of role-plays and the dramatization of stories.

Descriptive pantomimes. In this form of pantomime the teacher or peer leader gives a series of descriptive statements, starting with a statement that cues them that they will be pretending, such as "Imagine you were. . . ." The children respond by inventing facial expressions and motions that reflect what is being described. Topics for descriptive pantomimes include sensory experiences, expression of emotions, characterization, and fantasy.

Begin with simple one-sentence descriptions, such as "Imagine you are smelling a flower" or "Imagine you swimming in the sea." Be careful not to overwhelm the children by trying to do a whole string of them at once. It is better to do one activity a day, perhaps as a warm-up for a morning meeting.

More involved pantomimes can consist of extended descriptions that take the group on a journey or through a process. For example, the leader could think of a place and then guide the group around it. The popular *Going on a Bear Hunt* is an example of this kind of activity. A trip through a castle might start by imagining crossing over the moat on a shaky drawbridge, stomping across a dusty courtyard, banging on the huge wooden doors, climbing the steps to the throne room, and bowing to the giant ogre king. Such pantomimes provide an ideal context, particularly in the primary grades, to review facts and concepts children have learned. If the children have been learning how grain becomes the cereal they eat, a pantomime might have them imagine they are a grain of wheat and go through the process of being harvested, milled, cooked, and shaped into cereal, then boxed, trucked to the supermarket, placed on the grocery shelf, and finally, bought and eaten.

For more ideas for pantomimes, see *Ideas for Simple Descriptive Pantomines* on CourseMate.

Planning pantomimes. Brief pantomimes for young children can be spontaneous or even child-initiated; others will require a measure of preplanning. In planning pantomimes, consider the following:

〰️ Is the space adequate? Be sure there is enough room for the children to move actively. If necessary, outline the boundaries for movement or use hula hoops or marks on the floor to keep the children in place.

〰️ Do you know your audience? Be aware of the physical abilities and feelings of the children. Who is shy? Who tends to overreact physically? Adjust the activity to fit the needs of these children so that everyone can be successful and potential

Making Plans

GROUP ACTIVITY PLAN: IMAGINING IT

WHO?   Group composition age(s): Preschool and up

Group size: Preferably four to five preschoolers, but can be the whole group if the children are experienced at pantomiming.

WHEN?   Time frame: 5 to 10 minutes

WHY?   Objectives: Children will develop

- physically, by using their bodies to hold a position. (Bodily-Kinesthetic)
- socially, by working together to create a unified aesthetic event. (Interpersonal)
- emotionally, by gaining confidence to express ideas through pantomime. (Intrapersonal)
- language skills, by describing how the experience felt. (Linguistic)
- cognitively, by seeing that a whole is made up of parts. (Logical-Mathematical)
- dramatic skill and knowledge, by improvising a pantomime and modulating body movements to fit a role. (Content Standards 1 and 2)

WHERE?   Setup: Large, open carpeted area

WHAT?   Materials: Chart paper and markers

HOW?   Procedure:

Warm-Up: Go outside and observe a car or truck. Put the car in park with the emergency brake on and look under the hood when it is running. If possible, take a ride in it. If that is not possible, talk about how it would feel to ride in it. (Option: This could be a fire truck and be done after a visit to the firehouse.)

What to Do: Have the children brainstorm a list of all the parts of the chosen vehicle. Have the children stand up and imagine they are that vehicle, and then have them pretend to drive it around the circle. Next, ask the children to work in a group. Assign each child in the group a role, such as being the engine, the wheels, the driver, the steering wheel, and so on. Have group members take turns being each of the parts. Have them add sound effects like an engine, horn, and so forth, if desired.

What to Say: Use questions to guide problem solving. "How do you think the _____ would move? How will the parts join together? Where should the driver, wheels, and so forth be?" Provide control. "Let's imagine we are driving. Go around in a circle until you are back in your starting spot." Give positive feedback. "You solved the problem of how to stay together in a workable way by holding hands."

Transition Out: Return to the rug and ask them: How did it feel when just you were the vehicle? Was it hard to get everyone to move together? What are some ways you used? Do you think it is hard to get all the parts of a real vehicle to work together? Follow up this pantomime with others that reinforce the idea that a whole is made up of parts, such as a computer (monitor, keyboard, mouse, plug) or cake (flour, sugar, milk, eggs). For primary students, try pantomiming systems being studied, such as the solar system, an ecosystem, or the human body.

ASSESSMENT OF LEARNING

1. Do the children work together cooperatively to make a working vehicle?
2. Can the children describe the differences in the two pantomimes?
3. Do the children understand the concept that the whole is made up of parts?

For more examples of dramatic activity plans, see *Open-Ended Dramatic Arts Activity Plans* on CourseMate.

discipline issues are avoided. Pantomime should be fun for all.

🎵 Are there enough materials or props for everyone and are they safe? If a prop is part of the pantomime, such as a hat or flower, be sure to have one for every child. Make sure all surfaces are smooth and there are no sharp points. Avoid using sticks with active young children because even with care, accidents can happen.

🎵 Can you see everyone? Pantomime has an element of spontaneity and can be adjusted as needed. By watching the children's reactions you can decide whether to expand the activity or stop it. You can also note any children having difficulty and simplify or clarify as needed.

🎵 Can everyone see and hear you? Pantomime leaders, whether teachers or children, should be active participants. Use a loud and clear voice with plenty of enthusiasm.

🎵 Do the pantomimes build on each other? Start simple. Build on the children's skills. When they can follow a one-sentence pantomime, add an extension as in this example: Imagine you are licking a delicious ice cream cone in your favorite

Pantomime forces children to think of new ways to communicate concepts and ideas. What message do you think these two children are signaling each other?

flavor (let them lick for a while)—suddenly a big dog jumps up and knocks it out of your hand. Show how you feel.

🎵 Have you made the rules clear? Practice the start, listen, stop, and relax signals before beginning. Make sure the children know what is acceptable and what is not. Point out the boundaries in which they must stay.

The Pantomime Experience for Infants and Toddlers

Pantomime is strongly related to gesture, which is the earliest form of communication. We naturally use pantomime as we work with infants and young toddlers. We pantomime feeding ourselves when we want them to eat. We pantomime going to sleep, blowing kisses, being a pretend animal "eating" them up, and more. To make the experience more meaningful it is important to be aware of how we can use this most basic of the dramatic arts to reinforce learning and to develop creative thinking.

Doing things. Pantomiming familiar things helps children develop vocabulary and concepts. Together with the children, act out ordinary actions, such as brushing teeth, eating soup, and shoveling snow. Make the activity playful by exaggerating the movements and making silly sounds, such as slurping the soup.

Being things. Pantomiming objects in action helps children learn how things work. Together pretend to be inanimate objects. Be a clock, using your arms as the hands. Be a pencil and write with your feet. Be a car, steering the wheel with your hands as you drive around the room.

Being silly. Pantomiming with the total body helps develop physical control. Together act in exaggerated ways. Be a floppy rag doll or puppet that cannot stand up. Roll up into a ball and roll around the floor. Be a balloon blowing away in the wind. Be popcorn popping. Add music to enrich the experience.

Playing with props. Attach a short string to a piece of paper or a box and have the children interact with the dangling object as if it were a living thing. It can be anything the children imagine or make suggestions, such as a bird, kite, butterfly, or bee.

The Pantomime Experience for Preschoolers and Kindergarteners

For children between the age of three and six, simple pantomimes that ask them to pretend to be something or do something fit well with their normal fantasy play. These experiences should be short and very open-ended. At the same time, engage in pantomime often and encourage the children to contribute ideas for pantomime time.

How would? Ask the children how different things, with which they are familiar, might move or behave. How would a snowflake fall to the ground? How would a bird build a nest? How would a tall person fit under a low bridge?

Inside the picture. Have the children study a work of art and then pantomime what they would do if they were inside the picture, or select a piece of music and pantomime how it makes them feel.

Re-vision it. Take an ordinary object and pantomime using it in an unusual way. For example, use a shoe for a telephone or a hairbrush for a toothbrush. Pass it around and have each child think of a different thing to do with the prop.

Be someone. Have the children act out different jobs and sports activities.

Statues. Have the children move about as if they were animals, spaghetti, or made of gelatin. At a pre-established signal have them freeze and hold their positions. Walk around admiring their poses.

The Pantomime Experience for Primary Age

There is no question that pantomime offers a critical way to reinforce what is being taught across the disciplines. By first and second grade, children can create complex scenarios and can effectively take on the role of leader.

Messages. To develop reading skills, put the children in pairs and ask them to imagine they cannot talk. Give each child a written message to communicate solely through gesture, movement, and facial expression. Have primary children write their own messages to act out.

Invisible objects. To develop focus and physical control have the children sit in a circle. Describe an object while acting as if you are holding it in your hands.

Then pass the object to the child sitting next to you, who then passes it to the next and so on, each trying to hold it in a way that would be appropriate so that it retains its proper size, shape, and weight. For example, passing an invisible bowling ball will look very different from passing a slippery fish. Vary the activity by having the children change the object each time it is passed or do not say what the object is and have them try to guess it. Have children take turns being the leader.

Who or what or where am I? Increase reading comprehension by having the children pantomime an object, character, or setting from a story that is familiar to everyone and then try to guess who, what, or where they are. Extend the activity by having groups pantomime a scene from the story.

Slow motion. Develop focus and physical control by acting out familiar activities in slow motion. Challenge the children to line up, write their name, or eat their snack moving as slowly as they can. Vary the activity by asking them to move while shaking violently or bouncing up and down.

Tableaus. Another way to develop focus and physical control is to study a work of art or an event in history and re-create the scene holding the pose for a minute without moving. Be sure to record the tableau on camera.

Verbs. Learn about action words by writing verbs, such as *swim, jump,* and *hop,* on index cards and giving each child a card. Have the children act out the verb.

Did You Get It?

Which of the following pantomime activities can be used to develop creative thinking among preschoolers?

a. acting out ordinary actions with the children, such as brushing teeth and eating soup

b. passing a prop around in a group of children and asking them to think of different ways to use the prop

c. asking the children to pantomime familiar activities, such as writing their name or playing basketball in slow motion

d. having a child pantomime a character from a familiar story and asking the rest of the children to guess the identity of the character

Take the full quiz on CourseMate

The Improvisation Experience

Like pantomime, **improvisation** is the representation of an idea through movements, but with the added attraction of using words as well. Like pantomime, improvisation has a spontaneous quality and calls on the creativity of the children to respond to the open-ended problems set by the teacher or peer leader. Role-playing is the most common form of improvisation, but most pantomime activities can also be turned into improvisation with the addition of words.

Descriptive improvisation. As in descriptive pantomime, this form of improvisation begins with a leader describing a situation, event, character, or problem and then having the rest act it out. Simple dramatic activities such as these give children a chance to try out different ways of communicating with language and help develop their ability to think on their feet.

For ideas for improvisations, see *Ideas for Open-Ended Improvisations* on CourseMate.

Although for infants and toddlers one-on-one activities work best, in designing descriptive improvisations when working with an older group it is better to have the children perform in small groups or pairs because they will naturally be noisier than when pantomiming, which is done in relative silence. Alternatively, children can take turns performing their improvisation in front of their peers. Another effective method for some activities is to have the children form two concentric circles facing each other.

Radio or readers' theater. In this type of improvisation children use only their voices to create the characters. They can make up their own radio program complete with news, weather, ads and talent, retell a story, or in the primary grades act out the part of a character in a book by reading that character's words. A center can be set up to be a radio studio or children can go behind a real or fake radio and pretend to be on air for their peers. For inspiration have children listen to some old radio programs and discuss how different sound effects were made. Old time radio shows can be downloaded for free from the *Internet Archive* http://archive.org/details/oldtimeradio.

Role-plays. Role-plays are more involved than simple improvisations. They are most appropriate for kindergarteners and up who are able to work together in a small group.

Role-plays take more preparation than simple improvisation. In a role-play a pair or small group of children assume particular roles to play. For example, one child could be a current student and the other a new student to the school. Once roles are assigned the group is given a **scenario** or situation and each child acts how they think their character would. Role-plays can be used to help children develop dramatic skills, assist children in solving social problems, and help present concepts being studied in a fun and visible way. For example, children can act out a story they have read, or imagine they are traveling to a country they have studied.

For suggested ideas for role plays, see *Ideas for Role Plays* on CourseMate.

In designing role-plays try to make sure that the roles are equal in importance. When a role choice has to be made, a fair method is to write the roles on pieces of paper and have the children draw them out of a hat. This eliminates difficulties that can arise when children feel one part is more attractive than another. As children learn how to be more cooperative, they can be given the choice of roles.

Using Props for Improvisation and Role-Play

Props play an even more important role in improvisation than in pantomime. Children may feel more self-conscious when speaking a role than they did in pantomime in which they had to think only about what to do with their bodies. As in creative movement, props draw attention away from the performer and make the action clearer. For example, children who are asked to take the roles of different community workers will feel more confident if they can wear a piece of clothing or hat that reflects that occupation. Prop boxes can be an important resource for role-plays. In addition, children can use their imaginations and choose objects they find around the room to be props, such as substituting a yardstick for a cane. Art materials can be used to create masks, hats, paper costumes, and simple scenery as well.

Masks

Masks, like props, allow children to express themselves in ways that they might not otherwise. Behind

Making their own masks and props allows children to express their creativity. Large eye openings, such as the ones in this paper-bag mask, not only make the mask safer, but also allow children to feel less enclosed.

a mask, children can feel like they are someone else; they may try acting in a new way or attempt things that might be too frightening barefaced.

Commercial masks have sanitary problems when used by more than one child, and often feel suffocating. Instead, encourage the children to make their own masks. Mask-making activities can be done with small groups working at a center, or by individual children who need to create masks to meet some particular requirement of their own self-selected dramatic play activities or for a role-play.

Materials for masks. Masks can be made from stiff construction paper, tag board, cardboard, or large paper bags in which eyeholes have already been cut. Chapter 9 explains how to make a papier-mâché mask. Paint, marker, and materials from the collage center, such as yarn for hair, can enhance the character.

Type of masks. Children can make three basic masks independently, requiring only a little assistance for the fitting.

1. **Stick mask.** Provide children with face-sized pieces of construction paper or tag board pre-cut into circles, ovals, and other geometric shapes. Eyeholes should be pre-cut. Create the character using crayon, marker, collage materials, or paint. Then glue the mask to a sturdy strip of cardboard or rolled-up tube made from tag board. To use, the child holds the mask in front of his or her face.

2. **Paper bag mask.** Use large paper grocery bags with pre-cut eyeholes. Cut up the side slightly so that the bag rests comfortably over the child's shoulders. Tempera paint works well on the brown paper surface.

3. **Wrap-around mask.** Cut eyeholes in the center of a 12-inch-by-18-inch sheet of construction paper. After it is decorated, wrap it around the child's head, adding an extension strip of paper if needed, and staple it in place so that it rests on the child's shoulders and is loose enough for the child to lift off easily.

Eyeholes. Because few young children can manage to locate eyeholes in a safe, usable place, it is helpful if the teacher does this for children up to kindergarten age.. It is important that the eyeholes be large enough to provide safe visibility for children. Make eyeholes circle shaped, not eye shaped, and at least 2 inches in diameter, separated by half an inch. For primary students make a cardboard template they can use to trace eyes for a mask. Show them how to fold the paper and make a snip to start the hole. Note: Mouth and nose openings are unnecessary and can weaken the mask, making it more likely to tear. Draw these on instead.

Using the masks. Try to encourage the children not to take their masks home right away after making them. That way they will be able to develop richer dramatic play through interacting with the other children. By using their mask ideas, teachers can find related literature and themes to expand their play. For example, if several children have made animal masks then an interesting zoo or circus could result. A group of robots could lead into dramatic play about outer space.

Ask questions that will help the children develop their characters. What character will you make? How will you show your character's special features? What will its eyes, ears, and so on be like? Think about how your character will talk and move.

Special Needs

• DEALING WITH A FEAR OF MASKS •

Adults or strangers wearing masks often frighten young children. Mask-making activities help them deal with this fear. To reassure children who are easily frightened, adults should

- make their own masks using the same materials available to the children.
- avoid masks that show gruesome features.
- always put the mask on and take it off in front of the children.
- play peek-a-boo games with simple masks.

Children may also be frightened or uncomfortable when wearing masks that cover their own faces. Allow them to hold masks up to their faces rather than tying them on. Tie them on only when requested. Always keep eyeholes very large. Some children may not want their full faces covered or may want to make goggles. Have available rectangular pieces of paper or tag board, about 4 by 9 inches, with pre-cut eyeholes. These can be worn by fastening a paper strip around the back of the head.

When several masks are finished, invite different characters to interact with each other. Have them role-play different situations. Which characters do you think have similar characteristics? Which ones are very different from each other? How would this character talk to that one? Do you think they would like each other? How do you think they would shake hands, sing together, go on a trip together, and so forth? How would these characters play together or how would they work together to build something? Talk about how they feel wearing the masks. Ask: "Does wearing a mask change how you act?"

The Improvisational Experience for Infants and Toddlers

Infants and toddlers will naturally add sounds and words to their dramatic play. The best approach is to enter into their play and model ways to change and control the voice while matching it to one's actions.

Faces and sounds. Together, explore making faces showing different emotions with matching sounds and words. For example, laugh for happy or whimper for sad.

Picture perfect. Clip interesting pictures of people and animals from magazines. Show a picture to a toddler and ask him or her to act the way that person or animal might act. These pictures can be made part of a dramatic play center.

The Improvisational Experience for Preschoolers and Kindergarteners

Retain the spontaneous nature of children's play by adding improvisational experiences to play centers where the children have open-ended choices or introduce improvisation while reading a book aloud.

Clown around. Make a collection of large, safe, colorful, and fun objects such as a hula hoop, bug net, plastic ladle, child's umbrella, pocketbook, silly sunglasses, and giant elastic tie, and keep them in a box labeled "Inspiration." Children can select an object and improvise a brief performance using words and movement. This box can be kept in a dramatic play center. Add a clown costume to the box for added fun.

Sound effects. Add sound effects and motion to the reading of any book. If the book is about a duck, have the children quack and waddle in place every time you say "duck." This is a great way to develop listening skills.

The Improvisational Experience for Primary Age

As children mature, they become more capable of taking a role in a group improvisation. Role-plays provide a child-pleasing way to integrate subjects.

Card readers. Write a familiar word and action on index cards, such as *swim*, or *going in a door*. Pass the cards out at random and have the children say and do what the card says. Start by doing it normally. Then, after the children are familiar with what to do, challenge them to use funny voices, exaggerate motions, or do things backwards. Let them suggest other ways to act out the cards as well. This activity is a great way to practice reading skills, new vocabulary, and spelling words.

Do as I say. Have one child describe an action or character while another acts it out.

Talk back. Hand out index cards on which is written a character such as a reporter, clown, king,

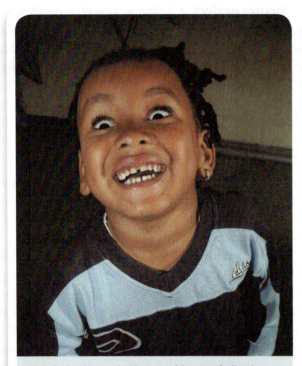

Descriptive improvisation combines verbalization and action. Imagining an emotion and acting it out helps children develop control over their facial expressions and vocal quality while at the same time providing emotional release.

or troll and have the children pair up and take turns acting out their characters and trying to guess who the partner is. Characters can also be selected from stories being read.

The Story Play Experience

Story play or **narrative drama** is based on children's own stories or on stories children have read or heard. Story play can be very simple. **Finger plays** and nursery rhymes are some of the first stories children learn. It can also be very complex. Primary age students can make up their own **story scripts,** assign roles, and act their story out using their developing reading and writing skills.

No matter what the level, narrative drama contains the following components:

- *Characters*—There may be one or more people, animals, or fantastical characters.

- *Verbal expression*—Stories may be told using words, sounds, or a combination of both as well as through mime.

- *Use of the body*—The characters must act out their roles through carefully planned movements.

- *Plot*—The story is presented in a sequence, the simplest being beginning, middle, and end.

- *Conflict*—Stories are most interesting when there is a problem or conflict that needs to be solved.

- *Setting*—Stories usually occur in a particular time and place.

- *Mood*—Throughout a story the characters may exhibit a variety of moods that relate to what is happening to them and around them.

- *Theme*—This is the main idea or purpose of the story.

Finger Plays

Finger plays are little stories acted out with the hands and fingers. These are usually accompanied by catchy rhymes. The words either give directions or suggest ways for the children to move their fingers, making the fingers the characters in the story. Because children can learn these when very young and because they involve both language and motion, finger plays are important ways to develop literacy skills. Finger plays can be found in books or learned from others.

TeachSource Video Case 12.2

Infant & Toddlers: Emotional Development

What techniques do the caregivers use to engage infants with finger plays? What other ways could these infants be introduced to story rhymes?

Watch on CourseMate

For some examples of finger plays, see *Finger Plays* on CourseMate.

Finger plays help children develop their language and fine motor skills.

Storytelling

The next level of narrative drama is storytelling. Just like finger plays, storytelling is an ancient art form. Before there were printed books, it was the main way that history and culture were preserved and passed down to the next generation. Today storytelling remains an important practice in some cultures, but has been replaced by books, television, and movies in many others.

Vivian Paley (2004) has developed ways to inspire storytelling by young children. Her method begins with her own invented stories, which she shares daily with the children. In her stories she incorporates real events and problems that occur in the classroom in a fictional format. Next she sets up a storytelling center where her kindergarten children can come and dictate stories to her or another adult. At whole group time she reads the story while other children take the roles of the characters and act the story out in the middle of the circle. Paley finds that children who have participated in this process are likely to write more stories. She has also found that this is an excellent way to include children with

special needs and second-language learners in the group. Aeliki Nicolopoulou, Judith McDowell, and Carolyn Brockmeyer (2006) found that with low-income children, Paley's method transformed the existing journal-writing activity into one that was much more engaging for the children, and in doing so increased their literacy development.

Storytelling and Literacy

Vivian Paley's model is an important one for teachers of young children to understand and incorporate into their classrooms. Dictation has been shown to be a powerful tool for early literacy development (Cooper, 1993). During the one-on-one time with the child, the teacher can work on many aspects of literacy that best meet the needs of that child. The child gets to watch his or her words turn into letters that can be read back to others. The teacher can suggest words, model how a writer thinks, and ask questions that help the child develop the plot. The teacher can also assess the child's language development and comprehension of narrative elements. However, dictation is a time-consuming process. Elizabeth Kirk (1998) suggests limiting children to one page of dictation by gently saying to the child: "We are getting near the bottom of the page. How do you want to end your story?" That way everyone gets a turn at least once a week to dictate and act out a story.

Retelling Stories

Narrative drama features the physical retelling of familiar poems, fables, nursery rhymes, and stories. Enacting stories enriches children's language and develops reading comprehension (Bromley, 1998; Furman, 2000). Research by Brian Cambourne and Hazel Brown (1990) shows that retelling stories improved children's vocabulary, comprehension, and writing skills.

Children can retell stories in a variety of ways. Toddlers often make up stories using toys or objects. Preschoolers dress up and become characters in the story, acting it out, and adding their own creative twists. Older children can write their own version of the story, creating scripts, props, costumes, and even scenery.

Puppetry

Using puppets is another way to retell or create stories. A puppet is really any inanimate object brought

Dress-up clothes allow children to try out new roles, imagining they are community workers or characters in the books they have read.

Across Cultures

Storytelling for Dual Language Learners

Storytelling and reading aloud can be used to promote language development in children who are learning English (Gillanders & Castro, 2011). Select a nursery rhyme or a traditional story, or write one of your own, that will allow the addition of hand or body movements and that has many repetitious phrases such as the *Gingerbread Boy* or *Going on a Bear Hunt*.

- To develop vocabulary, select three to five core words and one repetitive phrase essential to the story to emphasize. Before telling the story introduce these words, review their meaning and show pictures or objects illustrating them. Have children repeat the words and suggest gestures to go with them. For example, in the *Gingerbread Boy* every time the phrase "run, run as fast as you can" is said, children could make their fingers run up and down their leg. Alternatively give out the pictures or objects for children to hold up at the appropriate time.

- Tell the story in the child's home language first. If you don't know the language, ask a parent or native speaker to translate for you and tell it with you or make a recording.

- Then repeat the story in English.

- Send home a recording of the story in both English and the home language for the child to share with his or her family.

- Arrange the play centers so that the words and phrase will be repeated and used in new ways throughout the coming days. For example, after telling the story of the *Gingerbread Man*, set up a race course on the playground for children to practice running fast.

to life through the active manipulation of a child's hand. Introduce children to the world of puppets by including purchased or adult-made puppets as regular visitors to the program. Most young children do not truly see the actual puppet, but rather the imaginary being it becomes through their play. Puppets can share secrets, read stories, and play with the children. They allow the adult to enter the child's world. Many of the most successful early childhood television programs, such as *Mr. Roger's Neighborhood* and *Sesame Street,* depend heavily on the use of puppets.

In addition to using commercial puppets, children can make their own. Making a puppet should not be a one-time activity, but something the child will re-turn to again and again in order to create a character or persona with which to face the world. After intro-ducing puppet-making supplies at the art center, they should be available on a regular basis for whenever a child wants or needs to create a puppet. It is im-portant, therefore, to keep the design of the puppets quite simple, and within children's ability to create independently, without step-by-step instruction. Try stick puppets, shadow puppets, hand puppets and more.

For more information on making and using puppets, see Puppetry Resources *on CourseMate.*

Storytelling Experiences for Infants and Toddlers

For children who are just beginning to talk, storytell-ing experiences should foster a love for story and a development of descriptive language.

Family stories. Children's favorite stories are the ones about their own lives, such as when the car broke down on the trip to Florida, getting caught in a thunderstorm while boating on the lake, or grand-ma's remembrance of her first day of school. Care-givers can share stories about themselves and their families as well as learning some of the child's own stories.

Read, read, read. Introduce the world of chil-dren's literature to infants from birth. It is never too early to read to a child. Read nursery rhymes, folk-tales, fairy tales, and traditional stories from the child's ethnic heritage. Based on oral traditions these simple stories provide an introduction to the basis of storytelling—character, setting, and plot. Knowing these also prepares children for reading the great lit-erature of the world, which often is based on or incor-porates elements from these traditions.

Tell me. Encourage young children who are talk-ing to tell about something they just did. Cue them to use the three part story structure through your ques-tions with a "What happened when you . . . ? What happened next? How did it end?"

Storytelling Experiences for Preschool and Up

Storytelling is so much a part of the play of young children that the list of possible activities is endless. Here are a few to try:

Family and school stories. Continue to tell and retell stories about events in the life of the chil-dren and their families. Add stories about happenings in school, such as "Remember the day when the paint spilled all over my pants?"

Retell. Model the art of storytelling by retelling fa-miliar tales from memory. Add props, finger movements, and actions. Speak with intensity, using voices to match the characters. These things will help you remember the story and keep the focus of the children as well.

Puppets. Put out commercial or handmade theme- and story-related puppets at the puppet theater. For example, animal puppets can be used when studying habitats.

Masks. Make masks to represent the different characters in a story and as you read the book hold up the mask at the appropriate time and speak in the character's special voice.

Take a role. Give each child a prop, mask, or puppet that goes with the story. As you tell the story have the child do something related to the tale using the prop, mask, or puppet. For example, give out bowls and spoons to go with a telling of Goldi-locks. When the bears eat their porridge, the child with the appropriate size bowl stands up and mim-ics eating.

Draw it. As you tell a story illustrate it by draw-ing simple line drawings. To emphasize story structure

Puppets come to life in children's minds. They provide a safe way for children explore new ways of interacting with others.

divide the paper into three parts for beginning, middle, and end.

Illustrate it. Use a felt board to show the setting and characters in the story. Encourage children to make their own felt board pictures to tell stories of their own.

Storytelling Experiences for Primary Age

By the primary grades, children are developing vocabulary at a rapid rate and learning how to read and write. These new skills can be reinforced and enhanced through dramatic activities.

Story jar. Place a number of small objects equal to the number of children in the group in a jar or box, such as toy figurines, jewelry, and pieces of fabric. Have the children sit in a circle and start off a story with an exciting sentence. Pass the jar around the circle and have each child remove one object and add a sentence to the story that includes that item.

Odd pairs. Select two words for things that are not usually associated together, like fish and tricycle, and challenge children to invent a story that includes both things.

Everyone's story. Sit in a circle and start off a story with an exciting sentence. Each child adds on to the story in turn.

One word. Say a word, such as *dog*, and have the children think of other words that mean close to the same thing or go with it, such as puppy, collie, mutt, collar, leash, dog bone, and so forth. Record the words on chart paper and then challenge children to make up a story using all the words.

"What would happen if. . . ." Develop imaginative stories by asking "What would happen if . . ." completed with a fantastical occurrence, such as the sky suddenly turned red, the school started to float, or all the fish in the sea started walking around on land. Let the students invent their own "what if" story starters, too. Make up cards with "what if" ideas for times when someone needs a creative spark and keep them at a storytelling center.

Describe it. To introduce the use of descriptive language, have the children name different kinds of people, animals, or objects, such as a detective, panda, or pencil. Then on separate paper have them brainstorm a list of descriptive words, such as angry,

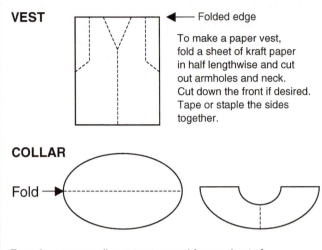

VEST

Folded edge

To make a paper vest, fold a sheet of kraft paper in half lengthwise and cut out armholes and neck. Cut down the front if desired. Tape or staple the sides together.

COLLAR

Fold

To make a paper collar, cut out an oval from a sheet of kraft paper or construction paper. Fold in half and cut out the neck hole. Add a slit for easy on and off.

FIGURE 12–2 Making Paper Costumes

Did You Get It?

Story or narrative play is based on

a. stories the teacher selects.

b. stories from other cultures.

c. children's improvisations and pantomimes.

d. stories children have invented, read, or heard.

Take the full quiz on CourseMate

sneaky, or broken. Put the lists together and have each child select a character and a descriptive word and then tell a story that includes that character. Try two or more of the descriptive words.

Setting easel. Make a class collection of settings. On large pieces of tag board, have children draw possible settings, such as a farmyard or an ocean. Then share the settings with the whole group. Ask, "How would you act if you were in one of these places?" Place the settings in turn on an easel and have pairs of children come forward and act out an appropriate event or animate a puppet in front of the scenes.

Making costumes, hats, and jewelry. Making costumes, hats, jewelry, and other body decorations is another way that art and dramatic play interact. As with puppets and masks, body-wear items should be simple enough for children to make on their own using simple art supplies.

For directions for making these items, see Making Costumes, Hats, and Jewelry on CourseMate.

How Do We Introduce Children's Theater?

Besides creating their own dramatic play scenarios, young children should have the opportunity to attend drama performances done by older children and adults. Exposure to this level of dramatics will inspire children to expand their own dramatic play and narratives. A backstage tour will introduce children to the role of lighting, stage sets, and costuming in creating the illusion of reality. Being able to see actors in their character roles and as themselves helps them distinguish between fantasy and reality. They will also learn how to behave as an audience.

Finding performances. Children's theater is especially designed to meet the attention span and need for interaction that young children require. Often a local drama group or a high school dramatics club will be willing to perform a program especially for young children.

Local and state arts-in-education programs can often provide information, links to performers, and grants to school groups. More information on these programs can be found at the Arts Education Partnership http://www.aep-arts.org. Many states have Councils for the Arts, which provide grants to groups who perform for schools. Performances geared to children can also be found at street fairs and arts festivals such as the First Night events held in many cities on New Year's Eve.

Theater Experiences for Toddlers

For children who have only seen recorded performances, a live performance in which they can interact with the actors provides a wonderful model of what the dramatic arts can be. At the same time, we need to remember that young children believe that what they are seeing is real. If possible, have the actors talk to the children first and then put on their costumes. At

Children can respond to dramatic performances in many ways. Paige, age seven, has drawn the characters in a children's play she has seen with herself and her friends in the roles of the actors.

the end actors can remove the costumes and answer children's questions about what they were wearing, why, and how the costumes were made.

For a positive experience we need to make sure the children are comfortable. Because of their high activity levels, initial theater experiences for toddlers should be no more than 20 to 30 minutes long. Holding performances in the classroom or another familiar place is helpful as chairs in an auditorium or theater may be too large and visibility difficult. Having children sit on the floor is one possible alternative. The ideal performance for this age has only one to three actors with minimal staging who carry out their show very close to the children.

Theater Experiences for Preschoolers

With their longer attentions spans, most preschool age children can attend longer performances about 30 to 60 minutes in length. They particularly enjoy stories and characters they are familiar with and will notice any changes that have been made in the narrative. Like toddlers, preschoolers may still be too small to sit comfortably in adult size seating. Before going to a performance make sure to ask about seating. Some theater groups let the children sit in a circle on the stage or on simple risers. Puppet shows work well because small children can get a good view of the raised up puppet stage.

Theater Experiences for Kindergarteners and Primary Students

By the age of 5 or 6 children are ready for lengthier performances. They are better able to sit in adult-size theater seats and have a longer attention span. Most children by this age have heard many stories, seen many television shows and movies, and will be aware of the story elements in the play they see. Wanting to know the ending of the story will motivate them to sit through the play to the end.

Theater Etiquette

Susan Fishman (2010) recommends that adults model how to be good audience members. This begins before the performance during which children are shown how to listen, when to participate, and how to show appreciation by clapping at appropriate times. These skills can first be practiced when viewing performances by peers. Later, when taking a group to a show, invite parents to accompany the group so there is a high adult to student ratio, and be sure to go over audience skills with both children and volunteers. Advise children to watch an adult if they are not sure what to do. If a child cannot sit still and pay attention, or is plainly uncomfortable during a performance, rather than disciplining the child and making the experience unpleasant, just quietly leave early with the child, and then try another performance when the child seems more ready.

With a little bit of effort the wonder of live theater can be shared with children.

Responding to Dramatic Performances

Books provide an ideal way to introduce the vocabulary of drama and to practice discussing how the elements are used. Books model the narrative structure of beginning, middle, and end essential to all story making and demonstrate how conflict and tension are built to maintain interest. We can look for setting, discuss the characters, and decide on the theme and mood of the story.

Retelling and re-enacting stories from books will enhance children's natural play and develop their comprehension and story writing skills while making them more critical viewers of live and recorded dramatic productions. The story *Hey, Little Ant* (Hoose & Hoose, 1998) is an excellent example of a book that serves multiple purposes. The story tells about a boy who is considering whether or not to step on an ant. The book illustrates a clear beginning with the boy ready to step on the ant, a middle in which the ant defends himself, and an ending where the boy makes his decision. The conflict and tension build as we all wait to find out what the boy will do. Follow up reading similar stories by having preschoolers and older children act it out or retell it in a different way. Ask children to identify the dramatic elements. Ask questions such as

- Did your retelling have a beginning, middle, and end?
- Why did you choose to start there?
- How did you create conflict and tension?
- What mood did you create?
- What was your message?
- What is another way you might have told this story?
- What other ending could you have?

Provide opportunities for them to record their responses in their journals or at the art center using pictures and words. Videography of the dramatic play of the children provides an excellent way for children to see themselves as actors.

Expand on what children are exposed to on television and in movies by showing videos and DVDs of stories from other places that they are less likely to see home. Videos of storytellers and pantomime performed by both professionals and children can be found on the Internet. Show short excerpts that relate to children's dramatic play interests and integrated units.

Making Connections through Drama

Bring the stories of children's home cultures into the classroom by having families share favorite stories. Create class books featuring these stories and share with families and the school community, such as displaying them in a public library. Bring in storytellers and dramatic performances that reflect different

Classroom Technology

WAYS TO USE TECHNOLOGY TO ENHANCE CHILDREN'S PLAY

The most obvious way to use technology is to show videos, DVDs, and recordings of dramatic performances and retellings of children's literature for children to watch and discuss. Here are some other things to try:

- Use an old slide projector or overhead to project a background image or colors on a wall to create a setting and mood for children's play.

- Photograph the children at play and use the photographs to inspire journal entries, make a class book, or presentation panel to share with families.

- Videotape the children at play and use the recording to show children their performance, to create digital presentations, and to share with families.

cultures, and provide opportunities for children to compare similarities and differences in the various stories, finger plays, puppet shows, and performances they see. Primary children can research and report on famous actors or folktales using the Internet, a teacher-prepared Web quest, or personal interviews and then teach their peers about what they learned or create their own dramatic act in response.

Did You Get It?

Theater experiences for toddlers should

　a. be at about 20 to 30 minutes long initially.

　b. be in a large auditorium or theater.

　c. include more than five actors to keep the toddlers interested.

　d. be viewed on TV or video.

Take the full quiz on CourseMate

How Do We Use the Dramatic Arts to Assess Growth?

Because dramatic play integrates so many of the growth areas, it provides an ideal situation in which to observe and evaluate children's learning.

Content knowledge. Teachers can observe the subject matter and concepts being used in children's play. For example, following a trip to the firehouse, a group of kindergartners playing in the dramatic play center might be observed play acting the safety practice of "Stop, Drop, and Roll" when pretending the food they are cooking is burning or children acting out the metamorphosis of a butterfly can be watched to see if they repeat the life stages in the correct order.

Critical and creative thinking. Decision making plays a key role in dramatic play. Teachers can observe the choices children make as they act out their ideas. For example, are the events in a logical order? Do the props and costume choices relate to the children's purpose? Are their choices unique and reflective of creative thinking?

Physical control. In order to play a role or imitate a behavior, children must exhibit both gross and fine motor control. Pretend play provides a noncompetitive setting in which children can explore the extent of their body motion. A toddler wiggling around pretending to be a worm, or a first grader stretching as high as possible to reach imaginary apples on a tree, are moving their bodies in ways not commonly found in ordinary events. Careful observation of how children handle props and move as they play can provide feedback on general physical development.

Language development. Teachers can also assess children's interest in stories and how well they have comprehended them by observing which stories are chosen for retelling and how they are reenacted. They can also note vocabulary usage and sentence structure.

Did You Get It?

Which of the following is a way to use dramatic arts to assess children's growth in critical and creative thinking?

　a. by assessing their comprehension of a story

　b. by observing if they have improved their fine motor control

　c. by asking them to identify a character in a story

　d. by noticing the types of decisions they make in their play

Take the full quiz on CourseMate

Conclusion: Imagine It!

The dramatic arts are the world of story and imagination with its roots in children's natural fantasy play. Through dramatic play, pantomime, improvisation, and storytelling, children can learn to control their bodies and words to create personas. They can become anything and anybody. Literacy skills are nurtured and developed as children become enthusiastic storytellers and scriptwriters. Music, dance, and visual art play a role in children's dramatic work.

The processes of pantomime, improvisation, and storytelling can be used to enhance everyday teaching and make facts and concepts more meaningful for students.

Teachers must also be performers. The skills of drama can also enhance how we teach. We can add flair to what we say, intensity to how we move, and story to what we tell.

For additional information on teaching the dramatic arts to young children, *see Chapter 12 Online Resources* on CourseMate. Visit our Web site at http://www .cengagebrain.com.

Teaching In Action

Puppets: Transcript of a Student Observation

When I entered the three- and four-year-olds' room, I saw the teacher's aide working with a small group of children. They were sitting on a rug, and the aide was using a puppet made of a cardboard tube and a piece of round paper with a simple face on it. She was using a funny little voice and singing a song that described something about each child. When she said the child's name, she would lightly touch the child's hand with the puppet. The children seemed delighted. They giggled whenever the puppet touched them. Then she asked them if they would like to make a puppet, too. The children seemed very excited by the idea.

She had paper circles in a basket, and she let the children each choose a circle and gave them each some markers in a small tray. The children drew a face for their puppets. I noticed that some of them were already talking in little, high-pitched puppet voices as they drew. When they were done, they went to a table and glued a cardboard strip to the back of the face. The aide had moved to the table and assisted them by asking if they had put on enough glue and reminding them to hold the paper to the cardboard until it was stuck.

Next, the children began to have their puppets talk to each other. Two of them took them to the housekeeping area and fed them and pushed them in the carriage. Several others joined the aide in singing the song again, this time using their own puppet to touch a friend. When it was time to go home, the teacher asked the children to put their puppets to sleep in the puppet house [a decorated box that looked like a house]. I thought it would be hard to get them to leave the puppets, but the way she said, "Tomorrow you can wake them up to play again" seemed to fit with how the children thought about the puppets—like real playmates—so they all came over and carefully laid their puppets in the box to sleep. When their families picked them up, some children took family members over to see the puppets sleeping. They were so cute. They would say, "Shhh. . . . Don't wake them up."

Reflection Page

The Importance of Play

For each of the developmental growth areas, give an example of how dramatic play facilitates skill development.

Social

_____

_____

_____

_____

Physical

_____

_____

_____

_____

Language

_____

_____

_____

_____

Cognitive

_____

_____

_____

_____

Emotional

_____

_____

_____

_____

Reflection: Based on the skills developed by dramatic play, how much time should be devoted to children's play during the school day?

_____

_____

Digital Download   **Download from CourseMate**

Reflection Page

Using Guided Imagery

Select one of the guided imagery suggestions in this chapter or on CourseMate or make up a scenario of your own. Write a script for this experience that you could use with young children.

Step 1: Relaxation

_____
_____
_____
_____
_____
_____

Step 2: The Journey

_____
_____
_____
_____
_____
_____

Step 3: The Return

_____
_____
_____
_____

Reflection: What will children learn from participating in this activity?

_____
_____
_____

Reflection Page

Designing a Play Center or Prop Box

Select a developmental age level, an appropriate topic, and learning objectives, and then write a plan of what you would include in a dramatic play center or prop box. Be sure to include a book or two, and multicultural and antibias materials.

Children's ages: _____

Topic: _____

Objectives: Using this center or prop box the children will develop

physically _____

socially _____

emotionally _____

language skills _____

cognitively _____

dramatic skill and knowledge_____

Describe what materials will be in the center or prop box.

_____

_____

_____

_____

_____

Refelction: What will be the greatest benefit of having this prop box or center prepared and ready to use at a "teachable moment."

_____

_____

Reflection Page

Telling a Story

Prepare yourself for telling a simple story to a group of children.

1. Select a folktale, fairy tale, or create an original story. Write a brief summary of it.

   _____

   _____

   _____

   _____

   _____

   _____

   _____

2. List the props you will use to enhance your presentation.

   _____

   _____

   _____

   _____

   _____

   _____

3. Describe how the children will actively participate as you tell the story. For example, how will they move or what sounds will they make?

   _____

   _____

   _____

   _____

Reflection: Do you feel confident about telling a story to young children? What can you do to prepare yourself beforehand?

   _____

   _____

   _____